INDIA'S WORLDS AND U.S. SCHOLARS

1947 – 1997

Dr. Rajendra Prasad and Governor-General Lord Mountbatten
entering the Chamber of Parliament House on 15 August 1947
(Photo courtesy: Maureen Patterson).

India's Worlds and U.S. Scholars

1947 – 1997

Editors

JOSEPH W. ELDER, EDWARD C. DIMOCK, JR.,
AINSLIE T. EMBREE

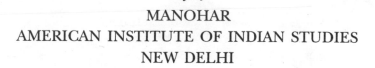

MANOHAR
AMERICAN INSTITUTE OF INDIAN STUDIES
NEW DELHI

First published 1998

Hardback: ISBN 81-7304-235-7
Paperback: ISBN 81-7304-257-8

Published by
Ajay Kumar Jain for
Manohar Publishers & Distributors
2/6 Ansari Road, Daryaganj
New Delhi 110002

Lasertypeset by
A J Software Publishing Co. Pvt. Ltd.
305 Durga Chambers
1333 D.B. Gupta Road
Karol Bagh, New Delhi 110005

Printed at
Thomson Press (India) Ltd.
New Delhi 110001

Contents

PART II. CONTRIBUTIONS OF THE STUDY OF INDIA
TO VARIOUS ACADEMIC DISCIPLINES

Abbreviations

AAB	American Academy of Benares
AAS	Association for Asian Studies
ACLS	American Council of Learned Societies
ACM	Associated Colleges of the Midwest
ACSAA	American Committee on South Asian Art
AIA	Archaeological Institute of America
AIBS	American Institute of Bangladesh Studies
AIIS	American Institute of Indian Studies
AIPS	American Institute of Pakistan Studies
AISLS	American Institute for Sri Lanka Studies
AOS	American Oriental Society
ARCE	Archives and Research Center for Ethnomusicology
ASI	Archaeological Survey of India
BHU	Banaras Hindu University
BULPIP	Berkeley Urdu Language Program in Pakistan
CAA	Center for Art and Archaeology
CAORC	Council of American Overseas Research Centers
CIA	Central Intelligence Agency
CIC	Committee on Institutional Cooperation
CONSALD	Committee on South Asian Libraries and Documentation
CRL	Center for Research Libraries
CSA	Committee on South Asia
EITA	*Encyclopaedia of Indian Temple Architecture*
FEA	Far Eastern Association
GLCA	Great Lakes Colleges Association
IGNCA	Indira Gandhi National Centre for the Arts
LC	Library of Congress
NDEA	National Defense Education Act (1958)
NEH	National Endowment for the Humanities
NMERTA	Near and Middle East Research and Training Act (1991)
NRC	National Resource Center
NRI	Non-Resident Indian

NSF   National Science Foundation
ORC   Overseas Research Center
OSS   Office of Strategic Services (1942-1945)
PL 480   Public Law 480 of 83rd U.S. Congress
SAC   South Asia Council
SAC-East   South Asia [Library] Consortium-East
SAC-West   South Asia [Library] Consortium-West
SITA   South India Term Abroad
SSRC   Social Science Research Council
UP   United Provinces/Uttar Pradesh
USEFI   United States Educational Foundation in India
USIA   United States Information Agency
USIF   United States-India Fund

Preface

This volume has been prepared by a group of U.S. scholars with three purposes in mind: (1) To felicitate the people of India and their government on the fiftieth anniversary of India's independence; the title of this volume reflects this first purpose. (2) To acknowledge some of the many ways in which the study of India has stimulated U.S. scholars and scholarship during those fifty years. (3) To express our gratitude, on behalf of the American Institute of Indian Studies (AIIS), to the people of India and their government for the many ways in which, during the past fifty years, they have helped in those scholarly endeavors.

During the past half century the American Institute of Indian Studies (AIIS) — a non-governmental consortium of U.S. colleges and universities interested in India — has emerged not only as a sponsor of bi-national research in architecture and the arts, and music and ethnomusicology, but also as the major channel for research and study of India by students and scholars in the U.S. The story of that emergence is itself worth telling. Maureen L.P. Patterson, scholar, historian, and long-time South Asia bibliographer at the University of Chicago, tells that story in Part I of this volume. Her account makes it clear how indebted the community of U.S. scholars are to scholars, institutions, and governmental agencies in India for enabling the AIIS to come into existence and to facilitate the on-going study of India by U.S. scholars.

The idea for this volume goes back to various AIIS meetings in 1994 and 1995. A consensus began to emerge that it would be appropriate for the AIIS to acknowledge 1997 and the first fifty years of India's Independence by publishing a volume. The AIIS Executive Committee asked the three living past presidents of the AIIS to form the editorial board, define the volume's theme, and select contributing authors. In May 1995 we three met on Cape Cod and wrote the following statement:

The main purpose of this volume is to identify ways in which, during the past fifty years, scholars, by working with data and systems of conceptualization and articulation in India, have been led to reconsider western-based theories, classification schemes, disciplines, and methodologies for organizing knowledge. This volume is not intended to be a review of what scholars have learned about India during the past fifty years (although that is not entirely ruled out). This volume IS intended to be an analysis of how, during the past fifty years, scholarship throughout the world has been affected by interchange with India.

Originally we identified twenty academic disciplines, each of which we wished to represent with a chapter in the volume. However, we soon found it necessary to introduce further distinctions within disciplines. For example, a discipline we originally defined as *Religious Studies* we eventually re-defined as six separate disciplines, each beginning with the heading *Religious Studies* followed by a sub-title. This in itself reflects how the study of India has affected academic conceptualizations and articulations in the United States.

Suggestions regarding possible authors came from many sources including members of the AIIS Executive Committee and the AIIS Board of Trustees, former AIIS Fellows, and members of various academic disciplines. By November 1995 we three editors had drawn up our list of potential authors and had sent them letters describing the volume's purpose and theme and inviting their contributions. We are most grateful to those scholars who responded to our invitation. All the scholars are distinguished in their fields. All have many commitments. And all were willing to set aside other projects to provide us with the contributions we requested. We feel that the quality of their contributions does credit to them, to the AIIS, and to colleagues and scholars in India.

As editors, we have tried, on the whole, to let the scholars speak for themselves. As editors, however, we also assume responsibility for whatever errors and shortcomings may be found in this volume.

It has been a pleasure working on this volume with our academic colleagues in the United States, with Dr. Pradeep Mehendiratta, Director General of the AIIS in India (with whom all three of us continue to have warm associations as past presidents of the AIIS), and with Ramesh Jain and Manohar Publishers and Distributors who, in publishing this volume as well as other books in the past, have provided so much assistance to the AIIS.

We, and the current president of the AIIS, Frederick M. Asher, hope that this volume, in its own small way, contributes to bridges of scholarship.

JOSEPH W. ELDER   EDWARD C. DIMOCK, JR.   AINSLIE T. EMBREE

PART I

History of the Study of India in the United States

Institutional Base for the Study of South Asia in the United States and the Role of the American Institute of Indian Studies

MAUREEN L.P. PATTERSON

INTRODUCTION

India achieved its independence on the 15th of August 1947. This was the culmination of six decades of Indian National Congress' mainly non-violent struggle to eject the British Raj. In 1997 we celebrate these fifty years of Indian freedom and parliamentary democracy.

The year 1947 holds special significance for me. I was then living in New Delhi with an Indian family, and together we experienced the climactic final days of colonial rule and the euphoria of independence. This was my second trip to India. Before that, in 1942, shortly after the Japanese bombing of Pearl Harbor that precipitated the United States into World War II, I enrolled in an intensive course in the Japanese language at the University of Michigan in the hope of contributing in some way to the war effort. With that suddenly acquired—though admittedly limited—new tool, in 1943 I landed a job with the U.S. Office of Strategic Services (OSS) and in early 1944 was sent to New Delhi, where I was attached to the headquarters of the American army's China-Burma-India theater of operations. There I helped to evaluate and translate Japanese-language materials captured in Burma during the Allied campaign to prevent Japanese military incursions into northeast India. For two years I lived in New Delhi and in my spare time made friends with Indian students, daughters of prominent Indian families. From these young women I heard much about Indian life and culture, and began to learn a bit of Urdu along the way.

After World War II ended, and after a short time back in the United States, I returned to India on my own as a student determined to learn much more about the intriguing civilization I had stumbled into a couple of years before. Putting aside the Japanese language that had served a limited wartime purpose but that in the process had introduced me to India, I began to study Sanskrit during the few months I spent at home in 1946. As soon as I returned to New Delhi, I plunged into studies of Hindi.

Between 1944 and 1947 Indian friends had whetted my interest in Indian history and politics, and on many occasions I was able to meet nationalist leaders. These included Mahatma Gandhi, Pandit Jawaharlal Nehru, Dr. B.C. Roy, Begum Shah Nawaz, Maulana Azad, and Mohammed Ali Jinnah. Capping it all, on 15 August 1947 I marched in a student procession to Parliament House to watch the Indian National Congress flag replace the Union Jack. That was indeed a day to remember.

A second event of great personal significance occurred later in 1947. That was my first meeting with W. Norman Brown, professor of Sanskrit at the University of Pennsylvania. He was in New Delhi on one of his many trips to India, at that time preparing to establish a program of South Asian studies at his university. When he learned that I planned to go to Allahabad University to study in its famous Hindi Department, Brown asked me to prepare a list of Hindi books for his proposed department's library at Penn. That was my first venture in bibliography. Brown also invited me to join his new program as a graduate student. But first I had to carry out my self-directed Hindi studies in Allahabad and finish my long-delayed B.A. in the U.S. Following that, in 1950, taking up Brown's suggestion, I went to Penn.

My wartime experience in the Allied effort to forestall Japanese military aggression gave me an unintended introduction to India during its momentous transition. This, together with the fortuitous meeting with W. Norman Brown in 1947, are the two events that determined my life for the subsequent fifty years. Thus I count it both a privilege and a pleasure to prepare this historical review at this historic time. It honors India's epic struggle to nationhood and is offered as *guru-dakṣaṇa* to W. Norman Brown, the man who, beginning in the early 1920s, led the long effort to establish the American Institute of Indian Studies thirty-five years ago.

These seventy-five years of planning and eventual operation of an institute, together with Brown's central role in them, must be seen against the backdrop of nearly two centuries of U.S. contact with, and incipient academic interest in, India.

I should like to thank the American Council of Learned Societies-Social Science Research Council Joint Committee on South Asia for awarding me grants in 1986 and 1988 that enabled me to carry out research on the development of South Asian studies in the United States. Similarly I am indebted to the American Institute of Indian

Studies for funding assistance in preparation of a history of the AIIS, based on research in the U.S. since 1991, and in India in 1992.

The statements made here do not represent the official views of either the AIIS or any other institutions described herein. I alone am responsible for selection and interpretation of the facts presented in these pages.

Constraints of space have forced me to minimize reference throughout the text to American individuals and specific academic institutions in favor of general statements and mention primarily of *leaders* both of South Asian studies in the U.S. and of the American Institute of Indian Studies. Omission of individuals' names is not intended to downplay their many contributions to the field but is simply a function of space in this historical overview. My aim has been to present highlights of the development of the institutional base of South Asian studies during the past fifty years, and to place them within broad contexts in both India and the United States decade by decade from 1947 to 1997.

EARLY CONTEXT OF AMERICAN ACADEMIC INTEREST IN INDIA

NINETEENTH CENTURY: DEVELOPMENT OF INDOLOGY

U.S. interest in India began on a commercial note after the Revolutionary War, when ships began to sail from New England to Indian ports with cargoes of ice and other supplies for British residents of Calcutta and other settlements in Bengal. Then after the British East India Company discouraged Christian missionary activity in India fearing it would interfere with the Company's primary interest in trading, many British missionaries came to New England to take passage to India on American ships so as to circumvent Company restrictions. Soon newly-established American missionary societies joined the British in sending members to proselytize for their various Protestant denominations. By 1818 a reverse religious flow began when Unitarian church members brought to the U.S. the writings of Raja Rammohun Roy, the Bengal religious reformer. His brand of Hinduism provided the sophisticated and intellectual group of Unitarians in New England with a positive view of Indian civilization, counteracting the derogatory descriptions of Hindu religion and society imported by some of the missionaries of the evangelical churches. Thus from the early part of the nineteenth century most information about India came to America along these two tracks.

Unitarian activities in the Boston area sparked the influential philosophical and literary movement known as Transcendentalism, whose best known members were Ralph Waldo Emerson and Henry David Thoreau. Their writings were influenced by Rammohun Roy's teachings as well as by the European Romantic movement, which had in turn been influenced by translations into English of Sanskrit classics newly available from the Asiatic Society of Bengal, established by Sir William Jones in 1784. In the first quarter of the nineteenth century in both France and Germany, these translations of Indian literature stimulated interest in the original Sanskrit, and in 1814 a Chair of Sanskrit was established in Paris, followed in 1818 by similar chairs set up in several German universities.

In the early nineteenth century, many American students began what was to be a long tradition of traveling to Europe to enroll in the research-oriented German universities. There some encountered the new discipline of comparative philology that had developed after the relationship of Sanskrit to the languages of Europe had been postulated by Sir William Jones at the Asiatic Society of Bengal. One of these students was Edward E. Salisbury who, after learning Sanskrit in Germany, returned to Yale where he was appointed in 1841 to a newly established position to teach Sanskrit. This first American Sanskrit Chair was followed gradually by others set up at the Johns Hopkins University in 1876, Harvard and Columbia in 1880, Chicago in 1892, and Pennsylvania in 1904. Early offerings through these positions usually consisted of classical Indian literature as well as the language itself, and, depending on the interests of the professor, provided instruction in aspects of Indian religion and philosophy as well. The number of students in indology always remained small, and the field was seen as esoteric. However, Sanskrit and its allied subjects gained a foothold in eight of America's leading universities and served as the groundwork for the multi-disciplinary South Asian studies that came about in the mid-twentieth century in several dozen American universities.

The content, locus, and personnel of the first century of American indology came from German universities, concentrated on Vedic and classical Sanskrit texts, and was primarily armchair in nature—few Sanskritists ventured to do fieldwork in India, the land of their studies. Indology emphasized classical languages (Sanskrit, Pali, and the Prakrits) and their literatures, philosophy and religion (primarily Hinduism and Buddhism), and to some extent related art and architecture of the classical period.

INTERWAR YEARS, 1918 TO 1939

The interwar years from 1918 to 1939 saw an increase in general American consciousness of India. Foreign correspondents and the rapidly developing media of still and motion picture photography brought to Americans words and pictures of India's struggle for independence from British rule. Americans were particularly fascinated with the personality and strategies of Mohandas Karamchand Gandhi, the Mahatma, who had first developed his powerful techniques of non-violent resistance and civil disobedience in many years of fighting for civil rights in British-ruled South Africa at the turn of the century. A small number of Indians who had visited or come to settle in the United States in the first quarter of the twentieth century used America as a sympathetic base from which to promote the nationalist cause.

North American academic work in Indian studies in the period between the World Wars was carried on primarily by scholar-missionaries resident in India for extended periods. "Scholar-missionaries" were persons with advanced degrees mainly in religion or theology who went to India to teach in a church-run college or school or to work in a mission station. The number of U.S. citizens so involved was probably less than a hundred, out of several thousand American missionaries who worked in India in the nineteenth and early twentieth centuries.

A surprising number of North American scholars—humanists and social scientists—managed to make visits to India and Ceylon for research in the interwar period, even during the Depression. James B. Pratt, a philosopher from Williams College, made three trips to India in the course of studying Buddhism and its place of origin—he was there in 1913-14, 1923-24, and 1931-32. Helen Moore Johnson, who became an accomplished scholar of Jainism, made four research trips to western India over a period of more than 30 years. Quaker political scientist William T. Hull spent a year gathering materials for his book on the Indian political scene in 1927-29. In 1934 the philosopher George P. Conger made the first of his three research visits to India. Sanskritist Franklin Edgerton first went to India in 1926-27, and then stayed there for the year 1938. W. Norman Brown carried on a variety of teaching and research in India in 1922-24, 1928-29, and 1934-35. Brown's half-brother, John Clark Archer, professor of comparative religion at Yale, spent 1937 at Khalsa College in Amritsar researching his book on the Sikhs.

In 1935 Murray Emeneau began his three-year linguistic investigation in the Nilgiri Hills, and in 1937-38 David Mandelbaum followed him to the same area for ethnographic work. Meanwhile, historian Holden Furber had explored colonial archives in Southeast Asia and Ceylon in 1934, and then spent 1936-37 locating historical source materials in many parts of India. In 1939 the anthropologist, Dorothy Spencer, went to Chota Nagpur to work on the Munda tribes. After Sanskritist Horace Poleman was appointed the first Indic specialist at the Library of Congress in 1938, the Library sent him to India for a year (1939-40) on an acquisitions trip that included location and microfilming of Sanskrit manuscripts.

Much of present-day South Asian studies in North America had its roots in this key period. Organizations were set up, men began to study and do research (with one or two exceptions, women entered the field later), and interests broadened from classical studies of earlier generations to include more contemporary concerns.

FROM INDOLOGY TO SOUTH ASIAN STUDIES: W. NORMAN BROWN'S ROLE

W. NORMAN BROWN'S BACKGROUND, TRAINING IN SANSKRIT

Beginning in the twenties, scholar-missionaries and academics in a number of disciplines taught and wrote about India in a scattering of seminaries, colleges, and universities in the United States. But those new offerings did not go much beyond courses in Sanskrit and allied subjects available in a few universities or the specialized training for missionaries at seminaries. And at that time only two academic organizations, the Archaeological Institute of America (AIA) and the American Oriental Society (AOS), expressed interest in developing facilities for American scholars to carry out research in India. It was these two organizations with which the young W. Norman Brown began to work in the twenties, effectively launching him onto his six-decades-long career in promoting study and research of India and in India.

While Brown was not alone in this concern, he was the most persuasive and untiring of all who shared his concerns and objectives. Through the years leading up to the establishment of the American Institute of Indian Studies, Brown's colleagues depended on his drive, contacts, and leadership capacity as evidenced by their choice of him as chairman or president of every group he was involved in. Without a doubt, for decades, W. Norman Brown was the most important person in the U.S. in driving American academic interest in India. How he attained this position is central to this story.

W. Norman Brown was born in 1892 in Baltimore, near which his father farmed and ran a small grocery store before deciding on a teaching and missionary career. After his ordination in 1900, George William Brown's church sent him to teach in a small town in British India's Central Provinces (now Madhya Pradesh). He soon became principal of a theological school in Jabalpur. Young Norman was 8 years old when he accompanied his parents to India. He quickly learned Hindi and absorbed folktales as well as stories from the epics. His father was a well-read man who encouraged Norman to converse with *pandits* who came to teach at the school. The family ambience was intellectual, and the elder Brown soon became a serious student of Indian philosophy and Sanskrit, eventually winning his Ph.D. at the Johns Hopkins University in 1910. After five formative years in India Norman was sent back to the U.S. to finish schooling. In 1909 he entered Johns Hopkins as a freshman just as his father was finishing his graduate studies. The younger Brown took many courses in Greek, Arabic, Sanskrit, comparative philology, and folkloristics, and presented his doctoral dissertation in 1916: a study of the relationship between the classical Sanskrit collection of tales, the *Pañcatantra*, and modern Indian folklore.

AIA, AOS, AND ACLS: ORGANIZING RESEARCH IN INDIA

After a stint with United States Naval Intelligence during World War I, and then several post-doctoral fellowships in Sanskrit, Brown returned to India in 1922 to study with a *paṇḍit* in Banaras, and then to teach English for a year at the Prince of Wales College in Jammu. During his 1922 trip to India, W. Norman Brown began his association with the first of two organizations that proposed development of an American research center in India. This was the Archaeological Institute of America (AIA), whose officers were stimulated by reports of exciting pre-Aryan finds in the Indus Valley and hoped to extend their work to India. When the AIA president learned that W. Norman Brown was about to visit India for study and teaching in 1922, he authorized Brown to act as AIA representative and make enquiries about the best place to locate a possible American School of Classical Studies in India. The AIA hoped to join British archaeologists in Indus Valley excavations, as they earlier had on various Near Eastern sites. Brown's mission was significant. It was the first proposal for establishment of an American "school" in India. While the AIA did not achieve its goal, its attempt was of lasting importance because it determined W. Norman Brown's future. From then on, Brown never swerved in working toward setting up an American research center in India.

When Brown returned to the U.S.A. in 1924, he could not find a teaching position, but Johns Hopkins gave him the honorary status of Fellow and Associate in Sanskrit while he worked at compiling an alumni directory to facilitate university fund-raising. Brown's big break came in 1926 when he was suddenly recommended for the Sanskrit professorship at the University of Pennsylvania. At the age of 34, W. Norman Brown stepped into that position, and it was his for the next forty years.

The American Oriental Society was the second organization eager to develop a U.S. scholarly center in the subcontinent. In 1926, as soon as Brown was secure in his professorship at Penn, the AOS chose him to chair its new Committee on the Establishment of an American School of Indo-Iranian Research. The proposed AOS School was designed to carry out archaeological work in India for which it planned to team up with the AIA. The eight U.S. universities that maintained departments of Indic or Iranian studies made pledges of financial support to the scheme, but ultimately the Committee could not raise adequate funds and had to postpone setting up an Indian counterpart of the successful American schools in Athens, Rome, Jerusalem, and Baghdad.

In 1930 the Committee on the Establishment of an American School of Indo-Iranian Research was transferred from the American Oriental Society to the American Council of Learned Societies (ACLS), and became its Committee on Indic and Iranian Studies. W. Norman Brown followed the Committee into the ACLS and retained its chairmanship. In 1931 the Committee was charged with organizing and incorporating an American School of Indic and Iranian Studies. The School was incorporated in June 1934, and its Board of Trustees chose W. Norman Brown as Chairman. Within a short time he was designated President of the American School of Indic and Iranian Studies.

The School hoped to set up headquarters in India, renting accommodations in Banaras. While this plan never materialized, the School successfully secured a concession from the Government of India to excavate in the Indus Valley. With funds provided mostly by the Boston Museum of Fine Arts, the School excavated at Chanhu-Daro in the province of Sind during the 1935-36 season, marking an important beginning of U.S. archaeological involvement in the subcontinent that was to increase dramatically in the last quarter of the twentieth century. Unfortunately, the School was unable to obtain funding for a second season at Chanhu-Daro, but it sponsored several individual research projects in linguistics and anthropology between 1935 and 1939. Ever the optimist, W. Norman Brown wrote in 1938 that at some point "the School will establish headquarters in Benares, where it will serve as a center of training for younger American scholars, [and] provide a radial point for the use of Americans conducting humanistic research in India." However, the outbreak of World War II in 1939 precluded any further School activity. Nearly a decade passed before planning resumed for an American research center in India.

W. NORMAN BROWN'S SYMPATHY FOR THE
INDIAN NATIONALIST MOVEMENT

W. Norman Brown was interested in all aspects of Indian civilization, in all eras. His bibliography reveals writings on archeology and the Indus Valley culture, on minutiae in Vedic poetry, studies of art history and folklore, and dozens of articles and reviews in popular journals and newspapers on India's contemporary political and social problems. Beginning in the 1920s, Brown expressed his passionate belief in the cause of Indian independence in publications such as the *Baltimore Sun, Asia,* and *The Nation.* He made countless speeches to a variety of U.S. audiences on India's long-lived civilization, essential unity, and need to be free of foreign domination. One such speech, for example, to the august American Philosophical Society in 1931, was a lengthy argument he titled "India's Will to Be a Nation." In an article Brown wrote in the Indian journal *Prabuddha Bharata* in 1938, he lamented the low level of information on India's cultural eminence and ancient civilization in U.S. educational curricula. Sadly, as Brown put it, "The fact is that it is scarcely studied," and he determined to remedy the situation. Books such as his *The United States and India, Pakistan, Bangladesh* (issued in three revised editions: 1953, 1963 and 1972) demonstrate Brown's comprehensive grasp of South Asia's social, cultural, and political background in the context of contemporary international relations. No other U.S. indologist of that era revealed such breadth of understanding and sympathy for the subcontinent. Determined to further U.S. study and research in all aspects of India, ancient and modern, Brown energetically planned structures that would realize that objective, and in the 1940s he impatiently awaited the end of wartime obstacles.

In 1947 India's achievement of independence, along with partition and the creation of Pakistan, stimulated academic interest in the subcontinent. In that year, W. Norman Brown succeeded in garnering foundation funds to carry out experimental summer programs on South Asia in 1947 and 1948, and then to open a full-fledged program of South Asian studies at the University of Pennsylvania in the fall of 1948.

THE STRUCTURE OF HIGHER EDUCATION
IN THE UNITED STATES

Before we look at the development of South Asian studies in the years following World War II, it will be useful to review the overall context of U.S. higher education within which this field grew.

It is not always remembered in the U.S., and not well understood overseas, that U.S. higher education is a complex structure, a mosaic of diverse colleges and universities spread across fifty states and the federal District of Columbia. The United States has no unitary system of education. Each individual state in the union has developed and maintains its own public institutions, be they, for example, research universities, two-year community colleges, or technical institutes of many kinds. These exist alongside private universities and colleges. Complex and ever-changing ties have been developed between public and private institutions themselves, and between such institutions and federal educational authorities for a limited set of purposes and functions.

Privately-run, endowed, church-related colleges were established on English and Scottish models in the original British colonies that became the first thirteen states of the union. Many of these developed into secular—public and private—universities, for example Harvard, Yale, King's (which became Columbia), and Queen's (which became Rutgers: the State University of New Jersey). Early on, a few privately-run, non-sectarian institutions existed, such as the College of Philadelphia, which became the University of Pennsylvania, still a private institution.

State-run and publicly-financed secular institutions—the state universities—were founded in the early nineteenth century, beginning with the University of Virginia in 1825. The Universities of Michigan (1837), Wisconsin (1848), and Minnesota (1851) followed. Eventually all states established their own universities, many of them on land granted by the federal government at the time the state entered the union.

In the latter part of the nineteenth century U.S. educators, impressed by the advanced methods and scientific rigor they had observed in German institutions, imported German approaches and set up graduate, research-oriented educational structures. The Johns Hopkins University was the first American mainly graduate institution, with just a small undergraduate college base. The Johns Hopkins' graduate school experiment, with German-style seminars, large lectures, and laboratory sessions, stimulated other colleges to superimpose the German model onto existing English-type college structures, or to create entirely new institutions. Thus Tulane (1884), Clark (1891), Stanford (1891), and Chicago (1892) were established as private universities with top-heavy graduate enrollments.

The German connection also brought to the U.S. the new discipline of comparative philology and the science of linguistics as well as indology based on the study of Sanskrit. These new fields were welcomed at the outset at private universities, which did not have to justify study of such exotic subjects to a state legislature. Of the eight chairs of Sanskrit established early on, only one was at a state school, the University of California, Berkeley. Indological studies introduced at many of these universities formed the base of later broad-ranging programs on South Asia. While the early centers of classical indology, with the exception of California and Chicago, were on the East Coast, postwar South Asian centers have developed on both coasts and in many Midwestern states. They are distributed almost equally between private and public institutions, with those at private institutions enjoying greater flexibility with less sudden financial constraints than those under the watchful eye of a state legislature. All South Asian studies centers have been funded by a mix of internal, federal, and philanthropic foundation grants.

Higher education in the United States has spawned many voluntary cooperative groupings over the past fifty years. Such groupings of public and private, large and small institutions of higher learning focus on specific activities or concerns. For example, the American Institute of Indian Studies, which is highlighted in this historical summary, is a consortium, established in 1961 with fourteen charter members, that has grown as of 1997 to fifty institutional members. It is a very successful example of cooperation among U.S. colleges and universities, dedicated as it is to study and research in India, as well as to bi-national Indo-American collaboration. By and large, though, in the hundreds of higher educational institutions in the United States there has not been great receptivity to international studies in general or to South Asian studies as a fragment of the larger field.

POST-WORLD WAR II EXPANSION OF AMERICAN STUDIES OF SOUTH ASIA

WARTIME AMERICAN PRESENCE IN INDIA

Some 100,000 U.S. troops had been stationed or passed through India during World War II in support of the fight against Japanese aggression in Burma—aggression during which the Japanese army invaded parts of northeast India and dropped some bombs on Calcutta and Madras. U.S. soldiers built airfields in northern India and Bengal in the east, from which to ferry men and equipment "over the Hump" into China where the war against Japan was raging. But these four years of contact with India led a very few Americans to an interest in India itself. Those who became interested probably numbered only a couple of hundred or so. Most stationed there seemed threatened by India's strangeness and appalled by the rampant poverty they observed. Besides, authorities of the British Raj discouraged Americans from making contacts with Indians in an effort to minimize possible contagious discussions of America's successful war of independence from Britain nearly two centuries earlier.

Some few dozen of us stationed in India managed to avoid British restrictions on our contacts and were able to learn something of India's history, culture, and current political situation during our tour of duty. When the war ended, we returned to our campuses in America and plotted means to expand our knowledge and pursue our attraction to India.

In the fifty years of Indian independence, thousands of U.S. citizens have travelled to India for study, research, and work of many kinds under the auspices of dozens of programs and agencies. Agricultural and technical departments in a number of American universities sent teams of specialists to set up new institutions in independent India or to add such courses as agricultural planning, engineering, home economics, or educational training methods to existing Indian institutions. India thus became a familiar destination for professors from many Midwestern state universities, intriguing many who had perhaps previously heard of the subcontinent only from Protestant missionaries or returning GIs.

THE FULBRIGHT FELLOWSHIP PROGRAMS IN INDIA

The Fulbright programs, beginning in India in 1950, provided the first large batch of postwar scholars the opportunity to study and do research in India and sent a number of U.S. professors to India to teach their specialities or advise on projects in agricultural or community development or river valley multipurpose irrigation schemes. Many individuals were supported to go and teach English, incidentally learning about India by living there.

Since the Fulbright program was designed to be a two-way street, it also brought many Indian scholars to the United States to study or teach. Critics of the Fulbright program's Indian component have charged lack of preparation or commitment to serious scholarship of India on the part of Americans selected in the early days of the program. Indeed a disadvantage of the early Fulbright program was its concentration on providing many scholars with somewhat superficial single visits, discouraging the repeated and intensive visits specialists need for long-term research. The Fulbright program's lack of planned contribution to fundamental area research, especially in such a complex civilization as India's, led W. Norman Brown—who experienced the Fulbright program in action as a grantee in 1954—to redouble his efforts to establish a highly selective and intellectually rigorous program of studies in India for Americans. Nevertheless, the Fulbright programs played an enormously successful part in awakening U.S. academic interest in India, sending in its first twelve years some 534 scholars of several levels—from graduate student to veteran professor. Fulbright programs are models of bi-national cooperation, not only in India but also all over the world.

DEVELOPMENT OF AMERICAN INFRASTRUCTURE
FOR SOUTH ASIAN STUDIES

If W. Norman Brown's efforts immediately after the war were primarily towards programs at the University of Pennsylvania and for the hoped-for overseas research center, U.S. philanthropic foundations began to fund a wide variety of activities to support South Asian studies. The Carnegie Corporation of New York had taken the lead in 1948 with grants to Penn for Brown's area studies program and to Cornell University for anthropology and language work on India. Later Carnegie subvented special conferences such as "India in Liberal Education" in 1957, and programs such as Wisconsin's pioneering College Year in India in 1961. The Rockefeller Foundation set up specialized programs such as the linguistics program in Poona where, beginning in 1954, U.S. linguists trained Indians in modern linguistics and explored ways of teaching many Indian languages. Rockefeller also sponsored dozens of leading Indian historians and social scientists for limited terms as visitng professors in the U.S. These visitors helped to stimulate study of South Asia by observing the American educational environment and advising on ways to teach about India. These visitors included S.M. Katre, D.R. Gadgil, and Iravati Karve from Poona; Nirmal Kumar Bose, Suniti Kumar Chatterji, and R.C. Majumdar from Calcutta; and K.A.N. Nilakanta Sastri from Madras.

Meanwhile the Ford Foundation, with its Foreign Language and Area Training Fellowships, had in 1952 begun supporting individual scholars for dissertation and post-doctoral research in India, as well as contributing to the field's organizational infrastructure.

The Far Eastern Association (FEA)—established in 1948 by scholars of China and Japan—by 1955 had begun to include persons interested in India. In that year, urged on by the Rockefeller and Ford Foundations, the FEA established a Committee on South Asia (CSA) to accommodate this new clientele. With W. Norman Brown as chairman, and using Rockefeller and Ford funds, the new committee set about identifying language and area studies needs and planning library resource requirements for the new field. When it became clear that South Asia was a valid and viable sub-field of Asian studies as a whole, the Far Eastern Association (with some hesitation but with prodding in the form of financial inducement from the Ford Foundation) changed its character and constitution and in 1957 became the more inclusive Association for Asian Studies (AAS). This proved to be of great significance since it gave the embryonic South Asia field a home base from which to build further its institutional infrastructure.

DEVELOPMENT OF LIBRARY RESOURCES

As one of its first moves and with foundation support, the Committee on South Asia concerned itself with developing badly needed specialized library resources in U.S. universities. To identify needs and plan detailed steps, the Committee on South Asia held a major conference at the Library of Congress (LC) in Washington in 1957 and established a high-level group to monitor progress. In 1961 millions of Indian rupees (owed to the U.S. in payment for shipments of wheat and other food-grains to India in the 1950s to avert famine) were made available under an amendment to Public Law 480 of the 83rd Congress to American agencies and institutions in India for a variety of educational and other purposes. The Committee on South Asia lobbied hard and successfully to set up a program whereby eleven American university libraries, in addition to the Library of Congress, could tap this reservoir of American-owned rupees. Accordingly LC established a large-scale office in New Delhi to select and buy twelve sets of Indian publications deemed to be of research value on all subjects and all Indian languages. LC established a similar office in Pakistan to buy Pakistani publications. These publications were processed and in 1962 began to be shipped to the participating libraries in the U.S. To date over thirty American libraries have participated in this program—later extended to Nepal and Sri Lanka—which has lasted for thirty-five years. This library program, quickly dubbed the "PL 480 Program," has built a resource base in the U.S. that makes possible research, writing, and training on India undreamt of in earlier scholarly generations. By 1969 when the AAS' Committee on South Asia became the South Asia Regional Council—later the South Asia Council—this new elective body formed its Committee on South Asian Libraries and Documentation, among other things, to monitor the Library of Congress South Asia program, proferring reactions and requests from America's South Asianists.

LANGUAGE PROGRAMS

As the new field of South Asian studies began to take shape in the U.S. in the 1950s, it was faced with a complex problem. What languages should be taught as entrée to India's diverse cultural traditions? The classical languages—Sanskrit, Pali, and the Prakrits—had served indological study well for the past century, but those who were developing centers for the study of modern India knew that courses in modern languages would be necessary. But which one or one's from among India's fifteen major literary languages, each spoken by millions of people? The fact that most educated Indians spoke English and wrote many scholarly works in English was deceptive. It represented but the tip of the iceberg. Many Americans seemed to believe they could study Indian subjects primarily through the medium of English. Though this may have been true for a subject such as international relations or economics, it most certainly was not true for history at the regional level, most modern literatures, or local religious traditions.

Beginning at Penn in 1948, courses were offered in Hindi, India's official language along with English. Then Bengali was added, with provision for one or another of the major Dravidian languages. Cornell University, with Carnegie funds, began in 1948 to study culture change in India. In 1949-50 it sent a team of anthropologists for field study in a village near Allahabad, in the State of Uttar Pradesh. Following that, a larger Cornell group worked with Lucknow University anthropologists on a study of another Uttar Pradesh village. This was funded by the Ford Foundation and set out to study processes of change prior to introduction of Government of India community development projects. Cornell's decade of concentrated anthropological work in U.P. (1948-58) required intensive use of Hindi, so from the early 1950s Cornell's South Asianists placed great emphasis on language training and developed a whole array of teaching materials. Thus Penn and Cornell took the lead in teaching Hindi in America.

The Cornell experience made it clear that U.S. fieldwork in India—especially in anthropology, the most popular discipline for Americans in the first postwar decade—required intensive language training, and not only in Hindi.

The Penn and Cornell programs quickly made it obvious that the U.S. urgently needed to develop both teaching materials and personnel for South Asian languages. By 1954 the Rockefeller Foundation recognized that it could possibly contribute to India's need for better inter-regional communication and what was called "national integration" by supporting a program of modern linguistics. Accordingly the Foundation established a broad program of linguistics training at the Deccan College, Poona, offering funds for U.S. linguists to go to India to teach and learn an Indian language, and for Indian scholars to go to the U.S. for advanced training in linguistics and language pedagogy.

In the U.S. an independent American Committee on South Asian Languages was formed in 1954 to advise the Rockefeller Foundation and select scholars for the Deccan College program. This committee was affiliated in 1956 with the FEA's (later AAS's) Committee on South Asia. In 1958, when the U.S. Congress passed the National Defense Education Act (NDEA), the South Asia Language Committee worked with federal language development officials in determining national needs for training in heretofore neglected South Asian languages and in recommending programs of development and research.

Veterans of the Deccan College linguistics program soon began to teach Indian languages at many of the newly-funded South Asian centers in America. No longer was Hindi the major, or only, language offered, but Bengali, Telugu, Kannada, Tamil, Marathi, Sinhala, Oriya, and Urdu became available to U.S. students. Other languages such as Malayalam, Gujarati, and Nepali were offered on an individual basis to students who planned research in regions where those languages were spoken.

After its establishment in 1961, the U.S. Peace Corps further stimulated and developed language training for those rural areas off the beaten track in India where it was sending its volunteers. Between 1961 and 1976, when the Government of India requested termination of Peace Corps operations, 4,413 volunteers had worked in India in development projects in agriculture, education, health, and nutrition. Many volunteers, inspired by their experience in India, entered graduate schools for advanced work in Indian studies upon their return. U.S. university programs of South Asian studies profited greatly from the infusion of a new brand of scholar who had had two or more years of grassroots involvement with Indian life and who had acquired substantial language skills in the process.

In its early years, recruitment to South Asian studies in the U.S. came in large part from three sources: children of U.S. missionaries, persons stationed in India during World War II, and former Peace Corps volunteers. Many of these people brought some level of language competence to their new academic work.

Within the first two decades of South Asian studies in the U.S., the crucial means of access to many cultural arenas in the subcontinent had been developed. Since the 1960s the number of language programs available to American students proliferated, and language pedagogy became more effective and technically sophisticated.

Undergraduate study in India, with language at its center, came to the fore in the early sixties with such programs as the University of Wisconsin's College Year in India that offered intensive Hindi, Urdu, and general area studies. In 1969 the Great Lakes Colleges Association (GLCA) consortium launched a yearly program of Tamil language training and area studies in Madurai for U.S. undergraduates. The Associated Colleges of the Midwest (ACM) consortium of thirteen (later fourteen) private liberal arts colleges in 1969 started its yearly program of Marathi language training and general Indian studies in Poona after orientation sessions at a selected college in the U.S.

The Committee on Institutional Cooperation (CIC), a voluntary organization of twelve Midwestern research universities, in 1963 developed a "traveling scholar" plan so that a graduate student from any CIC member institution could travel to another school for special study and research. This was particularly useful for language training where only a few universities were beginning to offer South Asian languages. In 1967 the consortium expanded this program for individuals to provide a fully structured and coordinated approach. This was the CIC Summer Institute for South Asian Language and Area Studies. Planned to be held on a different CIC campus each year on a rotating basis, the federally-funded summer institutes offered intensive courses in Hindi, Bengali, Tamil, Kashmiri, Sanskrit, etc., plus seminars, films, and lectures on a variety of subjects such as art history, literature, and sociology. These Summer Institutes, begun at the University of Illinois in 1967, greatly enhanced the opportunities for study of Indian languages and proved the value of cooperative programs. Unfortunately, with the withdrawal of federal funding in 1973, the CIC Summer Institutes came to an end. But their seven-year existence had been significant for the development in the U.S. of training in leading Indian languages during what was still an experimental phase. The University of Wisconsin, in order to meet the needs of its College Year in India Program, continued to offer summer language training in elementary Hindi-Urdu, Telugu, and eventually Tamil. Other programs, such as those run by the American Institute of Indian Studies, eventually took over the important function of advanced training in Indian languages in India.

Another ingredient in American language training has been the intensive Urdu program held annually in Lahore, Pakistan, and run by the University of California, Berkeley. Since its inception in 1974, this program has trained a large number of students who have gone on to do advanced work in Urdu literature both in India and Pakistan.

FEDERALLY-FUNDED AMERICAN LANGUAGE AND AREA CENTERS

It will be recalled that one U.S. reaction to the successful Soviet feat of launching its first satellite, Sputnik, into space in 1957 was passage of the National Defense Education Act (NDEA) in 1958 to spur study of so-called "critical" or strategic areas and subjects. For studies of India this meant modern languages, anthropology, and other social sciences. And India's fledgling democracy stimulated studies of political parties and elections.

Administrators at the U.S. Office of Education invited research universities to apply in national competition for funding under Title VI of the National Defense Education Act of 1958 to establish language and area centers focused on the nine major world regions identified under the Act. At the highest point in this funding history, over 100 such centers for all world regions existed. Of these, between 1959 and 1976, sixteen were Title VI centers for South Asian language and area studies. A subsequent shakeout reduced the number when a university either could not sustain the cost if often-unpredictable federal funds were cut, or was unable to measure up to shifting government criteria and policies in the periodic national competitions.

The Higher Education Act of 1965 succeeded the National Defense Education Act (HEA) of 1958, and under its Title VI continued crucial support of centers. With changes in the legislation under amendments passed in 1980, HEA Language and Area Centers were renamed National Resource Centers (NRCs) with a broader mandate and more stringent criteria built into the three-year competitive cycle. Nine NRCs were designated for South Asian studies, one of which—in a departure from precedent—was shared jointly by two universities. As of 1996 the ten institutions chosen were: University of California, Berkeley (begun as NDEA Title VI center in 1959); University of Chicago (1959); University of Pennsylvania (1959); Cornell University (1960, joint with Syracuse University in 1985); University of Texas at Austin (1960); University of Wisconsin-Madison (1960); University of Washington (HEA Title VI center in 1974); University of Virginia (1976); and Columbia University (1977).

SUMMARY OF POSTWAR DEVELOPMENTS
IN SOUTH ASIAN STUDIES

This infrastructure, in the making for just over a decade following the benchmark Conference on Southern Asian Studies in 1949, completely changed the parameters of the study of India in the United States. And with the sudden availability of "PL 480" funds in 1961, the nationwide academic structure was in place for the inter-university consortium that established the American Institute of Indian Studies in that year. The field had evolved from the elite eight chairs of indology and Sanskrit, with very few students in the first half of the twentieth century, to several dozen programs at universities and colleges across the country, with ten or twelve major centers offering wide-ranging humanistic and social science courses to hundreds of students. This then was the context for the establishment of the American Institute of Indian Studies.

STEPS TOWARDS THE AIIS:
FROM "SCHOOL" TO "INSTITUTE"

REVIVAL OF PROPOSAL FOR OVERSEAS CENTER, 1946

The development of broad-based South Asian studies in the U.S.A. after World War II serves as the setting within which we focus on the emergence of the long-planned American research center in India. This is the story of the revival in 1946 of the dormant American School of Indic and Iranian Studies and its transformation into the American Institute of Indian Studies in 1961.

As soon as practicable after World War II ended, and even before India's independence, W. Norman Brown, chairman of the American Council of Learned Societies' Committee on Indic and Iranian Studies, convened a meeting of this group. On 26 April 1946 the Committee called for reactivation of the American School of Indic and Iranian Studies, with proposed headquarters in Banaras. The School's focus was the encouragement of humanistic and social science research in India, in cooperation with scholars at Indian institutions. The ACLS Committee felt that development of the School in India would greatly further Indic studies in the United States, which it deemed to be of paramount importance. But lack of funds prevented progress on the project for a couple of years.

However, the ACLS' Committee on Indic and Iranian Studies, with Brown at the helm, met in late-1948 to plan the nationwide development of South Asian studies. In addition, the committee was eager to discuss further plans for the long-awaited overseas research center. Committee members spent considerable time debating its name: Should it be called "school," "academy," or "institute?" At this meeting, furthermore, in order to assist in developing South Asian studies in the United States, the humanistic American Council of Learned Societies' Committee on Indic and Iranian Studies decided to add a social scientist to its membership. Thus in April 1949 the American Council of Learned Societies and the Social Science Research Council agreed to form a Joint Committee on Southern Asia. The new Committee dropped the earlier focus on Iranian studies and extended its geographic purview to Southeast Asia.

When the Joint Committee on Southern Asia was formed in 1949, with W. Norman Brown as its chairman, it decided as its first major action to survey American academic resources and needs of the region, which it understood to be South and Southeast Asia. The Committee's second major action was to ask the U.S. Department of State to inquire of the new government of independent India what its attitude would be toward the establishment in India of an American Institute of South Asian Studies, as it was termed at that time. The Department of State conveyed the Government of India's favorable response to the Joint Committee in November 1949, with the suggestion that such an institute not be located in New Delhi because of the capital's housing shortage. The Government of India's positive reaction spurred the Joint Committee to renewed efforts to realize the long-planned overseas center envisioned by U.S. scholars led by W. Norman Brown.

The Joint Committee's third major action was to convene a

nationwide conference on Southern Asian studies in the U.S. For three days in December 1949, under W. Norman Brown's chairmanship, sixty-six representatives of American educational institutions, libraries, museums, learned societies, and foundations, as well as U.S. government officials and delegates from foreign embassies, met at the University of Pennsylvania in Philadelphia. Data papers and roundtable discussions, plus the results of the Joint Committee's national survey, contributed to a lengthy assessment of the state of the field. It resulted in a ten-year development plan for Southern Asian studies in the U.S. The report of this plan was published in 1951. The establishment of an American research facility in India was a central topic at the Conference and in its published survey.

Over the preceding three decades, proponents of an American research center in India had pondered its location and form. Banaras and New Delhi had long been favored as location. But when the Government of India discouraged New Delhi as its site, the U.S. scholars had to look elsewhere. After the successful Rockefeller Foundation experience of running its linguistics program at the Deccan College in Poona, and with the encouragement of Deccan College authorities, Brown and his colleagues saw Poona as a possible site.

The form of the proposed center was something else. As far back as 1929, the American Oriental Society's committee believed that the Indian center should be similar in scope, character, and objective to the American schools in Athens, Rome, Jerusalem, and Baghdad, and the French institute at Hanoi in Indochina. These were the precedents and models that Brown and others considered. They were particularly taken with the idea of a research and residential campus, complete with a substantial library. The Deccan College premises came close to the Athens model. But while the American scholars could dream of locations and models, they had first to face reality. They needed funds.

POSSIBLE FUNDING SOURCE: "PL 480" RUPEES

It was 1960 before proponents of an American institute in South Asia got wind of a potential funding source. By this time, Henry Hart, University of Wisconsin political scientist, had introduced a program on Indian studies on his campus. And in mid-1960 Hart and his colleagues decided to expand that program by developing an undergraduate-year-abroad component in India, with funds from the Carnegie Corporation of New York. Also at that time, Hart learned of U.S. Department of State agreements with certain countries to use for educational purposes in those nations local currencies the State Department owned. The Department of State solicited proposals from

U.S. institutions for the use of these "PL 480" rupees. The University of Wisconsin group submitted a proposal to teach faculty at Indian universities courses in American history and American literature, and to set up a center in India to provide a year's post-doctoral training in Indian languages and culture to non-specialist U.S. faculty members who were already teaching courses on India. Accordingly, in December 1960 Henry Hart and his team went to India with State Department funding to determine which Indian universities would welcome U.S. studies, as well as to locate a place where U.S. faculty might acquire proposed language and area knowledge.

Meanwhile, W. Norman Brown arrived in India, also on State Department funding, to present the U.S. Embassy in New Delhi with the detailed plans for an American overseas research center developed by a group of scholars over the previous twenty-five years. This proposal seemed to be an appropriate use of the U.S.-owned rupees. Apparently up to this point Henry Hart had not known of the proposal Brown and his colleagues had labored over for a quarter-century. When U.S. Embassy officials were confronted with both the Brown and Hart proposals, they suggested consolidation of the two plans. Thus in mid-January 1961 in New Delhi, Henry Hart and W. Norman Brown proceeded to merge their proposals.

CREATING THE AMERICAN INSTITUTE OF INDIAN STUDIES, 1961-1962

PROPOSAL TO DEPARTMENT OF STATE FOR "PL 480" FUNDS, 1961

By late-January 1961 the two principals, W. Norman Brown and Henry Hart, had consolidated their proposals and presented the joint document to U.S. Embassy officials. The joint document was approved and transmitted to the Government of India for its approval. Shortly thereafter Brown submitted the proposal for comments to two other American scholars then in India: Richard Park of the University of Michigan, and Milton Singer of the University of Chicago. Brown and Singer favored naming the research facility "American Institute for *South Asian* Studies" [my emphasis] if that would be acceptable to the Government of India. U.S. Embassy officials in Karachi, Pakistan, had discussed the proposal with Brown when he stopped over on his way home, and they asserted that Pakistan would agree to the more inclusive name. Brown felt strongly that the Institute should reflect the historical civilizational entity of the subcontinent, with India at its center—despite recent political changes in national boundaries. However, the fact that the final agreement on establishing the Institute had to be bi-national—between the U.S. Government and the Indian Government—led to restricting the focus of the center to India, hence the "American Institute of *Indian Studies*" [my emphasis].

W. Norman Brown returned to the U.S. in late-February 1961 and presided over several meetings called to discuss the sudden developments of the Institute. South Asianist scholars welcomed the proposal worked out in New Delhi, and on 30 April 1961 an "Interuniversity Conference to Establish an American Institute for [*sic*] Indian Studies" was held in New York. Representatives of fifteen universities and colleges attended and formed an organizing committee to arrange for incorporation and drafting of by-laws. This became the Executive Committee charged with working out the legal details over the summer. W. Norman Brown was chosen its Chairman.

INCORPORATION (1961), ESTABLISHMENT OF
POONA HEADQUARTERS (1962)

The American Institute of Indian Studies was incorporated on 4 October 1961, and fourteen educational institutions were declared to be charter members. When the newly-formed Board of Trustees met on 7 October 1961, W. Norman Brown was named President of the Institute, Milton Singer was Vice-President, and Henry Hart became Secretary. Immediately, notice of the Institute's legal standing was sent to the U.S. Embassy in New Delhi. On 3 March 1962 President Brown received written approval from his old friend P.N. Kirpal (Secretary in the Ministry of Education) and assurance that the Government of India welcomed the new organization.

By that date the Deccan College Council and Board agreed to host the AIIS on its Poona campus. On 18 June 1962 the Institute signed a contract with the U.S. Department of State for a grant of U.S.-owned rupees. This agreement triggered promised dollar funding from the Ford Foundation for Institute expenses in the United States.

When all the pieces were in place, the Institute set about establishing its Poona headquarters staff. While awaiting selection of an American Resident Director, the AIIS chose D.D. Karve as its first Executive Officer, taking charge on 1 August 1962. Karve, retired professor of chemistry and former Principal of Ferguson College in Poona, was well-known to many American scholars since he had visited the U.S. several times with his wife, the anthropologist Iravati Karve, when she lectured at a number of U.S. universities in the 1950s.

D.D. Karve ran the Poona headquarters for a year, and made all the arrangements for the first batch of Institute Fellows who began to arrive in late August 1962. When the first American Resident Director, McCrea Hazlett, came in 1963, Karve presented him with a fully functioning operation that had successfully negotiated its first year. D.D. Karve in Poona and W. Norman Brown at AIIS headquarters in Philadelphia formed a remarkable team that worked together for the first crucial decade in the life of the Institute. As a skilled educational administrator in India, and one well experienced in U.S. ways, Karve was just what the Institute needed as it began to function.

THE INSTITUTE'S FIRST DECADE OF OPERATION, 1962-1972

ARRIVAL AND ACTIVITIES OF INSTITUTE FELLOWS

With its structure in place, funding secured, and personnel selected, the American Institute of Indian Studies moved toward its major long-awaited operating goal: selection and dispatch of Fellows for research and training in India.

Beginning at the end of August 1962, D.D. Karve, fresh in his job as Executive Officer, welcomed the first Fellow to arrive for research. Within a couple of months twenty-four more Fellows arrived, representing both Senior and Junior levels, that is, faculty and graduate students. After orientation for some of them at Poona headquarters, the Fellows proceeded to their chosen research sites in various regions of India. Over the first decade (1962-72), 417 Fellows came for research and language training.

Between 1962 and 1972, the number of institutions with membership in the American Institute of Indian Studies rose from the original fourteen charter members to twenty-six—it totals fifty in 1997. Competition for fellowships has always been open to any student or faculty member at any U.S. college or university, and is not restricted to those institutions that are members of the American Institute of Indian Studies.

President Brown firmly believed that Institute Fellows of all levels should get together once midway during their one-year fellowship tenure to discuss research activities, exchange information, pose questions, and air grievances. Thus, in February 1964, at the time of the Institute's formal dedication ceremonies, all Fellows in India at that time were invited to Poona for the first annual meeting. Seven such annual meetings were subsequently held between 1964 and 1970 while the American Resident Director's office remained in Poona on the hospitable Deccan College campus. The annual meetings were discontinued in 1971 when Institute headquarters moved to New Delhi into a non-academic physical setting.

ESTABLISHMENT OF REGIONAL CENTERS

From the outset, the Institute determined to set up Regional Centers in other parts of India to assist Fellows who might have problems far from Poona headquarters. These Regional Centers could arrange for Fellows' instruction in the local language and help Fellows locate housing and gain access to scholars, institutions, and facilities in some of India's distinctive cultural regions. Each Regional Center was designed to be headed by an American Senior Fellow who added Center administration to his or her own research duties. Accordingly, in 1963 American Senior Fellows were appointed for Poona, New Delhi, and Calcutta Regional Centers, and in 1967 for Madras. These Senior Fellows were encouraged to conduct seminars and bring Indian scholars and specialists together with Fellows who shared similar interests. This Senior-Fellow arrangement lasted with varying degrees of success until 1972 when the Government of India prohibited U.S. scholars, as well as other foreigners, from administering foreign academic programs in India. This meant the end of American Senior Fellows heading regional centers. The AIIS Regional Centers thenceforth were run by Indian administrators.

THE INSTITUTE'S LANGUAGE PROGRAM

One of the Institute's oft-stated major goals was imparting advanced and specialized training in Indian languages to be carried out in India for Fellows who had already studied Indian languages in the U.S. However, some Fellows from U.S. institutions other than the established South Asia centers arrived without adequate language background. To assist them, the Institute started to offer, on an *ad hoc* basis, introductory and intermediate language training. Beginning in 1963, for example, Hindi was offered in New Delhi and Bengali in Calcutta.

In 1964 the Institute determined to develop an ambitious and more satisfactory language program and appointed Debi Prasanna Pattanayak its Chief Linguist in Poona. Pattanayak was a product of the early Rockefeller linguistics program in Poona, and had then gone on to take his doctorate at Cornell. The goal of the new program was to prepare teaching materials in a number of languages, to upgrade the existing Hindi and Bengali courses, and to start a Marathi course in Poona. After having visited long-running overseas language programs in places such as Cairo and Beirut, Pattanayak set about collecting all available texts for teaching Indian languages and began to develop language teaching methods appropriate to the Indian context. He produced substantial spoken language materials and tapes in several languages, and in 1967-68 expanded his work to cover the reading and writing of Tamil.

In 1969 Pattanayak's innovative work attracted the attention of the Indian Ministry of Education, and he was shortly made Director of the Government of India's newly-established Central Institute of Indian Languages in Mysore. While the Government of India's choice of Pattanayak for this prestigious position reflected well on the American Institute, it was a great loss to the AIIS program in Poona. President Brown praised Pattanayak's signal contributions to Institute activities and noted their lasting value. The Institute's language program languished for several years but eventually recovered, as we shall see, under different directors and in different places.

AIIS FELLOWSHIP PROGRAM

Administration of the Fellowship Program has always been the central activity of the Institute. The Selection Committee, composed of scholars from a balance of disciplines and representing a number of member institutions, in its first decade (1962-1971) chose 348 Fellows (at various levels, including those for the language program) for study and research in India. Most Fellows came from one or other of thirteen disciplines, with history, political science, anthropology, linguistics, and religious studies by far the most popular. This more or less continued the discipline representation of scholars in the preceding two decades of South Asian studies. In the Institute's first decade it is significant that Fellows were drawn from nearly a hundred American institutions. The AIIS had, by 1971, twenty-seven institutional members. It is not surprising that each of the twenty-seven members had provided at least one Fellow, but it is noteworthy that Fellows were also drawn from sixty-nine non-member institutions. This demonstrates the very broad reach of the Institute even in its first decade and its role as the major means through which scholars from American colleges and universities were funded for research in India.

AMERICAN INSTITUTE OF CEYLONESE STUDIES AS AIIS AFFILIATE

The initial success of the American Institute of Indian Studies prompted scholars who had research interests in Ceylon—it did not become the Republic of Sri Lanka until 1972—to urge W. Norman Brown to extend the idea of a research facility to India's island neighbor. After some legal wrangling, Brown succeeded in establishing the American Institute of Ceylonese Studies in late-1967. It was set up as an affiliate of the AIIS and was controlled directly from Institute headquarters in Philadelphia.

This accorded with the Government of Ceylon's refusal to have such an organization directed from the Institute's Indian headquarters in Poona, since doing so would suggest the Colombo operation was just one of the Indian Regional Centers of the AIIS, rather than an entity of an independent nation-state. Once this diplomatic problem was solved, and it was deemed to be "an affiliate of the AIIS," bypassing Poona's jurisdiction, the AICS was able to use U.S.-owned Ceylonese rupees to support half-a-dozen fellowships. The AICS functioned for five years, ending in 1972 when the supply of U.S.-owned rupees ran out, and when a less friendly revolutionary government took power. No attempt was made during the next two decades of often turbulent regimes in Sri Lanka to rekindle the idea of a U.S. research institute on the island until 1994 when preliminary discussions on this goal among American Sri Lanka scholars began in earnest. These discussions led to the establishment in August 1995 of the American Institute for Sri Lanka Studies (AISLS), under the umbrella of the Council of American Overseas Research Centers (to be described below).

CONTRIBUTIONS OF INDIAN SCHOLARS TO
EARLY AIIS ACTIVITIES

At the outset, and throughout the Institute's first decade, many Indian scholars, advisers, and dedicated staff played major roles in AIIS affairs. In addition to the outstanding role of D.P. Pattanayak in fashioning the language program, scholars at many of Poona's well-known educational institutions contributed to the launching of the AIIS. S.M. Katre of the Deccan College stands out because he made it possible for the Institute to set up its headquarters on the splendid Deccan College campus. D.R. Gadgil, Director of the Gokhale Institute of Politics and Economics; D.V. Potdar, Vice-Chancellor of the University of Poona; Iravati Karve, Professor of Anthropology at the Deccan College; and R.N. Dandekar of the Bhandarkar Oriental Institute were among Poona scholars who had long been friends of W. Norman Brown and who strongly supported the idea of a U.S. academic center. In 1962 the AIIS was most fortunate in persuading D.D. Karve, member of one of Poona's most illustrious families, to be its first Executive Officer, a post he held for ten years.

The star-studded roster of academics who joined the Institute's first Indian Advisory Committee set up in 1964 included: D.R. Gadgil; V.S. Agrawal; S.K. Chatterji; C.D. Deshmukh; V. Raghavan; M.N. Srinivas; and G.D. Parikh. And the Institute's formal dedication, on 7 February 1964, featured the chief welcoming address by the Governor of Maharashtra State, Madame Vijayalakshmi Pandit, sister of India's Prime Minister Jawaharlal Nehru, as well as a speech by U.S. Ambassador Chester Bowles.

PRADEEP MEHENDIRATTA'S FIRST ASSOCIATION
WITH AIIS, NOVEMBER 1963

When the New Delhi Regional Center of the AIIS was set up in 1963, Pradeep R. Mehendiratta was hired as its full-time Office Secretary. His education in accounting and management, and his good background in English quickly led him to become indispensable to the smooth running of the New Delhi Center. On several occasions, and for months on end, the Center did not have an American Senior Fellow at the helm. Mehendiratta came to be effectively in charge of the New Delhi office, in the absence of a Senior Fellow, rendering help to scholars, and establishing contacts with government ministries for the processing of visas and income-tax matters for research Fellows. In no time, Mehendiratta was upgraded to Administrative Assistant, and by June 1969 he was named Deputy Executive Officer in New Delhi. He was promoted to Executive Officer when the last American Resident Director of the Institute, Robert Miller, settled in New Delhi in 1970 for a two-year term. D.D. Karve remained in Poona as Co-Director and supervised the gradual move of Institute headquarters' functions from Poona to New Delhi. By the end of the Institute's first ten years, in 1972, the Government of India required administration of foreign organizations to be in Indian hands, and Mehendiratta was there to assume that responsibility.

The story of the Institute's first decade is incomplete without highlighting the rapid rise of the capable and dynamic Pradeep Mehendiratta to the top job in AIIS Indian headquarters. We shall in due course follow Mehendiratta's promotion to Director (March 1975) and then finally to Director-General in 1994, capping an extraordinary march up through the AIIS ranks. Suffice it to say here that he played a crucial role in the Institute's first decade.

GOVERNMENT OF INDIA RESTRICTIONS ON
FOREIGN ORGANIZATIONS

The Government of India promulgated new guidelines in 1969 restricting the conduct of all foreign educational enterprises in India. The Government imposed close supervision of scholars and their research, requiring that Fellows be affiliated with Indian institutions in order to gain greater scrutiny of research projects. U.S. scholars were hit particularly hard because of allegations that some American projects were funded by the CIA, and because of general charges that U.S. scholars were perpetrating what was called "academic colonialism." Monitoring and responding to the new Government of India policies demanded close attention of the American Resident Director. Thus when a new—and the last—Resident Director was appointed in 1970, his office was moved from Poona to New Delhi in order to maintain the closest possible touch with both the U.S. Embassy and the relevant Indian Ministries. All headquarters' functions were moved within a couple of years.

Meanwhile, Indo-U.S. relations in general deteriorated rapidly in 1971 after official U.S. policy tilted towards Pakistan when a civil war between the western wing and the eastern Bengali-speaking wing resulted in the creation of the nation of Bangladesh. Interestingly enough, many American academics at home and in India favored India's support for the liberation of Bangladesh from the autocratic military rule emanating from Pakistan's western wing. But that stance of the American academic community did not counteract the Indian perception of official U.S. policy. Radical Indian students—and sections of the press—saw CIA involvement everywhere, and several years of anti-Americanism ensued. It did not help that the U.S. was engaged in the Vietnam War, unpopular at home, and seen as imperialist abroad.

When the AIIS appointed a new American Resident Director in 1972, he was denied a visa, and the Government of India decreed complete Indianization of the Institute administration. After W. Norman Brown retired from the Institute presidency in June 1971, Ainslie Embree was elected to the post. He presided over the reorganization of the Institute's administration and, aided by Pradeep Mehendiratta, was able to maneuver the Institute through this bad patch. But it was a tumultuous end to the Institute's first decade.

THE 1970s: CHANGES IN SOUTH ASIAN STUDIES AND IN THE AIIS

QUESTIONS OF FUNDING FOR SOUTH ASIAN STUDIES

The unsuccessful conclusion to the Vietnam War brought financial constraints on the academic community in the United States and disillusionment with aspects of international studies. The era of substantial funding for Title VI Centers was over, and many universities found it impossible to continue broad programs of South Asian studies. The Ford Foundation changed its focus from institutional support for area studies in the U.S. to support for institutions in India engaged in education of women, development of legal services, and the like. Ford's International Training and Research program which, during its fourteen-year life, had made possible dramatic advances in international studies, had come to an end in 1966 with a change of foundation presidents, and funding of that magnitude was not forthcoming from any other source. Ford grants had supported creation of half-a-dozen major

South Asian centers, but these centers now had to seek other sources of funding to continue. Nevertheless, U.S. studies of the subcontinent had taken root in the 1960s and began to flourish during the 1970s despite changes in the funding situation.

REGIONALIZATION OF SOUTH ASIAN STUDIES

Increased sophistication in U.S. studies of South Asia grew apace in the 1970s. There was a shift away from general studies in many disciplines of national, all-India problems, and the early anthropological emphasis on individual village-isolates to research on cultural, social, political, and historical questions at the regional or sub-regional level. Because of the vastness and complexity of Indic civilization, a major thrust of the past thirty or so years developed toward concentration of research on one or other of the subcontinent's cultural-linguistic regions. This brought about the need for scholars to learn one or another of India's major literary languages, or sometimes other languages such as Rajasthani, Tulu, Konkani, or Bhojpuri.

This regionalization of South Asian studies greatly complicated the curricula of U.S. programs, requiring greater depth of instruction and diversity of resources. But no one university could support specialized faculty, offer courses, and provide library resources in more than one or perhaps two regions. Students had to move around if they fancied work on a particular area, and flexible fellowships and consortium arrangements such as those pioneered in Midwestern states—for example, the CIC and ACM programs described above—made that possible.

REGIONAL AND DISCIPLINE COMMUNICATION
NETWORKS IN THE U.S.

To facilitate communication among scholars with particular regional or national interests, Americans have formed organizations, published newsletters and directories, held periodic conferences, or have met annually at the Association for Asian Studies' convention. The earliest such organizations were the Bengal Studies Conference (1965), that bridged West Bengal in India and East Bengal in Pakistan (now Bangladesh), and Research Committee on the Punjab (1966) that similarly bridged Indian and Pakistani components. Then came the Maharashtra Studies Group and Society for South Indian Studies formed in 1968; Nepal Studies Association (1971); North India Studies Association (1974); Sri Lanka Studies Group (late 1970s); Rajasthan Studies Group (1981) and Gujarat Studies Association (1988). It is important to note that by and large U.S. scholars first and foremost identify as South Asianists or Indianists, and are practitioners of a discipline, and are not narrowly or exclusively focused on their region of choice. In addition, while they have created regional organizations as communication mechanisms, many scholars of the subcontinent are involved in more than one regional, country, or discipline association in order to keep abreast of a variety of research.

A number of organizations focusing on a discipline or field have also emerged. A particularly active group is the American Committee for South Asian Art (ACSAA) incorporated in 1967. It grew out of the American Committee for the History of South Asian Art, started in 1963, which was responsible for the establishment of the American Academy of Benares in 1965. Another flourishing group is the Conference on Religion in South India which began in 1970 and has held two-day annual conferences devoted to a single topic ever since. Other such groups include the Society for Tantric Studies (1986), South Asian Language Analysis roundtable (1979), South Asian Language Teachers Association (1995), and South Asian Muslim Studies Association.

NATIONAL CONFERENCES FOR SOUTH ASIAN STUDIES

Professional organizations such as the Association for Asian Studies and special interest groups organized around regions, disciplines, and topics are arenas where South Asianists get together to give papers and interact with colleagues. But one arena has taken pride of place among all others. This is the University of Wisconsin Annual Conference on South Asia, which held its first meeting in May 1973. Every year since then it has grown remarkably in size and quality, and now attracts some 500 participants, making it the most popular and important of all meeting places for South Asianists. With upwards of 60 panels, several embedded mini-conferences and meetings of associated groups over a three- or four-day period, the autumn Wisconsin Conference has become *the* place to try out new ideas, catch up with old friends, and make new ones. Panelists, drawn from a wide range of institutions in the U.S. and Canada, and often from overseas as well, are not only from the dozen or so major centers of South Asian studies, but also include graduate students and young faculty from smaller or less well-known colleges and universities across the land, thus affording them a valuable experience in presenting their research and mingling with the recognized leaders in the field. More and more, the roster of participants shows Indo-Americans as paper-givers and discussants. This reflects a general trend in the whole field of South Asian studies in the U.S., as children of last generation's immigrants from the subcontinent enter into studies of their cultural heritage. These same young scholars are now estimated to constitute about a quarter of AIIS Junior Fellows.

PROLIFERATION OF FIELDS OF STUDY

By the 1970s U.S. scholars extended their concerns to newly developing areas of study and research in South Asia. While history and anthropology were still the chosen disciplines of the largest number of AIIS Fellows, fields such as art history, archaeology, and the various performing arts attracted many. But the field of history of religions showed the steepest rise in numbers of fellowships awarded in the seventies. In this burgeoning field scholars veered away from all-India classical Sanskrit-based Vedic and Brahmanic subjects and delved into regional religious traditions expressed in a variety of languages. *Bhakti* devotional cults of the medieval era often established by non-Brahmans, and sometimes by women, became the subject of many research projects. Developments in the Dravidian language regions in south India showed that the south was no longer seen as an appendage of the Aryan and northern Ganges Valley Civilization, but was a coherent, integrated cultural entity in itself, yet part of overall Indic civilization. In terms of research focus, American scholars were developing a balance of interest between the gangetic valley "classical" and Indo-European language area and the many manifestations of the several Dravidian-speaking cultural-linguistic regions of the peninsular south. U.S. South Asian centers began the teaching of Tamil in a big way, and within a few years Tamil joined Hindi as the most popularly studied Indian languages in the United States.

Fewer U.S. scholars from political science applied for, and were awarded, Institute grants in the 1970s, and well into the following decades as well, since the Government of India was at that time critical of the thrust of many research projects in this field, and did not always approve scholars' proposals. In addition, the academic market in America for area-specific political scientists began a downward slide in favor of transnational projects with a particular bent such as dependency theory. Thus Government of India restrictions and demands of the market combined to reduce student interest in this previously popular field.

Himalayan studies have undergone a steep rise in interest in the U.S. beginning in the 1970s. In particular, scholars have focused on Nepal. Cornell and Columbia universities as well as the University of Wisconsin and the University of California, Berkeley, have led in developing language and area training on Nepal. By 1980 Wisconsin was ready to begin a popular College Year in Nepal program.

A general burgeoning interest in Buddhism in the U.S. has resulted in the building of many academic centers of Tibetan studies. Since so many Tibetans, including the Dalai Lama (who was forced out of Tibet when the Chinese took over that country in 1950) took refuge in India, studies of Tibetan Buddhism have become a subset of South Asian studies in the U.S. The universities of Wisconsin, California, Berkeley, and Virginia, along with Columbia University have developed particularly strong centers of Tibetan culture and language. The Library of Congress field office in New Delhi has greatly supported these studies through its large-scale acquisition and distribution to American research libraries of printed copies of the many manuscripts on a myriad of topics that Tibetan refugees brought with them to India.

In addition to studies of Tibetan Buddhism, U.S. scholars have incorporated Theravada (or southern) Buddhism into South Asian studies. Several centers offer study of Pali, the medium of transmission of Theravada Buddhism, the majority religion in Sri Lanka, as well as in Thailand. U.S. students can study Buddhism in India, the land of its birth, by enrolling in a variety of institutions in Sarnath and Bodh Gaya through such programs as that organized by Antioch College.

The conversion of the "untouchable" leader B.R. Ambedkar and thousands of his fellow Mahars to Buddhism in 1956 was a symbol of protest against the Hindu majority's age-old discrimination against this lowest rung of India's society. U.S. scholars began to focus on Ambedkar the man, on his and other downtrodden castes, and on his "new Buddhism". The "new Buddhists"—*nava bauddhas*—saw their step as a way out of an existence of oppression. Beginning in Maharashtra, this step was gradually taken by similar groups in other parts of India. After a conference in the U.S. in 1967 on untouchables and untouchability, U.S. scholars increased their study of these groups. As the Ambedkar movement spread, its "new Buddhist" character became incorporated in many parts of India into a broader socio-economic, political, and literary movement dedicated to the uplift of India's 125 million *dalits*. The term *dalit*, meaning "downtrodden" or "depressed," now is commonly used for these segments of Indian society. Increasingly since the 1970s, U.S. scholars are studying various aspects of the Dalit Movement, including its original "new Buddhism".

The seventies saw the development in the U.S. of innovative interdisciplinary approaches to various social and cultural phenomena in South Asia. The Social Science Research Council's Joint Committee on South Asia in 1975 proposed exploration of South Asian conceptual systems, those frames of thought that define and create meaning for individuals and society. Scholars were encouraged to identify indigenous South Asian analytical frameworks, using them in place of western concepts in research on a number of subjects. For example, to do that, scholars looked at studies of classical and modern South Asian literature, ethnographic and linguistic descriptions, and work in other disciplines. The SSRC sponsored a number of workshops and conferences in both the U.S. and India at which scholars—both South Asian and American— explored concepts of the person, the self, and the life-cycle in South Asia; the concept of *karma* and the mechanisms through which an individual's actions are believed to influence his or her future; economic and social concepts dealing with topics such as labor, property rights, and definitions of the family; and, sparked especially by the work of A.K. Ramanujan, the value of folklore as a source of conceptual material and the way to describe the folk/classical continuum in India. These conferences have resulted in a number of influential publications that contribute to a new comparative way of looking at both South Asian and western society and culture.

MUSLIM CULTURES IN SOUTH ASIA:
ISLAM, URDU, PAKISTAN STUDIES

Muslim cultures and Islam in India have long been of interest to American scholars. For a thousand years a variety of kingdoms, sultanates, and principalities grew and thrived for longer or shorter periods in most parts of the subcontinent. Arab, Persian, Afghan, Turkic, and Mongol families and tribes set down roots in India, intermarrying and converting many Hindus to various traditions of Islam. The lingua franca that came out of these encounters—Urdu, "the language of the camp", which was a kind of Persianized Hindi—came to be used all over urban India, and not only by a sizeable proportion of the Indian Muslim community that now totals some 100 million. With Urdu speakers in the millions in India, and with similar numbers in Pakistan where it is the official language, Urdu and its renowned poetic literature have gained many U.S. students. Two events in the 1970s have facilitated the study of Urdu and its literature and provided an entrée into subcontinental Islam and Muslim culture. In 1973, after a decade of false starts because of political instability in Pakistan, a group of U.S. scholars succeeded in establishing the American Institute of Pakistan Studies, modelled on the successful American Institute of Indian Studies. The AIPS consortium originated with 22 U.S. university members, of which Duke, Columbia, and Harvard universities were the major players. The principal function of the AIPS has been to award fellowships at the graduate student and faculty level. The second major event in the 1970s was the inauguration of the Berkeley Urdu Language Program in Pakistan (BULPIP), run by the University of California, Berkeley. Set up in 1974, the program provides intensive training in several levels of Urdu at its headquarters in Lahore. Widely praised, it has encouraged a large number of U.S. students to proceed with studies of Urdu literature and aspects of Muslim culture in both India and Pakistan.

A MAJOR CONTRIBUTION: *A HISTORICAL ATLAS*
OF SOUTH ASIA, 1978

A significant U.S. contribution in the 1970s to South Asian studies in general was the 1978 publication of the magisterial *A Historical Atlas of South Asia.* The chief editor, Joseph E. Schwartzberg, professor of geography at the University of Minnesota, assembled a dedicated staff of experts and contributors. Representing many disciplines and regional specialities, they labored on the project for well over a decade. The resulting book, now in its second impression (1992), was extremely well received all over the world. The AIIS and Ford Foundation joined in sponsoring a symposium on the *Atlas* in New Delhi in January 1979 on the occasion of the distribution—with Ford Foundation funding—of copies of the *Atlas* to each of one hundred selected Indian universities and educational institutions.

THE 1970s: CONTEXT AND RESULTS OF
AIIS REORGANIZATION

THE POLITICAL SCENE IN INDIA

Against a backdrop of institutional developments in South Asian studies in the United States and political developments in India, the AIIS spent most of the decade reorganizing itself both in the U.S. and in India.

In India the 1970s were marked early in the Nixon years by bad Indo-U.S. relations. These resulted primarily from the official U.S. "tilt to Pakistan" over the Bangladesh War, and by anti-U.S. sentiments brought on by alleged CIA activities. Within India there were unsettling events on the domestic political stage.

However, after the 1971-1973 low point in bi-national relations, the general atmosphere improved considerably with a solution to the "PL 480" problem. It will be recalled that, beginning in 1954 when India faced severe food shortages, the United States enacted Public Law 480 of the 83rd Congress. Through this law, millions of tons of food-grains were sent to India to avert famine. The Government of India agreed to pay for this food aid with rupees, which, because they could not be exported, accrued with interest to U.S. government accounts in India. Since these monies could be used only for U.S. governmental expenses in India, or later on, for certain educational and scientific operations, it was possible to expend only a fraction of the rupee accounts. In fact, the U.S. could make only a small dent in the overall debt. Many Indians worried that India would remain forever in thrall to the U.S., since, even in 1971, the U.S. owned one-fifth of all of India's currency, and day by day was acquiring an even larger proportion through interest on the debt. Observers—both U.S. and Indian—realized that it was very dangerous for one country to have so much of its currency controlled by another. Thus the "PL 480" problem had become a major political and psychological problem for India.

In 1973, when Daniel Patrick Moynihan became President Nixon's ambassador to India, he set about to solve the problem in order to improve Indo-U.S. relations. After an acrimonious battle in the U.S. Congress, Moynihan was empowered to propose to the Government of India that the U.S. write off $2.2 billion in rupees, keeping $1.1 billion in rupees for U.S. use, a sum that would gradually be drawn down. Both governments were satisfied with this solution and commended Ambassador Moynihan's achievement. The ambassador thereupon presented a check for $2 billion in rupees to the Indian government. Both sides were greatly relieved. By 1998 it is expected that all remaining U.S.-owned rupees will have been expended.

Just when, to India's relief, that problem had been solved, President Gerald Ford was prevailed upon in March 1975 to lift the embargo on U.S. arms sales to Pakistan, which had been in effect since the Indo-Pakistan War of 1965. Indian public opinion and the government of Prime Minister Indira Gandhi were enraged by this U.S. act, and Indo-U.S. relations once again plummeted.

Meanwhile Indira Gandhi's domestic political position became jeopardized by a legal judgment against her involving technical irregularities in her previous election campaign. Unpopular at the time for failure to improve general living standards, and with her own campaign activities called into question, Indira Gandhi feared that mass demonstrations by an aroused opposition could force her out of office. Her reaction was dramatic. She persuaded the Indian President to declare a national emergency, which he did on 25 June 1975. Opposition leaders were jailed, newspapers censored, and thousands of persons were put under surveillance. The "Emergency" remained in effect until March 1977.

Americans were dismayed at Indira Gandhi's autocratic trampling of India's vaunted and hard-earned democratic tradition. With the Cold War at its height, India's and Indira's close and cordial relations with the U.S.S.R., and Soviet failure to condemn the "Emergency", further rankled Washington. U.S. scholars of South Asia—by and large a liberal group within American academe—had a hard time understanding how the Indian leader, whose exploits they had extolled when she supported the liberation of Bangladesh just a few years before, could have taken such undemocratic and drastic measures against her own people.

Almost as suddenly as she had imposed the "Emergency," Indira Gandhi eased up on it in December 1976 and called for new elections. She terminated the "Emergency" on 21 March 1977, and elections were quickly held. After she and the Congress Party suffered a stunning defeat, the veteran and respected former Congress—now opposition— leader, Morarji Desai, was released from detention, became Prime Minister in the spring of 1977, and served until July 1979.

Morarji Desai's two years in office coincided with the first two years of Jimmy Carter's presidency in the U.S. Carter had long been sympathetic toward India—his mother had been a Peace Corps volunteer in a suburb of Bombay in the late 1960s—and in due course he made a triumphal tour of India in 1978.

Eager to improve relations with India, President Carter selected Robert F. Goheen to be his ambassador, and Goheen presented his credentials in New Delhi on 26 May 1977, less than two months after Indira Gandhi was soundly defeated. Robert Goheen, long-time President of Princeton University, had been born in India to missionary parents and maintained strong ties with his place of birth. When the Indo-U.S. Joint Commission was established in 1974, and held its initial meeting in October 1975, Goheen served as the first U.S. co-chairman of the bi-national organization's Subcommission on Education and Culture. In that position he worked closely with Edward C. Dimock, Jr., then President of the American Institute of Indian Studies and ex officio a member of the Subcommission. Goheen took with him to the U.S. Embassy post understanding and strong support for the Institute's work in India. This relationship came at a crucial point in AIIS history and went a long way toward counteracting the difficulties the Institute had encountered in the early 1970s. All these elements combined to produce a positive two-year interval in a long and often prickly relationship between India and the United States.

AIIS ADMINISTRATION RESTRUCTURED IN BOTH
THE U.S. AND INDIA

W. Norman Brown's retirement, after ten years as President of the AIIS, came in 1971 at the height of the bad patch of Indo-U.S. relations. The Institute then chose Ainslie Embree, historian at Duke University, to guide it through a traumatic period. While Brown's was a hard act to follow, Embree succeeded in leading the Institute through the troubled waters both at home and abroad. What with the aftermath of the 1960s student unrest and the deep rifts in the U.S. academy brought on by the Vietnam War, Embree's task was not easy, and he stepped down after two years as Institute President. During Embree's presidency the Institute's Board of Trustees was greatly conflicted over the organization's character and direction. This combined with contentious Indo-U.S. relations and Indian government restrictions on foreign organizations' administrative policies and foreign scholars' research proposals, made the very future of the Institute seem problematic.

During the Embree term, 1971 to 1973, U.S. administration of the Institute was split, with its Secretariat in Philadelphia and President Embree for a time at Duke University before he moved to Columbia. This situation was clumsy and inefficient, to say the least, and communications between the President and his Secretariat inadequate, especially given the turmoil at the Indian end. The solution came in 1973 when Embree stepped down, and the Trustees chose Edward C. Dimock, Jr., Professor of Bengali at the University of Chicago, as his successor. Immediately the Secretariat moved to Chicago, and Dimock took charge.

While Brown was President, control and authority emanated from Philadelphia, but after reorganization and "Indianization," following Embree's term, the Institute's center of gravity gradually shifted to India.

In India, Institute headquarters moved from Poona (after 1975, spelled "Pune") to New Delhi in 1972, in a step designed to increase needed contacts with a variety of Indian government agencies and officials. D.D. Karve, named AIIS Co-Director during the term of the last U.S. Resident Director who was in New Delhi, tied up loose ends in Poona but remained Co-Director until 1973. After the American Resident Director left, effective control of the Institute at New Delhi headquarters was in the hands of Executive Officer, Pradeep Mehendiratta, beginning in late 1972. When Dimock became President in July 1973, Mehendiratta was named Officiating Director in September 1973 and was promoted to Director in March 1975. Between 1973 and July 1986—when Joseph Elder took over as President—Dimock and Mehendiratta functioned through thick and thin as an effective team that led the Institute to stability and the renown it now enjoys. As of 1997, Mehendiratta continues to lead the Institute in India as its Director-General, and is now serving with his fifth President, Frederick Asher.

INSTITUTE LANGUAGE PROGRAM:
UPS AND DOWNS IN THE 1970s

The AIIS from the beginning took seriously the need to offer advanced language training in India to U.S. students who had had substantial prior instruction at their home universities. The Institute's experience in the 1960s had been largely experimental and developmental in nature under D.P. Pattanayak in Poona. He had introduced instruction in Hindi and Marathi in Poona, while Bengali was offered in Calcutta, and later Tamil was started in Madras.

After Pattanayak's resignation in 1969 to become director of the Government of India's Central Institute of Indian Languages in Mysore, and after AIIS headquarters moved to New Delhi, and under new Government of India guidelines, the Institute's language program was drastically reorganized. Prior to his first year as president, Embree had spent several months in 1971 in New Delhi in an effort to revitalize the language program. But he had to contend with lack of effective staff, diminished funding, and increased governmental restrictions. The new guidelines required that Indian language programs for U.S. students be set up in collaboration with an Indian university. This was less than satisfactory in terms of teaching methods students had been used to in the U.S. Nevertheless, the Institute arranged for its students to take special courses at the University of Delhi for Hindi, and at Madurai University for Tamil. This arrangement lasted until 1977-1978, when the Government of India relented, in the wake of general improvement in Indo-U.S. relations, and the Institute was permitted to establish its own independent language programs for which U.S. participants could receive student visas from the Government of India.

The ups and downs in the Institute's language program in the 1970s mirrored difficulties in other parts of Institute operations during this decade of crisis and change. But favorable developments in its final years presaged smoother sailing on all fronts later on.

FOCUS ON ART HISTORY: FROM ACADEMY TO AIIS CENTER

Breakthroughs in contentious Indo-U.S. relations came in 1977-1978 during Jimmy Carter's presidency and the prime ministership of Morarji Desai, which followed Indira Gandhi's authoritarian two-year "Emergency." For the AIIS, this period brought the legitimizing of the American Academy of Benares as the Institute's Center for Art and Archaeology at Varanasi in April 1978. To understand the significance of this event, we need to retrace our steps to the early 1960s. (It should be pointed out that "Benares" was the British rendition of the city's name, while "Banaras" was the Hindi version of the ancient "Varanasi". All three versions are used in this account.)

In 1963, Pramod Chandra—scion of a well-known Banaras scholarly family—was appointed to teach Indian art history at the University of Chicago. Disturbed by what he saw as Indians' lack of attention to their own artistic heritage, Pramod Chandra sought to interest U.S. scholars in setting up a learned academy in India for the history of South Asian art. He organized the American Committee for the History of South Asian Art, and invited W. Norman Brown, who had just succeeded in establishing the AIIS, to be one of its members. Chandra next convened an international conference in New Delhi in 1964, chaired by Brown. This gathering endorsed the idea of setting up an independent learned academy for Indian art, comparable to the British, French, Italian, and German institutions that had long focused on Near and Middle Eastern art. With general scholarly support, Pramod Chandra was able to obtain funds from U.S. funding agencies, and in September 1965 the American Academy of Benares (AAB) was established, with Chandra as its director. When the Government of India objected that the Academy, as an independent and unincorporated entity, could not receive foreign funds, Chandra and Brown reached an agreement whereby the AIIS, as an accredited body in India, would receive these funds and channel them to the AAB. In the process the AAB became, *de facto*, an AIIS affiliate. However, the Government of India refused to accept this situation. While the government did not terminate the AAB, or prevent the Academy from functioning, it did not recognize the institution as legitimate. This stalemate of non-recognition and non-approval went on for years. For a while the Academy carried out much highly-regarded research in its center on the campus of Banaras Hindu University (BHU). But the problem came to a head in 1969 when BHU officials would not renew the Academy's lease. At that point AIIS Trustees agreed to take over the Academy and moved it across the Ganges to Ramnagar, renaming it the Center for Art and Archaeology (CAA). Nevertheless, the Government of India still refused to approve the change, but neither did it disapprove it. In the eyes of the Indian government it was still the Academy, but for AIIS Trustees it was the Center. The legal limbo continued from 1970 to 1978 when, during President Carter's state visit to India, the stalemate was broken, and Indian government approval was given to the CAA.

Despite the legal uncertainties, the art history center continued to operate throughout the 1970s, albeit at a somewhat reduced level. The photo-documentation center for Indian art, special reference library, and publication program—all initiated at the American Academy of Benares under Pramod Chandra's direction—made great strides. The Academy/Center's facilities early on proved to be a magnet for Indian scholars and students who flocked to use its excellent library and photographic archive.

The AAB-CAA has been run in its day-to-day operation by a number of Indian scholars of great repute. Pramod Chandra (son of Moti Chandra, director of the Prince of Wales Museum in Bombay) educated and well-connected in the U.S., was the moving force at the outset. He assembled a competent staff and persuaded well-known scholars such as Pratapaditya Pal and M.A. Dhaky to join the Academy. Madhusudan A. Dhaky, who came from the Gujarat State Department of Archaeology, has been with the AAB-CAA since 1965 and is the leading scholar in the on-going monumental *Encyclopaedia of Indian Temple Architecture*, a project he had originated before he joined the Academy. Contributors to the *Encyclopaedia* project since the days of the Academy have included scholars associated with the Archaeological Survey of India, such as K.R. Srinivasan, Sri Krishna Deva, and K.V. Soundara Rajan. When the CAA took over, M.A. Dhaky continued to lead work on the *Encyclopaedia* in collaboration with U.S. art historians, especially Michael Meister of the University of Pennsylvania who edited the first published volume of the project.

As soon as the Center for Art and Archaeology was officially recognized in 1978, it was able to begin organizing a number of international conferences on archaeology, epigraphy, and art history. In the 1960s the Academy had hosted several important conferences, but government restrictions prevented holding any more until the permissive years beginning in 1979.

The major thrust of the Center for Art and Archaeology at Varanasi, as indeed of the Academy before it, has been documentation. Teams of well-trained photographers and research scholars have made extensive tours all over India to photograph and measure art historical and architectural remains and monuments. Center teams, always working with government permission, have supplemented the work of the Archaeological Survey of India, which was begun in the nineteenth century under the British Raj. The Government of India requires that the Center give the Archaeological Survey of India copies of all negatives made in exchange for permission to make the documentation tours. The Center's documentation teams, composed of Indian nationals, have been able to work at many sites in areas of the country where foreign researchers are not permitted.

In over two decades of work the Institute's Center for Art and Archaeology has assembled a fully documented and indexed research collection of over 125,000 black-and-white photos, and over 16,000 color slides. In 1978, after intensive negotiations and in the new climate of bettered Indo-U.S. relations, AIIS Director Pradeep Mehendiratta succeeded in persuading the Government of India authorities to permit export of a duplicate set of CAA photos and slides to the University of Pennsylvania, which agreed to set up a special South Asia Art Archive for research scholars in the United States.

The CAA photo-archive, directed and maintained by Indian scholars and locally-trained technicians and computer experts for a recently-instituted digitization project, has emerged as a model of bi-national collaboration. Funding, policy determination, and some technical training have come from the U.S. end, with Smithsonian Institution and National Endowment for the Humanities officials providing funds and working closely with the AIIS Committee on Art and Archaeology. The Ford Foundation has been generous with dollar support for needed equipment.

The Center has been involved in archaeology, in addition to art history, insofar as one of its major research projects has been compilation of *The Gazetteer of Archaeological Sites and Ancient Monuments.* Two of the six chairpersons of the Institute's Committee on Art and Archaeology, serving for a total of ten out of the Committee's twenty-five years' existence, have been trained archaeologists. However, since 1986 no archaeologist has been on the Committee.

The operations of the Center for Art and Archaeology are supervised in India by a special Bi-National Advisory Committee. This was established in February 1977 pursuant to an agreement between Institute president Edward Dimock and Anil Bordia, then Joint Secretary in the Ministry of Education and Social Welfare. This was the agreement that led within a year to the resolution of the legal problem of Government of India recognition. From the Indian side, members of the Bi-National Advisory Committee come from the Ministry of Education, the University Grants Commission, the Archaeological Survey of India, and, in its first years, the director of Banaras Hindu University's Kala Bhavan (Center for the Arts). This Bi-National Advisory Committee was expanded in 1982, as we shall see, to include oversight of the Institute's new ethnomusicology center.

AIIS VENTURES IN ARCHAEOLOGICAL EXCAVATION

While the Institute's Center for Art and Archaeology includes archaeology within its title, the Center has not been involved in any traditional excavation. Rather, the AIIS became involved with archaeological projects in 1979 when it started to administer Smithsonian-selected-and-funded group projects such as those of Gregory Possehl and Mark Kenoyer in Gujarat; John Fritz and others at Vijayanagara; Vimla Begley in Tamilnadu; and Jimmie Shaffer in Karnataka. These projects do not go through the normal AIIS fellowship selection process, and have not been connected in any way with either the AIIS Committee on Art and Archaeology or its Center for Art and Archaeology.

The largest on-going Smithsonian-selected group project administered by the AIIS is that at Vijayanagara, under the direction of John Fritz and George Michel, in collaboration with the Karnataka State Department of Archaeology. In addition, the half-dozen seasons of excavation on Harappan Civilization sites in Gujarat, directed by Gregory Possehl, have been conducted in cooperation with the Gujarat State Department of Archaeology. Other projects, mainly in Madhya Pradesh, have involved collaboration with teams from such universities as Sagar, Banaras Hindu, and Allahabad. Such collaboration not only facilitates and expedites excavation through the local knowledge brought by the Indian teams, but it also accords with Government of India mandates on joint operations.

THE DECADE IN RETROSPECT

During the 1970s the American Institute of Indian Studies' institutional membership increased from twenty-seven American colleges and universities in 1971 to thirty-six in 1981. Some 500 fellowships were awarded in thirteen major and some minor fields, with history, anthropology, religious studies, linguistics, and art history in the lead. While there were only fourteen Fellows in art history between 1962 and 1970, fellowships in that discipline rose to forty-five in the second decade of the Institute's operation. Fellows came from all member institutions as well as from eighty-nine non-members. This represented a wider spread of Fellows' home institutions than in the first decade.

Despite drastic reorganization, changes in leadership, Government of India restrictions, and an unstable funding climate in the U.S., the Institute entered the 1980s as a thriving organization, dedicated to the maintenance and development of South Asian studies in the U.S. Most importantly, the Government of India and the Indian scholarly community welcomed the Institute. The hard work and imagination of the Institute's staff in New Delhi and at its Regional Centers paid off.

EFFLORESCENCE OF SOUTH ASIAN STUDIES:
CONTEXT IN THE 1980s

ASPECTS OF FEDERAL AND FOUNDATION FUNDING IN THE U.S.

The new decade opened with a welcome sense of optimism in both the United States and India. In the U.S. the worst of the anti-government furor of the Vietnam War days was over, and the federal government once again funded programs of international studies that had languished for several years. A growing global dimension to many aspects of U.S. life—increased tourism, academic exchanges, trade, and commerce, in addition to national security needs—drove both government and educational institutions to accumulate knowledge about far-flung areas of the world and to train specialists on those areas. After the Vietnam debacle, Americans began to realize the dangers of ignorance, especially in the context of a Cold War-induced climate of suspicion between the super-powers and their respective allies.

After 1980, the new U.S. Department of Education (upgraded in 1980 from Office of Education within a more general department) channeled funds to National Resource Centers (NRCs). Until repeal of Title VI of the National Defense Education Act (1958) by sections of the Education Amendments of 1980, NRCs were called NDEA Language and Area Centers for major world areas. The nine NRCs for South Asian studies were at the universities that had developed the most substantial teaching and research programs as recipients of Title VI grants under both NDEA and its successor Higher Education Act of 1965. The NRCs constituted central hubs that produced the greatest number of South Asia-focused doctorates in a wide array of disciplines— and hence the source of teachers who would fan out to institutions all over the country. These were, in order of establishment as earlier NDEA centers: California, Berkeley, Chicago, and Pennsylvania (all set up in 1959); Cornell, Texas, and Wisconsin (1960); Washington (1974); Virginia (1976); and Columbia (1977). In 1985, Syracuse was added to form, with neighboring Cornell, the first joint NRC.

Periodic outside reviews and competitive re-applications on a three-year cycle with stringent, frequently changed guidelines enable the Department of Education to ensure subject coverage and quality of instruction at NRCs. South Asian programs at these centers operate with a mix of federal, institutional, and foundation grants. Individual faculty members at NRCs, as indeed at other universities and colleges, carry out their own overseas research with the aid of grants from a variety of sources, one of the most important of which is the American Institute of Indian Studies fellowship program for work in India.

In the fourth decade of South Asian studies as a developing field in the U.S., the establishment of the network of NRCs—those centers that have gained national recognition at the apex of the field— demonstrates the way in which the institutional base for South Asian studies has achieved a modicum of permanence within American higher education. Five of the ten institutions that have South Asia NRCs are private universities, and five are supported by their states. All are members of the AIIS, nine at the Class A level, with an annual fee of $2,500, and representation by two Trustees on the Institute's Board. The tenth—Syracuse—is a Class B member, paying $500 a year and entitled to one Trustee.

Department of Education funding for South Asian studies is supplemented in many cases by grants from other federal agencies.

The National Science Foundation (NSF), for example, has supported such projects as the ACLS/SSRC Joint Committee on South Asia's conferences on South Asian political economy, and has funded the preparation of reference grammars of several Indian literary languages, as well as basic research on Mundari and other tribal languages. And NSF generously contributed in the 1980s to some social science projects of AIIS Fellows, as well as to many AIIS activities in India. In these projects NSF has drawn on its own allotment of U.S.-owned rupees.

The National Endowment for the Humanities (NEH), established in 1965, began in the 1970s to fund South Asian projects. Through its Research Materials Division, for example, NEH supported preparation of Joseph E. Schwartzberg's *Historical Atlas of South Asia* (1978), my own *South Asian Civilizations: a Bibliographic Synthesis* (1981), and a major compendium of Sanskrit and other classical volumes, *Indological Books in Series*, prepared in the late 1980s by James H. Nye at the University of Chicago. Throughout the decade, NEH has supported in the United States projects of translation from several South Asian languages, a variety of summer institutes on South Asian topics, cooperative programs for preservation of fragile library materials, and in addition a whole range of AIIS activities in India.

By far the largest source of American funding for overseas South Asia-related activities is the Smithsonian Institution, an independent federal agency established in 1846 that now comprises a large number of museums and arts facilities, as well as the National Zoo. It holds in trust for the nation over 100 million artifacts and specimens, and constitutes one of the world's leading research centers in science, the social sciences, and the humanities. Smithsonian's offices of International Activities and Fellowships and Grants have supported numerous South Asian projects, particularly in the 1980s and 1990s. With special Congressional authority to draw on U.S.-owned rupees in South Asian nations, Smithsonian has used these funds for support in India to U.S. projects in art and archaeology, physical and cultural anthropology, linguistics, and ethnomusicology. Most of these projects have been administered or otherwise connected with the AIIS.

Throughout the 1980s the Smithsonian Institution continued to provide the AIIS with most of the rupees the Institute needed both for its fellowship programs and its operating costs in India. Of particular significance in the early 1980s was Smithsonian's establishment of a supplementary AIIS "forward fund" deposited in the U.S. Treasury to be drawn upon by the AIIS after the PL 480 U.S.-government-owned Indian rupees ended. In January 1987, when the PL 480 funds came to an end, they were succeeded for another decade by the U.S.-India

Rupee Fund for Educational, Cultural and Scientific Cooperation, i.e., the United States-India Fund (USIF). In the fall of 1990, through an act of Congress, the AIIS "forward fund" was made convertible into an AIIS rupee interest-bearing account managed by the U.S. Embassy in New Delhi. During the next few years, over five million "forward fund" dollars were transferred from the U.S. Treasury in Washington to the AIIS-owned rupee interest-bearing account in India. This interest-bearing account guarantees the survival of the AIIS into the twenty-first century.

All in all, U.S. federal funding has been critical to the orderly development of South Asian studies in the U.S. and to the execution of exciting and productive research in India under the aegis of the American Institute of Indian Studies.

The private philanthropic foundations continued in the 1980s to support South Asian studies in the U.S., and, through the AIIS, in India. While the Ford Foundation gave, for example, dollar grants for equipment needed at the two AIIS research centers in India, other foundations in the U.S. stepped in to support projects where government or other funding suddenly evaporated. Among these organizations were the Andrew W. Mellon and William and Flora Hewlett foundations, and the Pew Memorial Trust. Some of the funds that enabled the ACLS/SSRC Joint Committee on South Asia to convene its trailblazing seminars and conferences on important and innovative topics came from foundations such as these.

EXPANSION OF SOUTH ASIAN LIBRARY RESOURCE BASE IN AMERICA

The huge U.S. Library of Congress (LC) book procurement program, headquartered in New Delhi for India, and in Karachi for Pakistan, continued in the 1980s to provide over thirty American research libraries with publications from South Asia. At the beginning of the program in 1962, participants received sets of books and serials LC acquired in multiple copies. These materials covered most subjects (except, for example, technical engineering and agriculture, and some legal areas) and included publications in all major South Asian literary languages as well as those in minor languages and dialects. If the recipient library did not wish to keep a particular title, it was free to discard (but not sell) it.

Over the years the Library of Congress (LC) book procurement program gave a boost to the Indian book industry. Many new publishers sprang up. Some specialized in bringing out reprints of invaluable volumes produced in the nineteenth century by officials of the British Raj and other European residents of the subcontinent. The range and number of publications LC acquired for program participants skyrocketed. Some American libraries were overwhelmed by materials they did not want to add to their collections. Although the books were free and cataloging information was provided, participating libraries paid an administrative fee to cover postage, local-staff salaries, rent, light and heat, etc. Over time some South Asia librarians asked LC to be more selective. Thus in 1985 the Library of Congress devised a complex profile of subject and language categories for participants to fill out and return to the New Delhi office. Each library's staff, in consultation with their South Asianist faculty, pored over hundreds of categories and submitted their choices to LC. Computer technology and an expert staff in New Delhi made this selective mechanism a great success. In the long-run everyone benefitted.

The comprehensive LC acquisitions program has, over thirty-five years, changed the nature of the resource base for South Asian teaching and research in the U.S. Of the nearly thirty language categories offered in the late 1980s, some libraries chose only one, namely English, while only one, the University of Chicago library— other than LC itself—opted to continue receiving materials in all languages. The average number of languages selected by the other two dozen libraries was eleven. Some attempt was made during this period to coordinate selection by language to minimize duplication of resources in adjacent collections. For example, the two participants in New York City—Columbia University and the New York Public Library—decided that Columbia would not collect materials in Dravidian languages, leaving that to its midtown neighbor, the New York Public Library. This is not an ideal solution for scholars who wish to browse, but from an administrative point of view it made sense. Computerized information on holdings and interlibrary loan to some extent make up for lack of immediate on-site access.

In fact, despite such shortcomings, and because of the ready availability of most program receipts on interlibrary loan (although often a transaction fee is levied) and the easy identification of titles on increasingly sophisticated databases, the resource base for South Asian studies in the U.S. has been transformed. Scholars now take the program for granted. They will be shocked when it is drastically curtailed as the rupee funding reservoir runs dry.

This has been a truly collaborative venture between Indian entrepreneurs and the LC establishment in New Delhi. In New Delhi a large number of Indian librarians and technicians are led by Americans deputed from the U.S. Library of Congress in Washington. According to U.S. law, Indian institutions cannot participate as recipients of publications, but many Indian libraries profit from the technical by-products of the operation, especially from the periodic Accessions List,

South Asia and from readily available computerized cataloging information.

Nearly twenty years of comprehensive acquisitions on India made it possible in the 1970s to prepare a substantial guide to publications on South Asia. In the late 1970s, in association with William J. Alspaugh at the University of Chicago Library, I selected over 28,000 books and journal articles, primarily in English, on virtually all aspects of India and its neighbors, and organized them into a unique conceptual framework that outlined events, ideas, and persons through time and space. With funding largely from the National Endowment for the Humanities, this was published in 1981 as *South Asian Civilizations: A Bibliographic Synthesis*. This project, along with other projects of substantiated scholarship, depended to a very large degree on the infusion into an already strong library base of books and journals received under the LC cooperative program.

PROFESSIONAL PROSPECTS IN THE 1980s FOR SOUTH ASIANISTS

The rapidly growing field of South Asian studies in the 1960s and 1970s, and the availability of AIIS fellowships for research in India, brought about production of a large number of scholars in many disciplines who had focused on Indian topics. When these newly-minted Ph.D.'s went to get jobs in the 1980s, their number exceeded appropriate appointments at the major centers. The production of historians and anthropologists in particular exceeded available and desirable openings. Many were forced to become generalists rather than specialists, and the jobs they obtained were often in colleges and universities where they would be the sole South Asianist. These "loner scholars," as they came to be dubbed, at institutions off the beaten track of South Asian programs, actually managed to inject South Asian materials into broader courses they were asked to teach. Thus teaching about India went on in an increasingly large number of schools, but it tended to be hidden under more general rubrics such as nationalism, British Empire history, or non-western literature. Outside observers bemoaned the decrease in the number of centers but failed to notice that Indian studies were often subsumed under broader labels, in other words, at some level they had become part of mainstream U.S. curricula.

Even with this dispersion of highly trained South Asianists, quite a few talented scholars were unable to teach their specialty. Many were forced to enter other fields or leave academia altogether. Some took library work, while others went into administrative positions. While retaining a lively interest in South Asian affairs, these scholars were frustrated at the lack of opportunities to practice what they had been trained in. Nevertheless, they continued to add to the general discourse with understanding and sympathy for India's position in the world and the contributions of Indic civilization throughout history. And they were avid supporters of Indian cultural events such as concerts and museum exhibits.

Some fields appear to have prospered in the 1980s even as the more traditional ones languished. For instance, religious studies—or the history of religions as it is often called—along with women's or gender studies, are two fields that blossomed in the 1980s and continue to expand today. India provides a seemingly inexhaustible pool for dissertation topics and conference papers on these two fields, and they form the subject of untold new publications by U.S. scholars on South Asia.

POLITICAL CONTEXT IN INDIA AND BILATERAL
RELATIONS IN THE 1980s

Ambassadors may or may not leave much of a mark on bilateral international relations. Of those who made a mark, we may note Nehru's sister, Vijaya Lakshmi Pandit, who played an important role as India's ambassador to Washington from 1949 to 1952 after her part in establishing the United Nations. K.R. Narayanan represented his country with distinction from 1980 to 1984, as did his popular successor, K. Shankar Bajpai, between 1984 and 1986. Bajpai—son of Sir Girja Shankar Bajpai, who was British India's Agent-General in Washington in the days just before India's Independence—was a familiar and knowledgeable figure on U.S. campuses during his term. He was well-versed in U.S. ways since as a teen-ager he had lived in Washington with his ambassador-father in the very residence he himself later occupied as his country's representative.

Memorable and effective U.S. ambassadors to India were Chester Bowles (1951-1953 and 1963-1969), along with J. Kenneth Galbraith (1961-1963) during the Kennedy administration, and Daniel Patrick Moynihan (1973-1975), who was Nixon's appointee. Gerald Ford, who succeeded Nixon in 1974, chose William S. Saxbe in 1975. Saxbe served a short and often undiplomatic term during the difficult days of the "Emergency." Following Saxbe came two U.S. ambassadors who had important influence on Indo-American relations: Robert Goheen and Harry G. Barnes.

Robert Goheen (1977-1980)—noticed earlier as the first chair of the Indo-U.S. Subcommission on Education and Culture—helped bring about improved relationships between the U.S. and India. As President Carter's emissary, Goheen managed to calm Washington's reactions to the Soviet Union's intervention in Afghanistan. And when

Indira Gandhi returned to power in May 1980 after a nearly four-year interval, Ambassador Goheen, who had pointedly maintained friendly relations with her after she lifted the "Emergency" in 1977 and during the subsequent non-Congress regimes, found that her support of the Soviet action was less than had been thought by Washington. Despite Goheen's efforts and personal good terms with Mrs. Gandhi, and despite Carter's initial sympathy, the four Carter years did not experience always smooth bilateral relations. For example, the period saw Congressional refusal to send further supplies of fuel for India's atomic energy plant at Tarapur, legally owed to India under terms of the 30-year agreement drawn up when a U.S. agency cooperated in building the facility in 1963. In addition, U.S. policy began to favor arming Pakistan in an effort to counter Soviet moves in Afghanistan. If the Carter presidency started out on 'an upbeat note, it ended without improvement in relations on the official level. While Goheen's efforts did not result in high-level rapprochement, the environment he fostered eased the situation for academics in general and in particular for the AIIS, as the Institute was soon able to expand its activities.

Ironically, events in the Reagan years, beginning in 1981, led to warmer relations between the U.S. and India. President Reagan appointed a career diplomat, Harry G. Barnes, to be his ambassador to India. Earlier postings in Bombay and Nepal had provided Barnes with a good introduction to the subcontinent, and his warm personal style assured Indians of his sympathetic approach. Barnes quickly decided to focus on areas of cooperation between India and the U.S. rather than to remain obsessed with the admittedly thorny, if not intractable, issues of Pakistan, the Cold War, and nuclear proliferation. The new ambassador presented his credentials in New Delhi in November 1981, just a month after President Reagan met Prime Minister Indira Gandhi in Cancun, Mexico, at a summit of developed and developing nations called to discuss global economic matters. While the two nations espoused radically differing views, their leaders unexpectedly got on well together, with the personal chemistry between them widely reported to be positive. This was the breakthrough that enabled Ambassador Barnes to proceed towards his goal of incremental improvement in bilateral relations. To begin with, he suggested that the President invite Prime Minister Indira Gandhi to Washington on a state visit. The visit in July 1982 was a marked success, with important promises of cooperation on several levels. For instance, Washington agreed to let France supply India with the enriched uranium needed for the Tarapur plant, thereby avoiding a Congressional fight over American export of the fuel. On the science front, the two leaders agreed to promote technological and scientific cooperation through mechanisms already existing in one branch of the Indo-U.S. Joint Commission. And most significantly, for our present concerns, Reagan and Indira Gandhi designated 1985 as "The Year of India," during which exhibitions and conferences on Indian culture were to be held all across the U.S. According to the Barnes plan, these public displays of Indo-American cultural cooperation, plus enhanced scientific exchanges, would surely constitute firm steps towards the larger goal he envisaged: a solid and lasting environment of understanding between the world's two major democracies. As we shall shortly see, the American Institute of Indian Studies was to play an important role in what came to be called the "Festival of India, 1985-86." Ambassador Barnes' calculations were well made.

Indira Gandhi, tragically, was not to live to experience the fruits of these accords. She was assassinated in New Delhi on 31 October 1984 by some of her own Sikh bodyguards, incensed by her order to Indian army units to storm Sikhism's holiest shrine in June 1984 in an attempt to quash widespread anti-government violence by Sikh separatists in Punjab. President Reagan sent his Secretary of State and four former ambassadors to Mrs. Gandhi's funeral, and to meet Rajiv Gandhi, Mrs. Gandhi's son, who was immediately and unamimously chosen by the ruling Congress Party to succeed her. Elected Prime Minister in December, 1984, Rajiv Gandhi remained Prime Minister until December 1989 when he and his Congress Party were forced out of office in regularly scheduled elections. Despite a promising start as a reformer, Rajiv had not proved himself capable of governing a complex and often fractious nation. Lack of popularity and allegations of widespread corruption led to his defeat at the end of the decade. When he attempted a comeback in 1991 after the new government collapsed, he like his mother, was assassinated. This time the assassins were sympathizers with the Tamil separatists in Sri Lanka.

Even though many issues continued to divide the U.S. and India, Ambassador Barnes' sensitivities to the bones of contention, and his bureaucratic skills in persuading the U.S. Congress that India was due a more positive approach than heretofore, made rapprochement possible between the two nations. Indira Gandhi had been ready in 1982 to get closer to Washington, and the Reagan administration began to realize the advantages of closer trade and business ties with "the sleeping giant," as Eleanor Roosevelt had characterized India many years before. In addition, by the mid-1980s a sizeable segment of the American population consisted of well-educated, well-heeled Indian professionals, fluent and articulate in English. This ethnic group, whose children were flooding into American colleges and universities, was a rising force in science, medicine, and business. Retaining strong ties with their homeland, these new Americans became increasingly concerned that Indo-American official relations improve. Events and policies in both Washington and New Delhi were discussed and highlighted in numerous newspapers targeted to this growing affluent community, estimated in 1980 at 500,000 and spread across the United States. Indian cultural and religious organizations sprouted in major urban areas, and by the mid-1990s hundreds of temples and mosques had been built to cater to a community now over one million strong.

The Indo-American community was slow to appreciate the development of South Asian studies in the U.S. But by the end of the 1980s, as more and more of their children began to study in a serious manner aspects of their cultural heritage, community leaders started to explore ways of underwriting Indian studies, in serious academic settings, not just in the many temples that by then were flourishing. We shall describe below the mechanisms devised to enable local Indian communities to support South Asian studies in higher education in the U.S. However, in many ways it was the Festival of India that served as the take-off point for incipient support and participation by Indo-Americans in academic studies of their roots.

Before the end of his tenure as ambassador, Harry Barnes successfully persuaded the U.S. Secretary of State to set up a collaborative fund using some of the rupees remaining after the conclusion of the 1974 PL 480 rupee agreement that gave the bulk of American-owned rupees to India. As luck would have it, Daniel Patrick Moynihan who, in 1974 as U.S. Ambassador, engineered that critical agreement, was in 1983 a member of the U.S. Senate. His legislative skill helped win approval for the establishment of Title IX of Public Law 164 of the 98th Congress, which set up the United States-India Fund for Cultural, Educational, and Scientific Cooperation.

The U.S.-India Fund (USIF), signed on 7 January 1987 by the Indian Finance Minister and the new American Ambassador, John Gunther Dean, held $100 million worth of rupees. Its life was pegged at ten years, which means that by 1997 the entire corpus of the fund and interest on it should have been fully committed for purposes agreed to by both governments. The Department of State was named to administer the fund on behalf of the U.S. One stipulation of the agreement was that adequate funding be provided for three existing American educational programs in India: the U.S. Educational Foundation in India (USEFI) which administered the Fulbright programs; the American Studies Research Centre in Hyderabad, the premier organization in India presenting opportunities for Indian scholars to work on U.S. history and culture; and the American Institute of Indian Studies, the leading organization through which

U.S. scholars were enabled to go to India for advanced research on its culture. The USIF also provided funds for continued operation of the Library of Congress cooperative acquisitions program along with several other library-related projects.

The concept of the USIF, and its passage through the U.S. Congress, can be directly traced to the inspired and successful labors of Ambassador Barnes. The whole enterprise of U.S. South Asian studies owes a huge debt of gratitude to Barnes for master-minding this funding operation, capping his extraordinary ambassadorial tenure. The viability of the AIIS as the leading grantor of research fellowships for specialized studies of India was guaranteed until the mid-1990s. And that was no mean achievement. At least, on the cultural, educational, and scientific levels, the U.S. and India were working in tandem by the end of the 1980s.

THE FESTIVAL OF INDIA, 1985-86: ACADEMIC CONTRIBUTIONS
AND STIMULUS TO SOUTH ASIAN STUDIES IN AMERICA

It is worth reviewing the Festival of India in some detail. Based on proposals made as early as 1979 by the Subcommission on Education and Culture of the Indo-U.S. Joint Commission, a major cultural exchange between the U.S. and India entered the active planning stage in 1982 and received the hearty endorsement of President Ronald Reagan and Prime Minister Indira Gandhi at their meeting that year in Washington. They named 1985 "The Year of India." The Subcommission then requested the American Institute of Indian Studies in New Delhi, under the direction of Pradeep Mehendiratta, to play a leading role in carrying out this collaborative cultural effort. The AIIS formed a special liaison group to coordinate the participants for the performing arts segment of what came to be called "The Festival of India, 1985-86." This entailed considerable work by Institute representatives in both India and the United States.

While billed as exchange, the Festival in effect was a celebration in America of Indian culture, with only a few exhibitions of American culture in India. Some 300 cultural organizations from both nations put on performances of Indian music, dance, drama, and film, with dozens of exhibitions of arts and crafts in over ninety American cities in thirty-one states and the District of Columbia. The gala official opening on 13 June 1985 was held at Washington's Kennedy Center for the Performing Arts, along with inauguration of a major exhibit of books, manuscripts, and maps, called "Discovering India," at the Library of Congress. Later on, the Library of Congress hosted a symposium on the American scholarly understanding of India followed by an exhibit on "The Book in India." Another major exhibit on Indian books was organized by the New York Public Library. Titled "The Printed Book in India: The First 300 Years," the exhibit was shown in the spring of 1986. In addition, the New York Public Library prepared "The World of Jainism" exhibit, presenting fifty rare illustrated Jain manuscripts held in one of its special collections and never before shown in public.

A further AIIS contribution to Festival activities involved collection of a set of publications by U.S. scholars on India for display in New Delhi and subsequent donation to a research library in India. This project was initiated by the Ford Foundation, which had asked Professor N.G. Barrier of the University of Missouri, and Chair of the AIIS Publications Committee, to gather the materials for the exhibit as well as to prepare an accompanying guide to U.S. publishing on India. This guide, released in India in 1986 by the AIIS with Ford Foundation support, was called *India and America: American Publishing on India, 1930-1985*, and listed 4,500 publications. The Ford Foundation funded the purchase of 3,000 selected titles and paid for their dispatch to New Delhi, where they were exhibited in April 1986. Following the exhibit, the collection was presented to the Nehru Memorial Museum and Library. A few years later the AIIS negotiated with the Ford Foundation to put together three smaller sets of U.S. titles that were distributed to regional libraries. Once again N.G. Barrier directed the project. With these book projects, the Ford Foundation and the AIIS joined in presenting something of the Festival of India to an Indian audience in New Delhi.

Unfortunately Indira Gandhi did not experience the fruits of her meeting with Ronald Reagan in 1982. But the cultural and academic collaboration that meeting symbolized and set in motion did much to enhance public knowledge of India and represented welcome mutual cordiality on the official level. Studies of India proceeded apace in the United States, and under AIIS auspices research and training in India by U.S. scholars increased in scope and quality. The AIIS itself rode the wave of optimism and confidence, judging by its institutional membership, which climbed from thirty-six in 1981 to forty-six by 1990.

The Festival of India evoked a sense of cultural pride in the burgeoning and prosperous Indo-American communities across the nation, particularly strong in the major metropolitan regions of New York, Chicago, the Bay Area, Los Angeles, and Houston. This cultural pride would eventually translate into the community-based endowments for Indian studies that are becoming a phenomenon of the 1990s. The Festival coincided with the emergence of a newly confident Indo-American community that was ready, willing, and able to begin to contribute to intellectual pursuits and serious Indo-American academic cooperation. What was cause and what was effect remains to be determined.

SCHOLARLY CONFERENCES: REFLECTIONS OF
THE FIELD IN AMERICA

The Festival of India, coming from the effort to foster greater understanding of India on the public level in the U.S., organized many conferences to further this aim. But while they were primarily conferences of a general nature, the decade witnessed an explosion of academic events that fit the definition of conference, symposium, or workshop. A recent tally shows that 146 such events took place in the United States in the 1980s, up dramatically from 68 such events identified for the previous decade. The tally does not include South Asia-related panels at regularly scheduled conventions such as those of the Association for Asian Studies or of discipline organizations like the American Anthropological Association. Nor does it include sessions at the annual Wisconsin Conference on South Asia.

During the 1980s, occasional ad hoc conferences addressed humanistic topics in such fields as art history, the performing arts, literature, and folklore. Many meetings focused on standard subjects such as international relations, the economic situation in India, and political developments in the subcontinent. New topics for discussion included health care and Indian medical systems. Historical subjects ranged from the Mughal monetary system to the social history of Banaras, and, in 1985, several conferences commemorated the centennial of the Indian National Congress.

Migration overseas from the subcontinent, along with what has come to be known as "the Indian diaspora," were the focus of some academic conferences. And at least eight substantial conferences on women in South Asia occurred in this decade. This rapidly-developing field of interest produced discussions on, for example, widowhood, divorce, dowry, women's religious rites, and *sati*.

This period saw major conferences on issues in several of India's cultural linguistic regions. U.S. scholars presented papers in a trail-blazing conference on many aspects of Dravidian-speaking regions of South India held in 1983, while the first international conference on culture and society in Maharashtra took place in Toronto in 1984. In 1987, under joint U.S. and Indian direction, the Rajasthan Studies Group convened its first international conference in Jaipur on conservation of the environment and culture in Rajasthan.

In addition to these 146 one-shot conferences and symposia, in the

U.S. regional organizations such as the Bengal Studies Conference, Research Committee on the Punjab, and Maharashtra Studies Group continued to hold their annual meetings.

A new entrant on the periodic conference scene, joining the Association for Asian Studies and the Wisconsin Conference on South Asia, came in 1986 when the University of California, Berkeley, inaugurated its Annual South Asia Conference. Since 1986, the California meeting has attracted hundreds of scholars from near and far for a two-day get-together to address aspects of a selected South Asia-related topic. These have included gender issues, international power relations, and historical migration patterns. This Berkeley affair has become a lively spring term counterpart to Wisconsin's autumn academic meeting.

Such conferences—both periodic and occasional ad hoc events— are important parts of the institutional infrastructure of South Asian studies in the U.S. The tightly-focused ad hoc meetings mark beginnings, set agendas, help to define fields, pose questions, reveal accomplishments, and point to the future. As means of person-to-person communication, with resultant important networking—now greatly enhanced by new technology—these conferences are invaluable tools in academe. Their number and scope are remarkable. Over 350 have been identified for the first five decades of South Asian studies, with 146 in the 1980s alone.

MAJOR AIIS DEVELOPMENTS IN THE 1980s

The favorable atmosphere in bilateral relations—albeit with a few major issues unresolved—brought about additions, and some changes, to the American Institute of Indian Studies' activities in India. In the 1980s, with Pradeep Mehendiratta at the helm as Director in New Delhi, and under two strong and highly-regarded scholar-presidents based in the U.S.—Edward C. Dimock, Jr. (1973-86) and Joseph W. Elder (1986-94)—the Institute matured, built a strong financial base, and earned the respect and cooperation of the Government of India. It became by far the most important and influential educational organization carrying out serious advanced academic research and training in India by scholars from U.S. institutions.

With funding primarily from the Smithsonian Institution, and grants from the National Science Foundation, National Endowment for the Humanities, and the Ford Foundation, supplemented later in the decade by rupees allocated to it by the U.S.-India Fund (established in 1987), the AIIS embarked on new projects and strengthened old ones.

The Archives and Research Center for Ethnomusicology. The success of the AIIS Center for Art and Archaeology directed by a group of U.S. art historians led another group of specialists to propose organization of a parallel center for their field. This was ethnomusicology, with a rapidly growing number of Americans involved with the music and other performing arts of India. They aimed to set up in India a documentation and collection facility on the lines of the art history center in Varanasi. Originally the impetus for this came from Indian scholars resident in the U.S. As early as 1971, Nazir Jairazbhoy discussed with Professor T. Visvanathan—the great South Indian music teacher at Wesleyan University—the need to establish an archive in India where copies of recordings of Indian music made over the years by foreigners, and taken from India, could be tracked down, copied, and the resulting tapes collected at a central place and made available in the country as part of its musical heritage. Such recordings were known to be in England and several other countries. In 1978 a number of U.S. ethnomusicologists joined with Jairazbhoy to discuss the idea and draw up a proposal that, after much refinement, was submitted to the AIIS Board of Trustees in March 1981. After Director Mehendiratta, in New Delhi, testified that the proposal was sound and would be acceptable to the Government of India, the Board authorized establishment of the AIIS Archives and Research Center for Ethnomusicology (ARCE). The Ford Foundation and Smithsonian Institution provided appropriate funding, and in August 1982 the ARCE was formally dedicated. At the outset, its main documentation office was in Pune, with a smaller unit in New Delhi. A senior Indian scholar from the University of Bombay, Ashok Ranade, was named Associate Director, with Mehendiratta in New Delhi the overall Director.

The core of ARCE activities is to collect, catalog, preserve, and make accessible sound, visual, and video records and recordings of a broad array of India's performing arts. Its main focus is the collection of recordings made by scholars as part of their field research. Ethnomusicologists and other scholars from many countries are asked to offer ARCE the opportunity to copy their materials after they complete their research and before they head home. These are then cataloged and entered into a computerized database and, under specified conditions, will be available to fellow researchers. Within ARCE's first fourteen years, over 7,000 hours of such primary materials have been collected and processed and are constantly being consulted by visiting scholars. The existence in New Delhi of a copy of their precious research materials serves as insurance to scholars should their originals in some way be damaged on the way home.

ARCE has succeeded in collecting copies of many aural and visual recordings made in the past by western scholars, and these important documents of Indian performing arts are now back in India. Another large project has put on tape hundreds of performances of Indian music formerly only available on fragile 78 rpm disks. As more collections of these records are located, they will be preserved for posterity in this way.

Since 1986 all ARCE activities have been centralized in New Delhi. After Ashok Ranade's resignation in 1984, the ARCE has been led by Shubha Chaudhuri, a Ph.D. in linguistics from Jawaharlal Nehru University. With her command of technical, academic, and public relations operations of the Center, Shubha Chaudhuri has developed an international reputation both for ARCE and herself. She is well supported by a group of dedicated Indian specialists and technicians.

The AIIS now boasts two world-renowned academic centers in India: for art and archeology, and for ethnomusicology. Under policies emanating from the Institute's Board of Trustees, these centers are operated by Indians and overseen by the Bi-National Committee for Art and Archaeology and Ethnomusicology Centers. The Bi-National Committee is composed of leading Indian officials and academics, along with U.S. officers and scholar-administrators of the Institute, all coordinated in this effort by Director-General Pradeep Mehendiratta. The committee meets annually to exercise its oversight responsibilities and to chart the future course of the centers.

The AIIS Language Program Reorganized. The Institute's language program underwent another reorganization in 1985 to bring it in line with language teaching methods developed in the U.S. Screening techniques were improved, and proficiency and competency tests adopted so that the AIIS could compete successfully for continued U.S. Department of Education funding. The Government of India aided the reorganization by permitting the Institute to establish two integrated language teaching centers where the new approaches would be applied, and where improved audio-visual equipment would be installed. One center, for Hindi, was moved from New Delhi to Varanasi, and the second, for Tamil, remained in Madurai.

The 1980s saw the professionalization and consolidation of the Institute's Advanced Language Program in India. Its ongoing success in its two centers is due in large part to dedicated and imaginative work on the part of the Indian staff, many of whom are sent to the U.S. to discuss curricular improvement and the rapidly evolving methods of proficiency-based language instruction being developed there. Special mention must be made of the many contributions to the Tamil program by the late Dr. K. Paramasivam.

An Andhra philanthropist, B.V.S.S. Mani, made a significant gift to the AIIS by establishing a special fund for instruction in Telugu. For three years, 1989-1992, stipends from this fund have been given to three U.S. students to study Telugu in either Waltair or Hyderabad. Their work is under the general supervision of Professor V. Narayana Rao of the University of Wisconsin-Madison. The Institute hopes that similar arrangements can be made from time to time for instruction of U.S. students in other Indian languages that are less frequently offered in the U.S.

AIIS workshops are held periodically to bring its Indian language teachers up to speed on new teaching methods, materials development, use of media, and proficiency testing. These are shared with a wide range of Indian specialists and constitute an important type of interchange among persons concerned with enhancing communication in the multilingual country that is India. It goes without saying that such collaboration could not occur without the encouragement of the Government of India, and without the administrative acumen of AIIS Director Mehendiratta in New Delhi, whose ability to work with the government and through the layers of its bureaucracy has become legendary.

The AIIS Publications Program. From its beginning, the American Institute of Indian Studies planned to publish a wide range of works written by scholars associated with the Institute as Fellows, language teachers, scholars at its Research Centers, or conference participants and organizers. The program began in 1965 with a major work by the founding president, W. Norman Brown. That was followed with innovative language teaching materials by Senior Linguist Debi Prasanna Pattanayak. The 1970s produced a dozen titles, including the first in a series of state-of-the-field volumes, *American Studies in the Anthropology of India* (1978).

The publication program picked up speed in the 1980s, with twenty-six titles including more state-of-the-field volumes detailing U.S. scholars' work on Indian art, archaeology, paleoanthropology, and studies focused on South India. Several works honored individual scholars: Edward C. Dimock, Jr. (1986), J.A.B. van Buitenen (1988), and Gerald Kelley (1992), while a volume for W. Norman Brown had come out in 1978. Also in the 1980s, the first parts of the monumental *Encyclopaedia of Indian Temple Architecture* were produced, plus several other titles on art and archaeology.

The Institute's Publications Committee worked out very satisfactory arrangements for production of its volumes with several Indian publishers. Chief among these were the Delhi firms of Motilal

Banarsidass, Oxford & IBH, and Manohar Publications. Publication in India of significant volumes of research under U.S. auspices makes it possible for Indian scholars and institutions to acquire these works at reasonable prices rather than having to pay much more for foreign imprints. The leading Indian publishers have kept up with worldwide technological developments in the publishing industry and have achieved competitive standards. The volumes of the *Encyclopaedia of Indian Temple Architecture* are testimony to the quality of production now possible in India.

AIIS-Sponsored Seminars and Workshops, 1979-1989. In the 1970s, the Government of India imposed a variety of restrictions on AIIS—and other foreign educational organizations—that prevented scholars from these groups from organizing conferences either on their own or in collaboration with Indian colleagues at Indian universities or similar institutions. By mid-1977, after the "Emergency," AIIS made representations through its Indian Advisory Committee to the Government of India to lift these restrictions and permit the holding of academic seminars and workshops. By the end of 1978, along with relaxation of government restrictions on a number of fronts affecting foreign educational institutions in India, Institute Fellows were permitted to organize academic gatherings of various kinds, including presentation of public lectures and seminars on their specialities. Accordingly, because so many Fellows wished to participate in these activities, the Institute appointed a coordinator and set up a screening mechanism so that funds could be sought and allocated.

Starting in 1979, and occurring through the 1980s, the AIIS sponsored, in association with its two Research Centers, six substantial conferences and workshops, four on art and archaeology, and two on ethnomusicology. Each event, organized by an Institute Fellow, invited dozens of scholars from India and many foreign countries. The six international seminars covered the following: "Harappan Civilization in the Indian Subcontinent" (June 1979); "Indian Epigraphy and its Bearing on Art History" (December 1979); "The Ancient Culture of Mathura" (January 1980); "Documentation and Archiving in Ethnomusicology" (September 1984); "Text, Tone, and Tune" (December 1986-January 1987); and "Perceptions of India's Past from Ancient to Modern Times" (December 1989). Papers given at these events have been published under AIIS auspices.

AIIS Service to American Educational Organizations. The Institute's great success in maneuvering through layers of Indian bureaucracy to obtain project approvals and visas for its Fellows became well-known in the

1980s, and became the envy of other educational organizations. It can be directly attributed to the assiduous networking ability of Director Mehendiratta. Over the years, Mehendiratta learned whom to contact in the appropriate ministries, exactly what information was required, and when to proffer it. By the 1980s he had managed to streamline what had been a cumbersome process of application for needed permits, and his approach was greatly appreciated by Indian government officials. Gradually, representatives of U.S. grant-giving organizations such as Smithsonian, National Science Foundation, and the Indo-U.S. Subcommission on Education and Culture approached the AIIS Director for assistance. In due course, the Institute took on, for a small fee to cover administrative expenses, the task of obtaining visas and clearances for Americans associated with a number of organizations. Government of India officials were pleased at dealing with just one U.S. group rather than several. Everyone involved benefitted, and this service represented another feather in the Institute's cap.

AIIS Membership in the Council of American Overseas Research Centers. Discussions in Washington in 1978 among representatives of nine overseas research centers (ORCs as they came to known, paralleling NRCs, or national research centers, set up in 1980) with U.S. government and private foundation officials resulted in the incorporation in 1981 of the umbrella Council of American Overseas Research Centers (CAORC). The new body's major purpose was to speak in a unified voice to government and other funding agencies in support of overseas centers in a variety of countries, to expand their resource base, to foster inter-center collaboration, and to promote transnational research. In attempting to raise public awareness of the centers and obtain increased and sustained funding for them, CAORC aimed to bring about greater U.S. understanding of foreign cultures. The American Institute of Indian Studies was one of eleven charter members of CAORC, as was the American Institute of Pakistan Studies. The American Institute of Bangladesh Studies joined CAORC in 1989, and the American Institute for Sri Lanka Studies joined in 1995. The four South Asian institutes constitute a substantial South Asian presence on the Council, where they are associated with such venerable organizations as the American School of Classical Studies in Athens (1881), the American Academy in Rome (1894), and the American Schools of Oriental Research (1900). CAORC operates out of offices in the Smithsonian Institution in Washington, and works closely with that agency.

CAORC was designated to manage competition for funds for South

Asian studies promised under the post-Gulf-War Near and Middle East Research and Training Act of 1991 (NMERTA) whose jurisdiction was defined to include South Asia. The AIIS has for three years (as of 1996) received substantial funds from that source through the U.S. Congress-appropriated monies for the United States Information Agency's (USIA) Bureau of Educational and Cultural Programs. To bring that about, CAORC prevailed upon Congress in 1993 to add a section to Title VI of the Higher Education Act for support of ORCs such as the institutes in India, Pakistan, Bangladesh, and Sri Lanka.

The unified voice CAORC promised on behalf of sixteen organizations will be significant as long as Congress does not gut the ultimate source of crucial funds, namely the USIA. While, at this juncture, CAORC has proved successful in its effort to obtain needed funding for ORCs, even if that does not continue, all will not have been lost. CAORC's very existence, bringing together in a common cause the cream of American organizations dedicated to research overseas, has been an exercise in academic cooperation that will surely bear fruit in years to come. And, importantly, it has provided the context within which the long-time and highly respected U.S. scholarly outposts in Athens, Rome, and Jerusalem have had to expand their horizons and come to learn of the existence and ambitious aims of the younger U.S. institutes in South Asia.

AIIS Transitions in the 1980s. The decade was a period of welcome changes in the language program, of innovation represented by establishment of the ethnomusicology center, of an upsurge in the number of fellowships awarded, along with increased institutional membership of AIIS in the U.S. from thirty-four colleges and universities in 1980 to forty-six in 1990. The decade also included an important transition: Edward C. Dimock, Jr., president since 1973, was succeeded by Joseph W. Elder in 1986. Dimock's presidency had begun during the difficult days of the early 1970s and ended during the days of solid Institute achievements and increasing renown that characterized the mid-1980s. That these fourteen years brought about amazing growth and a well-deserved reputation for the Institute are generally attributed to President Dimock's devoted and inspired leadership, backed at every turn by the skillful management of AIIS on the scene in India by Director Pradeep Mehendiratta. When Joseph Elder took over as president in 1986, he was heir to a smoothly functioning organization that he and Mehendiratta worked together to maintain for the following eight years, with new opportunities to make the Institute even better as it matured.

REVIEWING THE DECADE

South Asian studies in general flourished in the United States during the 1980s after a somewhat uncertain and bumpy journey beginning with the end of World War II. And the dream of W. Norman Brown and his colleagues to establish an American academic presence for research in India was realized in 1961 with the organization of the American Institute of Indian Studies. This organization reached a high point in the 1980s and soon thereafter attained the wide recognition it now enjoys. This development was aided in no small measure in the eighties by positive and supportive policies of Government of India officials in key ministries.

The seriousness of U.S. scholars' purposes in carrying out advanced research on many aspects of Indian civilization, and their reaching out to Indian scholars in a host of collaborative ventures, contributed to the success of the AIIS mission. That in turn was reflected in the U.S. by increased (but not yet enough!) representation of Indian academic ingredients in the curricula of American higher education.

Despite the tragedies of assassination in India, and the subsequent contentious Indian political environment, India started its ascent, on the basis of its working and resilient democratic structure, to the ranks of emergent developing nations, and set the stage for the economic upturns to come. With greater confidence at home, bilateral relations between India and the United States in this period were easier to maintain on a cordial level, albeit with recurrence from time to time of misunderstandings and arguments. The Festival of India was important in improving the atmosphere, highlighting the significance of cultural relations in transcending political problems. The emergence of a large and articulate community of "new Americans"—the Indo-Americans—who retain strong ties to their homeland began in the eighties to be a factor that will more and more affect the development of South Asian studies in the United States.

THE 1990s: CHANGES AND CHALLENGES TO SOUTH ASIAN STUDIES IN THE U.S. AND THE AIIS IN INDIA

INTERNATIONAL SETTING AND INDIAN
DOMESTIC POLITICAL CHANGES

Forty years of the Cold War and incessant confrontation between the two superpowers wound down quite suddenly at the end of the 1980s, just as Ronald Reagan finished his second term as U.S. president. Soviet troops pulled out of Afghanistan, and the U.S. reduced its interest in Pakistan which, until then, had been designated a "frontline" state by the U.S. for containment of the perceived Soviet threat. However, Pakistan's reported nuclear program worried Washington, and under President Bush the U.S. took steps to forestall Pakistan's development of a nuclear bomb through the pressure of curtailing aid of all kinds to India's neighbor. While this pleased India, soon some anti-India members of the U.S. Congress alleged Indian human-rights abuses in its crackdowns on separatist movements in Kashmir and Punjab, and once again the achievement, of smooth Indo-American bilateral relations was thwarted. The anti-Indian atmosphere in Congress was exacerbated by a dispute over trade, by Indian government refusal to open its insurance industry to foreign concerns, and over the Indian approach to matters of protection of intellectual property, in this case its refusal to respect patents of pharmaceutical products.

In India, Prime Minister Rajiv Gandhi had been defeated at the polls in regularly scheduled elections in 1989, and his Congress Party government was followed by two short-lived non-Congress administrations. This coincided with the Persian Gulf crisis over Iraq's take-over of Kuwait, and the subsequent coalition—but primarily American—military intervention to rescue the oil-rich nation. While India initially hesitated to take a stand, it eventually backed United Nations resolutions concerning Iraq. If that was partly because the Soviets had gone along with the American action, India's support pleased Washington and erased some of the earlier tensions between the two nations.

The end of the Gulf War came while India was preparing for another round of elections after the second minority government collapsed. Balloting, set for May 1991, had to be delayed a month in the turmoil that erupted after Rajiv Gandhi was assassinated while campaigning in Tamilnadu in a comeback attempt. Nevertheless, Rajiv's Congress Party won the elections and formed a new government with P.V. Narasimha Rao named as prime minister.

In the wake of the Gulf War, the U.S. grew more involved with the Middle East and less involved with India. It has even been suggested that the U.S., seemingly unable to fathom India's international stance in the post-Cold War world after its long-standing friend—the Soviet Union—disintegrated, was ready to ignore India altogether.

But soon the economic liberalization policies Prime Minister P.V. Narasimha Rao quite unexpectedly instituted in 1991 shortly after he took office—repealing years of protectionism that had rejected foreign investment—led to the swift and widespread interest of U.S. firms in gaining a foothold in this country of some 900 million people. The huge rising middle classes in India's urban areas were becoming avid consumers, and U.S. business wanted part of the action. The Indian community in the U.S.—the Non-Resident Indians, or NRIs—quickly saw great opportunities for helping both the land of their birth and themselves. Thus the first half of the 1990s has witnessed an upsurge in interest and investment in India by U.S. corporations as well as by highly successful Indo-American businessmen.

While, for example, nuclear test ban treaties and the seemingly intractable Indian "problem" in Kashmir continue to be divisive issues in Indo-U.S. relations, liberalization on the economic front has produced a whole new atmosphere in which Indians and Americans join in mutually beneficial and fruitful ventures. Such a positive environment bodes well for the future in general, and suggests a favorable environment for official Government of India attitudes towards the AIIS that could continue despite periodic changes in Indian administration at the top.

SOUTH ASIAN STUDIES IN THE U.S.:
STATE-OF-THE-FIELD REVIEWS

A review of periodic reviews of the nature and status of South Asian studies in the U.S. will provide perspective on what has been accomplished in half a century and will aid in placing AIIS activities into that context.

Actually, evaluation of the field in the U.S. began in 1939, but the field was then indology, the crucial core that led to the composite of disciplines that is South Asian studies as we know it. It was in 1939 that the American Council of Learned Societies (ACLS) sponsored the publication, *Indic Studies in America,* whose 242 pages listed institutions that offered courses, identified library collections of books and manuscripts as well as art holdings in museums, and included a thought-provoking review of American humanistic studies on India by W. Norman Brown. While results of the ACLS survey revealed courses and resources primarily on Sanskrit and classical Indic culture, in his contribution Brown foresaw the need to fill in lacunae in the social sciences and contemporary affairs to construct a broad basis for understanding subcontinental civilizations.

The pioneering prewar overview was followed in 1949, after World War II ended, by the Conference on Southern Asian Studies whose 1951 report, called "A Survey and Plan," proposed "an integrated ten-year development plan for Southern Asia studies." W. Norman Brown, convener of the conference, wrote in its report that, "No region of commensurate area, population, and world significance is so little known in the United States," and he lamented that, "Our universities scarcely recognize it. Our government has only a handful of trained personnel to deal with it. Our newspapers and general public are uninformed about the living conditions and aspirations of its peoples, and are baffled by their actions." The plan, devised in the wake of the conference and energetically promoted by Brown, set about to remedy the situation he described.

The U.S. Library of Congress (LC) followed up on Brown's call by organizing in 1957 a national conference to identify existing library resources and their many gaps, and to design the all-important library base needed for teaching and study of South Asia. Papers at the conference underscored the inadequacy of U.S. library holdings and led to recommendations for a massive infusion of South Asian materials. This was translated into the American Libraries Book Procurement Program for selected U.S. research libaries that began in New Delhi in 1962 under the auspices of LC and with "PL 480" funding.

Ten years after the seminal 1951 "Survey and Plan," two more conferences, in 1960 and 1961, evaluated the decade's progress. Reports on development of language studies (1960) and broader South Asian area studies (1961) revealed impressive and encouraging progress. Most of what had been recommended in the 1951 report had been achieved or started, including the long-hoped-for overseas center, the American Institute of Indian Studies, organized in 1961. W. Norman Brown, who had played a leading role in these first five assessments, was justly proud of the accomplishments he had spearheaded. U.S. academic involvement with South Asia had really taken off, and it was to surge ahead through the AIIS.

A follow-up appraisal of the state of South Asian studies came in 1969 with a report on a series of meetings held in 1968 of nearly two dozen scholars representing a variety of disciplines. For the record, seventy-seven-year-old W. Norman Brown attended one of these meetings but no longer played a pivotal role. The South Asianists who presented reviews of progress in their specialities agreed that the whole field had been successfully launched, although at a much more modest level than the parallel fields of Russian and East Asian (Japanese and Chinese) studies. Participants particularly lauded the establishment and rapid development of the AIIS which, since it began operations in 1962, had become the prime agent dispensing grants for advanced research in India by scholars at U.S. institutions.

Two substantial reviews of South Asian studies took place in the 1970s. In 1974 the Association for Asian Studies' (AAS) special Committee on South Asian Libraries and Documentation (CONSALD) held a conference in Boston to assess the scope and development of South Asian library collections in North America. Some seventy librarians, bibliographers, library administrators, and scholars from the United States and Canada met to evaluate the impact of the first decade of the massive LC "PL 480" book procurement program on library collections and research and teaching by South Asianist users. The conferees discussed both the quality and quantity of publications chosen in the field by LC for program participants, and suggested means for improving selection and tailoring the program to the needs of individual libraries so that they would not be overwhelmed by unwanted publications. Emerging from this meeting, definition of national as well as local needs led to the formulation of plans for interlibrary cooperation and sharing of resources in the South Asian field.

In 1978 the AAS' South Asia Council (SAC) called a meeting to evaluate the field of South Asian teaching and research and to devise what it called, somewhat ominously, "strategies for survival and development in South Asian studies" in the 1980s. Members of the Council addressed questions of language training, access of scholars off the beaten track to major American library collections, and the role of the leading federally-funded centers in relation to smaller programs in the field. The South Asia Council's own funding had just been drastically cut, and it was no longer able to fund special bibliographic projects or conferences as it had in the past. Thus its role in the development of the field was diminished, reduced from an operational to an advisory role on the national scene.

To some extent the AIIS managed to take up the South Asia Council's representational role through annual meetings of Trustees, part of whose job was to publicize needs and activities of South Asianists when they returned to their campuses. The periodic meetings of the directors of the South Asian language and area centers also helped to maintain a national perspective. After changes in federal legislation in 1980 that brought about establishment of the National Resource Centers and the repeal of the National Defense Education Act, more mechanisms for outreach and communication from the hubs to outlying programs and loner scholars were put in place. The major centers were mandated to allot 15 per cent of their federal funding for such activities as providing teaching kits to local schools so that pre-collegiate students might have some access to materials on Indian history and culture. In addition, NRCs began to produce widely disseminated newsletters that reported on faculty and student activities, reviewed selected books, concerts, and art exhibits and began to develop contacts with the local Indo-American community.

South Asian studies did survive into the 1980s, and quite well, despite the forebodings of 1978. The Festival of India helped in this, as did the increasingly important communications role of the University of Wisconsin's Annual Conference on South Asia.

Continuing concerns over South Asian languages in U.S. higher education curricula prompted Department of Education officials to convene a meeting in February 1987 to assess progress, identify problems, and chart the future course of efforts to promote the study of these languages. In that month, a two-day conference of center directors and language specialists focused on "Purposes and Methods of Language Teaching at South Asia National Resource Centers in the 1990s."

In 1989 the AAS provided funds for its South Asia Council to prepare a lavish brochure titled *South Asian Studies in North American Higher Education,* destined for distribution to university and college administrators, to federal granting agencies, and to foundations. Its message was clear: the recent contraction in attention to South Asian studies on U.S. campuses and by federal granting agencies must be reversed. Colleges and universities must promote—not reduce—teaching and research on South Asia in order to counteract U.S. ignorance of regions and peoples of an increasingly interdependent world. The message had not changed from W. Norman Brown's warning issued a generation earlier. Thus, in the 1980s, the South Asianist scholarly community made a strong pitch in promoting the accomplishments and continuing needs of their field.

The latest state-of-the-field reviews began in 1993, sponsored once again by the South Asia Council of the AAS. The first session was held for three days in April 1993 at the University of Pennsylvania and dealt with "South Asian Languages in the Curriculum." By now it should be clear that teaching and learning the languages of the subcontinent have been enduring concerns over the past fifty years. Sanskrit for classical studies, and Hindi for the modern period, were early on seen to be far from the only languages needed for study of India's multi-regional landscape. Nineteenth-century Christian missionaries had found that out when training their people for work in the field, as did British colonial administrators. But somehow that reality was slow to be accepted in late twentieth century U.S. academe. "Simplistic thinking about the macrocosm of India," in Edward Dimock's 1967 words, had to be slowly replaced by examination "in necessarily minute detail [of] the single strands which make up the complex fabric of the subcontinental totality." Since those strands represent dozens of "exotic" linguistic entities in many cultural regions, enormous and on-going efforts have been made to provide U.S. students and scholars with the language tools needed to begin to comprehend areas within the macrocosm. The American Institute of Indian Studies has reflected this imperative with emphasis on its sophisticated language program, a program that is second only to the overall fellowship program that takes pride of place in the list of the Institute's priorities.

The April 1993 assessment of instruction in South Asian languages was followed in November 1993 by two sessions on the future of South Asian studies as a whole in the U.S. These were held in connection with the 22nd Annual Conference on South Asia at the University of Wisconsin. Some fifty conferees dealt with issues such as introduction of South Asian content into undergraduate education; infiltration of South Asian cases into regular courses in a variety of disciplines; and library collections and the dissemination of recorded knowledge. Most urgently, participants addressed the questions of institutional constraints on the part of deans and department faculty, funding from traditional and new sources, and suggested possible new modes of institutional cooperation.

Participants in the November meeting agreed to hold follow-up sessions annually on the final day of the regular Wisconsin conference. Accordingly, in 1994 the first "Sunday at Madison" event took place. This covered development of a national agenda for teaching South Asia studies, and a rational nationwide program of library acquisitions and access to them. In addition, a number of specialists described new syllabi designed to introduce South Asian topics into undergraduate curricula. If this could be accomplished at the collegiate level, it might serve to recruit a new crop of graduate students into the field.

The 1995 review on "Sunday at Madison" presented the latest developments in Internet access and other electronic resources for the South Asian field both within the U.S. and worldwide. By now, for example, U.S. scholars can obtain information directly from the AIIS' ethnomusicology center in New Delhi via an on-line address. Such innovations in comunication technology constitute changes and prospects for South Asian studies quite unimagined a few short years ago. In an era of tight money and shrinking resources, increased rapid communication among and between institutions and individuals is essential in order to avoid wasteful and costly duplication of effort.

Up to now, periodic face-to-face reviews of the field have constituted an important means of communication in the development and maintenance of the institutional base for South Asian studies. Perhaps they have been overtaken, or at least enhanced, by the newly available electronic networks. Be that as it may, the decade-by-decade assessments of the field's first fifty years presented here were crucial to its orderly, and quite remarkable, development. Whether face-to-face, or electronically, periodic reviews will need to be continued in the future, perhaps even more frequently than before, since technology undergoes rapid and unforeseen changes.

INSTITUTIONAL INNOVATIONS FOR
SOUTH ASIAN STUDIES IN THE 1990s

Funding constraints, experiments and challenges of cooperation, changes in constituencies, and technological advances in communication are the major institutional issues for South Asian studies programs at American colleges and universities in the last decade of the twentieth century.

Funding and Other Institutional Constraints. Without a centralized, national system of education that can determine language goals and overall plans with assured funding for more than a year or two at a time, adminstrators of most institutions of higher education in the U.S. spend an inordinate amount of time and energy—not to mention much of their money—on fund-raising. Few can mount major campaigns for enough funds to plan rationally for the long haul. This resultant piecemeal approach requires careful and constant scrutiny by small constituencies such as South Asian studies so that they can survive, let alone prosper, within the larger environment. Scholars of necessity become lobbyists, if not hunters and gatherers, in institutional, federal, and foundation jungles. It takes years for a relatively new and sparsely populated field such as ours to achieve any sort of permanence in an academic setting, and in many disciplines it is a constant struggle for a South Asianist practitioner to gain a solid footing. And when he or she moves or retires, it is another struggle at that institution to fill the empty slot with another South Asianist. Such is one of the realities of life within the ivory tower. Vigilance, determination, and optimism are all needed. What also may help is outside pressure from the AAS' South Asia Council and from the increasingly well-known AIIS.

Cooperation in the 1990s: Academic Consortia. There are many modes of cooperation among institutions. We noted earlier the CIC, the consortium of a dozen Midwestern universities that have banded together for specific functions. Among these functions were the summer language institutes of the late 1960s, and later "traveling scholar" arrangements that affected South Asian graduate students. New CIC programs for sharing library resources will be noted below.

At the national level, there are four consortia of American institutions for South Asia studies conducted overseas: AIIS (1961) for India; AIPS (1973) for Pakistan; AIBS (1989) for Bangladesh; and AISLS (1995) for Sri Lanka. The main function of these organizations is, in cooperation with the host countries, to provide fellowships for advanced graduate student and faculty research. In this historical survey we have focused on the AIIS, the oldest and most developed of this genre.

Regional cooperation is represented by the Triangle South Asia Consortium in North Carolina established in 1989, and formalized by creation of an executive committee in 1990. Its members are Duke University in Durham, North Carolina State University in Raleigh, and the University of North Carolina at Chapel Hill. The name "Triangle" refers to Research Triangle Park, a center for industrial and governmental research in the area bounded by the three major universities that support it and on which it depends for staffing and expertise. In 1977 the National Humanities Center, an independent organization with residential facilities for scholars in various humanistic disciplines selected in annual competition to carry out research and writing in their fields, chose to locate in Research Triangle Park.

The Triangle South Asia Consortium had grown out of a colloquium started in 1987 to provide a forum for presentation of work-in-progress by South Asianist faculty at the three universities, and from time to time by those at other institutions in a broader surrounding area reaching into South Carolina and eastern Tennessee. The ongoing colloquium rotates among the campuses and now includes graduate students as well as scholars who are visiting residents of the National Humanities Center.

In 1991 the Triangle Consortium introduced an experimental three-university team-taught course on South Asian cultures initially held at the Research Triangle Institute, a centrally located neutral site that offered accommodations. This core course has evolved into a teleconferencing format, with students participating on each of the three campuses, with all faculty present for all sessions. With the help of a 1995 U.S. Department of Education grant, the consortium is developing special techniques and modules for this innovative operation. The federal grant is also being used to design Hindi-Urdu language instruction through an advanced interactive televideo format for which appropriate new techniques are being developed. Within three years, the Hindi-Urdu program will be available to students of all three universities in the Triangle Consortium. These consortium activities are being carefully watched by other American institutions interested in adapting such new approaches to teaching about South Asia on their own campuses.

By pooling the substantial resources in the consortium, all manner of cultural events, lectures, and symposia are held jointly, thus minimizing costs. This is indeed a model cooperative approach to utilizing South Asianist talent, and it is a model that could be emulated in other regions of the U.S. where South Asianists work in neighboring universities. It is an imaginative institutional innovation that should lead to better use of resources. Since each of the three universities in the Triangle Consortium is a Class B Member of the AIIS, this strengthens the Institute's presence in an important and rapidly-growing region of the U.S. that has long been underrepresented on the national level of South Asian studies, and in the AIIS.

In 1993 the Triangle Consortium succeeded in garnering substantial Rockefeller Foundation funding to set up a four-year Residency Research Institute in the Humanities focused on "South Asian Islam and the Greater Muslim World." Each of the consortium members contributed to the major initial Rockefeller grant. This project runs from 1993 to 1997, with a fifth year planned. It gains for the consortium and its affiliated scholars considerable applause from their respective university administrations who have been impressed by the consortium's clout in attracting substantial funds.

Cooperation in Undergraduate Programs Overseas. While the major overseas institutes are geared towards pre-dissertation and faculty research in the field, a number of U.S. colleges and universities have devised programs for undergraduates to spend summers, semesters, or sometimes an entire academic year on introductory study tours in South Asia.

The pioneering program was developed at the University of Wisconsin in 1961 when the Carnegie Corporation funded a year-long pilot program affiliated with Delhi University. Wisconsin's full-blown College-Year-in-India began in 1962 under Joseph Elder's direction and was opened to nationwide competition. Over the years it established sites in Varanasi, Hyderabad, and Madurai. Requiring a summer of intensive language training (Hindi-Urdu, Telugu, or Tamil) on the Madison, Wisconsin campus prior to departure for an additional year of language training, tutorials, and fieldwork projects in India, by 1996 Wisconsin's program had enabled over 800 U.S. undergraduates to study for an academic year in India. This constituted a model for cooperation in developing studies of South Asia—and in South Asia—for undergraduates.

Study abroad, so common for generations of undergraduate students of western civilization who routinely went off to France, Italy and other European cultural destinations, did not get organized for India until Wisconsin's structured academic program was set up. Some less-academically-oriented programs had existed earlier, for example, the Experiment in International Living which took young Americans to various countries to stay with local families and experience the foreign culture. Many such attempts have been made to promote intercultural education, cross-cultural communications, and a global outlook. The School for International Training now runs college-semester-abroad programs for undergraduates in many countries, including India. But such programs seldom include the same level of intensive Indian language training as some of the college- and university-affiliated programs.

A few examples will illustrate the trend towards overseas programs for students selected in broad-based competition. The Associated Colleges of the Midwest (ACM) began its Program on India in 1969 for students from its thirteen (later fourteen) member colleges. Starting with orientation and intensive study of Marathi on an ACM campus, students proceed to Pune to complete a year's work on the Maharashtra region of western India. In 1977 Davidson College in North Carolina started its Semester-in-India program and established a collaborative relationship with Madras Christian College. In 1990 a consortium of colleges extending from Whittier College in California to Bowdoin College in Maine launched their fall-semester South India Term Abroad (SITA) program in Madurai, Tamilnadu. In 1992 Duke University inaugurated its Duke-in-India program that takes students to Bombay for six weeks each summer to focus on Indian history and, in India's film capital, to study the influence of modern media on contemporary Indian life. Penn-in-India began its six-week summer session in Pune in 1994, and its students, drawn from a variety of U.S. institutions, could choose from courses on such topics as cultural history, traditional medicine, the Indian economy, and various performing arts, all taught by University of Pune faculty. The University of Virginia started a more elaborate semester-long program at Jodhpur in Rajasthan, where students can study Hindi and the vibrant regional history and culture of this desert area of northwest India.

A highly distinctive and focused program was started by the University of Wisconsin in 1993. Emerging out of the long-standing special interest on the part of some Wisconsin faculty in South Asian martial and performing arts, the university established the Kerala Summer Performing Arts ten-week program open to graduate and undergraduate students chosen in a national competition. This program begins with an intensive orientation program in Wisconsin after which students fly to Thiruvananthapuram (formerly Trivandrum) in Kerala. There students receive ten weeks of training in one or two of Kerala's performing or martial arts. Students also take a cultural seminar that focuses on Kerala's history and culture and includes instruction in the Malayalam language.

While many other overseas programs exist for undergraduate study in India, these just described represent some of the best-established and the most innovative. Furthermore, all manifest a high degree of the inter-institutional cooperation that promotes variety and minimizes costly duplication of effort.

Cooperation among U.S. South Asia Library Collections. A key element in the development of South Asian library resources in the U.S. has long been cooperation. The LC acquisitions program, started in 1962, was based on joint participation of LC and major American research libraries. The latter agreed to pay LC an administrative fee and to make widely available the materials they received from New Delhi. Cooperation inhered in the fact that the participants entered into this scheme for the general national good of providing research materials for a growing scholarly field. Participants sometimes made recommendations to LC regarding selection decisions and a number of technical processing matters. Thirty-five years of this cooperative enterprise, in which over thirty libraries now take part, have successfully filled the glaring gaps in the national resource base that were identified at the 1957 conference hosted by LC.

In these thirty-five years the scale of the program can be seen in recent statistics from the University of Chicago Library, which, after LC itself, has accepted the publications sent from South Asia at the most comprehensive level possible. (Other libraries from the beginning rejected certain subject or language categories). Since 1962 Chicago reports that it has, as of 1996, received 234,136 books and 15,858 serial titles. It has added to its permanent collection 93 percent of the books received (7 percent were outside of its collecting guidelines) and 30 percent of the serials (many serials and periodicals have only a short life and disappear). Of the books received, an amazing number, 157,617 or 67 percent of the total, are in one or another of over thirty South Asian languages, including Sanskrit and other classical languages. English-language receipts total 76,519, or 33 percent. While not all libraries have collected at this comprehensive level, ready access to the University of Chicago collection is assured through interlibrary loan. Identification of what is available is now made easy by electronic databases.

The Center for Research Libraries (CRL) is a major independent cooperative enterprise situated in Chicago, that was designed to collect, store, and make available lesser-used materials that both complement and supplement collections of leading American research libraries. One of CRL's primary foci is on foreign materials, and, within that category, it has had a historical commitment over four decades to acquiring South Asian titles. Over 50 percent of the serials and official government documents it receives are from South Asia. CRL also receives numerous contributions from its more than 130 members, scattered across North America. These members, through their links with CRL, are afforded access to many South Asia publications not likely to be in local collections.

One of CRL's important functions in support of South Asian studies is administrating, housing, and loaning out a rapidly growing collection of microforms on subcontinental affairs. These are both current and retrospective. This special collection was initiated in 1969 by the independent South Asia Microform Project (SAMP), a consortium of over two dozen paid institutional subscribers in the U.S. and Canada. CRL has administered SAMP since 1967, houses its microform collection, and sends requested titles out on loan to member libraries. It grew out of a loosely organized group of South Asianist historians who, in the early 1960s, saw the need for building a collection in the U.S. of basic texts for study of nineteenth-century India. They urged collection of early newspapers, provincial administration reports, and other long-runs of documents needed for historical analysis. After a few years of attempts on the part of some individuals to bring this about, the group became an informal part of the AAS' Committee on South Asia. When that did not bring about the desired results, they became an independent consortium, with an elected board and carefully crafted rules. The SAMP board works with CRL to increase the consortium's holdings of often unique materials, chosen according to suggestions from its members. SAMP has thus become an important part of the library base for South Asian studies and reflects the wisdom of cooperation.

In the context of shrinking budgets in the 1990s, and anticipating a period in the near future when the LC program from South Asia will be drastically curtailed, members of the South Asia library community across the U.S. have begun to explore a wide array of additional cooperative arrangements for sharing information and conserving resources by reducing duplication. Three regional consortia have been formed to develop appropriate mechanisms to accomplish this. Each focuses on a different objective.

The first new body is the South Asia Consortium-West (SAC-West) made up of the University of Washington; University of California, Berkeley; University of California at Los Angeles; University of Texas at Austin; and the University of Hawaii. The five members have signed a five-year agreement to coordinate among themselves collection of subjects or languages deemed important for South Asian studies at their institutions. Collecting responsibilities will thus be shared and costs minimized in the post "PL 480" era.

The second group, the South Asia Consortium-East (SAC-East), consists of Columbia, Harvard, Cornell, and Syracuse universities, along with the universities of Pennsylvania and Virginia, the New York Public Library, and LC itself. SAC-East is devising a plan to distribute ongoing collection responsibilities among its members and to provide adequate coverage for South Asian studies on the East Coast.

Through the long-established Committee on Institutional Co- operation (CIC) in the Midwest, six of its members with special South Asian focus are developing special electronic resources for access to and sharing of their collections. The six libraries involved are at the universities of Chicago, Illinois, Iowa, Michigan, Minnesota, and Wisconsin.

In order to ensure a national approach, CRL has recently taken the lead in coordinating the three consortia by establishing a South Asia Working Group (SAWG). The group's charge is to determine the most efficient use of the LC Cooperative Acquisitions Program—the latest name of the New Delhi-based operation—when its rupee support is reduced or ended.

A variety of other cooperative ventures will inevitably be spawned, both for acquisitions and access. An example of a joint approach designed to address one important access problem is the recent formation of a cooperative project to index articles in a large number of English-language South Asian journals. Only a few such journals are indexed in western bibliographic sources. To make such literature accessible, and since several U.S. libraries hold these periodicals as a result of the LC acquisitions program, six South Asia NRCs have jointly funded a scheme to index carefully selected journals for the years 1972 to 1993. The entries will be computerized with eventual wide access. The South Asian NRCs that have joined in underwriting this project are at Columbia and Cornell universities, and the universities of Pennsylvania, Texas at Austin, Washington, and Wisconsin. This cooperative effort will go a long way toward bibliographic control of significant information. The resultant machine-readable database will eventually be available for scholars in South Asia itself.

These cooperative library developments may prove to be of immense importance for the continued building of the essential underpinnings of the institutional base for South Asian studies in the U.S. They are indeed the wave of the future.

THE INDO-AMERICAN COMMUNITY: PARTICIPATION IN
AND SUPPORT OF SOUTH ASIAN STUDIES

Indo-American Students and South Asian Studies. The well-established Indo-American community in the U.S. now numbers over one million persons, scattered across all the states, but with large concentrations in half a dozen metropolitan areas. Traditionally most active in such fields as business, the medical professions, and scientific research, Indo-Americans were not very aware until recently of the humanities and social science components of the academy. Now many second-generation Indo-Americans who have entered college seek out courses that will inform them of their cultural heritage. And they are finding many such courses at a large number of colleges and universities, either in major South Asian centers or offered by "loner" South Asianists in many institutions away from the centers. While their elders often maintained ties with their South Asian roots by forming associations based on region and language of origin and by building temples—often of a universal Hindu rather than a regional or sectarian orientation—the younger Indo-Americans are flocking to college courses on Indian traditional culture and especially to language courses.

South Asian language classes in America are now filled with Indo-American students who bring with them familiarity with the sounds of their parents' language, and perhaps with some rudimentary conversational skills. Students of non-South Asian descent do not have that advantage, and, as a consequence, the teacher is faced with the problem of two distinct groups within the class. The solution is usually to set up two sections and address their differing needs separately. While this works, it is time-consuming for the teacher. The Indo-American student section advances to reading and writing more quickly than the other group which first had to master the basics of a strange phonetic system and grammatical structure.

In South Asian studies classes other than language, Indo-Americans come with some prior knowledge of cultural concepts and historical events, but also sometimes with preconceptions inherited from their families. The challenge here for the instructor is to demonstrate the complexity and diversity of their cultural heritage, and to induce in them an objective approach that transcends any initial biases they may have brought to their study.

In recent years, about 25 percent of AIIS Junior Fellows have been of South Asian descent (some were Indian citizens, but most were U.S. nationals). They are highly motivated and well trained, and since the AIIS Selection Committee is "background-blind," a large number survive this strenuous competition.

Indo-American Community Endowment of South Asian Studies. As members of the Indo-American community came to know of the existence of South Asian studies in U.S. institutions of higher learning, perhaps through the participation of their children in the courses offered, they have been approached by university representatives eager to gain their support. Beginning in the 1980s, and gaining strength in the 1990s, community-based fund-raising campaigns have resulted in establishment of endowed chairs in South Asian studies. The development of this source of support is generally seen to be a major institutional innovation in recent years.

The first attempt to tap the South Asian immigrant population actually was made in Canada, which has sizeable communities originating in the subcontinent. While Hindi was already offered, students at the University of British Columbia pressed for instruction in Punjabi, the language of their families in the largely Sikh community in Vancouver. Discussions over several years resulted in a decision to establish a chair in Punjabi and Sikh studies. The Canadian government agreed to provide half the needed funds, with the other half coming from the large and well-to-do local Sikh community. This development fitted well into the official Canadian policy supporting multiculturalism. The chair was established in 1987 and is the first Indian community-based endowment in North America.

Buoyed by the success of the campaign in British Columbia, South Asianists at some American universities sought to follow suit. Sikhs in northern California offered to support a similar position at Berkeley, but the strings they attached to their offer forced the university to refuse it. Nevertheless, Punjabi language courses are routinely taught.

Following that failed attempt, the University of California, Berkeley, has been remarkably successful in tapping into the Bay Area's Indo-American community, with its very large presence in Silicon Valley. Between 1991 and 1996 three endowed chairs of South Asian studies have been established on the Berkeley campus. The first, established in 1991, is the Indo-American Community Chair in India Studies. It is designed to bring to the campus distinguished visitors from India for teaching and lectures in a variety of disciplines. The chair will soon be filled by a permanent appointee.

The second is the Sarah Kailath Chair in India Studies, endowed by Thomas Kailath, an Indo-American professor at Stanford University who named the chair for his wife. The chair is designed to support programs of Berkeley's Center for South Asian Studies. Appropriately, its first holder, chosen in 1995, is Robert Goldman, professor of Sanskrit and current chair of his department. The third chair at Berkeley was established with funds from Tamil-speaking Indians from all across the U.S. and Canada. This is the Chair in Tamil Studies, to which George Hart, long-time teacher and Professor of Tamil Studies at Berkeley, was appointed in 1996.

The success of the Berkeley endowment drives can be attributed to three factors: the energetic articulation of university needs by its South Asianist scholar-administrators, the enthusiasm of the local Indo-

American community, and the continued support and participation of Indian government officials from both the Embassy of India in Washington and the Indian Consulate-General in San Francisco. In addition, we may note that the University of California has a relatively low minimum requirement for funds necessary for establishing an endowed chair. In policy matters, neither community representatives nor Indian government officials exercise any say whatever over the way the endowments are used. That is the province solely of academic administrators.

Columbia University's currently active fund-raising campaign for South Asian studies began in 1991 and is steadily advancing towards the $3 million the university requires as minimum for establishing an endowed chair. Well over one thousand members of the large New York-area Indo-American community have contributed as individuals, and several benefit cultural events have added to the total. When the campaign achieves its goal, Columbia will establish a chair whose incumbent will focus on the political economy of India. In due course, a similar campaign is proposed for a humanities position.

Meanwhile, the influential Hinduja family, with business interests in many parts of the world, has made a major grant to Columbia through its Hinduja Foundation. In May 1994 these monies established the Dharam Hinduja Indic Research Center within Columbia's Department of Religion. It is a memorial to Srichand P. Hinduja's son Dharam, who had studied both at Columbia and the University of Pennsylvania's Wharton School of Business, but who died tragically in 1992. The Center's purpose is to explore outstanding features of India's ancient heritage, in an effort to build bridges between the past and the present, India and the world, and across generations. The initial Hinduja grant is for five years, and there is a possibility of renewal. This is an example of the way in which an eminent Indian family has seen fit to contribute to the study of India in the U.S.

A somewhat unexpected entrant onto the endowment scene is Indiana University in Bloomington—unexpected because this university has not had a program or center for studies of the subcontinent, rather just a small number of individuals in separate departments who have focused on the subcontinent. Beginning in the early 1990s, the local and regional Indo-American community—led by a Bengali-speaking professor of geology at the university—hatched the idea of encouraging more coordinated studies of India on the campus. They pressed the university to identify scholars in its midst who had expertise on India in such fields as literature, music, religion, folklore (one of Indiana's major strengths), and political science. The university agreed to do this and authorized its Institute of Religious Studies to start a fund-raising campaign to support Indian studies. Shortly thereafter the Indo-American group decided to aim at establishing the Rabindranath Tagore Chair in Indian Civilization as the central pillar of a larger program. The campaign was strongly supported with a publicity drive by the Indian Consulate-General in Chicago, which has jurisdiction over the Indiana section of the Midwest. By 1994 the requisite funds had been collected, and the university offered the new professorship to Gerald Larson, a well-known scholar of Indian religion, philosophy, and Sanskrit. He was appointed to the chair in July 1995. The university has also started an undergraduate India Studies Program, and plans are afoot to develop graduate work beyond what already exists. This activity spurred Indiana University to seek membership in the American Institute of Indian Studies, and it was accepted as a Class B Member in 1996. Such membership further highlights the university's determination to be an active player on the South Asian studies stage in the U.S. The Indiana University fund-raising brochure explains well the motivation of Indo-Americans in supporting studies of their cultural roots:

Indian families are becoming American families, [but] they do not want to lose sight of their origins. They want to pass on to their children the history, culture and religion of India. An India Studies Program in Bloomington will be a place where the children of Indian immigrants can examine their roots.

Another chair in the field has been established at the University of Michigan at Ann Arbor. A ten-year campaign to set up a Chair in Sikh Studies was successfully concluded in 1996. Funds for a $2 million endowment came from members of the large Punjabi-speaking Sikh community spread across southeastern Michigan. The project was organized by the Sikh Association, in cooperation with the university's Center for South and Southeast Asian Studies and its International Institute. Appointment to the chair, scheduled to occur in late 1996, will be made jointly by these universities' bodies and the appointee's department, which could be fields such as history, literature, political science, or religion. With course offerings in the Punjabi language since 1991, Michigan thus joins the University of British Columbia in having established specialized endowed programs of study in the language, history, and culture of one of India's most dynamic and distinctive communities, whose members can now be found throughout the world. Not to be outdone, Sikhs in the New York area are intent on joining to underwrite Punjabi and Sikh studies at Columbia University.

Major community-based fund-raising campaigns have been carried on since 1992 at two other NRCs, namely the University of Texas at Austin and the University of Virginia. Both aim to establish endowed chairs in South Asian studies. The Indian Consulate-General in Houston is cooperating in the Texas campaign to mobilize donations, as is the Embassy of India for the Virginia-Greater Washington area effort.

Meanwhile, on a smaller scale, Indo-American communities have contributed to South Asian studies at other institutions. For example, at the University of Washington the India Association of Western Washington in 1996 provided sufficient funds to start an endowment that will provide an annual scholarship award to students of the field. And at the Louisiana State University in Shreveport the local Indo-American community has collected funds to endow a modest program in Indian studies, the first such community-based effort in the South. This program will concentrate on developing intercultural under-standing through events in the performing arts, lectures by leading scholars brought from India, and some university courses. It is hoped this could be the basis for a more serious academic endeavor in the future.

These then are innovative developments that forge ties between the burgeoning and increasingly prosperous Indo-American community and that segment of the U.S. academic world that focuses on the subcontinent. Such ties have already resulted in substantial financial support to studies of India in several institutions, and the prospects are good that Indo-Americans will continue to contribute to teaching and research that highlight their cultural heritage. These activities represent a significant component in the promotion of general understanding between the world's two largest democracies.

THE AMERICAN INSTITUTE OF INDIAN STUDIES IN THE 1990s

This summary history of the development of South Asian studies in the U.S. in the past fifty years has touched on the leadership of that effort, together with the most important institutions where these studies are taking place, as well as with the all-important matter of funding. For thirty-five of these fifty years, the American Institute of Indian Studies has been the overseas extension for the growing network of South Asian studies' centers and programs as well as for scores of "loner" scholars. As a cooperative venture of Americans and Indians, the Institute has become the principal consortium dedicated to the advancement of knowledge and understanding of India in the U.S., and to providing the means to carry out research in India by U.S.-based scholars and students of many nationalities. It should be noted that, unlike many other U.S. organizations, the AIIS awards fellowships without discrimination by citizenship.

Having described the national context within which both the field we know as South Asian studies and the American Institute of Indian

Studies were born and grew to maturity, it is fitting in the final pages of this historical narrative to highlight, and sometimes to recapitulate, features and activities of the AIIS, and to bring the story up to the mid-nineties.

AIIS IN THE U.S.: RISING MEMBERSHIP, DIMINISHING FUNDS

The major change in administration of the Institute in the U.S. came in 1994 when Frederick M. Asher, professor of art history at the University of Minnesota was elected president to succeed Joseph W. Elder, professor of sociology at the University of Wisconsin, after the latter completed his two terms, 1986-1994.

Pressure on institutional budgets forced some colleges and universities to reconsider membership in the AIIS. Two dropped out in the 1990s, and Duke University found it necessary to change its level of membership from Class A (with an annual fee of $2,500) to Class B ($500 per year). However, between 1990 and 1996 eight institutions were admitted at the Class B level, making a net gain of six Class B Members in the first half of the decade. As of 1997 the total membership is fifty: forty-nine colleges and universities, plus the Independent Scholars of South Asia (ISOSA). ISOSA is an incorporated group of persons with South Asia scholarly interests who either do not have tenure-track academic positions or who continue active research on South Asia as unaffiliated individuals. Organized to represent the concerns of such individuals, ISOSA was admitted to the AIIS in 1989 as a Member at the Class B level. Its dues-paying members who receive Institute fellowships are entitled to the same financial and other benefits as though they were members of Class B institutions. The Institute's reach is increasing across the U.S., with an especially strong new membership component in the southeastern region of the country.

The popularity of AIIS fellowships and the consistently high quality of applications have been countered in the 1990s by the distressing decrease in availability of funds. AIIS administrators in the U.S. are constantly looking for further sources to tap and seeking ways to cut existing costs. Meanwhile, demands continue to escalate on an already hard-pressed staff at Chicago headquarters. With the exception of modest honoraria for Selection Committee members who shoulder a huge and time-consuming burden, and travel expenses to officers who have to attend policy-making committee meetings, the work of the Institute's scholar-administrators is volunteered as service to the profession. By and large, then, the Institute is, and always has been, a shoe-string operation on the U.S. side, with the voluntary labor of topnotch South Asianist scholars supporting the small paid administrative staff at U.S. headquarters.

AIIS OPERATIONS IN INDIA

The Fellowship Program. From the outset, the Institute has regarded the fellowship program as its central function and, indeed, its very reason for being. Close to 3,000 fellowships have been awarded over thirty-five years to more than 2,000 individuals. With an average of seventy-five or eighty fellowships per year, most have been made at junior and senior levels—that is, pre-dissertation graduate student and post-Ph.D faculty. A small number of fellowships have been professional development grants (for instance, to librarians). Beginning in 1988, a new category of performing arts fellowships was set up. (Prior to that many individuals had received grants for research, rather than performance training, in such fields as dance and music.) Institute fellowships are awarded by a rotating Selection Committee chaired by a past Vice-President of the AIIS and composed of seven scholars chosen to represent a balance of gender, disciplines, institutions, and national origins.

AIIS Fellows are selected "blind," that is without regard to discipline, nationality, or gender, and regardless of whether or not the applicant's home institution is an AIIS Member. The only criterion used in vetting applications is merit, according to the judgment of the seven-member Selection Committee. In one recent year, of a total of seventy-nine selectees, history was the discipline of fourteen; anthropology came in with twelve; religious studies accounted for ten; humanities, eight; art history, seven; sociology and performing arts, four each; while the number in political science, formerly a popular field, dropped to two. The balance of twenty selectees came from fifteen different disciplines. In that year's group, fifty-two were U.S. citizens, twenty-two were Indian nationals, with one each from five other nationalities. In terms of gender, forty-one were female and thirty-eight male. Finally, fifty-five grantees were from AIIS Member institutions, compared with twenty-four from non-members. Fellowships for the Institute's Advanced Language Program are awarded by the AIIS Language Committee in the U.S. rather than by the Selection Committee.

Institute Fellows (other than Language Fellows) have since 1969 been required by the Government of India to be affiliated with an appropriate department of an institution in the region in which the scholar intends to do research. An Indian faculty member is designated to meet the AIIS Fellow, follow his or her research progress, and submit quarterly reports to Institute headquarters in New Delhi, which forwards them to the appropriate government ministry. In the past, affiliation arrangements, made by AIIS headquarters or Regional Center staff in India, were free. But Indian universities have begun to charge substantial fees for these affiliations. Because of general AIIS belt-tightening measures, individual Fellows may have to pay affiliation fees out of their grants. This problem remains to be solved.

The question of research access to India, while a thorny issue in the past, now appears to be much less a problem. Institute Trustees set up a special committee in 1995 to draft a statement for submission to the Government of India stating the Institute's expectation of reasonable freedom of research access for its Fellows. The atmosphere of general Indian government liberalization towards foreign companies wishing to do business in India appears to have spilled over into an easing up of restrictions on research topics. With increasing sensitivity to what research is appropriate and acceptable on the part of both Institute Fellows and the Government of India, the 1990s have brought welcome rapprochement on this often contentious front. The academic appears to have prevailed over the political, and government approvals of research proposals submitted to it are at an all-time high.

The wise counsel of Director-General Mehendiratta to Institute officers and fellowship applicants, plus his inimitable rapport with key figures in the Indian bureaucracy, have played no small role in alleviating both suspicions and frustrations on questions of scholarly research access.

Funding constraints may bring about temporary reductions in the size of the AIIS fellowship program. But when a secure funding base is achieved, this central Institute function will be the first to be reinstated at an optimal level.

The Language Program. The Institute's language programs, both the summer, and the nine-month Advanced Language Programs, continued during the 1990s under the dynamic leadership of University of Texas Professor Herman van Olphen, chair of the AIIS Language Committee. The Hindi program in Varanasi was especially successful in producing students adept in conversation and capable of good writing skills in the language. Students have enjoyed the total immersion in Hindi afforded them by the Varanasi environment, a vast improvement over multilingual New Delhi. All have been enthusiastic over the audio-visual techniques used and have praised their instructors. For a while, student health problems in the summer prompted thoughts of moving the program because of river flooding and attendant environmental hazards. But the positive pedagogical results from the location of the Hindi Center in Varanasi have persuaded the Board of Trustees to retain the program there, with part of the summer program perhaps meeting in Mussoorie. Health hazards exist in many parts of India if proper personal precautions are not taken.

The Tamil program continues successfully in Madurai, despite its frequent under-utilization. This reflects the inherent unpredictability of enrollment in language programs and their easy vulnerability in belt-tightening situations. Ad hoc instruction in Telugu, Marathi, and Bengali continues as required.

In sum, the Institute's language programs have developed, dependent on skilled Indian teachers who have been instructed in the latest American pedagogical techniques, required under U.S. Department of Education guidelines for funding application on a nationally competitive basis. Beginning in 1996 the AIIS has been awarded a new three-year language-training grant; so the program can continue on a solid basis.

Looking back to the 1960s, it is remarkable to trace the advances in teaching materials, techniques, and technology for South Asian languages made since the pioneering days of D.P. Pattanayak and others in Poona as the Institute got under way.

The Publications Program. Of the seventy-one publications produced in some sort of association with the AIIS between 1965 and 1996, fifteen came out between 1965 and 1979, and twenty-six between 1990 and 1996. This compares with thirty, the total for the entire previous decade. The total for the whole decade of the 1990s will greatly exceed that when everything in the pipeline is published.

Overall, in terms of subject-matter, archaeology and art history, including volumes from the huge Vijayanagara project, account for twenty-nine titles, or nearly half of the grand total. The remaining publications cover a wide range of subjects including philosophy, literature, music, and a two-volume regional study of Rajasthan.

The Institute's Publications Committee, established in 1979, was dissolved as a standing body in 1993 and replaced by a Publications' Adviser. However, it has been revived in 1996 as an Ad Hoc Publications Committee, reverting to its form prior to 1979. The revived group is charged with assessing the current situation and considering future activities in the light of the Institute's straitened financial circumstances. The existence of good quality book production and energetic publishers in India has led many U.S. scholars to submit works, prepared while on AIIS grants, for publication in India. With faster production than U.S. firms, scholars gain time and the extra cachet from explicit Institute support, helpful in enhancing their own bibliography. Cooperation in this regard benefits everyone.

The massive *Encyclopaedia of Indian Temple Architecture* (EITA) project has long been a concern of the Publications Program as well as of the Institute's Committee on Art and Archaeology. Of the projected seventeen separate bindings (subdivisions of numbered volumes), twelve have been published up to 1996, four in the 1980s, and eight between 1990 and 1996. The end of the EITA publication project is reportedly in sight. To aid in the massive enterprise, the Indira Gandhi National Centre for the Arts (IGNCA) in New Delhi has proferred a heartening measure of cooperation by granting Rs.1,800,000 to underwrite publication costs of three parts of EITA. This is also a measure of the esteem in which the Government of India's IGNCA holds both the project and AIIS itself.

Through its Publications Program and the fact that production takes place in India, the Institute is underscoring its confidence in the Indian publishing industry, and making available to scholars in India the fruits of much Institute-sponsored research.

The Institute's Research Centers. The Center for Art and Archaeology in Varanasi and the Archives and Research Center for Ethnomusicology in New Delhi succeeded in the first half of the 1990s in meeting their main goals of collection, documentation, and service to the scholarly community, both in India and abroad. Both have, in a short period of time, carried out their mandates, and provided the American Institute of Indian Studies as a whole with enhanced visibility and credibility in the eyes of the Government of India. The Centers have built first-class library collections on their specialities, and these constitute permanent contributions to the Indian academic world.

Both Centers were initially conceived by Indians resident in the United States, there joined in their aspirations by a group of U.S. specialists in their respective fields. From the beginning, the Centers have been run and developed on the ground, both in Varanasi and New Delhi, by Indian scholars and technicians. With ongoing substantial Smithsonian Institution and Ford Foundation funding, both Centers have been able to set up state-of-the-art facilities for their photo, visual, and sound documentation operations. Under the scholarly direction of Madhusudan A. Dhaky—even after his recent official retirement—at the Center for Art and Archaeology in Varanasi, and the leadership of Shubha Chaudhuri at the Archives and Research Center for Ethnomusicology in New Delhi, these facilities have, in a couple of decades, enhanced the reputation of the AIIS as a serious and solid contributor to study and research of many aspects of India's complex cultural heritage.

Towards Permanence: the Institute's Own Building. Funding problems have plagued the AIIS throughout its existence. With the end in sight for rupee funding through the U.S.-India Fund, with a problematic future for support from Smithsonian, NSF, and other federal agencies, and in the context of escalating costs in India for rental of needed buildings, the Institute decided to implement its years-old intention to construct its own headquarters building. For over twenty years the AIIS had negotiated with the Delhi Development Authority and other governmental bodies for a plot of land at a concessional price usually offered to an educational organization. After several offers of unsuitable plots in inappropriate locations, the Institute looked outside Delhi State. It found a plot in neighboring Haryana State, near the town of Gurgaon in a rapidly growing industrial and commercial area some ten miles southwest of Indira Gandhi International Airport. While over twenty miles from downtown New Delhi, adequate land was available at a better price than in Delhi. So, in 1993, the Institute's Executive Committee gave the go-ahead to Director-General Mehendiratta to purchase this lot a few hundred yards off the main highway between Delhi and Gurgaon, a twenty-minute drive from the airport. On 20 January 1994 the AIIS held a Foundation Stone Laying Ceremony to which Government of India, Haryana State, and diplomatic officials were invited. Actual construction began in early 1996 according to designs drawn up by a well-known Indian architect, Vinod Gupta, and in consultation with Edward Dimock, a former Institute president and an architecture graduate in his years before South Asian studies.

The Institute's building will accommodate much of its administrative staff, with a substantial part of the structure designed to house both AIIS Research Centers. The art and archaeology documentation facility and library will be moved from Varanasi, where the lease on its premises is about to expire. The ethnomusicology center will be shifted from its present New Delhi site, where the rent has skyrocketed to the point where the Institute has found it difficult to meet the costs.

To tap potential donors to underwrite costs of various parts of the Institute's building, the AIIS is publicizing opportunities for benefactors to be named as contributors to construction of, for example, a room or some other facility. A "Friends of the Library" group has been formed for interested persons to join in exchange for a donation. A major start in this direction is the gift of Rs. 2,500,000 from the publishing firm of S. Chand and Company, designated for construction of the new library that will house the collections from both Research Centers. According to terms of this gift, the library will be named for Shyamlal Gupta, the father of the current president of S. Chand and Company. This represents a most encouraging and highly auspicious start for construction of a permanent home for the American Institute of Indian Studies.

Relocation of the Centers and consolidation of some of their operations will inevitably change their individual characters. But it is hoped that when the changes are completed in the next five or so years, the Institute's research capability will be streamlined and appropriately upgraded through technological advances so that the Institute can enter the twenty-first century in a strong position to continue its innovative work. The Gurgaon site will not be the quiet residential campus that W. Norman Brown had envisaged, an environment that actually existed at the Deccan College in Poona for the Institute's first ten years. But it will reflect the changed needs, conditions, and tools of a whole new information era.

A MOMENTOUS HALF-CENTURY, 1947-1997: RETROSPECT AND PROSPECT

India's advent onto the international stage in 1947 as a fully independent nation, about to become a vibrant democracy based on the Constitution of 1950, spurred American involvement during the country's early traumatic years. These years saw nation-building activities following massive population shifts in the wake of partition of the subcontinent into Pakistan and India. Later widespread food shortages brought wrenching poverty into sharp focus. Americans rushed to help through the Truman-era "Point Four" program of federal aid and through many private agencies such as the Ford Foundation. These events stimulated U.S. academics to try to understand India's manifold problems and aspirations and to put them into the perspective of the great civilization and complex history that preceded the freedom struggle of the modern era. This was the context for development of the new field of South Asian studies, an amalgam of disciplinary interests focused on the subcontinent.

The overview of these fifty years presented in these pages has traced the formation of the institutional base within U.S. higher education needed to introduce teaching and research on India, both of which help to bring about understanding between our two countries. The path has not been easy or straight, but that it has been successfully blazed should be clear from the descriptions provided above of outstanding academic programs established in the U.S. Dozens of mechanisms have been set in place since 1947 through which Americans can journey to India and embark on serious careers in South Asia-oriented fields.

With the cooperation of the Government of India and the Indian scholarly community, the American Institute of Indian Studies was established in 1961 under W. Norman Brown's inspired leadership, with its primary goal of sending students and scholars from U.S.

colleges and universities to do advanced research in India with all its often bewildering complexity.

The AIIS, in its thirty-five years, has become the apex of the pyramid of South Asian studies in the U.S. Through thick and thin, bad years in bilateral relations, and years of funding uncertainties—even crises—the AIIS has survived and prospered, led by dedicated volunteer scholar-administrators in the U.S. who determine the Institute's goals and policies, policies carried out in India by an exceptional, energetic, and devoted staff at headquarters in New Delhi as well as at the several Regional Centers. The AIIS, as an exemplary Overseas Research Center, has truly succeeded in just a few years in furthering intercultural understanding at the highest academic and intellectual levels, so desperately needed in an increasingly interdependent world.

INSTITUTIONAL MEMBERS OF THE
AMERICAN INSTITUTE OF INDIAN STUDIES, 1997

THIRTEEN CLASS A MEMBERS, WITH TWO TRUSTEES EACH

University of California, Berkeley
University of Chicago
Columbia University
Cornell University
Harvard University
University of Illinois at Urbana-Champaign, and at Chicago
University of Michigan
University of Minnesota-Twin Cities
University of Pennsylvania
University of Texas at Austin
University of Virginia
University of Washington
University of Wisconsin-Madison

THIRTY-SEVEN CLASS B MEMBERS, WITH ONE TRUSTEE EACH

American University
Amherst College
Arizona State University
Brown University
California State University, Hayward
Carleton College
Colby College
Colgate University
University of Colorado at Boulder
Duke University
Emory University
University of Florida
University of Hawaii at Manoa
Independent Scholars of South Asia
Indiana University
University of Iowa
Kansas State University
Loyola Marymount University
University of Maryland at College Park
University of Missouri-Columbia
New York University, Institute of Fine Arts
University of North Carolina at Chapel Hill
North Carolina State University

University of Northern Iowa
Oakland University (Rochester, Michigan)
Oberlin College
Ohio State University
Pennsylvania State University-University Park
University of Pittsburgh
Princeton University
Purdue University
University of Rochester
Rutgers, The State University of New Jersey at New Brunswick
Syracuse University
Temple University
Virginia Polytechnic Institute and State University
Yale University

REFERENCES

Adams, Robert McC. and Corrine S. Schelling, (eds.), 1979. *Corners of a Foreign Field: Discussions about American Overseas Advanced Research Centers in the Humanities and Social Sciences*. New York: Rockefeller Foundation.

Barrier, N. Gerald, 1986. *India and America: American Publishing on India, 1930-1985*. New Delhi: Manohar, for AIIS.

Brown, W. Norman, 1974. *The United States and India, Pakistan, Bangladesh*. 3rd edn. Cambridge: Harvard University Press.

————, 1978. *India and Indology: Selected Articles by W. Norman Brown*, (ed.), Rosane Rocher. Delhi: Motilal Banarsidass, for AIIS.

————, 1939. India and Humanistic Studies in America. In *Indic Studies in America*, ed. by Horace I. Poleman. ACLS *Bulletin* 28 (May): 1-26.

————, (ed. and trans.), 1965. *The Mahimnastava, or, Praise of Shiva's Greatness*. Poona: AIIS.

————, (ed.), 1960. *Resources for South Asian Language Studies in the United States*. Philadelphia: University of Pennsylvania Press.

Buitenen, J.A.B. van, 1988. *Studies in Indian Literature and Philosophy: Collected Articles of J.A.B. van Buitenen*, ed. by Ludo Rocher. Delhi: Motilal Banarsidass, for AIIS.

Case, Margaret and N. Gerald Barrier, (eds.), 1986. *Aspects of India: Essays in Honor of Edward Cameron Dimock, Jr.* New Delhi: Manohar, for AIIS.

Dawes, Norman, 1962. *A Two-way Street: The Indo-American Fulbright Program, 1950-60*. Bombay: Asia Publishing House.

Dimock, Edward C., Jr., Braj B. Kachru, and Bh. Krishnamurti, (eds.), 1992. *Dimensions of Sociolinguistics in South Asia: Papers in Memory of Gerald B. Kelley*. New Delhi: Oxford & IBH, for AIIS.

Dhaky, M.A. (ed.), 1996. *Encyclopaedia of Indian Temple Architecture*. New Delhi: AIIS, etc. [twelve separate parts published up to 1996].

Frykenberg, Robert E. and Pauline Kolenda, (eds.), 1985. *Studies of South India: An Anthology of Recent Research and Scholarship*. Madras: New Era; and New Delhi: AIIS.

Gould, Harold A. and Sumit Ganguly, (eds.), 1992. *The Hope and the Reality: U.S.-Indian Relations from Roosevelt to Bush*. Boulder: Westview.

Haithcox, J. Patrick and Bardwell L. Smith, 1982. "American colleges and the study of contemporary India." In *Contemporary India: Socio-Economic and Political Processes*, ed. by N. Inamdar: 355-64. Poona: Continental Prakashan.

Hart, Henry C., 1961. *Campus India: An Appraisal of American College Programs in India*. East Lansing: Michigan State University Press.

Hess, Gary, 1971. *America Encounters India, 1941-47*. Baltimore: The Johns Hopkins University Press.

Joint Committee on Southern Asia, 1951. *Southern Asia Studies in the United States; A Survey and Plan*. Philadelphia: University of Pennsylvania.

Kux, Dennis, 1994. *Estranged Democracies: India and the United States, 1941-1991*. New Delhi: Sage.

Lambert, Richard D., (ed.), 1962. *Resources for South Asian Area Studies in the United States*. Philadelphia: University of Pennsylvania Press.

————, (ed.), 1969. *The Development of South Asian Studies.* Ann Arbor: Association for Asian Studies' Committee on South Asia.

————, (ed.), 1984. *Beyond Growth: The Next Stage in Language and Area Studies.* Washington, D.C.: Association of American Universities.

McCaughey, Robert A., 1984. *International Studies and Academic Enterprise: A Chapter in the Enclosure of American Learning.* New York: Columbia University Press.

Meister, Michael, M.A. Dhaky, *et al.*, (eds.), 1983. *Encyclopaedia of Indian Temple Architecture.* New Delhi: AIIS, etc. [twelve separate parts published up to 1996].

Patterson, Maureen L.P., 1969. "The South Asian P.L. 480 Library Program." In *Journal of Asian Studies* 28 (August): 743-54.

Patterson, Maureen L.P. with William J. Alspaugh, 1981. *South Asian Civilizations: A Bibliographic Synthesis.* Chicago: University of Chicago Press.

Patterson, Maureen L.P., (ed.), 1975. *South Asian Library Resources in North America: A Survey Prepared for the Boston Conference, 1974.* Zug: Inter Documentation Company.

Patterson, Maureen L.P. and Martin Yanuck, (eds.). *South Asian Library Resources in North America: Papers from the Boston Conference, 1974.* Zug: Inter Documentation Company.

Poleman, Horace I., (ed.), 1939. *Indic Studies in America.* ACLS *Bulletin* 28 (May): 1-242.

Rahim, Enayatur, 1988. *Smithsonian Focus on India: A Guide to the Institution's Resources.* Washington, D.C.: Smithsonian Institution. [prepared as part of Smithsonian's participation in the Festival of India, 1985-6].

Rudolph, Lloyd I., Susanne Hoeber Rudolph, *et al.*, 1980. *The Regional Imperative: The Administration of U.S. Foreign Policy Towards South Asian States under Presidents Johnson and Nixon.* New Delhi: Concept Publishing.

Sakala, Carol, 1980. *Women of South Asia: A Guide to Resources.* Millwood, NY: Kraus International.

Schwartzberg, Joseph E., (ed.), 1978. *A Historical Atlas of South Asia.* Chicago: University of Chicago Press. (Second Impression, 1992) New York and Oxford: Oxford University Press.

————, (ed.), 1989. *South Asian Studies in North American Higher Education.* Ann Arbor: Association for Asian Studies' South Asia Council.

Singer, Milton, (ed.), 1957. *Introducing India in Liberal Education: Proceedings of a Conference Held at the University of Chicago, May 17, 18, 1957.* Chicago: University of Chicago.

Vatuk, Sylvia J., (ed.), 1978. *American Studies in the Anthropology of India.* New Delhi: Manohar, for AIIS.

Williams, Joanna G., (ed.), 1981. *Kaladarsana: American Studies in the Art of India.* New Delhi: Oxford & IBH, for AIIS.

PART II

Contributions of the Study of India to Various Academic Disciplines

Anthropology

SUSAN S. WADLEY

The U.S. anthropological study of India began after World War II
as anthropology was in the midst of a major shift away from the study
of so-called tribal societies to the study of complex societies. Aside
from being at the beginning of a burgeoning of anthropological
endeavors, the post World War II era was also for anthropologists a
time of great questioning: Were western paradigms valid (Leach
1963)? Were U.S. anthropologists imposing western models on an
Indian reality? Should anthropology be a science, or was anthropology
part of a humanistic endeavor (Redfield 1962-63, Evans-Pritchard
1965)? Fifty years later, anthropologists find themselves still in
turmoil, though asking different questions: What is the relationship
between anthropology and colonialism? Are western paradigms
valid? Should anthropological analyses be based on internal evidence
or external models (Marriott 1989, Milner 1994)? And what, indeed,
is an internal model (Madan 1995)? To what extent, and how,
should the anthropologist be self-reflective (Visvaram 1993)? And, to
mark that some things don't change, are anthropologists scientists
or are they humanists? At the same time, U.S. anthropology has
moved from a focus on issues of fate and caste in what were seen as
small, self-contained communities in India to issues of the nation
and its construction, to studies of modern media and their effects
on local constructions of self and India, to religious movements, and
to the South Asian diaspora in an increasing complex world system.

U.S. anthropology in India coincides almost exactly with India
as an independent nation. However, India had not been unknown
to other students of culture prior to 1947. In the 1800s, for example,
the American anthropologist Lewis Henry Morgan wrote on Dravidian
kinship, and in the early 1900s the German sociologist Max Weber
used Hinduism as a case study of the importance of ideology on
society. Scores of British colonial administrators studied India as
they ruled its inhabitants and wrote extensively on their findings
(e.g., Tod 1971, Crooke 1971). The English scholar W.H.R. Rivers

studied Toda kinship in the early 1900s, while the U.S. missionaries, William and Charlotte Wiser, did path-breaking work in India in the 1920s, authoring the influential *Hindu Jajmani System* (W. Wiser 1936) and *Behind Mud Walls* (Wiser and Wiser 1989). One of the first Americans who was an anthropologist by training to work in India was David Mandelbaum, who studied, according to the orientation toward primitive and tribal societies that was prevalent in the pre World War II era, the Kota of southern India. M.N. Srinivas, trained in England and pursuing British structural-functionalism, set a new standard for anthropologists with his work among the Coorgs in the 1940s and went on to influence anthropology in the U.S. and Europe. U.S. anthropologists, some of whom were motivated in part by their physical presence in India during World War II as well as by the shift to the study of "peasant" societies that was occurring in the U.S. under the leadership of Robert Redfield, began focusing on India in the 1950s. This interest continues, now increasingly from U.S.-taught students of Indian origin, perhaps in record numbers. Many of the resulting studies have been significant to the development of anthropology as a discipline, as well as to the development of other disciplines. Other less far-reaching studies have contributed to both the expansion of Indian anthropology in particular and the humanistic and social scientific understanding of South Asia in general.

Although it is difficult to mark boundaries, in the following pages I attempt to keep my focus on anthropologists trained or based in the United States, while locating their work amidst that occurring in Europe and India, for the flow of ideas across geographic boundaries is only increasing with time. This scanning is necessarily superficial, for the range of topics covered by modern anthropologists is vast, and the numbers of players are many. I regret that, despite my attempt to encircle the field and capture the key points, I may leave off some names that should be included.

THE INITIAL PARADIGM

In order to gauge more accurately the influence of U.S. anthropology as related to the study of India, it is worth noting where U.S. anthropologists were in the late 1940s at the time of India's independence. Bernard S. Cohn provided one summary of this 1940s paradigm, as developed over 200 years of European contact and study, in association with the anthropological thinking of the 1930s and 1940s:

These assumptions and methods can be summarized briefly. Anthropologists study isolated or circumscribed systems; such systems in India can be found in villages, in the self-sufficient Indian village community of Munro, Metcalfe, Maine and Baden-Powell. The anthropologist's model of change is based on the assumption of a baseline or zero point of change. There was a time, anthropologists argue, when the systems we want to study were stable or static, and the anthropologist studies change by studying what happened from the postulated period of stability. In India this was to be found in villages where "traditional India" existed. This is the orientalist's assumption of the unchanging character of Indian civilization. Caste is the central institution of rural Indian society; it governs behavior and values. This is the official view of caste as a "thing," as a set of attributes. The way you study caste is to observe it in action and ask people about it. (Cohn 1968, 25)

Writing about his own training in the 1950s in India, T.N. Madan defined the paradigm more concretely: First, in India, anthropology meant the study of tribals (the 'Other' to the Hindu scholars at Lucknow University); then, and if not tribals, anthropology meant the study of "karma, caste and renunciation" (Madan 1996, 258).[1] In the following discussion I shall explore largely what has happened to this initial paradigm of village, change, and caste, and the associated ideas of karma and renunciation, as these were issues that consumed the anthropologists of India in the 1960s and 1970s. And anthropologists still struggle with and about them.

Underlying this paradigm was an implicit assumption of a monolithic Indianness, an assumption that there was agreement across the social divisions of India about what being "Indian" or "Brahman" or "Kumhar" [potter] etc. meant, ignoring gender, class, and regional differences. As Cohn's work on the pasts of an Indian village (1961) itself showed, not only was there no static village community, there was no consensus about what the history of that community had been. The multiple voices first identified by Cohn and others writing in the 1950s increasingly demanded attention in two ways. First, there was the voice of the Indian anthropologist, by definition trained either in the West or with western conceptual tools (increasingly an Indo-American anthropologist or even a "haftie," see Narayan 1993). Second, there were the many voices of India itself—female, male, Brahman, untouchable, rich, poor, urban, rural. As anthropologists began to understand societies as constructed and imagined (rather than based in some never-changing primordial sentiments), these multiple voices with their varying constructions of what is "India" played an increasing role in the analyses and writings of anthropologists everywhere.

CHANGING THE PARADIGM: FROM VILLAGE TO CITY WORLD

Titles of anthropology books written in the 1950s mark the concerns of the time. Two of the most important books were *Village India* and *India's Villages*. The former, a U.S. endeavor, resulted from two major efforts: The work of Redfield and Singer at the University of Chicago on "civilizations" and the peasants who lived in rural villages; and the Cornell India Project, wherein two teams of social scientists were sent to two north Indian villages, each person assigned a different topic to investigate. Both efforts focused on village communities. At a time when many anthropologists were studying the relationships between more isolated communities and the adjoining cities, India became a setting in which new theories could be explored. Moreover, the complexity of Indian social systems led to new methodological and theoretical issues and immediately began to challenge working assumptions (although 50 years later some of those assumptions still seem remarkably entrenched).

Village India was part of a series edited by Robert Redfield and McKim Marriott titled "Comparative Studies in Culture and Civilizations." As Marriott stated in his introduction to *Village India*, the goal of the series was "to seek understanding of any great civilization and its enormously complex changes through anthropological studies of villages" (1955, xi). Further, Marriott questioned the role of the anthropologist: "What does this say about the interests and way of work of the anthropologist who wrote this paper: what did he [*sic*] try to find out and how did he [*sic*] go about it?" (Marriott 1955, xii).[2]

One paper that immediately challenged the paradigm of the isolated and unchanging village was Marriott's own paper on great and little traditions. Unlike Mexico, which provided the initial case study for Redfield's folk-urban continuum, India had villages, where most people were illiterate, and cities, where there were scholars, as well as texts thousands of years old and in a multitude of languages (though certainly, in the 1950s, scholarly attention focused almost solely on Sanskrit texts). [3] What was the relationship between the practices of the village and the texts of the Sanskritic scholar? What were the relationships between pan-Indian and regional forms of religiosity and village-level practices? Building on Redfield and Singer's discussions of the folk-urban continuum and the role of cities, Marriott provided a paradigm that spread far beyond the borders of South Asia, one that remains as a handy tool, though often ill-used, even today. He pointed to the continual interactions between great and little traditions and, more importantly, named the processes linking these with the terms universalization and parochialization, thus showing that the Indian village was not an isolate, but was continuously connected to other villages and to urban areas both intellectually and socially. As anthropology expanded its scope geographically into Europe, the Middle East, and Southeast Asia, this model of the interplay between local traditions, textual traditions, and urban traditions was increasingly used. Within the Indian context, it also struck a major blow against the idea of the isolated Indian village. Other articles in *Village India* by M. N. Srinivas and Alan Beals also highlighted the external forces that impinged on Indian villages, countering the image of the isolated, static Indian village.[4]

The focus on great and little traditions was also a mark of one of the most difficult issues facing anthropologists studying India. How are traditions (including textual traditions) constructed in the first place, whether by Brahman males, by colonial administrators, by nationalist leaders, or (increasingly) by politicians or film stars? And how are these traditions deployed and used by different kinds of people? Finally, how are these various kinds of cultural rhetoric influencing anthropological rhetoric? Whether discussing caste (Dumont 1980, Marriott 1968, Raheja 1996); prestations (Marriott 1968, Vatuk 1975, Raheja 1988); gender (Bean 1975, Gold and Raheja 1994, Wadley 1976 and 1994, Vatuk 1987); or religion (Narayan 1989, Gold 1988), U.S. anthropologists of South Asia have grappled with various claims to traditional authority and "tradition," while continuously redefining the meaning of tradition within the Indian context and exposing the multiple ways in which tradition is made. This tension emerged much later in anthropological studies of other world areas. Perhaps because of the enormous weight given India's ancient texts from the earliest scholars onwards, the claims to classical authority seemed more conflictual in India than elsewhere.[5]

Two other articles from *Village India* are noteworthy as we gaze backwards on the history of U.S. anthropology in India. Bernard Cohn, in an article that was a harbinger both of the emerging relationship between anthropology and history and of the concern for multiple voices, described the changes that had been occurring in a rural community near Banaras. Cohn noted that multiple versions of the community's past existed, each dependent upon the structural position of the teller. Kathleen Gough, in her discussion of a south Indian community (1955), analyzed the socio-economic transformations that led to lower castes acquiring land at the expense of Brahmans. Her work presaged the appearances of

Marxist and political economic analyses by the 1980s and marked, once again, the changing Indian village and the importance of economic status vis-a-vis Brahmanic ritual status.

Studies of local-level politics emerged from village and caste studies, especially after scholars like M.N. Srinivas (1959) dealt a death blow to the view that Brahmans were always dominant because of their ritual status, and often in spite of their economic and political inferiority. The fact that William Wiser wrote *The Hindu Jajmani System* about a village that happened to be economically and politically controlled by Brahmans did not help students of India to recognize the disjunctures between economic, political, and ritual status. Further, the fact that India did not give the same weight to economic status as the West did, especially after the Protestant revolution, made India even more exotic, more interesting.

In an early work, Bailey (1957) looked primarily at local politics and their economic relations, using a model that separated ideology and material relations. Somewhat later, Nicholas (1968) published a comparative study that provided a model of two prominent kinds of political divisions in rural communities, one based on horizontal ties between groups of more-or-less equal status, and the other based on vertical ties linking dominant/dominated groups. Nicholas noted that universal adult suffrage and land tenure reform would adversely affect the political dominance of minority "dominant" castes, as indeed they have (see Wadley 1994). Bailey's more recent book, *The Witch Hunt* (1994), provides a more nuanced and complex picture of caste and politics. While ostensibly about witches, his book is in fact more about economics, politics and the variant readings of one incident as (in one interpretation) a community seeks to control a man no longer content with his lowly economic position. Fox (1972) moved the study of political anthropology out of the village and to issues of region and then to issues of nationhood and nation-state. He accomplished this first with his examination of the historical development of local-level political groups based on clan and caste in northern India (1971) and then with his work on Punjabi politics (1985). In the latter, Fox linked the cultural construction of Sikh to historical processes and a view of culture as a constant struggle among groups, of culture as "always becoming." Moreover, Fox, along with Appadurai (1981), Cohn (1971), Dirks (1993), Rudner (1994) and others, has been significant in redefining the relationship of history and anthropology not just for India but for any region in the world.

Culture as contested and as continuously being made underlies more recent village monographs. While village life is still the locus of much anthropological research, it is no longer seen as isolated or self-contained. In a rare recent village monograph, Wadley's *Struggling with Destiny in Karimpur, 1925-1984* (1994) specifically tied change in the village community to political, social, and economic changes at the national and international levels.[6] Moreover, Karimpur social relations and "culture" (itself not homogenous) were seen as having changed continuously over time, while also always being contested by both individuals and groups.[7] Despite their propensity no longer to see the village as an isolate, anthropologists continued to work in villages, while asking different and often more focused questions.

During the past fifty years the questions have changed, but the anthropologists' methodology of participant-observation and close personal contact and exchange with those studied has led them to continue to situate their research in small communities, which in India often still means a village. What has changed is that the village is recognized as being located historically and structurally in a larger setting, frequently in a world political economy. So, for example, a recent dissertation on women's health in Tehri Garhwal was related to women's health in a Rajput village and to the imposition of western science and the westernization of Indian medicine, as well as to high-caste Gangetic plains' definitions of proper female behavior, reflecting both Brahmanic textual writings and British Victorian morality.[8] Similarly, a dissertation on a Kumaoni village's use of the forests related to issues of western forest management and the international funding of non-governmental organizations, as well as to national and state politics within India.[9] Gupta's recent work (1995) on state formation was grounded in data obtained in a rural north Indian community. The demise of the isolated village community is clear, but the village as a site for research continues to thrive.

DEBATING CASTE AND HIERARCHY

Caste and hierarchy grabbed the most attention of western anthropologists, especially as they moved away from the 'simpler' societies that had been the primary focus of anthropological research through the 1940s. Having initially sought out the seemingly simplest societies for investigation of the 'Other,' the Euro-American imagination was captured by the hierarchy found in India. Further, Hindu textual traditions such as the Puruṣa model supported the placement of the Brahmans at the top of the hierarchy, in marked contra-distinction to hierarchies based on economic superiority that were developing in the West. This same hierarchy led Murray Milner (1994), following in the Durkheimian tradition, to use India as the locus for his investigation of status relations. Further, caste spoke to Americans of the 1950s and 1960s who were fighting their own "caste" cum racial stereotypes and wars. Indian caste and U.S. caste were commonly contrasted, thus making us in the U.S. a little less strange, and perhaps, by comparison, seemingly a little better than India.

Under the British, caste increasingly became a "thing," marked by endogamy, specific customs, boundaries of exclusion and inclusion, and above all hierarchy based on ritual status. European investigations of caste were often tied to the exigencies of colonial rule; so it was not surprising that castes were seen as isolates, marked by customs that could guide British administrators in their rule, whether the British were differentiating groups to be recorded in a census, or were marking their habits to control them better (e.g., see Cohn 1968 and Raheja 1996).

Studies of caste in India focused on two issues: the role of ideology versus practice, and the role of the purity/pollution complex as contrasted with other rationales for ranking, particularly power (Wadley 1975, Dirks 1987) and suspiciousness (Marglin 1977, Raheja 1988). By the 1960s, U.S. anthropology was overwhelmed by Dumont's (1980) analysis of *homo hierarchicus*, with the attendant focus on ideology. Marriott initially countered Dumont with studies showing the relationships between caste hierarchies and economic and political power (Marriott 1968) as well as the relationships between caste heirarchies and transactions more generally (1989). Eventually, however, Marriott, too, moved to a more ideological focus, resulting in the seminal piece co-authored with Ronald Inden in the *Encyclopaedia Britannica* (1974). With its focus on the 'dividual-particle' Hindu self (more concisely captured by Kolenda 1985), this view saw caste as both ideology and practice, while at the same time seeking a Hindu view of caste, in contrast to the dominant model of ranking, endogamy, occupation and purity (a model still prevalent in U.S. high school textbooks and in the U.S. public's mind). Part of the debate on caste has been focused on the use of "native categories" as contrasted to the imposition of western models, seen in the works of both Ostor (1984) and Daniel (1984). The extent to which Marriott's model of the dividual self and a three-dimensional Hindu conception of the world, while claiming this "native categories" position, in fact imposed western models was criticized by scholars like T.N. Madan (1995, 99-107) who found it as western and arbitrary as the older model marked by endogamy and purity, despite Marriott's claims to merge ideology and observed behavior.

Yet other modifications of U.S. anthropologists' understanding of caste emerged. The ethnohistorian Nicholas Dirks saw caste as imbedded in local and regional politics, and gave greater prominence to the role of the king than did writers relying more heavily on ideologies found in Brahmanical texts. While their approaches were very different, Marglin (1977) and Raheja (1988) both addressed issues of auspiciousness and the maintenance of Hindu hierarchies. Finally, those viewing caste from the lower ranks of the hierarchies (Berreman 1968, Mencher 1974, Moffat 1979, Freeman 1979, Lynch 1969) criticized Dumont and others whose interpretations were too textual and not representative of the multiplicity of views found in India. Belatedly, the connection between caste and class was raised, as well as extra-village studies of caste politics (e.g., Lynch 1969, Fox 1972). These merged into urban studies, where the attempt to find a small community to replace the village often led to the study of a caste community (Lynch 1969, Mines 1984, Rudner 1990) or caste organization in urban areas (see, for example, the papers in *Urban India*, Fox 1970).

More recently, caste conflicts rather than caste harmony came to dominate anthropological studies (e.g., see Wadley 1994, Bailey 1994), especially as caste played an even greater role on the national political stage, whether in the Dalit movement, in responses to the Mandal Commission report, or in the rewriting of panchayat laws when lower-caste politicians gain ascendancy in states like Uttar Pradesh.

MOVING KINSHIP STUDIES FROM STRUCTURE TO PROCESS

Given the dominance of caste and issues of great traditions, other aspects of Indian anthropology developed more slowly. Kinship, in part due to its connection to legal systems but also because of its reputed role in anthropological models of evolution, was an early focus of anthropological attention. India initially came under the anthropological gaze because of tribal kinship patterns. It was not until the 1960s that non-tribal kinship studies gained a foothold. While India became a testing ground for various anthropological debates, it also provided examples of kinship patterns that attracted foreign observers, whether these be the dominance of the ideology of the joint family, the ban on widow remarriage (see Wadley 1995), dowry (Tambiah 1973), matrilineality (Gough 1959, Yalman 1963), or polyandry (Berreman 1968, Rao 1995).

Two major trends in kinship influenced this work: alliance theory, reaching India from Levi-Strauss via Dumont and focusing on the nature of exchange relationships rather than the constitution of unilineal descent groups, and the cultural approach to kinship associated with David Schneider (1968) and found in the work of Inden and Nicholas (1977). More recently, kinship studies have become concerned with the functioning of the family, rather than on the structural relationships of descent or exchange that form the family.

Kinship studies marked the clearest north-south divide, following the linguistic divisions between Indo-European languages and Dravidian languages. Anthropologists sought to explore the implications of hierarchy and caste in the hypergamous marriage patterns that dominate northern elite kinship structures contrasted to the cross-cousin marriage patterns of the south. Some U.S. anthropological work dealt with terminological systems (Fruzetti and Ostor 1976, Vatuk 1969, and a non-anthropologist, Trautman 1981). Others focused more clearly on the structural implications of alliance and hypergamy (see Ostor et al. 1983). Regional patterns of family structures, building on Karve's path-breaking work of family structures, were further elaborated by Kolenda (1968) and re-emerged in the work of geographers (Sopher 1980) and demo-graphers (Dyson and Moore 1983, Caldwell 1984). Later, Vatuk (1975) and Raheja (1988) both focused on exchange between affines, Vatuk looking at gift-giving and Raheja at the exchange of inauspiciousness. In Raheja's work, for example, we learn that auspiciousness and good fortune are not merely obtained through birth, but are maintained through the transference of inauspicious out of the family through the giving of gifts. Others examined marriage alliances as related to local political systems (Fox 1972), or the importance of family in economic transactions (Carter 1988). Finally, the household economy began to be examined, as in the work of Gough (1979) and Mencher (1966) on production and kinship patterns while Vatuk (1972) moved anthropologists' attention to urban kinship patterns and the negotiations involved in maintaining kinship networks in the absence of extended households.

The family as a cultural unit and as a unit raising children, while not topics of major concern to the structural functionalist or structuralist studies of kinship, was of vital concern to some anthro-pologists. Trawick's study of love in a Tamil family (1990) moved U.S. anthropologists toward the study of emotion as she demonstrated how a particular family acted out the culturally marked notion of love (*anpu*). Related is Lynch's important edited volume, *Divine Passions* (1994), where a number of authors argue that emotion is socially constructed and not a universal quality of human history. Using the female life and life cycle as a locus for understanding family dynamics, Roy (1975) and Fruzetti (1982) made important contributions to the understanding of family dynamics, especially of child-rearing and the social construction of femaleness.[10] Nuckolls (1993) directed scholars' attention to sibling relationships and added a psychoanalytic interpretation, as did the anthropologically-inclined psychoanalyst Sudhir Kakar (1981). Further, it was through kinship studies that gender concerns were first taken up by anthropologists, resulting in volumes such as Papanek and Minault (1982) on the nature of purdah and the rules for female behavior, or Wadley (1980) on women in Tamil society.

More recent kinship analyses were closely tied to issues of gender, whether of household economy (Das Gupta 1995), female autonomy (Dyson and Moore 1983), women's health and survival (Miller 1981, Das Gupta 1987), patterns of education (Seymour 1994), mental health (Ullrich 1987), or fertility (Wadley 1993). (See Forbes, this volume, for an extensive discussion of scholarship on women in India.) Following on S. Daniel's examination of multiple perspectives of Tamil marriage (1980), an important volume on marriage edited by historians of religion (Courtright and Harlan 1995) examined marriage "from the margins," that is, from the view of those who had crossed or transgressed its boundaries. This volume demonstrated that there was no monolithic view of marriage, but rather that there were multiple conceptions of what marriage is and that looking at marriage from those who have transgressed its borders provided an unusually deep understanding of this multidimensional human institution. Other recent works on women's views on marriage and sexuality include Raheja and Gold (1994) and Wadley (1994). In both of these books, women were seen as not merely objects of exchange, but also as advocates for their own positions and situations. Sax's work (1991) on the goddess in the Himalayas presented related issues, particularly focusing on the crucial role of the daughter (also a theme in Raheja 1988) who remained responsible for her natal family's welfare despite her marriage into another family and village.

Kinship studies focused increasingly on processes and various kin relations, and less on structure and rules. Rather than collecting the rules, anthropologists were now more concerned with the dynamics of kinship, the variability surrounding the "rules," and the ways in which various groups, whether defined by caste, urbanity, or gender, were negotiating and contesting these rules.

INTERROGATING KARMA, RENUNCIATION, AND POPULAR RELIGION

If caste were the social institution that most defined India for the Euro-American, karma was the religious belief that upheld it. Following on Max Weber, karma was seen as the cause for India's lack of progress (why would people work, when their life was defined by a previous life?). In marked contrast, renunciation and the associated spirituality were lauded by the West as a Hindu way of escaping from social-economic strictures (as much for westerners as the Indians). Both have given way only slowly to more nuanced interpretations. The anthropological encounter with karma was best seen in the articles collected in Keyes and Daniel (1983) and in Wadley and Derr (1989). Here it was argued that karma, or fate, was not a feature determined for all time at one's birth, but rather was part of one's continual remaking (see also Gold 1988). If one were not bound, in fact, to a predetermined fate, then one could "act." He or she could gain merit for this lifetime through pilgrimage, ritual, or meritorious acts. He or she could also seek a better lifestyle and challenge his/her position in caste and family structures, as did the washerwoman in Wadley (1994) who divorced her first husband, saying "that marriage was not in my fate."

The Hindu sadhu or renunciate as a spiritual preceptor for the materialistic West was also a figure whose prior image had been challenged by numerous recent scholars. In her examination of the guru who used stories to teach, Narayan (1989) captured the droll humor and inventiveness of a modern swami, resting in his lawn chair before his foreign guests. Moreover, both Narayan and Gold (1992), in her rendition of an epic of renunciation, captured the ambivalence by both swami and audience about the renunciate's role. In a related book, Babb (1986) examined the "Hindu religious imagination" through the lens of three markedly different modern religious movements, two of which had special roles for spiritual leaders or gurus: The Radhasoamis, whose living guru is an incarnation of the highest Lord, and the followers of Sai Baba, whose miracles impress a western-educated middle class audience. In both religious movements, the interpersonal encounter between guru and devotee was paramount to establishing religious identity.

The vision of the renunciate held by Madan's teachers in the 1950s was most directly challenged by the recent recognition of their political role. Three works stand out: van der Veer's *Gods on Earth*

(1988), Andersen and Damli's *Brotherhood in Saffron* (1987), and McKean's *Divine Enterprise* (1996). Taken together, these three books presented priests and sadhus actively engaged in profit-making and politicking. They described spirituality performed and manipulated for both spiritual and this-worldly ends. Further, these books spoke directly to issues of nation and nation-building, which in India, as elsewhere, implies socially-constructed identities, identities which some see as religious. Van der Veer addressed these issues of religious nationalism in another book (van der Veer 1994) where he argued that religious identity is constructed through ritual discourse and practice, i.e., that it is emergent in everyday religious life. (See also Kakar 1996.)

As American anthropologists gained a better grasp of the languages of India, popular textual traditions began to influence their work, especially in the realms of popular religion (Sax 1991) and oral traditions (Narayan 1989, Gold 1992, Gold and Raheja 1994, Blackburn et al. 1989, Blackburn and Ramanujan 1986). This intersection of anthropology and folklore studies (which tended to be pursued by those with anthropological training) was linked to the development of performance studies more generally, and to the recognition of culture as emergent in practice (see also Claus, this volume). Whether a study of goddesses (Preston 1982, Sax 1990), of women's interpretations of goddesses (Raheja and Gold 1994), of women's rituals of childbirth or the calendar (Hanchett 1988), of the relationship between Hindu divinities and humans (Babb 1975, Wadley 1975) of Jain ideas of divinity (Babb 1996),[11] of the content and role of oral epics and written epics in oral form (Beck 1982, Blackburn et al. 1989), or of the dynamics of storytelling and other folk forms (Blackburn and Ramanujan 1986, Henry 1988, Trawick 1988). Anthropological studies of the little traditions of Hinduism and Jainism and their complex relationships to the classical traditions of Sanskrit and other literate languages have been rich and rewarding, merging with the work of historians of religion and enhancing both. Taken together, these efforts capture innumerable traditions long ignored by textualists and unremarked by most (though some British colonial observers like Crooke and Tod are exceptions). These newly discovered tales, epics, and rituals force anthropologists to reexamine their assumptions about Indian tradition and to listen carefully to the multiple voices of Indians past and present as they reveal cultural constructions of everyday life long ignored or unseen.

Closely allied to studies of popular religion were explorations of traditional healing systems within South Asia. The original concern was to compare the use and efficacy of traditional and western medicine (e.g., Gould 1965). Charles Leslie's edited volume, *Asian Medical Systems* (1976), was crucial in legitimating Hindu traditions of healing for western academic audiences. Issues raised by South Asian healing range from the nature and forms of spirit possession, to the role of mother goddesses as historically constructed in response to specific disease paradigms, to definitions of mental and physical health and well-being. A second volume edited by V. Daniel and J. Pugh (1984) addressed a number of these issues, ranging from astrology, to smallpox and tuberculosis as they intersected with the Tamil goddess Mariamman, to folk concepts of mental disorder in Bengal, to spirit possession. Related is the work of Joseph Alter (1992) on Indian constructions of the body, especially as seen in the wrestler. As the West recognizes its own social constructions of medicine and the body, these works on India became increasingly valued outside the circle of Indianists.

Finally, Hindu patterns of food consumption gained the attention of scholars such as Khare (1992) and Toomey (1994). Toomey captured the relationships between ritual, religious experience and food in his study of the rituals of feasting at Krishna pilgrimage sites in Govardhan. He found that food practices associated with *prasād*, offerings to the deity, often contradicted and contested the normal strictures of Hindu society, and thus were used in practice to create and mark identities. Khare edited a volume in which the expressive aspects of food were examined in relation to regional and local ritual and religious practices, as well as sacred and secular texts. These two volumes highlighted the importance of food in formulating social relationships and identities within the South Asian world.

MOVING TO NATION AND WORLD

In a circular fashion, U.S. scholars of India are now recapturing their interest in India's indigenous peoples. While the tribals of India were the focus of English researchers, American anthropology has had little impact on "tribal" studies for two reasons. First, the shift to the anthropology of India marked the shift to the peasant, and ultimately to the city. Second, even·now it is difficult for U.S.-based researchers (including Indian nationals) to get research clearance from the Indian government to study so-called tribal peoples. Despite these drawbacks, and related to current trends in anthropological praxis as well as to the current concern among both academics and the public at large for indigenous peoples worldwide, U.S.-trained anthropologists, many of South Asian descent, reclaimed a space for tribal studies, especially as related to environmental issues (see Fisher 1996 and Parajuli 1995 for examples of this concern).

The 1950s also saw the development of a neo-colonial anthropology: Applied anthropology at the service of development agencies. In India, this was most visible in Albert Mayor's *Pilot Project India* (1958), which provided the blueprint for India's village-based community development program (constructed in part on the work of the U.S. missionaries and observers of Indian village life, William and Charlotte Wiser, at the India Village Service in Etah District, U.P.). More recently, anthropologists have supported the efforts of non-government organizations, especially those focusing on women, the environment or indigenous peoples.

Three South Asians have dealt directly with the problematic of development and traditions of knowledge among peasants and adivasis. Appadurai (1990) provided an ethnographic account of how a small change in water technology affected the sociality of a peasant community in Maharashtra. Akhil Gupta (1995) developed an ethnography of the state in a small community in Uttar Pradesh based on the everyday perceptions of development administration and bureaucratic corruption. Parajuli (1991, 1995) began the discursive analysis of development in relation to new social movements in India. Based on the ethnographic study of *ādivāsī* peasants' participation in various ethnic and ecological movements in Jharkand and other parts of middle India, Parajuli developed the notion of ecological ethnicity as a way of linking peasant and tribal traditions of knowledge, sustainability of their ecosystems, and their resistance to destructive development projects.

In the same tradition, the sociologically-trained Amita Bhaviskar (1995) drew attention to the delicate tribal-peasant connection and the articulation of resistance to development projects such as large dams in Narmada Valley. The anthropologist William Fisher edited a volume on Narmada (1995), while Anderson and Huber (1988) highlighted the contestation between World Bank-sponsored forestry programs and the *ādivāsī* ecological milieu in Madhya Pradesh. Apffel-Marglin (1995) situated rural Indian women in the debate on traditions of knowledge. She articulated the question of gender and its representation, and urged anthropologists not to reduce Indian women's cognition either to the liberal idea of 'subjecthood' or to the more elusive notion of "subaltern consciousness."

One of the most important developments coming out of Indian anthropology was the focus on public culture and the journal *Public*

Culture, initially sponsored by the Joint Committee on South Asia for the Social Science Research Council and the American Council of Learned Societies. Conceived by Arjun Appadurai and Carol Breckenridge, *Public Culture* focused on the transnational character of emerging cultural forms and on those aspects of culture that are neither folk nor mass, but related instead to propagation by/ through the media and other kinds of information systems, through consumer specialists. Sara Dickey's work (1993) was an exemplary piece in this mold as she examined the effects of cinema-going on the urban poor in Madras. Here she examines not the producers' intentions but the meaning imputed to Tamil films by the urban movie goers who she saw as using films to negotiate their disadvantages by seeing in the melodramas of a film personal solutions rather than collective opposition to their social situations. The relationship between mass media and identity formation was also the focus of Purnima Mankekar's work (1993) on television viewing in urban north India. Like Dickey, she focused on the ways in which viewers engaged with what they viewed, rather than acting as mere passive receivers. A more wide-ranging volume was Babb and Wadley's edited work (1995) on media and transformations in religious systems in South Asia. This volume included articles on the Amar Chitra Katha comic books and the social vision of Anant Pai, their creator; on the Sagar's *Rāmāyaṇa,* again as a particular cultural construct; on the transmission of religion through the new media of record and cassette; and on the pervasive "god posters" found in taxis and scooters, shops and homes, throughout India. These new media forms carried recognizable versions of old symbols, while reconstructing them for new audiences with increasing exposure to non-Indian ideas.

In addition to numerous attempts to comprehend the process of nation-building and nationalism, mentioned above, recent research often contends with the Indian diaspora, the dispersal of populations from India to Africa, Europe, East Asia, and the Americas. As with the studies of Indians in India, the first writings were about caste in overseas communities (Schwartz 1967). Now the focus is on Indian identity, song and political structures in Fiji (Brenneis 1984) or other contested identities of religion and nationality in Fiji (Kelley 1991); or the ethnoterritorial identities that link Sikhs in California and Canada to those in Punjab (Dusenbery 1989), as definitions of religious communities are reimagined for these modern times.

A NEW PARADIGM?

There is no doubt that the vision of Indian society held by anthropologists at the time of India's independence in 1947 has altered. Anyone now reading Ralph Linton's classic textbook from the 1950s would question his initial assumptions: "Indian culture was characterized by an extreme development of ascribed status and role, which made it the most static and most perfectly integrated culture so far developed" (1955, 515). It is possible to see a "perfectly integrated" society when one's vision is through the same glasses worn by the elite; when women's voices are not heard; when conflict is denied; and process unexplored. The many challenges to this vision have engrossed U.S. anthropologists for the last fifty years. But more critical has been the difficulty in marking the boundary of anthropology.

The often overwhelming interdisciplinary nature of the anthropology of India is breaking rigid boundaries set between sociology and anthropology, political and religious studies, or culture and nature. Witness the fact that recent anthropological writings draw on the work of non-anthropologists such as Vandana Shiva (1988) on feminism and ecology, Gadgil and Guha (1992) on history and political culture, Partha Chatterjee (1993) on nationalism and the subaltern consciousness, Gail Omvedt (1993) on social movements, Patricia and Roger Jeffery on gender and demography (1989), Bina Agarwal (1994) on gender and social justice issues, Lindsay Harlan (1992) on women's religious roles, and Sudhir Kakar (1979) and Ashis Nandy (1987) on the Indian consciousness. The list could continue. But perhaps the most important break in the paradigm created by Cohn, Marriott, Madan and colleagues in the early stages of the U.S. venture into the anthropology of India is that insights and paradigms are now coming increasingly from across the disciplines and, even more critical, from within India itself.

Without doubt, the paradigms of the 1940s and early 1950s are no longer seen as valid. The specifics of a new paradigm or paradigms are unclear, but I suggest that they are constructed around ideas such as contested identities, historical processes of continual change, imagined communities, subaltern voices, nationalism, the politics of space, gender (and gendered identities), and emergent in everyday practice. Certainly they are not "static" and "perfectly integrated."

NOTES

1. For readers who are interested in pursuing the issues raised here, I suggest these sources: Marriott (1995) *Village India*; Singer and Cohn (1968) *Structure and Change in Indian Society*; Mandelbaum (1970) *Society in India*, vols. 1 and 2, and various essays by T.N. Madan, especially those in *Pathways* (1995), as well as the volumes in the Oxford University Press series on the social anthropology of South Asia (Gupta 1991, Oberoi 1993).

2. It is important that anthropologists remind themselves that they are not the first to ask such questions. The passion with which their graduate students grab on to issues such as reflextivity makes it appear as if these are new questions, when they are not.

3. This is not to say that Mexico had no ancient textual traditions, but rather that in the 1950s, they were largely inaccessible and unstudied. Further, the colonial destruction of native traditions throughout the Americas was far-reaching, unlike India. There is also a vital connection between the availability of training in languages and the work done by anthropologists. Prior to the mid-1950s, aside from Sanskrit, no Indian languages were offered regularly in U.S. universities. Through the 1960s, the Ford Foundation provided language training for students in England before embarking to India. As Hindi, and then Bengali, Tamil, Telugu, and Malayalam began to be offered in U.S. universities (though often not regularly or in many locations), U.S. anthropologists had increasingly good language skills. (Note that, even today, one cannot study Kannada or Orissi, to take just two examples, in the U.S.) Where U.S. scholars do their work in India is closely tied to what languages were available where they were trained. Chicago students frequently worked in Bengal or, after Ramanujan's arrival, Tamilnadu, while Wisconsin students were more likely to work in Andhra Pradesh. More importantly, the kind of research they did changed as their linguistic skills improved. This was particularly important for the study of popular religion and oral traditions, as well as family dynamics, local politics, and the emerging field of the study of emotion. (I remain convinced that early scholars focused on such concrete "items" as kinship terminologies because their lack of language skills limited their access to the more complex processural issues now demanding attention, though not given the same elite status, even today, as the kinds of analyses found in *African Systems of Kinship and Marriage*. Note too that a major recent American piece on kinship terminologies is not by an anthropologist but by an historian; see Trautman 1981.)

4. See Singer 1972 for a key vision of the modernizing great tradition.

5. I must note the truly interdisciplinary nature of U.S. anthropology about India. Perhaps in Indian studies, more than any other field defined geographically, there is a remarkable exchange of ideas

across disciplines. On the positive side, the blurring of academic genres has happened particularly rapidly. On the negative side, the anthropology of India is not well-represented in forums like the American Anthropological Association or the American Folklore Society, with the best and more interesting panels about India being interdisciplinary in nature and found at the South Asian Studies meetings at places like Wisconsin or the Association for Asian Studies. This interdisciplinary collaboration is further reflected in the diversity of disciplinary backgrounds found in major edited volumes. See, for example, Singer (1959) *Traditional India*; Singer and Cohn (1968) *Structure and Change in Indian Society*; Babb and Wadley (1995) *Media and the Transformation of Religion in South Asia*; Harlan and Courtright (1995) *From the Margins of Hindu Marriage*; or Van der Veer (1995) *Nation and Migration: The Politics of Space in the South Asian Diaspora*.

6. The volumes produced by Ruth and Stanley Freed on a village on the outskirts of Delhi are a form of magnum opus, covering health, demography, family, religion, etc.

7. I recently presented a paper at the American Anthropological Association meetings in which continual change was reaffirmed in my own mind. Looking at women's self-representations over time, as seen in presenting themselves before a camera, I found myself struck by the changes in dress style and attire since 1967, aided by interviews that took change in women's dress back to the 1930s. Once we accept that change is and has been occurring, everything must be challenged including dress, food, and housing styles.

8. See Bhuvana Rao 1995. Her dissertation research was funded by AIIS.

9. See Shubra Gururani 1996. Her dissertation research was funded by AIIS.

10. It is noteworthy that nothing representing these approaches makes it into the Oxford volumes (see note 1).

11. There are as yet no major anthropological studies of Islam in India written by American anthropologists.

REFERENCES

Agarwal, Bina. 1994. *A Field of One's Own: Gender and Land Rights in South Asia*. Cambridge: Cambridge Univ. Press.

Alter, Joseph. 1992. *The Wrestler's Body: Identity and Ideology in North India*. Berkeley: Univ. of California Press.

Anderson, Robert and Walter Huber. 1988. *The Hour of the Fox: Tropical Forests, the World Bank and Indigenous Peoples in Central India*. Seattle: Univ. of Washington Press.

Anderson, Walter and Sridhar Damle. 1987. *The Brotherhood in Saffron: The Rashtriya Swayamsevak Sangh and Hindu Revivalism*. Boulder: Westview.

Apffel-Marglin, Fredrique. 1995. "Gender and the Unitary Self: Looking for the Subaltern in Coastal Orissa." *South Asia Research* 15: 78-130.

Appadurai, Arjun. 1981. *Worship and Conflict under Colonial Rule: A South India Case.* Cambridge: Cambridge Univ. Press.

————. 1990. "Technology and the Reproduction of Values in Rural Western India." In *Decolonizing Knowledge: From Development to Dialogue,* ed. Frederique Apffel-Marglin and Stephen A. Marglin, 185-216. Oxford: Clarendon.

Babb, Lawrence A. 1975. *The Divine Hierarchy.* New York: Columbia Univ. Press.

————. 1986. *Redemptive Encounters: Three Modern Styles in the Hindu Tradition.* Berkeley: Univ. of California Press.

————. 1996. *Absent Lord: Ascetic and King in a Jain Ritual Culture.* Berkeley: Univ. of California Press.

Babb, Lawrence A. and Susan S. Wadley, eds. 1995. *Media and the Transformation of Religion in South Asia.* Philadelphia: Univ. of Pennsylvania Press.

Bailey, Frederick G. 1957. *Caste and the Economic Frontier: A Village in Highland Orissa.* Manchester: Manchester Univ. Press.

————. 1995. *The Witch Hunt.* Ithaca: Cornell Univ. Press.

Blackburn, Stuart H., and A.K. Ramanujan, eds. 1986. *Another Harmony: New Essays on the Folklore of India.* Berkeley: Univ. of California Press.

Blackburn, Stuart H., Peter Claus, Joyce Burkhalter Flueckiger, and Susan S. Wadley, eds. 1989. *Oral Epics in India.* Berkeley: Univ. of California Press.

Bean, Susan. 1975. "Referential and Indexical Meanings of Amma in Kannada: Mother, Woman, Goddess, Pox, and Help!" *Journal of Anthropological Research* 31: 313-330.

Beck, Brenda E. F. 1982. *The Three Twins: The Telling of a South Indian Folk Epic.* Bloomington: Indiana Univ. Press.

Berreman, Gerald D. 1968. *Hindus of the Himalayas.* Berkeley: Univ. of California Press.

Brenneis, Donald 1984. "Grog and Gossip in Bhatgaon: Style and Substance in Fiji Indian Conversation." *American Ethnologist* 11.

Caldwell, John, P.H. Reddy, and P. Caldwell. 1984. "The Determinants of Fertility Decline in Rural South India." In *India's Demography: Essays on the Contemporary Population,* ed. Tim Dyson and Nigel Crook, 187-207. New Delhi: South Asian Publishers.

Carter, A.T. 1974. "A Comparative Analysis of Systems of Kinship and Marriage in South Asia." *Proceedings of the Royal Anthropological Institute for 1973,* 29-54.

————. 1988. "Land Transactions and Household Dynamics in Maharashtra." In *City, Countryside, and Society in Maharashtra,* ed. D.W. Attwood, M. Israel, and N.K. Wagle, 151-171. Toronto: Univ. of Toronto Press.

Chatterjee, Partha. 1993. *Nation and its Fragments.* Princeton: Princeton Univ. Press.

Claus, Peter. 1975. "The Siri Myth and Ritual: A Mass Possession Cult of South India." *Ethnology* 14:47-58.

Cohn, Bernard S. 1955. "The Pasts of an Indian Village." *Comparative Studies in Society and History* 3:241-249.

———. 1968. "Notes on the History of the Study of Indian Society and Culture." In *Structure and Change in Indian Society*, ed. Milton Singer and Bernard S. Cohn, 3-28. Chicago: Aldine.

———. 1971. *India: The Social Anthropology of a Civilization*. Englewood Cliffs, NJ: Prentice-Hall.

Crooke, William. 1971. *The North-Western Provinces of India: Their History, Ethnology and Administration*. Delhi: Indological Book House.

Daniel, E. Valentine. 1987. *Fluid Signs: Being a Person the Tamil Way*. Berkeley: Univ. of California Press.

Daniel, Sheryl. 1980. "Marriage in Tamil Culture: The Problem of Conflicting 'Models'." In *The Powers of Tamil Women*, ed. Susan S. Wadley, 61-91. South Asia Series No. 6, Foreign and Compa-rative Studies Program, Maxwell School, Syracuse University.

Das Gupta, Monica. 1987. "Selective Discrimination against Female Children in Rural Punjab, India." *Population and Development Review* 13: 77-100.

Dickey, Sara. 1993. *Cinema and the Urban Poor in South India*. New York: Cambridge Univ. Press.

Dirks, Nicholas. 1993 (2nd edition). *The Hollow Crown: Ethnohistory of an Indian Kingdom*. Ann Arbor: Univ. of Michigan Press.

Dumont, Louis. 1980 (rev. edition). *Homo Hierarchicus: The Caste System and Its Implications*. Chicago: Univ. of Chicago Press.

Dusenbery, Verne A. 1995. "A Sikh Diaspora? Contested Identities and Constructed Realities." In *Nation and Migration: The Politics of Space in the South Asian Diaspora*, ed. Peter Van der Veer. Philadelphia: Univ. of Pennsylvania Press.

Dyson, Time and M. Moore. 1983. "On Kinship Structure, Female Autonomy, and Demographic Behavior in India." *Population and Development Review* 9:35-59.

Erndl, Kathleen M. 1993. *Victory to the Mother: The Hindu Goddess of Northwest India in Myth, Ritual and Symbol*. New York: Oxford Univ. Press.

Evans-Pritchard, E. E. 1965. *The Position of Women in Primitive Societies, and Other Essays in Social Anthropology*. New York: Free Press.

Fisher, William. 1995. *Toward Sustainable Development: Struggling Over India's Narmada River*. New York: M.E. Sharpe.

Flueckiger, Joyce Burkhalter. 1996. *Gender and Genre in the Folklore of Middle India*. Ithaca: Cornell Univ. Press.

Fox, Richard G. 1972. *Kin, Clan, Raja and Rule: State-Hinterland Relations in Pre-Industrial India*. Berkeley: Univ. of California Press.

———. 1985. *Lions of the Punjab: Culture in the Making*. Berkeley: Univ. of California Press.

Fox, Richard G., ed. 1970. *Urban India: Society, Space and Image*. Monograph and Occasional Paper Series no. 10, Program in Comparative Studies on Southern Asia, Duke University.

Freed, Ruth. 1980. *Rites of Passage in Shanti Nagar*. New York: American

Museum of Natural History. Anthropological Papers of the American Museum of Natural History, 56:1.

———. 1981. *Enculturation and Education in Shanti Nagar*. New York: American Museum of Natural History. Anthropological Papers of the American Museum of Natural History, 57:2.

Freed, Stanley A. 1976. *Shanti Nagar: The Effects of Urbanization in a Village in North India*. New York: American Museum of Natural History. Anthropological Papers of the American Museum of Natural History, 53:1.

Freeman, James M. 1979. *Untouchable: An Indian Life History*. London: George Allen and Unwin.

Fruzzetti, Lina. 1982. *The Gift of a Virgin*. New Brunswick, NJ: Rutgers Univ. Press.

Fruzzetti, Lina and Akos Ostor. 1976. "Is There a Structure to North India Kinship Terminology?" *Contributions to Indian Sociology, new series* 10:63-96.

Fruzetti, Lina, Akos Ostor and Steve Barnett, eds. 1983. *Concepts of the Person: Kinship, Caste and Marriage in India*. Delhi: Oxford Univ. Press.

Gold, Ann Grodzins. 1988. *Fruitful Journeys: The Ways of Rajasthani Pilgrims*. Berkeley: Univ. of California Press.

———. 1992. *A Carnival of Parting*. Berkeley: Univ. of California Press.

Gough, Kathleen. 1955. "The Social Structure of a Tanjore Village." In *Village India: Studies in the Little Community*, ed. McKim Marriot, 36-52. Chicago: Univ. of Chicago Press.

———. 1959. "The Nayars and the Definition of Marriage." *Journal of the Royal Anthropological Institute* 89: 23-34.

———. 1979. "Dravidian Kinship and Modes of Production." *Contributions to Indian Sociology, new series* 13:265-291.

Gould, Harold. 1965. "Modern Medicine and Folk Cognition in Rural India." *Human Organization* 84: 201-208.

Gururani, Shubhra. 1996. *Fuel, Fodder, and Farmers: The Politics of Forest Use and Abuse in Uttarakhand, India*. Unpublished doctoral dissertation, Syracuse University.

Gupta, Akhil. 1995. "Blurred Boundaries: The Discourse of Corruption, the Culture of Politics and the Imagined State." *American Ethnologist* 22:375-402.

Gupta, Dipankar, ed. 1992. *Social Stratification*. Delhi: Oxford Univ. Press.

Hanchett, Suzanne. 1988. *Coloured Rice: Symbolic Structure in Hindu Family Festivals*. Delhi: Hindustan.

Harlan, Lindsay. 1992. *Religion and Rajput Women: The Ethic of Protection in Contemporary Narratives*. Berkeley: Univ. of California Press.

Harlan, Lindsay and Paul B. Courtright, eds. 1995. *From the Margins of Hindu Marriage: Essays on Gender, Religion and Culture*. New York: Oxford Univ. Press.

Henry, Edward O. 1988. *Chant the Names of God: Musical Cultures in Bhojpuri-speaking India*. San Diego: San Diego State Univ. Press.

Inden, Ronald B. and Ralph W. Nicholas. 1977. *Kinship in Bengali Culture*. Chicago: Univ. of Chicago Press.

Jacobson, Doranne and Susan S. Wadley. 1996 (3rd edition). *Women In India: Two Perspectives*. Delhi: Manohar.

Jeffery, Patricia, Roger Jeffery, and Andrew Lyon. 1989. *Labour Pains and Labour Power: Women and Childbearing in India*. London: Zed.

Kakar, Sudhir. 1981 (2nd edition revised and enlarged). *The Inner World: A Psychoanalytic Study of Childhood and Society in India*. Delhi: Oxford Univ. Press.

———. 1996. *The Colors of Violence: Cultural Identities, Religion, and Conflict*. Chicago: Univ. of Chicago Press.

Kelly, John D. 1991. *A Politics of Virtue: Hinduism, Sexuality, and Countercolonial Discourse in Fiji*. Chicago: Univ. of Chicago Press.

Keyes, Charles F. and E. Valentine Daniel, eds. 1983. *Karma: An Anthropological Inquiry*. Berkeley: Univ. of California Press.

Khare, R.S. 1984. *The Untouchable as Himself: Ideology, Identity and Pragmatism Among the Lucknow Chamars*. Cambridge: Cambridge Univ. Press.

———. 1992. *The Eternal Food: Gastronomic Ideas and Experiences of Hindus and Buddhists*. Albany: State Univ. of New York Press.

Kolenda, Pauline. 1968. "Region, Caste and Family Structure: A Comparative Study of the Indian 'Joint' Family." In *Structure and Change in Indian Society*, ed. Milton Singer and Bernard S. Cohn, 339-396. Chicago: Aldine.

———. 1985. *Caste in Contemporary India. Beyond Organic Solidarity*. Prospect Heights, IL: Waveland Press.

Leach, Edmund. 1963. *Rethinking Anthropology*. London: Athlone Press.

Leslie, Charles, ed. 1976. *Asian Medical Systems*. Berkeley: Univ. of California Press.

Linton, Ralph. 1961. *The Tree of Culture*. New York: Alfred A. Knopf.

Lynch, Owen M. 1969. *The Politics of Untouchability: Social Mobility and Social Change in a City of India*. New York: Columbia Univ. Press.

Lynch, Owen M., ed. 1990. *Divine Passions: The Social Construction of Emotion in India*. Berkeley: Univ. of California Press.

Madan, T. N. 1996. "Anthropology as Critical Self-Awareness." In *The Multiverse of Democracy: Essays in Honour of Rajni Kothari*, ed. D.S. Sheth and Ashis Nandy. New Delhi: Sage.

———. 1995. *Pathways: Approaches to the Study of Society in India*. Delhi: Oxford Univ. Press.

Madan, T. N., ed. 1992. *Religion in India*. Delhi: Oxford Univ. Press.

Mandelbaum, David G. 1970. *Society in India*. vol. one: *Continuity and Change*. Berkeley: Univ. of California Press.

———. 1970. *Society in India*. vol. two: *Change and Continuity*. Berkeley: Univ. of California Press.

Mankekar, Purnima. 1993. "National Texts and Gendered Lives: An Ethnography of Television Viewers in a North Indian City." *American Ethnologist* 20:543-563.

Marglin, Frederique A. 1977. "Power, Purity and Pollution: Aspects of the Caste System Reconsidered." *Contributions to Indian Sociology, new series* 11:245-270.

Marriott, McKim. 1955. "Little Communities in an Indigenous Civilization." In *Village India: Studies in the Little Community*, ed. McKim Marriot, 171-222. Chicago: Univ. of Chicago Press.

———. 1966. "The Feast of Love." In *Krishna: Myths, Rites, and Attitudes*, ed. Milton Singer, 200-212. Chicago: Univ. of Chicago Press.

———. 1968. "Caste Ranking and Food Transactions: A Matrix Analysis." In *Structure and Change in Indian Society*, ed. Milton Singer and Bernard S. Cohn, 133-171. Chicago: Aldine.

———. 1989. "Constructing an Indian Ethnosociology." *Contributions to Indian Sociology, new series* 23:1-40.

Marriot, McKim, ed. 1955. *Village India: Studies in the Little Community.* Chicago: Univ. of Chicago Press.

Marriott, McKim and Ronald B. Inden. 1974. "Caste Systems." *Encyclopaedia Britannica, macropaedia* 15th ed., 3:982-991.

Mayer, Albert and Associates. 1958. *Pilot Project India: The Story of Rural Development in Etawah, U.P.* Berkeley: Univ. of California Press.

McKean, Lise. 1996. *Divine Enterprise: Gurus and the Hindu Nationalist Movement.* Chicago: Univ. of Chicago Press.

Mencher, Joan. 1966. "Kerala and Madras: A Comparative Study of Ecology and Social Structure." *Ethnology* 5:135-71.

———. 1974. "The Caste System Upside-down, or the Not-so- Mysterious East." *Current Anthropology* 15: 469-493.

Miller, Barbara D. 1981. *The Endangered Sex: Neglect of Female Children in Rural North India.* Ithaca: Cornell Univ. Press.

Milner, Murray, Jr. 1994. *Status and Sacredness: A General Theory of Status Relations and an Analysis of Indian Culture.* New York: Oxford Univ. Press.

Mines, Michael. 1984. *The Warrior Merchants: Textiles, Trade and Territory in South India.* Cambridge: Cambridge Univ. Press.

Moffat, Michael. 1979. *An Untouchable Community in South India.* Princeton: Princeton Univ. Press.

———. 1996. "Village and Personal Agency in South Asia." *American Anthropologist* 98:172-174.

Nandy, Ashis. 1987. *Traditions, Tyranny and Utopia.* Delhi: Oxford Univ. Press.

Narayan, Kirin. 1989. *Storytellers, Saints, and Scoundrels: Folk Narrative in Hindu Religious Teaching.* Philadelphia: Univ. of Pennsylvania Press.

———. 1993. "How Native is a 'Native' Anthropologist?" *American Anthropologist* 95:671-686.

Nicholas, Ralph. 1968. "Structures of Politics in the Villages of Southern Asia." In *Structure and Change in Indian Society*, ed. Milton Singer and Bernard S. Cohn, 243-284. Chicago: Aldine.

Nuckolls, Charles W. 1993. *Siblings in South Asia: Brothers and Sisters in Cultural Context.* New York: Guilford Press.

Oberoi, Patricia, ed. 1993. *Family, Kinship and Marriage in India.* Delhi: Oxford Univ. Press.

Omvedt, Gail. 1994. *Reinventing Revolution: New Social Movements and the Socialist Tradition in India.* London: M.E. Sharpe.

Papanek, H. and Gail Minault, eds. 1982. *Separate Worlds: Studies of Purdah in South Asia.* New Delhi: Chanakya.

Parajuli, Pramod. 1991. "Power and Knowledge in Development Discourse: New Social Movements and the State in India." *International Social Science Journal* 127:173-190.

———. 1995. "Ecological Ethnicity in the Making: Developmentist Hegemonies and Emergent Identities in India." *Identitites: Global Studies in Culture and Power* 3:15-59.

Preston, James J., ed. 1982. *Mother Worship: Themes and Variations.* Chapel Hill: Univ. of North Carolina Press.

Raheja, Gloria Goodwin. 1988. *The Poison in the Gift.* Chicago: Univ. of Chicago Press.

———. 1996. "Caste, Colonialism and the Speech of the Colonized: Entextualization and Disciplinary Control in India." *American Ethnologist* 23.

Raheja, Gloria Goodwin and Ann Grodzins Gold. 1994. *Listen to the Heron's Words: Reimagining Gender and Kinship in North India.* Berkeley: Univ. of California Press.

Rao, Bhuvana. 1995. *"Is She or is She Not?" Female Sexuality, Gender Ideologies and Women's Health in Tehri Garhwal, North India.* Unpublished doctoral dissertation, Syracuse University.

Redfield, Robert. 1962-63. *Human Nature and the Study of Society; the Papers of Robert Redfield.* Chicago: Univ. of Chicago Press.

Roy, Monisha. 1975. *Bengali Women.* Chicago: Univ. of Chicago Press.

Rudner, David West. 1994. *Caste and Capitalism in Colonial India: The Nattukottai Chettiars.* Berkeley: Univ. of California Press.

Sax, William. 1991. *Mountain Goddess: Gender and Politics in a Himalayan Pilgrimage.* New York: Oxford Univ. Press.

Schneider, David. 1968. *American Kinship: A Cultural Account.* Englewood Cliffs, NJ: Prentice Hall.

Schwartz, Barton M., ed. 1967. *Caste in Overseas Indian Communities.* San Francisco: Chandler.

Seymour, Susan. 1994. *Women, Education and Family Structure in India.* Boulder: Westview.

Shiva, Vandana. 1988. *Staying Alive: Women, Ecology and Development.* London: Zed.

Singer, Milton. 1972. *When a Great Tradition Modernizes: An Anthropological Approach to Indian Civilization.* New York: Praeger.

Singer, Milton, ed. 1959. *Traditional India: Structure and Change.* Philadelphia:

American Folklore Society, Bibliographical and Special Series, vol. 10.

————. 1966. *Krishna: Myths, Rites, and Attitudes.* Chicago: Univ. of Chicago Press.

Singer, Milton and Bernard S. Cohn, eds. 1968. *Structure and Change in Indian Society.* Chicago: Aldine.

Sopher, David. 1980. *An Exploration of India: Geographical Perspectives on Society and Culture.* Ithaca: Cornell Univ. Press.

Srinivas, M. N. 1959. "The Dominant Caste in Rampura." *American Anthropologist* 61:1-16.

Tambiah, S. J. 1973. "Dowry and Bridewealth and the Property Rights of Women in South Asia." In *Bridewealth and Dowry,* ed. Jack Goody and S. J. Tambiah. Cambridge: Cambridge Univ. Press.

Tod, James. 1971. *Annals and Antiquities of Rajasthan or the Central and Western Rajpoot States of India.* New Delhi: K. M. N. Publishers.

Trautman, Thomas R. 1981. *Dravidian Kinship.* Cambridge: Cambridge Univ. Press.

Trawick, Margaret. 1988. "Spirits and Voices in Tamil Song." *American Ethnologist* 15: 193-215

————. 1990. *Notes on Love in a Tamil Family.* Berkeley: Univ. of California Press.

Ullrich, Helen. 1987. "A Study of Change and Depression Among Havik Brahmin Women in a South Indian Village." *Culture, Medicine and Psychiatry* 2: 261-287.

Van der Veer, Peter. 1988. *Gods on Earth: The Management of Religious Experience and Identity in a North Indian Pilgrimage Center.* London: Athlone Press.

————. 1994. *Religious Nationalism: Hindus and Muslims in India.* Berkeley: Univ. of California Press.

Van der Veer, Peter, ed. 1995. *Nation and Migration: The Politics of Space in the South Asian Diaspora.* Philadelphia: Univ. of Pennsylvania Press.

Vatuk, Sylvia. 1969. "Reference, Address, and Fictive Kinship in Urban North India." *Ethnology* 8:255-72.

————. 1972. *Kinship and Urbanization: White Collar Migrants in North India.* Berkeley: Univ. of California Press.

————. 1975. "Gifts and Affines in North India." *Contributions to Indian Sociology* 9:155-96.

————. 1987. "Authority, Power and Autonomy in the Life Cycle of North Indian Women." In *Dimensions of Social Life: Essay in Honor of David G. Mandelbaum,* ed. Paul Hockings, 23-44. Berlin: Mouton de Gruyter.

Visweswaram, Kamala. 1995. *Fictions of Feminist Ethnography.* Minneapolis: Univ. of Minnesota Press.

Wadley, Susan S. 1975. *Shakti: Power in the Conceptual Structure of Karimpur Religion.* Chicago: Dept. of Anthropology, Univ. of Chicago.

————. 1977. "Women in the Hindu Tradition." In *Women in India: Two Perspectives,* ed. Doranne Jacobson and Susan S. Wadley, 113-139. New Delhi: Manohar.

————. 1993. "Family Composition Strategies in Rural North India." *Social Science and Medicine* 37:1367-76.

————. 1994. *Struggling with Destiny in Karimpur, 1925-1984*. Berkeley: Univ. of California Press.

————. 1995. "No Longer a Wife: Widows in Rural North India." In *From the Margins of Hindu Marriage: Essays on Gender, Religion and Culture,* ed. L. Harlan and P. Courtright, 92-118. New York: Oxford Univ. Press.

Wadley, Susan S., ed. 1980. *The Powers of Tamil Women*. South Asia Series no. 6, Foreign and Comparative Studies Program, Maxwell School, Syracuse University.

Wadley, Susan S. and Bruce W. Derr. 1989. "Eating Sins in Karimpur." *Contributions to Indian Sociology, new series* 23.

Wiser, William H. (1936) 1958. *The Hindu Jajmani System*. Lucknow: Lucknow Publishing House.

Wiser, William H. and Charlotte V. Wiser. 1989. *Behind Mud Walls, 1930-1960*. With a sequel, "The Village in 1970" and a new chapter by Susan S. Wadley, "The Village in 1984." Berkeley: Univ. of California Press.

Yalman, Nur. 1963. "On the Purity and Sexuality of Women in the Castes of Ceylon and Malabar." *Journal of the Royal Anthropological Institute* 93:25-58.

Archaeology

GREGORY L. POSSEHL

The decades since Indian independence have seen significant progress in understanding the prehistoric past in India. Most of this progress is attributable to the archeological establishments in India: the Archaeological Survey, state departments of archaeology, and their colleagues in Indian universities. The founding and growth of archaeology in Indian universities unfolded in the post-colonial era, but as yet there has been little written on this subject. There has also been some cooperation between Indian institutions and research teams from other countries. The most prominent foreign teams have been from the United States and the United Kingdom, but there have also been teams from France (Casal, Francfort), Germany (Hartel), and Sweden (Rydh). Italian archaeologists have never had an independent project but have involved themselves in archaeology in other interesting and significant ways.

One of the early foreign archaeological projects in the sub-continent was conceived and sponsored by Dr. W. Norman Brown, a professor of Sanskrit at the University of Pennsylvania and the principal founder of the American Institute of Indian Studies. In the 1920s he was anxious to participate in the exploration of the newly discovered Harappan civilization and visited Mohenjo-daro in 1928, where he met Ernest J.H. Mackay, then in charge of the excavations. Brown later recruited Mackay to be the field director of the U.S. excavations at Chanhu-daro in Sindh. The excavation took place during the 1935-1936 field season. It was funded by the Museum of Fine Arts in Boston, but it was Brown's project.

Archaeologists from the United States are working on several projects in India today. The University of Pennsylvania's work at Rojdi is coming to an end, but excavations by Jim G. Shaffer at Watgal, a southern neolithic site in Karnataka, continue unabated. So does the work of the U.S. team at Vijayanagara under the direction of John Fritz, George Michelle, Carla Sinopoli, and Kathleen Morrison. U.S. archaeologists have also undertaken ethnoarchaeological research in India. Dr. Lee Horne of the University of Pennsylvania studies modern-day brass casters in Bihar and Bengal in an effort to further an understanding of ancient metallurgy. J. Mark Kenoyer and his Italian colleague, Masimo Vidale, teamed with archaeologists from the M.S. University of Baroda, have studied the modern bead makers and lapidary artisans in Khambat as part of their research on the crafts of the Indus civilization. The work that biological anthropologists Kenneth A.R. Kennedy and his colleague John Lukacs have done on the ancient peoples of the Indian subcontinent is a good example of continuity in research on ancient periods of South Asian history.

All of the research has been done in collaboration between U.S. and Indian scholars and has had strong support from the Government of India as well as from local bodies. Successes, such as they are, could never have materialized without this backing.

There are a number of ways that progress has been made in understanding India's ancient past. Two are methodological: (1) chronology and (2) archaeological exploration. Paleolithic archaeology, the Indus civilization, the early iron age and medieval archaeology are also important to this discussion, as are biological anthropology and human paleontology.

CHRONOLOGY

The chronology of the earlier eras of Indian history was clouded by doubt and debate as India became an independent state in 1947. There was a strong sense that the Indus civilization was contemporary with the Akkadian period in Mesopotamia, largely because of the presence in Mesopotamia of Indus materials brought by the adventurous mariners of India who sailed into the Gulf and the port of Akkad. There was also the journey of Alexander the Great into the Punjab in 326 BCE and the historical cross-references that emerged between Indians and westerners that helped, in some small way, to settle the chronology of the Mauryan dynasty. Finally, the discovery of Roman coinage at India sites, especially near the megaliths of the south, were extremely important in establishing the antiquity of at least the later megalithic monuments.

These chronologies were not precise, and there were many gaps between periods and across the immense distances that span the regions of India. There were a few chronological points, as with Alexander the Great, that were known, but the implications that flowed from them were not always clear, providing room for disagreement among the experts. The chronology of ancient India was not well understood from a scientific point of view, but India was not alone in this regard. The same held true for places like Mesopotamia with far richer documentation.

The revolution in understanding the chronology of ancient India is probably, for the most part, thought to begin in 1948, with the publication of Willard Libby's *Radiocarbon Dating*. This dating technique, based on the regular decay of the radioactive isotope of carbon (^{14}C), allowed archaeologists to date carbonized or burnt organic materials in their sites because carbon is such a prominent part of all organic matter.

The first dates from the subcontinent come from Kili Ghul Mohammad and Damb Sadaat in Baluchistan, the result of the excavations of Walter Fairservis. They were run at the Lamont Laboratory affiliated with Columbia University in New York, using the early, crude, laboratory technique that dates the solid carbon directly. These dates showed that the early farming communities in the Baluchi hills were at least 6,000 years old, and that Damb Sadaat was partially coexistent with the Indus civilization. Dates were also run at the University of Pennsylvania from archival samples from Mohenjo-daro and fresh excavations at Kot Diji, also in Pakistan. These confirmed the chronology that was derived from ties between Mesopotamia and the Indus valley.

In the late 1950s it became apparent that India needed its own radiocarbon laboratory, and D.P. Agrawal, a bright young archaeologist, was selected to make it a reality at the Tata Institute of Fundamental Research. This facility, which was later shifted to the Physical Research Laboratory in Ahmedabad, ran a series of dates on a host of excavations in the country. Date list number 1 had results from the following places: Ahar, Burzahom, Chandoli, Kalibangan, Lalitpur, Lothal, Navdatoli, Nevasa, and Rajgir. These dates were the first leads to the true date for the northern neolithic of Kashmir (Burzahom) and surrounding valleys and the central Indian chalcolithic (Chandoli, Navdatoli, Nevasa, Ahar), and they provided a cross-check on the chronology of the Mauryans (Rajgir). They also dated early Indian excavations on the Indus civilization sites of Kalibangan and Lothal.

My list of over 1,500 dates from the subcontinent includes 990 from India, 399 from Pakistan and 145 from Sri Lanka. Recent advances have added greater precision to the dating method, and, taken as a body, these dates have revolutionized our ideas concerning the chronology for prehistoric India. It is now known that the earliest food-producing peoples of the subcontinent date to c. 7,000

BCE, and that there is a long series of regional cultures that bridge the millennia between these early neolithic folk and the mature Harappan which can be securely placed at 2,500-1,900 BCE. We know that the bronze age peoples of Malwa and the Deccan overlap with the later centuries of the mature Harappan and continue on to the beginnings of the south and central India iron age. There are no historical gaps there. The same is true in north India, where the transition from the later Harappan peoples can be dated to the introduction of iron technology, which began in India and many other parts of Asia at 1,100-1,000 BCE.

These chronological issues are dependent on the fundamentals of archaeology: Careful excavation and detailed, intensive exploration. Excavation has grown to be a prominent and substantive pursuit in India, but archaeological exploration is not nearly as "flashy" an undertaking and receives far less notice. It is, however, a very important tool for understanding the past through settlement patterns and an analysis of the size, density, and longevity of human habitation.

ARCHAEOLOGICAL EXPLORATION

In the minds of many, the greatest of the early archaeological explorers was Sir Aurel Stein. His work in Chinese Turkistan is a significant part of the history of archaeology. His explorations in the Northwest Frontier and Baluchistan were for decades the best source of information on the prehistoric peoples there. Stein was also a pioneer in the exploration of the ancient Sarasvati river, which was pursued and expanded on by the great Director General of the Archaeological Survey of India, A. Ghosh, and even more recently by the Pakistani scholar M. Rafique Mughal.

It is fair to say that in 1947 India was poorly explored in terms of its archaeological heritage. Stein's work was there, but it was neither a dense area coverage, nor, by modern standards, was it systematic. Stein followed the well-worn roads and tracks of his exploration area, recording sites as he came upon them, which gives his work a linear quality, a distinct liability in the investigation of settlement patterns.

Over the years, in a patient program of correcting this serious deficiency, India has been explored. The job is not yet done, and many districts have not been given the attention they will eventually receive. But substantial parts of the Punjab, Haryana, Rajasthan, Gujarat, northern Madhya Pradesh, Maharashtra, and Tamilnadu have been well explored archaeologically. Some of the credit for this exploration goes to the Archaeological Survey of India and devoted explorers like Jagat Pati Joshi and his team, K.N. Dikshit, C. Marghabandhu, and R.S. Bisht. Indian universities have been active in this area as well. Kurukshetra University has produced a number of dissertations and MA theses with taluka and district exploration as their theme. The same has been true for the M.S. University of Baroda and Deccan College, where dissertations based on exploration projects and the analysis of settlement patterns have closed many of the gaps in this part of the archaeological record.

With support from the American Institute of Indian Studies I undertook one of these projects in northern Bhavnagar District of Gujarat in 1970-1971; so I am especially attached to this exploratory genre of archaeology. Several other U.S. scholars have also done this kind of work. More recently Kathleen Morrison spearheaded the exploration efforts around Vijayanagara, and Monica Smith undertook detailed site analysis in Madhya Bharat. A student from the University of Pennsylvania is scheduled to explore the Palghat pass that links coastal Kerala with Tamilnadu. Exploration aimed at understanding the Indian paleolithic was undertaken by Jeromy Jacobson. He addressed problems of paleolithic archaeology in Madhya Pradesh following the early explorations of paleolithic sites in the region made by biological anthropologist Theodore McCown on the Narmada river.

All of this work, and it is lonely, grinding toil, has begun to yield important results in understanding the distribution of ancient Indian populations and the cultural mosaic of different peoples who inhabited the subcontinent in prehistoric times. In one or two small areas archaeologists might even begin to work on the important issue of prehistoric demographics, which requires a sound, precise chronology and thorough exploration. These kinds of analyses are done only with bronze age periods, the Indus civilization, and contemporary cultures. Research on the peoples of the paleolithic in India has come a long way since 1947, but it still has a way to go before archaeologists can begin to deal reliably with demographics.

PALEOLITHIC ARCHAEOLOGY

The growth of paleolithic archaeology in India was modest. Stone tools were discovered, and reports were published by Robert Bruce Foote in 1866. He found Acheulian type hand axes and cleavers at Palavaram near Madras. Then there was the famous Yale-Carnegie project led by Helmut de Terra and T.T. Paterson. But progress was slow, and it was not until the last colonial administration of the Archaeological Survey of India, under Sir Mortimer Wheeler, that the Archaeological Survey of India established a prehistory branch dedicated to the study of the stone ages.

The Siwalik Hills and Potwar Plateau are known to be rich in Pleistocene fossils, dating to the age within which modern humans evolved. The real breakthrough in dating the early cultures of the subcontinent has taken place in Pakistan, in the Pabbi Hills near Jhelum, and at a site in that region called Riwat. If early stone tools are found in the Pabbi Hills, it is a virtual certainty that they will eventually be found in the Siwaliks of India.

Riwat is 10 kilometers southeast of Rawalpindi. It has a stream-cut section that is 70 meters deep. Twenty-four flaked tools of quartzite were found there in 1983 by a joint British-Pakistani team along with another single example in 1988. There is some controversy about the nature of these stones, but it is widely agreed that at least three of them are artifacts. One of these pieces is a core, from which smaller flakes were detached and used as tools. These flakes compare well with the tools found in the Olduvai Gorge in Tanzania that are approximately 1.75 million years old. The dating of these artifacts has generated considerable debate. The level at which they were found in the deep section was dated to 1.9 million years by earlier American-Pakistani research. The British-Pakistani team has added to this by noting that the sediments associated with the tools have reversed palaeomagnetic readings indicating that they belong to the matuyama chron that dates to between 780,000 and 2.6 million years ago. Moreover, the artifacts are just below a volcanic ash that has been dated to 1.8 ± 0.16 million years ago using one of the radiographic dating techniques. Therefore, the artifacts have to be older than about 1.9 million years. These tools are as old as any tools in the world, and there is every reason to believe that northern India has the potential to inform us about the very earliest evolutionary period of human existence.

No human fossils have been associated with the Riwat or Pabbi Hills tools, but by 1836 fossils of monkeys and apes had been discovered in the miocene-pliocene strata of the Siwalik hills, and this is a good environment for finding fossil hominids. An archaic *home sapiens* was found in the Narmada valley just east of Hoshangabad.

The later periods of the paleolithic have been further clarified since India's independence. Excavations at the complex of caves and ·rock shelters at Bimbhetka in Madhya Pradesh and research at Didwana in Rajasthan have produced dates and stratigraphic sequences of the lower, middle and upper paleolithic indicating that the middle and upper paleolithic date to c. 100,000 to 20,000 years ago. The joint Allahabad University-University of California-Berkeley team conducted several seasons of intensive survey and excavation in the Son and Belan valleys of northern Madhya Pradesh, at the point where the Vindhyas merge with the Gangetic plains. There is also a team of archaeologists from the Smithsonian Institution working with their colleagues at Deccan College seeking to date the paleolithic sequences in central and southern India. Taken together, this research has yielded more dates and good stratigraphy, all of which add to the building of a record for the time-space dimensions of the Indian paleolithic and tell something about the lifeways of the peoples who lived then.

India has a bounty of sites with microlithic tools. These are small chipped stone implements, sometimes less than a centimeter in their greatest dimension. Some excavated sites have produced a hundred-thousand or more of these artifacts that were used to make larger composite implements, such as spears and arrows. The earliest phases of this technology have been dated in Sri Lanka, where dates in the range of 25,000 years ago have surfaced. If this technology is as old as that in Sri Lanka, there is every reason to believe that a similar chronology will be found from south India sites, possibly from sites in all the regions of India. The interesting thing about this technology in India is that it lasts well into the historical periods. This is not true in Pakistan, Iran, Afghanistan, the Middle East, and Europe, where microlithic technology disappears with the advent of mature agricultural communities. But in India we have microlithic tools associated with historic pottery, iron tools, and coins, some of which might be Islamic. The people who made and used the microliths in India found them to be well adapted to their way of life. What was found to be an "archaic" form of adaptation in the West was a perfect fit for Indian conditions. B. Subbaro, the founder of the Department of Archaeology at the M.S. University of Baroda, once observed that India was a place of diversity and contrast, where coexistence of the bullock cart and the Boeing jet made perfect sense.

A great deal of research could be devoted to the cultural diversity of India during the time these microlithic tools were in use. There are probably connections between the peoples of these archaeological sites and the modern tribal populations, for example. But to date there has been little interest in the kind of archaeology that tries to find direct historical connections among disparate data sets, although I have done some research on the relations between the peoples of the Indus civilization and their hunter-gatherer neighbors.

INDUS CIVILIZATION

There have been vast changes in our knowledge of, and perspectives on, the Indus or Harappan civilization over the past fifty years. Exploration, excavation, and an expanded view of this fascinating ancient culture have revolutionized our thinking about this, the earliest phase of Indian history.

At one level, the interpretation of the civilization was guided by what has come to be called the "Wheeler-Piggott Paradigm." It began with the notion that the Harappan civilization was the same wherever it was found. Everything was orderly and regulated, a bit dull, and more than a trifle lacking in the stimulus of individuality. Wheeler found in Mohenjo-daro an absence or even a suppression of personality in its details from street to street, and a strong sense of regimentation. He frequently recalled being struck by the astonishing sameness of the civilization reflecting a kind of isolation. Recent research on the Harappan civilization, rather than thinking in terms of "sameness" and "isolation," has defined regional "polities" and interaction, and has sought to understand the long distance relationships between ancient India, the Horn of Africa, the Arabian Gulf, Central Asia, the Iranian Plateau, and Mesopotamia. The regional mosaic of early and mature Harappan remains, and it is seen as a proxy for ethnic diversity. The languages spoken by these people are not known. Nor does one know much about their social life and organization. But there is a feeling strong among archaeologists that the early and mature Harappan civilization represent many kinds of people.

Sir Mortimer Wheeler was not an admirer of Sir John Marshall, the Director General of the Archaeological Survey of India that gave the world its first glimpses of the Harappan civilization. Marshall's field methods were antiquated, and he seems to have promoted a kind of personality cult around himself that stifled innovation and change in the Survey. Wheeler was determined to rethink the Harappan civilization beginning with his first visit to Harappa in May of 1944. He approached the huge AB mound in the early morning and immediately imagined it to have been a fortress to defend the inhabitants of the city from attack. During times of peace the city's priests and god-head were proposed to have been there. Wheeler used his knowledge of Mesopotamian society to interpret the Indian material, since he believed that the bronze age of India recalled a social organization not altogether unlike that of the contemporary West. The concept of the priest-king in the Harappan civilization was appropriate because in Sumer the wealth and discipline of the city-state were vested in the chief deity, and the focus of the city was the exalted temple, center of an elaborate and carefully-ordered secular administration under divine sanction. Wheeler assumed that the source of authority in the Harappan civilization was religion. He also assumed that the lords of Harappa administered their city in a fashion not unlike that of the priest-kings or governors of Sumer and Akkad.

Stuart Piggott's position on mature Harappan society was much the same, but he was a little more cautious in his treatment of Sumerian matters. In his book *Prehistoric India* he describes the Harappan civilization as a state under priest-kings ruling the Harappan peoples autocratically from twin capitals of their vast empire. The whole civilization was linked by the Indus and other rivers of the Punjab.

The idea that there were priest-kings in the Indus cities has been abandoned, as has the notion of citadels, although these concepts linger on in secondary literature. Archaeologists are now thinking in terms of a more decentralized political system, with loose alliances between the major urban environments and regions. But there is no denying the presence of an artifactual style that covers about 1,000,000 square kilometers. It is now thought that the internal economics and trade of the Harappan civilization were useful in promoting adherence to this style, and that the style itself was deeply connected to the self-identification of the Harappan peoples. They used the style of their civilization, which we call the mature Harappan, because it identified them as a certain kind of people.

It is not known what the mature Harappan people called themselves, but the Sumerian word "Meluhha" may have been their name for this civilization. The Indus writing system has been studied by a number of scholars, several of whom have claimed to read the script. To date, none of these decipherments can be shown to be valid, and more work is needed on this important topic.

As August 1947 approached, Indian archaeologists became aware that there were virtually no sites of ancient India's first civilization on the Indian side of the Indo-Pakistan border. The premier sites of Mohenjo-daro and Harappa were in Pakistan, in Sindh, and in the West Punjab. Corrective measures were soon taken. Between 1950 and 1953 the Director General of the Archaeological Survey of India explored the now dry Sarasvati river system. He found a large number of sites there, stretching back to early Harappan times. The Survey undertook excavation at a number of these sites. The most important excavation was at Kalibangan, where the Archaeological

Survey of India worked for nine seasons, beginning in 1960. S.R. Rao, from the Archaeological Survey of India, began the exploration of Gujarat, looking for mature Harappan sites there. Pundit M.S. Vats had excavated Rangpur in the old Limbdi State in 1934-1935 and had determined that it had an affinity with mature Harappan remains, although he thought this was a rather late manifestation. Rao started his work at Rangpur, and then he found Lothal where he conducted the first of eight season in 1958. Thus, when faced with the challenge of Partition, the Survey sprang to action and was eminently successful in its exploration efforts, and subsequent by strategic excavations. My gazetteer of mature Harappan sites has records of 1,022 such places; 406 of these are in Pakistan; the balance, 616, are in India. Ninety-six of these mature Harappan sites have been excavated: 41 in Pakistan, the remaining 55 in India. Virtually all have been excavated since 1947. Some of the excavations have been small, but some reflect long-term commitments with substantial resources at stake. The work at Kalibangan and Lothal was in this tradition. So too is the research at places like Banawali (Haryana) and Dholavira (Kutch). My own site of Rojdi in central Saurashtra (Rajkot District) has been the scene of nine seasons of work, two by the Gujarat State Department of Archaeology and seven by a joint team from there and the University of Pennsylvania, with much needed support from the American Institute of Indian Studies and the Governments of India and Gujarat.

Publication of these materials is often perceived as a problem, and final reports are lacking on some of this work. But every site in my gazetteer carries a bibliographic citation; so the explored sites have been published somewhere. Major excavation reports are missing for important places (e.g., Kalibangan), but there is a program in place to publish them. Indian archaeologists are not alone in dealing with the gap between the closing of excavation work and the appearance of a written report. Good reports can take a decade, sometimes two, to write.

It was once thought that there was a "dark age" in northern India that separated historical times from the later phases of the Harappan civilization, the so called "post-urban Harappan." This idea promoted the thought that the end of the ancient cities of the Indus was mysterious. It is now known that this perspective is not viable. Thanks largely to the explorations and excavations of Jagat Pati Joshi and his team from the Archaeological Survey of India, there is a complete culture historical sequence in the Punjab that connects the mature Harappan with the early iron age of the painted grey ware. There is no "dark age" in northern India. Now, waiting for answers, there are new, important questions about the early iron age and the peoples who made and used the painted grey ware.

EARLY IRON AGE

The painted grey ware was defined by Krishna Deva in 1946 from the finds of the Archaeological Survey of India's excavations at Ahicchatra. This ceramic is associated with the earliest regular use of iron in northwestern India and dates to c. 1,100-500 BCE. In southern and central India the early regular use of iron is associated with the megaliths, and it occurs in those parts of India at about the same time as it does in the north.

This period is associated with the regular use of iron, because there is iron in the bronze age. This very early iron can be accounted for as part of the process of smelting copper in the presence of iron-rich materials, probably used as flux. Prior to about 1,100 BCE, iron was as much a curiosity as it was utilitarian. There was also very little of it, and from this we can suppose that the iron workers probably did not have full control over iron's production. But by about 1,100 BCE this changed, and there was a marked increase in the regularity with which iron was used, still occurring with copper and bronze. One of the unresolved problems in the archaeology of Asia is that this changeover took place in a broad belt extending from the Near East to South China at about the same time. Thus the change in India was not isolated but was part of a much larger process of technological innovation.

Following B.B. Lal's important excavations at Hastinapura, there was a vigorous, multipronged program of archaeological exploration that has led to the discovery of just over 1,000 painted grey ware sites. They are concentrated in the Punjab, Haryana, central and western Uttar Pradesh, and northern Rajasthan. There are fourteen painted grey ware sites in Cholistan but none in the other parts of the west Punjab. There have been two excellent studies of painted grey ware settlement patterns, one by Dr. Makkhan Lal, then of Deccan College, the other by Dr. George Erdosy, then of Cambridge University. They tell of increasing sedentarism in the western Ganges area, implying a clearing of forests and draining of swamps. There was also increased agriculture in this region, which spans the boundary between the wheat and rice growing regions of north India. As a whole, these studies place the painted grey ware peoples at the prelude to the second urbanization of north India.

Although exploration has revealed the presence of a large number of painted grey ware sites, excavation has been more spotty. There is still no complete plan for a building of this period, although B.B. Lal has described the foundation trench for a painted grey ware house that was never built. What is now needed is a good, horizontal excavation of several painted grey ware sites to show how the people lived.

There has been a great deal of speculation about who made the painted grey ware. Given the date and geography, there is a reasonable fit with the time and place of the events portrayed in the *Ṛg Veda*. But the *Ṛg Veda* makes reference to many different peoples in this region, and it has not yet been proven that the settlements of the Vedic Aryans were those we now associate with the painted grey ware. Moreover, the Vedic Aryans were mobile pastoral peoples who did some farming. The painted grey ware settlements seem to have been villages of sedentary farmers. It is clear that useful research is needed to clarify these important historical issues.

The early iron age of central and south India is associated with the settlements and interments of the megalithic peoples. The megaliths themselves are funerary monuments associated with large stone constructions of several types. The burials are usually fractional, secondary internments. There are also a few contemporary habitation sites, but the life style of the megalithic peoples of central and south India seems to have been based on mobile cattle pastoralism. Thanks in large part to the excavations of Deccan College in and around Inamgaon, and the central Indian chalcolithic site just east of Pune, the kind of culture historical continuity there compares with that which is available in the north. The Deccan College research has documented a late jorwe period with transitions into the early iron age and the megalithic monuments.

The megaliths of India have remained something of an enigma in spite of intensive explorations and selective excavation in several regions of the country. The investigation of these monuments began as early as 1823 when Babington presented a comprehensive description of the megalithic monuments of Malabar. Since that time, research has produced much evidence for them; however, a true understanding of these funerary and commemorative monuments and their creators is lacking.

Most of the megalithic sites are found in central and south India, especially in Andhra Pradesh, Karnataka, Tamilnadu, and Kerala, but they also occur in many other parts of the country. The only major regions without them are the Punjab, the Ganges plains, the

Thar desert, and North Gujarat. There are a few megaliths in relatively out-of-the-way places like Kashmir and Ladakh. Tamilnadu and Kerala have thousands of megalithic sites. S.B. Deo of Deccan College has noted that there is some variation in the material culture associated with the megaliths, and they come in an interesting typology of funerary monuments:

Menhirs or memorial stones occur singly or as rows of standing monoliths. This type has the largest geographical distribution, and they are still made and used by some tribal peoples in eastern India.

Dolmenoid cist or dolmen consist of a burial chamber constructed of stones for both the orthostats (vertical slab or stone) and capstone. The chamber is surrounded by a circle of stones and covered with stone rubble.

Slabbed cists are stone boxes made of four slabs arranged as a rectangle for the walls and a capstone. There is no surrounding circle.

Chamber tombs and long barrows are round or oval earthen mounds that may contain burial urns.

Pit-circles consist of a cairn or stone-circle concealing a pit-burial.

Cairns with urns are tumuli composed of large heaps of stone rubble covering an internment.

Multiple hood-stones or topikallu are made up of four quadrangular standing stones laid together in such a way as to form a slightly truncated pyramid. There is a dressed capstone on the top of this base.

, Rock-cut caves need no elaboration, other than the observation that the later Indian tradition of carving caves had its beginnings in the early iron age.

Many of these internments have terracotta sarcophagi in them. Some are relatively simple, but others are very elaborate therio-morphic affairs.

The study of settlement patterns of the megaliths of central and southern India has revealed a number of habitations near the meanders of perennial rivers or on streams. There is also a concentration of sites in areas with ready access to iron ores as well as to the rock outcrops that could provide material for funerary monuments.

Through excavations by the Archaeological Survey of India, Deccan College, and several universities in the south, it was learned that some megalithic villages were composed of clusters of circular huts. Occasional larger, rectilinear structures also occurred. These appeared to be the abodes of important families, indicating a degree of internal differentiation in these societies.

The megalith builders were skilled smiths and artisans. The range of iron objects was wide and included weapons such as daggers, lances, tridents, arrowheads, and spikes. Domestic articles included cauldrons, nail-parers, hooks and clamps, ladles, and lamps. Agricultural tools such as plowshares, hoes, adzes, forks, and sickles occurred, along with flat axes and chisels. These people also used the domesticated horse and made their bits and check pieces of iron. Bimetallic objects of copper and iron were also made. There were bowls, dishes, cups with handles, bangles, and lids with their finials beautifully decorated with figures of birds, flowers, and other animals. These people also continued the use of pure bronze, making horse trappings, cups, and other objects from this material. There is some gold associated with the megaliths: necklaces, earrings, rings, and pendants of gold leaf.

The complex typology of the funerary monuments and differences between artifactual assemblage suggests that there were many different kinds of people whom we lump together under the catchall "megaliths." Megaliths were built for over a millennium, and the early megaliths differed from the later ones, which were made during the period of Roman trade in the first and second centuries CE. Further support for this differentiation of megalith builders comes from physical anthropologist Kenneth A.R. Kennedy who has observed that the people interred in these structures were phenotypically variable, and it is not likely that they were members of a single population. This observation also implies that there was no sudden introduction of a new population at the beginning of the tradition of megalith building, strengthening the observations on the culture historical continuity.

There are many things still to be learned about these fascinating monuments, but progress has been made in their study. By the end of the period, we are on the threshold of history in central and south India, the study of which has also received attention from archaeologists.

EARLY HISTORIC, MEDIEVAL ARCHAEOLOGY AND
THE ARCHAEOLOGY OF LATER PERIODS

The archaeology of the Indian early historic and later periods has been of great concern to scholars interested in the roots of modern India. In the south there have been a number of important projects.

The joint American-Madras University excavations at Arikamedu, the Roman trading station, is an outstanding example of this and one that documents good international cooperation in archaeology. The co-directors of this work, Dr. Vimala Begley and Dr. K.V. Raman of Madras University, have begun to produce reports on this fascinating place, which might have been the home of at least one Roman family. The Arikamedu excavations are complemented by U.S. excavations on the Red Sea coast of Egypt, where Dr. Steven Sidebotham of the University of Delaware is investigating a port that is contemporary with Arikamedu. He has recovered some Indian pottery and actual peppercorns preserved in one of the storage rooms. The peppercorns were discovered by a student from the University of Pennsylvania, Shinu Abraham.

Perhaps the largest and most successful of the joint archaeological projects undertaken since India's independence has been the one at Vijayanagara. Drs. John Fritz and George Michelle, working with their counterparts in the Karnataka State Department of Archaeology, most notably Dr. M.S. Nagaraja Rao, have completely mapped this medieval city and have conducted studies of the ancient agricultural system, ceramic manufacturing, and trade. They have documented and salvaged hundreds, if not thousands, of documents and antique photographs of the site. They have been faithful publishers of their work, and a series of jointly produced books about the site have appeared.

Professor R.N. Mehta of the M.S. University of Baroda was a pioneer of medieval archaeology in India. His survey of the famous deserted city of Champanier in Gujarat is a model of careful archaeology work with a minimum of excavation. Mehta also mapped a huge area in great detail and brought Champanier to life in this interesting way. He also published a full book on medieval archaeology,

Perhaps the most important find from Sanghol was an accidental discovery made in 1985. Road repairs led to the discovery of a pit excavated in antiquity. The posts and railing of a miniature fence of red sandstone, the kind that usually surrounds a stupa, were in the pit. The pieces had been disassembled and carefully buried to keep them from being discovered. The 117 architectural pieces were complete and in very good condition. The posts are carved with medallions and figures, mostly females in transparent garments. The railings are ovoid in cross-section, typically ancient Indian. These stone architectural members are small, the posts being about one meter in height. Traces of wear and handling demonstrate that the fence from which these pieces came was once installed around a small-scale stupa, probably at or near Sanghol. The carving can be related to the Mathura school, and it may be that the pieces were carved there and then brought to Sanghol. They date to the early Kushana Dynasty (1st and 2nd centuries CE).

There has also been interesting excavation by the Archaeological Survey of India at Fatehpur Sikri. It is another huge city, and excavations had to be selective. But digging produced documentation of private houses, mostly of nobles, the presence of a bazaar, the structure of one set of stables, the form of Abul Fazal's bath, and much more.

A great deal of work has been done on historical archaeology since India's independence, and much more is being learned about the formative processes of Indian civilization. The material record is proving to be a useful complement to historical documents and epigraphic sources. Another complement to the archaeological record comes from biological anthropology, a fascinating topic.

BIOLOGICAL ANTHROPOLOGY AND HUMAN PALEONTOLOGY

Biological anthropologists who work with prehistoric human populations are dealing with a series of interconnected themes. One focuses on the evolution of biologically modern humans (*homo sapiens*). Others involve the study of palaeodemography, the age and sex ratios of ancient populations, rates of mortality, morbidity, fertility, and fecundity, and relationships of population migrations to habitat, trauma, stature, and body size and shape. The study of nutrition and diet is closely linked with the more general study of palaeobotany by archaeologists interested in the history of Indian agriculture. The study of ancient teeth has proven to be an important source of information on palaeo diet, stress, and trauma, as well as on biological affinities between populations.

Western science is no longer involved in describing and discussing the kinds of racial typologies that were popular earlier in this century. Human physical features rarely, if ever, form the large population clusters that the concept of race implies. The pattern of biological features within most regions is more characterized by variation in physical form than by homogeneity. When larger world patterns are studied, such as those of physical features between geographical regions, the patterns that emerge are not clusters of co-varying traits, but rather gradual clines of change for each trait analyzed. For example, there is a tendency for humans of light skin color to be found in the northern latitudes. This gradually gives way to humans of darker pigmentation as one moves south toward the equator. These clines are never wholly regular, and there are always a healthy number of exceptions, demonstrating that the clustering of human biological traits among significant numbers of people is itself the exception rather than the rule.

Although biological or physical anthropology is a well-established discipline in India, those who deal with ancient populations are relatively few. In fact, only one department of archaeology in India has such a position—the famous program at Deccan College. Much of this work has fallen to western scholars, working closely with Indian colleagues. The senior American is Kenneth A.R. Kennedy who has had a long and distinguished career in the field. His students, John Lukacs and Nancy Lovell, now established scientists on their own, have also increased our knowledge considerably.

One of the most important advances in biological anthropology took place in 1931 with the establishment of the Indian Statistical Institute under the direction of P.C. Mahalanobis. He developed a number of applied statistical tests that were useful in biological anthropology: the Coefficient of Racial Likeness, Student's T-test, and Mahalanobis D test. These are statistical manipulations that are widely used all over the world and have advanced science generally in a positive direction.

The best fossil human from the subcontinent was discovered in 1982 by Dr. Arun Sonakia, a scientist with the Geological Survey of India. He found a fossil human calvaria on the surface of a late middle Pleistocene deposit on the north bank of the Narmada river near Hathnora village, Madhya Pradesh. A good portion of the skull, or cranium, was recovered that included about three-quarters of the cranial vault and the right half of the frontal bone with its superior orbital border and portions of the cranial base. No teeth were recovered, or parts of the lower body.

Kenneth A.R. Kennedy says that Sonakia assigned it to a new taxon, *homo erectus narmadensis*. Later analysis by M.A. de Lumley and Sonakia in France and Kennedy of the United States, in collaboration with Indian colleagues, concluded that Narmada man was either an "evolved *homo erectus*" or represented an "archaic" *homo sapiens*. This interpretation is supported by the results of comparative analyses of the Narmada calvaria with fossil hominid specimens from other middle Pleistocene sites in Asia and Europe.

CLOSING REMARKS

The highlights of archaeological research in India since Independence have been covered in this short essay. A great deal of fieldwork has been done, and the scientific advances in dating have served to place these achievements in far more secure chronological frameworks. There is still work to be done, and exploration needs to proceed with the same vigor that has characterized the past fifty years of work. But Indian archaeology is a healthy discipline overall, and there are good lines of communication between Indians and their U.S. colleagues and other foreign researchers.

Indian archaeology in the United States is also healthy. In 1947 there were no prehistoric archaeologists with positions in U.S. universities or museums dedicated to this study. By 1973 there were two, with two others in positions that were more general anthropological appointments. Today there are six appointments dedicated to the study of South Asian archaeology in university departments in the United States, with three additional appointments of professors with full qualifications in this topic who teach more general archaeological curricula as well. It is hoped that the next fifty years will bring as much progress to understanding and international cooperation as have the last fifty years since Indian independence.

Art History (Islamic)

CATHERINE B. ASHER

I would like to think this essay was commissioned prematurely. That is, I predict that it will still be a decade before the impact of current South Asia scholarship on ways of thinking—western or Indian—about Islamic art is realized. Let me explain. To date, scholarship on Indian Islamic art can be divided roughly into two periods; the dividing line between them is the Iranian revolution of 1979. The impact of the Ayatollah Khomeini's revolution in Iran on many scholars who studied the Islamic world was profound. The closing of Iran to European and American art historians gave new scholarly significance to India, its art and culture; as a result, new attitudes toward an understanding of the Islamic world and its art have been developing.

Until very recently, Indian Islamic painting (and to a less extent other arts such as jades, jewelry, ivory carving, and textiles) were the domain of one set of scholars and connoisseurs, while architecture was largely the domain of archaeologists and epigraphers. Generally scholarship on painting was commonly published; scholarship on the other arts or architecture was less commonly published.[1] Both A.K. Coomaraswamy (1877-1947), a prolific writer and finally curator at the Boston Museum of Fine Arts, and Stella Kramrisch (1898-1993), formerly a lecturer at the University of Calcutta, later a curator at the Philadelphia Museum and professor at the University of Pennsylvania and the Institute of Fine Arts, wrote on Mughal and Deccani painting (although they were better known for their work on Buddhist and Hindu art).[2] Neither of them, however, ever wrote on Indian Islamic architecture. More recently Pramod Chandra, in his three Polsky lectures at New York's Asia Society published in 1983 under the title *On the Study of Indian Art*, dedicated about eight percent of the text to Mughal painting, but almost entirely excluded Indian Islamic architecture.[3]

Scholars generally considered Mughal and Deccani painting to be the most legitimate of Indian Islamic arts. Since the names of master artists were given in Mughal chronicles, and Mughal librarians had inscribed individual painters' names on the illustrated pages of manuscripts kept in the imperial libraries, it was not surprising that art historians studying Islamic painting tended to focus on individual artists. This was modeled on western approaches to painting and connoisseurship in which an artist's creativity is privileged. Close analysis of individual paintings could yield an understanding of style and date; the ultimate goal was, and remains for many scholars today, identifying individual artists and their handiwork.[4]

Many of the scholars whose work focuses on the contribution of individual Mughal artists are from the West or have access to western collections where the majority of Mughal paintings are held. Such scholars' work, widely available in the West, and often in the form of museum catalogues, went far in making Indian painting accessible and appreciated by a western audience (see Welch 1963, Desai 1985, Beach 1978 and 1981). Tracing the evolution of artists' styles allowed scholars to write the history of Mughal painting, especially in its formative stages (Chandra 1976, Beach 1987). Although this approach followed western methods, it found favor with scholars in India as well, as witnessed by the 1994 publication of S.P. Verma's *Mughal Painters and their Work: A Biographical Survey and Comprehensive Catalogue.*

While this sort of scholarship continues to be the focus of much research, other scholars have begun to seek new approaches to the study of Mughal and Deccani painting. One approach is to examine entire historical manuscripts and their illustrations as keys to understanding dynastic history. Manuscripts of the *Babur Nama* and *Akbar Nama* had been carefully examined earlier for style and the contributions of individual artists (Sen 1984, Beach 1978 and 1981, Smart 1973 and 1978). But only recently have illustrated Mughal histories been evaluated as statements of historical legitimizing events. Glenn Lowry and Michael Brand presented this view most succinctly in their catalogue to the 1985-86 exhibition on Fatehpur Sikri, *Akbar's India* (Lowry and Brand 1985, 70-79). They discuss Akbar's commissions of historical manuscripts as documents that position the Mughals and specifically Akbar in both their Islamic and their Timurid context. This approach to manuscript illustration, especially the illustration of historical texts, parallels the purpose for writing the histories.

Increasingly, entire historical manuscripts, not simply single pages, are considered from every angle – style, artists' hands, and also overall purpose. This sort of scholarship applied to Indian historical manuscripts has had an impact on the broader study of

Islamic art. For example, the Timurid specialist, Thomas Lentz, worked in collaboration with the historian of Indian art, Glenn Lowry, on *Timur and the Princely Vision* (1989) using such an inclusive approach. Their work is a significant and welcome contrast to much of the earlier work on the Timurid dynasty that focused on the style and subject matter of individual works of art. Lentz and Lowry, by examining the artistic output of all the Timurid rulers, recognized the dynastic significance of this patronage.

Recent scholarship on Indian illustrated historical manuscripts has had an impact not only on the study of Persian illustrated historical manuscripts, but also on subsequent studies of Indian manuscripts. A case in point is the upcoming exhibition of the *Padshah Nama* to be held in Delhi, London, and the United States.[5] An international body of scholars is writing the catalogue. They will probe various aspects of the *Padshah Nama* including its artistic style as well as the historical significance of the text and its illustrations. Studies such as these that utilize the expertise of a number of scholars and speak of international cooperation are a healthy growing trend.

Several young scholars are questioning approaches that privilege the artist and style. They ask: Was this the key issue for the artists, the patrons, or the audience? At a recent conference on South Asian art, John Seyller discussed the valuations included on the front page of Mughal manuscripts—that is, the monetary worth ascribed to the illustrations at the time of their creation.[6] Such notations, virtually ignored by earlier scholars, reveal Mughal attitudes toward the worth of physical objects of their own commission, as well as, in some cases, the actual price of the ink, paper, and other materials needed to produce the manuscript. Seyller is still working on this project; so its full implications are not yet apparent. But Seyller's work, which involves a careful reading of notes scribed on the pages of illustrations, is already changing our understanding of Indian painting (Seyller 1987).

Sharon Littlefield, currently working on her dissertation, is also probing issues of value and worth in aesthetic objects such as paintings, manuscripts, jades, and jewelry. Her work focuses on Indo-Iranian cultural exchange between the Mughal ruler, Jahangir, and the Safavid ruler, Shah Abbas. She is exploring how such fabulously wealthy and powerful connoisseurs of art as Jahangir and Shah Abbas perceive art as treasure, as political expression, and as commodity. More than a study about the aesthetics of two distinct Islamic empires, India and Iran, her work probes exchanges of religious, political, and cultural ideology. While anthropologists have studied gifting and its subsequent commodification, this has not been done before for elite art in India.

Indian Islamic painting is often considered secular in subject matter, in contrast to non-Islamic Indian painting, which is generally considered religious. Yet Deborah Hutton is reversing this attitude at least for the *ābri* marbled illustrations produced in the Deccan.[7] Her work, still in progress, shows that the very technique of *ābri* (meaning "cloud") mirrors the subject matter that is always Sufic, that is mystic, in nature.

It is premature to predict what impact studies such as these ones still in progress will make on our understanding of Indian art. I would venture to guess, in any case, that studies such as these herald new directions in art historical thinking and may even inform the work of our colleagues working on western art.

While painting may be the field currently deemed most esteemed in terms on Indo-Islamic art, architecture is the older field of serious study. Europeans from the 16th century on had read the writings of travelers describing India's spectacular mosques, tombs, and palaces; at times these writings were illustrated, though usually in amateur fashion. By the late 17th century professional artists were publishing large-scale illustrations of Indian monuments.[8] At the beginning of the 19th century images of the Taj Mahal could be found on European serving ware (Pal et al. 204). Throughout the 19th century, but especially after 1858, handbooks for tourists and gazetteers for administrators, all part of the colonial agenda, were written and illustrated, often with the newly emerging medium of photography (Taylor 1866, Cole 1872, Latif 1896). In these volumes architecture was emphasized over other courtly arts. The educated public could read about, and see the illustrations of, the Qutb Minar at Delhi, the Taj Mahal and tomb of Itimad ud-Daula at Agra, and the mosques and tombs of Bijapur. Most of these works were written by amateurs, but the newly formed Archaeological Survey of India began to produce monographs on important monuments written by trained archaeologists.[9]

Typically, the focus of all these works was a particular site or structure. The first (and, until the 1940s, the only) synthetic scholarly account of Indian Islamic architecture was James Fergusson's *History of Indian and Eastern Architecture* (1876). He dedicated about a quarter of his overall text to Islamic architecture and, importantly, to the architecture of non-Muslims constructed during periods of Islamic political domination (a type of architecture to which I shall return later). Fergusson's work (revised and enlarged by James Burgess in 1910) remained the classic; it was surpassed only for Sultanate materials with John Marshall's essay on pre-Mughal Muslim architecture in the *Cambridge History of India,* vol. 2 (1922), and by Percy Brown's contribution on Mughal architecture in the *Cambridge History of India,* vol. 4 (1937). In 1942 Brown published his *Indian Architecture (Islamic Period),* which was the first serious attempt since Fergusson to survey the corpus of Indian Islamic architecture. Brown remained the authority for the next thirty years. For example, when John Hoag's *Islamic Architecture,* a volume discussing Islamic architecture from Spain to India, appeared in 1977, his bibliography for India included only Brown's opus and a handful of monographs written anywhere from 75 to 30 years earlier.

In the late 1960s and 1970s a Japanese team under the auspices of the Institute of Oriental Culture at the University of Tokyo began careful documentation of the pre-Mughal architecture of Delhi (Yamamoto and Tsukinowa 1968-70, Ara 1977). The results were published in several magnificent volumes. They were, however, circulated only privately, and the text was in Japanese, a language accessible to few scholars working in India.

Beginning in the early 1980s this situation changed. But before I address that, we might want to ask why Indian Islamic architecture, in spite of the widespread knowledge of its existence through guide books and prints, was virtually ignored in Indian art historical studies. There appear to be several forces at work here. One is that the Archaeological Survey of India concentrated on non-Islamic material despite the fact that the Survey produced some monographs on Islamic architecture. This trend had commenced in the 19th century under the British, by the very founders of the Archaeological Survey of India. The British were more interested in the oldest (Buddhist, Jain, and Hindu) structures and less interested in the more recent monuments that included Islamic structures. This approach, coupled with the western notion that Indian history was divided into sectarian time frames—that is, first Buddhist, second Hindu, and third Muslim—essentially served to dismiss all but the most spectacular Islamic monuments. But attitude alone was not the reason that Indian Islamic architecture was rarely considered by serious western scholars and (except for Fergusson and Brown) never in an integrative manner. Accessibility was another reason. Few western scholars were in a position to traverse the subcontinent looking for scholarly data; they worked with what was near at hand. Access was also a reason why scholarship tended to focus on Mughal or Deccani painting; many such paintings were in collections outside of India, and therefore were readily accessible to western scholars. Rigorous field work in India was not a prerequisite for research.

By the 1970s a few scholars were turning to serious consideration of Islamic Indian architecture (Meister 1972, Asher 1977, Begley 1979) and its garden tradition (Crowe et al. 1972, Moynihan 1979). In India, R. Nath's, *History of Sultanate Architecture* (1978) examined Persian sources for information about specific structures. In North America, E. Merklinger's *Indian Islamic Architecture, The Deccan 1347-1686* (1981), followed the earlier French tradition of looking at individual components of a building in an attempt to understand its style. M. Ara in "The Lodhi Rulers and the Construction of Tomb Buildings in Delhi" (1981) argued that the appearance of Lodi tombs related directly to theories of kingship unique to this dynasty. Wayne Begley's article "The Myth of the Taj Mahal and a New Theory of Its Symbolic Meaning" (1979) used new methods to probe the meaning of the world's most famous building.

The year Begley's controversial article appeared, 1979, ultimately proved to be a turning point for the future of Indian Islamic art historical study. Events outside of India, most notably the Ayatollah Khomeini's revolution in Iran, forced many scholars, especially U.S. citizens but others as well, to reconsider where they did their research. With the closing of Iran, scholars and students, like the first Mughal ruler, Babur, looked eastward toward India as new fertile ground. Language was not a problem, for Persian was the language of most Muslim courts of the subcontinent. Seasoned scholars changed research direction to include India as part of their academic agenda. For example, Lisa Golombek, known for her work in Iran and Central Asia, included the Taj Mahal in an article on the legacy of Timurid art (Golombek 1981). Howard Crane, who had worked in Afghanistan and Turkey, collaborated with Anthony Welch, a noted specialist of Iranian painting, on an article on the Tughluqs (Welch and Crane 1983). Since then, Crane has done further work on the architecture of the first Mughal emperor, Babur (Crane 1987), and Welch has written several articles on Indian Islamic architecture, particularly on that of the Tughluqs (A. Welch 1985, 1993). Robert Hillenbrand, noted for his work on Iran, wrote a seminal article on political symbolism at the Ajmer mosque (Hillenbrand 1988). The American Institute of Indian Studies, with its superb Center for Art and Archaeology, was an important source of support for these scholars new to India.

Yet another stimulus was an enormous endowment given to

Harvard and the Massachusetts Institute of Technology (MIT) by the Aga Khan.[10] He was particularly interested in encouraging research in understudied countries such as India. Thus students, many supported by Aga Khan funding, who might otherwise have turned to Iran for fieldwork now opted for India. A series of dissertations, books, and articles appeared that transcended the earlier descriptive approach, placing an emphasis on analysis. For example, by relating Humayun's tomb to earlier Timurid tombs, Glen Lowry was able to probe the structure's dynastic symbolism (Lowry 1987). Ebba Koch's work on Shah Jahan's palaces gave new understanding to the metaphoric meaning of imperial Mughal forms (Koch 1982, 1983, 1988). Sher Shah Sur's architectural output came to be understood as a carefully-planned campaign aimed at fabricating a genealogy suitable for a king (Asher 1988). The South Asian garden tradition became a field almost of its own. Notable studies on the Mughal garden have appeared (Wescoat 1985, 1989, 1990, 1991; Wescoat and Wolschke-Bulmahn 1996), spurring at least two forthcoming studies that will examine Indian gardens and their contributions to gardens around the world.[11]

While these and other works focused on imperially-sponsored projects, others focused on regional and non-imperial works. Examples include monographs by Mehrdad and Natalie Shokoohy on architecture in Gujarat, Hisar, and Nagaur (Shokoohy 1988, Shokoohy and Shokoohy 1988, 1993), and by S. Parihar (1985) on monuments in Haryana and the Punjab. The Aga Khan Foundation sponsored a massive photographic archive for eastern India (Asher 1991). Two books on Mughal architecture that appeared almost in succession in the 1990s specifically addressed the issue of imperial and non-imperial patronage (Koch 1991, Asher 1992a). Studies such as these went far in breaking down the traditional belief that Indo-Islamic art was the exclusive product of imperial patronage. Such studies also raised intriguing questions about the compositions, funding sources, and ideologies of their non-imperial patrons.

Much credit for bringing international scholarly regard to Indian Islamic architecture must go to Wayne Begley and his earlier-mentioned article, "The Myth of the Taj Mahal and a New Theory of Its Symbolic Meaning." It appeared in the *Art Bulletin*, the single most prestigious art history journal in North America. While a few pieces on Indian Buddhist art had earlier appeared in this journal, Begley's article put on the scholarly map the Taj Mahal, until this time known to all almost as a cliche. Begley's article internationally legitimized the field of Indian Islamic art.

All these forces played into yet another important development, a changing definition of what constitutes the Islamic world. Scholars began to expand what was studied about the Islamic world outside of the traditional confines of the Middle East and Iran. Francis Robinson's *Atlas of the Islamic World Since 1500* (1982) featured a notable section on South Asian geography, history, art, and culture. Ira Lapidus's *A History of Islamic Societies* (1988) even includes a summary of then unpublished scholarship on Indian Islamic architecture.[12]

The classic surveys of Islamic art such as D.T. Rice's *Islamic Art* (1965) or K. Otto-Dorn's *Kunst des Islam* (1964) excluded India from their discussion.[13] To Rice and Otto-Dorn, India did not contain enough Islamic art to be worthy of scholarly consideration. But the new surveys that began to appear in the 1990s pay substantial attention to Indian Islamic art. B. Brend's *Islamic Art* (1991) indicates a slight discomfort with the inclusion of India since she lumps all Indian art together in a single final chapter, although the rest of the book is organized chronologically and geographically. The most recent and by far most ambitious project of this sort, Sheila Blair and Jonathan Bloom's *Art and Architecture of Islam, 1250-1800* (1994), has several carefully-written chapters on Indian Islamic art and architecture properly dispersed throughout the volume. These authors have gone to great lengths to consult all recent scholarship; thus the volume can be seen as a state-of-the-field presentation.

The original invitation to write this essay requested that I write on: Art History (Muslim). Note that I have rarely used the word Muslim, that is, a follower of the faith. Rather, I have opted for the word Islamic, which can refer to time periods without denoting explicit religious affiliations. I do so in order to counter the colonial construction that divided Indian history into sectarian time frames that is, first Buddhist, second Hindu, and third Muslim. Unfortunately, even today Indian history (and thus by extension India's art history) is often understood in exactly this antiquated sectarian manner. For example, all too often the scholar who studies a mosque of the 18th century will not think to examine its neighboring 18th century Hindu counterpart. Interestingly, it was James Fergusson, writing in the late 19th century, who included contemporary (19th century) Jain temples and Islamic monuments in his work, although one could not argue that his attitudes were free of ethnic prejudice (Fergusson 1876, 259-260).

The very recent writings of scholars working on artistic production between the 12th and 19th centuries, periods of Islamic political domination of certain regions of India, attempt to break down this artificial colonial construction. Phillip Wagoner and George Michell in their work on Vijayanagara follow the lead of the late historian Burton Stein by seeking to dispel the notion that there is a Hindu or Muslim style of architecture.[14] Scholars working in north India have made similar suggestions. Examples that might be cited include work on the patronage of Raja Man Singh, a high ranking Hindu noble who served the Mughal emperor Akbar (Asher 1992-b, 1993, 1995, 1996), and work on Fatehpur Sikri (Koch 1987). Studies such as these indicate the pitfalls of using sectarian terminology in referring to architectural forms. Currently research continues on Hindu temples in cities often assumed to be "Muslim" (such as Shahjahanabad) and on mosques in cities such as Jaipur that were constructed by Hindu rulers (Asher forthcoming-a, forthcoming-b). Not only will such research reveal much about early modern India; it will also stress the similarities among communities rather than the differences. In this sense, art history follows the lead of the subaltern school. That is, these recent studies attempt to get beyond an architecture of the elite to an architecture built and used by the populace.

Issues surrounding the communalist construction of India's history and art history may also be applicable to larger issues in art history outside of India. If there has been a politicization of art history in India, might there not also have been politicizations of art history in other parts of the world? When western art historians speak of Russian, or Italian, or Scandinavian, or U.S. art and architecture, are they including the art of the landless, the immigrant laborers, the fisherfolk, and the villagers? To what extent do scholars, by focusing on the creations of the elite, thereby ignore the creations of the non-elite? And if sectarian terminology can lead to pitfalls in discussing architectural forms in South Asia, can sectarian terminology not also lead to pitfalls in discussing architectural forms in the West? As mosques are being built in Manhattan, and Buddhist, Jain, and Hindu temples are being built in suburban Chicago, what building-code and zoning requirements are being met, and what architectural modifications are being introduced by diasporic communities that call for a rethinking of what has largely been sectarian terminology?

NOTES

1. This is true in the case of scholars not associated with the Archaeological Survey of India. But even the Archaeological Survey of India tends to consider Islamic art and architecture to be less important than

Buddhist or Hindu art and architecture.

2. Examples include Kramrisch's *A Survey of Painting in the Deccan* (1937) and Coomaraswamy's *Rajput Painting* (1916) where he addresses the fundamental differences between Mughal and Rajput art.

3. Chandra (1937, 87) mentions the Taj Mahal, but only in passing.

4. See Chandra (1983, 86-93) for an historigraphical sketch. Recent work in this vein includes Chandra (1976), Beach (1987, 1981), Welch (1961), Zebrowski (1983), and Verma (1994).

5. The Exhibition is entitled "King of the World." The entire *Padshahnama* housed in the Royal Library, Windsor Castle will be displayed. Because of recent conservation efforts, the manuscript is unbound so all pages can be shown. Once the exhibition is over, the volume will be rebound.

6. John Seyller presented "The Valuation of Manuscripts in Mughal India" at the American Committee for South Asian Art Symposium VII, University of Minnesota, May 10, 1996.

7. Deborah Hutton presented "The Marbled Drawings from Bijapur: 'Clouding' the Issue," at the Mid-West Conference on Asian Affairs, St. Louis, October, 1995.

8. The most famous artists were the uncle-nephew team of Thomas and William Daniell.

9. The first such monograph to appear was James Burgess (1878); other early monographs on Islamic art were Fuhrer (1889) and Smith (1894-98).

10. In 1980 the Aga Khan gave $7.5 million to Harvard and MIT. He subsequently gave additional monies to bring the total well into the teens.

11. James L. Wescoat, an expert on South Asian gardens, and D. Fairchild Ruggles, an expert on Spanish and North African gardens, each propose to write overviews of Indian gardens and their contributions to gardens around the world.

12. Lapidus (1988, 456) includes unpublished material presented at conferences that later appeared in Asher 1992-a.

13. Carel J. Du Ry van Beest Holle (1970) did include India in his volume but in a single chapter at the end, almost as an afterthought. No attempt was made to integrate the Indian material into appropriate chronological or geographical divisions of earlier chapters.

14. Asher (1985) was the first to suggest this, followed by Michell (1992) and Michell and Eaton (1992); Phillip Wagoner's work on this material is still in progress. He has presented two important papers on this topic: "Sultan Among Hindu Kings: Dress, Address, and the Islamicization of Hindu Culture at Vijayanagara," at a conference titled "Shaping Indo-Muslim Identity in Pre-modern India," Duke University, April, 1995; and "Understanding Islam at Vijayanagara: Representation and Practices" at the Association for Asian Studies meetings in Boston, March 1994.

REFERENCES

Ara, Matsuo. 1977. *Dargahs in Medieval India.* Tokyo: Institute of Oriental Culture, Univ. of Tokyo.

———. 1982. "The Lodhi Rulers and the Construction of Tomb Buildings in Delhi." *Acta Asiatica* 43:61-80.

Asher, Catherine B. 1992 a. *The Architecture of Mughal India.* Cambridge: Cambridge Univ. Press.

———. 1992-b. "The Architecture of Raja Man Singh: A Study of Sub-Imperial Patronage." In *The Powers of Art: Patronage in Indian Culture,* ed. Barbara Stoler Miller, 183-201. New Delhi: Oxford Univ. Press.

———. 1995. "Authority, Victory and Commemoration: The Temples of Raja Man Singh." *Journal of Vaisnava Studies,* 3:25-36.

———. 1985. "Islamic Influence and The Architecture of Vijayanagara." In *Vijayanagara: City and Empire—New Currents of Research,* 2 vols. ed. A.L. Dallapiccola and S. Zingel-Ave Lallemant, 188-195. Weisbaden: Steiner Verlag.

———. 1991. *Islamic Monuments of Eastern India and Bangladesh. Part 3.2 of South Asian Art,* Leiden: Inter Documentation Co. on behalf of the American Committee for South Asian Art.

———. 1996. "Kachhwaha Pride and Prestige: The Temple Patronage of Raja Man Singh." In *Govindadeva: A Dialogue in Stone,* ed. Margaret Case, 215-238. New Delhi: Indira Gandhi National Centre for the Arts.

———. 1988. "Legacy and Legitimacy: Sher Shah's Patronage of Imperial Mausolea." In *Shari'at Ambiguity in South Asian Islam,* ed. Katherine P. Ewing, 79-97. Berkeley: Univ. of California Press.

———. Forthcoming-a. "Piety, Religion and the Old Social Order in the Architecture of the Later Mughals and Their Contemporaries." In *New Perspectives on Early Modern India,* ed. Richard B. Barnett. New Delhi and Columbus, MO: South Asia Books.

———. Forthcoming-b. "Mapping Hindu-Muslim Identities through the Architecture of Shahjahanabad and Jaipur."

———. 1977. "The Mausoleum of Sher Shah Suri." *Artibus Asiae* 39:273-298.

———. 1993. "Sub-Imperial Palaces: Power and Authority in Mughal India." *Ars Orientalis* 23:281-302.

Beach, Milo C. 1987. *Early Mughal Painting.* Cambridge: Harvard Univ. for the Asia Society.

———. 1978. *The Grand Mogul: Imperial Painting in India, 1600-1660.* Williamstown, MA: Sterling and Francine Clark Art Institute.

———. 1981. *The Imperial Image: Paintings for the Mughal Court.* Washington: Freer Gallery of Art, Smithsonian Institution.

Begley, Wayne E. 1979. "The Myth of the Taj Mahal and a New Theory of Its Symbolic Meaning." *Art Bulletin* 61:7-37.

Blair, Sheila S. and Jonathan M. Bloom. 1994. *Art and Architecture of Islam, 1250-1800.* New Haven: Yale Univ. Press.

Brand, Michael and Glenn D. Lowry. 1985. *Akbar's India: Art from the Mughal*

City of Victory. New York: Asia Society Galleries.

Brend, Barbara. 1991. *Islamic Art.* Cambridge: Harvard Univ. Press.

Brown, Percy. 1942. *Indian Architecture (Islamic Period).* Bombay: Taraporevala and Sons.

———. 1937. "Monuments of the Mughal Period." In *Cambridge History of India,* vol. 4, ed. W. Haig and R. Burns, 523-576. Cambridge: Cambridge Univ. Press.

Burgess, James. 1878. *Report on the Antiquities in the Bidar and Aurangabad Districts.* London: W.H. Allen.

Chandra, Pramod. 1983. *On the Study of Indian Art.* Cambridge: Harvard Univ. Press for the Asia Society.

———. 1976. *Tuti-Namah.* Graz: Akademische Druck-u. Verlagsanstalt.

Cole, Henry Hardy. 1872. *The Architecture of Ancient Delhi.* London: Arundel Society.

Coomaraswamy, A.K. 1916. *Rajput Painting.* London and New York: H. Milford and Oxford Univ. Press.

Crane, Howard. 1987. "The Patronage of Zahir al-Din Babur and the Origins of Mughal Architecture." *Bulletin of the Asia Institute* 1:95-110.

Crowe, Sylvia et al. 1972. *The Gardens of Mughal India.* London: Thames and Hudson.

Desai, Vishakha N. 1985. *Life at Court: Art for India's Rulers: 16th-19th Centuries.* Boston: Museum of Fine Arts.

Fergusson, James. 1876. *History of Indian and Eastern Architecture.* London: John Murray.

Fergusson, James, James Burgess and R.P. Spiers, eds. 1910 (rev. edition). *History of Indian and Eastern Architecture.* 2 vols. London: John Murray.

Fuhrer, Alois Anton. 1889. *The Sharqi Architecture of Jaunpur.* Calcutta: Superintendent of Govt. Printing.

Golombek, Lisa. 1981. "From Tamerlane to Taj Mahal." In *Essays in Islamic Art and*
Architecture in Honor of Katharina Otto-Dorn, ed. A. Daneshvari, 43-50. Malibu: Undena Publications.

Hillenbrand, Robert. 1988. "Political Symbolism in Early Indo-Islamic Mosque Architecture: The Case of Ajmir." *Iran* 26:105-117.

Hoag, John. 1977. *Islamic Architecture.* New York: Harry N. Abrams.

Koch, Ebba. 1987. "The Architectural Forms," *Fatehpur Sikri,* ed. M. Brand and G.D. Lowry, 121-148. Bombay: Marg.

———. 1982. "The Baluster Column—A European Motif in Mughal Architecture and Its Meaning." *Journal of the Warburg and Courtauld Institutes* 45:251-262.

———. Forthcoming. *The Hunting Palaces of Shah Jahan.*

———. 1983. "Jahangir and the Angels: Recently Discovered Wall Paintings Under European Influence in the Fort of Lahore." In *India and the West,* ed. J. Deppert, 173-195. New Delhi: Manohar.

———. 1991. *Mughal Architecture: An Outline of Its History and Development (1526-1858).* Munich: Prestel.

————. 1988. *Shah Jahan and Orpheus: The Pietre Dure Decoration and the Programme of Shah Jahan's Throne in the Hall of Public Audience at the Red Fort of Delhi.* Graz: Akademische Druck-und Verlaganstalt.

Kramrisch, Stella. 1937. *A Survey of Painting in the Deccan.* London: India Society.

Lapidus, Ira. 1988. *A History of Islamic Societies.* Cambridge: Cambridge Univ. Press.

Latif, S.M. 1896. *Agra, Historical and Descriptive.* Calcutta: Calcutta Central Press.

Lentz, Thomas W. and Glenn D. Lowry. 1989. *Timur and the Princely Vision.* Los Angeles and Washington: Los Angeles County Museum of Art and the Arthur M. Sackler Museum.

Lowry, Glenn D. 1987. "Humayun's Tomb: Form, Function and Meaning in Early Mughal Architecture." *Muqarnas* 4:133-148.

Marshall, John. 1922. "The Monuments of Muslim India." In *Cambridge History of India,* vol. 3, ed. W. Haig, 568-640. Cambridge: Cambridge Univ. Press.

Meister, M. 1972. "The Two-and-a-Half-Day Mosque." *Oriental Art* n.s. 18(1):57-63.

Merklinger, Elizabeth S. 1981. *Indian Islamic Architecture: The Deccan 1347-1686.* Warminster: Aris and Phillips.

Michell, George. 1992. *The Vijayanagara Courtly Style.* New Delhi: Manohar.

Michell, George and Richard M. Eaton. 1992. *Firuzabad: Palace City of the Deccan.* Oxford: Oxford Univ. Press.

Moynihan, Elizabeth B. 1988. "The Lotus Garden Palace of Zahir al-Din Muhammad Babur." *Muqarnas* 5:135-152.

————. 1979. *Paradise as a Garden in Persia and Mughal India.* London: Scholar Press.

Nath, R. 1978. *History of Sultanate Architecture.* New Delhi: Abhinav.

Otto-Dorn, Katharina. 1964. *Kunst des Islam.* Baden-Baden: Holle.

Pal, Pratapaditya et al. 1989. *Romance of the Taj.* London and Los Angeles: Thames and Hudson, Los Angeles County Museum of Art.

Parihar, Subhash. 1985. *Mughal Monuments in the Punjab and Haryana.* New Delhi: Inter-India.

Robinson, Francis. 1982. *Atlas of the Islamic World Since 1500.* New York: Facts on File.

Rice, David Talbot. 1965. *Islamic Art.* London: Thames and Hudson.

Ry van Beest Holle, Carel J. Du. 1970. *Art of Islam.* New York: Abrams.

Sen, Geeti. 1984. *Paintings from the Akbar Nama: A Visual Chronicle of Mughal India.* Varanasi: Lustre Press.

Seyller, John. 1987. "Scribal Notes on Mughal Manuscript Illustrations." *Artibus Asiae* 48(3-4):247-277.

Shokoohy, Mehrdad. 1988. *Bhadresvar: The Oldest Islamic Monuments in India.* Leiden: Brill.

Shokoohy, Mehrdad and Natalie H. Shokoohy. 1988. *Hisar-i Firuza: Sultanate and Early Mughal Architecture in the District of Hisar, India.* London:

Monographs of Art, Archaeology and Architecture.

———. 1993. *Nagaur: Sultanate and Early Mughal Architecture in the District of Nagaur, India.* London: Royal Asiatic Society.

Smart, Ellen. 1973. "Four Illustrated Mughal Baburnama Manuscripts." *Art and Archaeology Research Papers* 3: 54-58.

———. 1978. "Six Folios from a Dispersed Manuscript of the Baburnama." In *Indian Painting.* ed. T. Falk et al., 109-132. London: Colnaghi.

Smith, Edmund W. 1894-98. *The Moghul Architecture of Fathpur Sikri.* 4 vols. Allahabad: Superintendent, Govt. Press.

Taylor, Meadows. 1866. *Architecture at Beejapoor.* London: J. Murray.

Verma, Som Prakash. 1994. *Mughal Painters and Their Work: A Biographical Survey and Comprehensive Catalogue.* Aligarh and Delhi: Centre of Advanced Study in History, Aligarh Muslim Univ. and Oxford Univ. Press.

Welch, Anthony. 1985. "Hydraulic Architecture in Medieval India: the Tughluqs." *Environmental Design* 2:74-81.

———. 1993. "Architectural Patronage and the Past: The Tughluq Sultans of India." *Muqarnas* 10:311-322.

Welch, Anthony, and Howard Crane. 1983. "The Tughluqs: Master Builders of the Delhi Sultanate." *Muqarnas* 1:123-166.

Welch, Stuart Cary. 1963. *The Art of Mughal India: Painting and Precious Objects.* New York: Asia Society and H. Abrams.

———. 1961. "The Paintings of Basawan." *Lalit Kala* 10:7-18.

Wescoat, James. L. Jr. 1985. "Early Water Systems in Mughal India." *Environmental Design* 2:57-79.

———. 1990. "Gardens of Invention and Exile: The Precarious Context of Mughal Garden Design During the Reign of Humayun (1530-1556)." *Journal of Garden History* 10:106-116.

———. 1991. "Landscapes of Conquest and Transformation: Lessons from the Earliest Mughal Gardens In India, 1526-1530." *Landscape Journal* 10: 105-114.

———. 1989. "Picturing an Early Mughal Garden." *Asian Art* 2: 57-79.

Wescoat, James L. Jr., and Joachim Wolschke-Bulman, eds. 1996. *Mughal Gardens: Sources, Places, Representations and Prospects,* Washington: Dumbarton Oaks.

Yamamoto, T., M. Ara and T. Tsukinowa. 1968-1970. *Delhi: Architectural Remains of the Sultanate Period.* 3 vols. Tokyo: Institute of Oriental Culture, Univ. of Tokyo.

Zebrowski, Mark. 1983. *Deccani Painting.* London and Berkeley: Sotheby Publications and Univ. of California Press.

Dance

JOAN L. ERDMAN

International recognition of Indian dance has expanded significantly
in the last fifty years to include performances in almost all countries
of the world, exchanges of artists and dance scholars, and influence
on the world-wide development of new dance styles, techniques, and
repertoires. The work of U.S. scholars on Indian dance, both as
participants and as observers, has contributed to this expansion and
development.

India's dance artists were first presented to a wide public
audience in the United States in the 1930s, when thousands of
Americans saw Uday Shankar and His Company of Hindu Musicians
and Dancers during tours sponsored and promoted by the great
Russian impresario Sol Hurok (Erdman 1987). Prior to that, U.S.
academics in general had not taken note of the 'oriental dance' in
their scholarship; non-Indian performers of Indian dance had taken
themes, rather than styles, from India's dance arts (Shelton 1981,
Erdman 1987). The "divine dancer" Ruth St.Denis had brought
ideas from Indian dance to the public in the beginning of the 20th
century. Three generations of dancers from one Indian family
played important roles in the dissemination of Indian dance in the
United States. Ragini Devi danced in the United States in the 1920s
and 1940s and published a book on Indian dance (Ragini Devi
1928). Ragini Devi's daughter Indrani appeared at Jacob's Pillow
with her company in 1960, and for many years provided guidance
to the Asia Society's performing arts program. And Indrani's daughter
Sukanya is currently dancing and teaching dance in the United
States. Nevertheless, U.S. audiences had little exposure to Indian
dances from the 1930s to the 1960s.

Two groups of events converged in the 1960s and 1970s to
interest U.S. dance scholars in India's dance. One was the intensified
immigration of Indian citizens into the United States, particularly
into university towns. These recent arrivals, often associated with
research centers, hospitals, and clinics, were also willing to teach
their music and dance to Americans and fellow emigres who were

interested in India's performing arts. The other group of events was
the wave of visiting artists from India who presented their classical
dances at universities and colleges and at such other U.S. dance
venues as Jacob's Pillow.

The Asia Society first promoted a tour by an Indian classical
dancer in 1961 when Isadora Bennett was Asia Society's director of
performing arts, and her advisory committee included eminent
dancers, musicians, ethnomusicologists, and scholars such as Mantle
Hood, Alan Hovhaness, Joseph Campbell, Martha Graham, Yehudi
Menuhin, and Ted Shawn. Beate Gordon, as performing arts director
at the Asia Society in New York, took as her mission the presentation
of Asian artists to U.S. audiences. Speaking on behalf of the Asia
Society, she said:

We try to build up an art and the name so it will be better known here. This
also helps artists to renew their fame in their own countries. The traditional
arts are facing away in many places, and after a successful tour in the United
States they really get new leases on life. Often their governments will help
support them when they return.[1]

In 1961-1962 the Asia Society launched a 78-city tour. The
University of Chicago was one of 85 educational institutions and
cultural organizations participating in that tour. Indrani danced at
the University of Chicago in the fall of 1961, preceded by a program
introducing sitarist Pandit Ravi Shankar, and followed in the spring
of 1962 by a performance of the Ceylon National Dancers (Erdman
1985). As a complement to these programs, artists were asked to give
lecture-demonstrations in the University of Chicago's Indian
civilizations course. Kathak dancer Birju Maharaj and Kumudini
performed at the University of Chicago's Mandel Hall in March
1962. During that same year, Balasaraswati, one of India's leading
Bharata Natyam dancers, performed for an elite invited audience at
the University of Chicago's Quadrangle Club, as the "leading
exponent of authentic Indian 'notch' dance" (Erdman 1985, 48) in
what was called a "lecture-demonstration." Shanta Rao came to
Mandel Hall in the 1963-1964 season, and Balasaraswati returned in
the 1964-1965 season. Their performances were accompanied by
illustrated lectures by art historians and music scholars, placing
Indian dance squarely in the academic domain of South Asia rather
than of dance departments. Nevertheless, universities with dance
departments occasionally received the Asia Society touring artists in
dance venues. In due course Balasaraswati began to come almost
annually to the United States, sponsored by Luise Scripps and the
American Society for Eastern Arts as well as by Mills College

(California) and by Robert Brown's budding Asian Arts program at Wesleyan University (Connecticut). At these sites, her workshops and lecture-demonstrations welcomed Americans interested in studying Bharata Natyam and showed them the expertise of an artist and traditional teacher.

In the 1970s immigrants from India began to open private dance schools in the United States. These schools were most often housed in local recreation centers, schools, or churches. They were usually organized by Indian women trained in dance in India, who immigrated to the United States (and Canada) with their husbands and subsequently found themselves unable to teach at colleges and universities in the U.S. that did not teach non-western dance.[2] In time, Indians cultivating an interest in their ancient heritage and Americans interested in promoting India's arts joined organizations and universities to produce programs that introduced a wide range of U.S. audiences to Indian dance.

In the 1980s and 1990s these organizations, run mainly by Asian Indian immigrants, have been the pivotal organizers of performances by India's musicians and dancers (and even some theatrical programs) in the U.S.A. Locally-based groups and a few national promoters have brought famous and less famous Indian dancers to U.S. theaters, universities, and high schools.

Departments of dance at U.S. universities were founded to teach and promote western dance practice (rather than scholarship) in ballet, modern, and sometimes tap dance, as well as ballroom dancing. In the 1970s such departments rarely considered the possibility of including non-western dance in their regular curricula, although some hired an occasional instructor to teach students in one or two courses. For many years programs of Indian dance were more often sponsored by university-wide offices, South Asian studies departments, and museums than by dance departments and dance practitioners. The University of California-Riverside's M.A. program in dance ethnology was one of the first to offer a degree in dance other than western forms.

Important contributors to Indian dance scholarship were the South Asia departments and centers established by the 1960s and 1970s on a number of U.S. campuses. Here dance and theater students, searching for programs in which to continue their interests in Indian dance, could learn Indian languages and study South Asian literatures, arts, and religions. These university departments and centers gradually began to legitimize the study of Indian dance as an academic subject in the United States.

The American Institute of Indian Studies (AIIS), as well as the Fulbright Program, played major roles in facilitating U.S. interests in Indian dance. While it was possible for Americans to gain initial access to India's performing arts through books and by studying with those few scholars who included information about India's performing arts in their courses, actual encounters with India's performing artists were limited. Traveling artists or companies on tour were not available to students seeking prolonged interaction and study. Indians trained in the dance in India but now living in the U.S. could teach Indian dance forms. But they could not provide the atmosphere or context in the same way as living in India automatically did. So, for students interested in India's performing arts, going to India was not only a dream. It was a necessity.

Dance scholarship has been both a sequel to, and an instigator of, the study and presentation of Indian dance outside of India. Students of Indian dance in the U.S. who wanted to see more of it often sponsored (or cajoled their institutions or organizations into sponsoring) programs by visiting Indian dancers. Some champions of Indian dance in the States became organizers and promoters, and performing arts scholars offered expert commentary on dance programs, especially for non-Indians who could not otherwise understand the songs or gestures. Seeing Indian dance, some scholars turned to its study, both as an addition to their study of western dance, and as a medium through which India's cultural heritage could become manifest. Like art historians who found that the great works of Indian art propelled them into the study of Indian languages, history, and religion, U.S. dance practitioners and scholars found that, unless they were familiar with the languages of the dance forms, the sources for the repertoire, and the techniques associated with movement in Indian styles, they could not hope to understand Indian dance.

The American Institute of Indian Studies (AIIS) recognized the need for dance practitioners to study in India and to acquire knowledge of Indian languages and civilizations paralleling that required by art historians and ethnomusicologists. During the initial decades of the AIIS, students wishing to study India's dance-drama (such as Kathakali and Kuttiyattam) had to apply for fellowships under the rubric of history of art and were ranked (to their disadvantage) in competition with art historians. In the 1990s, however, practitioners of Indian dance have acquired two avenues of financial support from the AIIS. AIIS Senior Performing Arts Fellowships were established for:

accomplished practitioners of the performing arts of India who demonstrate that study in India would enhance their skills, develop their capabilities to teach or perform in the U.S., enhance American involvement with India's artistic traditions, and strengthen their links with peers in India.[3]

And AIIS Senior Scholarly/Professional Development Fellowships, were established for professionals and scholars who had not previously specialized in Indian studies or worked or studied in India. AIIS fellowship support was also available to scholars whose interests in dance were directed towards scholarly research and writing. The AIIS has awarded both Junior (dissertation) and Senior Research Fellowships to academic and independent scholars of Indian dance whose research has led to publications, presentations at professional conferences and meetings, and other public dissemination of their findings.

Scholars and practitioners of dance from Canada, Great Britain, France, Germany, Italy, Holland, Belgium, Spain, Japan, Korea, Russia, and other nations as well as those from the United States have traveled to India and benefited from the learning that can take place only in the atmosphere of India's masters, dance schools, performance venues, and daily life. Elements of the atmosphere enter the dance in subtle but significant ways and include learning to wear and walk in a sari, observing pujas, and viewing architectural and festival sites for dance.

TO DANCE IS DIVINE: INDIAN DANCE AND DANCE SCHOLARSHIP

A key area in which Indian dance and U.S. dance scholars have influenced western-based theories of the dance is through the intimate connection between the spiritual and the dance in India's classical forms. In the 1920s anthropologist Radcliffe-Brown had found a basis for social organization in the dance patterns and practices of the Andaman Islanders, patterns and practices that were later re-examined by Institute scholar Vishwajit Pandya. In the post-Independence era, scholars recognized that in India the ties between dance and the divine were, as Ruth St. Denis had understood earlier in her attempt to recreate the power of Radha in dance, intimate and powerful (Shelton 1981). In post-war studies of Asian cultures, some scholars set out to understand, in a more profound way, the means by which particular performing arts produced *rasa* and its aesthetic potency. The scholars' goals were threefold: (1) to learn the practice of the art as a means of understanding how its techniques and repertoire induced communication with the divine; (2) to find techniques and repertoire in these arts that could be fused with, or imported into, western arts as innovations or interpretations; and (3) to contribute to scholarly study of the performing arts and to discussions of the significant and impressive knowledge of Indian culture in these areas.

In dance in particular, solo performances were rare in the West, with ballet and modern dance companies dominating the stages. Yet a solo performer of one of India's classical styles with only the musicians for accompaniment would hold an audience entranced for several hours. In addition, the association of ancient Indian texts, in particular the *Nātya Śāstra*, with India's classical dance forms raised issues of tradition and change as interrelated with, rather than opposed to, each other. Furthermore, India's multiple dance forms challenged nascent attempts to notate Indian dance, since they disputed western authority about movement and space, centers and balance.

Despite the fact that Indian dance practice has not yet found a permanent place in the curriculum of most U.S. universities, features of Indian dance have influenced non-Indian dancers, particularly modern dancers in the United States. U.S. universities, already ambivalent about performing in the arts as opposed to studying them as productions and texts, have, with some notable exceptions, preferred to support only occasional instructors in Indian dance, and these usually in non-tenured and part-time positions. The inclusion of dance as performance in many universities' curricula has been as problematic as the inclusion of musical performance, theater productions, and artists' studios. The western idea that the university is for the mind rather than for the body (an idea challenged by concepts from India) often left Indian dance practice on U.S. campuses relegated to occasional lecture-demonstrations, workshops, and extra-curricular and summer programing.

When India began to present its dance arts abroad in the 1960s and 1970s, audiences were delighted and excited to see the magnificent virtuosity, the compelling elegance, and the spiritual engagement with which these artists offered their presentations. Many of the early applicants to the American Institute of Indian Studies for fellowships to study Indian dance had been inspired by seeing one of the early performances by Balasaraswati or Shanta Rao or Indrani. The possibility of learning these ancient arts, of acquiring the skills in dance forms radically different from the ballet and modern dance forms taught in U.S. schools, and of understanding dance components integral to Indian culture presented an irresistible appeal to the early fellowship applicants. The AIIS and the Fulbright

Program provided two of the limited number of funding sources for young Americans wishing to study Indian dance in India.

During the past thirty years the American Institute of Indian Studies, the Fulbright Foundation, the Shastri Institute, and the Jon Higgins Fellowship have supported studies in Indian dance. These explorations by graduate students, professional artists, and advanced scholars have included a variety of Indian dance and dance-drama forms: Kathakali, Kuttiyattam, Krishnattam, Bharata Natyam, Kathak, Odissi, Manipuri, Chhau, Kuchipudi, Kalarippayattu[4], Shankarstyle, and new dance. Grantees have in some cases become professional performers of their chosen arts. A number of them have produced significant articles and books on India's dance forms, including their history and practice, development, re-evaluation, renaissance, and new directions. Some of the scholars' video and film productions are shown in schools, universities, and museums across the country. And their lecture-demonstrations of dance and dance-drama practice have informed U.S. audiences of the values and aesthetic achievements of Indian culture.

INFLUENCE OF INDIAN DANCE STUDIES ON U.S. SCHOLARSHIP

Many scholars of South Asia see dance as marginal to, or distant from, their studies of languages, literature, history, sociology, anthropology, and fine arts. But at conferences and workshops, dances of India have been brought to such scholars' attention through performances as well as through scholarly panels and academic discussions. Since India's dance arts are not separate from India's history, visual arts, literature, music, religion and philosophy, the western compartmentalization of dance into a separated topical area is challenged. This challenge has been intellectually fruitful for South Asian scholars. Images of India in the West have often purposely included the picture of a classical Indian dancer, in elaborate costume and makeup, posed often in the context of a temple or near a sculptured dancer. This representation reflects both the sophisticated culture of India's dance and the ancient heritage of which it is a part. The music that accompanies dance, for example, is analogous to the timing and emotions of the dance. The dance itself often preserves texts that elaborate upon the older historic relationships among men and women, human and divine, and India's varied communities. Religious rituals and celebrations include dance and dance-dramas that reiterate the connections between the worldly and the divine through classic epic stories and a language of movement. Each of these connections can be made because scholars who study India's dance arts have sufficient proficiency to present these connections to scholars in other fields and to illustrate the relationships to their work. The article entitled "Performance as Translation: Uday Shankar in the West" (Erdman 1987) was provoked by an audience of literature and translation experts at the University of Chicago's South Asia seminar who were shown how gesture and movement were necessary to translate as a language of dance for western audience appreciation.

Uday Shankar and subsequent Bharata Natyam proponents in India saw in Indian sculpture the stances and movements of the dance. Similarly U.S. and Indian art historians have come to see the sculptures and temple reliefs they study as connected to the dance. Dr. Kapila Vatsyayan, a scholar and advocate for dance studies as well as a distinguished public officer who has promoted dance scholarship and practice, contributed to this discourse through her own works, especially her *Classical Indian Dance in Literature and the Arts* (1968). Films that relate Indian dance and sculpture have proved enlightening to dancers as well as to museum audiences.

DANCE AND PUBLIC AWARENESS OF INDIAN CULTURE

In recent decades three outstanding efforts have been organized to promote U.S. public awareness of Indian culture: the India Return Tour (sponsored by the AIIS) that featured three American artists who were disciples of Indian masters; the Festival of India Performing Arts tours in the U.S. that presented renowned Indian artists in universities, museums, and public venues with commentary and management by India-trained U.S. artists; and the series of festival presentations originated and convened for many years in New Delhi to present *videshī* artists to Indian audiences. In all three cases former AIIS grantees were involved in organizing, performing, presenting, and commenting on these programs that introduced thousands of new viewers to India's dance arts.

U.S. proponents of India's dance arts often do a lot of "pollinating," even though it is difficult to assess the results quantitatively.[5] They enhance their dance programs with polished and knowledgeable lecture-demonstrations. Young audiences in schools (and their teachers) are fascinated to see ten movements of the neck, or five walks in Odissi dance, or to learn how a particular costume influences movement in a dance. They are amazed that India's classical dance arts are so intricate, so precise, so beautiful. Such experiences can remain embedded in children's minds, and may influence their later attitudes towards things Indian.

U.S. scholar-dancers who have become authentic exponents of India's dance arts are also teachers in dance schools, in colleges, in workshops for dance students, in short residencies at universities, and in video presentations. Such teaching influences the lives of their students, often a combination of U.S.-born Indians and other Americans. Teaching Indian dance involves a style of learning that is noticeably different from western dance training. Involvement with the emotions, facial expressions, movements of the limbs in patterned circles, extension and return, all encompass values that are inherent in Indian culture, but often are new ideas for western students. The groundedness of Indian dance styles, the centering of the body, and representations of nature and the divine all present Indian culture to students who otherwise would have no access to a deeper understanding of what is Indian.

Western-trained dancers find in Indian dance the opportunity to learn a repertoire that expands their view of what dance is, and gives them new ideas in movement, a new articulation, and a new vocabulary. Modern dance in the United States and Europe has benefitted from such cross-cultural learning. Asian dance forms introduce new energies, themes, and concepts of space and the cosmos. Such possibilities are now being explored in U.S. modern dance, especially by students trained in both an Indian classical form and in a school of modern dance.

CONTRIBUTIONS TO THE FIELD OF DANCE

The study of Indian dance has provoked changes in U.S. academic life. The field of performance studies, championed by Professor Richard Schechner (see also Schechner, this volume) and his colleagues at New York University, has been motivated by studies of Indian dance arts to consider the role of practice as central in theorizing about performance. The works of Phillip Zarrilli on Kalarippayattu and Kathakali (1984), and the work of Avanthi Meduri on Bharata Natyam (1996) are examples of this contribution to performance studies.

Dance historians, who focused for decades on ballet and modern dance in the West, have recognized that Asian dance, and particularly Indian dance, must be included and foregrounded in studies of the history of the art. One current scholarly project includes six months of interviewing key artists in India in order to include their lives in a major publication of dance biographies. The study of Indian dance has contributed to the relationships between dance, other movement forms, dance-drama, sculpture, painting, music, and voice. Anne-

Marie Gaston's work (1982) on representations of Shiva and on the history of Bharata Natyam, Frederique Marglin's study (1985) of the Orissa *devadāsīs*, Martha Ashton's books on Yakshagana and Krishnattam (1977, 1993), Joan Erdman's work on Uday Shankar (1987, 1993, 1996), and many other writings have introduced into the field of dance scholarship ideas that would have been unknown without the significant publications of both Indian and non-Indian authors. Because publications from India have a limited (but growing) distribution abroad, accounts and studies of Indian dance published by scholars outside India have had a disproportionate impact on the awareness of India dance scholarship around the world.

During the past decades, Indian dancers from India and outside of India have developed cooperative experiments with dancers of western forms, including tap, flamenco, salsa, ballet and modern. This is leading to a new florescence of "fusion" programs, very popular with audiences, and suggestive of cultural dialogues that promote integration rather than separation through the arts. Janaki Patrik's Ka-tap, Mekhala Devi Natávar's kathak-flamenco-salsa, V.P. Dhananjayan's Panchatantra with the Ohio Ballet, Matteo's longtime fusion programs, Uttara Asha Coorlawala's dance choreography, Mamata Nyogi's Pandanallur ballets, Anne-Marie Gaston's environmental themes, Hema Rajagopalan's collaboration with Hedwig Dances, and many other notable presentations have brought to western dance performance new ideas, new fluencies, and new repertoires that stem from knowledge and appreciation of the multiplicity and intricacy of India's dance arts.

INDIAN DANCE AND THE AMERICAN INSTITUTE OF INDIAN STUDIES

The role of the AIIS has been pivotal in the opportunity for U.S. scholars and practitioners interested in the serious study of India's dance arts to pursue their goals. Edward C. Dimock, Jr., when he was president of the AIIS, argued for inclusion of dance practitioners as well as traditional scholars in the fellowship granting process. Under the directorship of Pradeep Mehendiratta, the AIIS enabled U.S. dancers not only to study Indian dance forms during extended stays in India, but also to find presentation venues. The AIIS even sponsored some performances by AIIS grantees in India.

While there have been nearly sixty Institute grantees in dance and dance-related topics over the past 33 years, and many notable achievements, I will mention only a few artists as examples of the impact dance scholarship has had on the field of dance and theater, South Asian scholarship, dance history, and public awareness of

India's cultural treasures. Each story is unique, as is true for all artists. Every artist's perseverance has been notable, since the arts are not, traditionally, a way to provide reliable and continuing sustenance. However, all the artists have succeeded, in their own ways, in studying, learning, professionalizing, legitimizing, and authenticating their arts, and in presenting, promoting, educating, and publicizing India's arts in the process.

Sharon Lowen, a professional Odissi dancer who also performs Manipuri and Chhau as well as western modern dance, first became acquainted with Indian dance at the University of Michigan, where she was studying modern dance and found an Indian teacher for Manipuri. Early in the 1970s she applied for a Fulbright fellowship to study in India, and on reapplication received support for two years of study, after which she became a teacher at the American School in Delhi, enabling her to continue her Indian dance studies. When after five years in India she came back to the United States to offer some of the benefits of her grants to Americans and to see what she could do with herself as an Indian dancer, she taught Manipuri and Odissi in San Diego and gave dance performances on the west coast and a few hundred school programs from San Diego to Portland[b].

Returning to India for further study of dance as an AIIS Fellow in 1981 under the 'professional development' category, and on a second grant in 1986, Lowen opened the door to a deluge of proposals to the AIIS, which had by then become another source of funding, besides Fulbright and private funds, for dancers wanting to continue their studies in India. Sharon Lowen danced in the India Return Tour sponsored by the AIIS, toured the U.S. with her guru Kelucharan Mohapatra, danced with other dancers in Europe, in Africa, and in various countries in Asia, and now is settled in New Delhi. In New Delhi she helped found, and was convener for the critical initial years of, the Videshi Kalakar Utsav, which gives dancers of non-Indian nationalities the opportunity to perform for public audiences and critics in India, to gain reviews, and to enhance their credibility outside of India. The Utsav's annual festival, which includes seminars as well as performances, has opened up on-going discourses among dancers, gurus, critics, organizers, presenters, and others interested in Indian dance.

Martha Ashton was introduced to India's performing arts by Professor Farley Richmond at Michigan State University, where he was teaching. Ashton came to Michigan State from the University of Georgia, where she had seen and been excited by a Noh performance, to join a program in Asian theater[7]. But the expert with whom she had hoped to study Japanese theater and Kabuki had moved on, and Ashton became an assistant to Richmond, who suggested she search for a theater form in Balwant Gargi's texts on Sanskrit and folk theater. She chose Yakshagana, attracted to the southern climate, the seashore, and the lush greenery and flowers of the southwest coast of India, but also because Yakshagana had not been studied in depth, and it had music, dance, and extravagant costumes that appealed to Ashton's theatrical interests. She studied Kannada in a program that rotated among ten American universities, and was given an introduction to a local expert on Yakshagana, who introduced her in turn to her dance teacher, Hiriadka Gopala Rao, in the village of Hiriadka near Udupi in South Kanara district.

Not initially planning to study dance but rather to observe and record what she saw, Ashton knew after seeing a first performance that the only way to know how the Yakshagana performance worked was to experience it herself. She started with drumming but moved on to training in dance, after finding that her fingers were not large and strong enough for drumming. Martha first went to India on a Fulbright fellowship in 1969, and again before taking her Ph.D. and becoming an AIIS Senior Fellow. While Martha taught briefly, her major contribution to scholarship on Indian dance has been through publications and programs. For three months in 1979 she toured with a Yakshagana troupe for the Asia Society, presenting this art rarely seen outside of South Kanara districts in India, playing in museums and universities, and presenting, lecture-demonstrations as well as programs. Ashton was the speaker and wrote the program notes, explaining each number, introducing and providing a history of the form for the audience, and sometimes participating in question-and-answer sessions. Exchanges with audience members included visits backstage by children to see the costumes and makeup, meetings with the performers to learn hand gestures and songs, and visits of the performers to the homes of audience members before and after programs. Ashton toured again in 1977 with her teacher, Gopala, and as earlier they offered some high-school shows and lecture-demonstrations as well as concert performances. Her combination of practical and theoretical knowledge is demonstrated in her publications, and, though it is difficult to know the effects of texts on present or future scholars, her documentation of Yakshagana and its modern history is preserved for future generations.

Kay Poursine is one of the major disciples of famed Bharata

Natyam artist Balasaraswati[8]. At Michigan State University Kay was studying to be a graphic designer and dancing (modern and ballet) on the side when she was awestruck by a performance of Indian dancer Shanta Rao. Then she had the opportunity to attend a workshop on Kathakali and Kuchipudi by Betty True Jones[9], who advised Poursine to go to New York after her graduation and find a teacher for Indian dance with whom to pursue her fascination with Bharata Natyam. But in New York, studying with several teachers, Kay felt "something was missing," particularly in the separation of the dance from the music. Her confidence in her fascination was fulfilled when she became a student of Balasaraswati on the west coast in classes offered by the American Society for Eastern Arts, supported by Balasaraswati's U.S. disciple Luise Scripps. Poursine eventually moved to Middletown, Connecticut to study vocal music at Wesleyan University, as demanded by Balasarawati who fully recognized the integration of music with dance. There Poursine studied with Balasaraswati's brother Viswanathan, now a professor of music at Wesleyan. Poursine was already teaching in Wesleyan's dance department when Balasaraswati sent her an invitation to study with her in Madras, which was enabled by Poursine's first AIIS fellowship in 1982.

Mekhala Devi Natavar is a kathak dancer and a devotee of Lord Krishna. Raised in the U.S. and abroad, she developed a yearning to be in India and finally achieved this goal after high school. Spending many years in Jaipur and Brindavan, she became fluent in the local languages and a disciple of a traditional exponent and teacher of Kathak from Rajasthan, Madanlal. Eventually she returned to the U.S., completed her undergraduate degree, and entered a graduate program at the University of Wisconsin. There she became a Hindi teacher and deepened her knowledge of India and dance while continuing to expand her dance to include flamenco. In the U.S. she taught Kathak and performed in numerous venues, as well as presenting papers concerning the social organization and history of Kathak. Researching the *gharānā* of her teacher brought her back to India with an AIIS Junior Fellowship, where she gathered the data that formed the basis for her doctoral dissertation. An accomplished performer, Mekhala conveys communication with the divine through her dances for Krishna. Audiences everywhere are captivated by her Kathak and Rajasthani folk dances. In bringing India's folk dances to western audiences, she joined Ram Dayal Munda who, while teaching Hindi at the University of Minnesota, organized a folk dance group that performed at universities and eventually led to one group member becoming an ethnomusicologist of Indian folk music. In California, Medha Yodh has introduced U.S. students to Gujarati folk dances and has researched and written about *garba* and its many subtle meanings.

Although his departmental affiliation is theater and drama, Professor Phillip Zarrilli of the University of Wisconsin has been involved with the study of Indian dance in three ways. One is through his own study and practice of the Kerala martial art form, Kalaripayattu, which has become an integral part of new dance choreographies of Chandralekha (Chennai, Madras) and Daksha Sheth (Tiruvanathapuram). The second is through a Kerala summer performing arts program he launched that is administered by the University of Wisconsin. The third is through his extensive publications about Kathakali, which bring the dance and movement features of this dance-drama into scholarly discourse in new ways.

Many other artists and scholars are conducting research, writing about, promoting, organizing, dancing, and discussing India's dance arts and influencing western dance arts through their commitment to Indian dance. While each individual artist's contribution is significant, the totality is impressive. The study of Indian dance has come a long way from the few touring artists who were the only representatives of Indian dance for westerners fifty years ago.

WHAT THE FUTURE HOLDS

Towards the turn of the century, after fifty years of dance studies and dance scholarship, several trends are noticeable. Exchanges between Indian dancers and exponents of other dance forms within India and abroad are bringing a new vitality to the dance world-wide. The 1984 East-West Dance Encounter in Bombay was the first of a series of international and national dance gatherings in India that have provided meeting grounds for dancers, choreographers, and organizers from around the globe. In addition to the fusion projects and exchanges already mentioned, Jonathan Hollander is collaborating with Mallika Sarabhai and the Darpana Academy in Ahmedabad, as well as with Anita Ratnam of Chennai in a series of exchanges and interactions, currently represented in a tour of Hollander's company in India, incorporating Indian dancers into the performances. Recently Jacob's Pillow, a venerable American dance venue founded by Ted Shawn, has once again started inviting an Indian dancer or company each summer to a residency and performance at its site. And the Brooklyn Academy of Music will present a newly commissioned work of Chandralekha in 1997.

Exchanges have been fostered and supported by the United States Information Agency, as well as by the Smithsonian Institution and the Asian Cultural Council, and new supporters are on the horizon.

Through dance and dance scholarship Indian culture has been seen by millions of people in dozens of countries. Who knows the full effects of these encounters? Robert Gottlieb's film, *Circles Cycles Kathak Dance,* is an outcome of a viewing of Indian dance by his wife Lois, when Uday Shankar and Company toured the United States in the early 1960s. No doubt the next generations of dancers and dance scholars will come from those who have had the opportunity to witness and become fascinated with Indian dance through recent programs and lecture-demonstrations. *Sruti*, founded in 1983 under the guidance of its editor-in-chief, N. Pattbhi Raman, has brought a serious journal, published in India and distributed widely abroad, to the attention of scholars and the public interested in India's dance arts. This monthly magazine provides dance history and a record of dance events, as well as numerous photographs and biographical details about dancers and musicians. Indian dance art has become a public event, a prized performance, a pathway into India, and an enlightening source for Indian values and philosophy, as well as evidence of complex trans-nationalism.

Looking to the future, the beginnings of an infrastructure for dance in India will no doubt be developed into a full-blown professional support for dance during the early part of the next century, particularly as the market for dance increases with media possibilities and excitement about new directions in the dance. For Asian Indians living in the United States and Canada, classical Indian dance has become a cultural touchstone, bringing their children into contact with their heritage through practice and embodiment, as well as through home and parental examples. Perplexing and uncertain choices, which must be made when one lives in an adopted society, are often worked out through the stories of the dance repertoire and the dance teachers' guidance of their young students (Cunningham 1992).

Plans are also underway to integrate the scholarship on Indian dance into current dance histories and dance studies. The *Oxford Encyclopedia of Dance* will include a section on dance in Indian films, as well as on Indian classical and folk styles. A forthcoming collection of biographies of renowned dancers will include biographical sketches of important Indian artistes. Reports on dance research in India are being published (Ananya 1996). A project to create a history of Indian dance in the twentieth century is in progress, and several important critiques of the renaissance and revival of Indian dance in the 1920s and 1930s are awaiting publication.

With the development of a substantial infrastructure appropriate to the market economy of modern India and the maintenance of tradition while moving towards new dance for the twenty-first century, the contributions of Indian dance and dance scholarship to world dance studies and international exchanges promise to be as significant as in the past fifty years. There is little reason to doubt that Indian dance will continue to challenge and motivate change in western dance and dance scholarship, and to stimulate with its delightful performers and performances serious consideration of the values and realizations that it represents.

NOTES

1. McHugh, Mary. 1984. "Our Woman in Borneo...and Other Asian Limes." *Newsletter of the Asia Society.* 1:3 (November-December): 5.
2. Katherine Dunham and Selma Jean Cohen had earlier discovered at the University of Chicago that there was no place or dance departments for their interests; so they turned to anthropology and English departments, respectively.
3. From a 1990s American Institute of Indian Studies brochure.
4. This martial art of Kerala has been taught and adapted to western theater by Phillip Zarrilli at the University of Wisconsin-Madison. It is now becoming a key component of new dance choreographies in India.
5. Discussions with Sharon Lowen are the basis for some of these points, and I am grateful to her for interview time on July 16 and 24, 1996 during a brief visit to the United States.
6. This account is based on interviews with Sharon Lowen July 16 and 24, 1996 as well as on-going conversations over the years.
7. This account is based on a telephone interview on April 1, 1997, and on earlier meetings and discussions.
8. Ibid.
9. Betty True Jones and Clifford Jones studied Kathakali and other Kerala dance-drama forms from the 1960s, and were among the earliest western supporters of India's performing arts in the post-Independence era. In 1964, soon after its formation, the American Institute of Indian Studies supported Clifford Jones's dissertation study of Kathakali, the traditional theater of Kerala. Cliff and Betty Jones became noted scholars of Kathakali and influenced students and theater performers through their work in theater, their tours with Kathakali companies, and their writings. Other early students of Indian theater, which included dance-drama forms, were Farley Richmond and James Brandon, for whom India was part of a broader interest in Asian theater forms.

REFERENCES

Ananya. 1996. "Dance Research in India: A Brief Report." *Dance Research Journal* 28:1 (Spring): 119-124.

Ashton, Martha Bush and Bruce Christie. 1977. *Yakshagana: A Dance Drama of India.* New Delhi: Abhinav.

Ashton-Sikora, Martha Bush and Robert P. Sikora. 1993. *Krishnattam.* New Delhi: Oxford.

Blank, Judith. 1973. *The Story of the Chou Dance of the Former Mayurbhanj State, Orissa.* Unpublished doctoral dissertation, University of Chicago.

Coorlawala, Uttara Asha. 1994. *Classical and Contemporary Indian Dance: Overview, Criteria and a Choreographic Analysis.* Unpublished doctoral dissertation, New York University.

Cunningham, Jean. 1992. *Classical Dance of India in Canada: Adaptation, Play and Woman.* Unpublished doctoral dissertation, William Lyon University.

Erdman, Joan L. 1984. "Who Should Speak for the Performing Arts? The Case of the Delhi Dancers." In *Cultural Policy in India,* ed. Lloyd I. Rudolph. New Delhi: Chanakya.

————. 1985. "Today and the Good Old Days: South Asian Music and Dance Performances in Chicago." *Selected Reports in Ethno-musicology VI: Asian Music in North America.* 39-58. Los Angeles: Department of Music Program in Ethnomusicology, University of California.

————. 1987. "Performance as Translation: Uday Shankar in the West." *The Drama Review* (Spring) 31:1.

————. 1993. "Performance as Translation II: Shankar, the Europeans, and the Oriental Dance." In *Institute for Culture and Consciousness: Occasional Papers I,* ed. Susanne Hoeber Rudolph, Leela Fernandez, and Andrew Rotman, 34-47. Chicago: Committee on South Asian Studies, University of Chicago.

————. 1996. "Dance Discourses: Rethinking the History of the 'Oriental Dance'." In *Moving Words: Rewriting Dance,* ed. Gay Morris, 141-149. London: Routledge.

Gaston, Anne-Marie. 1982. *Siva in Dance, Myth and Iconography.* Delhi: Oxford Univ. Press.

Jones, Clifford R. and Betty True Jones. 1970. *Kathakali: An Introduction to the Dance-Drama of Kerala.* San Francisco: American Society for Eastern Arts and Theatre Arts Books.

Marglin, Frederique. 1985. *Wives of the God-King: The Rituals of the Devadāsīs of Puri.* Delhi: Oxford Univ. Press.

McHugh, Mary. 1984. "Our Woman in Borneo ... and Other Asian Limes." *Newsletter of the Asia Society* 1:3 (November-December).

Meduri, Avanthi. 1996. *Nation, Woman, Representation: The Sutured History of the Devadasi and Her Dance.* Unpublished doctoral dissertation, New York University.

Puri, Rajika. 1983. *A Structural Analysis of Meaning in Movement: The Hand*

Gestures of Indian Classical Dance. Unpublished master's thesis, New York University.

Ragini, Devi. 1928. *Nritanjali: An Introduction to Hindu Dancing.* New York: Hari G. Govil.

Shelton, Suzanne. 1981. *Divine Dancer: A Biography of Ruth St. Denis.* Garden City, NY: Doubleday.

Sruti. 1983- . *Indian Music and Dance Magazine.*

Vatsyayan, Kapila. 1968. *Classical Indian Dance in Literature and the Arts.* New Delhi: Sangeet Natak Akademi.

Zarrilli, Phillip. 1984. *The Kathakali Complex: Actor, Performance and Structure.* New Delhi: Abhinav.

Economics

ALAN HESTON

INTRODUCTION

This survey covers three major fields related to the economy and society of India: Economic History, Economics, and Economic Demography and Equity. Scholarship in the field of economic history most closely parallels the research findings of AIIS Fellows over the years, as reflected in their dissertations and monographs. The Fellows' research has often built upon shared research interests of scholars in India. During the past thirty years their joint efforts have built up a major institutional base in India, with the *Indian Social and Economic History Review* being the single most important journal in the field. Demography and related economic concerns have had large amounts of financial support from governments and international institutions both within and outside India. As a result much of the scholarship in demography and economics on India has been carried out within an international setting. The interactions between research in India and the cutting edges of demography and economics have been very close. These interactions have been enhanced by the significant numbers of demographers and economists from India who teach in U.S. academic institutions. This is the good news about two of the three major fields related to the economy and society of India. News about the third major field (Economic Demography and Equity) is less sanguine. Economics scholarship has tended to neglect the rich detail of India in order to try to reach more general and comparative results.

This survey intentionally emphasizes links between recent research on India with the disciplines as typically taught in the United States. On one hand, because of limitations of space, it may appear to those coming from an AIIS background that the research of a number of well-known scholars is overlooked. On the other hand, it may appear that descriptions of the work of a number of scholars not normally associated with Indian studies are given space. While the survey does have this orientation, it is hoped this will highlight how influential has been work on India for a variety of disciplines. And in my view it will show how indispensable have been the contributions of the area specialists who have called to the attention of the disciplines the rich economic fabric of India, an experience captured in the saying that if one has a theory that cannot find support in one of the 600,000 villages in India, it must be a poor theory, indeed.

International intellectual involvement with the Indian economy is hardly new. The names of British economists who were attracted to Indian problems is impressive indeed; a sampler would include Adam Smith whose favorite foil was the British East India Company, a monopoly illustrating all the reasons that free trade and competition would be preferred; James Mill and John Stuart Mill, both servants of the East India Company where they were able to put into administrative practice in India Jeremy Bentham's utilitarian principles; T.R. Malthus who, as the first professor of political economy at Haileybury, taught Ricardian rent theory to future civil servants in India; and John Maynard Keynes, who wrote on, among other matters, Indian currency problems. Indian economic problems in the 19th century also attracted an impressive group of political economists from India including Dhadabhai Naoroji, B.R. Ranade, and R.C. Dutt, and many more in this century. Given the very strong legacy of economic writing in and on India, it is not surprising that, despite declining interest in the interwar period, this tradition has continued after India's independence.

A principal use of the rich variety of Indian economic experience has been to test alternative theories. For example, an event like the Bengal Famine of 1943 may be used to test a theory of causes of famine as A.K. Sen (1981), Paul Greenough (1982), and others have done. Or India may be an observation in a cross section of countries used to test some hypothesis, like convergence of economies as in endogenous growth models of Paul Rohmer and Robert Barro. In the latter type of analysis, it is unlikely that specific aspects of the Indian experience will feed into more global analysis. However, in the Bengal Famine example the questions raised by this event have generated a substantial literature that continues to feed into the disciplines of demography, economic history, and economics. In the period since India's independence another major economic focus has been the set of planning policies that India has implemented, and a comparison, usually not in India's favor, between the outcomes of these policies and the policies of other countries, typically China, Korea, or other Asian tigers. This paper will describe many (but hardly all) such examples of scholarship of the past fifty years that are grounded in Indian economic experience.

ECONOMIC HISTORY

The Nobel Prize in economics awarded to Douglass C. North and Robert Vogel in 1993 was for their achievements in economic history. The contribution of North was to look at how institutional arrangements change in response to large movements in relative prices allowing economies to make more efficient uses of their resources. Vogel pioneered in quantitative economic history, especially in posing counterfactual questions that lent themselves to being empirically tested. North and Vogel did not work on Indian economic history, but in many of the areas in which they pioneered new scholarship on India arose. The discussion below deals with five subject areas: 1. The Price Revolution and Asia; 2. Industrial Organization and the Trading Companies; 3. The Impact of the British on the Indian Economy; 4. Rethinking the Indian Experience; and 5. Surplus Labor. The discussion is intended to be suggestive rather than exhaustive.

1. THE PRICE REVOLUTION AND ASIA

The price revolution in Europe of the 16th century that resulted in the rise in prices of commodities in terms of gold and silver was attributed by Hamilton to the influx of precious metals from the Americas into Spain and their spread north through Europe. A part of this story traditionally was that these precious metals subsequently spilled out of Europe into Asia and sank into the hordes of gold and silver in China and India. K. N. Chaudhuri (1968) attacked the notion of Asia as a sink for precious metals and argued that what happened in Asia was similar to what happened in Europe with some lag in time. Developments in monetary theory during the 1970s led to viewing the developments of the 16th century as part of a worldwide redistribution of precious metals increasing their supply throughout the world. As a consequence, a number of studies have looked at price behavior in various parts of India during the 16th and 17th centuries as well as at the monetary needs of India for circulating coinage: J. Brennig (1983), D. Flynn (1986), I. Habib (1963), Om Prakash (1995), and John Richards (1983).

These inquiries have provided a richer understanding of the interactions of the trading companies with India and the rest of Asia. As the trading companies tried to export to Asia, they were hindered not only because their manufactures were often unsuitable for the market (e.g., woolen clothing), but also because the prices of all their goods in Europe had risen in terms of gold and silver. Until the price revolution had also spread to Africa and Asia, it meant all of their exports were expensive, with the important exception of precious metals. So, to the dismay of the mercantilists in Europe, large initial amounts of silver and also gold were necessarily exported to India and the rest of Asia. Scholarship on India has provided an important part of the story of monetary integration of the world in the period 1500-1700 that has, in turn, produced monographs by international and monetary economists, e.g., Kindleberger (1989), and Goldsmith (1987).

2. INDUSTRIAL ORGANIZATION AND THE TRADING COMPANIES

A major development of the last fifty years that has involved many of the social sciences is organization theory. Often organizations have evolved in the view of economic historians like Douglas C. North as responses to arrangements that previously prevented the efficient use of economic resources. The emergence of the Dutch and British East India Companies in Asia in the 17th century is often viewed as a major break with the parasitical organization of the Portuguese trading empire. As an organizational form these joint stock companies were clearly an important innovation. But what is of more interest in recent literature is the internal organization of these companies and the way in which they dealt with the agency problem. The "servants" of these companies were the agents of their directors; but how does one build a system of incentives that induces agents six months out of the directors' reach to undertake the activities and decisions that will be in the interests of the directors and perhaps even the stockholders and the trading companies? These are the kinds of questions that have led to a reexamination of the experience of the activities of the factors, the shipping interests, the local finance of inventories, and the relationships of the trading companies with private Indian and European interests. Building on the work on the trading companies beginning with Holden Furber (1948), K.N. Chaudhuri (1965), Anderson, McCormick and Tollison (1983), and others have, for example, looked at the British East India Company as a model for corporate decentralization and for management of the agency problem that General Motors might do well to study.

3. THE IMPACT OF THE BRITISH ON THE INDIAN ECONOMY

The research of Vogel, North, and many other proponents of the new economic history (where "new" is post-1960) was to confront received historical scenarios with facts. Frequently the confrontation was framed in terms of formal models tested on previously unused data sets, often under the name of cliometrics. But it could also involve a much less formal use of the facts. For example, Dharma Kumar (1964) questioned the received scenario that the large group of landless laborers in India were a consequence of the de-industrialization of India resulting from the industrial revolution in England and the decline of Mughal administrative centers and urban markets. Kumar simply asked if there were evidence that the extent of landless labor in India in the latter half of the 19th century could have been generated by a society that had no landless labor circa 1800. The answer she found was that it seemed likely there was substantial landless labor at the time of British hegemony. She also found fragmentary data for parts of south India early in the 19th century that confirmed from direct evidence the existence of landless groups at that time.

Morris D. Morris has similarly reinterpreted the 19th century economic history of India, arguing that there was substantial economic expansion in India at least during the 1800-1870 period. His article and a set of responses were published in a symposium (Morris 1969). This skirmish did not resolve the different interpretations of the colonial experience in India, but it did bring to Indian economic history an increasing quantitative focus. An early example of this was the work of Meghnad (later Lord) Desai (1971) in which he tested an argument of Morris about the handloom weavers. Morris had pointed out that while the exports of cotton cloth from England clearly cut into Indian export and local markets, the exports of cotton thread to India provided handloom weavers with a cheaper input than had previously been available. Since the industrial revolution did not immediately lead to mechanical weaving driving out handloom weaving, this meant that weavers in India could now satisfy local demand at lower cost than before, so that, on net, the employment of weavers could have gone down if lost export markets exceeded expanding domestic sales or vice versa. Empirical work on this question continues, including regional studies that examine weaver employment, as well as alternative models for examining the impact of the expansion of British industry. It should also be mentioned that the re-examination of economic relations between

England and India in the 17th and 18th century provides one of the clearest illustrations of how trade barriers and infant industry protection of final product imports can have positive effects for at least some groups. The case in point is the prohibition of imports of printed cotton under the Navigation Acts that led to innovations in other stages of manufacture, namely cotton spinning and weaving that, in turn, were the core of the industrial revolution in England.

The general push in economic history towards quantification is also apparent in the various contributions to the *Cambridge Economic History of India* (1982). An important precursor of this work was the study of agricultural production trends in British India by George Blyn (1966), a student of Daniel Thorner who, with Alice Thorner, carried out important quantitative studies of the labor force from Indian census data (1962). Another recent direction of research follows up Vogel's work that uses heights of populations from historical periods as a proxy for nutritional status of populations. In this context the heights of cohorts of indentured servants in Fiji have been used as an indicator of levels of nutrition in areas of recruitment in eastern India in several decades of the late 19th century (see Brennan, McDonald and Shlomowitz 1994).

4. RETHINKING THE INDIAN EXPERIENCE

The imperialism-exploitation tradition of Marx and Lenin has played a minor role in U.S. economics during the last fifty years in part because of its suppression in academe in the name of the Cold War.[1] However, in India Marxian analyses of the Indian economy have been important for the past century, with many Indian scholars providing Marxian perspectives to writings on Indian economic problems and actively contributing to the international communist intellectual scene. While this strand of economic thought has not fed much into U.S. universities, the general themes of imperialism, exploitation, and dependence have had major impacts on economic thought. The "drain" theory that Naoroji evolved in the 1860s can be found in much of the core-periphery analysis of writers like Raul Prebisch, who was extremely influential a century later, and whose influence continues today under names like neo-imperialism.

Another strand of thought has sought to explain the slow growth of India under the British as due to specific policies of the British, such as free trade and the relative neglect of education and irrigation expenditures by the British government. These policies meant that India did not converge with more-rapidly-growing countries during the ninety years before Independence. These or related observations have been incorporated into theories that emphasize relationships between dependency and development, and have offered alternative, views of why India may have responded less to economic stimuli than some of its Asian neighbors in the past forty years.

A related but somewhat different interpretation of the Indian experience is the notion of multiple equilibria. At the center of mainstream economics is market or aggregate equilibrium. One of the unwelcome facts that tended to be observed for India was that Indian markets were often in equilibrium, but at a very low level of overall economic activity. These observations have led to consideration of the possibility of multiple equilibria, a possibility considered in some of the early development literature under names like the low-level equilibrium trap. In such a view, the different initial conditions facing an economy may lead to different outcomes even if the responses to given stimuli are the same.

The British East India Company territorial acquisitions, combined with the emergence of James Mill and others sympathetic to utilitarian ideology as administrators, provides an amazing period of experimental administrative practice in India. The utilitarian influence was very strong from 1820 to 1850, but it plateaued and came under increasing attack after 1857. The parallels between this style of policy making and the rational-expectations mode of analysis of the 1970s is evident in many ways. The practice of setting the land revenue demand in ryotwari areas as the average of good and bad years, with the peasant expected to set aside from good years to provide for shortfalls in the bad years, is a typical utilitarian model of the rational peasant. The rational investor and consumer of recent rational-expectations models clearly draw from the utilitarian tradition of a century and a half earlier. The reaction to this in India was an equally influential mode of thought, namely the development by Henry Maine and others of an appreciation of the wide variety of rural communities in India where implementation of a single set of administrative principles might not achieve uniform results. This line of thought generated many official ethnographic studies that helped lay the foundation of modern anthropology in India.

5. SURPLUS LABOR

One of the distinguishing characteristics of models of developing countries was the assumption that, for a large number of such economies, there was surplus labor that could be removed from the agricultural sector without reducing agricultural output. This labor pool was also termed disguised unemployment because the workers might in fact be working on a family farm but be underemployed, so that it was thought possible to rearrange family labor and free up labor that could be employed elsewhere. Since these models were applied to countries like India, where there was a positive wage for hired agricultural labor, economists who were uncomfortable with markets that did not clear did not find the notion of surplus labor attractive. One of the earliest economists to make clear why disguised unemployment in a country like India was different from involuntary unemployment in industrial countries, as described by Keynes, was V.K.R.V. Rao (1964). What Rao argued was that expansionary fiscal policies used to reduce unemployment in industrial economies assumed idle industrial capacity, and that assumption was not valid for countries like India; so such policies would be inappropriate.

In the context of Indian economic history, Theodore Schultz, another Nobel laureate, used the 1919-1921 influenza epidemic in India as an example to illustrate that surplus labor did not exist in Indian agriculture. A.K. Sen (1967) argued that the influenza epidemic was not an appropriate test of the surplus labor assumption because the labor removed from agriculture by deaths was very different than might be experienced in a program consciously designed to mobilize surplus labor. In particular, the epidemic tended to hit whole families and areas so that often fields were not planted during this period, but not because a number of workers from different families migrated outside the village to take on non-agricultural work.

Another important strand of research related to surplus labor is that of Sen and others on intensity of cultivation of larger and small farms. The stylized fact, based upon the Farm Management Surveys and the work of M.L. Dantwala (1986) and others that required explanation, was that output per acre was higher on smaller rather than larger farms. Sen explained this by saying that when holdings were large enough to require hiring of labor, employers would hire workers only to the point where their extra output was at least equal to the wage. Smaller farms relying solely on family labor would not use this marginal calculus and would only send out family labor if employment opportunities were plentiful. This type of family enterprise labor-use behavior was also embedded in the work of Chayanov on peasant agriculture in Russia, which Thorner (1986) and others brought to the attention of a much wider audience. The Sen analysis explained the higher output per hectare on small farms, and also explained why, if one costed family labor at the wage for unskilled labor, smaller farms were less profitable than larger farms.

This analysis was important, but it left a number of loose ends that will be discussed below.

ECONOMICS[2]

This section on economics must be savagely selective both in neglecting some of the margins of economics and in neglecting a number of ways in which Indian issues have fed into the field of economics. One institution, the Indian Statistical Institute (ISI), must at least be mentioned. ISI has been a premier center for both theoretical and applied statistics since the 1930s, beginning its activities in Calcutta. Its longtime director, P.C. Mahalanobis, was a confidante of Nehru and is considered the architect of the second Five Year Plan in India and an advocate of long-term planning. As a part of Indian economic planning, the ISI was involved operationally as a unit within the Perspective Planning Division of the Planning Commission and interacted with leading economists throughout the world. Another venerable institution is the Indian Council of Agricultural Research which, like ISI, made theoretical and applied contributions that were widely known outside of India and which fed into areas like econometrics, agricultural economics, and economic planning. This discussion is divided into three sections; the first discusses contributions from India in three areas of general economics, (efficiency wages, entrepreneurship, and interlinked rural markets); the second discusses contributions from India in two areas of agricultural economics (sharecropping and rural credit); while the third section briefly discusses contributions from India in economic planning.

1. CONTRIBUTIONS FROM INDIA IN
THREE AREAS OF GENERAL ECONOMICS

Efficiency Wages. One issue in the surplus labor debate has been the existence of unemployment in a labor market where there are workers who would willingly work at the existing wage for unskilled labor. A related observation, also often noted for India, is that there are jobs in other sectors of the economy, including government and foreign firms, where the salary paid is above what is necessary to attract applicants. Two types of explanation tend to be offered. One explanation is that employers, like governments, because they do not face competition, can set wage scales on the basis of other considerations than profitability. This line of analysis has been offered as an explanation for why education is often used as a screening device for positions, in turn leading to large demand by households for higher education.

A second and usually complementary line of analysis sees the higher wage as justifying itself in terms of the higher productivity it induces from the labor hired. At the level of manual labor the argument is that the relation of nutrition and productivity is direct, and that often wages are well above the minimum necessary. This permits workers to be better nourished and therefore to be more productive, justifying their higher "efficiency" wage. It is illustrative of how much analysis of the Indian economy has become part of mainstream economics that the efficiency wage argument grew out of Indian experience and was put forward by Stiglitz, who was Chair of the Council of Economic Advisors under U.S. President Clinton and is now Vice President for Research at the World Bank. In terms of white collar workers, the argument is that by paying a premium above what is necessary to attract workers, those hired are more loyal to the firm and are more productive, therefore justifying their salaries.[3]

Entrepreneurship. The rich variety of Indian business communities continues to feed into studies of the entrepreneurship function and theories of industrial leadership. The social divisions in India and the de-emphasis of the material world in many of India's religions led Max Weber and others to regard India as lacking the social framework to produce a dynamic business leadership class. As Morris and others have made clear, far from inhibiting business activity, Hinduism and its traditional *varna* system provided a role for trading activity. Further, there were important Muslim business communities, such as the Bohras and Khojas, and immigrant business communities like the Jews and Parsis. None of these facts fit neatly into theories like those of Tawney and Weber that would give priority to the Protestant Ethic as a key to the growth of capitalism.

Further, the ability of Indian business groups to merge the corporate form and the managing agency system with their own family-based business networks suggested their easy adaptability to modern business practice. Bert Hoselitz and David McClelland, who have contributed in very different ways to our understanding of what leads individuals to undertake entrepreneurial activities, have both used India as a case study. Blair Kling has examined the integration of the managing agency system into Indian business; Tom Timberg has carried out a major study of the Marwari community; and Trivedi has fostered a number of studies of Indian business communities in both an historical and contemporary setting. Another interesting issue with respect to Indian business is how important a factor was British discrimination against Indian entrepreneurs in explaining patterns of investment, and particularly the preponderance of British capital in eastern India and Indian capital in western India, a subject explored by A. Bagchi, Morris, Sen and others.

With respect to caste, rather than viewing it as a peculiarly Indian institution, there have been attempts to see caste, whatever its origins, as operating like many other discriminatory systems. Ackerlof (1984), for example, has suggested that the type of statistical discrimination following from the assumption that all members of a group will display average characteristics of the group can be applied to caste. And the system of outcasting as a sanction shares many features with modern groups, like professional associations, or corporate and government bureaucracies.

Interlinked Rural Markets. The relationships between those who control agricultural land and those who till it, and between both these parties and the government, has been a continuing focus of study in the context of India and other countries of the world. Many of the earlier studies such as those of D. Thorner, W.C. Neale, F.T. Januzzi, and Jan Bremmer did not believe that land reform legislation and other rural programs would change the economic position of the landless without an accompanying upheaval in the power structure in rural India (see R. Herring 1983). These studies varied from detailed analyses of how land reform legislation evolved in particular states of India in the 1950s to nonrandom collections of vignettes of how the positions of those at the bottom or top of the rural power structure were usually not touched by the legislation. A remarkable journalistic account of these and other agricultural programs in India was provided by Kusum Nair in *Blossoms in the Dust.* The publication of this book and the work of Francine Frankel provided one of the many attacks on the notion so often expressed by the Congress Party and other Indian political parties that somehow equality could be legislated or, more often, if an ideal became a political resolution, it also became fact.

2. CONTRIBUTIONS FROM INDIA IN TWO AREAS OF AGRICULTURAL ECONOMICS

A parallel set of agricultural studies had looked at individual behavior of farmers based upon surveys collected by university scholars and other groups, such as the Farm Management Studies, as well as the continuing rounds of the National Sample Survey. In our selective approach, only two aspects of these later developments are examined, sharecropping and rural credit, both of which have had major influences on mainstream economics.

Sharecropping. Why should sharecropping be a prevalent institution in agriculture throughout the world, when, as Alfred Marshall observed a century ago, it appears very inefficient? Why should a tenant want to put out additional effort if the gains in terms of additional production had to be shared with the landowner, asked Marshall. Wouldn't total agricultural output be less under such an arrangement as compared to, say, owner-operation or a fixed land rent? Since sharecropping is widespread in India, one can also raise the question of why it exists, frequently alongside fixed rents and owner-operated holdings.

Stiglitz, T.N. Srinivasan, and G.A. Ackerlof (1984), among many others, have examined this question, frequently using Indian data. A way of restating the Marshall question emerged, and that was to view the sharecropper as an agent of the owner. In this view, there are likely to be owners who are good supervisors and monitor labor well, and other owners who would be better off letting out their land to others. On the supply-of-labor side, there are those wishing to cultivate on the land of others who are good and poor farmers. The quality of labor available gives a range of choice to the owner. Ideally, a good cultivator would be a preferred sharecropper, but a good cultivator would prefer a fixed rent for land so that any surplus would accrue to him. Poor cultivators would be willing to sharecrop, but owners would not wish to take them on, so they are more likely to work as hired labor.

The sharecropping question has been formulated by Ackerlof into a model where time and effort of labor are distinct variables, the effort of labor being only observed as cost to the landowner. While evidence of the wide difference between average and best practice in agriculture is often anecdotal, such as Ackerlof cites for Punjab and Uttar Pradesh, this does appear a quite general problem.

The combinations of owners and potential cultivators may thus produce arrangements where owners choose to (a) cultivate their own land using hired workers, (b) lease out land on fixed rent, or (c) enter into sharecropping agreements. The rich set of rural surveys available in India, including those of the International Center for Research in the Semi-Arid Tropics (ICRISAT) in Hyderabad, have permitted much more detailed analysis of the widely varying practices of land use in India. Jodha, for example, has shown that a large proportion of leasing of land is based upon the variations in the current family labor force size and that the market for land is often related to the credit market in rural areas, an area to which we now turn.

Rural Credit. The villain of many a rural drama is the moneylender. Often rural credit policy has been directed at breaking the vicious circle of indebtedness that binds the small rural borrower to the village moneylender. As the Rural Credit Surveys of the Reserve Bank of India and other studies were to show, the moneylender often made unsecured loans for marriages and other rites of passage, with no forms to fill out or explicit assets to pledge, that would not be granted by other credit channels. The moral hazard of default by peasants without assets was not something that mainstream financial institutions could monitor; whereas those with assets at the local level could qualify as intermediaries as described with customary humor by R.K. Narayan in the *Financial Expert.* However, if large farmers-cum-moneylenders had access to additional credit from agricultural lending agencies, this ought in principle to trickle down to make for lower borrowing rates in informal credit markets.

By extension, one could ask how well rural credit markets in fact functioned and what was the relationship between credit, labor, land markets, and risk. For example, if credit markets operated well, then in choosing what crop to produce, cultivators should not be concerned to grow food for their own consumption if there are more profitable cash crops to grow and it is possible to borrow funds to finance consumption between harvest seasons. Bardhan (1989) and Bell and Srinivasan (in Bardhan) have described a number of the links between the needs for an insurance and credit market that may be linked to tenancy or labor contracts. In a similar vein, Rosenzweig and Wolpin (1993) and others have examined how the desire to smooth consumption, given seasonal production fluctuations and credit constraints, is interlinked with the investment in bullocks.

3. CONTRIBUTIONS FROM INDIA IN ECONOMIC PLANNING

The First Five Year Plan in India was an impressive document that was extremely important because, when it was published in 1951, little was available in print on the practice of Soviet Planning. As a result the growth and investment goals of the first Plan captured the attention of economists throughout the world and in turn influenced planning in many countries. The second Plan, with the long term frame of P.C. Mahalanobis as its centerpiece, became the subject of much discussion and criticism over the years because of its emphasis on heavy industry. India's third Plan had perhaps the most lasting intellectual impact because it sought for the first time to set national goals to reduce poverty that were made operational by use of a poverty line. The interactions of Indian economists and economists in other parts the world with respect to economic planning was extensive during most of the 1950-1970 period, and it is not possible to do justice to this large subject here. However, two areas (rent-seeking activities and international trade restrictions) are singled out for discussion because they have had a general impact on how economists think about economic interventions by government.

Rent-seeking activities are illustrated by import quotas, licenses, or foreign exchange allocations, all of which create a difference between the quantity available on the market and quantity demanded at the official price, as in the case of foreign exchange or cement in India at various times. Those who can obtain quotas or licenses will make the difference between the parallel market and official price, which earns them not only a substantial rent but also the wherewithal to lobby lavishly to maintain their privilege. While rent-seeking behavior has been widespread through all economies, its importance in India has attracted many to its study and to spelling out how pervasively it internests with the rest of the economy.

Jagdish Bhagwati and T.N. Srinivasan have studied the impacts of international trade restrictions. They have been particularly critical of how India's planning created opportunities for rent seeking of a Himalayan dimension. They have also analyzed the limitations of the effective rate of protection and other measures associated with interventions in foreign trade as a guide to policy. Bhagwati has built on Indian experience in foreign trade interventions to analyze the second-best aspects of smuggling, the dubious benefits of export subsidies or other measures creating multiple exchange rates, and the invidious character of exchange controls including under-invoicing of imports and the like.

ECONOMIC DEMOGRAPHY AND EQUITY

This section is organized around the Human Development Index (HDI) that forms the core of the Human Development Report of the United Nations Development Fund. The HDI has been published since 1990 and, despite widespread criticism, has grown in use and influence. It began as a way for one international organization to break ranks with the World Bank and International Monetary Fund and question the value of structural adjustment policies of the 1980s that were the condition of loans to countries not able to meet their international debts. The origins of the HDI are heavily bound up with the experience of India as seen through the analysis of demographers and economists in India and abroad. The discussion is interpretative and describes how the various dimensions of the HDI have been developed from Indian experience, though the experience of many other countries played a role too. The HDI itself is currently constructed from a measure of real per capita GDP of a country, a literacy measure, and a measure of its health status (life-expectancy at birth). The resulting HDI can then be constructed for countries and within countries by gender, region, or socio-economic group.

1. CONTRASTS BETWEEN KERALA AND PUNJAB

One of the regularities assumed in the early development literature was that higher incomes are associated with improved health status and usually with higher levels of education. What emerged from many studies in India was the finding that this generalization simply did not hold. The life expectancy in Kerala, a middle-income state, was higher than in Punjab, the state with the highest per capita income. And the education level in Kerala was the highest in all of India.

Another striking contrast between Kerala and Punjab was the ratio of males to females in the population. Typically the male/female ratio in a given population is 1.0 by age one and has often declined in later years so that for many countries the average is below 1.0. In India the ratio has been around 1.1 for most of this century. This finding was often explained away as a probable statistical anomaly in the 1950 and 1960 censuses. Then serious studies were made of the internal variations in India, particularly the very high masculinity ratios in Punjab and other northern states and more "normal" male/female ratios in South India. Among others, Narinder Uberoi Kelley and Pravin Visaria contributed to this literature which was given wider notice by Pranab Bardhan (1974) and A.K. Sen (1988). These findings led to a number of studies of intra-household allocations of food and education and health investments in boys versus girls (see M. Rosenzweig and T.P. Schultz, 1982). A major finding of these studies was that those areas with high masculinity ratios were areas where the ratio of female to male literacy was low.

Much of this research coincided with worldwide discomfort with the level and growth of income per capita as measures of economic well-being and progress. This discomfort was due both to the fact that average per capita income neglected distribution and that, when comparing incomes across countries, the use of exchange rates to bring currencies to a common denominator appeared to lead to implausibly low incomes in India and similar countries. One way to address this issue was to construct indices based upon various physical indicators of economic and social well-being. Many of these indices involved large numbers of variables put together by methods less than transparent. A very simple index constructed by Morris D. Morris (1979), based heavily upon Indian experience, was the Physical Quality of Life Index (PQLI). This index had a great deal of appeal because of its transparency and its ease of construction for many countries and other groupings. It combined an overall literacy measure with infant mortality and life expectancy at birth as its three ingredients. In a later effort with Michelle MacAlpin, Morris (1982) constructed this index for the different states of India, again confirming the lack of association of state income and the PQLI.

2. INCOME MEASUREMENT

While Gross Domestic Product (GDP) remains the standard national accounts aggregate constructed by over 150 countries, it continues to be criticized for its failure to include women's work or to take account of environmental degradation, to give but two limitations. However, most international agencies do use a GDP measure in evaluating the well-being of countries and are reluctant to rely on a measure like the PQLI that covers only a limited part of human economic activity. The two issues associated with the use of an income measure, namely its comparability across countries and its distribution within countries, were also extensively addressed after 1970. With respect to comparability, the International Comparison Programme (ICP) of the United Nations was inaugurated in 1968. It undertook conversions of incomes from national to a common international currency for a sample of ten countries including, naturally, India.[4] Later these ICP benchmark studies were extended to about 100 countries, and extrapolated over time and space for over 150 countries (see Summers and Heston 1991), and formed the income variable used in the Human Development Index.

With respect to the distribution of income, it is fair to say that both Indian and foreign social scientists were important in pointing out the extremely low living standards of those at the bottom of the

Indian income distribution. These concerns led India, paralleling the war on poverty in the U.S. and the efforts of Mollie Orshansky to define a U.S. poverty line, to take the lead in the developing world in generating a poverty line that for the Third Five-Year Plan was Rs. 20 per person per month. This income was judged to be the minimum necessary to purchase basic human needs in terms of nutrition, shelter, clothing, and medical supplies. Sen was to sharpen this concept, and his writings stimulated a large literature on conceptualizing and measuring poverty and inequality. This initial Indian poverty line was combined by the World Bank with the purchasing power conversion factors of the ICP to obtain a comparable poverty line across most developing countries to allow a count of all persons in poverty. Thus far two of the World Bank Development Reports have been devoted to the theme of poverty.

3. THE HUMAN DEVELOPMENT INDEX (HDI)

When the Human Development Index (HDI) was initiated, Mahbub ul Haq was made special advisor in charge of preparation of the reports. Haq was well known for his exposure of the forty families who controlled most of the industrial wealth in Pakistan and for his championing of income distribution with growth at the World Bank. Among Haq's influential consultants were Paul Streeten, Amartya Sen, and Megnad Desai. The initial shape of the HDI was a marriage of the PQLI and the real-income measure derived from the International Comparison Programme studies, with the latter given very little importance for high income countries. One advantage of the HDI was that it allowed one to look at the ranking of countries at different points in time, and the Human Development Report frequently pointed out not only that the rank of countries on the HDI is often different from that based simply on income, but also that a country's rank can easily rise or decline over time. And, in fact, for a number of countries undergoing structural adjustment, the HDI rank of countries did decline.

Again following some of the within-India studies, the Human Development Report showed how the gender-based HDI was quite different across countries. This supported what had been found in India, namely that the education and health status of females was much lower in north India than in south India. The HDI has been computed for the states of India and subdivisions of other countries, and for particular socio-economic groupings, like rural versus urban groupings, Scheduled Castes, and Scheduled Tribes.

4. SOME RELATED STUDIES

Some of the findings about the masculinity ratio in Indian censuses were supported by detailed household fertility surveys such as were carried out by the Harvard and Johns Hopkins Schools of Public Health in Punjab in the 1960s. These studies were also important for establishing that rural families in Punjab had large families because they wanted large families, not because they were ignorant of how to control family size. And these rural families tended to favor boys over girls in feeding, education, and health care, in part because boys would stay in the home and work on the farm while girls would move to another village at marriage. This in turn led mothers to favor sons because sons, not daughters, would be in the home to look after them in their old age. Many of these family patterns remain a subject of active research. One comparative note may be added, namely that the high masculinity ratio characteristic of north India is common not only in Pakistan, as one might imagine, but also in north China prior to the Revolution and subsequent to the 1978 reforms.

Another China-India comparison that Sen has stressed is the relationship of democratic institutions and particularly of a free press to economic issues. Sen, whose famine analysis in terms of entitlements has already been mentioned, contrasts the post-1950 experiences of China and India. Even though India had no safety nets like the iron rice bowl of China, China experienced a famine involving at least 15 million excess deaths in 1959-1961, while India had some minor outbreaks of famine but nothing of the magnitude of China. Sen attributes this to the free press in India putting pressure on governments to move grains to deficit areas and to provide entitlements to those unable to find work. Since the 1978 reforms, the freedom of China to move grains to deficit areas through the market has greatly improved, but the iron rice bowl has become much less widely available. The interactions of democratic institutions and economic development will continue to be a fascinating area of comparative study in China and India.

CONCLUSION

This survey has emphasized a limited number of studies based in India that have been incorporated into economics and, to a lesser extent, demography and economic history. In looking back, I am painfully aware of areas of neglect. The industrial policies in India as discussed by George Rosen, Padma Desai and Jagdish Bhagwati, Stanley Kochanek and others is one such area. The contrast of the

East Asian Tigers and India and the role of government is another such area. The relationship of economic performance and election results, the role of the Marxist parties, the aid and development literature, the performance of nationalized industries, the Green Revolution, the relation of nutrition to productivity, and agricultural pricing policies are some others. The centralized character of the Indian federal system, the regional imbalances and the Fiscal Commissions, the specialized financial institutions, the nationalized banks and their failures, the poor export performance up to the 1980s, the operation of exchange control and eventual freeing up of the rupee on current account, and the various experiments with economic reform are all subjects that have held a wider interest than simply Indian economic publications. However, it is hoped that the topics covered are enough to indicate the truly important role that the Indian economic experience has played in how these disciplines now view the world.

NOTES

1. One well-known casualty of the Joseph McCarthy era was Daniel Thorner, who was forced in the 1950s to seek his academic fortunes outside the United States. This he successfully did in France and India. Karl Wittvogel, in his book *Oriental Despotism,* reinterpreted Asian history in relation to contemporary communist governments. Thorner dealt with these "oriental mode of production" arguments in the 1960s in interchanges that were important in Europe at the time.
2. This section draws heavily on Pranab Bardhan (1993).
3. Henry Ford's heretofore unheard of wage of $5 a day in 1924 has been analyzed in recent years as an efficiency wage. For a fuller discussion of the contributions of India to the development of this concept, see Bardhan (1993).
4. This first study was published (Kravis et al. 1975) and showed that on a purchasing power basis there was much less difference in real GDP between countries than on an exchange rate basis. The methodology of this study was influenced by the work that had been carried out at the Indian Statistical Institute by Moni Mukerjee and his colleagues. While academics used these data almost immediately, it was another fifteen years before the World Bank and International Monetary Fund embraced them in their publications.

REFERENCES

Ackerlof, G.A. 1984. "The Economics of Caste and of the Rat Race." In *An Economic Theorist's Book of Tales.* ch. 3. Cambridge: Cambridge Univ. Press.

Anderson, G.M., R.E. McCormick, and R.D. Tollison. 1983. "The Economic Organization of the English East India Company." *Journal of Economic Behavior and Organization* 4.

Bardhan, Pranab. 1974. "On Life and Death Questions." *Economic and Political Weekly* (August): Special Number.

———. 1993. "Economics of Development and the Development of Economics," *Journal of Economic Perspectives* (Spring).

Blyn, George. 1966. *Agricultural Trends in India, 1891-1947.* Philadelphia: Univ. of Pennsylvania Press.

Brennan, L., J. McDonald, and R. Shlomowitz. 1994. "The Heights and Economic Well-Being of North Indians Under British Rule." *Social Science History* (Summer).

Brennig, J. J. 1983. "Silver in Seventeenth Century Surat: Monetary Circulation and the Price Revolution in Mughal India." In *Precious Metals in the Later Medieval and Early Modern World,* ed. R.F. Richards. Durham, NC: Academic Press.

Chaudhuri, K.N. 1965. *The English East India Company: The Study of an Early Joint-Stock Company, 1600-1640.* London: Cass.

———. 1968. "Treasure and Trade Balances: The East India Company's Export Trade, 1660-1720." *Economic History Review* (December).

Dantwala, M.L. 1986. *Indian Agricultural Development Since Independence.* Bombay: Asia.

Desai, Meghnad. 1971. "Demand for Cotton Textiles in Nineteenth Century India." *The Indian Economic and Social History Review* (December).

Flynn, Dennis O. 1986. "The Microeconomics of Silver and East-West Trade in the Early Modern Period." In *The Emergence of the World Economy, 1500-1914,* ed.W. Fischer, R.M. McInnis and J. Schneider. Stuttgart: Steiner Verlag Wiesbaden.

Frankel, Francine R. 1978. *India's Political Economy, 1947-1977: The Gradual Revolution.* Princeton: Princeton Univ. Press.

Furber, Holden. 1948. *John Company at Work.* Cambridge: Harvard Univ. Press.

Goldsmith, Raymond. 1987. *Pre-Modern Financial Systems: A Historical Comparative Study.* New York: Cambridge Univ. Press.

Greenough, Paul. 1982. *Prosperity and Misery in Modern Bengal: The Famine of 1943-44.* New York: Oxford Univ. Press.

Habib, Irfan. 1963. *Agrarian System of Mughal India.* Bombay: Asia.

Herring, Ronald J. 1983. *Land to the Tiller: The Political Economy of Agrarian Reform in South Asia.* New Haven: Yale Univ. Press.

Kindleberger, Charles P. 1989. *Spenders and Hoarders: The World Distribution of Spanish American Silver 1550-1750.* Singapore: Institute of Southeast Asian Studies.

Kravis, I.B., A. Heston, Z. Kennessey, and R. Summers. 1975. *A System of International Comparisons of Gross Product and Purchasing Power.* Baltimore: Johns Hopkins Univ. Press.

Kumar, Dharma. 1964. *Land and Caste in South India.* Bombay: Asia.

Kumar, Dharma and Meghnad Desai. 1983. *Cambridge Economic History of India*, vol 2. New York: Cambridge Univ. Press.

Morris, Morris D. 1969. *Indian Economy in the 19th Century*. Delhi: Hindustan.

———. 1979. *Measuring the Condition of the World's Poor: The Physical Quality of Life Index*. New York: Pergaman.

Morris, Morris D. and Michelle MacAlpin. 1982. *Measuring the Condition of India's Poor: The Physical Quality of Life Index*. New Delhi: Promila.

Nair, Kusum. 1961. *Blossoms in the Dust: The Human Factor in Indian Development*. New York: Praeger.

Prakash, Om. 1995. *Precious Metals and Commerce: Dutch East India Company in the Indian Ocean Trade*. U.K.: Aldershot Hawkins.

Rao, V.K.R.V. 1964. "Investment, Income and the Multiplier in an Underdeveloped Economy." In *Essays in Economic Development*, ed. V.K.R.V. Rao, Bombay: Asia.

Richards, John F. 1983. "Outflows of Precious Metals from Early Islamic India." In *Precious Metals in the Later Medieval and Early Modern Worlds*, ed. J.F. Richards. Durham, NC: Academic Press.

Rosenzweig, M.R. and T.P. Schultz. 1982. "Market Opportunities, Genetic Endowments and the Intra-family Distribution of Resources: Child Survival in Rural India." *American Economic Review* (September).

Rosenzweig, M.R. and K.I. Wolpin. 1993. "Credit Market Constraints, Consumption Smoothing, and the Accumulation of Durable Production Assets in Low-Income Countries: Investments in Bullocks in India." *Journal of Political Economy* (March).

Sen, Amartya K. 1967. "Surplus Labour in India: A Critique of Schultz's Test" and exchange. *The Economic Journal* (March).

———. 1981. *An Essay on Entitlement and Deprivation*. New York: Oxford Univ. Press.

———. 1988. "Family and Food: Sex Bias in Poverty." In *Rural Poverty in South Asia,* ed. T.N. Srinivasan and Pranab Bardhan. New York: Columbia Univ. Press.

Summers R. and A. Heston. 1991. "Penn World Table (Mark 5): An Expanded Set of International Comparisons, 1950-88." *Quarterly Journal of Economics* (May).

Thorner, Daniel and Alice. 1962. *Land and Labour in India*. Bombay: Asia.

Thorner, Daniel, R.E.F. Smith, and Basile H. Kerbley, eds. 1986. *A.V. Chayanov on the Theory of Peasant Economy*. Madison: Univ. of Wisconsin Press.

Folklore

PETER J. CLAUS

It must be admitted from the outset that India has never played much of a role in U.S. folkloristics, and in fact India does not do so even today. But what I hope to show is that the folklore of India has encouraged us—at least those U.S. scholars who *have* studied it—to fulfill some of the original ideals and goals of the discipline of folklore. Over the past hundred-odd years, the study of folklore by Americans has been shared by several disciplines, and has been taken in various direction by its dominant interest groups, primarily anthropologists and students of literature. What follows is, first, a discussion of the historical estrangement of anthropologists and students of literature, and, then, their reunification on more solid ground through studying India's folklore.[1]

The study of folklore in the U.S.A. was conceived at the outset as an interdisciplinary endeavor. At its inception its major professional body, the American Folklore Society, and its official voice, the *Journal of American Folklore* (*JAF*), tried to provide a meeting ground for students of literature, anthropologists, historians, linguists, and a smattering of other social scientists. It has struggled through much of its existence to maintain this synthesis and to provide a healthy forum for debates in which data are emphasized and tolerance for diverse disciplinary perspectives is encouraged.

Not without difficulty, however. The U.S. mind often defines things in opposition. The perennial arguments within the discipline about how to define the term 'folklore' themselves exemplify this tendency, but it would not serve my purpose to elaborate on these usually fruitless debates. Without realizing that perhaps it was the activities of the elites, not the folk, that needed special categories and continual redefinition, folklorists seem compelled to define *their* special area of interest in opposition to something else: classical, literary, elite, urban, etc. The expressive culture of the folk, 'the people,' might reasonably be considered the baseline for such a study. Such culture of 'the people,' with their special interests and social classes, at particular times, and in association with particular ideological movements opposed to an existing standard, might well appear to need defining labels and explanations. Among the early folklorists, those who belonged to the humanities felt the greatest need to define folklore, suggesting that their home discipline in the humanities was already associated with the elite (cf., Bourdieu 1984, 1993). The anthropologists within the American Folklore Society, drawing from their experience in classless (and, as they thought, also timeless) Native American societies, have usually been less concerned than those in the humanities with defining a class of expressive culture to call 'folklore.'

While anthropologist Franz Boas, one of the *Journal of American Folklore's* founding members and later its editor, and Boas' students dominated the journal, it maintained an interdisciplinary character. Anthropology itself, after all, is very much an 'interdisciplinary discipline.' Anthropologists tend to divide themselves over theoretical issues. And it was Boas' theoretical interests that had a greater effect on the form U.S. folklore took than did questions about folklore's subject matter. Boas was strongly opposed to concepts of unilineal evolution and favored, instead, studies of historical diffusion. This was, by and large, in line with the major trends in both American and European folklore studies, too. But European anthropology was still dominated by ardent evolutionists who saw folklore as a survival of an earlier stage of evolution. Sir James Frazer,[2] whose *The Golden Bough* served generations of colonial missionaries and administrators as a guidebook for cataloging native superstitions, in a lecture delivered before the University of Liverpool in May 1908, defined the relationship between anthropology and folklore as follows:

Thus the sphere of Social Anthropology as I understand it, or at least as I propose to treat it, is limited to the crude beginnings, the rudimentary development of human society ... The study might accordingly be described as the embryology of human thought and institutions, or, to be more precise, as that enquiry which seeks to ascertain, first, the beliefs and customs of savages, and, second, the relics of these beliefs and customs which have survived like fossils among peoples of higher culture ... (161) The one department may be called the study of savagery, the other the study of folklore. (1908, 167)

By the turn of the century, the compartmentalizing tendencies of U.S. academic institutions meant that most of the disciplines that started during the middle of the nineteenth century had to specify themselves. Boas managed to preserve anthropology by emphasizing its scientific basis. Boas tried to emphasize the scientific study of folklore too, but this was a harder job, at least as far as trying to find a place for folklore in academia. Universities regarded 'folklore' and 'higher education' as oxymoronic, and, to this day, folklorists find it hard to establish a department to call their own. Folklore has usually had to resign itself to the interstitial areas of academic institutions. Since folklore is usually taught in other departments, folklorists have to do double duty in departments of language (teaching English) or literature (American) or music (American genres), etc. Because America is a land of immigrants, American folkloristics has been inherently international in its orientation, tracing the dominant strains of American traditions from their European and African roots.

The fledgling discipline of anthropology, in which Boas also served an important role, had its own history of institutional divisiveness. Lewis Henry Morgan, often called the father of American Anthropology, had framed the scope of the discipline around the theory of cultural evolution. At the time, cultural evolution was questioned only in its particulars by European anthropologists such as E.B. Tylor and Sir James Frazer. But in the U.S.A., for many years, Boas and his students at Columbia University and A.L. Kroeber and Robert Lowie at the University of California, Berkeley vigorously opposed this conception of anthropology. Nevertheless, with biological evolution gaining ground as the background explanatory theory in biology, cultural evolutionism persisted in anthropology at other U.S. universities, notably the University of Michigan under the tutelage of Leslie White.

Then, shortly after World War I, A.R. Radcliffe-Brown revolutionized British social anthropology with Durkheimian functionalism with its strongly anti-historical mode of studying society. For Radcliffe-Brown, anthropology could retain its natural science credentials on the analogy of comparative physiology. When Radcliffe-Brown came to teach at the University of Chicago, he saw little value in either Boas' historical diffusionism or the ideas of the American cultural evolutionists. As a result, a deep rift formed between native-born cultural anthropology (with its own internal schools) and British social anthropology. Anthropologists focused these debates in the *American Anthropologist*, and gradually the *JAF* was turned over to scholars specializing in Euro-American literature (Stith Thompson)[3] and history (Richard Dorson) and the incessant debates over what folklore was.

By mid-century the long-standing alliance between anthropology and literature within American folklore was broken. Radcliffe-Brown's functionalism swept through U.S. anthropology. He disdained pseudo-historical speculation and relegated the study of folklore to historians, linguists, and amateurs for whatever use they might see in it. There were few anthropologists left in the American Folklore Society. In anthropology, to call oneself a folklorist was an embarrassment.

As interest in folklore declined in anthropology, the American Folklore Society was left to those specializing in oral traditions, American regionalism, and European roots. India was out of their territory. Up to this point in the history of the *JAF*, only a single full-length article—by Murray Emeneau on the Toda in 1944—had been published on India.[4] The only major work done on Indian folklore by U.S. scholars was done by Sanskritists and linguists who favored a textualist approach.[5] True, folklorist Stith Thompson was at work organizing several invaluable catalogues of Indian folktales, but this material, too, was largely textualist in nature and derived from secondary sources (Thompson and Balys 1958, Thompson and Roberts 1960, Kirkland 1966).[6]

TRADITIONS

When, at the close of World War II, new nations were being born, and the U.S. was rapidly realigning its world-interests, anthropologists turned their attention from the study of small, isolated tribes to the study of peasants in civilizations. India, naturally, aroused the attention of a new breed of anthropologists. Based on his work in Mexico, Robert Redfield had already conceptualized the study of large-scale civilizations along his now famous folk-urban continuum. Together with his colleagues at the University of Chicago, where he was dean of the social sciences, Redfield organized a far-reaching project, the comparative studies in culture and civilizations (for discussion of these developments within anthropology, see also Wadley, this volume). Anthropologists began the project by pursuing the institutional dimensions of civilization through village studies. While not ignoring the cultural dimensions of civilization, their focus was societal and structural.[7]

Attention to the more humanistic, cultural side of civilization picked up in 1957. With India's independence still in recent memory, Milton Singer organized a symposium directed at assessing India's cultural traditions. He published the papers in a seminal collection of essays entitled *Traditional India: Structure and Change*. Its preface began collaboratively by pointing out that "... modern nationalism in India ... has always shown a strong interest in the recovery or reinterpretation of India's traditional culture," and suggested that "The professional student of culture and civilization may contribute something to this inquiry through an objective study of the variety and changes in cultural traditions ..." (Singer 1959, ix).

Milton Singer, Redfield's colleague and collaborator on the comparative civilizations project, having had first-hand experience in India, recognized the need to restate the relationship between the great tradition and the little tradition, the whole and the parts, not only on more concrete grounds, but also on grounds that might link the vast accumulated knowledge of western indology to the anthropologists' village data. The difference between the two data sets (orientalists' and social scientists') presented to the newcomer (as many U.S. social scientists were), as well as to those familiar with India through its ancient texts, a contradiction increasingly difficult to ignore but equally difficult to reconcile.[8] A major assessment of our knowledge of Indian civilization was clearly in order, one that would allow us to grasp the nature of India's past as well as its present, its parts at all levels (villages, regions) as well as its whole in all forms (civilization, tradition).

Still working within the opposition between the social sciences and the humanities, Singer chose to operationalize the "abstract, generic conception of a structure of tradition" along two lines: the social organization of tradition, on one hand, and cultural performances and cultural media on the other.[9] The study of cultural performance, as Singer saw it, was analogous to the analysis of social structure, "... except that the data in this case are the cultural constituents of performances, i.e., the cultural media of song, dance, instrumental music, verbal texts, plots and themes, the scene of the performance, etc. rather than the statuses and roles that occur in social organization" (Singer 1959, xii). Characteristic of anthropological fashion at the time, Singer avoided the term folklore to characterize this list of contents.[10] Nor did he draw upon the then-standard folkloristic approaches to the study of tradition. Folklore and anthropology had defined themselves in such opposition by this time that each tended to concentrate, as Singer noted, on particular aspects of a performance: oral texts in the case of the former, social function in the case of the latter. Singer merged these two approaches in his consideration of Indian cultural traditions by including in his focus the texts and contexts, performers and their audiences, and the sequence of events within the performance time-frames. Further, perhaps in choosing to avoid the term folklore, Singer sought once again to bring together the students of literature and the anthropologists—both as students of folklore—and encourage them to take to the field.

Singer was by training neither an anthropologist nor an indologist but a philosopher, specializing in symbolic logic and the philosophy of science. This perhaps explains why he was less influenced by the identity-opposition that separated others who studied India at the time.[11] When Singer went to India, he went with a fresh, from-the-ground-up, pragmatist approach, and he came back with a suspicion that in India oral and written did not distinguish the elite from the folk in the same way as in the West. Oral tradition (the medium that distinguished folklorists from students of literature) was by no means confined to a particular class or caste. Brahmans and merchants, farmers and shepherds, high castes and low all had a wealth of folklore peculiar to their group. Nor were Redfield's two traditions clearly separate. According to Singer, "Little and Great traditions are not neatly differentiated along a village-urban axis" (1959, 171). Even the concept of elite presented a confused picture; there were many distinct elite traditions. In his own research on the cultural traditions of Madras, Singer was able to survey a broad array of different traditions, from village folk and ritual traditions to the rapidly accelerating popular, classical, and secular traditions of the city. When organizing the conference papers, and modeling its structure after his own research, choosing not to pin the idea of cultural performance to "just folklore," Singer enabled everyone to see broader connections than they might have seen under the simpler dichotomies of the disciplines involved.

All of the papers in the Singer volume, and Singer himself at most times, discussed India's cultural media in broad generalizations and in terms of familiar, unquestioned dichotomies: the folk-urban continuum, little and great traditions, and folk-classical distinctions, supported by such Indian intelligentsia's categorizations as *mārga* and *deśī*.[12] The various genres were, perhaps, being recognized for the first time and needed to be placed into broad categories. There was value, however, in focusing on specific forms and genres. Unfortunately, few who studied India had any connection with the discipline of folklore in the United States. During this period Indian folklore was being studied in structural and institutional terms, without much regard for the detailed historical and thematic considerations (historical reconstruction and dissemination) being encouraged at the time by folklorists.

In India, beginning even before the turn of the century, interest in folklore had linked up with the nationalist movement. Indian intellectuals, who a generation or two earlier might have emulated western literary forms, began to find their common roots in the revival of folklore. Not only did they collect folklore, but some of them drew what they found in folklore into their own creative efforts. Tagore, for example, argued vehemently that nationalistic sentiment needed a 'national literature' constructed on a foundation of folk traditions in order to link all Bengalis into one chain of collective patriotic consciousness.[13] Tagore's personal patronage of research, his prefaces for Bengali books on folklore, his own writings on the subject, as well as his artistic indebtedness to the itinerant mystic bards, the Bauls of Bengal, stimulated and shaped the field of Bengali folkloristics. In doing so, however, he inadvertently cast Bengali folklorists with an urban, aristocratic version of the Bengali folk, infused with the romantic vision of the peasant as a simple, peaceful, and harmonious individual. This was true not only of Tagore's work but also of his whole generation and the subsequent generations that they influenced.[14]

The literary creation of the folk and the literary enthusiasm for folklore were necessary steps in the history of Bengali nationalism, but in some ways they were problematic steps in the development of Indian folkloristics. As Blackburn and Ramanujan have noted:

... the nationalist movement spurred new respect for and interest in folk traditions. The search for ancient origins and the desire to present a 'pure' heritage, which accompanies such nationalistic movements everywhere, cast this research in a decidedly antiquarian and chauvinistic mold. (1986, 7)

After Independence folklore continued to be the domain of writers and literary scholars, but it gravitated increasingly to regional interests. As Ramanujan has characterized this era:

In India, the literature departments have begun to include linguistics and folklore, and become interested in notions of 'region', 'tradition', and 'folk'. Mārga and deśī, an old Indian pair—loosely translated as 'classical' and 'folk', technical terms in native discussions of literature, music, drama and dance—have been linked to, or reincarnated as, 'Great and Little Tradition'. These interest have naturally led to the collection and analysis of regional folk-materials. For instance, in a language like Kannada, over 200 books were published in the field of folklore in the last two decades (Nayak 1974); all the three major universities in the Kannada area have opened special departments and publication series for folklore. The data is piling up ..." (Ramanujan 1987, 79-80)

Folklore was also a part of Indian anthropological studies, which, both before and after Independence, focused their attention on the so-called tribals. In India, even more than in the United States, interest in folklore by students of literature and anthropology was dichotomized. So deep was the divide that not only was the type of folklore each concentrated on very different, but also each tended to treat folklore in special ways.[15] Students of literature collected peasant lore; students of anthropology and linguistics collected tribal myth. Selective pressures imposed by their respective disciplines emphasized the differences between, rather than the variations within, the two categories, and the considerable overlap in the traditions of what was called tribal and what was called folk was rarely seen.

None of the Indian contributors to *Traditional India: Structure and Change* called themselves folklorists. M.N. Srinivas, A.M. Shah, R.G. Shroff, Surajit Singh, Indera Singh, T.B. Naik, and Nirmal Kumar Bose were all anthropologists. Of these, Surajit Singh, Indera Singh, and N.K. Bose perhaps leaned more toward the U.S. school of cultural anthropology. V. Raghavan, representing the most humanistic side with his training in Sanskrit literature and the classical arts, spoke from within the culture. Although Singer drew heavily on Raghavan's distinction between classical and folk—derived from *mārga* and *deśī*—and linked these to the notion of great and little tradition, Singer began to see that these simple dichotomies were inadequate to account for the five different kinds of performances (folk, ritual, popular, classical, and modern urban) he was trying to trace (Singer 1959, 169-174).

Singer's ecumenical vision brought together a wide range of scholars within a single volume; nevertheless, for the next two decades interests in India's cultural traditions were pursued largely within the confines of separate disciplinary discourses.[16] Anthropologists' fieldwork brought them into proximity to the little tradition; Singer turned their attention to the study of tradition itself.[17] Soon they began to explore this new resource for what it might teach them in terms of the folk exegesis of the indigenous categories they sought to understand and explain.

Since at least the 1940s anthropologists have taken ethnomethodology (or ethnoscience, or 'emic') as their own special approach to non-western cultures (see the classic examples of Evans-Pritchard 1939, 1940, 1953; for application to village study see, e.g., Pitt-Rivers 1961) and tried to construct society and the world in which it exists out of the conceptual categories of that culture.[18] There are several ways one might go about doing this. Aside from just being there doing fieldwork (often defined as 'participant observation'), the most obvious way is through interviews. Another way is to query the vocabulary people use in describing their world-view. But one problem with such interactive approaches is that, unless you already know what terms and concepts are potentially important, you cannot explore them. Another method exists. Many folklore genres contain the very kinds of implicit cultural assumptions that anthropologists seek to understand. The fact that these assumptions are embedded in unintended, pre-existing ritual and textual contexts, not predicated by foreign inquiry and assumptions external to the cultural scheme of things, make them ideal sources for understanding broad cultural and relational systems.

One of the first American scholars to use this method was Brenda Beck. In a paper published in 1974 she explored the general theoretical relationships between descent groups, marriage alliances, and family units (nuclear kin) by examining Tamil folklore:

... Tamil folklore rarely mentions larger, opposed groupings of cross and parallel males. Instead one can say that the folklore complements the above analysis by placing a marked stress on the relationships between immediate family members. Such a finding suggests that the folklore itself acts as a kind of counterweight to the formal exchange relationships of everyday experience. (Beck 1974, 3)

Central to the divergence between the lived-in experience of social life and the folk-ritual and oral-narrative traditions was the position of women:

At the center of the kin nucleus ... is a female who is surrounded by males.... Their śakti lies behind everything .... The power of the female can cause a male to be successful, strong and prosperous, or it can cause him to suffer defeat, misfortune and poverty. (Beck 1974, 7)

Beck and other scholars pursued the implications of the tension she found in the complementarity between oral tradition and social life—as well as the tension's particular embodiment in the image of women—through a number of subsequent studies (Beck 1980, 1982, 1986; see also Babb 1975, Wadley 1980, Obeyesekere 1984, Trawick 1990). Such images encountered in folklore and contextualized by village life soon led researchers to re-examining literary sources and larger contexts where they found a seamless transition of traditions, a network of associated meanings extending in all directions.

In a similar vein (not yet explored to the extent it should be) in another paper titled "The Human Body Image: Its Popular Description in Tamil Proverbs" Beck found that, although the body and body parts occur frequently in Tamil proverbs, they do not do so in equal frequency, and some body parts are missing altogether (notably the breasts and genitals). According to Beck, "The most striking thing about the statistics, ... is the extreme emphasis given to the head ... there is a rapid fall off of emphasis on the body's anatomy as one progresses downward from the head to the feet." (n.d. [c. 1975], 5). Surprisingly, the body's image in Tamil proverbs is used overwhelmingly in negative parallels. In this and other regards, Beck noted, contemporary Tamil proverbs are like passages from the ancient but still universally revered *Tirukkural*, in that they present the body as a transitory container. If Beck's observations are correct, then relationships between folk genres and even the most sophisticated philosophical traditions may exist in dimensions both subtle (unconscious) and abstract, as well as in terms of themes and motifs (see also Ramanujan 1986, 1987, 1989).

Other anthropologists at the time, too, began to look to various genres of folklore in order to sharpen their understanding of Indian culture. Together with their colleagues in literature and religious studies they began to explore the distinctive Indian concepts of the hero (Beck 1978, Blackburn 1978, Claus 1978, Narayana Rao 1986) and hero worship (Blackburn 1985), political ideologies (Beck 1978b, Claus 1978, 1979), and philosophical and religious concepts such as karma (Beck 1977, Wadley 1983). These concepts had all been noted as important features of traditional Hindu culture, but little detailed data had been gathered on these concepts at the village level. Because anthropologists had been working with folk genres, they were able to add to almost any topic of discussion perspectives from indigenous oral literature.[19]

Wadley's 1975 more extended study of *śakti* may be put into the category of folk exegesis. Wadley's overall goal was to understand the concept of *śakti* (female power) within the conceptual system of north-Indian village life. The methods (linguistic and structural) she employed toward that end drew from up-to-date theoretical developments in anthropology at large, and what she found out about *śakti* added new understandings of the concept. In addition, her work was a major innovation in at least two other respects. The one that is most important to my present essay was the way in which, as well as the extent to which, she drew upon a wide range of folklore to explore *śakti*. The other was her observation that the concept of *śakti* played such a key role in such varied everyday contexts in village life. This observation provided a rich counterpoint to the abstract, philosophical, and religious exegesis of *śakti* already elaborated by indologist and other students of India's high traditions (see also Wadley, this volume, for reference to subsequent studies of gender and authority).

Wadley's was one of the first recent studies of Indian culture to view folklore as an integrated system. She placed less importance on the division between great and little traditions than she did on the unity of Indian traditions. She described the place of Karimpur within those traditions as a "local-level," diffusing past dichotomies. Furthermore, in treating folklore (like any other societal or cultural phenomenon) as a conceptual system rather than as a miscellany of derivatives (as the notion of peasants as 'part society' suggests) or as survivals (as cultural evolutionism suggests), she viewed folklore holistically, as a term pervading an ideology, forcing her to look beyond particular motifs, genres, or institutions and beyond the heuristic dichotomy of practice (the organization of behavior) and media (culture). This approach not only led us to understand local tradition as genre systems, but also suggested to us that there was in Indian tradition 'another harmony.'

ANOTHER HARMONY

In the early 1980s the flurry of research employing Indian folklore prompted a round of conferences on "indigenous terminology" sponsored by the Joint Council on South Asia of the Social Science Research Council and the American Council of Learned Societies. The first conference, called "Models and Metaphors in South Asian Folklore," was exploratory, bringing together those who had been working on folklore, independently for the most part, in different regions of India.[20] During this conference those studying folklore began to transcend the great and little tradition divide, looking instead at the relationship between genres within systems and trying to understand the genres themselves and the power they held in particular contexts. A.K. Ramanujan steered participants in the direction of examining India's folklore more directly and more resourcefully. What could be done with this material (folklore)? What does it mean? How can one frame its rich and distinctive qualities?

In a paper titled "The Relevance of South Asian Folklore," Ramanujan distinguished some of the key concepts that would set the future for the study of Indian folklore. He suggested that within society different genres do not belong to different cultural worlds or divided traditions (such as great and little) but are themselves implicit cultural categories with different contextual functions.[21] At all levels, traditions are:

... coexistent, context-sensitive systems ... held and used deftly and persuasively to perceive and solve the culture's special dilemmas ... They may contradict each other (as different proverbs do, within a language) when treated as a single facetless system, but they would be seen as viable, flexible "strategies" when treated in context. In cultures and in languages, there are rules of structure and there are rules of use: novel is only one-half of creativity; appropriateness is the other half. (1987, 82)[22]

New, deeper, more intense genres—crying songs, possession cults, competitive games, sacrificial epics, and ambiguously-gendered heroes—were introduced and presented in their performance contexts, provoking new ideas and directions of inquiry. In these more specialized genres (as well as in the other, more familiar genres) there are often themes and emphases that give expression to emotions not found in other realms of Indian culture. Indeed, this is reason, perhaps, why these genres exist. But while these genres provide us with a wider and fuller understanding of Indian culture as it is lived by participants of all kinds and levels, it is also important to understand that there are variants of themes and stories in other genres with which these genres have inherent intertextual relationships, and with which they stand in implicit contrast.

The next conference took up the intensive investigation of a particular genre: oral epics. Several of the participants at the Models and Metaphors conference had done extensive work on regional epics; so oral epics, in their regional variants, served as common ground.[23] These participants were joined by other U.S. scholars whose work focused on India's epic traditions as well as by J.D. Smith from England, and Komal Kothari, J.S. Paramashiviah, R.V.S. Sundaram, and S.M. Pandey from India. The regional variants discussed were regionally representative: Pabuji, Devnarayan, Alha, Guga, Dhola, Candaini of northern India; and Annanmar, Palnadu, Ellamma, Bow Songs, Paddana of the south.[24] The performances were as varied as shadow puppet shows and possession cults, and each performance was seen to be something of great complexity, embedding oral text in aesthetic forms of all kinds, sponsored by patrons of all sorts, and addressed to audiences from all classes. It quickly became apparent to everyone that when taken as a performance tradition, not simply as a collected text, the oral epic genre had both tremendous variability and previously unrecognized importance to the idea of Indian civilization. The performances themselves needed new approaches to analyze their structure—approaches that would also discover how the oral epic performers managed to produce and orchestrate them (Wadley 1989, Goldberg Belle 1989, Blackburn 1986, 1981). Some epics had to be looked at as stories in relation to a whole system of regional epics (Flueckiger 1989, 1996; Claus 1989, 1991; Blackburn 1989), while others, consisting of a single story, constituted a genre unto themselves.

Taken together, the studies of Indian folk epic (many not cited above) generated a distinct interdisciplinary field of performance studies. Stuart Blackburn recently summarized the importance of Indian folklore to this development:

The study of performance in South Asian folklore is inseparable from the history of the concept in international folkloristics. Drawing on the pool of anthropological, literary, linguistic, and theater studies that coalesced into a performance-centered approach to folklore in the 1970s, performance studies in South Asia have produced a new literature that has changed the textual orientation of Indology. Although no sustained theory of performance has yet emerged, this new approach has demonstrated that the meanings of folklore are not confined to words but are encoded also in events, such as speech acts, behavior, music, song, and dance. Despite differing emphases, vocabularies, and conclusions, the numerous monographs published since 1970 have extended the definition and enriched our understanding of text, audience, and genre in South Asian folklore. (Blackburn, forthcoming)

What makes India such a marvelous place to study oral epics is that one can trace their numerous thematic threads through a vast network of intertextual linkages, and through every conceivable performance context, both within a given tradition and between given traditions. My own research on a Tulu oral epic tradition called *pāḍḍana* revealed to me some of the subtle kinds of links village traditions entail. The Tulu epics are at once both a macro-genre and a performance tradition. Within the genre there are a number of distinct stories, but many of those stories exist in context-sensitive variants. Furthermore, the stories and their variants make frequent intertextual reference to one another. When I was contemplating the relationships between distinct, named epic traditions in Tulunad, it became clear to me that there was a larger 'epic' that "exists in the minds of the performers and audience" (1989, 57). That is, any particular story:

... exists in a number of different forms, is identified by different terms in different contexts, and is performed by different groups. Each performance configuration in its own way elaborates on a different aspect of the story. The Kordabbu story itself is an elaborated excerpt from a larger pool of characters in a larger story. This larger story, however, is never told in its entirety. It is in this sense—that is, as a large repertoire of loosely connected and variable stories—that we may speak of the *pāḍḍana* as a multi-story epic tradition. (Claus 1989, 71)[25]

What is characteristic of the many regional epics is also writ large in the *Mahābhārata* and *Rāmāyaṇa*, the flagships of Indian civilization. Both are compilations of what had at one time been many independent story traditions that, throughout history, performers and literati alike have reworked in innumerable versions. Ramanujan identifies these many *Rāmāyaṇas* as a "pool of signifiers" (1991, 46), while Narayana Rao characterizes the *Rāmāyaṇa* as "... not just a story, but a language with which a host of (ideological) statements may be made" (1991, 114). Blackburn sees it as an oral tradition containing many forms: "... the diversity of the tradition—the many *Rāmāyaṇas*—is a function of the many genres, the many languages, and the many occasions on which the Rama story is orally performed" (1991, 156). For all who contributed to Paula Richman's volume *Many Rāmāyaṇas: Diversity of a Narrative Tradition in South Asia*, there was no question that the study of regional oral epics, epics such as the *Rāmāyaṇa* or many others, provided valuable insights into even the often-studied pan-Indian epics. What has been achieved in the transformation of India's folkloristics has been not only papers and books and improved research, or even better scholarship, but also a community of scholars who can better appreciate the relevance of one another's work, and who now regularly share in the surveillance of a wider perspective.

THE FUTURE

What I have tried to focus on in this essay is not India's folklore but rather how, in studying this dimension of India's culture, U.S. scholarship has reached a broader, more unified view of a civilization—Indian civilization. One last sub-theme needs to be discussed. I began this essay with the observation that U.S. folkloristics was, since its inception, a broadly interdisciplinary endeavor. While this is true, it was not because the individual folklorists were necessarily so broad minded. Folkloristics at the time (but to use terminology of the present) could be divided into two groups: those who studied the lore of 'Others' (anthropologists), and those who studied from a perspective within their own culture a segment of tradition other than their own (mostly students of literature). Although these two perspectives sometimes came together in a single individual, one of the two perspective generally subjugated the other and always with unproductive results such as evolutionism or romanticism. The

unification of Indo-American folkloristics will come about, I would
predict, when at an international level these two perspectives come
together within a community of scholars including U.S. and Indian
scholars. In fact, significant efforts in this direction have been
taken.[26]

The Models and Metaphors conference had another dimension
not as well-known publically. Shortly after the meeting in Berkeley,
a number of the participants presented versions of their papers at
a similar gathering of Indian folklorists in Mysore. Indian folklorists,
as mentioned earlier, had been busy collecting folklore. Because
what they had collected was published in regional Indian languages,
most of it was unknown to western scholars. By this time, Indian
folklorists were also developing their own folkloristics, with discourses
based in theories, ideologies, and concerns distinctly different from
those prevalent in U.S. folkloristics. Like U.S. folkloristics at home,
Indian folkloristics presents an insider's view of itself. The hope of
the Mysore conference was that a final dichotomy might be bridged.
At the time it was thought—rather naively and patronizingly, in
retrospect—that the U.S. participants might benefit greatly from
learning about the rich database of material collected by their
Indian colleagues, while the Indian participants might benefit from
the recent developments and theoretical orientations of the
Americans.

In fact, forging a bi-national discipline proved to be more of a
challenge than originally anticipated. The difficulty stems from the
different discourses in which the folklorists are enmeshed: U.S.
folklorists address themselves to audiences who are outsiders to the
Indian traditions. The works of Indian folklorists are read by
insiders. While I cannot, in this essay, pursue the great significance
of this difference, I would like to show why it is important to
understand that an international folkloristics has some valuable
common grounds in a perspective made up of both outsiders and
insiders.

An outsider's perspective is sometimes the only way that people
from within a tradition become aware of features they are culturally
conditioned to ignore, whether because they are too familiar or
because they are inappropriate to discuss openly. As an example,
one might point out that there are no indigenous terms for folklore
in most Indian languages. Terms recently coined to encompass this
realm—*jānapada*, *lok versa*, etc.—are Sanskritized translations of the
English 'folklore.' The indigenous term *deśī* is not an equivalent. Not
all that is *deśī* is what is meant by folklore. For centuries up to the

present era, that which is now studied in India as folklore had been completely ignored or reworked into literary styles before considered appropriate for inclusion in scholarly discourse.

An insider's perspective enables one to acknowledge and appreciate that, as my earlier citation of Ramanujan suggests, in folklore, like language, there are levels of competence and rules of appropriateness. While outsiders may study "folklore in context," they do so abstractly through observations of events. To understand the performers' intentions—"choosing a path," as Susan Wadley (1989) has called it—that predicate these events, or the audiences' evaluation of the outcome, folklorists must turn to experts, the performers and audiences themselves (Flueckiger 1988), or to connoisseurs. Alan Dundes long ago coined the term "folk literary criticism" to encourage precisely this, but few folklorists have explicitly done so.[27] Here is where collaboration with Indian folklorists could be constructive. Raised in the culture, Indian folklorists cannot escape an evaluative perspective on folklore, whether or not they share particular folk-abilities to produce it. At Indian folklore conferences many participants, coming as they do from departments of literature, wax eloquently on the distinctive beauty of folk expression, even to the extent of using the podium as a stage for their own performances of it.[28] If they were able to develop a dialogue with their Indian counterparts, American folklorists might be able to tap into this kind of experiential sensitivity and appreciation of the material.

Distractions and difficulties lie in the path of forging an international discipline of Indian folkloristics. One distraction (however well-intended) is, as Singer recognized in the early years of U.S. collaboration in the study of Indian culture, the existence of regional and national governments. Academic colleagial ties, however, need not be bound by national identities. Without ignoring the very different interests Karnataka folklorists may have in Kannada folklore, or the different relationships that Kannada folklore may have to any Kannada literary traditions the folklorists might wish to explore, or the different constituents they must address, there must be much that Karnataka folklorists can share only with other folklorists of the world. A folkloristics that is so culturally bound as to be pertinent only to the folklorists of one culture is unlikely to become anything other than folklore itself.

In the years that followed the Mysore conference, the Ford Foundation provided support for a series of international conferences and workshops and several Indian archives and Indian folkloristic research projects. Through these, some U.S. and Indian participants have formed lasting ties, and some joint ventures have been launched. Still, the efforts toward internationalizing Indian folkloristics have been experimental and exploratory. Only time will tell whether or not these efforts will be successful and a truly international discipline will emerge.

NOTES

1. For a more detailed, but sometimes differing, interpretation see Zumwalt 1988.
2. Although his work is rarely cited in connection with the development of any of the modern disciplines today, the immense intellectual impact Frazer's writings had in the colonies must still be kept in mind. For reasons that, hopefully, will be clearer later in this essay, one still finds *The Golden Bough*, and its defining concepts, methodologies, and theoretical orientation used as a handbook for the study of folklore in Indian departments of literature where 'the anthropological' approach is in vogue.
3. It must be said, however, as his classic, *The Folktale*, bears abiding testament, Stith Thompson developed a deep interest in international folklore in general, and Indian folklore in particular. See also below.
4. That the exceptional work by Murray Emeneau on India is poorly represented in the pages of the *JAF* perhaps encapsulates all that I have thus far said about the dichotomies within U.S. folklore. As a student of linguist-anthropologist Edward Sapir, Emeneau was also an intellectual descendant of Franz Boas. Neither of Emeneau's monumental works on folklore, *The Songs of the Todas* (1937) and *Kota Texts* (1944), were published primarily as contributions to folklore.
5. The *JAF* also published a two-page note on demon-worship by the missionary, Dr. Bulmer (1894), and most major publications of Indian folklore were at least reviewed in the *JAF*. Several generations of European colonial administrators and anthropologists had gathered vast quantities of oral tales from the Indian countryside, and these had found popularity in European anthologies. For U.S. folklorists, India, the land of stories, was not altogether ignored. But interest in India's literary traditions had been taken up earlier by text-oriented indologists rather than folklorists. It seemed not to occur to U.S. folklorists that these literary traditions might have current oral counterparts, or that relationships between the written and the oral traditions might be fruitful ground for investigation. Until relatively recently, India was represented in world epic studies only by the literary versions of the *Mahābhārata* and the *Rāmāyaṇa*, despite the existence of dynamic independent regional oral epic traditions and a bewildering array of folk *Mahābhārata* and *Rāmāyaṇa* traditions,

each with fascinating peculiarities not found in the literary forms. U.S. folklorists may have considered India too distant, or they may have been too preoccupied with North American Indian and Euro-American continuities. Whatever the reasons, U.S. folklorists showed little interest in the rich possibilities inherent in India's oral traditions.

6. Stith Thompson also did the tale-type index for Emeneau's *Kota Texts*. Emeneau's acknowledgment speaks to the separation between folklorists and the group of social scientists to which linguist-anthropologist Emeneau saw himself belonging: "My thanks are due to him [Thompson] for what will undoubtedly be of great value to workers in that field." (1944, vi)

7. The anthropologists associated with this project had received diverse training representing several contemporary schools of anthropological thought: M.N. Srinivas (Oxford), McKim Marriott (Chicago), David Mandelbaum (Yale), Alan Beals (University of California, Berkeley), Oscar Lewis (Columbia), Kathleen Gough (Cambridge), and John Hitchcock (Cornell), to mention a few. They were all, nonetheless, deeply affected by British social anthropology and the functionalism of Radcliffe-Brown and Malinowski. Whatever their differences, they saw themselves as social scientists.

8. In a mixed collection of papers published in 1966, McKim Marriott described the naivete of an anthropologist invited to 'play Holi' in a UP village: "I asked how it was to be played ..." In the foreword to the same volume, and in reference to how Marriott subsequently came to grips with what he initially experienced, the Sanskrit scholar Daniel Ingalls articulated the ineffable wonderment of his indological colleagues over the ambition of the U.S. social scientists: "How does one bring the diverse facts of literature, of society, of religion, as one finds them in different ages and areas, into a single understandable system? What system shall we use for the evaluation even of contemporaneous phenomena? It may be said, of course, that systematizing is just what we should not yet do, for it has been the experience of the sciences, social as well as natural, to begin with description and to come to systems only when they are full grown. Let us first, then, gather the facts. But still, one must be aware of an ultimate goal, and one yearns for it. Personally, I tend to think of such a goal as a system of history, for such has been my training. But I recommend to the reader the very different systematization offered by McKim Marriott. Although the author is a scholarly man, his is the least academic of the contributions. And yet, from the disreputable phenomena of the Holi festival he builds, in bold strokes and in a very American way, a system that seems to me not inapplicable to much that is Indian, old as well as new, noble as well as mean." (Ingalls 1966, x-xi)

9. The idea of 'cultural performances' was Singer's own, one that developed within his own paper for the conference and then applied

more generally to the particularization of a tradition in different media, carried by human agents and performed on certain occasions. Among the special connotations he captured with this term was his observation that "... people think of their culture as encapsulated in such discrete performances, which they can exhibit to outsiders as well as to themselves. For the outsider these can be conveniently taken as the most concrete observable units of the cultural structure..." (Singer 1959, xiii). In part, perhaps, Singer was thinking of the operational aspects of collecting folklore. In part he may also have been trying to justify outsiders' study of contemporary Indian culture, and to situate this interest in relation to his introductory remarks: "Those cultural traditions that become symbols of national identity ... take on a life of their own, quite different from their life as regional and local traditions. They become the chosen representatives of a national tradition ... The professional student of culture ... can contribute something ... through an objective study ... freed from the immediate necessity of choosing among them a single pattern of existence." (1959, ix)

10. Despite the fact that this volume of collected papers was published by the American Folklore Society, the term 'folklore' does not even occur in the index. Apparently this did not bother the *JAF*'s editor, Thomas Sebeok, himself a master of several disciplines and known to have favored interdisciplinary approaches.

11. The source for these biographic details is Singer (1984, vii).

12. The two exceptions are Norvin Hein's article on Ram Lila and Murray Emeneau's article on Toda songs.

13. For further details see Claus and Korom 1991, where we attempt at various places, and in relation to several theoretical constellations, to reconstruct the development of the discipline of folkloristics in India.

14. Tagore's idealistic world-view is in part derived from the cultural evolutionary perspective that dominated British anthropological scholarship in India during Tagore's lifetime.

15. As in the United States, anthropology in India was divided between those who regarded themselves as cultural anthropologists and those who regarded themselves as social anthropologist. The former have tended to focus on tribal groups, the latter on village peasant societies. While it has been standard in tribal ethnographies to include, as folklore, a collection of tribal myths, folklore has often been ignored in village studies. Increasingly, however, both types of anthropologists have been leaving the collection of folklore to linguists and adventurous literary scholars.

16. Another issue Singer touched upon must be mentioned. Between the interests of "modern nationalism" and "the professional student of culture" lay areas of potential conflict. To forward the goals of national integration, Singer stated, "Theoretically, any element of traditional culture is a potential candidate for selection, but in fact

only a small number are so chosen at any given time. In this selective process, cultural traditions take on a fluidity and self-consciousness that reflects constantly changing moods and aspirations, and changing conceptions of national identity." Cultural traditions are the constructions of an illusion in national scholarship no less than in governmentally-orchestrated cultural displays. Until recently, collaboration between Indian and U.S. folklorists has been minimized by their different relationship to the material. While both have been working hard since India's independence, their goals have been quite different. Indian folklorist have sought their traditional moorings in the common ground of folklore and have concentrated on collection. U.S. folklorists have seen themselves in the role of dispassionate pursuers of theoretical issues.

17. Another ingredient to this successful formula was dramatic improvement in South Asia language training at U.S. universities.

18. U.S. anthropology has consistently seen culture and society reflected in, if not embodied in, its language (Morgan 1871, Boas 1911, Kroeber 1909). During the 1960s there were various attempts at developing rigorous methods—ethnosemantics—for revealing a people's reality by semantic analysis of their vocabulary (Frake 1964, 1980).

19. For the difference folklore brought to the anthropological study of village India, compare, for example, the studies on the concept of karma cited above with similar studies based on traditional anthropological methods as in Lewis (1958, 253-259) or Kolenda (1964).

20. None of those who worked on folklore at this time had formal training in either folkloristics or classical studies. Guiding the neophyte students of Indian folklore as advisors and discussants at the first conference were Wendy O'Flaherty and Alan Dundes. Dundes and O'Flaherty, in their realms of written and oral texts, were masters of comparative analysis and interpretation. They continually reminded us that much of what we had been treating as exclusively regional folklore (India's little tradition) had counterparts in other, world-wide, domains, some of which already had a wealth of scholarship upon which we could draw.

21. Similar discomfort with the dichotomies of great and little traditions had been expressed earlier at a more abstract, social, and cognitive level (Obeyesekere 1963).

22. An expanded sub-set of this paper by Ramanujan was published in *Another Harmony* (Blackburn and Ramanujan 1986), while this version, closer to the original read at the conference, was published by the Central Institute of Indian Languages, Mysore in *Indian Folklore II* (Claus, Handoo and Pattanayak 1987). The paper was further reworked and published by the University of Hawaii.

23. The works of two of the participants, Beck and Roghair, were

published in 1982, the same year of the oral epics conference. At the time the conference was planned and held, however, these books were not yet available.

24. The *Mahābhārata* and *Rāmāyaṇa*, in a variety of regionally performed incarnations, were frequently discussed for the background influences they had on regional epics. But for the first time discussion was not dominated by these favorites, and certainly not by their textual form. Indeed, from the evidence presented at this conference, it might even be suggested that the popularity of the *Rāmāyaṇa* and *Mahābhārata* owes much to the regional performance forms in which they are embedded, i.e., that it is the performed *Rāmāyaṇas* and *Mahābhāratas*, not their textual versions, that have made them emblems of Indian civilization (for the follow-up of this suggestion, see Richman 1991).

25. Inspired by U.S. research on India's oral epics, Scandinavian folklorists focused a series of workshops and panels on oral epics around the similar themes of variant forms in a "pool of tradition" (Honko 1996, 1). One of the organizers of the project, Lauri Honko, working on the Tulu Siri epic collected during specially arranged sittings, compared dictated to recorded variants of the text. Drawing upon the work of U.S. scholars, he, too, postulated the existence of a 'mental text' consisting of "... such elements loosely organized around a larger topic ... a kind of general storyline with a store of obligatory, alternative and optional textual possibilities to be accepted or rejected by the singer at the moment of performance ..." (Ibid. 1). Earlier folklorists often worked from texts that had been dictated, and their focus was largely on the content of the text. While my own research used the concept of mental text to understand better the relationship of texts to live performance contexts, Honko used the concept to· identify elements in an artificially induced text. Although the induced text of an individual raconteur has little ethnographic significance, Honko used the material to evaluate the kinds of epic texts folklorists in the past have collected in the name of epic tradition.

26. It is worth noting that the development of Indo-American folkloristics has been blessed by highly productive collaborative efforts between individual Indian and U.S. scholars, and with the presence of several bi-cultural scholars such as A.K. Ramanujan, V. Narayana Rao, and Kirin Narayan, to mention only three. It is also worth noting that throughout the history of folkloristics international collaboration has often worked well when the two cultures are historically related as homeland and immigrant ethnic group. It may be that in the future rewarding insights into Indian culture will come from U.S. folkloristics along these lines, too, although at present the folklore of the Indian diaspora in the U.S. has been very limited.

27. A notable exception is Kirin Narayan (1989, 1995). In the process of their work, most folklorists probably acquire a degree of insiders' appreciation of the aesthetic differences between performances, but

that is a different matter. A folklorist's evaluative understanding is usually generalized to the culture as a whole, and it is rarely put to test.

28. The American Folklore Society's annual meetings have this delightful feature, too, with the difference that talented folk-folklorists usually postpone their performances until after-hours.

REFERENCES

Babb, Lawrence. 1975. *The Divine Hierarchy: Popular Hinduism in Central India.* New York: Columbia Univ. Press.

Beck, Brenda E.F. 1974. "The Kin Nucleus in Tamil Folklore." In *Kinship and History in South Asia,* ed. Thomas Trautman, 1-27. Ann Arbor: Center for South and Southeast Asian Studies, University of Michigan.

————. n.d. [c. 1975]. "The Human Body: Its Description in Tamil Proverbs." Unpublished.

————. 1977. "The Concept of Karma in a Contemporary Folk Epic from Tamilnadu." Unpublished.

————. 1978. "The Hero in a Contemporary Local Tamil Epic." *Journal of Indian Folkloristics* 1(1):26-39.

————. 1978b. "The Authority of the King: Prerogatives and Dilemmas of Kingship as Portrayed in a Contemporary Oral Epic from South India." In *Kingship and Authority in South Asia,* ed. John Richards, 169-191. Madison: Center for South Asia, University of Wisconsin.

————. 1980. "The Role of Women in a Tamil Folk Epic." *Canadian Folklore* 2:7-29.

————. 1982. *The Three Twins: The Telling of a South Indian Folk Epic.* Bloomington: Indiana Univ. Press.

————. 1986. "Social Dyads in India Folktales." In *Another Harmony: New Essays on the Folklore of India,* ed. Stuart H. Blackburn and A.K. Ramanujan, 76-102. Berkeley: Univ. of California Press.

Blackburn, Stuart H. 1978a. "The Folk Hero and Class Interests in Tamil Heroic Ballads." *Asian Folklore Studies* 37:131-149.

————. 1985. "Death and Deification: Folk Cults in Hinduism." *History of Religions* 24:255-274.

————. 1989. "Patterns of Development for Indian Oral Epics." In *Oral Epics in India,* ed. Stuart H. Blackburn, Peter J. Claus, Joyce Burkhalter Flueckiger, and Susan S. Wadley, 15-32. Berkeley: Univ. of California Press.

————. 1991. "Creating Conversations: The Rama Story as Puppet Play in Kerala." In *Many Rāmāyaṇas: The Diversity of a Narrative Tradition in South Asia,* ed. Paula Richman, 156-172. Berkeley: Univ. of California Press.

————. Forthcoming. "Performance." In *South Asian Folklore: An Encyclopedia,* ed. Peter J. Claus and Margaret Mills. New York: Garland Press.

Blackburn, Stuart H., Peter J. Claus, Joyce Burkhalter Flueckiger, and Susan S. Wadley, eds. 1989. *Oral Epics in India.* Berkeley: Univ. of California Press.

Blackburn, Stuart H. and A.K. Ramanujan, eds. 1986. *Another Harmony: New Essays on the Folklore of India.* Berkeley: Univ. of California Press.

Boas, Franz. 1935. *Kwakiutl Culture as Reflected in Mythology.* New York: American Folklore Society.

———. 1911. "Handbook of American Indian Languages, Part I." Washington, DC: *Bureau of American Ethnology, Bulletin* 40.

Bourdieu, Pierre. 1993. *The Field of Cultural Production: Essays on Art and Literature.* (ed. Randal Johnson) New York: Columbia Univ. Press.

———. 1984. *Distinction: A Social Critique of the Judgement of Taste.* Cambridge: Harvard Univ. Press.

Bulmer, Dr. 1894. "Demon-Worship in Southern India." *Journal of American Folklore* 7:153-154.

Claus, Peter J. 1978a. "Oral Traditions, Royal Cults and Material for the Reconsideration of the Caste System in South India." *Journal of Indian Folkloristics* 1(1):1-25.

———. 1978b. "Heroes and Heroines in the Conceptual Framework of Tulu Culture." *Journal of Indian Folkloristics* 1(2):28-42.

———. 1979. "Mayndala: A Myth and Possession Cult of Tulunad." *Asian Folklore Studies* 38(2):94-129.

———. 1989. "Behind the Text: Performance and Ideology in a Tulu Oral Tradition." In *Oral Epics in India,* ed. Stuart H. Blackburn, Peter J. Claus, Joyce Burkhalter Flueckiger, and Susan S. Wadley, 55-74. Berkeley: Univ. of California Press.

———. 1991. "Kinsongs." In *Gender, Genre, and Power in South Asian Expressive Traditions,* ed. Arjun Appadurai, Frank J. Korom and Margaret Mills, 136-177. Philadelphia: Univ. of Pennsylvania Press.

Claus, Peter J. and Frank J. Korom. 1991. *Folkloristics and Indian Folklore.* Udupi: Regional Resource Centre for Folk Performing Arts.

Dundes, Alan. 1966. "Metafolklore and Oral Literary Criticism." *The Monist* 60:505-516.

Emeneau, M.B. 1944 *Kota Texts.* Berkeley: Univ. of California Press. Univ. of California Publications in Linguistics 2:1.

———. 1943. "Studies in Folktales of India II: The Old Woman and Her Pig." *Journal of American Folklore,* 56:272-88.

Evans-Pritchard, E.E. 1939. "Nuer-Time Reckoning." *Africa,* 12(2):189-216

———. 1940. *The Nuer.* Oxford: Clarendon.

———. 1953. "The Nuer Conception of Spirit and its Relation to the Social Order." *American Anthropologist,* 55(2):201-214.

Finnegan, Ruth. 1969. "Attitudes to the Study of Oral Literature in British Social Anthropology." *Man* 4(1):59-69.

Flueckiger, Joyce Burkhalter. 1988. "He Should Have Worn a Sari: A 'Failed' Performance of a Central Indian Oral Epic." *The Drama*

Review: A Journal of Performance Studies, 32(1): 159-169.

————. 1989. "Caste and Regional Variants in an Oral Epic Tradition." In *Oral Epics in India,* ed. Stuart H. Blackburn, Peter J. Claus, Joyce Burkhalter Flueckiger, and Susan S. Wadley, 33-54. Berkeley: Univ. of California Press.

Frake, Charles O. 1964. "Notes on Queries in Ethnography." *American Anthropologist,* 66(3) (Part 2): 132-45.

————. 1980. *Language and Cultural Description.* Stanford: Stanford Univ. Press.

Frazer, James George. 1890. *The Golden Bough.* London: Macmillan.

————. 1927 [1908]. "The Scope of Social Anthropology." In *Man, God and Immortality: Thoughts on Human Progress,* ed. James George Frazer, 159-176. London: Macmillan.

Goldberg Belle, Jonathan. 1989. "Clowns in Control: Performances in a Shadow Puppet Tradition in South India." In *Oral Epics in India,* ed. Stuart H. Blackburn, Peter J. Claus, Joyce Burkhalter Flueckiger, and Susan S. Wadley, 118-139. Berkeley: Univ. of California Press.

Honko, Laurie. 1996. "The Quest for Oral Text: The Third Wave?" *FF Network for the Folklore Fellows,* 12(1):6.

Ingalls, Daniel H. H. 1966. "Forward." In *Krishna: Rites, Myths and Attitudes,* ed. Milton Singer, v-xi. Chicago: Univ. of Chicago Press.

Kirkland, Edwin Capers. 1966. *A Bibliography of South Asian Folklore.* Bloomington: Indiana Univ. Press. Indiana Univ. Folklore Series, 21.

Kolenda, Pauline Mahar. 1964. "Religious Anxiety and Hindu Fate." In *Religion in South Asia,* ed. Edward B. Harper, 71-82. Seattle: Univ. of Washington Press.

Kroeber, A.L. 1909. "Classificatory Systems of Relationship." *Journal of the Royal Anthropological Institute* 39:79.

Lewis, Oscar. 1965. *Village Life in Northern India.* New York: Vintage.

Marriott, McKim. 1966. "The Feast of Love." In *Krishna: Rites, Myths and Attitude,.* ed. Milton Singer, 200-212. Chicago: Univ. of Chicago Press.

Morgan, Lewis Henry. 1871. *Systems of Consanguinity and Affinity of the Human Family.* Washington, DC: Smithsonian Institution.

Narayan, Kirin. 1989. *Saints, Storytellers and Scoundrels: Folk Narrative in Hindu Religious Teaching.* Philadelphia: Univ. of Pennsylvania Press.

————. 1995. "The Practice of Oral Literary Criticism: Women's Songs in Kangra, India." *Journal of American Folklore,* 108:243-265.

Narayana Rao, Velcheru. 1986. "Epics and Ideologies: Six Telugu Folk Epics." In *Another Harmony: New Essays on the Folklore of India,* ed. Stuart H. Blackburn and A.K. Ramanujan, 131-164. Berkeley: Univ. of California Press.

————. 1991. "A Rāmāyaṇa of Their Own: Women's Oral Tradition in Telugu." In *Many Rāmāyaṇas: The Diversity of a Narrative Tradition in South Asia,* ed. Paula Richman, 114-136. Berkeley: Univ. of California Press.

Nayak, H.M., ed. 1974. *Kannaa Janapada Grantha Suci.* Mysore: Univ. of Mysore Press.

Obeyesekere, Gananath. 1963. "The Great Tradition and the Little in the Perspective of Sinhalese Buddhism." *Journal of Asian Studies*, 22(2):323-342.

―――. 1984. *The Cult of the Goddess Pattini*. Chicago: Univ. of Chicago Press.

Ramanujan, A.K. 1986. "Two Realms of Kannada Folklore." In *Another Harmony: New Essays on the Folklore of India*, ed. Stuart H. Blackburn and A.K. Ramanujan, 41-75. Berkeley: Univ. of California Press.

―――. 1987. "The Relevance of South Asian Folklore." In *Indian Folklore, II*, ed. Peter J. Claus, J. Handoo and D.P. Pattanayak, 79-156. Mysore: Central Institute of Indian Languages.

―――. 1989. "Is There an Indian Way of Thinking? An Informal Essay." *Contributions to Indian Sociology* 23(1):41-58.

Ramanujan, A.K. 1991. "Three Hundred Ramayaas: Five Examples and Three Thoughts on Translation." In *Many Rāmāyaṇas: The Diversity of a Narrative Tradition in South Asia.*, ed. Paula Richman, 22-49. Berkeley: Univ. of California Press.

Richman, Paula, ed. 1991. *Many Rāmāyaṇas: The Diversity of a Narrative Tradition in South Asia*. Berkeley: Univ. of California Press.

Roghair, Gene H. 1982. *The Epic of Palnadu: A Study and Translation of Palnuti Virula Katha, a Telugu Oral Tradition from Andhra Pradesh, India*. Oxford: Oxford Univ. Press.

Singer, Milton B. 1959. "The Great Tradition in a Metropolitan Center: Madras." In *Traditional India: Structure and Change*, ed. Milton B. Singer, 141-182. Austin: Univ. of Texas Press.

Singer, Milton B., ed. 1959. *Traditional India: Structure and Change*. Austin: Univ. of Texas Press.

Singer, Milton B., ed. 1966. *Krishna: Myths, Rites, and Attitudes*. Honolulu: East-West Center Press.

Thompson, Stith and Warren Roberts. 1960. *Types of Indic Oral Tales: India, Pakistan and Ceylon*. Folklore Fellows Communications, No. 180. Helsinki: Suomalainen Tiedeakatemia Academia Scientiarum Fennica.

Thompson, Stith and Tony Balys. 1958. *The Oral Tales of India*. Indiana Univ. Folklore Series, 10. Bloomington: Indiana Univ. Press.

Wadley, Susan S. 1983. "Vrats: Transformers of Destiny." In *Karma: An Anthropological Inquiry*, ed. Val Daniel and Charles Keyes, 147-162. Berkeley: Univ. of California Press.

―――. 1989. "Choosing a Path: Performance Strategies in the North India Epic Dhola." In *Oral Epics in India*, ed. Stuart H. Blackburn, Peter J. Claus, Joyce Burkhalter Flueckiger, and Susan S. Wadley, 75-101. Berkeley: Univ. of California Press.

Wadley, Susan S., ed. 1980. *The Powers of Tamil Women*. Syracuse: Foreign and Comparative Studies, South Asian Series, No. 6, Maxwell School of Citizenship and Public Affairs, Syracuse University.

Zumwalt, Rosemary Levy. 1988. *American Folklore Scholarship: A Dialogue of Dissent*. Bloomington: Indiana Univ. Press.

Geography

JOSEPH E. SCHWARTZBERG

INTRODUCTION

To be human is to be, in various senses, a geographer. Each of us, in the course of our maturation, learns to make sense of the world around us, to impart order to the spaces of which that world is comprised, and to navigate through those spaces. We imbue certain spaces with personal meanings that flow from our individual life experiences and thereby turn them into places. As members of social collectivities, we also classify the spaces in which we function as friendly or hostile, sacred or profane, useful for specific purposes or relatively lacking in value. We devise rules as to how and by whom particular spaces may be utilized and how they should be taxed. On the political plane, we may develop a strong patriotic bond with the territory of a nation state or, alternatively, more parochial emotional attachments to a particular region within a state.[1]

Three types of questions are habitually asked by professional geographers: What is where? Why are things where they are? And, so what? Lay persons must also ask such questions; but when professional geographers seek to provide their answers, they do so in distinctive ways. For example, the 'What is where?' question is often most effaciously answered through the medium of maps. Answers to the 'Why?' question are, to the extent possible, sought within the framework of general laws or principles thought to be at work in determining variations among places over the surface of the earth, or, where universal generalizations cannot be advanced, over a particular portion of that surface. Analyses and syntheses of the phenomena studied are likely to be presented within a framework of regions, that is, intellectually-constructed or legally-instituted portions of space (or, more precisely, out of the space-time continuum) differentiated from other portions of the space-time continuum on the basis of one or more defining characteristics.[2]

The ways in which societies deal with space are, of course,

culturally mediated, and they are conditioned also by the physical conditions under which decisions must be taken. It is only natural, therefore, to expect spatial perceptions and decisions to vary from one culture region to another and from one physical geographic environment to another. Despite the universalizing tendencies that accompany the process of globalization that is sweeping our planet, a cultural realm such as India, which draws inspiration from a heritage of nearly five millennia of civilized society, may be expected to present a unique set of ways of dealing with space and environment; and it is—or ought to be—among the essential tasks of professional geographers concerned with India to comprehend those ways and to elucidate them for other scholars and for society at large.

This essay, then, examines how Indians and scholars working on India have treated space in general and Indian space in particular, how the content and practice of Indian geography have varied over time, and how geographers concerned with India have interacted, or failed to interact, with scholars in other disciplines who are working on space-related problems. This essay pays particular attention to changes in the post-Independence period.

EVOLUTION OF INDIAN GEOGRAPHY IN
THE PRE-INDEPENDENCE PERIOD

In the literary heritage of India we find a plenitude of evidence of keen awareness among early Aryan-speakers and later peoples of the varying physical natures of their geographic milieus and of the diverse peoples and polities therein. To cite but a few examples, the *Nadi-stuti* of the *Ṛg Veda* lauds many of India's life-giving rivers; the *Mahābhārata* provides a rich account of the regions, peoples, cities, polities, natural features, and sacred places extant at the time of the epic war that forms its central theme; and Panini's *Aṣṭādhyāyī* and Kautilya's *Artha Śāstra* abound in similar geographic allusions. Exceptionally rich sources of spatial information are the *Mahā-Purāṇas*. Of particular importance within these texts are sections known as *bhuvana kośa*, (which provide detailed descriptions not only of the sacred land of Bharat, but also of the encompassing cosmos) and the *tīrtha māhātmyas*, (which indicate the blessings to be derived from pilgrimage to specific sacred sites in all parts of the subcontinent).[3] Although the literature of subsequent periods may not be quite so rich as that of ancient India, there is no epoch without its sources of literary and epigraphic data on geography, and there can be little question that in all ages India's Hindu literati had a keen sense of the sacred geography of Bharat.

Following the arrival of Muslims in north India, written geographic knowledge assumed a wide range of new forms. Because of space constraints we here note only a few relevant works. A singularly impressive achievement was Al-Biruni's *Ta'rīkh al-Hind* ("Account of India," c. 1030), a remarkably objective description of India, based in no small measure on materials provided by Hindu informants.[4] Following the consolidation of Mughal rule in north India, Abul Fazl's *Ā'īn-i-Akbarī* ("Institutions of Akbar," 1603) provided a systematically arranged compendium of the peoples, military resources, cropped area, and revenue assessments of the major and minor administrative divisions of the Mughal Empire.[5] Shortly thereafter, the *Shāhid-i Ṣadiq* of Sadiq Isfahani of Jaunpur (1647) provided not only encyclopedic coverage of the world, but also a world atlas in thirty-three sheets of which six related in whole or part to India.[6]

With the coming of European colonialism, indigenous Indian knowledge of geography was, to a remarkable extent, devalued and subliminated. While it undoubtably continued to inform and guide behavior at the folk level, decision-making at the district, provincial, and national levels was based on new scholarly paradigms. The fact that James Rennell, the first Surveyor General of Bengal and author of the estimable *A Bengal Atlas* (1780 and later editions) and *Memoir of a Map of Hindoostan* (1785 and later editions) should be widely—but erroneously—acclaimed as "the father of Indian geography" testifies to the new, Eurocentric perspective. In a word, whatever understandings of space and place India possessed prior to Rennell were simply not regarded as geography. Moreover, many British simply could not believe that Indians possessed any sense of nationhood rooted in shared knowledge of their own land. Thus, Sir John Strachey, a late 19th century bureaucrat, in a dictum that was to influence many subsequent administrators, proclaimed, "This is the first and most essential thing to learn about India, that there is not and never was an India, or even any country of India, possessing, according to European ideas, any sort of unity, physical, political, social and religious, no people of India of whom we hear so much."[7]

Following Rennell, thanks to the combined efforts of the Survey of India and the Great Trigonometrical Survey (launched in 1800), surveying and mapping of India proceeded apace.[8] By the close of the 19th century topographic mapping of India was virtually complete at the quarter-inch scale (one inch = four miles), and, by the time of India's independence, the vast majority of the country was mapped at the scale of one inch to the mile or larger.[9] In numerous other respects, knowledge of the geography of the Indian subcontinent also expanded at a remarkable rate. Pioneers in this process included Sir Colin Mackenzie and Francis Buchanan Hamilton, who established models for the systematic compilation of gazetteers at the district, provincial, and national levels. Inasmuch as many gazetteers were published in two volumes per district and most went through several editions, the total published pre-Independence volumes number in the thousands.[10] Supplementing the gazetteers as aids to the efficient administration of India were a host of settlement reports that provided a plethora of data (much of them at the village level) on people, resources, property regimes, land use, etc. that were not elsewhere available.[11] These reports, complemented by cadastral maps (frequently at scales of up to twelve inches to the mile), provided additional bases for the assessment and collection of land revenue.

Apart from the surveys needed for mapping India, other projects also had important geographic dimensions. Among those monumental undertakings were the Linguistic Survey of India, organized by Sir George Grierson; the Archaeological Survey of India, headed by Sir Alexander Cunningham; numerous epigraphic and numismatic surveys; provincial, state, and regional surveys of castes and tribes; the anthropometric surveys that discredited early British theories on the nature of Indian races; surveys of fauna and flora; forest surveys; the Geological Survey; and magnetic, marine, and climatological surveys.[12] Finally, one must note the detailed and, on the whole, reasonably accurate decennial censuses which, since their inception in 1871-1872, have been indispensable for social-science research, as well as for a wide range of administrative decision making.[13]

Virtually all of the aforementioned activities were carried out primarily to serve the practical ends of administration and were in the mainstream empirical mode of western rational positivist science. The data collected were, as a rule, carefully classified and systematized, and, to some extent, they provided the bases for new theories. But the underlying principles and classificatory schemata on which those theories were based were derived, for the most part, from developments in the then newly-burgeoning academic disciplines evolving in Europe, rather than being rooted in categories meaningful to the Indian populations to which they were to be applied. The beginnings of modern academic geography in India came relatively late. Although the Bombay Geographical Society was founded (as a branch of the Royal Geographical Society in London) as early as

1926, it was not until 1931, with the launching of the first postgraduate program at Aligarh Muslim University, that geography became established as a university-based academic discipline. Five other departments were founded by the time of Independence: Calcutta (1941), Panjab (1944, originally in Lahore), Banaras Hindu University (1946), Allahabad (1947), and Agra (1947).[14] With few exceptions, the senior faculty of these initial departments had completed their postgraduate studies in the United Kingdom, or, in one or two cases, on the European continent. The sole Ph.D. in geography granted in India prior to Independence was awarded in 1941. It was, therefore, hardly surprising that the early programs—as in the case of many other university subjects—closely followed western models. This was true not only in respect to the types of courses offered, but also in respect to their content. What was fashionable in British academic geography (and soon afterward in the U.S.A. as well) more or less automatically became the fashion in India. The texts used in Europe, the theories that were debated, and the research methods that were employed were initially adopted with little change. In regard to texts, there was no practicable alternative, since appropriate Indian geographical publications scarcely existed. The situation with respect to geographic journals was slightly better. In Madras *The Indian Journal of Geography* commenced publication as early as 1926, and *The Geographical Review of India* was launched in Calcutta a decade later.

DEVELOPMENTS SINCE INDEPENDENCE

The post-Independence period in India has seen a remarkable burgeoning of academic geography as well as a continuation and expansion of other geographic activities, primarily by government agencies, and also the inception of professional geography in the private sector.

Outside academe, growing numbers of geographers are employed in mapping, planning, and research agencies. Prominent among these are the Survey of India; the National Atlas and Thematic Mapping Organization (established in 1956 and headquartered in Calcutta); the Office of the Registrar General, which oversees India's censuses (including the preparation of All-India and State Census Atlases); the Regional Planning Unit of the Indian Statistical Institute; and the National Council of Applied Economic Research. Planning offices employ geographers at the national, state, and municipal levels as well as on studies related to specifically delimited regions such as the Calcutta Metropolitan Planning Region, and various river basin development and resettlement projects. Although larger in scale than many comparable undertakings in the pre-Independence period, the types of activities under consideration are motivated by similar practical concerns, and the manner of their execution shows no marked break from the old British bureaucratic traditions. In the private sector, professional geography has yet to make substantial inroads; however a few mapping companies and publishing houses do employ a handful of geographers.

Today scores of Indian university and college departments offer degrees in geography. Postgraduate work up to the Ph.D. level can be pursued at virtually every major university. Possibly as many as a thousand doctoral degrees in geography have by now been granted, and holders of master's degrees are probably at least twice as numerous. Geography figures prominently in university programs in planning and is taken as an optional course in conjunction with many other programs, especially those leading to commercial degrees.[15] Regrettably, the quantitative expansion in geography has not been matched by a comparable improvement in quality. Although individual Indian geographers have won international recognition and have served in many capacities on commissions within the International Geographical Union, of which Shiba Prasad Chatterjee was President from 1964 to 1968, geography remains, overall, a relatively low-status discipline. A significant proportion of students majoring in the field, if my own informal inquiries may be taken as a credible guide, have done so because of their failure to be accepted in other programs, especially economics. All too many curricula continue to be slavishly modeled on those developed in the West. And to compound the problem, in not a few departments a distressingly large number of doctoral dissertations are formulaic recastings of previous works, especially those of the department's founding chair (though carried out in different geographic settings), with tables of contents that scarcely differ from one thesis to another.[16]

Along with the proliferation of academic departments in India has come a dramatic explosion in the number of geographical societies and journals. As of 1980 no fewer than fifty-three such journals had commenced publication, though with varying frequency. Most were associated with individual departments or with societies that they created.[17] Regrettably, as in so many endeavors, quantity and average quality are inversely related in respect to their published research, methodological statements, and reviews.

Outside India, the growth of interest in Indian geography has been less dramatic, and many spatial questions that might well be addressed by geographers have, as we shall see, been more seriously pursued by scholars in such other disciplines as anthropology, history, art history, and political science. I am not aware of a single course in any U.S. university focusing on the geography of India (or South Asia) prior to the mid-1950s, and the total number of such courses in the United States today is probably fewer than two dozen. Although W. Norman Brown, the founder of the AIIS, had a keen appreciation of geography, due perhaps to his having worked closely with geographers in the Office of Strategic Services during World War II, and although he saw to it that the faculty of the Department of South Asian Regional Studies at the University of Pennsylvania (the first of its kind) included a geographer, relatively few major centers of Indian/South Asian studies in the United States presently have any such position. In other countries the situation is substantially better. Geography has long been held in high esteem, for example, in South Asian programs at Cambridge, Heidelberg, Hiroshima, and Moscow, each of which has produced numerous excellent monographs and research papers on various aspects of the geography of the subcontinent. Nevertheless, the total number of non-South Asian geographers specializing in the region would not likely exceed two hundred worldwide.

The first university level text on the subcontinent as a whole, O.H.K Spate's *India and Pakistan: A General and Regional Geography*, was published in England only in 1954.[18] While exceedingly well written and enhanced by excellent maps, this work was based almost entirely on material culled from published government reports and on such limited individual independent research as was then available. Even so, no comparable work has ever been published in the United States. Within India, the first attempt at compiling a university-level text came in response to the International Geographical Congress being held in New Delhi in 1968. The belatedly completed work, *India, A Regional Geography*, did not appear until 1971.[19] A poorly integrated pastiche of submissions from several dozen contributors, the result is far from felicitous. Yet it does contain much information, especially on caste and settlement patterns, that is not to be found in other texts. Among other general university texts published in western-European languages, the one that clearly stands out from the rest is *Sudasien*, a work by eleven contributing authors, published in Germany in 1977.[20] Unlike Spate's text, this one is well grounded in original field research.

Contributions to Indian Geography, under the general editorship of

R.P Misra, aspires to be a general survey of the discipline, each of its thirteen volumes covering a specific sub-discipline (e.g., Applied Climatology, Resource Geography, etc.).[21] Many of the works included, by both Indian and foreign authors, are excellent; but the fact that many other selections are only of ephemeral interest and/or of questionable value indicates that Indian geography has yet to emerge from its formative stage. The emphases in *Contributions*, as in the discipline as a whole, are on various branches of physical and economic geography. These are fields whose research methods tend to be—not always wisely in the latter case—little affected by the culture of the region under consideration. What geographers do in one part of the world (for example, factorial analysis of complex systems) can be applied mechanistically to any other major world region, with little or no regard to its cultural distinctiveness. While some of the results do have utilitarian or pedagogical value, the studies in which they are presented are typically formulaic and not intellectually stimulating. As a rule, they do little to enhance regional studies. Notable lacunae in *Contributions to Indian Geography* are volumes dedicated to historical, cultural, and social geography. It is these fields, in the present writer's view, that offer the widest scope for significant statements that will be read avidly by area specialists approaching the region from other disciplinary perspectives.

Happily, over the past two decades a number of more specialized anthologies in the fields of cultural and social geography have appeared. Of these, *An Exploration of India*, edited by David Sopher, stands out for its originality, its methodological sophistication, its topical breadth, and its judicious blending of all-Indian, regional, and local perspectives.[22] Among other collected works worthy of mention, despite the uneven quality of their contents, are those edited by Aijazuddin Ahmad, Robert C. Eidt et al., A.B. Mukerji and Aijazuddin Ahmad, Allen G. Noble and Ashok K. Dutt, and R.L. Singh and Rana P.B. Singh.[23]

Exemplary monographic studies are not numerous, given the number of geographers working on the region.[24] Especially noteworthy works include those by Bhardwaj, Blaikie, Dupuis, Farmer, Harris, Lodrick, Michel, Schwartzberg, Simoons, Rana P.B. Singh, and Wanmali.[25] Obviously, a list this short must exclude many works that have considerable merit; and in drawing it up I have been guided by my preferences not only for works embodying direct experience of the subject in the field, but also for those that speak to specifically Indian issues in culturally sensitive ways. It may here be appropriately noted that few Indian geographers have shown a propensity to undertake extensive and life-long field investigations. For all too many their last research was that associated with obtaining their terminal degree. Inadequate funding and severe logistical difficulties are largely to blame for this serious shortcoming. Those two related problems urgently need to be addressed by the University Grants Commission and other agencies funding Indian geographical research.

Apart from field research, one of the most characteristic activities for geographers is the preparation of atlases. In this respect, contributions from both India and abroad are numerous and often of high quality. Atlases covering a remarkably wide range of subjects have been prepared by various ministries and branches of the Indian government and also by the governments of most of India's states and various municipal bodies. In 1957 the National Atlas Organization, now the National Atlas and Thematic Mapping Organization (NATMO), issued the first substantial atlas of India using the Devanagari Script.[26] Since then NATMO has been continuously at work adding fascicles to an ever-expanding *National Atlas of India* and has also prepared more specialized, large-format atlases related to agriculture, climate, forestry, irrigation, population, tourism, and other subjects. These works typically combine all-India maps at the scale of 1:6 million, regional maps at a scale of 1:2 million; and very detailed sectional maps at 1:1 million.[27] Also especially worthy of note are the decennial Indian census atlases (already cited), the state planning atlases prepared by the National Council of Applied Economic Research, and numerous additional planning atlases prepared by individual states.

Atlas preparation is also a common activity in university departments of geography. The range of works created therein is too broad to discuss in this brief account. Additionally, individual scholars or small teams of scholars in India and abroad have prepared a variety of small, usually paperback atlases to serve the needs of high school and college students.

INTERACTION BETWEEN GEOGRAPHERS AND SCHOLARS IN OTHER
DISCIPLINES AND GEOGRAPHY DONE BY NON-GEOGRAPHERS

By far the most ambitious non-governmental atlas project ever undertaken with respect to India occupied a team of geographers, historians, and other scholars at the University of Minnesota over the period 1964-1978. The result was *A Historical Atlas of South Asia*, a large-format work that seeks to portray the political, cultural, social, economic, and demographic history of the region from the old stone age to the contemporary period.[28] A distinctive aspect of this atlas is that, in addition to its attempt to provide the most objective cartographic reconstruction of history that the available primary and secondary sources will allow, it also maps India as it was seen and described by its own inhabitants and by foreign visitors from both the East and the West and from classical antiquity to the modern era.

Although *A Historical Atlas of South Asia* provides a remarkably successful example of interdisciplinary cooperation, it must be admitted that mutually beneficial interaction between geographers and South Asian specialists in other disciplines has not been as extensive as it ought to be. As has been noted, few major centers of South Asian studies in the United States include geographers among their faculty. Furthermore, the numbers of geographers in attendance at annual meetings of the Association for Asian Studies or at meetings on South Asia held each autumn at the University of Wisconsin have never been especially great. More pointedly, in a large and prestigious international conference held in New Delhi in 1986 to discuss conceptions of space in Indian as well as in other cultures, one might have expected a good representation of geographers; yet not a single one was present.[29] There have, however, been other important conferences dealing largely with constructions of space in which geographers have played prominent roles. Among these, several sponsored by the Program in Comparative Studies on Southern Asia at Duke University are especially worthy of mention: the first on regions and regionalism in South Asian Studies, held in 1966; a second on society, space, and image in urban India in 1970; and a third on realm and region in traditional India in 1973.[30]

The conferences just noted were, perhaps, exceptional in respect to geography, in that they addressed the subject of space and region in India from a distinctively area studies perspective, with an emphasis on a humanistic approach with which most geographers are not yet particularly comfortable. In other conferences stressing issues of development, planning, and ecology, geographers of South Asia have felt more at home. The number of such conferences is large. I shall here single out only one in which the role of geographers was large, namely the one on urbanism held in Berkeley, California in 1960, which was noteworthy because of the contrast between the essentially practical themes it addressed and those addressed at Duke a decade later.[31]

Three conferences are especially worthy of mention because of their comprehensive approach to a discrete area, rather than to India as a whole. The first of these, held in 1979 under the auspices of the French Cultural Center in Calcutta in cooperation with several local Indian agencies, considered the whole of the Calcutta Metropolitan Region and prompted vigorous subsequent debate in academic, governmental, and planning circles.[32] The second and third conferences, held in Jaipur and Udaipur in 1987 and 1991 respectively, explored the "idea of Rajasthan" with a view to the conservation of its distinctive environment and culture.[33] The initial essay of the resultant two-volume work, "Rajasthan, as a Region: Myth or Reality" by Deryck Lodrick, a geographer raised in Rajasthan, is a masterful analysis of the various ways in which the region has been viewed from within and without over the course of history.

It is, of course, not merely in academic conferences that geographers working on South Asia have interacted with colleagues in other disciplines. Of equal or greater value, arguably, have been multi-disciplinary research projects, such as that conducted jointly by the Centre of South Asian Studies at Cambridge University, the Universities of Madras and Sri Lanka, and the Agrarian Research and Training Institute, Colombo to study the workings of the Green Revolution in various areas of Tamilnadu and Sri Lanka.[34]

Outside an essentially academic domain, I have already noted a number of Indian governmental agencies in which geographers regularly work with others on applied projects, largely in the realm of documentation and planning. But multi-disciplinary teamwork extends also to research projects sponsored by international agencies (the World Bank, World Health Organization, International Rice Research Institute, International Food Policy Research Institute, etc.), foreign governments (largely in respect to development assistance and non-restricted intelligence activities), and foundations (Ford, Rockefeller, etc.), in a number of which academic geographers have played significant roles.[35]

Paradoxically, some of the best modern work on Indian geography has been done by scholars who are not normally thought of as geographers. Although the forms in which they present their findings may differ somewhat from those which geographers might employ, one can document in many cases—and can sense in others—that their work has been influenced, in varying degrees, by direct or indirect contact with geographers. We may here indicate, if only in passing, a somewhat arbitrary sampling of the non-geographers in question and the noteworthy areas in which their contributions have enriched our understanding of the regional complexity of India: on the physical geographic foundation of pre- and proto-historic history, by Bendapudi Subbarao; on contemporary cultural regions, by

Clarence Maloney; on India as a linguistic region, by Colin Masica; on the jajmani system, by Thomas O. Beidelman; on patterns of caste hierarchy, by McKim Marriott; on kinship, by Irawati Karve; on family structure, particularly in respect to the joint family, by Pauline Kolenda; on the treatment of females and on the resultant sex ratio, by Barbara Miller; on demographic zones, by Anish Bose; on material folk culture, by Richard Huyler; on land tenure systems and reform, by Daniel and Alice Thorner; on agrarian political culture, by Joan Mencher; on regional responses to development initiatives, by Kusum Nair; on meso-scale territorial organization, by Brenda E.F. Beck; on integrated river basin development, by B.G. Verghese; on electoral politics, by Harry Blair; on migration and nativist movements, by Myron Weiner; on separatist movements, by Selig Harrison; on spatial aspects of inter-familial transactions within a single village, by Jean-Luc Chambard; and on historical geography, by Irfan Habib.[36] This suggestive list, drawn mainly from works on my own bookshelves, could easily be greatly expanded. While, as noted, many of the cited authors have benefitted substantially from contacts with geographers, it is not equally clear that geographers have benefitted to a comparable degree from the relevant contributions of those in other disciplines in what is, after all, the shared enterprise of understanding the regionally complex reality that is India.

NEEDED: A NEW PARADIGM

Commenting on the contemporary practice in the social sciences in India, Marriott observed:

It is an anomalous fact that...[social sciences in India] have developed from thought about Western rather than Indian cultural realities. As a result, although they pretend to universal applicability, the Western sources often do not recognize and therefore cannot deal with the questions to which many Indian institutions are answers. ... Attending to what is perceived by Indians in Indian categories should at least promote a more perceptive Indian ethnography.[37]

What Marriott had to say about the social sciences in general applies with particular force, in my view, to the practice of geography as it relates to India, and quite possibly—and paradoxically—more so in respect to work being done by Indians within India than to work done on India by non-Indian scholars.

Although virtually all of the studies cited thus far in this essay, irrespective of authorship, do have considerable merit and, in many cases, practical utility as well, relatively few have been predicated on cultural categories derived from India's own heritage, whether from Brahmanical Hinduism or some other tradition. While I would certainly not call for an end to studies based on western social science paradigms, I would argue that, for geographical studies of quintessentially Indian themes, geographers wishing to provide new insights appealing to regional specialists in other disciplines would do well to try to analyze their subjects in ways that draw on Indian conceptions of cultural reality. To illustrate the foregoing point, I will refer to three different subjects that have elicited markedly different studies when pursued by means of western and Indian paradigms: rural settlement patterns, regionalization, and cartography.

In the case of rural settlement patterns, numerous studies have been published that focus, following German classificatory schemata, on the shapes of settlement, as might be seen on a large-scale topographic or cadastral map. Thus, in Bose's *Peasant Life in India*, for example, the terms used to describe village forms include: "shapeless agglomerate" (predominant over perhaps half the country), "linear assemblage," "linear and square agglomerate," "dispersed cluster," and "isolated homesteads."[38] Although these characterizations are undoubtably objectively true and valid generalizations for the areas so mapped by Bose, one may safely assert that not one Indian villager in a thousand would respond, if asked to describe his village, that it was a "shapeless agglomerate." And one may even question whether the external shape of villages is of any particular importance to Indian peasants. A much more important question would be whether the village was settled according to principles that are cosmologically sound and in keeping with views related to the caste hierarchy. In a forthcoming study by Jaipal Singh and Mumtaz Khan, whose work—in contrast to that of most other Indian geographers— is consistently rooted in Indian notions of cultural reality, note is taken of various studies of rural settlement geography which, while recognizing the characteristic segregation of caste and religious groups within villages, fail to appreciate and call attention to the rules by which the patterns of settlement and segregation are determined.[39] Singh and Khan note such rules as set forth in the *Purānas*, the *Mānasāra* (a guide to architectural practice), and other sacred texts. They also discuss the cosmological principles and the directionally situated tutelary deities that determine the relative auspiciousness and moral character of different directions from the village center and establish a social gradient (essentially from the most favored northwest to the least-favored southeast). Furthermore, they illustrate, for particular villages, circumstances that lead to departures from the ideal patterns based on adherence to traditional norms.

An excellent illustration of the non-correspondence between internal perceptions (mental maps) of a village and an externally-imposed reality is provided by the anthropologist E. Valentine Daniel, who performed a series of experiments in which he asked inhabitants of the pseudonymous Tamil village of Kalappur to sketch for him maps of their *kirāmam* (revenue village) and of their *ūr* (the village space with which they identified as a group). The results were remarkably different. Whereas the former maps were recognizably similar to the existing cadastral map, emphasizing its external legal boundary as a revenue unit, the latter emphasized places based on their importance (the temple, the priest's house, etc.) and took as markers of the periphery of the village "the shrines of the sentinel deities, the points at which roads or the village stream enter the village, and the haunted tamarind trees that dot the edge of the village."[40]

Just as the external (etic) and internal (emic) views of villages differ, so too do western and indigenous modes of perceiving Indian regions. Virtually without exception, geographic descriptions of India divide the country into a few broad physiographic macro-regions, which are then subdivided, depending on the level of the text, into smaller and smaller physically-defined subdivisions. Thus, the text by Spate and Learmonth, which many geographers still regard as a canonical work, presents, for the whole of South Asia, a five-tier hierarchy, beginning with three macro-regions, (The [Northern] Mountain Rim, The Indo-Ganetic Plain, and The Peninsula); proceeds to thirty-seven second-order regions; and ultimately reaches several hundred divisions, some as localized as, for example, "Dindigul Col."[41] But no Indian, asked what region he or she hails from, would say from Dindigul Col, or from the Upper Vaigai Basin of which it is a part, or from the Dry Southeast, to chose the next highest level of Spate's hierarchy.

To what areas, then, do Indians themselves refer when asked to identify the regions from which they come? In an attempt to answer this question, I and a group of students in a seminar on field methods that I conducted when teaching at Jawaharlal Nehru University actually put the question to 272 informants (139 males and 133 females) in twenty-one villages scattered over an area of roughly 20,000 square miles straddling the borders of Rajasthan, Haryana, Uttar Pradesh, and Delhi. Informants were asked to name the region (*ilāqā*) to which they belonged and to specify the differences between it and neighboring regions in respect to ten variables: men's dress, women's dress, diet, house type, speech, religious/other customs, folklore, important castes, crops, and physical environment. Although the degree of consensus among the responses varied significantly from one village to another, and from males to females, there was sufficient agreement to enable us to map, over most of the study area, the first contemporary map of Indian regions as seen by their own inhabitants.[42] The differences between our map and those relating to the same area in the published geographic texts of which I have knowledge are so great that one would hardly suppose that they were referring to the same geographic space. For example, while most published texts map the Ganga-Yamuna Doab as a region, referring to it simply as "the Doab," not a single informant in our two study villages within that presumed region specified, or even recognized, such a regional designation.

In respect to cartography, received wisdom had long been that India had no indigenous tradition of map-making. Bagrow's once standard *History of Cartography* asserts that "India had no cartography to speak of" and that "no one in India seems to have been interested in cartography."[43] The only indigenous map cited in that volume is identified simply—and erroneously—as a seventeenth-century Persian work. Even as recently as 1972, Bagrow's dismissive judgement was echoed by Raza and Ahmad who, in an extensive *Survey of Research in Geography*, wrote of "the absence of...maps prepared in India during the ancient and medieval periods," adding that "there exists no evidence of an indigenous tradition of mapmaking."[44] This is but another instance of Indians taking on faith the *obiter dicta* of presumably reputable western scholars and not looking to the evidence around them in museums, libraries, and private collections, not to mention published works.

To explain the remarkable neglect of Indian cartography, one is forced to conclude that a great many works that did not closely conform to what had become the prevailing European view of what a map ought to look like were simply overlooked by geographers and early historians of cartography. A new, less Eurocentric definition of a map, however, is now becoming accepted, namely that maps "are graphic representations that facilitate a spatial understanding of things, concepts, conditions, processes, or events, in the human world."[45] Art historians, students of religion, and others have recently brought to light, analyzed, and described hundreds of works of Indian provenance that fit this expanded definition.[46]

Among the early publications to deal with what would now be regarded as an Indian map (though its author did not so describe it) is an essay by W. Norman Brown, founder of the American Institute of Indian Studies (AIIS), and the preeminent pioneer of South Asian studies in the United States. Writing for a 1947 Festschrift in honor of Ananda K. Coomaraswamy, Brown provided a richly informed, even if incomplete, analysis of a mid-eighteenth century depiction of a Jain pilgrimage held by the Brooklyn Museum on New York, that appears here as Figure One.[47] Figure Two is a graphic summary of Brown's deconstruction of the map. The two paragraphs below illustrate numerous points of difference between "proper" maps seen from the Eurocentric perspective of modern, scientific cartography, and traditional Indian maps of the type illustrated in Brown's essay.

"Modern" Eurocentric Map. (a) Drawn to a fixed scale; scale is indicated on map. (b) Size of features presented is proportional to their physical extent. (c) Has particular orientation, usually to the north. (d) Drawn to a particular projection. (e) Normally has a discreet boundary. (f) Typically is impersonal. (g) Typically depicts a moment in time. (h) Employs conventional signs and symbols. (i) Is limited to terrestrial features visible or otherwise sensible in the "real world." (j) Frequently contains large blank areas. (k) Overall aim is to portray "objective" scientific reality.

"Traditional" Indian Map. (a) Drawn to a variable scale; no scale is indicated on map. (b) Size of features presented is proportional to their perceived importance. (c) May have multiple orientations or no particular orientation at all. (d) Not drawn to a particular projection. (e) Boundary is often indefinite (though not so in the case of Figure One). (f) Patron or other individual is often insinuated into the map. (g) Often has a narrative quality covering a period of time. (h) Employs idiosyncratic signs and symbols. (i) Often combines features from the terrestrial world and the extra-terrestrial cosmos and includes other mythological elements. (j) Typically fills in entire available surface. (k) Overall aim is to convey some moral or spiritual message.

CONCLUSION

Geography in India has a long, rich, and distinctive culturally-rooted history. With the coming of western colonialism, that history was not only denigrated but also, in time, rendered virtually invisible.

European authorities introduced into India a completely new way of viewing the world and of dealing with the variegated spaces and places comprising it. While the ostensibly objective new geography that they thereby created was and remains exceedingly useful for administrative purposes, it was not, as supposed, free from pronounced cultural bias. The cultural values that informed it were those of the West, rather than of the inhabitants of the land to which the new geography related.

Academic geography was introduced to India late in the period of colonial rule. Those who established the first academic departments of geography were, almost without exception, western educated and uncritically accepted the western academic paradigm for doing geographic research. The same held and remains true for those practicing geography within government agencies. While there can be no denying the utility of the western paradigm for many purposes, the geographic research to which it has so far led in India has been, for the most part, lacking in originality and of limited interest to scholars in disciplines other that geography. There is, however, much scope from Indian cultural traditions. What is now needed is to enrich geographic research in India through a skillful blending, in appropriate cultural contexts, of the rigor of the western scholarly paradigms and greater application of indigenous culturally relevant concepts.

Figure One. MAP OF A JAIN PILGRIMAGE: India, Rajasthan, Mewar or Jodhpur c. 1750. Opaque watercolors on cotton. 30 x 37.5 in. (77 x 96 cm.), Brooklyn Museum of Art, 31.746. This pilgrimage map is painted on cloth, comes from Gujarat or southern Rajasthan, and is believed to date from the mid-eighteenth century. The painting is colored in red, yellow, two shades of blue, white, silver, light purple, black, and dark brown. The border around the edge of the cloth is mainly yellow with a green and red vine motif. For a key to details of this map, see *Figure Two*.

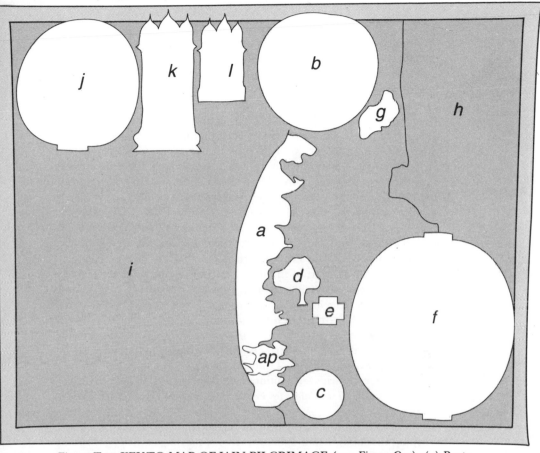

Figure Two. KEY TO MAP OF JAIN PILGRIMAGE (see *Figure One*). (a) Party of Jain pilgrims. (Actual number was probably far more than those shown here; members of party depicted in subsequent portions of route are not indicated in this key.) (ap) The patron of the pilgrimage mounted on a white horse. (He appears at least nine more times in the right half of the painting and once in the upper left.) (b) Group of five Jain *tīrthaṅkaras* (preceptors). (c) Kuṇḍagāma, the city of birth of the *tīrthaṅkara* Mahāvīra (in Bihar). (d) The tree under which Mahāvīra took *dīkṣā* (initiation). (e) The *samavasaraṇa* (place of first preaching) of Mahāvīra (in Bihar). (The order of visit to c, d, and e is not clear.) (f) Pāvā, the city of Mahāvīra's nirvana (in Bihar). (g) A Jain monk preaching a sermon seated under a tree. (h) Conference scene. (i) Sammetaśikhara (Parasnath Peak), in Bihar, where twenty of twenty-four *tīrthaṅkaras* are said to have died; fifteen, not all individually identified, are shown, along with mango and aśoka trees and piles of pots (symbols of luck). (j) Satrunjaya (Shatrunjaya), in Gujarat, place of death of the *tīrthaṅkara* Ṛsabha (tentative identification). (k) Un-identified *tīrthaṅkara*. (l) Five unidentified *tīrthaṅkaras*.

NOTES

1. Within geography the theoretical literature on space and place is very extensive. For a good summary, see Sack, Robert David. 1980. *Conceptions of Space in Social Thought, A Geographic Perspective.* London: Macmillian and Minneapolis: Univ. of Minnesota Press.

2. The most complete and widely cited methodological statement is Hartshorne, Richard. 1939. *The Nature of Geography: A Survey of Current Thought in the Light of the Past.* Washington, DC: Association of American Geographers. Reprinted 1977. Westport, CN: Greenwood Press; and further elaborated in Hartshorne, Richard. 1959. *Perspectives on the Nature of Geography* (AAG Monograph Series, no. 1). Washington, DC: Association of American Geographers. Major alternative views were presented in, *inter alia*, Gergory, Derek. 1978, 1979. *Ideology, Science, and Human Geography.* London: Hutchinson, and New York: St. Martin's Press; and Harvey, David. 1969. *Explanation in Geography.* London and New York: Edward Arnold.

3. The geographic content of the texts referred to, and of other texts as well, is mapped in Schwartzberg, Joseph E., ed. 1992 (second impression). *A Historical Atlas of South Asia.* New York: Oxford Univ. Press. An easily comprehended general introduction to Indian cosmography is provided in Gombrich, R.F., "Ancient Indian Cosmology," in Blacker, Carmen and Michael Loewe, eds. 1975. *Ancient Cosmologies.* 111-142. London: George Allen and Unwin.

4. For a modern abridged edition, see Embree, Ainslie, ed. 1971. *Alberuni's India, Translated by Edward C. Sachau.* New York: W.W. Norton.

5. Detailed, richly annotated maps based on the data of this work are provided in Habib, Irfan. 1982. *An Atlas of the Mughal Empire: Political and Economic Maps with Detailed Notes, Bibliography and Index.* Delhi: Oxford Univ. Press.

6. Described in Habib, Irfan. 1977. "Cartography in Mughal India." In *Medieval India: A Miscellany.* 4: 122-134; also published in 1979. *Indian Archives.* 28: 88-105.

7. Cited in Eck, Diana L. 1996. "Rose-apple Island." *The India Magazine.* (February-March): 6-16, quotation from 8, 10.

8. For works produced up to the early 19th century see Gole, Susan. 1983. *India Within the Ganges.* New Delhi: Jayaprints. For Rennell onward, the definitive history is Phillimore, Reginald Henry (comp.). 1945-1968. *Historical Records of the Survey of India,* 5 vols. (of which vol. 5 is officially suppressed), Dehra Dun: Office of the Geodetic Branch, Survey of India.

9. It will come as a surprise to most readers of this volume that India today (as it was also prior to Independence) is better mapped than the United States. For an index map showing the extent of topographic map coverage at various scales, see Schwartzberg, *A Historical Atlas of South Asia* (see note 3), 142.

10. The most complete guide is Scholberg, Henry. 1970. *The District Gazetteers of British India: Bibliography.* Zug, Switzerland: Inter Documentation. Also useful are the essays in *The Indian Gazetteers.* New Delhi: Govt. of India, Ministry of Education, 1967.

11. Barrier, N. Gerald. 1976. "Land Settlement Reports and Rural India." In *The Indian Archives,* and Barrier, N. Gerald and Robert I. Crane, eds. 1981. *British Imperial Policy in India and Sri Lanka, 1858-1912: A Reassessment.* New Delhi: Manohar.

12. An account of most of these surveys will be found in 1909. *The Imperial Gazetteer of India.* Oxford: Clarendon, vol. 4, *Administrative,* especially 481-507.

13. For critical commentaries see Barrier, N. Gerald, ed. 1987. *Census in British India: New Perspectives.* New Delhi: Manohar. Also Cohn, Bernard S. 1987. "The Census, Social Structure and Objectification in South Asia." In *An Anthropologist Among the Historians, and Other Essays,* ed. Bernard S. Cohn, 224-254. Delhi: Oxford Univ. Press.

14. A very useful source of information on the formative phase of Indian academic geography is Chatterjee, S.P. 1964. *Fifty Years of Science in India: Progress of Geography.* Calcutta: Indian Science Congress Association.

15. See listings of programs in the annual *Commonwealth Universities Yearbook,* London; and *Handbook of Universities of India,* New Delhi.

16. Lest these and subsequent comments seem excessively severe, it may be noted that a number of comparably harsh, if not harsher, criticisms have been set forth by Indian geographers. See, for example, Bhardwaj, Surinder M. 1987. "Toward an Indian Geographic Agenda." *National Geographic Journal of India,* 33(3): 327-334; Misra, R.P. 1983. "Introduction." *Concepts and Approaches,* vol. 1, 1-10 of *Contributions to Indian Geography.* New Delhi: Heritage; Mukherji, A.B. 1991. "What Ails Indian Geography?" In *Indian Geography,* ed. J. Diddee, vol. 1, 135-155. Pune: Institute of Indian Geographers. Reprinted in Singh, R.L. and Rana P.B. Singh, eds. 1992. *The Roots of Indian Geography: Search and Research,* 205-218. Varanasi: National Geographical Society of India.

17. Harris, Chauncy D. and Jerome D. Fellman (compilers), 1980 (3rd. edition) *International List of Geographical Serials.* Chicago: Univ. of Chicago, Dept. of Geography Research Paper No. 193.

18. Spate, O.H.K. 1954. *India and Pakistan: A General and Regional Geography.* London: Methuen. A second edition appeared in 1957, and a third, co-authored with A.T.A. Learmonth, appeared in 1967.

19. Singh, R.L., ed. 1971. *India, A Regional Geography.* Varanasi: National Geographical Society of India.

20. Blenk, Jurgen, Dirk Bronger, and Harald Uhlig, eds. 1977. *Sudasien.* Frankfurt am Main: Fischer Taschenbuch Verlag. This work, little known in the English-speaking world, saw four printings by 1983, by which time 35,000 copies had come off the press. The remarkable

recent expansion of relevant German scholarship on South Asia (especially on India) can be gauged from the fact that the bibliography of this work cited 134 geographical works on the region in German as against 75 in English. Lest one assume that this merely reflects a predictable linguistic bias, the comparable figures for non-geographic works cited were 116 and 238.

21. Misra, R.P., gen. ed. 1983-1984. *Contributions to Indian Geography* (thirteen vols.). New Delhi: Heritage. It is likely that additional volumes will appear in this series.

22. Sopher, David E., ed. 1980. *An Exploration of India: Geographical Perspectives on Society and Culture.* Ithaca: Cornell Univ. Press. Apart from Soper himself, all nine of the other authors were his former students.

23. Ahmad, Aijazuddin, ed. 1993. *Social Structure and Regional Development: A Social Geographic Perspective, Essays in Honour of Professor Moonis Raza.* New Delhi: Rawat; Eidt, Robert C., Kashi N. Singh, and Rana P.B. Singh, eds. 1977. *Man, Culture, and Settlement, Festschrift to Prof. R.L. Singh:* New Delhi: Kalyani; Mukherji, A.B. and Aijazuddin Ahmad, eds. 1985. *India: Culture, Society, and Economy: Geographical Essays in Honour of Prof. Asok Mitra.* New Delhi: Intra-India; Noble, Allen G. and Ashok K. Dutt, eds. 1982. *India: Cultural Patterns and Processes.* Boulder: Westview; and Singh, R.L. and Rana P.B. Singh, eds. 1987. *Trends in the Geography of Pilgrimage: Homage to David E. Sopher.* Varanasi: National Geographical Society of India.

24. More complete, yet selective, critical bibliographies than we can provide here may be found in Schwartzberg, Joseph E. 1983. "The State of South Asian Geography." *Progress in Human Geography,* 7(2): 232-253 (along with critical discussion), and in his 1985 "South Asia." In *A Geographical Bibliography for American Libraries,* ed. Chauncey D. Harris, 325-331. Washington, DC: Association of American Geographers and the National Geographic Society. Less up-to-date but more inclusive works are Indian Council of Social Science Research, ed. 1972. *A Survey of Research in Geography.* Bombay: Popular Prakashan; and Indian Council of Social Science Research, ed. 1984. *A Survey of Research in Geography, 1972-75.* Bombay: Popular Prakashan; and Sukhwal, B.L. 1974. *South Asia: A Systematic Geographic Bibliography.* Metuchen, NJ: Scarecrow. The most recent overview is provided by Ahmad, Aijazuddin, ed. 1996. *Progress in Indian Geography, 1992-1996: A Country Report.* New Delhi: Indian National Science Academy (prepared for the 28th International Geographical Congress, the Hague, the Netherlands, August 4-10, 1996).

25. Bhardwaj, Surinder Mohan. 1973. *Hindu Places of Pilgrimage in India: A Study in Cultural Geography.* Berkeley: Univ. of California Press; Blaikie, Piers M. 1975. *Family Planning in India: Diffusion and Policy.* London: Edward Arnold; Dupuis, J. 1960. *Madras et le Nord du Coromandel, Etudes des Conditions et de la Vie Indienne dans un Cadre*

Geographique. Paris: Librairie d'Amerique et d'Orient; Farmer, Bertram Hughes. 1974. *Agricultural Colonization in India Since Independence.* London: Oxford Univ. Press (for the Royal Institute of International Affairs); Harriss, John. 1982. *Capitalism and Peasant Farming: Agrarian Structure and Ideology in Northern Tamil Nadu.* Bombay: Oxford Univ. Press; Lodrick, Deryck O. 1981. *Sacred Cows, Sacred Places: Origins and Survivals of Animal Homes in India.* Berkeley: Univ. Of California Press; Michel, Aloys A. 1967. *The Indus Rivers: A Study of the Effects of Partition.* New Haven: Yale Univ. Press; Schwartzberg, Joseph E. 1969. *Occupational Structure and Level of Economical Development in India: A Regional Analysis.* New Delhi: Office of the Registrar General, India (Census of India, 1961, Monograph 4); Simoons, Frederick J. 1968. *A Ceremonial Ox of India: The Mithan in Nature, Culture and History, with Notes on the Domestication of Common Cattle.* Madison: Univ. of Wisconsin Press; Singh, Rana P.B. 1977. *Clan Settlements in the Saran Plain (Middle Ganga Valley): A Study in Cultural Geography.* Varanasi: National Geographical Society of India; Wanmali, Sudhir. 1981. *Periodic Markets and Rural Development in India.* Delhi: B.R. Publishing Co. Among these, the monographs by Bhardwaj, Farmer, Harris, and Michel have been much used and cited by workers in disciplines other than geography.

26. 1957. *National Atlas of India, Hindi Edition.* Calcutta and Dehra Dun: Govt. of India, Ministry of Scientific Research and Cultural Affairs.

27. A listing of the more important government atlases published up to the year 1963 can be found in Chatterjee, S.P. *Fifty Years of Science in India: Progress of Geography* (see note 14), 261-262. The number of significant titles will have increased several-fold since this list was prepared.

28. Schwartzberg, Joseph E., ed. 1978. *A Historical Atlas of South Asia.* Chicago: Univ. of Chicago Press. An updated second impression of this work was published in 1992. New York: Oxford Univ. Press.

29 . The proceedings of this conference are presented in Vatsyayan, Kapila, ed. 1991. *Conceptions of Space, Ancient and Modern.* New Delhi: Abhinav (for Indira Gandhi National Centre for the Arts). Papers at this conference were presented by art historians, practitioners, and critical scholars of a wide range of graphic and performing arts, architects, archaeologists, anthropologists, philosophers, physicists, mathematicians, and others.

30. The published volumes presenting the transactions of these conferences were: Crane, Robert I., ed. 1967. *Regions and Regionalism in South Asian Studies: An Exploratory Study;* Fox, Richard G., ed. 1970. *Urban India: Society, Space, and Image;* and Fox, Richard G., ed. 1977. *Realm and Region in Traditional India;* all published in Durham, NC by the Duke Univ. Program in Comparative Studies in Southern Asia, as Monographs 5, 10, and 14 respectively.

31. Selected papers presented, including some submitted by persons unable to attend, are published in Turner, Roy, ed. 1962. *India's*

Urban Future. Berkeley: Univ. of California Press.

32. The proceedings appear in Racine, Jean, ed. 1990. *Calcutta 1981: The City, Its Crisis, and the Debate on Urban Planning and Development.* New Delhi: Concept (in collaboration with Maison des Sciences de l'Homme, Paris and French Institute, Pondicherry). The title is misleading in at least two respects: First, because it does not indicate the historical dimension of many of the papers presented, and, second, because the substantive issues addressed went well beyond those relating to planning and development. The geographer, Racine, was the guiding spirit behind the conference, which was a direct outgrowth of the first Indo-French Seminar on the problems of urban growth held in New Delhi in 1978 under the joint auspices of the Centre for the study of Regional Development at Jawaharlal Nehru University and the Centre for Studies in Tropical Geography of the French National Centre for Scientific Research.

33. Ultimately, these conferences led to a two-volume work, including many of the papers prepared for the conferences as well as a number submitted by scholars unable to attend: Schomer, Karine, Joan L. Erdman, Deryck O. Lodrick, and Lloyd I. Rudolph, eds. 1994. *The Idea of Rajasthan: Explorations in Regional Identity.* Columbia, MO: South Asia Publications (in collaboration with Manohar, New Delhi). The two volumes are subtitled "Constructions" and "Institutions" respectively.

34. The results are presented in Farmer, B.H., ed. 1977. *Green Revolution? Technology and Change in Rice-Growing Areas of Tamil Nadu and Sri Lanka.* Boulder: Westview. Additional findings appear in Bayliss-Smith, Tim P. and Sudhir Wanmali, eds. 1984. *Understanding Green Revolutions: Agrarian Change and Development Planning in South Asia.* Cambridge: Cambridge Univ. Press.

35. Space limitations preclude citation of individual projects, which are quite numerous.

36. In order of mention of authors, the following works may be cited: Subbarao, Bendapudi. 1958. *The Personality of India: Pre- and Proto-Historic Foundation of India and Pakistan.* Baroda: Faculty of Arts, Maharaja Sayajirao Univ. of Baroda (M.S. University Archaeology Series No. 3); Maloney, Clarence. 1974. *Peoples of South Asia.* New York: Holt, Reinhart, and Winston; Masica, Colin. 1976. *Defining a Linguistic Area, South Asia.* Chicago and London: Univ. of Chicago Press; Beidelman, Thomas Q. 1959. *A Comparative Analysis of the Jajmani System.* Locust Valley, NY: J.J. Augustin (Association for Asian Studies, Monograph 8); Marriott, McKim. 1965. *Caste Ranking and Community Structure in Five Regions of India and Pakistan.* Poona: Deccan College Postgraduate and Research Institute; Karve, Irawati. 1968 (3rd edition). *Kinship Organization in India.* New York: Asia; Kolenda, Pauline. 1987. *Regional Differences in Family Structure in India.* Jaipur: Rawat; Miller, Barbara D. 1981. *The Endangered Sex: Neglect of Female Children in Rural*

North India. Ithaca and London: Cornell Univ. Press; Bose, Ashish. 1994. *Demographic Zones in India.* Delhi: B.R. Publishing Co.; Huyler, Richard. 1962. *Village India.* New York: Harry N. Abrams; Thorner, Daniel and Alice. 1962. *Land and Labour in India.* Bombay: Asia; Mencher, Joan P. 1978. *Agriculture and Social Structure in Tamil Nadu: Past Origins, Present Transformations and Future Prospects.* New Delhi: Allied; Nair, Kusum. 1961. *Blossoms in the Dust: The Human Factor in Indian Development.* London: G. Duckworth; Beck, Brenda E.F. 1972. *Peasant Society in Konku, A Study of Right and Left Subcastes in Southern India.* Vancouver: Univ. of British Columbia Press; Verghese, B.G. 1990. *Waters of Hope, Himalaya-Ganga Development and Cooperation for A Billion People.* New Delhi: Oxford Univ. Press; Blair, Harry. 1979. *Voting, Caste, Community, Society: Explorations in Aggregate Data Analysis in India and Bangladesh.* New Delhi: Young Asia; Weiner, Myron. 1978. *Sons of the Soil: Migration and Ethnic Conflict in India.* Princeton: Princeton Univ. Press; Harrison, Selig S. 1960. *India: The Most Dangerous Decades.* Princeton: Princeton Univ. Press; Chambard, Jean-Luc. c. 1980. *Atlas d'un Village Indien: Piparsod, Madhya Pradesh.* Paris: Laboratoire de Graphique de l'Ecole Pratique des Hautes Etudes en Sciences Sociales and Mouton; and Habib, Irfan. *An Atlas of the Mughal Empire: Political and Economic Maps with Detailed Notes, Bibliography and Index* (see note 5).

37. Marriott, McKim. 1990. "Constructing an Indian Ethnosociology." In *India Through Hindu Categories,* ed. McKim Marriott, 1-39. New York: Sage, quotation from 1.

38. These are mapped for the whole of India in Bose, N.K. 1961. *Peasant Life in India: A Study of Unity in Diversity.* Calcutta: Anthropological Survey of India, map one, with seven pages of accompanying illustrations and text (not all numbered). An elaboration of this map extending to the whole of South Asia appears in Schwartzberg, Joseph E, ed. *A Historical Atlas of South Asia* (see note 3), 131, with supplementary maps of villages, by type, on 131-132.

39. Singh, Jaipal and Mumtaz Khan. Forthcoming. "Cosmology and the Orientation and Segregation of Castes." *Annals of the Association of American Geographers.*

40. Described in Daniel, E. Valentine. 1984. *Fluid Signs: Being a Person the Tamil Way.* Berkeley: Univ. of California Press, discussion, 72-79, quotation from 74.

41. The regional scheme, by Spate, is presented in Spate, O.H.K. and A.T.A. Learmonth. 1967. *India and Pakistan: A General and Regional Geography* (see note 18), 407-423. So far as I am aware, the first map to show the regionalization of South Asia within an essentially cultural, rather than physical, framework appears in Alsdorf, Ludwig. 1955. *Vorderindien: Bharat-Pakistan-Ceylon, Eine Landes-und Kulturkunde.* Braunschweig, Germany: Georg Westermann Verlag, 178. Alsdorf shows twenty-one regions in all and does not resort to a hierarchical

arrangement in his presentation. Although he describes his work, in part, as geography, Alsdorf is known primarily as an indologist. A much more detailed cultural regional presentation than Alsdorf's is provided by Schwartzberg, Joseph E. 1967. "Prolegomena to the Study of South Asian Regions and Regionalism." In *Regions and Regionalism in South Asian Studies: An Exploratory Study*, ed. Robert I. Crane (see note 30), 89-111. This map arranges regions in a four-level hierarchy. Whatever pedagogical merit the map may have, it cannot, as a rule, claim to present a set of regions that would be clearly recognized as such by their respective inhabitants.

42. Survey results are provided in Schwartzberg, Joseph E. 1985. "Folk Regions in Northwestern India." In *India Culture, Society, and Economy*, ed. Aijazuddin Ahmad and A.B. Mukerji (see note 23), 205-235. The map printed with this article, regrettably, was badly butchered in publication; however, a proper version, along with a critical analysis, appears in Lodrick, Deryck O. 1994. "Rajasthan as a Region: Myth or Reality?" In *The Idea of Rajasthan: Explorations in Regional Identity*. ed. Karine Schomer et al. (see note 33), 1-45, map on 26. Another map of what might be considered folk regions, based essentially on dialect, will be found in Bhatt, Bharat L. 1980. "India and Indian Regions: A Critical Overview." In *An Exploration of India: Geographical Perspectives on Society and Culture*, ed. David E. Sopher (see note 22), 35-61, map on 59. However, this map, relating to the state of Gujarat, lacks boundaries and is not based on fieldwork. More impressive is Brenda E.F. Beck's cartographic reconstruction of the twenty-four traditional *na-Tus* (sub-regions) of the Tamil *mandalam* (region) of Konku, in her 1972 *Peasant Society in Konku* (see note 36), 64.

43. Bagrow, Leo. 1964 (rev. and enlarged by R.A. Skelton). *History of Cartography*. Cambridge: Harvard Univ. Press. Reprinted and enlarged 1985. Precedent, 207-208, quotation from 207.

44. Raza, Moonis and Aijazuddin Ahmad. 1972. "Historical Geography: A Trend Report." In *A Survey of Research in Geography*, ed. Indian Council of Social Science Research (see note 24), 147-169, quotations on 148 and 153.

45. Harley, J.B. and David Woodward, eds. 1987. *The History of Cartography*. Chicago: Univ. of Chicago Press. vol. 1, xvi.

46. See, in particular, Schwartzberg, Joseph E. 1992. "South Asian Cartography." Part Two of *Cartography in the Traditional Islamic and South Asian Societies*. In *The History of Cartography*, ed. J.B. Harley and David Woodward, vol. 2, book 1, 293-509. Chicago and London: Univ. of Chicago Press; Gole, Susan. 1989. *Indian Maps and Plans, From Earliest Times to the Advent of European Surveys*. New Delhi: Manohar, a more popular exposition; and Bahura, Gopal Narayan and Chandramani Singh. *Catalogue of Historical Documents in the Kapad Dwara, Jaipur*. Part 2: *Maps and Plans*, an annotated catalogue of 372

Indian maps recently discovered in the city palace in Jaipur. All three works are copiously illustrated.

47. Brown, W. Norman. 1947. "A Painting of a Jaina Pilgrimage." In *Art and Thought: Issued in Honour of Dr. Ananda K. Coomaraswamy on the Occasion of His 70th Birthday*, ed. K. Bharatha Iyer, 69-72 and plate XIV. London: Luzac. Reissued in Brown, W. Norman. 1978. *India and Indology: Selected Articles*, ed. Rosanne Rocher, 256-258 and plate XLVII. Delhi: Motilal Banarsidass (for the American Institute of Indian Studies). Brown assigned the work to "the late 17th or early 18th century, more likely the latter." Schwartzberg discusses the map in his work on "South Asian Cartography" (see note 46), 440-442.

History (Pre-Colonial)

DAVID LUDDEN

A century before the founding of the Indian National Congress, indologists and orientalists—Indians and Europeans—were composing texts that would change India's national imagination. India's emerging modern intelligentsia would thus discover their own historical identity in old accumulations of academic research about ancient and medieval India. History defined nationality and informed its self-awareness. With Dadabhai Naoroji, Bankim Chandra Chattopadhyay, and R.C. Dutt, history joined the national movement, and, ever since, historiography and nationalism have moved together, interacting and changing the content of history. The modern practice of reading history as a guide to the experience of collective identity has encouraged historians to project national sensibilities into their interpretations of data from pre-colonial centuries. Scholars work painstakingly to decipher and critically interpret texts, and they engage in technically specialized research. Yet the Indus valley, Vedic hymns, Sanskrit epics, Mauryas, Kushanas, Guptas, Delhi sultans, and Mughal emperors first came to life for readers of history who became India's first modern historians—and they still come to life for many readers of history—as evocative icons of Indian nationality.

The nation implicates modern and pre-modern histories somewhat differently. Modern history officially begins with colonialism, and its writing began with British accounts of the rise of the raj. As a field of study, colonial history remained predominantly British until 1947, and, at Independence, academic research concerning Indian nationalism had barely begun. In fifty years we have seen a steady historiographic displacement of foreigners from modern history. Native activity and experience have become the core concern, and the master narrative of modern history is the epic of nationalism. By contrast, pre-colonial history continues to encode the origins and evolution of Indian nationality, to chronicle the nation before the rise of modernity and nationalism.

By 1920 scholars had a good collection of data with which to construct the history of India's pre-colonial identity, and Indian scholars were prominent among pre-colonial historians. Dyarchy made education a "native subject" and further enhanced efforts to document India's indigenous character. Distinctive schools and divisions arose within Indian historiography. In Madras, for example, south India became a separate historical territory, centered on the Tamil country. Historians reconstructed a separate history of south India from evidence in sangam literature (discovered in the 1890s) and in Chola and Vijayanagar inscriptions (organized in volumes by the Archaeological Survey of India and the Madras Government). Historians spawned debates—which continue today—about Dravidian culture, south Indian kingdoms, medieval Hindu institutions, and the impact of invasions from the north. In the 1920s, Madras University's *Tamil Lexicon* helped to make the language of sangam literature "classical Tamil," and a classical (sangam era) south India thus emerged in the literature that could be set alongside classical Greece, Rome, and north India. The Cholas became to the south what the Guptas were to the north. Vijayanagar became the south's last indigenous empire, analogous to the Mughals. Sakkottai Krishnaswami Aiyangar's 1921 book, *South India and her Muhammadan Invaders*, depicts the resulting north-south division of India history, and also its communal division. By 1920 literary Urdu and Hindi had been separated from one another to mirror separations of Muslim and Hindu cultures. Separate electorates had been established. Muslim history was in its own realm, with its own separate sources, scholars, chronology, and geography. Readers of history would thus find "Muslim history" injected into Indian history at moments of medieval "invasions" and "conquests," so that even freedom fighters who worked for Indian unity would read histories that bolstered the two-nation theory. Scholars divided pre-colonial millennia into the hoary, ancient, and classical Hindu epochs and the more recent centuries of Muslim power; and in the process, they accomplished a totalizing, anachronistic, backward projection of modern communal identities onto pre-colonial history. In the history books, rulers labeled "Hindu" represented modern Hindus; "Muslim" conquerors came to personify Islam. Bankim Chandra produced early historical fiction on these lines in *Ananda Math*, and in the 1890s, when Romesh Chunder Dutt composed *Ancient India, 2000 B.C.-800 A.D.*,[1] he clearly identified the indigenous culture of India with the age of "classical" Hinduism, before Muslim influence.[2] History became a national site for debate and exhortation. Authors discussed all types of issues in history books. As a pedagogical tool for national self-analysis, historiography thus became a repository for competing accounts of India's national character. In 1944, in this vein, Jawaharlal Nehru wrote *The Discovery of India* during five months of imprisonment in the Ahmadnagar Fort. As Gandhi used philosophy, Nehru used history, and the lessons he took from history pertained above all to problems of national leadership: In his extended account of ancient India, for instance, Nehru lionized Ashoka, and he argued that India lost its vigor whenever it had become too preoccupied with national self-defense, closing itself off from the world.[3] If India's past was a guide to its future, for Nehru, independent India promised to be a fulfillment of India's imperial past. He thus duly reminded the reader that Akbar's communal tolerance built the Mughal empire, which Aurangzeb tore apart. Because the validity of his discovery depended upon scientific history, Nehru appreciated the authority of scholars. National identity and national progress needed studious leadership, in his view, and accurate history provided the best guide to freedom and prosperity.

1947 altered the character of Indian nationality and historiography. Partition hardened old separations. The phrase "Muslim rule" had long been applied to the period after 1290, when dynasties led by Muslims proliferated. Historians had long used "Hindu" and "Indian" with facile interchangeability, as a matter of convention. International scholarship had set Muslim history and Islamic studies apart, following the British model. Muslims everywhere were defined by Islam and attached historically to its point of origin rather than to the regions of their own social life, reflecting an implicit diaspora theory that continues today to dominate histories of the Muslim world. "Indian civilization," on the other hand, was taken to be confined within its modern borders and defined by cultural traits that were documented before "Muslim influence," as in A.L. Basham's *The Wonder that Was India* (1954), which is subtitled *A Survey of the History and Culture of the Indian Subcontinent Before the Coming of the Muslims*. The arrival of Muslims in India, like the arrival of the British, thus appeared to represent a major historical turning point in the history of the nation, and Partition further institutionalized the practice of projecting national and communal identities into the pre-colonial past. Independence also separated the territories of historical studies. Research increased rapidly as scholars in India, Pakistan, and Bangladesh worked separately; and India's linguistic states also developed diverging historical identities. New research and debates have redefined pre-colonial India very dramatically in fifty years, but there is still no one central academic institution within which to view the entire scope of pre-colonial historiography.

After 1947 India's international stature rose dramatically, and so did the influence of Indian historians and new research in pre-colonial Indian history. Under the raj, pre-colonial India had become a centerpiece of world history dramatizing the inexorable progress of European hegemony. Since 1947 scholars have fundamentally rewritten the history of pre-colonial India, and, in doing so, they have made a serious impact on studies of world history. During these fifty years many Indian historians have worked or settled abroad; many foreign scholars have done research in India; and many scholarly institutions have reoriented their thinking toward the authority of Indian scholars, to make places like Cambridge, Canberra, Chicago, Heidelberg, Paris, Singapore, and Tokyo parts of a worldwide Indian intellectual network. The political and cultural project of transforming India under conditions of national independence also inspired historians to study social, economic, and cultural change in pre-colonial times, and the historical dynamics of social inequality, social power, and economic development became particularly prominent themes in history. Nehru's own words helped to set the stage. In 1931, as President of the All-India Congress Committee, he argued that:

the great poverty and misery of the Indian People are due, not only to foreign exploitation in India but also to the economic structure of society, which the alien rulers support so that their exploitation may continue. In order therefore to remove this poverty and misery and to ameliorate the condition of the masses, it is essential to make revolutionary changes in the present economic and social structure of society and to remove the gross inequalities.[4]

FOUNDATIONS

Building on previous research and working within a broad chronology that was already established in 1947, historians in the Republic of India have produced the modern fields of ancient, medieval, and early modern Indian history. This small chapter can barely begin to do justice even to the part of their work that most pertains to Indian influence in the study of comparative and world history. The corpus of pre-colonial Indian historiography that we read today has been composed substantially by three scholarly generations, and a small number of very eminent historians have played pivotal roles, notably

D.D. Kosambi and Romila Thapar (ancient history); R.C. Majumdar, K.A. Nilakanta Sastri, and R.S. Sharma (early medieval history); Irfan Habib, M. Athar Ali, and Satish Chandra (Mughal history); and Tapan Raychaudhuri and K.N. Chaudhuri (early modern economic history).[5] The fields that surround these scholars share a broadly materialist orientation to core themes of state formation, political economy, and social power. Encouragements in this direction are many. Unlike modern (colonial) history, which covers barely two-hundred years using a vast official archive in English; pre-colonial history covers three-thousand years and scores of dynasties, and it uses sources scattered in many archives in many archaic languages. Important documents are of uncertain provenance. Pre-colonial history combines disparate data from many (often uncertain) sources and from many disciplines—religion, philology, linguistics, literature, art, folklore, archaeology, numismatics, epigraphy, and metallurgy— to address big questions about long-term changes. Because dynasties provide dates and locations for sources, historians tend to orient their work along lines drawn by states, and they learn most directly about issues that concerned the people who wrote their sources, mostly state elites. To integrate data and to reason across lacunae in documentation, comparative theories of state formation, class differentiation, and pre-capitalist modes of production have proved to be most valuable, and these theories center on social power in political economies, conceived in abstract terms that do not refer only to India. Using such theories allows pre-colonial historiography to move beyond the intellectual confines of nationality, and puts pre-colonial India into international discourse concerning pre-modern world history.

This comparative theoretical orientation has become an integral part of professional historiography in India since 1947. D.D. Kosambi—not himself university trained as an historian—helped to set the standard by garnering an impressive array of technical skills, writing about ancient India in comparative terms, developing a flexible and distinctively Indian form of Marxian theory, criticizing the habit of reading national identity into ancient history, and eschewing racial ideas about the definition of social groups.[6] Using history to fire national emotions, and using nationality to discipline historiography may be universal features of modernity; and disentangling history from myth, ideology, prejudice, propaganda, communalism, and nationalism is certainly fundamental for historical professionalism.[7]

The expansion of historical knowledge has continued to

accelerate since 1947. Regional research has generated a new multiplicity of Indian histories and changed our geographical orientation to pre-colonial territory.[8] Historical themes and theoretical orientations have diversified. D.D. Kosambi, R.S. Sharma, and Irfan Habib made agrarian political economy prominent. Urban history became a distinctive field.[9] Economic history is most luxuriant for later medieval and early modern periods, when statistical data improve, providing additional information on Mughal and Maratha inland economies and on the conduct and impact of overseas trade. Compendia of Mughal economic data by Irfan Habib and Shireen Moosvi, as well as the first volume of the *Cambridge Economic History of India*, have put later medieval India in the mainstream of Old World economic history.[10] European trade put the history of economic networks on the map, initially, but networks of exchange, finance, migration, and social relations that organized India's own expansive economies for many centuries became part of pre-colonial Indian history in the 1960s, beginning with the work of S. Arasaratnam, K.N. Chaudhuri, and Om Prakash. Scholars have now analyzed Indian economic networks that intersected in temples and towns (R. Champakalakshmi and Burton Stein), followed trade along routes of medieval state expansion (Kenneth Hall), traced merchant travels into central Asia and China (Xinru Liu, Stephen Dale), shown the intersection of European and Indian Ocean world economies (Sanjay Subrahmanyam), and described circuits of commercial capital formation and monetary history (J.F. Richards, Frank Perlin). Social history—as distinct from political and economic history, or literary and cultural studies—has developed under Romila Thapar's steady influence, so that tracing the history of social identities, ideologies, movements, conflicts, solidarities, and mobility is now a field of study in its own right, with recent notable books by Muzaffar Alam, Brajadulal Chattopadhyay, Richard Eaton, and Burton Stein. Foundations for new fields of environmental (Chetan Singh) and gender (Kumkum Roy) history have been laid recently by scholars working at the intersection of social, political, and cultural history.[11]

REVISIONS

Indian historians have influenced international scholarship by bringing new research from India into studies of comparative and world history. I cannot do justice to all their contributions, and I will be able to touch only four related themes that give some sense of how pre-colonial Indian history has changed since 1947. Indian writing on 1. State Formation, 2. State-Society Interaction, 3. Modes of Production, and 4. Early Modernity has changed ideas about pre-colonial India and about world history among scholars not only in South Asia but also in the U.S., Europe, Japan, and Australia. Because the preponderance of English-language historiography on the pre-modern world concerns Europe, India, China, Japan, and a few areas in the Middle East; because India is the only world region outside Europe for which most new empirical studies are in English; and because Indian scholars address themselves convincingly to international audiences, Indian history has made a very deep impression on historical studies of pre-modern Eurasia.[12]

1. State Formation. Fifty years ago, history textbooks everywhere reflected the old view that India's ancient states had developed logically from the progress of Aryan conquest, Aryan elite differentiation, and the incorporation of native peoples into an Aryan political and social order that was described in Sanskrit texts. The discovery of the Indus sites had revealed a pre-Vedic culture that either was destroyed by invaders or died by natural causes, but this did not disrupt the linear narrative that began with the influx of the Aryans and led to the rise of Aryan monarchies roughly in the seventh century BCE. Scholars have now discarded this narrative in its entirety. There were in fact no Aryan people (defined either as a race or as a linguistic or ethnic group). Rather, we have a number of texts that reflect the spread of linguistic elements that we combine to fit the classification of an Indo-Aryan language group; and these texts, spread over many centuries and locations, convey a number of ritual, prescriptive, descriptive, and narrative messages, whose authorship, audience, influence, and cultural coherence remain debatable. Archaeological evidence constitutes an increasing proportion of our evidence on ancient India, and it indicates that a great many cultural formations were developing. Many chronological lines of historical change can be proposed now using available evidence, and many of these would have intersected to produce the rise of ancient states. Variously connected and disconnected processes of change visible in archaeological data also implicate the formation of pre-Harappa sites and Indus valley culture. So the timeline of change leading up to the formation of ancient historical societies has been extended back deeper and deeper into prehistory. The rise of "Vedic society" (that is, the many dispersed social settings in which the Vedas were composed) occurred over many more centuries than imagined in 1947, and we now appreciate more fully that the Vedic corpus represents only one set of outcomes of this process, presenting the perspective of one group among many. Showing exactly how these texts pertain to the rise of ancient monarchies is a very difficult task, full of uncertainty (which Kumkum Roy has unraveled masterfully). For ancient India—as for ancient Eurasia as a whole—causal connections and temporal sequences represent historical hypotheses about patterns of change that involved many forces—like climate change—that we cannot see clearly in our evidence. Old assumptions of linear development are quite arbitrary and do not have much support today. Ancient India's many histories involved many different peoples; some intersected, and some remained relatively independent; and they variously implicated different regions.

D.D. Kosambi put ancient history on its current footing by abandoning the search for all-inclusive linear models that account for all our evidence. He began a search that continues today for multiple, open-ended narratives that can account for shifts among various forms of socio-political order. Certainly, increasingly complex forms of order—most importantly, powerful kingdoms and empires—did evolve in the last half of the first millennium BCE, but the shift from "lineage to state" (Romila Thapar) did not constitute a general or comprehensive evolutionary shift toward state formation and away from older forms in India as a whole. Very old and very new forms of social, political, and economic organization coexisted and interacted with one another throughout pre-colonial history. Social change and continuity can and do occur at the same time. Now, instead of seeing ancient India as a unitary territorial entity in which a single civilization evolved as a whole into a single, classical formation, historians focus on its regional and social diversity, on interactions across boundaries, and thus on a multiplicity of concurrent Indian histories. Vedic India was itself a migratory and a regional phenomenon; it moved from the northwest eastward down the Ganga plain. Ancient states arose in the eastern flood plains at the intersection of trade routes. Territorial markers in ancient texts indicate various regional societies, cultures, and political economies interacting with one another. Scholars today highlight their multiplicity and interaction, and especially the role of trade and mobility among regions. In fact, one historical feature that does seem to connect the rise of the Indus valley with the rise of the Mauryan empire is the continuous influence of connective trading activity amidst diversifying regional economies in India, Central Asia, and in the Indian Ocean basin.[13]

2. *State-Society Interaction.* Trade, mobility, and interaction among

specialist groups of various kinds during the production of early states has received increasing attention, and the resulting regional formations of political and social power in ancient India now appear to have developed in what we might call semi-autonomous regions, loosely connected by networks of interaction. This imagery contrasts sharply to that of the 1950s, when the centralized power of the Mauryan empire was the dominant image of ancient India, and Indian civilization appeared to evolve as a unified whole over a millennium following the first Mauryas, reaching its maturity under the Guptas. This traditional formation of a classical India rested on the idea that a consolidation of state elite military power accompanied an entrenchment of Brahmanical socio-cultural power. This idea has been radically modified. Numerous discontinuities disrupted what became known in the nineteenth century as the classical age. Institutions and political territories changed dramatically, and they took on the appearance of classical stability only for relatively short periods—most effectively perhaps in prescriptive texts themselves— and even then only in regions of the northern plains. Many people, regions, and historical trends in ancient India fall outside the scope of this classical narrative, and trends in urban development and social change even in the core imperial territories of the Mauryas and Guptas moved in various directions. Even granting that classical texts might reflect social reality for some people under the Guptas, as Romila Thapar observed in 1966, the idea of a "Classical Age .... is true only in so far as we speak of the upper classes, amongst whom living standards reached a peak never before attained..."[14] This elite clearly achieved its new power and wealth through state institutions that commanded revenues from agriculture, war, manufacturing, pastoral groups, and trade. How states elites achieved their power and reproduced it in their relations to other social groups remains a subject of debate.

Inscriptional evidence permits new empirical precision in early-medieval history, beginning with the Guptas. Hundreds of thousands of stone and copper-plate inscriptions have been collected and catalogued by the Archaeological Survey of India. Each is a fragment of an institutional discourse; it represents a single moment in a chain of statements and transactions. Each requires that a scholar bring to its reading a framework of analysis that is not described in any contemporary text, to reconstruct the transactional complex in which the inscriptions were composed. Who wrote this text? Why? Who were they talking to and for what purpose? Was anyone listening and to what effect? Such questions lie at the base of primary research in medieval Indian history. Most inscriptions record land

and revenue grants to temples and Brahmans by dynasts and officials, and their statist, imperious language bolsters the idea that the answers to these basic questions lie in the operational interior of medieval states. The territorial spread of inscriptions and thus of transactions that they record indicate a rapid multiplication of states after the Guptas, and, by roughly 1000 CE, inscription-producing states covered most of India's agrarian lowlands. How were these states organized, and how did they transact with the various groups that lived within reach of their power? That is the central issue in medieval history, today as it was in 1920.

In the 1950s K.A. Nilakanta Sastri argued that the Cholas had built a strong—"almost Byzantine royalty" (1955, 447)—following the disappearance of the Guptas. The Chola state, he argued, administered its territory with a combination of bureaucratic taxation, feudatory control, and Brahman and temple land grants, forming an imperial system of state power derived from a Gupta model that might have migrated south via the Pallavas of Kanchipuram, who had been Gupta vassals. In the 1960s R.S. Sharma argued to the contrary that post-Gupta states represented a medieval formation of Indian feudalism, that might presuppose a strong state in the past, as under the Guptas, but comprised an array of feudal regimes based on land grants to Brahman landed elites, who were the Indian analogue of European feudal lords. This concept of Indian feudalism was intended to encompass the Chola case and to produce an all-India model that included many regional variants. Its superiority to the model proposed by Nilakanta Sastri lay in its grasp of state-and-society within one formation of power that included both ritual-religious and coercive-political elements, and in its adaptability to all medieval settings in which Brahmans and kings joined forces. Since the 1970s regional historians have developed alternatives to R.S. Sharma s model, but they have not replaced it. Herman Kulke (1995, 1-47) has rightly concluded that today there is no consensus concerning the plausibility of an "Indian model" of medieval state organization. Social forces that influenced state-society relations—and complicate any definition of the institutional boundaries that would enclose what we might want to call "the state" in the medieval period—differed markedly among regions and over time. In Rajasthan, warrior lineages constituted states. In Tamilnadu, gentry farming clans were powerful. In Orissa ritual centers seem to have held the balance of power at times. In Chhattisgarh and Chotanagpur tribal chieftains held sway. A shifting diversity of social forces produced states of different kinds in the many regions of medieval

India, and, as a result, India is beginning to look much less like a unified, traditional civilization and much more like a rapidly changing, differentiated, and mobile medieval territory, at least as diverse internally as western and eastern Eurasia in its range of institutional forms and historical dynamics.

3. Modes of Production. The concept of Indian feudalism covers more than state power; it refers to a "mode of production," a theoretical construct in Marxian theory, a historical structure of social relations, coercive powers, and physical means of production in which the state is but one institutional component. To say that "feudalism" applies to India's medieval mode of production implies that India potentially could have participated in the same developmental trajectory as Europe, thus that India had the possibility of moving into a capitalist mode of production on its own, as did Europe during the centuries after 1500 in what is now called the early modern period. Marx denied this potentiality. Instead, he theorized that India, like China, was constrained from making autonomous progress toward capitalism by the presence of overbearing Asiatic states that, he thought, dominated India's native mode of production, repressed commercial groups, usurped property rights, and thus prevented a structural transformation in a capitalist direction. The invention of "Indian feudalism" thus marks a break with old Marxian theory and seems to open the historical possibility that India could have generated capitalism on its own, rather than having to wait for the British empire, as Marx envisioned. But R.S. Sharma and Irfan Habib have combined to show why this potentiality did not materialize. They argue that Indian feudalism expanded its reach during centuries of declining trade and urbanism following the end of Gupta imperium. They maintain, furthermore, that the rise of urbanism and commercialism after 1200 was accomplished by massive state revenue extraction from subsistence cultivating communities. The Mughal state thus formed an approximation to Marx's Asiatic mode of production, preventing the indigenous rise of capitalism in India.

All the empirical supports for this understanding of conditions in medieval India are today under vigorous reconsideration, which opens the door to a most lively academic discourse concerning India's historical dynamism and its position in the world economy. To what extent did traditional social organization, caste strictures, and Brahmanical, temple-centered ritualism stifle economic, political, and social dynamism in India? How much power did states wield over productive resources, and to what effect? In discussing these questions, regional diversity in economic and political development and the relative autonomy of social forces working outside state control—merchants, farmers, pastoral groups, tribals, warrior lineages, and religious sects—play a much larger role than they did ten years ago. India's medieval political economy seems to have been much more dynamic, adaptable, and changeable than would appear possible in the models of pre-modern state and culture that we inherited. Harbans Mukhia has argued, for instance, that India did not have any version of feudalism, because peasant farmers in India were, in general, relatively free of state control—certainly as compared to their counterparts in Europe, China, and Japan. The land was fertile and relatively open for peasant colonization, and peasants could simply move to set up communities if they felt burdened with state demands. In 1600 *Ā'īn-i-Akbarī* statistics indicate that about half the land that would be farmed three centuries later, in 1900, was under the plow in the Mughal heartland, with great variations among regions: highs in Mughal Uttar Pradesh, Gujarat, and Panjab ran over 85%, and lows dipped under 29% in Champaner, 28% in Rohilkhand, and 8% in Sindh Sagar. For the Gangetic plain and Bengal as a whole, James R. Hagen argues that the proportion of cultivated land to total land area was approximately 30% in 1600, 50% in 1700, 50% in 1800, 65% in 1910, and 70% in 1980, so that cultivated acreage more than doubled between 1600 and 1910, with more than half of that increase occurring before 1700.[15] Such figures indicate a very dramatic change in agrarian conditions after 1500, which may well have been propelled more by aggressive peasant farming communities and by expansive commercial and manufacturing groups than by overbearing states. Such dramatic changes are hard to imagine within the traditional structures of Indian feudalism. Other models help to imagine the possibilities. Burton Stein for instance argues that, in the peninsula, medieval peasant communities formed the structural segments of medieval political systems, held together in state territories as much by ritual and commercial networks surrounding temples and towns as by dynastic military power. In this view, religious institutions and state power did not combine to form the "almost Byzantine" system described by Nilakanta Sastri. Rather, peasant, merchant, warrior, tribal, manufacturing, and other groups maintained significant degrees of autonomy and freedom of action. Surjit Singh, Amalendu Guha, and others have now made it clear that social forces in the hills and other territories outside the control of inscription-producing medieval states had their own dynamism and contributed significantly to the historical process of change in regions of medieval India.[16]

4. Early Modernity. Precolonial history is breaking out of its mold. Everyday social, political, and economic life in ancient and medieval India now seem less rigidly controlled by rulers and religious traditions than they appeared to be twenty years ago. As a result, the habit of dividing pre-colonial millennia into the hoary, ancient, and classical Hindu epochs and the more recent centuries of Muslim power is now archaic. In politics, the interactive powers of mobile warrior lineages created a strong continuity between state organization under the Gurjara-Pratiharas and the Mughals, and it also defined a political territory running from central India up into central Asia that remained salient for Indian history all across the medieval centuries. In religion, clear lines between "Muslim" and "Hindu" were not established until the colonial period, and both these labels cover a vast and changeable diversity of cultural forms in medieval centuries. Dividing "Hindu" from "Muslim" periods of history is therefore inappropriate.

A new period of Indian history is also emerging—not without opposition—to capture conditions of change roughly from 1500 to the nineteenth century and the colonial period. Indian early modernity is being discussed increasingly in the context of an early modern world system that embraces both India and Europe. The advantage of this periodization is that it allows historians to focus on the interaction of forces that transformed India so dramatically from the beginning of the Mughal era to the rise of the Company raj. Until recently, the end of "medieval India" came in three phases: the rise and fall of the Mughal empire, the eighteenth century interlude, and the expansion of British conquest. Today, as change in the conditions of everyday life attract more attention, the eighteenth century is appearing less as a period of imperial transition and more as a period of maturing, long-term transformations. Regional histories began to produce modern social and economic conditions. Muzaffar Alam and Chetan Singh have shown how regions of political economy in Mughal Punjab, Awadh, and Bengal interacted with changing urban and rural societies to form territories of history that span the Mughal age and the eighteenth century. Histories of Rohilkhand, Bihar, Marwar, Karnataka, and Bengal (by Iqbal Husain, Kumkum Chatterjee, G.D. Sharma, K.S. Sivanna, Richard Eaton, and Sushil Chaudhuri) have put imperial histories into a new, long-term, regional perspective. Now the fall of the Mughals seems much less catastrophic because the eighteenth century has been discovered to have been an age of social and cultural creativity and, in places, efflorescence. The empire did not collapse leaving disorder behind.

Rather, it gave way to regional formations of power that developed under its administration and on its periphery. Eighteenth century history has stimulated a most lively scholarship in the past fifteen years, in part because it benefits from documentation in many languages and witnessed the rise of regional polities that bridge the Mughal and colonial periods. V. Narayana Rao, David Shulman, and Sanjay Subrahmanyam have combined their diverse linguistic skills to explore the multi-lingual source materials that abound for early modern history, which make its historiography most challenging and rich. Early modern social forces developed not only under the influence of the Mughals, but also within expanding circuits of trade and migration that connected India and Europe within a new world economy (Sugata Bose). Eighteenth century political and economic innovations, as well as social and cultural change, may indeed comprise the onset of Indian modernity and nationality before colonialism.

NOTES

1. 1896. London and New York: Longmans Green.
2. For more detail, see Romila Thapar (1997); also David Ludden, ed. 1996. *Making India Hindu: Community, Conflict, and the Politics of Democracy in India*. Delhi: Oxford Univ. Press.
3. 1946. *The Discovery of India*. New York and Calcutta: John Day and Signet Press.
4. Zaidi, A. Moin, ed. 1985. *A Tryst With Destiny: A Study of Economic Policy Resolutions of the Indian National Congress Passed During the Last 100 Years*. New Delhi: Publication Dept., Indian Institute of Applied Political Research, 54.
5. See *References* for citations. To accommodate this essay to its size constraints, I limited myself to monographs and the most critical collections of essays.
6. Thapar, Romila. 1992. "The Contribution of D.D. Kosambi to Indology." In *Interpreting Early India*, ed. Romila Thapar, 89-113. Delhi: Oxford Univ. Press.
7. Its value has been accentuated since 1984 during struggles over the past and the future of sacred sites. See Neeladri Bhattacharya. 1991. "Myth, History, and the Politics of Ramjanmbhumi." In *Anatomy of a Confrontation: The Babri Masjid-Ramjanmbhumi Issue*, ed. Sarvepall Gopal, 122-137. Delhi: Viking. M. Athar Ali spoke for his profession when he said in his Presidential Address to the Indian Historical Congress, "We should not try to read back our present-national sentiments into those of the people of a millennium earlier." 1990. "Encounter and Efflorescence: Genesis of the Medieval Civilization." *Social Scientist*, 1:14-28.

8. Notable contributions include those by Indu Banga (Punjab), Sushil Chaudhuri (Bengal), P.M. Joshi, A.R. Kulkarni, and Hiroshi Fukuzawa (the Deccan), Amalendu Guha (Assam), A. Appadorai, T.V. Mahalingam, A. Krishnaswami, Noboru Karashima, and Burton Stein (the southern peninsula), G.D. Sharma (Rajasthan), Surjit Sinha (central India), K.S. Sivanna (Karnataka), K. Veluthat (Kerala), and M.R. Tarafdar (Bengal).

9. See the work of Indu Banga, R. Champakalakshmi, and Satish Chandra.

10. See also the work of A. Appadorai, D.N. Jha, R. Champakalakshmi, A.I. Chicherov, and Burton Stein for other important contributions in earlier medieval and peninsular economic history.

11. I have not included the literary or art history in this survey of the field, because they are typically not represented within university departments of history.

12. See recent books by Janet Abu-Lughod, Henri Claessen, and Immanuel Wallerstein.

13. Joseph Schwartzberg s atlas is the best compendium of geographical information.

14. *A History of India*, vol. 1. London: Pelican. 136.

15. Habib (1995, 91-92) and Moosvi (1987, 39-73). See also James R. Hagen. 1988. "Gangetic Fields: An Approach to Agrarian History Through Agriculture and the Natural Environment, 1600-1970." Unpublished.

16. For some debates see Mukhia (1993), Karashima (1992), and Narayanan (1976).

REFERENCES

Abu-Lughod, Janet L. 1989. *Before European Hegemony: The World System A.D. 1250-1350*. New York: Oxford Univ. Press.

Alam, Muzaffar. 1986. *The Crisis of Empire in Mughal North India, Awadh and the Punjab, 1707-1748*. Delhi: Oxford Univ. Press.

Appadorai, A. 1981. *Economic Conditions in South India (1000-1500 AD.)*. New York:

Arasaratnam, S. 1994. *Maritime India in the Seventeenth Century*. Delhi: Oxford Univ. Press.

Athar Ali, M. 1968. *Mughal Nobility Under Aurangzeb*. Bombay: Asia.

Banga, Indu. 1978. *Agrarian System of the Sikhs: Late 18th and Early 19th Century*. New Delhi: Manohar.

Banga, Indu, ed. 1991. *The City in Indian History: Urban Demography, Society, and Politics*, New Delhi: South Asia.

Basham, A.I. 1954. *The Wonder That Was India: A Survey of the Culture of the Indian Sub-Continent Before the Coming of the Muslims*. New York: Macmillian.

Bose, Sugata, ed. 1990. *South Asia and World Capitalism*, Delhi: Oxford Univ. Press.

Champakalakshmi, R. and S. Gopal, eds. 1996. *Tradition, Dissent, and Ideology: Essays in Honor of Romila Thapar*, Delhi: Oxford Univ. Press.

Chandra, Satish. 1986. *The Eighteenth Century in India: Its Economy and the Role of the Marathas, the Jats, the Sikhs, and the Afghans*. Calcutta: Centre for Studies in Social Sciences.

———. 1979. *Parties and Politics at the Mughal Court.* New Delhi: People's Publishing House.

Chatterjee, Kumkum. 1996. *Merchants, Politics, and Society in Early Modern India: Bihar 1733-1870*. Leiden: Brill.

Chattopadhyaya, Brajadulal. 1994. *The Making of Early Medieval India*. New Delhi: Oxford Univ. Press.

Chaudhuri, K.N. 1990. *Asia Before Europe: Economy and Civilization of the Indian Ocean from the Rise of Islam to 1750*. Cambridge: Cambridge Univ. Press.

———. 1985. *Trade and Civilization in the Indian Ocean: An Economic History from the Rise of Islam until 1750*. Cambridge: Cambridge Univ. Press.

Chaudhuri, Sushil. 1995. *From Prosperity to Decline: Eighteenth Century Bengal*. New Delhi: Manohar.

———. 1975. *Trade and Commercial Organization in Bengal, 1650-1720*. Calcutta: Firma K.L. Mukhopadhyay.

Claessen, Henri J.M. and Peter Skolnik, eds. 1981. *The Study of the State*, New York: Mouton.

Claessen, Henri J.M. and Peter van de Velde, eds. 1986. *Early State Dynamics*, Leiden: Brill.

Dale, Stephen Frederic. 1994. *Indian Merchants and Eurasian Trade, 1600-1750*. Cambridge: Cambridge Univ. Press.

Eaton, Richard M. 1978. *The Sufis of Bijapur, 1300-1700: Social Role of Sufis in Medieval India*. Princeton: Princeton Univ. Press.

———. 1994. *The Rise of Islam and the Bengal Frontier, 1204-1760*. Berkeley: Univ. of California Press.

Fukazawa, Hiroshi. 1991. *The Medieval Deccan: Peasants, Social Systems, and States (1500- 1700)*. New Delhi: Oxford Univ. Press.

Gokhale, B.G. 1977. *Surat in the 17th Century: A Study in Urban History of Pre-Modern India*. London: Curzon.

Guha, Amalendu. 1991. *Medieval and Early Colonial Assam: Society, Policy, Economy*. Calcutta: Bagchi.

Habib, Irfan. 1963. *The Agrarian System of Mughal India: (1556-1707)*. Bombay: Asia.

———. 1982. *An Atlas of Mughal Empire: Political and Economic Maps with Notes, Bibliography, and Index*. Delhi: Oxford Univ Press.

———. 1995. *Essays in Indian History: Towards a Marxist Perception*. Delhi: Manohar.

Husain, Iqbal. 1994. *The Ruhela Chieftaincies: The Rise and Fall of Ruhela Power in India in the Eighteenth Century*. Delhi: Oxford Univ. Press.

Jha, D.N. 1980. *Studies in Early Indian Economic History*. Delhi: Anupama.

Karashima, Noboru. 1992. *Towards a New Formation: South Indian Society Under Vijayanagar Rule*. Delhi: Oxford Univ. Press.

Kosambi, D.D. 1965. *The Culture and Civilization of Ancient India*. London: Routledge and Kegan Paul.

Krishnaswami, A. 1964. *The Tamil Country Under Vijayanagar*. Annamalainagar: Annamalai University.

Kulkarni, A.R., M.A. Nayeem, and T.R. de Souza, eds. 1996. *Medieval Deccan History: Commemoration Volume in Honor of Purshottam Mahadeo Joshi*, Bombay: Popular Prakashan.

Kulke, Hermann, ed. 1995. *The State in India, 1000-1700*, Delhi: Oxford Univ. Press.

Liu, Xinru. 1988. *Ancient India and Ancient China: Trade and Religious Exchanges, AD 1-600*. Delhi: Oxford Univ. Press.

Mahalingam, T.V. 1955. *South Indian Polity*. Madras: Univ. of Madras.

Majumdar, R.C. 1968. *Expansion of the Aryan Culture in Eastern India*. Imphal: Atombapu Research Centre.

Majumdar, R.C., gen. ed. *The History and Culture of the Indian People*, Bombay: Bharatiya Vidya Bhavan.

Malloo, Kamala. 1987. *The History of Famines in Rajputana*. Udaipur: Himanshu.

McLanc, John R. 1993. *Land and Local Kingship in Eighteenth-Century Bengal*. Cambridge: Cambridge Univ. Press.

Moosvi, Shireen. 1987, *The Economy of the Mughal Empire, c. 1595: A Statistical Study*. Delhi: Oxford Univ. Press.

Mukhia, Harbans. 1993. *Perspectives on Medieval History*. New Delhi: Viking.

Mukhia, Harbans, ed. 1985. *Feudalism and Non-European Societies*, London: Frank Cass.

Narayana Rao, Velcheru, David Shulman and Sanjay Subrahmanyam. 1992. *Symbols of Substance: Court and State in Nayaka Period Tamilnadu*. Delhi: Oxford Univ. Press.

Narayanan, M.G.S. 1976. *Reinterpretations of South Indian History*. Trivandrum: College Book House.

Nehru, Jawaharlal. 1946. *The Discovery of India*. New York and Calcutta: John Day and Signet Press.

Nilakanta Sastri, K.A. 1955. *The Cholas*. Madras: Univ. of Madras.

Perlin, Frank. 1993. *Invisible City: Monetary, Administrative, and Popular Infrastructures in Asia and Europe, 1500-1900*. Aldershot: Variorum.

————. 1994. *Unbroken Landscape: Commodity, Category, Sign and Identity: Their Production as Myth and Knowledge from 1500*. Aldershot: Variorum.

Raychaudhuri, Tapan. 1969. *Bengal Under Akbar and Jahangir*. Delhi: Munshiram Manoharlal.

Raychaudhuri, Tapan and Irfan Habib, eds. 1982. *The Cambridge Economic History of India*, vol. 1, Cambridge: Cambridge Univ. Press.

Richards, John F., ed. 1987. *The Imperial Monetary System of Mughal India*, Delhi: Oxford Univ. Press.

Roy, Kumkum. 1994. *The Emergence of Monarchy in North India, Eighth-Fourth Centuries B.C.: As Reflected in the Brahmanical Tradition.* Delhi: Oxford Univ. Press.

Sarkar, Jadunath. 1978. *Glimpses of Medieval Bihar Economy: Thirteenth to Mid-Eighteenth Century.* Calcutta: Ratna Prakashan.

———. 1979. *House of Shivaji: Studies and Documents of Maratha History.* New Delhi: Orient Longman.

———. 1952. *Shivaji and His Times.* Calcutta: Sarkar.

Schwartzberg, Joseph E., ed. 1978. *Historical Atlas of India,* Chicago: Univ. of Chicago Press.

Sen, S.N. 1976. *Administrative System of the Marathas.* Calcutta: Bagchi.

Sharma, G.D. 1977. *Rajput Polity: A Study of Politics and Administration of the State of Marwar, 1638-1749.* Delhi: Manohar.

Sharma, R.S. 1980. *Indian Feudalism.* Delhi: Macmillan.

———. 1983. *Material Culture and Social Formations in Ancient India.* Delhi: Macmillian.

Shivanna, K.S. 1992. *The Agrarian System of Karnataka (1336-1761).* Mysore: Prasaranga.

Siddiqui, Iqtidar Husain. 1983. *Mughal Relations with the Indian Ruling Elite.* New Delhi: Munshiram Manoharlal.

Singh, Chetan. 1991. *Region and Empire: Panjab in the Eighteenth Century.* Delhi: Oxford Univ. Press.

Sinha, Surajit, ed. 1987. *Tribal Polities and State Systems in Precolonial Eastern and North Eastern India,* Calcutta: Bagchi.

Stein, Burton. 1980. *Peasant State and Society in Medieval South India.* Delhi: Oxford Univ. Press.

———. 1989. *Vijayanagara.* Cambridge: Cambridge Univ. Press.

Subrahmanyam, Sanjay. 1990. *The Political Economy of Commerce: Southern India 1500-1650.* Cambridge: Cambridge Univ. Press.

Tarafdar, M.R. 1965. *Husain Shahi Bengal, 1494-1538 A.D.: A Socio-Political Study.* Dacca: Asiatic Society of Pakistan.

Thapar, Romila. 1961. *Asoka and the Decline of the Mauryas.* London: Oxford Univ. Press.

———. 1966. *A History of India,* vol. 1. London: Pelican.

———. 1978. *Ancient Indian Social History.* New Delhi: Orient Longman.

———. 1984. *From Lineage to State: Social Formation on the Mid-First Millennium B.C. in the Ganges Valley.* Bombay.

———. 1997. *The Tyranny of Labels.* New Delhi: Hashmi.

Veluthat, Kesavan. 1993. *The Political Structure of Early Medieval South India.* New Delhi: Orient Longman.

Wallerstein, Immanuel. 1989. *The Modern World-System III; The Second Era of Great Expansion of the Capitalist World-Economy, 1730-1840.* San Diego, CA: Academic Press.

Wink, Andre. 1990, 1997. *Al-Hind: The Making of the Indo-Islamic World.* vol. 1 *Early Medieval and the Expansion of Islam 7th - 11th Centuries.* vol. 2 *The Slave Kings and the Islamic Conquest 11th - 13th Centuries.* Leiden: Brill.

History (Colonial and Post-Colonial)

FRANK F. CONLON

"Historians of the peoples of the sub-continent have in the past performed rather like isolated guerrilla fighters in a jungle, often performing feats of individual brilliance, but lacking discipline and only vaguely aware of the part they should play in a general campaign."

C. H. Philips, 1961[1]

"Modern Indian history offers God's plenty to the scholar since the subject is so important, the material so abundant and the accepted version so improbable."

John Gallagher, 1963[2]

"But the day of the fake Indian history is over."

Ashin Das Gupta, 1976[3]

"There is a particular vigour in the Indian history-making of our day that is marvellously stimulating."

Burton Stein, 1990[4]

History has been described as a conversation—a dialogue between the present and the past and, by extension, between historians and their evidence, and their audience as well.[5] In the case of the history of modern India, that conversation has been transformed during the past half-century with growing numbers of participants and broadening range of subjects, sources, and interpretations. The very vigor of this development has meant that the analogy of dialogue has sometimes been supplemented by that of argument, occasionally of a shouting match.

History matters for modern India, yet modern Indian history has not mattered very much for history as a discipline.[6] On the one hand concepts of India's history have provided powerful symbols for the cultural politics of Indian nationalism and the consequent "nationalist" celebration of the uniquely Indian past. For Jawaharlal

Nehru the very idea of the Indian nation was grounded in history: "Nationalism is essentially a group memory of past achievements, traditions and experiences" (Nehru 1959, 391). Furthermore, the practice of India's history has raised reflective questions. The historian Ranajit Guha has argued that the idea of an Indian nation itself had required the production of an *Indian* historiography to serve as a means for autonomous reclamation of India's past (and future) from colonial power (Guha 1988, 56-58). According to Guha, such a history was not merely a common-sense shared memory of the past, but an intellectual exercise of power utilizing the creation of knowledge as a means to domination and self-rule. Nehru's conception was a thoughtful example of a popular conventional appreciation of history, a reading of the past in order that there might be a "discovery of India." Guha's insights display an advanced critical consciousness of historiographical practice and epistemo- logical analysis. Both perspectives are part of history, but Nehru's perspective is associated with the conventional interest in India's past, while Guha's will be of greater concern to professional academic historians.[7]

This essay surveys the development of the academic historical study of modern India and reflects on its career and significance in India and abroad. What Nehru entitled the "discovery of India"—a growing realization among Indians of a historical heritage—was paralleled in the half-century since India's *swaraj* by a rise in India, and elsewhere, of an academic discipline of historical research and teaching focused upon modern India, particularly on the phenomena of colonialism and nationalism.

Most of this historical efflorescence represented applications of the methodology of a discipline imported from the West to the South Asian field. Modern Indian history remained almost entirely at the margins of a still Euro-American-centered historical discipline, contributing perhaps a diversity of subject matter but no profound alteration to general historiographical practice until, at least, very recently.

During the nineteenth century in western Europe the discipline of history had developed as a distinct intellectual enterprise divorced from literature and philosophy. The concepts and institutions of history as a professional academic practice were transferred to India only gradually. At the same time, apart from a presence in some chapters in the history of European colonial expansion, Indian history remained little studied in the West. Prior to this century, most historical writings on India either were produced by British colonial officials preparing official papers (Guha 1988, 9), or by retired colonial officials re-visiting issues of policy through chronicles of politics: The "men and events" of the British *raj* (Philips 1961, 2, 8-9; Spear 1961, 408; cf. Stokes 1961). In British-ruled India, history as a subject did enter education during the nineteenth century, but formal instruction in the subject was limited, and then focused principally upon the past of England or pre-colonial India. Indian teachers of history were encouraged to follow metropolitan models of instruction. For example, in 1914 the University of Bombay hosted Professor Ramsey Muir, of Manchester, who "gave a series of lectures and also held a number of conferences with college teachers in Bombay on the subject of the teaching of history (Dongerkery 1957, 60)." Historical research on modern India did not flourish. British Indian administrators neither appreciated nor encouraged applications in India of the professional conventions of critical study and writing when the topic was colonial history. Official defensiveness against nationalist critique was compounded with stereotypes of Indians—in particular educated Indians—as self-seeking and parochial. Research access to archives thus was regarded as a potential source of "abuse" and was discouraged. In 1921, for example, the Government of Bombay in a new handbook of archival records stipulated that only "*bona fide* historical research workers" could obtain access to the Secretariat Record Office, and then with constraints:

"The Government of Bombay will do all that lies in their power, due regard being had to the public interest, to facilitate researches in their records *for proper purposes* (emphasis added). But such researches can, of course, be allowed only for the scientific study of historical facts, and not for investigations directed toward personal objects." (Kindersley 1921, i.)[8]

Institutionally, the study of modern Indian history emerged rather slowly in the latter decades of British rule in India. The government-sponsored (and dominated) Indian Historical Records Commission commenced in 1919. An all-Indian organization for Indian professional historians, which would become the Indian History Congress (IHC), commenced only in 1935. The IHC contributed to an institutionalization of academic historical study by encouraging a sense of community among academic historians in India and planning publication of a comprehensive history of India (Prasad 1963, 153; Sen 1963, 24-26).[9] Indian history found no more support in Britain itself; by the late 1930s "there were still no departments or posts in British universities offering a career specifically in Indian history." (Philips 1995, 7-8)

Perhaps because history was received in India as a western discipline, an emphasis upon transferring to Indian subjects the presumed rigor of European practice continued well beyond the end of colonial rule. K.A. Nilakanta Sastri's *Historical Method in Relation to Indian History* (1956) opened with invocations of noted nineteenth century European historians.[10] A decade later, R.C. Majumdar commenced his lectures on Indian historiography with praise of the German historians Niebuhr and Ranke. In emphasizing their "scrupulous regard for truth," Majumdar seemed to suggest that that quality was wanting among some Indian members of the profession (Majumdar 1970, 4). Colonial habits of mind did not die easily.

The coming of *swaraj* in 1947 did not produce immediately a new history of modern India, but it created the setting for an expansion of historical studies and the possibility of new approaches. Free India's development included the growth of higher education, which included an opening of fresh opportunities for academic posts that stimulated a demand for Ph.D. degrees in history. Young Indian scholars could pursue studies in Indian universities or, at greater cost, in Britain, particularly at the University of London's School of Oriental and African Studies (SOAS). C.H. Philips, the modern India historian at SOAS envisioned a conjunction of necessity and benefit in such educational ties for Indian history:

Above all we have come to appreciate that in their urgent task of creating a stronger sense of historical consciousness the new nations of the sub-continent will need more trained historians, and that in the thin years immediately ahead, when their nation-building services will continue to absorb all the trained men and women who can be found, it is a primary responsibility of historians and university departments of history in western countries to help to train and to encourage and support their Indian, Pakistani and Ceylonese colleagues (Philips 1961, 3).

Perhaps Philips was speaking really to a British academic audience rather than potential "customers" in the subcontinent since Indian history continued not to occupy a very prominent place in the British academy in the years after 1947. As one British historian remarked in retrospect, "Overseas history, as a *parvenu*, was still obliged to validate itself through a minute analysis of the lapidary prose of India's law-givers and proconsuls. The people of India often emerged simply as a stage rabble, to be speedily defeated and pacified" (Bayly 1979, 22). "Foreign" connections and degrees could convey advantages to ambitious "London-returned" Indian academics, yet a fair number of their research projects on modern Indian history were conventional in conception and based primarily upon English-language records, whether read at the India Office Library in London or the National Archives of India. The prestige of the English language, and the relative lack of research apparatus in most Indian languages, tended to perpetuate this pattern.

Robert Crane, himself a pioneer advocate of Indian history in the United States, observed, "...there has been all too little writing [by Indians] of Indian history." Crane thought it "more or less understandable that western scholars have tended to be confined to English-language sources" but "not at all understandable that Indian scholars should be tied to the same kind of language materials" (Crane 1963, 46).[11] Crane's comments were directed at the Indian students of modern Indian history. Indian historical scholarship on the pre-modern fields demonstrated a sophisticated use of indigenous sources, as in the emerging center of Mughal studies at Aligarh Muslim University. New centers of modern Indian historical study did emerge in India, particularly in the new Jawaharlal Nehru University and in Calcutta under Professor N.K. Sinha. In the 1960s Sinha, disturbed by what he saw to be a continuation of the emphasis on British administrative history, observed that now Indian historians "should not have the feeling that we have gathered after the reapers. The climate of values, ideas and opinions is now so very different that Indian historians could write Indian history anew" (Sinha 1963-64, 36).

In North America, Australia, and Britain, the study of modern Indian history began to grow from the mid-1950s in conjunction with a broader phenomenon of higher education expansion. The opening of new universities and government support for non-western area studies created new opportunities for historical research and teaching on India. Initially, in the United States, this extension coincided with a trend in the historical discipline of accommodating insights and questions from the social sciences, a process that was reinforced with the establishment of area studies programs with the support of major foundations and the U. S. Department of Education Title VI funding. Graduate training in Indian history became increasingly marked by cross-disciplinary linkages to social sciences, including social and cultural anthropology, sociology, political science, and economics. For the most part this did not mean that young historians merely tried to appropriate, for example "modernization theory" or concepts of "development," rather historical enquiry was broadened. The late Burton Stein once said to his seminar: "You don't become an anthropologist; you just let anthropology lead you to ask new questions of the evidence."[12] Some years later, in a prospectus introducing a seminar for college teachers on "Anthropological Models and the Study of Indian History," Bernard Cohn observed: "Without history, social scientists cannot deal with social and cultural variations found in South Asia, nor develop adequate theories of change to comprehend what is happening in the successor states which emerged out of colonial India. Without anthropological models the historian can only deal with surface features of the societies of South Asia or narrowly restrict himself to western based conceptions of economics and politics, which obfuscate and mislead students wishing to understand modern South Asia"(Cohn 1980).

The re-thinking and disaggregating of received conceptual models extended even to India's geography. The sheer size and complexity of India proved a daunting challenge to detailed historical research. While lectures and seminars continued to be designed with a focus on "India" or "South Asia," historians manifested a growing concern in research and publication concentrating upon one of the linguistically defined regions of the subcontinent. This may have reflected India's own recent realignment of state boundaries on linguistic lines as well as illustrated a growing knowledge of Indian languages. In the United States, the introduction of the Title VI fellowship programs meant that young scholars were expected to study modern Indian languages (Lambert 1962). The scholars, at least in theory, would no longer have to wait until reaching India to utilize these languages because the new U.S. Library of Congress program under Public Law 480 began supplying a broad range of Indian publications in all major Indian languages to American university libraries. Although not all newly minted historians fully exploited this training in Indian languages, the dominant expectation in the 1960s was that most new research projects would have a regional emphasis and at least some documentary basis in Indian-language materials. Regions had captured the scholarly imagination. Regions, it was felt, were somehow more "real" as venues for understanding Indian society and history.[13]

This "search for the real" in social science and historical studies of India in the 1950s and 1960s was sometimes too dominated by the influence of various theories that were fashionable at the moment.

The contemporary interest in the 1950s of foundations and governments in the process of "modernization" of "traditional societies" held implications for the study of history (cf. Lerner 1958, Black 1960). Given the influence of concepts of modernizing transformations of non-western societies, presumably in a shape recognizably western in style, studies of colonial India might turn on themes of "British impact" and "Indian response." The potential distortions that such themes might suggest of a dynamic and active "West" stimulating an inert and stagnant "East" were, however, limited by two complementary factors. The residual empiricism of conventional historiography encouraged investigations of "what really happened," which soon uncovered Indian actors as subjects. Research appearing in the early 1960s by Bernard Cohn (1987) and Robert Frykenberg (1965) called into question the degree to which British rule had changed India at all. Also, in the context of inter-disciplinary area studies training, historians were, as Burton Stein had suggested, asking new questions about Indian society and culture in the colonial period, and thus introducing a research shift from colonial policy and administrative initiatives to indigenous institutions and relationships. If there were a weakness in this shift, it lay in the under-development of academic historical research on India. Too few scholars were conducting too few studies. A few, highly visible, influential studies of specific localities and regions were made to stand for the entire subcontinent.[14]

As the multi-disciplinary area studies paradigm evolved, it manifested a distinctive concern for the diversity of India and a growing sense that western models and conceptual categories were insufficient to comprehend the richness of India's historical experience. Did the fact that there was "so much to learn" about India then present western scholars with a risk of becoming enmeshed in "Indian exceptionalism" and becoming distanced, if not alienated, from the core of discipline of history and its European roots? At the time of my training in the early 1960s, the history department of the University of Minnesota required that all graduate students complete a year-long pro-seminar on "Readings in the Great Historians." Needless to say, no non-European historians turned up in our readings. Those of us specializing in the history of India or China were expected to come to terms with such great historians of the West as Ranke, Stubbs, Michelet, and Croce. It was an interesting experience, not unlike visiting another culture. But it was an important visit since, in North America, few academic appointments offered a chance to teach exclusively Indian history. Most young India scholars anticipated that future academic employment would include the "opportunity" of lecturing also on European history or "western civilization."[15]

Academic expansion in Australia also enlarged the study of

modern Indian history. A research program at Australian National University, commencing in 1960 under Professor D.A. Low, addressed all-Indian history through the regional prism:

It is only at a rather rarefied level that modern Indian history may be said to comprise a single all-Indian story. At other levels marked variations exist, and if we are to proceed to understanding it further, regional studies, within the orbit of an awareness of the overall story, are now quite vital (Low, ed. 1968, 5).[16]

In Britain modern Indian history grew during the 1960s, also in a context of academic expansion. Although training in modern languages was available at SOAS, the emphasis in doctoral studies upon getting on with the research project itself provided a contrast with American practice, where often two or three years of course-work (including language) preceded the dissertation research and writing. The India Office Library was not far away.

British historiography of modern India was also taking "the regional turn." C. H. Philips expressed reservations about a "prevailing tendency ... to view India's history from the center and through the eyes of the central government, neglecting the development of society in the provinces, districts and towns" (Philips 1961, 3). New history projects focused on regions or localities, particularly when exploring the vagaries of Indian nationalism. In 1963 the historian John Gallagher had mentioned in passing that the methods that Lewis Namier had applied to eighteenth century English politics "might well be applied to the study of the Congress" (Gallagher 1963, 50). He prescribed region-based analysis since "the basic factor in modern Indian political history is that the country has been developing at uneven rates of change. This is true of one region as compared with another, and it is true of one group in a region as compared with another" (55). Gallagher concluded "in terms of power and change combined, nationalism appears as the continuation of imperialism by other means" (56). This represented an early statement of the underlying thesis of what came to be labeled, somewhat inaccurately, as "the Cambridge school." The recognized opening of this new perspective came with publication of Anil Seal's *Emergence of Indian Nationalism: Competition and Collaboration in the Later Nineteenth Century* (Seal 1968). Seal proposed a disaggregation of Indian nationalism and, in the tradition of Namier, found competing interests underlying much of what had till then been regarded as the foundation building of that nationalism. Simultaneously, the work by younger historians trained at Cambridge, including Francis Robinson, David Washbrook and Christopher

Baker, plus, from Oxford, Christopher Bayly, began to explore the implications of the Seal-Gallagher insights. (Baker 1976, Bayly 1975, Robinson 1974, Washbrook 1976.) Seal had announced that his book would be the first of a multi-volume set of studies on Indian politics up to the 1940s. In fact no further volumes appeared. As regional studies were completed, the stories became more complicated and the analyses less congruent with Seal's interpretation. When a series of essays from these scholars appeared in 1973, the attributed unity of viewpoint could already be seen to be eroding (Gallagher et al., eds. 1973). While "the Cambridge school" provoked an extensive critical reaction, stimulated fresh research on Indian nationalism(s), and perhaps had an impact on the study of pluralist politics generally, it must be conceded that it did not provoke a substantial rethinking of the historical discipline generally (Spodek 1979, Raychaudhuri 1979, Habib 1988, 55-57).[17] The "academic generation" of "Cambridge" historians moved on in new and separate paths where they have made distinctive contributions. Since "History," as John Webster reminds us, "is an unending conversation between the past and the present" (Webster 1981, 15), no given "school" or interpretation, however widely embraced or celebrated, will provide a convincing closure to historiographical exploration—there will be no "end of history" for modern India (cf. Lelyveld and Subrahmanyam 1995, 428-430).

Marxism, another "western" historiographic perspective, also became influential in interpretations of modern India. The best-known center of Marxist research, at Aligarh Muslim University, made the Mughal period its principal focus. Marxian interpretations of imperialism and emphases upon economic explanations for perceived distortions in India had a wide appeal among nationalist intellectuals both before and after *swaraj* (Chakrabarty 1992, 49-50). An extensive domestication of Marxian thought in Indian historiography seems to have resulted in a trend of assimilating Marxian terminology without necessarily an accompanying rigor of Marxian analysis.[18]

Teaching and research on modern Indian history thus entered the final quarter of the twentieth century in an expansive mode and with a variety of approaches to an increasingly complex subject. In 1976 Ashin Das Gupta identified three developing and related trends among Indian historians (Correia-Afonso 1979, 79):

1. They were moving away from narrative history centered on individuals toward study of structures within which those individuals functioned.

2. They were attempting "to dig down to the grass-roots of the Indian past by work in regional and local history."

3. They had begun to work with an awareness of similar work in the international arena.

In the twenty years since Professor Das Gupta's observations, another conversation between Indian and foreign historians began to be heard, as Indian historians moved from awareness of an international arena to active participation in it. In the process, modern Indian history—at least one form thereof—has begun to have an impact on the shape of the broader historical enterprise, albeit without a concomitant enlargement of awareness of the substance of that history.

Well before any impact, however, important publications had sought to link questions of India's modern history with wider debates within the discipline of history. For example, the works of Eric Stokes (1959) and Ranajit Guha (1963) articulated with European studies of ideology and policy. However, the "balance of trade" remained skewed, as these valuable studies primarily enriched historical awareness in the India field itself, with less impact beyond.

Das Gupta's perception was, in effect, that within India, Indian history had existed in a condition not unlike that of the Indian economy. There was a *swadeshi* mode that emphasized Indian history as an Indian subject, often understood by historians, both Indian and foreign, largely in terms of Indian institutions and relations. This must not be taken to imply in any way a lack of energy or acuity in practice, but to acknowledge that the conversation of Indian history, apart from some comparative aspects of colonial rule and resistance thereto, was being conducted primarily in terms of the subcontinent's own history.[19] This should not be cause for surprise. Most specialists in European history interact with other European historians; many American history specialists remain placidly parochial and insular in outlook. A view that Indian specialists must somehow remain always engaged with external sources of methods and concepts seems to reproduce the colonial relationship that situates India's history at the margins.

This *swadeshi* effect also had implications for foreign scholars of India within their home institutions in the West. Over the decades, a number of U.S. scholars working on Indian history have expressed frustration at a sense of being marginalized in their profession. My impression, based on a recent review of annual conference programs from 1962 to 1994, is that more historians of India working in the

United States actively participated in the "area studies" organization of the Association for Asian Studies than in the American Historical Association, the central professional association of historians in the United States.

If modern Indian history may be compared to a protected and circumscribed (*swadeshī*) marketplace, it must be conceded that the intellectual tariff walls have been relatively porous. New problems, concepts, and approaches have been appropriated and extended by both Indian and foreign scholars in the field. European social history, for example, provided stimulus in fresh studies of public life (cf. Freitag 1991). The extraordinary flowering of feminist history has rapidly contributed to historical explorations of gender and the lives of Indian women (Ramusack 1990).[20] K.N. Chaudhuri's explorations of the trading world of the Indian Ocean represents the first significant application of the *longue duree* historical investigations associated with the *Annales* school of French historians, particular Fernand Braudel (Chaudhuri 1985). The modern India of historians is marked by diversities of method and subject. Conventions of academic empiricism grounded in analysis and narration of selected past events and human lives, based upon a critically employed body of evidence, have continued to predominate. But in the past decade new winds have blown through, or sometimes past, the dusty archives. The practice of the historiography of modern India has undergone a critical reexamination.

A fundamental tenet of historical practice is that all sources must be critically evaluated. As the enterprise of modern Indian historiography began to grow, scholars such as Burton Stein and Bernard Cohn were pushing their students to greater consciousness of implications of how sources of colonial evidence had been constituted. Cohn's interest in the process of "objectification" in colonial Indian census data may serve as an example (Cohn 1987, 224-254; Cohn 1996, esp. 3-15).[21] Modern Indian historiography was subject to a further significant "turn" in the period around 1980, between the publication of Edward Said's *Orientalism* (1978) and the appearance of the first volume of *Subaltern Studies* (Guha 1981).

Said's critique of European scholars' representations of "the Orient," particularly the Islamic Middle East, provided an opening to a profound questioning of the authority of western knowledge as it had been applied to the East. Said was concerned with "representation" grounded in "a style of thought based upon an ontological and epistemological distinction made between 'the Orient' and (most of the time) 'the Occident' " (Said 1978, 2).

"*Orientalism*" as a concept, or merely a term, was rapidly appropriated in literary, social scientific, and historical discourse.[22] The congruence of the Saidian framework with the so-called "linguistic turn" of western literary and historical scholarship provided a strong stimulus to re-thinking how India had been "represented" and how its history might be reconceived (cf. Breckenridge and Van der Veer 1993). Now some historians of modern India saw the need for employing discursive analysis and for reevaluating historical and cultural categories that had presumably been produced by colonialist descriptions of Indian "reality." Indeed *Orientalism* seemed to subvert the disciplinary boundaries themselves (Prakash 1995). For some historians this has led to the expectation of a "post-colonial" liberation from the "Eurocentric discourse" of "the historicism that projected the West as History" (Prakash 1994, 1475n; Prakash 1990). The implications of this perspective for modern Indian history and the degree to which this perspective would establish its origins in an Indian historiography and recast Indian history remain to be realized.[23]

One focal point of innovation in modern Indian historical studies during the recent past has been the collective production of a group of Indian, Australian, European and American scholars publishing, thus far, eight volumes of essays under the title of *Subaltern Studies.* The term "subaltern," when first encountered, suggested to an older generation some evocation of Kipling and the British army; nothing could have been further from the mark. Subaltern studies built upon the Italian Marxist Antonio Gramsci's concept of subalterns as the subordinated strata of society, dominated by hegemonic elites in a condition of oppression. Ranajit Guha offered a manifesto in the inaugural volume with a critique of the state of historiography of modern India (Guha 1981, 1-7). Guha criticized previous historiography as having been dominated by elitism—both colonial and bourgeois-nationalist elitism—that excluded or marginalized the masses of subalterns of India (Guha 1981, 1-4). Like Said, Guha was concerned with the position of the historian and the sources of evidence employed by the historian, particularly the colonial archives. Such awareness was not an exclusive possession, however. Kenneth Ballhatchet, scarcely a candidate for membership in the subaltern collective, had, for example, observed that if studies of Indian nationalist leaders by D.G. Tendulkar, B.N. Pandey and Sarvepalli Gopal tended to underestimate the significance of socio-economic factors, this might be expected "when high-caste authors are writing about members of the high-caste elite" (Ballhatchet 1984, 36).

In a fundamental sense, the subaltern studies project was a specific example of a broader and older historiographical concern that sought to avoid teleologies of events and movements that conferred an inevitability upon a privileged narrative (in this instance, what the subalterns would term "bourgeois nationalism"). The broader concept also sought to avoid evaluating historical events only in terms of a later product, such as the Indian nation state. If this meant another disaggregation in the manner of the "Cambridge school," it differed by commencing with a more explicit political stance. The subaltern collective manifested sympathy with the predicament of the non-elite or subaltern peoples of India and sought to document, and thereby restore, the agency and potential of these "subalterns" in history. Whether or not Edward Said was accurate in calling the project "an attempt to wrest control of the Indian past from its scribes and curators of the present" (Said 1988, vii), the subaltern scholars produced research on relatively unstudied subjects while raising critical methodological questions for all historians. The collective aspects of the enterprise sometimes seemed more apparent than real; disagreements occurred over alternative paths of emphasis and interpretation. One member, David Hardiman, reported in 1986 that the project was "standing at something of a crossroads" with two possibly incompatible directions: "One road leads towards greater concentration on textual analysis and a stress on the relativity of all knowledge; another towards the study of subaltern Consciousness and action so as to forward the struggle for a socialist society" (Hardiman 1986, 288).[24]

If the explicit goal of restoring the subaltern and the autonomous world of the subaltern to Indian history was not fully realized, the scholars who were admitted to the subaltern collective did produce a rich and varied range of essays that provoked a wide introspection in the historiography of modern South Asia.[25] Subaltern studies also gained a small foothold for the history of modern India in the wider worlds of the discipline of history in the West, as well as in cultural and other interdisciplinary studies. Recently a Latin American subaltern studies group launched its own project.[26] Some scholars have perceived, incorrectly, the subaltern collective to offer a uniquely authentic Indian voice, grounded in a subaltern third-world position vis-a-vis the metropolitan elite academic world. But, in fact, the enterprise has always been multi-national, and some of its members enjoy highly privileged positions in elite universities both in India and the West. Furthermore, the romantic image of a collective project confronting the rest of the historical profession never rang true—the essays published in the *Subaltern Studies* volumes could easily have found publication in professional journals. It is my impression that outside the South Asian history field itself the subaltern mode is more celebrated for its intellectual and political position than for its roots and research in Indian history.[27] Within South Asian history, critics have questioned the significance and impact of subaltern scholarship (Sarkar 1994, Perusek 1992, Chakrabarty 1995). Notwithstanding the stimulating subaltern and post-colonial critiques of the universalizing claims of particular modes of thought, the interest thereby generated may risk, in some, a certain presentist amnesia either unaware, or incapable of recognizing, that even *before* the dissemination of the newly received theories or perspectives, some historians were actively pursuing research on the subject.[28]

The term "subaltern" has taken on a life of its own; thus the celebrated cosmopolitan writer Salman Rushdie has been labeled a "subaltern author" (Callahan 1995). Perhaps as the Prince of Wales said of socialists in 1895, we could say "we are all subalterns nowadays." But we aren't really. Within the world of academic history of modern India, however, there may be true subalterns, members of the subordinated strata of society, dominated by hegemonic elites, those women and men who lecture in the colleges of the subcontinent without adequate institutional libraries, opportunities for research, or respect from their better-placed colleagues.[29]

In this rapid overview of dimensions of the academic field of modern Indian history, I have been unable to note all of the many significant new directions of research and their consequences. Nor have I been able to cite the work of more than a handful of the many professional historians who have labored in this international enterprise. In each generation of historians, critical insights offer fresh interpretations and, sometimes, rather sharp dismissals of previous scholarship. The impatience of the young with the inadequacies of their elders has been long with us in human affairs, not the least in academic history. Impatience of the elders with the enthusiastic energies of the young is also well established.

Perhaps there is just a bit too much impatience all around. I once served on a fellowship selection committee in which one member would have preferred not to support a young scholar whose proposal was well conceived but insufficiently informed by a particular theory. My colleague seemed to think that it would be better to turn back the candidate and hope that some scholar in the future might do a better job with the subject. This led me to wonder if "history" is one of those unusual commodities that is more valuable unprocessed and unused. So long as "history" remains in its "raw" form of documentation, it has the potential to provide the basis for "scholarship of enduring value." But in most instances, once "history" has been mined from the evidence and processed, it yields just another competent article or monograph.

Fashions of interpretation have had their hour: modernization, regions, Namierite splitting, nationalist lumping, anti-orientalism and, most recently, the subalterns. We have to recognize that each interpretive frame and critical perspective has had its contributions and its criticisms of previous work. Each interpretation has gained a hearing, enriched our understanding, and then has begun being digested into the on-going historiographical synthesis. Perhaps history is—like India itself—a variegated fossil bed of ideas and practices from many sources. Some social scientists, wary of the narrative conventions and apparent conservatism of historical practice, might enjoy that reference to fossils. Their pleasure would be misplaced. Each professorial generation can look forward with satisfaction (or distaste) to the fruits of the prodigious energies of the next generation of younger scholars.

However, those new historians seeking to advance the frontiers of modern Indian history face many hurdles: funding for graduate training and post-doctoral research, acquiring (and maintaining) command of appropriate languages and auxiliary disciplines, academic appointments, research access, and publication venues. Contraction of public higher education adds the further challenge of reproduction of another new generation of scholars. Yet, thinking our cup to be half-full rather than half-empty, we must acknowledge the burgeoning energy with which the study of modern India has grown during the past fifty years. Scholars have opened entirely fresh vistas in which modern India's history has been found to contain new questions, new themes, and, most importantly, people—not "new" people, but newly-included people, women, peasants, and laborers—in the conversation of history. Maintaining that conversation of history will require sympathy and support from governments, universities, and colleges, and the public of many countries where the modern Indian epoch has been, or ought to be, taught and explored.

I opened this essay with an observation on the significance of history for modern India. I will close with the expectation that with the creative energies, particularly of India's own historians, modern India will increasingly matter for history.

NOTES

1. Philips, C.H. 1961. *Historians of India, Pakistan, and Ceylon*. 3.
2. Indian International Centre. 1963. *Problems of Historical Writing in India*. 50.
3. Das Gupta, Ashin. 1979. "The Future of Historical Research in India: The International Context." 76.
4. Stein, Burton. 1990. "A Decade of Historical Efflorescence." 138.
5. Webster, John C.B. 1981. *An Introduction to History*. 15.
6. Although this *is* an essay about the history of modern India, I find the frequent occurrence herein of phrases such as "modern India," "history of modern India," or "modern Indian history" to be a source of distraction and regret the reader's inconvenience. I have been unable to discover suitable alternatives.
7. Ravinder Kumar observes, "It would, therefore, be legitimate to define myths as the historiography of pre-industrial societies and history as the mythology of industrial societies" (Kumar 1989, 30).
8. When I first applied to consult the Maharashtra State Archives in Bombay in 1965, it appeared that official caution concerning admittance of research scholars had not eroded significantly with *swarāj*. By the 1970s India scholars faced fewer obstacles than earlier.
9. A critical history of the growth and development of the academic disciplines in Indian higher education, to my knowledge, has yet to be written.
10. Given his own interests, it may not be surprising that Nilakanta Sastri's list of great historians of India included only specialists on pre-modern history, mostly Indian and European orientalists (Nilakanta Sastri 1956, 159-181).
11. A notable exception to Crane's criticism of Indian scholars was Shankar Ganesh Date who, by 1943, had completed and published his bibliography of Marathi printed books from 1800 to 1937. However, the majority of Marathi history writing cited in the bibliography focused on the pre-modern period of Maratha rule or earlier.
12. At the University of Minnesota, Minneapolis, January 16, 1963. Stein reiterated this point in a comment published by the Indian University Grants Commission: "Serious training in some social science certainly would alert historians to possibilities in the fields of social and economic history which have been neglected" (University Grants Commission 1964, 33). Not all practitioners of modern Indian history were equally enthusiastic at this prospect. John Gallagher complained that "all sorts of preposterous demands are pressed upon us that we should work out the history of the Indian family and kinship systems ... the nineteenth century evolution of income structure and of occupation structure. But since next to nothing is known about these matters in the history of Russia, Britain and the United States, where the material lies readier to hand, and the scale is less daunting,

perhaps we may leave these physicians to cure themselves" (Gallagher 1963, 50). Eleven years later Tom Kessinger demonstrated that, at least for one village in one region, such a study could be done (Kessinger 1974).

13. During the later 1960s scholarly groups with seminars and conferences and occasional publications had been launched concentrating on Bengal, Punjab, Maharashtra, and South India. Others followed (Crane 1967).

14. Frykenberg's impressive study of Guntur district in Andhra Pradesh, for example, has not been replicated for other regions of the Indian subcontinent. Nevertheless, it has been used for generalizations for all of India. By contrast, study of aspects of rural economy in, say, Burgundy, would not support generalizations for Germany or Spain, much less for the entire subcontinent of Europe.

15. Even as I struggled with Croce, there had appeared a "classic" guide that I discovered a year too late: Bernard Cohn's 1962 essay "An Anthropologist among the Historians," (reprinted in Cohn 1987, 1-17) which offered an academic ethnography of the historical tribe that was not so essentialized as to obscure recognition.

16. See also Kumar ed. (1971) and Low ed. (1977) For critical Indian response see De (1978).

17. Burton Stein once noted that the "Cambridge school" had gained fresh prominence and an unrealistic appearance of coherence in critiques written by Ranajit Guha within the subaltern studies framework (Stein 1985, 129).

18. Tapan Raychaudhuri once lamented that the acceptance of the Marxist framework of analysis could have been a useful tool, at least up to a point. But, by and large, the consequences of this influence have been disappointing. The Marxist framework has been generally applied without a full understanding of its implications in the context of modern knowledge or of the sophisticated use, satisfying strict academic standards, to which it has been put by several western historians (Raychaudhuri 1963, 139).

19. Another side of this coin is to be glimpsed in the publication of major reference works in Indian history including a historical atlas (Schwartzberg 1978) and a biographical dictionary (Sen 1972-73).

20. See Sangari and Vaid (1989), O'Hanlon (1994).

21. See also the various essays by historians such as Jones and Conlon in Barrier, ed. (1981).

22. Sumit Sarkar (1994, 205), while recognizing the benefits of the post-Said focus on colonial domination and power relations, comments that, nevertheless, "it has become obligatory in many intellectual circles to begin with a critique of Orientalism, of colonial discourse, if one wants to acquire or retain a radical reputation."

23. The critique of "orientalist discourse" has been noticed in India by

enthusiasts of Hindu revival who apply it to reinforce their project of rewriting the subcontinent's history along lines that might give Saidians pause.

24. Hardiman noted the view that questioned the fruitfulness of literary textual analysis as an end in itself. "It can furthermore be argued that subaltern studies sets out with a constructive rather than a deconstructive aim, for it seeks first of all to make the subaltern classes the subject of their own history. From this flows the critique of existing historiography. Deconstruction for its own sake leads down a slippery path to pure relativism" (Hardiman 1986, 290). Notwithstanding these strictures, the analytical tools of literary deconstruction have continued to be employed in many of the subaltern studies essays.

25. Among significant comments and critiques of the subaltern studies project see Masselos (1992), O'Hanlon (1988), and Stein (1990). For a spirited response to critiques of the subaltern's post-modern aspect see Chakrabarty (1995).

26. See Latin American Subaltern Studies Group (1993, 110); see also Mallon (1994). I have been told that Russian historians are very keen to learn more about subaltern history, but they have some difficulty in understanding who subalterns are (personal communication, Oct. 18, 1996, Professor Gregory Koslowski).

27. The history of the subaltern studies project itself can get lost. A literature seminar at a major U.S. university in 1995 described subaltern studies as "the movement *begun by Gayatri Chakravorty Spivak* (emphasis added) to de-center colonial history by documenting the mentalities of the oppressed peoples of India through their own documents of history."

28. The editors of a *History Workshop's* special thematic issue on "Colonial and Post-Colonial History" wrote, "In the last fifty years, colonialism has received surprisingly little attention from British historians of both conservative and radical traditions" (Burrell and Chrisman 1993). Burrell and Chrisman do allow for "notable exceptions," but what is conveyed to this reader is a sense that a particular agenda exists for how "colonialism" must be explored.

29. These conditions were noted by Sinha (1963-64, 38).

REFERENCES

Baker, Christopher John. 1976. *The Politics of South India, 1920-1937.* Cambridge: Cambridge Univ. Press.

Ballhatchet, Kenneth. 1984. "The Rewriting of South Asian History by South Asian Historians after 1947." *Asian Affairs* 15 (February): 27-38.

Barrier, N. Gerald, ed. 1981. *The Census in British India: New Perspectives.* New Delhi: Manohar.

Bayly, Christopher A. 1975. *The Local Roots of Indian Politics: Allahabad, 1880-1920.* Oxford: Clarendon.

———. 1979. "English-language Historiography on British Expansion in India and Indian Reactions since 1945." In *Reappraisals in Overseas History: Essays on Post-war Historiography about European Expansion.* ed. P.C. Emmer and H.L. Wesseling, 21-53. Leiden: Leiden Univ. Press.

———. 1994. "Returning the British to South Asian History: The Limits of Colonial Hegemony." *South Asia* n.s. 17:2 ii (December): 1-25.

Black, Cyril E. 1960. *The Dynamics of Modernization: A Study in Comparative History.* New York: Harper and Row.

Burrell, John and Laura Chrisman. 1993. "Editorial." *History Workshop* 36 (Special Issue on Colonial and Post-Colonial History). (Autumn): iii-v.

Breckenridge, Carol A. and Peter van der Veer, eds. 1993. *Orientalism and the Postcolonial Predicament: Perspectives on South Asia.* Philadelphia: Univ. of Pennsylvania Press.

Callahan, Allen D. 1995. "The Language of the Apocaplypse." *Harvard Theological Review* 88 (October): 453-471.

Chakrabarty, Dipesh. 1992a. "Marxism and Modern India." *History Today* 42 (March): 48-51.

———. 1992b. "Postcoloniality and the Artifice of History: Who Speaks for 'Indian' Pasts?" *Representations* 37 (Winter): 1-26.

———. 1993. "Marx after Marxism: History, Subalternity and Difference." *Meanjin* 52 (Spring): 421-434.

———. 1995. "Radical Histories and Question of Enlightenment Rationalism: Some Recent Critiques of Subaltern Studies." *Economic and Political Weekly* 30 (April 5): 751-759.

Chatterjee, Partha. 1992. "History and the Nationalization of Hinduism." *Social Research* 59 (Spring):111-149

———. 1995. "Alternative Histories, Alternative Nations: Nationalism and Modern Historiography in Bengal." In *Making Alternative Histories: The Practice of Archaeology and History in Non-Western Settings,* ed. Peter R. Schmidt and Thomas C. Patterson, 229-251. Santa Fe: School of American Research Press.

Chaudhuri, K.N. 1985. *Trade and Civilization in the Indian Ocean: An Economic History from the Rise of Islam to 1750.* Cambridge: Cambridge Univ. Press.

Cohn, Bernard S. 1980. "Anthropological Models and the Study of Indian History." Prospectus: National Endowment for the Humanities Summer Seminar, University of Chicago.

———. 1987. *An Anthropologist among the Historians and Other Essays.* Delhi: Oxford Univ. Press.

———. 1996. *Colonialism and Its Forms of Knowledge: The British in India.* Princeton: Princeton Univ. Press.

Cooper, Frederick. 1994. "Conflict and Connection: Rethinking Colonial

African History." *American Historical Review* 99 (December): 1516-1545.

Correia-Afonso, John, ed. 1979. *Historical Research in India*. New Delhi: Munshiram Manoharlal.

Crane, Robert I. 1963. "Problems of Writing Indian History: The Case of Indian Nationalism." In *Problems of Historical Writing in India*, ed. Indian International Centre, 30-34. New Delhi: Indian International Centre.

Crane, Robert I. ed. 1967. *Regions and Regionalism in South Asian Studies: An Exploratory Study*. Durham, N.C.: Duke Univ. Program in Cooperative Studies in Southern Asia.

Das Gupta, Ashin. 1979. "The Future of Historical Research in India: The International Context." In *Historical Research in India*. ed. John Correia-Afonso, 67-79. New Delhi: Munshiram Manoharlal.

Date, Shankar Ganesh. 1943. *Marathi Grantha Suci, 1800-1937*. Pune: Shankar Ganesh Date.

De, Barun. 1963-64. "A Preliminary Note on the Writing of the History of Modern India." *Quarterly Review of Historical Studies* 3: 39-46.

―――. 1978. "A Canberra Outlook on the Indian Freedom Struggle." *Indian Historical Review* 4 (January): 405-417.

Dongerkery. S.R. 1957. *A History of the University of Bombay, 1857-1957*. Bombay: Univ. of Bombay.

Education Commission (India). 1971. *Education and National Development: Report of the Education Commission, 1964-66*. New Delhi: National Council of Educational Research and Training.

Freitag, Sandria B. 1991. "Introduction: Aspects of the 'Public' in Colonial South Asia." *South Asia* n.s. 14: 1 (June): 1-13.

Frykenberg, Robert E. 1965. *Guntur District, 1788-1848: A History of Local Influence and Central Authority in South India*. Oxford: Clarendon.

Gallagher, John. 1963. "Imperialism and Nationalism in Modern Indian History." In *Problems of Historical Writing in India*, ed. Indian International Centre, 50-56. New Delhi: Indian International Centre.

Gallagher, John, Gordon Johnson, and Anil Seal, eds. 1973. *Locality, Province, and Nation: Essays on Indian Politics, 1870-1940, Reprinted from Modern Asian Studies*. Cambridge: Cambridge Univ. Press.

Guha, Ranajit. 1963. *A Rule of Property for Bengal; An Essay on the Idea of Permanent Settlement*. Paris: Mouton.

―――. 1981. "On Some Aspects of the Historiography of Colonial India." In *Subaltern Studies I: Selected Writings on South Asian History and Society*, ed. Ranajit Guha, 37-44. Delhi: Oxford Univ. Press.

―――. 1988. *An Indian Historiography of India: A Nineteenth Century Agenda and Its Implications*. Calcutta: K.P. Bagchi for Centre for Studies in Social Sciences, Calcutta.

Guha, Ranajit, ed. 1981. *Subaltern Studies, I: Selected Writings on South Asian History and Society*. Delhi: Oxford Univ. Press.

Guha, Ranajit and Gayatri Chakravorty Spivak, eds. 1988. *Selected Subaltern Studies*. New York: Oxford Univ. Press.

Habib, Irfan. 1988. *Interpreting Indian History.* Shillong: North-Eastern Hill Univ. Publications.

Hardiman, David. 1986. " 'Subaltern Studies' at Crossroads." *Economic and Political Weekly* 21 (February 15):288-290.

Indian International Centre, ed. 1963. *Problems of Historical Writing in India.* New Delhi: Indian International Centre.

Indian History Congress. 1966. *Indian History Congress: Proceedings of the Ranchi Session-1964.* Aligarh: Indian History Congress.

Johnson, Gordon, ed. 1985. "Review of The Cambridge Economic History of India and Beyond." *Modern Asian Studies* 19 (July): 353-732.

Kessinger, Tom G. 1974. *Vilyatpur: 1848-1968: Social and Economic Change in a North Indian Village.* Berkeley: Univ. of California Press.

Kindersley, A.F. 1921. *A Handbook of the Bombay Government Records.* Bombay: Government Central Press.

Kumar, Ravinder, ed. 1971. *Essays in Gandhian Politics: The Rowlatt Satyagraha of 1919.* Oxford: Clarendon.

Kumar, Ravinder. 1989. "The Past and the Present: An Indian Dialogue," *Daedalus: Journal of the American Academy of Arts and Sciences* 118:4 (Fall): 27-49.

Lambert, Richard D. 1962. *Resources for South Asian Area Studies in the United States* (Report of a Conference on the Strengthening and Integration of South Asian Language and Area Studies. New York: 1961). Philadelphia: Univ. of Pennsylvania Press.

Latin American Subaltern Studies Group. 1993. "Founding Statement." *Boundary 2* 20 no. 3 (Fall): 110-121.

Lelyveld, David and Sanjay Subrahmanyam. 1995 (3rd edition). "South Asia." (Introductory Essay to Section 15) In *The American Historical Association's Guide to Historical Literature,* gen. ed. Mary Beth Norton. 1: 427-430. New York: Oxford Univ. Press.

Lerner, Daniel. 1958. *The Passing of Traditional Society: Modernizing the Middle East.* Glencoe: Free Press.

Low, D. Anthony, ed. 1968. *Soundings in Modern South Asian History.* Berkeley: Univ. of California Press.

————. ed. 1977. *Congress and the Raj: Facets of the Indian Struggle, 1917-47.* London: Heinemann.

Majumdar, R.C. 1970. *Historiography in Modern India.* (Heras Memorial Lectures, 1967) New York: Asia.

————. 1973. "Indian Historiography: Some Recent Trends." In *Historians and Historiography in Modern India,* ed. S.P. Sen, 17-23. Calcutta: Institute of Historical Studies.

Mallon, Florencia E. 1994. "The Promise and Dilemma of Subaltern Studies: Perspectives from Latin American History." *American Historical Review* 99 (December): 1491-1515.

Masselos, Jim. 1992. "The Dis/Appearance of Subalterns: A Reading of a Decade of Subaltern Studies." *South Asia* n.s. 15:1 (June): 105-125.

Nehru, Jawaharlal. 1946. *The Discovery of India.* New York and Calcutta: John Day and Signet Press.

Nilakanta Sastri, K.A. 1961. *Historical Method in Relation to Indian History.* Madras: S. Viswanathan.

O'Hanlon, Rosalind. 1988. "Recovering the Subject: Subaltern Studies and Histories of Resistance in South Asia." *Modern Asian Studies* 22 (February): 189-224.

————. 1994. *A Comparison between Women and Men: Tarabai Shinde and the Critique of Gender Relations in Colonial India.* Madras: Oxford Univ. Press.

Perusek, Darshan. 1992. "Subaltern Consciousness and the Historiography of the Indian Rebellion of 1857." *Novel* 25 (Spring): 286-301.

————. 1993. "Subaltern Consciousness and Historiography of Indian Rebellion of 1857." *Economic and Political Weekly* 28 (September 11): 1931-1936.

Philips, Cyril H. 1995. *Beyond the Ivory Tower: The Autobiography of Sir Cyril Philips.* London: Radcliffe.

Philips, Cyril H, ed. 1961. *Historians of India, Pakistan and Ceylon.* (Historical Writing on the Peoples of Asia, volume I) London: Oxford Univ. Press.

Prakash, Gyan. 1994. "Subaltern Studies as Post-Colonial Criticism." *American Historical Review* 99 (December): 1475-1490.

————. 1995. "Orientalism Now." *History and Theory* 34:199-212.

Prasad, Bisheshwar. 1963. "Recollections." In *Indian History Congress Silver Jubilee Souvenir Volume,* ed. S.P. Sen, 151-154. Calcutta: Indian History Congress.

Ramusack, Barbara. 1990. "From Symbol to Diversity: The Historical Literature on Women in India." *South Asia Research* 10 (November): 139-157.

Raychaudhuri, Tapan 1963. "Teaching and Research in History in the Indian Universities." In *Problems of Historical Writing in India,* ed. Indian International Centre, 135-143. New Delhi: Indian International Centre.

————. 1979. "Indian Nationalism as Animal Politics." *The Historical Journal* 22: 747-763.

Robinson, Francis. 1974. *Separatism among Indian Muslims: The Politics of the United Provinces' Muslims, 1860-1923.* Cambridge: Cambridge Univ. Press.

Said, Edward. 1978. *Orientalism.* New York: Random House.

————. 1988. "Foreword." In *Selected Subaltern Studies,* ed. Ranajit Guha and Gayatri Chakravorty Spivak, v-xiv. New York: Oxford Univ. Press.

Sangari, Kumkum and Sudesh Vaid, eds. 1989. *Recasting Women: Essays in Indian Colonial History.* New Delhi: Kali for Women.

Sarkar, Sumit. 1994. "Orientalism Revisited: Saidian Frameworks in the Writing of Modern Indian History." *Oxford Literary Review* 16: 205-224.

Schwartzberg, Joseph E., ed. 1978. *A Historical Atlas of South Asia.* Chicago: Univ. of Chicago Press.

Sen, S.P. 1961. "Editorial." *Quarterly Review of Historical Studies* 1 (April-June): 3-8.

Sen, S.P., ed. 1973. *Historians and Historiography in Modern India.* Calcutta: Institute of Historical Studies.

Sen, S.P., ed. 1963. *Indian History Congress Silver Jubilee Souvenir Volume.* Calcutta: Indian History Congress.

Sen, S.P., ed. 1972-73. *Dictionary of National Biography.* 4 vols. Calcutta: Institute of Historical Studies.

Sinha, N.K. 1963-64. "Indian History Which is Emerging Today." *Quarterly Review of Historical Studies* 3: 36-38.

Spear, T.G.P. 1961. "British Historical Writing in the Era of the Nationalist Movements." In *Historians of India, Pakistan, and Ceylon,* ed. Cyril H. Philips, 404-415. London: Oxford Univ. Press.

Spodek, Howard 1979. "Pluralist Politics in British India: The Cambridge Cluster of Historians of Modern India." *American Historical Review* 84 (June); 688-707.

Stein, Burton. 1990 "A Decade of Historical Efflorescence." *South Asia Research* 10 (November): 125-138.

Stokes, Eric. 1959. *The English Utilitarians and India.* Oxford: Clarendon.

Stokes, Eric. 1961. "The Administrators and Historical Writing on India." In *Historians of India, Pakistan, and Ceylon,* ed. Cyril H. Philips, 385-403. London: Oxford Univ. Press.

University Grants Commission (India). 1964. *Report of the Seminar on Postgraduate Teaching and Research in History.* New Delhi: University Grants Commission.

Washbrook, David A. 1976. *The Emergence of Provincial Politics: The Madras Presidency, 1870-1920.* Cambridge: Cambridge Univ. Press.

Webster, John C. B. 1981 (2nd edition). *An Introduction to History.* New Delhi: Macmillan.

Languages

HERMAN H. VAN OLPHEN

Western interest in the study of Indian languages goes back much further than just the last fifty years; India has a long tradition of affecting the conceptualization and articulation of language. In ancient India the study of language that culminated with Panini's description of Sanskrit was much more developed than anywhere else in the world. And the report by Sir William Jones to the Oriental Society in London in 1786, which documented the relationship of Sanskrit to other ancient languages and thus the later identification of the modern languages of north India as members of the Indo-European group of languages, is considered the beginning of modern comparative linguistics. As a result, the study of Sanskrit and the Indian grammatical tradition was an important part of western scholarship for more than a century prior to Indian independence in 1947.

Since other chapters in this volume discuss the study of linguistics and Sanskrit, I will focus here on the modern languages of India. Here, also, there is a long tradition of western study, particularly Hindi-Urdu. Beginning with Ketelaar's grammar of Hindustani, written in Dutch in 1608, a large number of grammars and dictionaries were produced by westerners for many of the languages of India. Although a major goal was utilitarian, i.e., the British had a need to learn Indian languages to communicate and carry out their colonial objectives, many works reflected high standards of scholarship. The landmark of the colonial period was Sir William Grierson's *Linguistic Survey of India* (1903-1928) that utilized the widespread network of colonial governance to produce an extensive documentation of the languages of India. The *Linguistic Survey of India* still retains its usefulness today.

When India gained independence in 1947, there was little awareness in the West of modern Indian languages. They were taught in few institutions, and little was known about their geopolitical status. They were often dismissed as "vernaculars" or "dialects." It would be tempting to say that after fifty years of independence the situation has greatly improved, and indeed a large number of westerners have had contact with Indian languages, and many have even learned them. However, these numbers are still minuscule compared to the number of those who have studied other "less-commonly taught" languages, especially when we consider the number of speakers of even lesser-known Indian languages. Whereas little-studied languages such as Turkish, Rumanian, or Albanian are at least associated with well-known national groups or nations, such is not the case for many major Indian languages such as Tamil, Marathi, or Telugu. Although most westerners would be able to identify Hindi, Hindustani, and perhaps Bengali as modern Indian languages, they would be able to say little else about them and would certainly be puzzled by Hindi's status as the third most-spoken language in the world. In this same context, a school superintendent in a major U.S. city, while discussing immigrants in the city's schools, expressed puzzlement that so many of the students had given Urdu, a language he had never heard of, as their home language.

We can, of course, regret this lack of awareness, but it is not surprising. Although Hindi and a number of other Indian languages have had official recognition in the Indian constitution from the earliest days of independence, the continued use of English in those situations with which outsiders are most likely to come into contact has limited the visibility of these languages. The original plan to replace Hindi with English by 1965 could not be realized; opposition by non-Hindi speakers made that change impractical. Nevertheless, Nehru's decision to delay the change was more likely a result of the lack of progress that the use of Hindi had made since Independence. In fact, the use of English had increased in India since Independence, both in commerce and in the government. And the decades since 1965 have given little indication that Hindi will replace English in those registers where English has retained its predominance. At the central government level and in commerce, English is still the most important medium for communication, while at the state level, the regional languages also compete with English. In addition, English-medium education from the primary level on continues to gain in popularity, even in rural areas.

One major area of western influence is in the area of classification of the Indian languages and the identification of the four major language families represented in India: Indo-Aryan (which is the easternmost branch of Indo-European), Dravidian, Munda, and Tibeto-Burman. For the Indo-Aryan languages, most of the work of classification was done during the British period, first by Beames in 1872-1879 and then by Grierson in 1903-1928. Western scholars tended to apply the traditional Indo-European family-tree model to the Indo-Aryan branch . Thus in the same way that Latin led to Vulgar Latin and then to the modern Romance Languages, it was believed that Sanskrit developed into Middle Indo-Aryan languages, which in turn developed into the New Indo-Aryan languages such as Marathi, Hindi, and Bengali. As Shapiro and Schiffman (1981) point out, the linguistic situation of the Indo-Aryan languages in India demonstrated the shortcomings of this approach. Shared phonological, syntactic, and lexical features among the various Indo-Aryan languages and, indeed, between the Indo-Aryan languages and other groups in India makes the relationship between languages in India much more complicated. In addition, linguistic features have spread throughout the Indo-Aryan languages, causing the greatest affinity between languages or dialects that are geographically close rather than most closely related genetically. This sharing of features means that there is a continuum of speech forms throughout north India with a gradual transition between dialects. Across the northern part of India there are only minor differences between adjacent dialects. Mutual intelligibility between speech forms decreases, however, as the distance between them increases. On the other hand, there are regional dialects or languages such as Bhojpuri in Bihar and eastern U.P., in addition to the regional languages, such as Hindi and Bengali, that are superimposed on the local dialects.

For Dravidian languages, initial work on classification was again done prior to Independence by Grierson, who built on the earlier work by Caldwell (1856), who first identified the Dravidian group of languages as a separate language family. Both western scholars (such as Emeneau and Zvelebil) and Indian scholars (such as Bh. Krishnamurti and Subrahmanyam) have refined the classification considerably since then. Most of the work on classifying the languages of the other linguistic families spoken in India has been done by western scholars, such as the classification of Munda by Zide and Pinnow, and the classification of Tibeto-Burman by Shafer and Miller.

Subsumed in this entire discussion is the difficulty in India of distinguishing between languages and dialects, compared with areas such as Europe where national boundaries have often served to make the distinction clear. First of all, there are no clear-cut linguistic definitions that allow us to distinguish the concepts of

"language" and "dialect." Every linguistic or geographical area seems
to require its own definition. In China the various forms of Chinese
such as Cantonese and Hakka are commonly referred to as dialects;
the main reason seems to be that they all share a common written
form. In one sense, a language has many dialects that are subvarieties
(sense A according to Masica 1991). In another sense, languages and
dialects coexist with dialects not having a written standard (sense B
according to Masica). Caldwell (1856), in a way clearly similar to
sense A above, divided the Dravidian languages into cultivated
dialects and uncultivated dialects. Grierson states that both
grammatical structure and nationality must be taken into account
when distinguishing dialects from languages. In fact, every modern
Indian language included in the constitution in the early years had
a distinctive writing system with the exception of Marathi, which is
written in the Balbodh script that is almost identical to the Devanagari
script used for Hindi. Political and cultural factors as well as the
number of speakers made the inclusion of Marathi indispensable,
and Marathi did have a script that was different from that of
languages in contiguous areas, such as Gujarati and Kannada. The
creation of linguistic states and the enumeration of scheduled
languages in the Indian constitution, even if it did not resolve the
problem of distinguishing between language and dialect in India,
did at least define an upper tier of languages that would play a larger
role in Indian nation-building than the languages not listed. Although
this list has been amended over the years (most recently in 1993 by
the addition of Nepali and Konkani), there is clearly a group of
languages analogous to the national languages of Europe and other
parts of the world. The eighth schedule of the constitution currently
lists fifteen languages as official.

Only one of the official languages listed in the constitution does
not have an indigenous writing system derived from the ancient
Brahmi script, and that language is Urdu. Since Urdu is not
associated with a specific territory, it would not seem to qualify for
inclusion using the same criteria. In addition, there is no inherent
linguistic difference between Urdu and Hindi. Both languages are
based on the same "khari boli" speech form, which originated in the
Delhi area, and they share common vocabulary, grammar, and
pronunciation. Only the importation of Sanskrit vocabulary into
Hindi and Perso-Arabic vocabulary into Urdu differentiates the two.
Thus here script is not just one linguistic criterion for distinguishing
two languages; it is the only one. Both Indian and western scholars
have had difficulty in explaining this phenomenon, which is

apparently unique in the world. The Serbo-Croatian dichotomy would seem to be somewhat similar, since the two varieties have different writing systems and are spoken by different religious groups. Recently the similarity has become even greater as a partition has also made Serbian and Croatian the national languages of two separate countries, and efforts are being made to differentiate the languages further through lexical borrowing from different sources. Still Serbian and Croatian both have a definite territorial identity and are also based on separate dialects, thus producing different pronunciation patterns that do not exist in Hindi-Urdu. Also, Hindi and Urdu are not the only national languages of two different nations; they also coexist within India and most of the Indian states. They both have official status at the center and in several states as well. In his 1960 article "Formal and Informal Standards in Hindi Regional Area" included in his 1971 volume, Gumperz describes the speech differences among speakers of Hindi or Urdu that depend to a large extent on differences in religious and educational background. In his 1969 article "Language, Communication and Control in North India" in the same volume, Gumperz describes the differentiation that has occurred between formal Hindi and the more Urdu-like spoken language because of government language planning. The Hindi-Urdu dichotomy is one of the examples of the importance of sociological factors in Indian languages, and the study of such relationships between language and society all over the world has been influenced by such situations in India.

In the context of language dialect, we should mention the concepts of diglossia and the related functional bilingualism as described by Ferguson (1959) and Fishman (1967). Diglossia was initially defined as the coexistence of two forms of the same language, one a literary form, such as modern standard Arabic, the other a colloquial non-written form, such as the various Arabic "dialects" spoken in the Arab world. Functional bilingualism is a similar relationship, except that the two forms are not considered a single language. An example would be the use by an educated Indian of English at work and other formal contexts and of an Indian language at home, a language he would rarely write. There is a tendency to overuse the term diglossia in the context of India, since almost all of the major languages have strongly differentiated formal and informal forms. But in India the difference is usually of a different kind, between the spoken style and the written style, as described for *sādhu* and *calit* Bengali by Dimock (1960), and between formal Hindi and colloquial Hindustani, where formal Hindi is characterized mainly by extensive use of Sanskritic vocabulary.

The main example of true diglossia in India is Tamil, where a single literary standard coexists with various colloquial forms (Shanmugam Pillai 1960). Still many other kinds of diglossia exist in India, where many people use at least two forms of the same language. Thus in Varanasi and other areas of eastern Uttar Pradesh and Bihar the language of the home and much street conversation is Bhojpuri, but the language of education and other formal contexts is Hindi. This situation exists in most of India where regional standards coexist with local dialects of the regional standard. Sometimes the local dialect is promoted to regional standard; thus many speakers of Punjabi once considered Punjabi to be their local form of Hindi. Sometimes the regional standard is demoted to the status of local dialect as happened with Awadhi and Brajbhasha, which were once regional standards but are now considered merely local varieties of Hindi in Uttar Pradesh.

Most studies of language in India emphasize the great variety of languages found in India. There are four distinct language families even though the major languages listed in the constitution belong to only two families, Indo-Aryan and Dravidian. Still, these languages have distinctive writing systems and are for the most part mutually unintelligible. During the last fifty years there has been a tendency to emphasize the differences even more. Thus in the first two decades after Independence Punjabi and Hindi were both spoken in Punjab, and although Punjabi was written using the Gurmukhi writing system and had liturgical status in the Sikh religion, the linguistic differences between Hindi and Punjabi were minor. Still, the Sikh movement in Punjab, as described by Brass (1974), led to the division of Punjab into two states: a Punjabi-speaking Punjab and a Hindi-speaking Haryana. Hindi and Urdu represent the most striking example of this tendency to differentiation. Their differentiation was one of the major issues in the partition of India at the time of Independence. The differentiation has continued in India during the last 50 years with much controversy in the north Indian states about the official status of Urdu along with Hindi.

It is interesting that much study of the languages of India by western scholars has focused on India as a single linguistic area, i.e., what is striking about Indian languages is that, in spite of their seeming heterogeneity in the Indian subcontinent, in all their diversity there is a basic unity. India can be described as a single linguistic area with all the languages sharing certain common features. Prior to Independence, Caldwell, Grierson and Jules Bloch had already noted this. The first clear enunciation of this phenomenon was by Murray Emeneau in 1956. Bloch had mentioned features shared by Indo-Aryan and Dravidian languages, such as the presence of an absolutive construction, the absence of prepositions, and the existence of retroflex consonants that contrast with dentals. Emeneau first used the term linguistic area with reference to India and pointed out that similarities made the Indo-Aryan languages more similar to genetically unrelated languages in India such as the Dravidian languages than to other Indo-European languages outside the Indian subcontinent. He added the features of echo-word constructions and the use of classifiers to the features shared by the languages of India. Masica (1976) enumerated other features of South Asian languages that are generally shared by all South Asian languages, such as causative verbs, explicators, dative constructions, and the absence of the verb "to have."

The most significant development that relates to western scholarship and the modern Indian languages is the development of instructional programs in those languages over the last fifty years. At the beginning there was little expertise available in any of those languages, and young Indian scholars traveled to the U.S. to provide instruction. In many cases they also earned degrees while teaching and brought western scholarship in language and linguistics back to India. Thus much of the scholarship in Indian languages both in India and the West was the result of this give-and-take between Indian and western scholarship. Every decade since Indian independence has produced an evolution in the study of Indian languages in the West. In the 1950s the first instructional programs in modern Indian languages were established, usually as part of the emphasis on uncommonly-taught languages in linguistics programs. In addition, scholars like Hacker in Germany and Lienhard in Sweden, who were primarily Sanskritists, turned their attention to the modern Indian languages with linguistic studies of the Hindi verb. The compound verb, i.e., a helping verb used in the same way that prefixes are used in European languages (such as English and German) to alter the meaning of the main verb, became a subject of interest for the first time. Modern Indian languages were incorporated in the curriculum of universities in the Soviet Union, Czechoslovakia, and East Germany. With the advent of the 1960s, the study of modern Indian languages increased greatly, especially in the United States, where the National Defense Education Act began a program of federal support for the study of "critical" languages that included the languages of India. The establishment of federally-supported South Asia Centers at universities like Pennsylvania, Chicago, Wisconsin, Berkeley, and Texas was a great impetus for the increasing study of Indian languages. By the end of the 1960s many students had been trained in Indian languages, especially Hindi-Urdu, and a number of these students were subsequently hired at the various South Asia Centers to guide their Indian language programs to the present time. U.S. government support was also provided for the creation of teaching materials. In several Indian languages (such as Hindi-Urdu, Bengali, and Tamil) materials produced at that time are still the basis for teaching these languages today.

By 1970 the teaching of modern Indian languages in the United States was well established. Undergraduate students were drawn to Indian language courses because of the increased interest in Indian culture and, in some cases, because of the opportunity to earn academic credits in India under some recognized study-abroad program. Graduate students preparing for research in India were now routinely studying Indian languages with financial support in the form of language fellowships. The American Institute of Indian Studies (AIIS) augmented its fellowship program with the establishment of an advanced language program that, from 1969 on, received support from the U.S. Office (later Department) of Education. Under this program the AIIS provided advanced language training in India to a number of graduate students each year. An in-India summer program was also available until funding for this program ended in the mid-1970s. The summer program resumed in 1990. Most of the advanced language training in India was provided in Hindi and Tamil, but from time to time there was also instruction in other languages such as Telugu.

From 1985 to the present, Indian language instruction underwent yet another transformation. An increasing number of students in Indian language classes were the children of immigrants from India, who already had some latent knowledge of the language. In addition, new emphases on proficiency-based instruction and the availability of videos in the classroom generated increased emphasis on language skills that could be used in the real world. Examinations were developed that tested oral proficiency on a scale defined by the American Council on Teaching of Foreign Languages (ACTFL). Other measures were developed to test ability to comprehend texts without use of the dictionary and to test listening comprehension using authentic materials such as Indian television programs and films.

In the fifty years since Independence language has been a vital part of the Indian scene. Even though the casual visitor may think that everything of any importance in India revolves around English, the indigenous languages of India play a much more important role as is evident to those who study India. These languages are an important aspect of political identity; they are listed in the constitution and are the basis for identifying various political divisions such as the states. In addition, they are a key to identity, culture, and social groups. During the last fifty years western scholars have studied Indian languages as a key to the discovery of India in a variety of fields, such as political science, anthropology, folklore, literature, religion, and history. Others have continued in the tradition of William Jones and George Grierson and have studied language itself. The major contributions of western scholarship have been in language classification and analysis, while Indian scholarship has provided much of the data and lexicographic material so necessary for this work. The ever-increasing emphasis on language study as a necessary prerequisite for scholarly work on India during the last fifty years is, therefore, likely to continue in future years.

REFERENCES

Beames, John. 1872-79 (reprinted 1966). *Comparative Grammar of Modern Indo-Aryan Languages of India.* 3 vols. Delhi: Munshiram Manoharlal.

Bloch, Jules. 1934 (reprinted 1965). *Indo-Aryan: From the Vedas to Modern Times.* Paris: Librairie Adrien-Maisonneuve.

Brass, Paul R. 1974. *Language, Religion and Politics in North India.* New York: Cambridge Univ. Press.

Caldwell, Robert. 1856 (3rd edition, 1961). *A Comparative Grammar of the Dravidian or South-Indian Family of Languages.* Madras: Univ. of Madras.

Dimock, Edward C., Jr. 1960. "Literary and Colloquial Bengali in Modern Bengali Prose." In *Linguistic Diversity in South Asia: Studies in Regional, Social, and Functional Variation,* ed. Charles A. Ferguson and John J. Gumperz. Bloomington: Indiana Univ. Research Center in Anthropology, Folklore, and Linguistics. *International Journal of American Linguistics* 26:3 (part 3).

Emeneau, Murray B. 1956. "India as a Linguistic Area." *Language* 32(1):3-16.

Ferguson, Charles A. 1959. "Diglossia." *Word* 15(2): 325-340.

Fishman, Joshua A. 1967. "Bilingualism With and Without Diglossia; Diglossia With and Without Bilingualism." *Journal of Social Issues.* 23(2):29-37.

Grierson, George A. ed. 1903-1928 (reprinted 1967-1968). *Linguistic Survey of India.* Delhi: Motilal Banarsidass.

Gumperz, John J. 1971. *Language in Social Groups: Essays by John Gumperz.* Stanford: Stanford Univ. Press.

Hacker, Paul. 1958. *Zur Funktion Einiger Hilfsverben im Modernen Hindi.* Mainz.

Lienhard, S. 1961. *Tempusgebrauch und Aktionsartenbildung in der Modernen Hindi.* Stockholm.

Masica, Colin P. 1976. *Defining a Linguistic Area. South Asia.* Chicago: Univ. of Chicago Press.

Masica, Colin P. 1991. *The Indo-Aryan Languages.* Cambridge: Cambridge Univ. Press.

Miller, Roy Andrew. 1969. "The Tibeto-Burman Languages of South Asia." In *Current Trends in Linguistics,* vol. 5, *Linguistics in South Asia,* ed.Thomas A. Sebeok, 431-449. The Hague: Mouton.

Pinnow, Heinz-Jurgen. 1963. "The Position of the Munda Languages Within the Austro-Asiatic Language Family." In *Linguistic Comparison in South East Asia and the Pacific,* ed. H.L. Shorto, 140-152. London: School of Oriental and African Studies, University of London.

Shafer, Robert. 1955. "Classification of Sino-Tibetan Languages." *Word.* 11:94-111.

Porizka, Vincenc. 1963. *Hindstina: Hindi Language Course.* Prague:

Shanmugam Pillai, M. 1960. "Tamil-Literary and Colloquial." In *Linguistic Diversity in South Asia: Studies in Regional, Social, and Functional Variation,* ed. Charles A. Ferguson and John J. Gumperz. Bloomington: Indiana Univ. Research Center in Anthropology, Folklore, and Linguistics. *International Journal of American Linguistics* 26:3 (part 3).

Shapiro, Michael C. and Harold F. Schiffman. 1981. *Language and Society in South Asia.* Delhi: Motilal Banarsidass.

Zide, Norman H. 1969. "Munda and Non-Munda Austroasiatic Languages." In *Current Trends in Linguistics,* vol. 5, *Linguistics in South Asia,* ed. Thomas A. Sebeok, 411-430. The Hague: Mouton.

Zvelebil, Kamil. 1970. *Comparative Dravidian Phonology.* The Hague: Mouton.

Linguistics

JAMES W. GAIR

Modern U.S. linguistics, though it developed a character of its own in the twentieth century and especially in the post World War II period, nevertheless owes its origins to European linguists of the nineteenth century who were largely, but not exclusively, located in Germany. The role of a knowledge of Sanskrit in the foundation of Indo-European historical linguistics, especially as it was triggered by the work of Sir William Jones, is famous, and it was from those beginnings that the modern science of linguistics, whether historical or synchronic-descriptive, developed. The progress of linguistics was also fed by a knowledge of the ancient Indian grammatical tradition that exceeded in precision and formal elegance anything that had been known in Europe up to that time. The role that this knowledge played was clearly and forcefully stated by Murray Emeneau in his presidential address "India and Linguistics," delivered to the American Oriental Society in 1925:

It is clear that, however much may have been added by Western scholars to the general phonetic inventory and to an exact knowledge of the articulatory processes, the first long but slow steps away from the awkward fumblings of early European scholarship were taken only when Hindu phonetics had come to be generally known to Sanskrit scholars and had been introduced by them into the stream of European scholarship.[1]

Emeneau's statement refers to what might be called the content of linguistics, but it was also the case that India played a vital role in the organization of the field in terms of institutions or leading scholars. Thus a recent historian of U.S. linguistics pointed out:

... it might be said (and has often been said) that Indianism provided the impetus for the whole linguistic enterprise of the nineteenth century. The first professional society devoted exclusively to language was the Asiatic Society of Calcutta (founded in 1783) and the first professional journal was *Asiatic Researches* (founded in 1788). Researchers in the United States saw fit to follow suit. The first professional linguistic society was the American

Society of Oriental Studies, founded in 1842, and the first linguistic journal, the *Journal of the American Oriental Society* (1849). Indianism, furthermore, was to play a profound role in William Dwight Whitney's thought and reputation, both at home and abroad.[2]

The American Oriental Society was modeled on the Calcutta Society, and its interest was not limited to strictly oriental languages but was extended to languages in general.[3] Beyond his work in Indian languages that included the grammar still familiar to every U.S. student of Sanskrit, Whitney was a major influential figure in American general linguistics, who produced, among other important works , a pioneering book on general linguistics, *The Life and Growth of Language: An Outline of Linguistic Science* (1875).[4]

In the 19th century, the German scientific approach to linguistics led the field, and the route by which it was integrated fully into U.S. linguistic theories in the late 19th and early 20th century also involved an Indian connection. A great deal of this integration was fostered by Maurice Bloomfield, a student of Whitney's, who followed the Sanskritist William Lanman as chair of Sanskrit studies at Johns Hopkins University, and who served as the second president of the new Linguistic Society of America, following Hermann Collitz, also a Sanskritist. [5]

It was, however, Maurice Bloomfield's nephew, Leonard Bloomfield, who became a towering figure in American linguistics and arguably the most influential figure in shaping the field. His book *Language*, published in 1933,[6] became in effect the Bible of successive generations of largely young and enthusiastic U.S. linguists (extending up to the present author). The U.S. school of structural-descriptive linguistics that often bore Leonard Bloomfield's name was the dominant school in America and, to a significant extent, abroad as well up to the end of the 1950s.[7] It was that school that was, in a sense, "exported" to South Asia, (and especially to India) in the 1950s and 1960s and informed much of the linguistic work that was carried out there. Bloomfield reflected the Indian grammatical tradition to a generally unrecognized degree—a reflection that was stated clearly by Emeneau in his presidential address referred to above:

With Leonard Bloomfield, however, we come to a scholar who was intimately acquainted with Panini and the commentaries on Panini, and who expressed deep admiration for the results and the methods of the Hindu grammarians. His review of Liebich's *Konkordanz Panini-Candra* in *Language*, vol. V (1929), pp. 267-76, is a most explicit statement of what he found in Panini and what he thought other linguistic scholars ought to find there; this essay should be better known to all linguistic scholars and students than it is. More important: linguistic method as stated by Bloomfield in his book *Language* shows much that is the result of his readings of the Hindu grammarians. It is not too much to say that his methods in phonemic analysis, and in morphology and syntax would hardly have been stated as they were, if Bloomfield had not been steeped in Hindu grammar, so that he became such a firm admirer of its "scientific condensation, which places every feature into its proper settings" and of its "completeness,"[8] as well as of its striving for brevity and stringency of statement ...There is no need to go beyond the bounds of discretion and point out in detail the influence of Bloomfield on most of the younger American linguistic scholars. It is enough to say that most of the specific features that are taken at the present day to distinguish an "American" school of linguistics from others are Bloomfieldian, and, if I am correct, many are Paninean. Such Paninean features can hardly be said to be characteristic of any other group of linguistic scholars.[9]

In the 1950s, extending into the 1960s, western and predominantly U.S. structural linguistics returned the favor when then current western linguistic approaches were fostered in India and to some extent in Pakistan and Sri Lanka (then Ceylon). This was accomplished with considerable Foundation support for mounting workshops and programs, for aiding in the creation of centers and departments (for an account, see Patterson, this volume), and for the movement of scholars and students between the U.S. and India.

Although the introduction of U.S., and especially Bloomfieldian, linguistics into India was in a sense a re-importation and could be seen, as one commentator has remarked, to be "carrying coals to Newcastle" (see Patterson, this volume), the effect was significant in several directions. In addition to the descriptive and historical work that resulted, a whole generation of linguists concerned with South Asian languages, both Indian and foreign, was created. And many lasting collegial and personal relationships were forged that eventuated in further productive and often path-breaking work. There was also an important organizational effect. Many of the alumni of those programs ultimately staffed, to a great extent, the major South Asian linguistics programs in India and the U.S., and they figured prominently and productively in the language-related (and, in fact, more general) activities of the AIIS (again, see Patterson, this volume for details).

When the participants in those programs and their students obtained academic positions in the U.S., it was often in connection with language-teaching programs. One important byproduct of this was the application of linguistics to the creation of new teaching materials for South Asian languages, since there were few or unsatisfactory teaching materials currently available. The preparation of language-teaching materials was given a further boost when the U.S. Congress passed the National Defense Education Act of 1958, which was replaced in 1965 by Title VI of the Higher Education Act. This legislation provided support for teaching materials in "critical languages," including those of South Asia. The subsequent teaching materials were produced largely by those linguist language teachers connected with the university area centers also supported under that legislation. Between the introduction of the act and 1993, approximately 150 works, including teaching materials, reference grammars or handbooks, and dictionaries were supported in this way. Many of them are still in use in language programs, and some of them still constitute major sources of information for some of the languages.[10] Much of the work was carried out with graduate students. That, together with graduate fellowship support (also provided by the Act), helped to attract and produce a new generation of South Asian linguists.

In a 1969 paper in the major *Current Trends* survey of South Asian linguistics, Ashok Kelkar characterized the 1950s U.S.-linked efforts in India, and specifically the language project at Deccan College and the subsequent summer schools of linguistics, as inaugurating what he called the "contemporary phase of South Asian linguistics," stating:

Indian linguistics was finally ready to catch up with the Saussure-Sapir-Bloomfield revolution in linguistics... Linguistics has been put back on the map of Indian scholarship.[11]

Though the dominant theoretical paradigm involved was the Bloomfieldian-Saussurean one, by the time Kelkar made his remarks the seeds of change had already been sown and were, in fact, well sprouted. Kelkar also noted that:

In the third or contemporary phase we have become so accustomed to the competition of rival models of linguistic description that younger linguists are apt to forget the vastly different picture that prevailed when these models did not hold the stage. Of course, South Asian Linguistics does have its exhibits of classical American descriptions, Pike-tagmemics, Longacre-tagmemics, Harris-transformationalism, Chomsky-generative presentations, Firthian studies, Halliday-inspired systemic grammars, even glossematic studies. Structuralism has some historical-comparativist work to its credit in the Indo-Aryan, Dravidian, and Munda fields.[12]

Though now scarcely a quarter-century old, Kelkar's account

already has a rather archaic ring. The competition among models that he described devolved in the United States into the increasing dominance of one school of generative grammar, especially within syntactic theory, i.e., the increasing dominance of whatever Noam Chomsky and his followers at MIT or elsewhere were developing. This trend extended to a great extent to other countries as well. (Whatever one's own theoretical persuasion and hence view of this development may be, I believe this observation to be sociologically correct. There is no lack of either celebration or condemnation of it in the relevant literature.) The shift to generative grammar and subsequent developments within that theory were destined to have important effects on both the carrying out of linguistics in India and the extent and manner that Indian linguistics affected linguistics in the U.S.

When the earliest versions of transformational-generative grammar appeared, including both Chomsky's published work and that of his teacher, Zellig Harris, they seemed to many structural-descriptive linguists to provide a much needed and hence welcome set of powerful devices to account for data that had eluded or resisted description within previously available syntactic theory. As a result, a number of grammatical treatments of South Asian languages were produced in the transformational-generative paradigm ranging from Chomsky's 1957 *Syntactic Structures*[13] to his 1965 *Aspects of the Theory of Syntax*.[14] Studies of this kind appeared both in India and abroad and included, among others, published works such as those by Manindra Verma and Yamuna Kachru for Hindi, Franklin Southworth and Mahadeo Apte for Marathi, Agesthialingom and Harold Schiffman for Tamil, and James Gair for Sinhala, along with a number of theses and a quantity of circulated works by A.K. Ramanujan, James Lindholm, Colin Masica and others in "purple ink" or cyclostyled form.

This considerable body of productions and the enthusiasm that drove it slowed, however, and its results never entered the mainstream to the extent that they might have to the benefit of general theory. For one thing, generative grammar from the 1960s until recently was, to a great extent, English-driven by problems of English syntax. Work in other languages was, for much of the period, to a great degree marginalized and invoked only to a limited extent in the general literature. Though there were scholars working in South Asian languages who continued to be productive in the generative paradigm, they did not in general form part of the interacting group of scholars who were developing the dominant theory—or perhaps, more accurately, theories, since this time has been referred to by Harris (1993) and others as the "Linguistics Wars."[15]

Also, and perhaps more importantly, a reaction (or perhaps disillusion) set in among researchers in South Asian languages. This was especially marked in South Asia itself, though generative linguistics continued actively in some locations there. In the U.S. as well as in India productive work on South Asian languages (including that by a number of the earlier practitioners of generative-transformational grammar in South Asian languages) shifted to a great extent to other kinds of linguistics, especially sociolinguistics and applied linguistics, which already had a good beginning in India, and in which there were stimulating new developments.

There were a number of reasons for this shift; among them was the changing face of generative theory itself. Chomsky's interest was always theory and Universal Grammar (UG) in some form. Even at the beginning, the work that he considered important was his *The Logical Structure of Linguistic Theory*, which, though written in the mid-1950s, was delayed in general publication until 1975.[16] Chomski preferred *The Logical Structure of Linguistic Theory* to his *Syntactic Structures* (1957) through which most of us were introduced to the theory. Over time, presentations within generative grammar, whether in published form or in panels at relevant conferences, increasingly centered on theoretical rather than descriptive concerns. This reflected a shift from a theory that held that a specific language was a (presumably possible) device for generating all (and only) its possible sentences (though linked to a general explanatory theory of language) to a theory in which individual language systems and structures played a diminishing role, and the concern was with arriving at a conception of Universal Grammar. This eventuated in a theory in which specific language grammars became epiphenominal and, in fact, essentially nonexistent, except as reflections of Universal Grammar. Even before that final point, however, this rapidly developing and changing Universal Grammar theory appeared to many scholars to be becoming less and less relevant to descriptions of specific languages and at the same time technically and terminologically more complex and arcane. Moreover, it was difficult to keep up with the changes unless one were well connected with the network, and for many of those in India this was a formidable task. Also, as mentioned earlier, the evidence invoked by theorists was largely from English, with some attention to familiar European languages. This was an allowable practice under the assumption that, since Universal Grammar was reflected in all languages, work on any one language could be revealing. More recently, however, it has been recognized that arriving at a sound conception of Universal Grammar (UG) as a characterization of the structured human capacity for languages necesssarily requires cross-language information, since it must be able to account for forms of apparently radically different languages. As Chomsky himself remarked in 1986 ("I-language" here can be understood as the language as internalized by the speaker-hearer):

It is important to bear in mind that the study of one language may provide crucial evidence concerning the structure of some other language, if we continue to accept the plausible assumption that the capacity to acquire language, the subject matter of UG, is common across the species ... If we are interested in discovering the real properties of the initial state of the language faculty and of its particular realizations as potential or actual I-languages... we must regard a theory of one language as subject to change on the basis of evidence concerning other languages (mediated through a theory of UG), or evidence of other sorts.[17]

As a result of this recognition and of other developments leading to the growth of a new generation of scholars with interests both in current theory and in South Asian languages, along with renewed collaboration between Indian and western scholars, there are hopeful signs that South Asian languages will again receive the attention that they deserve within the general field.

If linguistic studies of Indian languages have played as yet a regrettably limited part in the formulation of linguistic theory (narrowly conceived as the formation of current linguistic theory within the dominant paradigm in the U.S.), their effects in other directions, specifically in those approaches that link language with socio-cultural or socio-historical factors, have been considerable. In retrospect, this is a result of the nature of the Indian language scene and the interaction of scholars with it. India, with its multiplicity of languages representing four major families along with some others, and replete with social, functional, and geographic varieties, forms a natural laboratory for work on such socio-cultural and socio-historical linkages and, in fact, virtually forces them on the investigator. In addition, there are significant commonalities underlying that diversity, so that as with other aspects of culture and society, India presents a picture of unity in diversity, a situation that invites investigation by linguists as well as by scholars in other areas of inquiry.

As William Bright, a scholar prominently involved in the first-hand study of Indian languages, remarked:

South Asia was an area where the phenomena of language contact and linguistic area were impossible to ignore ... and it was also an area where the sociolinguistic phenomena of language variation were impossible to ignore.[18]

Important research in two major, and to some extent interlinked, directions has marked the scholarly scene in India: 1. Research into linguistic areas and languages in contact, and 2. Research into language varieties and their locus and use.

1. Research into Linguistic Areas and Languages in Contact. Historical linguists had recognized for some time the existence of linguistic areas, or *sprachbunds,* defined by Murray Emeneau in his 1956 "India as a Linguistic Area" as "an area which includes languages belonging to more than one family but showing traits in common which are found to belong to the other members of (at least) one of the families."[19] While some common or partially common features of South Asian languages had been noted by earlier observers, the paper that set out the situation programmatically (and most inspired research along that line in the past four decades) was the 1956 Emeneau one just cited which built, as the author acknowledged, on work by Jules Bloch in the 1930s. Further work on this topic, though centering on India, extended to South Asia in general, and sub-areas within South Asia. It was carried forth by a number of scholars in the U.S. including Colin Masica, William Bright, and Franklin Southworth. By now a considerable literature has developed on the topic.[20]

The delineation of a linguistic area led to the question of the processes that enter into its formation. This was addressed to varying degrees in the work of the scholars mentioned, as well as by others. A number of studies based directly on Indian evidence entered the mainstream of work on the topic. One such study, for example, was a 1971 paper by Gumperz and Wilson[21] in which they gave an account of the convergence between Urdu, Marathi, and Kannada in a village (Kupwar) near the (then) Mysore-Maharashtra border that exhibited extensive contact between those languages. Similarly, a 1971 paper by Franklin Southworth[22] proposed a model by which pidginization played a role in the formation of the Indian linguistic area, with special reference to Marathi, and a 1975 paper by Mangesh V. Nadkarni[23] proposed a central role for specific kinds of bilingualism and their relation to the social framework in linguistic convergence.

These and other scholars produced further work on linguistic areas, contact, and convergence in South Asia.[24] The papers mentioned, however, were prominent among those that attracted attention beyond the community of South Asian linguists, inspiring discussion, extension to other areas, and in some cases, disagreement and counter-proposals. The extent to which such work has entered the general stream of research in that field in a significant way can be judged, for example, by the extent to which the work on India and wider South Asia has been incorporated into a recent comprehensive volume on language contact and creolization by Thomason and Kaufman.[25]

2. Research into Language Varieties and Their Locus and Use. Another area in which work in India has influenced and, to an important degree, inspired research in a wider sphere is the investigation of varieties of language, both functional and social. Both structural-descriptive and generative linguistics centered on language as both a formal system and as a system of forms, abstracting away from social settings and usage (although many of the structural-descriptive linguists did double duty, consonant with the partially anthropological roots of their field; see, for example, Chomsky's famous characterization of the object of investigation linguistics as the language of an ideal speaker-hearer in a homogeneous speech community).[26]

Chomsky's view represents a legitimate approach that underlay much descriptive work that had preceded him as well. It has greatly increased our knowledge of the nature of language and of specific languages, and it has informed, and continues to inform, much important work on Indian languages. Necessarily, however, the abstraction to the ideal native speaker is an abstraction to uniformity. It purposefully sets aside other inescapably-linked aspects of human language activity as a whole, and particularly those aspects relating to use and function and the sociocultural setting. Individual or socially linked variation thus becomes a peripheral and, in fact, intrusive concern. Such variation, to the extent it is treated at all, is treated as "free variation" without regard to those linkages and to any determining social discourse or interactional conditions.

However, the rich and complex language scene in India virtually forces the investigator to come face-to-face with, and deal with, questions of language varieties and their social settings and uses. The notion of competence widens to encompass the appropriate use of language relevant to participants, settings, purposes, and functions. One specific and more widely-construed sub-area of linguistics that takes this as the object of inquiry is "the ethnography of speaking," characterized in the words of one of its founders (and the apparent source of the term) as follows:

... what appears as variation from the standpoint of a single, homogeneously defined code may show patterning of its own. Analysis of the ways in which linguistic features covary with other factors of speech events shows that such variation is not random, but follows rules of use. If the generality of the concept, speech habits of a community, is exploited, and taken to include the formulation of such rules, then one moves from the realm of variation (largely statistical in conception) to a realm of structure and to the constitution of a new, second, qualitative and descriptive science of language, beside that of the linguistic code per se. In so moving, one breaks sharply with the widespread view that assigns structure exclusively to language (la langue) and only variation to speech (la parole), replacing it by the assumption that the full range of a community is structured. The patterning of language, as manifested in grammar, is but one phase, and to some extent, a dependent one, of the patterning of speech activity in general. Research based on the new approach (which may be termed the ethnography of speaking ...) brings into focus a good deal that has escaped attention, not being caught up in the frame of reference of either linguistics or ethnography as usually practiced. The whole of behavior is approached from the point of view of discovering the relevant classes of speech events, the factors constituting them, the range of functions served by speech in the particular community, and the relations existing among them.[27]

What is of special relevance in the present context is that this approach, which has since been actively and productively followed in many different settings, owes much of its beginnings to the confrontation between the variegated Indian linguistic scene and the scholars, particularly the foreign ones (primarily from the U.S.), who came into close contact with it.

Stephen O. Murray, a recent chronicler of the history of linguistic investigation in the U.S., has expressed this connection clearly:

While the ethnography of speaking developed in California, the foundation of socially-explainable variation in speech was laid in India. Several scholars who were to become prominent organizational and intellectual leaders in sociolinguistics as it emerged were at Deccan College in Poona during the mid-1950s. Confronted with linguistic diversity even within villages, they explored the sources of the variability that they observed.[28]

We can note here the connection of this development with the U.S. linguistic efforts in India in the 1950s. There was a large overlap between the participants in those 1950s activities, the scholars who investigated Indian linguistic areas, and the scholars referred to by Murray in the above quote. One pioneering work in the investigation of variation in India was a volume edited by Ferguson and Gumperz,

Linguistic Diversity in South Asia: Studies in Regional, Social, and Functional Variation,[29] that developed from a 1957 American Anthropological Association session. Charles Ferguson called it, "... the first thing you would label 'sociolinguistics,'"[30] and Stephen Murray referred to it as "the first exemplar of what would be dubbed the ethnography of speaking."[31] As Murray further noted, the collaboration on that volume began in Pune in the 1950s. Another pioneering volume in sociolinguistics was the one so titled edited by William Bright in 1966,[32] which proceeded from a conference held in 1964. It made use of Bright's extensive South Asian experience and included a provocative study by Gerald Kelley entitled, "Hindi as a Lingua Franca." Kelly's article addressed the important issues of official language, its implementation, and its standardization, articles that have occupied the attention of numerous scholars in South Asia and beyond.

In 1959 Charles Ferguson published an article titled "Diglossia" in which he characterized diglossia as follows:

... a relatively stable language situation in which, in addition to the primary dialects of the language (which may include a standard or regional standards) there is a very divergent, highly codified, often grammatically more complex superposed variety, the vehicle of a large and respected body of written literature, either of an earlier period or in another speech community, which is learned largely by formal education and is used for most written and formal spoken purposes, but is not used by any sector of the community for ordinary conversation.[33]

Ferguson's paper inspired a great deal of research and discussion attempting to define, modify, and further characterize diglossia and to apply it to other languages. This was by no means limited to South Asian languages. In fact, Ferguson (somewhat ironically, given his close acquaintance with South Asian linguistics, including his extensive prior work on Bengali) did not include any South Asian languages among his four major exemplary languages (Arabic, Greek, Haitian Creole, and Swiss German). Ferguson did include a brief characterization of diglossia in Tamil, but he could have drawn additional illustrations from a number of South Asian languages that exhibit diglossia or closely allied phenomena in their full forms. Subsequently, a great deal of work in this area has been carried out inside and outside India as well as abroad, especially concerning Bengali, Tamil, and the Sri Lankan language of Sinhala.

Research regarding diglossia has continued actively up to the present, incorporating, to varying degrees, currently available linguistic and sociolinguistic theory. One recent major work on the general topic of diglossia focused on Tamil.[34] Other work on diglossia has appeared in volumes such as *Linguistic Diversity in South Asia* (1960)[35], *South Asian Languages: Structure, Convergence and Diglossia* (1986),[36] and in various journal articles and dissertations. By 1993 diglossia had inspired a 472-page bibiography.[37] The relevant point here is that diglossia and the study of language varieties in general necessarily incorporate work in India and other areas of South Asia to an inescapable degree. Diglossia and the study of language varieties have constituted highly productive and active areas of research, with significant implications for linguistics, sociolinguistics, and applied linguistics and language planning in the U.S. and elsewhere.

Work in sociolinguistics relating to Indian languages has continued actively up to the present, as evidenced by numerous journal papers and conference proceedings as well as by volumes such as the 1992 *Dimensions of Sociolinguistics in South Asia*.[38] This volume included papers developing the notion of a sociolinguistic area[39] complementary to that of a linguistic area described earlier.

Another area of research that requires mention here is the study of Indian English as a distinctive variety or cluster of varieties, associated with Braj Kachru and others.[40] This is obviously an area of interests to scholars of South Asia, and one that holds important social and educational implications as well. Its importance in the present context is its place within the wider domain of historical linguistics and socio-linguistics. The topic is of relevance to those interested in English as a world language, but its contribution to the field extends well beyond work specifically devoted to English. Like the work on language contact and convergence characterized earlier, the study of Indian English serves as an important example of change under conditions of contact, and it has figured as such in the literature (see, for example, Thomason and Kaufman 1988).

While it is true that the study of Indian and other South Asian languages has affected the U.S. and international linguistic scene, it is also true, in the opinion of this writer, that Indian and other South Asian languages have been seriously underutilized and under-represented in the field at large. This has been especially marked in the case of linguistic theory formation. In the forward to a bibliography on Indian linguistics in 1978, D.B. Pattanayak remarked:

... the research in India has been data-oriented rather than theory-oriented. Unless theoretical insights are developed on the basis of indigenous data, Indian linguistics will continue to play second fiddle to the west and will remain irrelevant to the multilingual and multicultural countries of Asia, Africa, and Latin America.[41]

Pattanayak was actually referring here to work in cross-disciplinary fields, such as sociolinguistics and language planning, in which work in India has continued and has had a significant impact. But his words can also be applied with greater force to theory formation in structural fields such as phonology, syntax, and semantics. The development of theoretical insights on the basis of South Asian languages is still very much a desideratum. Not only must the necessary work be done, the insights gained thereby must also enter into the international mainstream of active linguistic research. Numerous proposals that have reached general acceptance in the theoretical literature could have been more robustly formulated had they faced and incorporated phenomena manifested in some languages of India and wider South Asia. In part this is the fault of the community of scholars most active and visible in theory formation, who based their work on their own languages or the readily accessible more familiar European ones. However, until recently this neglect has also been in part a function of the very limited number of Indian and other South Asian apprentice linguists who have been trained at institutions abroad noted for their leadership in theoretical formation, and whose research thus might most easily achieve notice partly by being brought to public attention by their mentors and fellow students. This in turn is at least in part traceable to the narrowness of admission policies at those same institutions, and contrasts with the situation described earlier when a number of linguists who were to become leaders in the field both in India and abroad were trained as a result of the collaboration between Indian, U.S., and other foreign scholars and institutions.

Another contributing factor lies in the failure of scholars of South Asia, both in India and abroad, to make their work more widely available in relevant publications. At present there is some fine work being carried out in India in the form of theses and presentations in local journals and collections. This work is known only by those with special interests in the area, but the work deserves wider notice. In fairness, it must be noted that the road to such publication is commonly not an easy one, and that the number of outlets offering both general access and wide distribution and prominence in the field has been limited. Nevertheless, more efforts are called for on the part of the concerned scholars to see that their work enters into wider channels of distribution. An interesting and instructive study of the degree to which Indian work has entered the international scene (with an analysis of the causes for its limited visibility) has recently appeared in the form of a paper by B.L. Sarada and L. Devaki.[42] These researchers surveyed a leading abstracting journal for language behavior, linguistics, and related fields,[43] searching for works by Indian authors residing either in India or abroad. Their study, though it is restricted to authors of Indian origin, illustrates the underrepresentation of work on Indian languages, especially by Indian authors residing in India. Sarada and Devaki suggest a number of ameliorative measures that might be undertaken to achieve greater prominence for Indian work.

There has recently been an awakened interest within generative theory in a wider range of languages, including those of South Asia. Work has already appeared in dissertations in the U.S. (as well as in India) and in published works and conference proceedings. Publications within the U.S., in particular, no longer take the character of "A Transformational-generative analysis of language L, or of some aspect of L." Now they tend to be more theory-centered and likely to be of the form "The X principle in language L," or "Such-and-such movement in L." As of now, there have been relatively few such publications. It is to be hoped that they will contribute significantly to increased recognition of the important contributions that South Asian languages can make to linguistics in general to the benefit of the field at large.

A new generation of theoretically sophisticated and dedicated younger South Asian linguists appears to be emerging both abroad and in South Asia, especially in India. One encouraging sign of this is the appearance of relevant dissertations produced at major U.S. institutions whose authors are generally contributing to the field through conferences and journal articles. A further indication of this development can be gained by inspecting the lists of participants and their topics at South Asian Language Analysis (SALA) and other linguistic conferences. Happily, this development is proceeding in India as well as abroad.

This increased activity is not confined to work linked to grammatical theory narrowly defined as it relates to formal structure in areas such as phonology, syntax, and formal semantics. Interesting and original work is also being carried out, much of it by younger scholars, in domains such as discourse, interaction, and social and functional correlates to language phenomena in South Asian languages. This work is providing a veritable mine of relevant data.

Organizationally, what will be of importance is renewed and increasing collaborative efforts between Indian and U.S. and other foreign scholars. This can have the effect of not only integrating Indian findings into the mainstream of current work, but also (and probably more importantly) of educating U.S. and foreign linguists into the richness of the Indian linguistic scene. Some recent events have looked promising. One was the 1996 international workshop at Delhi University on anaphora (the use of a grammatical substitute to refer to a preceding word or group of words) in South Asian languages, which produced detailed studies on a general plan of the relevant phenomena in fourteen languages of South Asia. The extensive volume resulting from that effort is now reaching completion.[44] Another event was the very successful and largely attended return of the South Asian Language Analysis (SALA) conference to India at Jawaharlal Nehru University in January 1997 after a long interval during which the conference had circulated among institutions in the U.S. The fact that it met in India enabled increased attendance by Indian scholars and students. This was followed immediately by another international workshop on null elements (phonetically unrealized forms—a matter of great interest in current syntax and semantics) in South Asian languages at Delhi University. It is to be hoped that these signal a renewal of the kind of lively interaction between Indian and U.S. scholars, as well as other international scholars, that characterized the efforts of the 1950s and 1960s.

Heartening developments are now taking place in the dissemination of South Asian work in the wider scene. *A Yearbook of South Asian Languages and Linguistics* is underway.[45] *A South Asia Syntax and Semantics Newsletter* listing and summarizing work in those areas in South Asian languages has also been appearing for the last few years, and it is now appearing in electronic form.[46] There are also now several lively lists and groups devoted to South Asian languages and linguistics in cyberspace.[47] Although it remains to be seen what effects e-mail and the Internet will have on our area of interest, these hopeful developments, as well as the opportunity of scholars of South Asian linguistics to participate in wider groups and make their work known there, have the potentiality for greatly expanding the dissemination of South Asian linguistics work and increasing its impact on the general field of linguistics.

We can appropriately end this brief account with another quotation from Murray Emeneau, a scholar who as much as anyone has served as a conduit for transmitting South Asian material into the wider stream and formulating the directions that stream has taken. In the 1955 presidential address quoted earlier he said:

Meanwhile, I shall sum up what I have presented by referring to the Society's seal with its insistence on "light" and its symbolic reference to the motto "Ex oriente lux." In the dawn of western linguistics, light certainly came from India. With the present resurgence of interest in linguistics in India, we can look forward to a new flood of light from India...[48]

Though his hopes might have been realized less than he envisioned in 1955, there are encouraging signs that another resurgence may well be under way, and that the light is becoming both wider and more intense.

NOTES

1. Emeneau, Murray B. 1967. "India and Linguistics." In *Collected Papers*. Linguistics Dept. Publication # 8. 187-200. Annamalainagar: Annamalai University. (Originally appearing in *Journal of the American Oriental Society* 75, 145-155). The quotation here is from 194.

2. Andresen, Julie Tetel. 1990. *Linguistics in America 1769-1924*. London and New York: Routledge, 44.

3. Ibid. 122.

4. Appleton, D. 1979. New York: Dover Publications. Republished with an introduction by Charles F. Hockett. Whitney's book was largely based on his earlier (1867) *Language and the Study of Language. Twelve Lectures on the Principles of Linguistic Science*. New York: Scribner's.

5. Andresen, op. cit. 181.

6. New York: Henry Holt.

7. As an example, see the 1957 volume *Readings in Linguistics*, ed. Martin Joos, which was published by the American Council of Learned Societies and intended to be a representational summary of the field.

8. *Language* 5:274.

9. Emeneau, op. cit. 195-196.

10. Gair, James W. 1995. "Impact and Importance of Title VI Funding for South Asian Languages: South Asian Languages Under Title VI." Prepared as part of a larger project conducted by Richard T. Thompson evaluating Title VI funding.

11. Kelkar, Ashok. 1969. "General Linguistics in South Asia." In *Current Trends in Linguistics*, vol. 5, *Linguistics in South Asia*, ed. Thomas A. Sebeok, 532-542. The Hague: Mouton. The quotation is from 535.

12. Ibid. 538.

13. The Hague: Mouton.

14. Cambridge: MIT Press.

15. See Randy Allen Harris. 1993. *The Linguistic Wars*. New York: Oxford Univ. Press.

16. New York: Plenum.

17. Chomsky, Noam. 1986. *Knowledge of Language: Its Nature, Origin, and Use*. New York: Praeger, 37-38.

18. Bright, William. 1976. *Variation and Change in Language*. Stanford: Stanford Univ. Press. 271. Quoted in Stephen O. Murray. 1994. *Theory Groups and the Study of Language in North America: A Social History*.

Amsterdam/Philadelphia: Benjamins, 291.

19. "India as a Linguistic Area." *Language* 32(1): 3-16. Reprinted in *Collected Papers*, op. cit., 172-286. The quotation is from 186 (footnote 28).

20. See especially Colin R. Masica. 1976. *Defining a Linguistic Area: South Asia.* Chicago: Univ. of Chicago Press. Also, for a comprehensive account of works relating to language and society up to the time of its publication, see Michael C. Shapiro and Harold F. Schiffman. 1981. *Language and Society in South Asia.* Delhi: Motilal Banarsidass.

21. Gumperz, John J. and Robert Wilson. 1971. "Convergence and Creolization: A Case from the Indo-Aryan/Dravidian Border in India." In *Pidginization and Creolization of Languages*, ed. Del Hymes, 151-167. Cambridge: Cambridge Univ. Press.

22. Southworth, Franklin. 1971. "Detecting Prior Creolization: An Analysis of the Historical Origins of Marathi." In Ibid. 255-273.

23. Nadkarni, Mangesh V. 1975. "Bilingualism and Syntactic Change in Konkani." *Language* 51: 672-683. This followed upon his 1970 *Embedded Structures in Kannada and Konkani.* Unpublished doctoral dissertation, University of California at Los Angeles.

24. Here, too, see Shapiro and Schiffman (1981) for an account. Unfortunately we lack a more recent comprehensive survey.

25. Thomason, Sarah Grey and Terence Kaufman. 1988. *Language Contact, Creolization and Genetic Linguistics.* Berkeley: Univ. of California Press.

26. Chompski, Noam. 1965. *Aspects of the Theory of Syntax.* Cambridge: MIT Press, 3.

27. Hymes, Del, ed. 1964. *Language in Culture and Society.* New York: Harper and Row, 386.

28. Murray, Stephen O. 1993. *Theory Groups and the Study of Language in North America: A Social History.* Amsterdam/Philadelphia: Benjamins.

29. 1960. Bloomington: Indiana Univ. Research Center in Anthropology, Folklore, and Linguistics. *International Journal of American Linguistics* 26:3 (part 3).

30. Quoted in Murray, op. cit. 307.

31. Ibid. 293.

32. Bright, William. 1966. *Sociolinguistics: Proceedings of the UCLA Conference.* The Hague: Mouton.

33. *Word.* 15(2): 325-340. Reprinted in 1964. *Language in Culture and Society*, ed. Del Hymes, 429-439. New York: Harper and Row. The quotation is from 435.

34. Britto, Francis. 1986. *Diglossia: A Study of the Theory with Application to Tamil.* Washington: Georgetown Univ. Press.

35. Ferguson, Charles and John Gumperz, eds. 1960. *Linguistic Diversity in South Asia: Studies in Regional, Social, and Functional Variation.* Bloomington: Indiana Univ. Research Center in Anthropology, Folklore, and Linguistics. *International Journal of American Linguistics* 26:3 (part 3).

36. Krishnamurti, Bh., Colin R. Masica and Anjani Sinha, eds. 1986. *South Asian Languages: Structure, Convergence and Diglossia.* Delhi: Motilal Banarsidass.

37. Fernandez, Mauro. 1993. *Diglossia: A Comprehensive Bibliography.* Amsterdam/Philadelphia: Benjamins.

38. Dimock, Edward C., Jr., Braj B. Kachru and Bh. Krishnamurti, eds. 1992. *Dimensions of Sociolinguistics in South Asia: Papers in Memory of Gerald B. Kelley.* New Delhi: Oxford.

39. A notion apparently initiated by Prabodh Pandit in 1968 in a series of lectures in Pune. Pandit, a pioneer in Indian sociolinguistics, was very much connected with the U.S.-linked activities in the 1950s and 1960s.

40. See, for example, Kachru, Braj B. *The Indianization of the English Language in India.* Delhi: Oxford Univ. Press. See also various issues of the journal *World Englishes* from 1985.

41. Sakuntala Sharma, J. 1978. *Classified Bibliography of Linguistic Dissertations on Indian Languages.* Mysore: Central Institute of Indian Languages, v-vi.

42. "Indian Linguistics at the International Scene.". *International Journal of Dravidian Linguistics.* 25(2):100-117.

43. *Language and Language Behavior Abstracts.*

44. Lust, Barbara C., K.V. Subbarao, Kashi Wali and James W. Gair, eds. In press. *Lexical Anaphors and Pronouns in Some South Asian Languages.* Berlin: Mouton-De Gruyter.

45. Edited by Rajendra Singh, with associate editors Probal Dasgupta and K.P. Mohanan.

46. This was begun by Veneeta (Srivasta) Dayal at Rutgers University. It is now edited by her and Rajesh Bhatt. Information is available at <bhatt@babel.ling.upenn.edu>.

47. Among these are "indology" with a web page at <http://www.ucl.ac.uk/~ucgadkw/indology.html> that can lead to wider links; "Vyakaran" at <VYAKARAN@email.uni-kiel.de>; as well as the South Asia Gopher at Columbia University: <gopher://gopher.cc.columbia.edu:71/1/cliopus>.

48. Emeneau, op. cit. 200.

Literature

VELCHERU NARAYANA RAO

I remember reading Shakespeare's *Hamlet* for the first time. My acquaintance with English literature was minimal. I had heard that Shakespeare was considered a great poet in English—as great a poet as Kalidasa was in Sanskrit. I was terribly disappointed after my first reading. I wondered how on earth a theme like that of Hamlet could ever be considered the subject of a great play. I thought, "What do we have here? An immoral incident of a woman falling in love with her husband's brother; the brother then kills her husband and marries her. A grown up son who passively suffers through the whole experience and kills himself at the end. Intrigue, murder, immorality, and a total lack of courage on the part of the hero." Barring some parts of the play that read like good poetry, I was ready to dismiss the text as an exercise of an incompetent author extolled for uncivilized reasons. It took a long time for me to learn the English language, its nuances, its beauties, and the culture that uses this language for its literary expression, before I began to appreciate the greatness of Shakespeare and the gift he conferred on the English-speaking peoples and on humanity at large.

Similar to my entering into a new literary culture and not knowing how to appreciate it, the English came to India and found themselves faced with a body of new literature in a bewildering variety of languages. The task of making sense of this body of literature was by no means small. It needed an army of scholars, linguists, poets, and literary critics to explore this new area, making their own mistakes in the process of coming to grips with it. When two great, complex civilizations meet, they rarely meet as equals. History tells us that such a meeting often takes place not in terms of a friendly handshake, but in the context of a religious war, military conquest, or colonial subjugation. The meeting of the English-speaking world and Indian culture was more the latter. English intellectuals of the time were adamantly convinced of their cultural superiority; some believed that the greatness of their civilization even gave them a certain divine sanction to civilize India. The story has been told over and over again (so it is unnecessary to restate it here), but we know that some of the finest British scholars of Indian literature were, at best, patronizing.

Most of the British interest in Indian literature was limited to Sanskrit and its "great tradition." The *Vedas*, the *Purāṇas*, and the "Law Books" like the *Mānava Dharma Śāstra* attracted the attention of the colonial scholars. Even after Sir William Jones identified Kalidasa and produced a translation of *Śakuntalā*, it took a while for western scholars to recognize that Sanskrit had literature and literary theory as well. India's regional languages and regional literatures remained almost totally unknown to the western scholars who had spent their lifetime specializing in Sanskrit. Even as late as 1922, literatures in Indian regional languages occupied only about thirty pages of an appendix in Winternitz's three-volume *History of Indian Literature*. The author, however, recognized the presence of a vast literature in popular, modern Indian languages but regretted his lack of competence to deal with these works adequately.[1]

U.S. interaction with India's regional literatures arose out of a context significantly different from the colonial-orientalist, nineteenth-century British interaction with India. All over Asia and Africa the years immediately after World War II saw the birth of new, independent nations freed from colonial powers. India's emergence as an independent nation in 1947 marked an end to India's formal colonial history and the beginning of India's history as a free nation, an event welcomed in the United States. U.S. university scholars were significantly free from the backlog of colonial memories and were open to the opportunity to embark as free entrepreneurs in a largely new and challenging world of scholarship and intellectual adventure in Indian literature. Even though methodologically building on the foundations of indology, which in itself was largely a product of orientalism, American scholars were relaxed and open to possibilities of a genuine interaction of mind with their Indian counterparts. U.S. universities in the early 1950s were still heavily oriented toward Sanskrit as a means to study India. Major universities such as Harvard, Pennsylvania, and Chicago had Sanskrit chairs. Sanskrit was a language of a civilization and culture comparable to any great civilization of the world. Regional languages were nowhere near as significant.

For over a century most Americans dealing with India's regional languages had been missionaries. The first serious encounter of significant numbers of Americans in independent India with India's regional languages occurred with the Peace Corps. Peace Corps volunteers needed crash courses in Indian languages to work with ordinary people in villages. Linguists took the responsibility for organizing spoken language courses in modern Indian languages, using native informants. This was also a time when linguists, methodologically trained in theories of structural linguistics, were confident that descriptive grammars of foreign languages could be written by trained linguists with the assistance of native informants, even if the linguists themselves had not learned the languages. Whatever may be the methodological weaknesses of this belief, the combination worked, inasmuch as it taught minimal competence in spoken languages to eager, mostly-young American men and women preparing to live in Indian villages as Peace Corps volunteers. When those men and women returned to the United States, many brought back with them a love of the language they had learned and the environment in which they had used it. A good number of them returned for further study and looked for opportunities to continue their language education. Several U.S. universities opened Indian Studies departments supported by federal funds for instruction in some of the less-taught languages of India. The U.S. government, determined to win the cold war against the Soviet Union, was eager to train young people in the languages of South Asia and other Third World countries. The National Defense Education Act provided generous grants for modern language instruction and for producing teaching materials. The study of modern Indian languages, however, did not stop with a linguistic understanding of Indian languages, their spoken uses, and their functional applications in anthropology and other social sciences. Humanistic interests of individual students and faculty led to a study of the literatures of these languages. Gradually a sizable body of experts in India's major regional languages came to occupy permanent positions in U.S. academic centers.

The American Institute of Indian Studies (AIIS) has been a key player in shaping U.S. academic expertise on India's regional languages .and literatures. With its support for field research by faculty and graduate students and, more significantly, for instruction in some of the so-called less-taught languages, AIIS has provided the much needed facility for generations of American scholars to work in Indian languages and literatures in their living environment.

This made an important difference in the history of regional language scholarship. While scholarship in Sanskrit had been textually and philologically focused right from the beginning, scholarship in regional languages began with the spoken forms of the languages and the study of literary texts in context. This difference had an important impact on the study of Indian regional literatures. Sanskrit texts were treated by European scholars as literary artifacts. They were ancient/classical to begin with and were available, for example, in palm leaf manuscripts. Few questions were asked about the uses of the text, its impact on the audiences, and its reception in different contexts. The study of Indian regional texts, however, was exactly the opposite. Scholars often found texts being performed for specific audiences, and from there the scholars traced their way to a manuscript of palm leaf, tree bark, or paper, or to a printed edition. To such scholars who were working from a text in performance toward a text in writing, the context of a text's use and its impact on audiences was far too strong to overlook.

Each major regional language on which U.S. scholars worked yielded a rich harvest of highly lyrical texts, most of them loosely categorized under *bhakti*, devotional poetry. These texts represented a high literary achievement of the languages under study. Many scholars attempted to reproduce in their translations the devotional lyricism of the text. A large body of *bhakti* lyrics from the major languages were translated into expressive modern English. Unlike the case of Sanskrit, where scholars were interested primarily in religious ritual and linguistic issues and only marginally in the literary quality of the text, translators of regional language texts were primarily interested in the literary qualities of their texts. The results have produced an extraordinary variety of translation practices.

PRE-MODERN LITERATURES

Scholars translating from Indian languages inevitably recognized that Indian texts have a high degree of orality. Theories of orality, beginning with those of Albert B. Lord (1960. *Singer of Tales*, Cambridge: Harvard Univ. Press), have influenced our understanding of non-literate societies. One can identify a small industry of scholarly production on the problems of orality and literacy. The U.S. scholars working in Indian literatures quietly recognized that Indian orality was unlike Yugoslavian orality or its African counterparts. In India, the relationship between oral and written texts was more subtle. The syllabary of Sanskrit (*varṇa-samāmnāya*), which was borrowed by all Indian languages except Persian and Urdu, was conceptualized as a broadly defined set of sounds (*varṇas/akṣaras*) based on the place of articulation and manner of articulation of each sound. This has freed the letter from its graphic form and made it possible for Sanskrit to be inscribed in more than one script. Also, a person could be "literate" without knowing how to write; he could compose orally—like any illiterate oral singer—and yet produce scholarly compositions. This situation, which I have called a state of oral-literacy, eliminated the opposition between orality and literacy so widely observed in the West.[2] This has given rise to important consequences in translating Indian texts. Texts that appear oral, with formulaic features, repetitions, and euphonic texture dominating translatable meaning, demanded far more detailed attention than translators were usually willing to pay to oral texts. Perhaps no translator understood this in practice better than A.K. Ramanujan. The texts he chose for his translations are largely oral ones like the songs of Nammālvar or the hymns of Basaveśwara.[3] His translations preserve the tone of orality without losing it; his chosen tone is clean and pure, elevating the text to speak through him with precision and authenticity. The work of Edward Dimock,[4] John Hawley and Mark Juergensmeyer,[5] Linda Hess,[6] Philip Lutgendorf,[7] Usha Nilsson[8] and a number of others made accessible to the English-speaking world a selection of devotional literature from a range of languages such as Maithili, Avadhi, Brajbhasha, and Rajasthani. Together they communicated to English readers the literary power of the spoken word and the sung narrative. Their translations and their literary critical statements, included in the introductions and separate books and essays,[9] made strong statements about the power of regional languages throughout the subcontinent during the medieval period. The sheer presence of a sizable body of translation from regional languages demonstrated the shift in power from Sanskrit to these languages. Each *bhakti* text has a story to tell and a context in which it arose. Stories about the author and the contexts of composition often represented a conflict between the devotional, lyrical *bhakti* text and the ritualist, distanced, scholarly Sanskrit text. The conflict of hierarchies between Brahmans and the lower castes appears again and again in powerful legends about low-caste poet singers.

Here is a story John Hawley tells about Ravidas, a Chamar leather worker and Untouchable. The queen of Jhali travels to Banaras to honor this great saint-poet as her guru, but the Brahmans of her court do not accept her choice. They report to the king, hoping he will intervene. The king brings together the Brahmans and Ravidas and asks them to stand before the image of the god. The king's decision will favor the party in whose direction the god's image turns. The Brahmans chant the *Vedas*, and Ravidas sings his poetry. The image jumps directly into the poet's lap. However, the battle is not won yet. The Brahmans still refuse to eat with Ravidas sitting beside them and insist that he eat across the hall from them. As they lift the first morsel of food to their mouths, however, they see that seated between each of them a Ravidas has miraculously materialized on their side of the room. They are horrified to see this Untouchable sitting beside each of them and challenge him. He peels back the skin from his chest and reveals a golden sacred thread lying within.[10]

Stories very different from the above are told about poets who wrote in a courtly style—poets like Kalidasa and Bhavabhūti, well known in Sanskrit scholarly tradition. According to one such story, Kalidasa was an illiterate shepherd. A king's minister, after he failed in his attempt to marry his son to the princess, vowed revenge against the princess. Searching for the most stupid man in the kingdom, the minister found Kalidasa sitting on a tree in the forest, trying to cut the very limb he was sitting on. The minister tried to warn Kalidasa that Kalidasa would fall with the cut limb, but Kalidasa would not listen. Seeing that he had found the right person for his scheme, the minister presented Kalidasa to the king as the best suitor for the princess, declaring that Kalidasa was the greatest scholar in the kingdom who, for very special reasons, was under cover, pretending to be an idiot. Every word Kalidasa uttered had profound inner meaning, even though it seemed to be an illiterate utterance. On the wedding night, the princess discovered the true nature of her imbecile bridegroom and devised a plan. Kalidasa was to sneak into the goddess Kali's temple during the middle of the night and lock the temple doors. The goddess Kali would return just before dawn, seeking entrance into her temple. Kalidasa was not to admit her until he received a boon from the goddess. Kalidasa did exactly as the princess instructed. Just before dawn the goddess Kali did return to her temple. Kalidasa followed the princess' orders and refused to unlock the doors until he received a boon. Finally, Kali yielded and instructed Kalidasa to open the doors a crack and stick out his tongue. On his tongue she wrote the seed-syllables (bījakṣaras), and Kalidasa was instantly transformed into the famous poet.

Legends like this also tell of poets from different centuries and distant lands meeting with each other—thus invariably creating problems of chronology and textual authenticity. Literary historians, with their penchant for dating and identifying the authorship of texts with as much positive historical evidence as possible, have thrown out these stories in despair, as unhistorical products of literary fancy. However, the power of these legends and their aesthetic impact on large communities of people over centuries of time cannot be easily dismissed.

David Shulman and I have worked on a number of such stories and poems circulated orally about poets and their poetry and their patrons. We have suggested that in India's literary traditions poets become legends. Released from their chronological limitations and biographical boundaries, authors acquire the freedom of existing purely as creators of the poetry attributed to them. Thus it becomes wholly natural for Kalidasa (4th century) and Bhavabhūti (8th century) or Dandin (8th century) to meet in these stories, to exchange poems, and to offer criticisms of one another's work. Indeed, there is a sense in which the *cāṭu* world (the world or community in which oral presentations circulate) aims precisely at this effect, bringing major voices into active relation to one another, establishing the dense fabric of intertextual resonances that allows for a new form of literary criticism to emerge.[11]

Premodern poetry from most Indian languages is inseparable from religious experience. Most literary texts of premodern India are therefore extensively used by historians of religion, discussed as religious texts, and used in religious studies courses. It is not always easy to separate the religious from the literary. But a few scholars have analyzed the poetics of religious texts and presented significant theoretical possibilities in literary criticism. Ramanujan discusses the structure of a Kannanda *vacana*, showing that the innocently simple spontaneity of the oral poem has a complex rhetorical structure. At a time when oral poetics were considered applicable only to long epics sung by illiterate bards, Ramanujan's discussion showed that oral poetics were equally applicable to shorter literary texts. The famous *vacana* of Basaveswara about the temple in the body is one of the examples Ramanujan chose in order to demonstrate the complex and carefully constructed quality of an Indian oral poem. Ramanujan's analysis of the *vacana* in his introduction to *Speaking of Siva* carefully unpacks the poem and illuminates its complex structure.[12]

Ancient Tamil poetry of the sangam period has perhaps fared better than any classical poetry of ancient India. In the beautiful translations of A.K. Ramanujan and George Hart we have a substantial selection from the classical Tamil anthologies. Superb translations as they are, the poems have attracted the attention of literary scholars beyond South Asia area studies. Especially noteworthy is the afterward A.K. Ramanujan wrote to his anthology, *Poems of Love and War*, in which he presented an elegant analytical discussion of classical Tamil poetics. With this essay the Tamil concepts of *akam* and *puram* (interior and exterior) entered literary critical discourse and have been applied both by Ramanujan himself and by a number of others to extensive literary uses in other contexts. Attention to Tamil poetry in translation extended to other Tamil classics. The *Rāmāyaṇa of Kampaṉ* was translated in part by George Hart and Hank Heifetz.[13] An excellent translation of *Cilappatikāram*, the great Tamil epic, was done by R. Parthasarathy, who also wrote a long postscript to his translation.[14] Other translators from Tamil classics include Indira Peterson, Paula Richman, and David Shulman.[15]

At least two literary languages of South India claim that their literatures were produced only after a foundational grammatical text was created or discovered (*Akattiyam* and *Tolkāppiyam* for Tamil, Nannayya's *Āndhra-śabda-cintāmaṇi* for Telugu). These supposed "first grammarians," invariably characterized as great sages or poets gifted with extraordinary creative power, play complex and well-defined roles in the internal perspective of these literary worlds. An examination of the cultural functions and images of grammar in these and other south Indian traditions, in relation to the classical culture of grammar in Sanskrit, reveals a significant role for grammar not so much as a description or prescription of language use but as a regulator of literary production. Here is a legend about the first grammarian in Telugu:

One evening in 1656, Appakavi, poet-grammarian of Kamepalli, had a dream. God appeared in the dream and revealed the existence of a Telugu grammar, *Āndhra-śabda-cintāmaṇi*, written by none other than Nannayya (11th century), the first poet of Telugu literature and the composer of the first three books of the Telugu *Mahābhārata*. Nannayya, the god said, first wrote the Telugu grammar and then, following the rules he himself had made, wrote the three books of the *Mahābhārata*. However, conditions were not conducive to the propagation of his grammar. Nannayya's rival Bhimakavi, who was jealous of Nannayya, destroyed Nannayya's grammar book by throwing the only copy in the Godavari river. However, Nannayya's grammar was not wholly lost. The long-lived Siddha Sarangadhara, the son of king Rajarajanarendra of Rajahmundry and a disciple of Nannayya, had memorized the whole book, had written it down in Sanskrit, and had given it to a Brahman at Matanga hill near Vijayanagara. This Brahman, god said, would bring this book of Nannayya's grammar the next day. Still in this dream, the god instructed Appakavi to write a commentary to Nannayya's grammar in Telugu. Naturally, the next morning the Brahman did turn up with the book. And Appakavi did write a Telugu commentary on Nannayya's grammar.

We miss the point of the story if we begin to discuss the historicity of Nannayya's authorship of this Telugu grammar. The point of the legend is the cultural role of grammar and the ideological power of the first grammarian in the course of the development of a literary language in Telugu. The images and uses of grammar generally have profound implications for the conceptualization of language and literature in pre-modern south India, where normative claims for language and grammar have distinct and privileged status in determining the modes of culture. What is interesting in this context is the claim made in the Telugu tradition that grammar generates literature (rather than the usual historical-linguistic hypothesis that reverses this order and says that literature generates grammar). Recent scholarly interest in the grammatical traditions of regional languages, as distinct from modern linguistic studies of regional languages, promises to open an entirely new field of study in Indian languages.

MODERN LITERATURES

American scholarly interest in modern literatures of India began with Rabindranath Tagore's work, which was available in translation, or with the work of other Indian writers who wrote in English such as R. K. Narayan and Rajarao. For a long time, both the popularity and the literary acceptability of these authors profoundly influenced the U.S. view of modern Indian literature. Comparable only to Sanskrit, which influenced western scholars' understanding of great Indian literature of the past, English writings by Indian writers constituted a dominant mode within which Indian literary modernity was perceived. The recent emergence of a new generation of Indian writers in English shows that the trend has matured into a tradition and is here to stay. Indian authors writing in English have an overpowering presence partly because of their accessibility and availability; they are published by commercial publishers and are heavily advertised and reviewed in the national press. They are also extensively discussed in English departments of U.S. colleges and universities. Furthermore, the Indian-English authors represent an emerging modern India with entirely new contexts of social relations in urbanized industrial cities, relatively free from regional linguistic identities, and closer to an emerging international idiom. Selections from Indian literature published in international journals celebrating fifty years of India's independence demonstrate the prominence of India's English writers as representatives of India's modern writing. The special issues of *Granta*[16] and the *New Yorker*,[17] which carried almost exclusively Indian writers in English, illustrate the new prominence Indian English writing acquired in recent years.

When *Granta's* editor, Ian Jack, was asked in a recent interview whether there was room for more Indian fiction, especially from Indian languages, he answered:

The translations that came to us didn't simply work, maybe these were poor translations. Many people will say that in other Indian languages, say in Bengali, there are books worthy of one hundred years of celebration. These books may exist, but on the evidence of the translation, they don't.[18]

"Contemporary Indian literature," wrote Salman Rushdie in the *New Yorker,* "remains largely unknown in the United States, in spite of its considerable present-day energy and diversity."[19] He even wondered if there is writing in regional languages in India today that is as good as there was during the time of Rabindranath Tagore. It appears that major literary personalities active on the world scene are no better informed about major regional literatures of India than were their late nineteenth-century counterparts . English, as a dominant language in the world, does give them a sense of comfort about their ignorance of what they consider minor literatures; they expect translations to be delivered to them before they recognize any merit in other literatures. However, this is not a matter of mere translations. If English literature had depended on translations into Indian languages—as for example the Bible has—for its impact on the Indian mind, it would have made a poor show. After more than two centuries of English learning in India, I cannot think of a single good translation of any major English poet in any Indian language. Translations into Indian languages of Indian novelists who wrote in English—R. K. Narayan, for instance—did not make a mark in India. Virtually all the impact English literature has exercised on the Indian mind has been a result of Indians reading the texts *in English.* Appreciation comes from translating the reader into the text, not translating the text for the reader.

It is still significant that a range of modern Indian poets from regional languages are being introduced to American literary circles. Vinay Dharwadker and A.K. Ramanujan's *Oxford Anthology of Modern Poetry* is the first of its kind, introducing modern poetry from fourteen languages. Another anthology by Vinay Dharwadker consists of a selection of twenty-nine modern Indian poems from Hindi and Marathi.[20] The coverage is not entirely adequate, and there are large gaps in our understanding of the vast regional literary traditions of India. However, the presence of a body of poetry from many of the modern regional languages from the subcontinent has made an impact on U.S. students quite distinct from the impact the body of poetry would have made had it been in a single language.

Interpreting India's modern literatures poses challenges very different from interpreting India's pre-modern literatures. In the case of the pre-modern literatures, the problem is one of bridging the difference in texture and genre between western/modern and pre-modern Indian sensibilities. India's pre-modern literature stands doubly distant from the western experience of literature. The oral abundance of sounds, the proliferation of synonyms, the density of compounds, and the varieties of metrical graces stand so far away from anything the English language does for its readers, that a literary interpreter's first task lies in narrowing the gap. However, when it comes to India's modern literatures, the surface appearance can be quite similar to modern literatures anywhere in the western world. The short story, the novel, and the prose poem are internationalized forms of literary modernity. Many of the political, social, and literary movements of the West have been transported to the Indian literary scene. A well-translated modern poem from an Indian language does not present an unfamiliar literary universe. The problem, therefore, is to show how modern literature from Indian languages is a product of its own context, a context both closely related to the pre-existing literary modes in a specific language and influenced by transferred sensibilities across continents. English and European poets are read by Indian literati. Literary movements that have an impact on the West mark their presence on the contemporary Indian mind. English is the most widely-used intellectual language of India. Books published in English all over the world are read and assimilated. The question, however, is how they are perceived and what particular local impact they make. While it is easy to treat all Indian modern literary productions as an inseparable part of international modernity, the role of the modern translator/interpreter consists specifically in showing how the Indian modern literature is different from other literatures, responding to a particular local context.

Pre-modern literary texts carried public statements of social and political ideologies. Often they included eulogies of kings, descriptions of the ideal social order, directions regarding respectable behavior, and codes of appropriate conduct for people in different stages of life. In brief, pre-modern texts did more than provide aesthetic pleasure. A poet in pre-modern India often represented the public voice with the power and authority that went with the status and respect accorded a poet. Some of these features carried into the literature of the modern period even after the old patronage system had been completely replaced by a book-buying public and publishers' royalties. India's modern poets and writers inherited the social responsibilities and concerns of pre-modern makers of literature. Readers' expectations also continued to a large extent the styles of pre-modern text communities. Just as the poet had status and respect in pre-modern Indian society, the modern writer, too, deserves respect and status in the public eye. To be a poet or writer is not just to engage in one more profession to make a living. To be a poet or a writer carries with it a moral and social responsibility to speak out for what is right and to denounce what is wrong. This has given modern Indian literature a public voice. Most modern literary movements in India look like literary versions of political movements. In nearly all major Indian literatures, each language has experienced a Marxist literary movement, a romantic/nationalist literary movement, a feminist literary movement, and most recently a Dalit literary movement. Poets and writers have been expected to pick up themes related to political movements.

A strong case in point would be the poetry of protest written by a large number of poets, in all regional languages, during the period when Prime Minister Indira Gandhi declared a national emergency and suspended personal freedoms and freedom of the press. While the press was muzzled and individuals were crippled, poets fearlessly went on writing poetry against the Emergency. John Perry's edited volume *Voices of Emergency: An All India Anthology of Protest Poetry of the 1975-77 Emergency* (1983. Bombay: Popular Prakashan) is a stunning demonstration of the voice of poets representing the public good. Sometimes a public statement from poetry is also constructed post facto by editing an anthology of writings by poets of a particular gender or caste order. Feminist poetry and Dalit poetry in many Indian languages are increasingly translated and made available to U.S. readers. Translations from modern poetry clearly demonstrate that the poet in modern India is much more than a poet; he/she is a social critic, a theorist and activist, and a policy-maker in addition to one who shapes the aesthetic world of his/her community.

Two journals dedicated to literature have done a valuable service in providing a forum for publication of translations, discussions, and critical comments on contemporary literature. One is Carlo Coppola's *Journal of South Asian Literature* (originally *Mahfil*), and the other is the *Annual of Urdu Studies*, edited by Muhammad Umar Memon. Both journals were founded by C.M. Naim. Coppola has edited a number of special issues on literatures in several languages. Memon has made the *Annual of Urdu Studies* a journal of superior standards of literary taste and scholarship.

The evolution of Urdu literature on the Indian subcontinent could well provide a study in itself. Unique among Indian languages, Urdu belongs to no specific region but is used in scattered locations throughout northern India as well as in more southern cities such as Hyderabad.

Urdu emerged around the fifteenth century as a language of army camps in north India (Urdu = "camp"). Using the Perso-Arabic script, Urdu looked to Persia and Arabia for many of its initial forms and vocabulary. In time Urdu developed distinctive features of its own. Its poetic references to the dream-like nature of the real world and to poetry leading toward mystical union with the ever-sought beloved convey particularly Indian-subcontinent qualities.

By the latter half of the eighteenth century Urdu had supplanted Persian as the poetic language of many northern Indian courts. Subsequently Urdu flourished under the patronage of Lucknow. The development of Urdu printing, usually by lithographic reproduction rather than typesetting, gave a further impetus to the spread of Urdu. Sir Syed Ahmad Khan used Urdu as his chief medium of expression, and Urdu became increasingly associated with Muslim cultural identity. Until Independence, Hindu writers (such as Prem Chand) as well as Muslims wrote acclaimed poems, short stories, and novels in Urdu as well as Hindi. Urdu has continued to be a vigorous form of literary expression used by Hindus, Christians, and Muslims in post-Independence India.[21]

The nineteenth-century impact of the ideas of western history and historiography have had a dominant impact on the production of India's literary histories. Scholarly energies in both India and the United States were directed toward positivist, chronologically-oriented histories of literature. Just as it was assumed that Indians lacked a sense of history before the impact of Islam and western civilization, it was also assumed that Indian literatures did not have a history. It appeared unsatisfactory that many of India's major texts did not give any indication when they were written. Legends about poets, prevalent throughout India, sounded like fantastic fairy tales. Any attempt to make chronological sense of this fairy-tale material seemed totally impossible. Early scholars concluded that what India needed was a responsible literary history for each language. They set about in earnest to determine, with the available tools of positive historical evidence, who wrote what when. Manuscripts in the libraries and memorized versions of texts differed extensively from each other, and it appeared that singers and scribes were taking liberties with the written texts of the original author. The right thing in this context was to produce critical editions, to reconstruct the ur-text with the best of text-critical methodological skills developed in the West. American scholars of Sanskrit and regional languages participated in these monumental enterprises, significantly advancing the quality of edited texts and critical editions. We have practiced reading texts critically for accuracy, coherence, and integrity. This practice has created a sustained and solid text culture in which the text as it appears on the palm leaf or tree bark and the scholar who works with it are the only two participants. The project of critical editions has given us a body of well-edited, carefully-restored texts in practically all disciplines of learning.

South Asia is the world's largest geographic area with a continuous literary tradition, with multiple languages and dialects. Such an area offers a unique opportunity for writing a rich literary history and producing an even richer theory of literary history. Nationalist ideas of a glorious India with a great past fueled the desire of nationalist literary historians to locate the use of regional languages as far back as possible. Contrary to the practices of pre-modern India, where multiple literary languages were available to poets, in post-Independence India nationalist concepts have marked tight boundaries between newly-invented regions and mother-tongues and have generated artificial competitions for superiority among them. Linguistic nationalism generated new political agendas that have empowered new regional literary histories.

Even after reasonably-connected narratives in the history of the literature of each regional language have been painstakingly produced, questions remain. Why does a language become a literary language at a certain moment of time? What were the reasons why the poets of a certain period chose one language over another? What were the roles of transregional languages like Sanskrit and Persian in the formation of regional literary cultures? How did the concept of the 'literary' change from time to time with the invention of new technologies of text production and with the emergence of new regional elites who used the language for cultural mobility? In the area of text production, why, despite critical editions, does allegiance to regional variations still persist among the Indian people? Some of these questions are receiving attention by an international group of scholars working under the leadership of Sheldon Pollock.

The future of scholarship in the literatures of regional languages of India depends largely on two factors. One factor is the availability of instruction and facilities for advanced study of regional languages in both India and the United States. India does not have a history of teaching its languages as second languages. For the most part, tools for learning India's languages have been produced by the scholars interested in learning those languages. In this area, the services provided by the American Institute of Indian Studies (AIIS) have been invaluable. In the United States, departments of South Asian Studies have been performing an admirable service in teaching major Indian languages, despite small numbers of students. However, these facilities and programs of instructions depend heavily on the continuing availability of federal funding , something that is always uncertain. A second factor that affects U.S. interest in the regional literatures of India is the degree of respect accorded by the U.S. academy to scholarship in the "little-known" languages of India . The study of India's regional literatures has so far been the occupation of specialists in area studies departments and centers. Indian literatures still remain largely outside comparative literature departments. We can be optimistic that the study of Indian literatures will fare better in the next century than it has during the first fifty years of India's independence.

NOTES

1. Winternitz, Maurice. 1985. *History of Indian Literature.* Delhi: Motilal Banarsidass, vol. 3, 703-704.
2. For another discussion of this situation see my paper "Purana as Brahminic Ideology" in Wendy Doniger, ed. 1993. *Purana Perennis: Reciprocity and Transformation in Hindu and Jaina Texts,* 85-100. Albany: State Univ. of New York Press.
3. Ramanujan, A.K. 1981. *Hymns for the Drowning: Poems for Visnu by Nammalvar,* Princeton: Princeton Univ. Press; Ramanujan, A.K. 1973. *Speaking of Siva.* Harmondsworth, England: Penguin.
4. Dimock, Edward C., Jr. and Denise Levertov. 1967. *In Praise of Krishna: Songs from the Bengali.* Garden City, NY: Doubleday.
5. Hawley, John Stratton and Mark Juergensmeyer. 1988. *Songs of the Saints of India.* New York: Oxford Univ. Press.
6. Hess, Linda and Shukdev Singh. 1983. *The Bijak of Kabir.* San Francisco: North Point.
7. Lutgendorf, Philip. 1995. "Ramacaritmanas: From Book Five. The Beautiful Book." In *The Norton Anthology of World Masterpieces,* gen. ed. Maynard Mack, vol. 1, 2316-2332. New York: W.W. Norton. For a full version of this translation see: 1994. "Sundar kand" (translation). *Journal of Vaisnava Studies.* 2(4): 91-127.
8. Nilsson, Usha S. 1969. *Mira Bai.* New Delhi: Sahitya Akademi; Nilsson, Usha S. 1982. *Surdas.* New Delhi: Sahitya Akademi.

9. For example, see John Stratton Hawley. 1984. *Sur Das: Poet, Singer, Saint.* Seattle: Univ. of Washington Press; see also Philip Lutgendorf. 1991. *The Life of a Text: Performing the Ramcaritmanas of Tulsidas.* Berkeley: Univ. of California Press.

10. Hawley and Juergensmeyer, op. cit. 15.

11. Narayana Rao, Velcheru and David Shulman. 1998. *A Poem at the Right Moment: Remembered Verses from Premodern South India.* Berkeley: Univ. of California Press.

12. Ramanujan, A.K. 1973. *Speaking of Siva.* 19-22.

13. Hart, George L., III and Hank Heifetz. 1988. *The Forest Book of the Ramayana of Kampan.* Berkeley: Univ. of California Press.

14. Parthasarathy, R. 1992. *The Cilappatikaram of Ilanko Atikal: An Epic of South India.* New York: Columbia Univ. Press.

15. Peterson, Indira Viswanathan. 1989. *Poems to Siva: The Hymns of the Tamil Saints.* Princeton: Princeton Univ. Press; Richman, Paula. 1988. *Women, Branch Stories, and Religious Rhetoric in a Tamil Buddhist Text.* Syracuse: South Asian Series no. 12, Foreign and Comparative Studies Program, Maxwell School, Syracuse University; Shulman, David. 1990. *Songs of the Harsh Devotee: The Tevaram of Cuntaramurttinayanar.* Philadelphia: Dept. of South Asia Regional Studies, University of Pennsylvania.

16. 1997. *Granta,* 57 (August).

17. 1997. *New Yorker* June 23 & 30.

18. From an interview with Hasan Suroor published in *The Hindu* (Chennai) April 20, 1997 and circulated on the Internet.

19. Ibid. 50.

20. Dharwadker, Vinay. 1989/90. "Twenty-nine Modern Indian Poems." *Tri Quarterly,* Winter, 119-228.

21. For further information about the evolution of Urdu literature see the following: Faruqi, Shamsur Rahman. 1995. "Constructing a Literary History, a Canon, and a Theory of Poetry: *Ab-e Hayat* (1880) by Muhammad Husain Azad (1830-1910)," *Social Scientist* 23:10-12 (October-December): 70-97; Matthews, David J., Christopher Shackle, and Sharukh Husain. 1985. *Urdu Literature.* London: Urdu Markaz, Third World Foundation for Social and Economic Studies; Memon, Muhammad Umar, ed. 1991. *The Colour of Nothingness: Modern Urdu Short Stories.* New Delhi: Penguin; Memon, Muhammad Umar, ed. 1997. *The Seventh Door: Selected Stories: Intizar Husain.* Boulder: Lynne Reinner; Pritchett, Frances W. ed. 1994. *Nets of Awareness: Urdu Poetry and Its Critics.* Berkeley: Univ. of California Press; Russell, Ralph, ed. 1972. *Ghalib: The Poet and His Age.* London: George Allen & Unwin; Russell, Ralph. 1992. *The Pursuit of Urdu Literature: A Select History.* London: Zed; Russell, Ralph and Khurshidul Islam. 1968. *Three Mughal Poets: Mir, Sauda, Mir Hasan.* Cambridge: Harvard Univ. Press; Shackle, Christopher, ed. 1989. *Urdu and Muslim South Asia: Studies in Honour of Ralph Russell.* London: School of Oriental and African Studies, University of London.

REFERENCES

The Annual of Urdu Studies. Madison: University of Wisconsin.

Dehejia, Vidya. 1990. *Antal and her Path of Love: Poems of a Woman Saint from South India.* New York: State Univ. of New York Press.

Desai, Anita. 1989. "Indian Fiction Today." *Daedalus.* 118(4): 207-232.

Dharwadker, Vinay. 1989/90. "Twenty-nine Modern Indian Poems." *TriQuarterly.* Winter: 119-228.

Dharwadker, Vinay, Barbara Stoler Miller, A.K. Ramanujan, and Éric A. Huberman. 1993. "Indian Poetics." In *The New Princeton Encyclopedia of Poetry and Poetics,* ed. Alex Preminger and T. V. F. Brogan, 582-600. Princeton: Princeton Univ. Press.

Dimock, Edward C., Jr. and Denise Levertov. 1967. *In Praise of Krishna: Songs from the Bengali.* Garden City, NY: Doubleday.

Doniger, Wendy, ed. 1993. *Purana Perennis: Reciprocity and Transformation in Hindu and Jaina Texts.* Albany: State Univ. of New York Press.

Hart, George L., III. 1979. *Poets of the Tamil Anthologies: Ancient Poems of Love and War.* Princeton: Princeton Univ. Press.

Hart, George L., III and Hank Heifetz. 1988. *The Forest Book of the Rāmāyaṇa of Kampaṉ.* Berkeley: Univ. of California Press.

Hawley, John Stratton. 1984. *Sur Das: Poet, Singer, Saint.* Seattle: Univ. of Washington Press.

Hawley, John Stratton and Mark Juergensmeyer. 1988. *Songs of the Saints of India.* New York: Oxford Univ. Press.

Hess, Linda and Shukdev Singh. 1983. *The Bijak of Kabir.* San Francisco: North Point.

Hutt, Michael James. 1991. *Himalayan Voices: An Introduction to Modern Nepali Literature.* Berkeley: Univ. of California Press.

Journal of South Asian Literature. East Lansing, MI: Michigan State Univ.

King, Bruce. 1987. *Modern Indian Poetry in English.* Delhi: Oxford Univ. Press.

Lutgendorf, Philip. 1991. *The Life of a Text: Performing the Ramcaritmanas of Tulsidas.* Berkeley: Univ. of California Press.

Matthews, David J., Christopher Shackle, and Sharukh Husain. 1985. *Urdu Literature.* London: Urdu Markaz, Third World Foundation for Social and Economic Studies.

Memon, Muhammad Umar, ed. 1991. *The Color of Nothingness: Modern Urdu Short Stories.* New Delhi: Penguin.

———, ed. 1997. *The Seventh Door: Selected Stories: Intizar Husain.* Boulder: Lynne Reiner.

Misra, Vidya Niwas, ed. 1965. *Modern Hindi Poetry: An Anthology.* Bloomington: Indiana Univ. Press.

Munda, Ram Dayal, David Nelson and Paul Staneslow, Jr. 1981. *The Sun Charioteer.* By Ram Dhari Singh 'Dinkar'. St. Paul, MN: Nagari Press.

Narayana Rao, Velcheru. 1990. *Siva's Warriors: Basava Purana of Pakluriki Somanatha.* Princeton: Princeton Univ. Press.

———. 1992. "Kings, Gods, and Poets: Ideologies of Patronage in Medieval

Andhra." In *The Powers of Art: Patronage in Indian Culture*, ed. Barbara Stoler Miller, 142-159. Delhi: Oxford Univ. Press.

————. 1993. "Purana as Brahminic Ideology." In *Purana Perennis: Reciprocity and Transformation in Hindu and Jaina Texts*, ed. Wendy Doniger, 85-100. New York: State Univ. of New York Press.

Narayana Rao, Velcheru and Hank Heifetz. 1987. *For the Lord of the Animals: Poems from the Telugu Kalahastisvara Satakamu of Dhurjati*. Berkeley: Univ. of California Press.

Narayana Rao, Velcheru, and David Shulman. 1998. *A Poem at the Right Moment: Remembered Verses from Premodern South India*. Berkeley: Univ. of California Press.

Naim, C.M. 1992. "Mughal and English Patronage of Urdu Poetry: A Comparison." In *The Powers of Art: Patronage in Indian Culture*, ed. Barbara Stoler Miller, 259-276. Delhi: Oxford Univ. Press.

Nilsson, Usha S. 1969. *Mira Bai*. New Delhi: Sahitya Akademi.

————. 1982. *Surdas*. New Delhi: Sahitya Akademi.

Parthasarathy, R. 1993. *The Cilappatikāram of Ilanko Atikal: An Epic of South India*. New York: Columbia Univ. Press.

Perry, John Oliver, ed. 1983. *Voices of Emergency: An All India Anthology of Protest Poetry of the 1975-77 Emergency*. Bombay: Popular Prakashan.

Peterson, Indira Viswanathan. 1989. *Poems to Siva: The Hymns of the Tamil Saints*. Princeton: Princeton Univ. Press.

————. 1992. "In Praise of the Lord: The Image and Tradition of the Royal Patron in the Songs of Saint Cuntaṭamurtti and the Composer Tyagaraja." In *The Powers of Art: Patronage in Indian Culture*, ed. Barbara Stoler Miller, 120-141. Delhi: Oxford Univ. Press.

————, ed. 1995. "India's Heroic Age" and "India's Classical Age." In *The Norton Anthology of World Masterpieces*, gen. ed. Maynard Mack, vol. I, 837-984, 1161-1280. New York: W.W. Norton.

Pritchett, Frances W. ed. 1994. *Nets of Awareness: Urdu Poetry and Its Critics*. Berkeley: Univ. of California Press

Ramanujan, A.K. 1973. *Speaking of Siva*. Harmondsworth, England: Penguin.

————. 1981. *Hymns for the Drowning: Poems for Visnu by Nammalvar*. Princeton: Princeton Univ. Press.

————. 1985. *Poems of Love and War: From the Eight Anthologies and the Ten Long Poems of Classical Tamil*. New York: Columbia Univ. Press.

Ramanujan, A.K. and Vinay Dharwadker. 1989. "Sixteen Modern Indian Poems." *Daedalus*. 118(4): 295-330.

Ramanujan, A.K., Velcheru Narayana Rao, and David Shulman. 1994. *When God is a Customer: Telugu Courtesan Songs by Ksetrayya and Others*. Berkeley: Univ. of California Press.

Richman, Paula. 1988. *Women, Branch Stories, and Religious Rhetoric in a Tamil Buddhist Text*. Syracuse: South Asia Series no. 12, Foreign and Comparative Studies Program, Maxwell School, Syracuse University.

Roghair, Gene H. 1982. *The Epic of Palnadu: A Study and Translation of*

Palnati Virula Katha, a Telugu Oral Tradition from Andhra Pradesh, India. Oxford: Clarendon.

Rubin, David. 1993. *The Return of Sarasvati: Translations of the Poetry of Prasad Nirala, Pant and Mahadevi.* Philadelphia: Univ. of Pennsylvania.

Russell, Ralph, ed. 1972. *Ghalib: The Poet and His Age.* London: George Allen & Unwin.

———. 1992. *The Pursuit of Urdu Literature: A Select History.* London: Zed.

Russell, Ralph and Khurshidul Islam. 1968. *Three Mughal Poets: Mir, Sauda, Mir Hasan.* Cambridge: Harvard Univ. Press.

Shackle, Christopher, ed. 1989. *Urdu and Muslim South Asia: Studies in Honor of Ralph Russell.* London: School of Oriental and African Studies, Univ. of London.

Schomer, Karine. 1983. *Mahadevi Varma: And the Chhayavad Age of Modern Hindi Poetry.* Berkeley: Univ. of California Press.

Social Scientist. 1995. 23:10-12 (December).

Shulman, David. 1990. *Songs of the Harsh Devotee: The Tevaram of Cuntaramurttinayanar.* Philadelphia: Dept. of South Asian Regional Studies, University of Pennsylvania.

Shulman, David. 1992. "Poets and Patrons in Tamil Literature and Literary Legend." In *The Powers of Art: Patronage in Indian Culture,* ed. Barbara Stoler Miller, 89-119. Delhi: Oxford Univ. Press.

Tharu, Susie and K. Lalita, ed. 1991. *Women Writing in India.* New York: Feminist Press.

Walsh, William. 1990. *Indian Literature in English.* London: Longman.

Winternitz, Maurice. 1985. *History of Indian Literature.* Delhi: Motilal Banarsidass. 3 vols.

Mathematics and
Mathematical Astronomy

DAVID PINGREE

It is proving to be particularly difficult for historians of science to grasp the significance of traditional Indian science for their discipline and the changes in attitude and in concepts that the existence of this Indian science and of other non-western sciences indicates to be necessary. Science, as the dominant element in the western intellectual enterprise, is narrowly conceived of by most of its historians as a genus having only one species, so that, even when they by chance stumble upon a specimen of an exotic type, they dismiss it as a member of a different genus because it lacks the external marks of authentification. As social scientists become interested in the odd behavior of contemporary scientists who develop and deploy methods of increasing their authority within their scientific disciplines, within the community of academics, and within society at large, some attention is being paid to the very different modes of behavior and means of legitimization followed by scientists in cultures other than our own, and comparisons are being made.[1] But it remains extremely rare, if not non-existent, for social scientists to study non-western science deeply enough to grasp the intellectual challenge posed by Indian and other sciences to the commonly held concept of the uniqueness of western scientific methodology as a means of discovering "the truth." In this paper I wish to address the question of the differences between the Indian search for scientific "truth" in mathematics and in mathematical astronomy and that of the ancient Greeks, and to point to two facts: that Indian scientific discoveries, though arrived at by a very different methodology, were incorporated into Islamic and western science and thus are part of the heritage of modern science; and that Indian scientists, using non-Western methods, arrived at valid conclusions, some of which could not initially be correctly understood in the West simply because these conclusions can be properly grasped only by persons familiar with

Indian culture, and willing to discard the notion of western methodologies being the only ones that are authentic in science.

Before entering into these demonstrations, however, I need to dispel two common misconceptions. Westerners tend to look upon the Greeks as the world's chief students of science in antiquity. From a quantitative point of view, however, many more works on scientific subjects were written in India between 500 BCE and 1500 CE than in ancient and medieval Greece, in Western Europe, and in the Islamic world combined.[2] India did *not* have a culture dominated by religion and interested only in nirvana or *mokṣa*; the Indians who wrote and read millions of surviving manuscripts on science were interested in the answers to questions about this world. The questions they asked were not necessarily those that our scientists ask, for the questions that both their and our scientists become involved in are determined by the culture to which each group belongs and by the rules for furthering knowledge adapted by those cultures. But the Indians sought answers based on reason just as westerners did. Their answers, of course, might involve non-physical forces such as souls in both India and the West, e.g., the demons propelling the planets on the deferent from rotating positions on their epicycles in the *Sūryasiddhānta*, the souls of the planets propelling their epicycle mechanisms in the second book of Ptolemy's *Planetary Hypotheses*, and the soul of the universe propelling the planets in their elliptical orbits in Kepler's *Harmonice Mundi*.

The Indians, then, were just as interested in the natural world as the westerners and just as rational in their investigations of it. What differentiated them from the Greeks in mathematics was that they were pragmatic while the Greeks treated geometry as almost divine, as a sure path to sure knowledge. What differentiated them from the Greeks in mathematical astronomy was that they were more interested in clever approximate solutions and mathematical short-cuts while the Greeks worried about precision and mechanics.

In mathematics the differences are visible in both arithmetic and geometry. Arithmetic for the Pythagoreans among the Greeks constituted a theory of numbers, but for the Indians arithmetic constituted practical rules for adding, subtracting, multiplying, dividing, squaring and cubing, taking square and cube roots, dealing with fractions, and using proportions.[3] The Greeks also could perform all of these tasks, but their approach to arithmetic was abstract and theoretical. In fact, it was more rigid. In geometry the Greek ideal was to "prove" the truth of a relationship by showing how it could be deduced from a very limited number of generally accepted axioms, while Indians again sought pragmatic means—often approximative—to solve particular problems.[4] By many Greek philosophers numbers were regarded as the constituent elements of the universe. By other Greek philosophers the geometry of the heavenly bodies and their motions was the only manifestation of the workings of the mind of God visible to man. No Indian that I know of ever held such extreme views about the position of mathematics. Mysticism in this case lies on the western side, not on the eastern.

Given these different views of the function and status of mathematics, the Indians were more satisfied by approximations and therefore more ready to tackle problems that might permit only an approximate or an equivocal answer. Thus the Indians can offer solutions to arithmetical problems involving zero and irrationals and, in algebra,[5] to indeterminate equations of the first degree (by Aryabhata c. 500 CE) and of the second degree (by Jayadeva c. 1000 CE), and to problems in permutations and combinations (summarized and expanded by in 1356[6]): While some of the problems (e.g., irrationals and indeterminate equations) were familiar to the Greeks, they were not able to advance as far as the Indians did. Indeed, a number of the Indian solutions were rediscovered in the west only during the Renaissance.

In part, at least, the success of the Indians was due to their non-recognition of mathematics as a system of logic. They were always ready to experiment with methods, (even involving guess-work) that led to acceptable results. None of this Indian arithmetic or algebra is abstract; it all has (or pretends to have) practical applications; and the desire to satisfy practical needs was undoubtedly an important element in what motivated the mathematicians to discover the means.

In geometry this also was, in general, true. But Brahmagupta in the early seventh century CE gives a series of extraordinary theories concerning cyclic quadrilaterals and concerning right triangles which in India at least had no practical applications. Many of these theories, like many of the algebraic solutions referred to above, were independently discovered in western Europe in the seventeenth and eighteenth centuries. But the Indians never tackled subjects like conics or spirals. Nor were they challenged by famous set problems like squaring the circle, trisecting an angle, and duplicating a cube, though some of the mathematicians of Kerala in the fifteenth and sixteenth centuries dealt successfully with related problems. To some extent this lack of interest in solving difficult set problems in India must have been due to the facts that mathematics and philosophy were not linked in India, that there was no axiomatic method in Indian geometry, and that mathematics was never a profession in India in which fame and authority could be gained by a clever solution to a well known, classic problem.

This is not to say that cleverness was not valued by Indian mathematicians. There is every sign that the desire to win admiration for the solution of difficult problems was a prime motive for many of the innovations in Indian mathematicians, but this admiration would be granted by only a few students or later mathematicians who might come upon the evidence of someone's cleverness; there was no chorus of educated afficionados who might applaud the mathematician's efforts. While there were many persons using and writing about mathematics throughout India, each worked in virtual isolation. A striking instance is the fact that Brahmagupta's amazing geometrical theories were explained and first extended more than seven hundred years after their original publication.

In summary of the remarkable results of this non-Euclidean, Indian approach to geometry we can cite the following achievements.

1. The formula for the area for a cyclic quadrilateral given by Brahmagupta in 628, with the rationale by Jyesthadeva c. 1500.
2. The theories about the diagonals of a cyclic quadrilateral, also given by Brahmagupta, and rediscovered by W. Snell in 1619.
3. The formula for the circumradius of a cyclic quadrilateral given by Paramesvara c. 1400, with the rationale provided by Sankara c. 1550; rediscovered by Lhuilier in 1782.
4. Infinite series for pi given by Madhava c. 1400 with the rationale provided by Nilakantha c. 1500; rediscovered by Leibniz in the 1670s.
5. Infinite power series for sine and cosine given by Madhava c. 1400, with the rationale by Sankara c. 1550; rediscovered by Newton in 1660.[7]

When Madhava's work was first discussed in English by Whish in 1830, it was mistakenly believed to indicate that the Indians knew the calculus. Only in recent years has it been shown that Madhava reached his brilliant results without the calculus.

In addition to these very precise results in some cases, especially in the work of Madhava and his school in Kerala, based on unproven but essentially correct assumptions and on approximations—Indian mathematicians brilliantly modified trigonometrical functions so that they approximated curves needed to solve complex problems with three variables, and indeed invented simple but close approximations to the trigonometrical functions themselves.[8] These achievements emphasize the contention of this paper that Indian mathematics, by routes quite different from those of the West, made many extraordinary and valid discoveries that should challenge the historians and the philosophers of western mathematics to reconsider their fundamental assumptions about what mathematics is and how it is done. Let me emphasize that if western historians and philosophers, look at some of the recent work done on Indian mathematics referred to in the *Notes,* they will find real, recognizable mathematics. I am not arguing that Indian mathematics is preferable to its western cousin, just that it is different and yet often highly successful.

In mathematical astronomy, where the historical connections among Babylonian, Greek, Indian, Islamic, and western forms of this science are now much more refined and clear than in the past,[9] the variety in expressing almost identical mathematical formulae and geometrical models points to the truth of the opinion that culture strongly influences science even when it is borrowed by one culture from another. Indian astronomy beginning in the second century CE. consists to a large extent of adaptations of Greek originals. Greek adaptations of Babylonian "linear" astronomy mixed with Hipparchan elements in the *Yavanajātaka* of Yavaneśvara (149/150 CE) and in the *Vasiṣṭhasiddhānta, Romakasiddhānta,* and *Paulisasiddhānta* summarized by Varāhamihira c. 550 in his *Pañcasiddhāntikā.* And pre-Ptolemaic Greek spherical astronomy appeared in the *Paitāmahasiddhānta* of the *Viṣṇudharmottarapurāṇa* c. 425 and numerous later *siddhāntic* texts.[10]

The *siddhāntic* tradition initiated by the *Paitāmahasiddhānta* differs from the Hellenistic tradition that is its ancestor in its assumptions about the nature of the geometrical models that were introduced into India from the West. For the Greeks of the Platonic tradition the geometry of the celestial spheres and their motions are the only reflections of the activity of the mind of God that are perceptible to us. For the Greeks of the Aristotelian tradition, celestial motions are by nature uniform and circular. The Greek geometrical models were expected somehow to conform to an interpretation or modification of Aristotelian celestial mechanics, and the planetary positions that resulted from the motions of their parts were expected to be computed by Euclidean means. Such restraints did not operate in the Indian tradition, where the geometric models were simply calculating devices; for the solutions of geometric models, sine, cosine, and versine functions were invented and iteration techniques were developed. These trigonometrical functions and the iteration techniques found many other applications in mathematical astronomy, as did analemmata in the solution of problems in spherical trigonometry. Many of these substitutes for Greek methods were employed to find not precise, but approximate answers; the Indians did not employ observations as the Greeks did, to measure the component parts of the celestial mechanisms, so that approximations were more readily tolerated. The Indians, then, applied great ingenuity over the centuries to the invention of approximations even when the accurate solutions were known.

Much of this early Indian mathematical astronomy was transmitted to Islam in the late eighth century, and exercised a long and profound influence on Near Eastern astronomy as well as on that of Andalusia and its western European offshoot. Indian mathematical astronomy forms an important component in the traditions from which modern western positional astronomy has evolved; its historical contributions again demonstrate that one cannot fully comprehend the nature of scientific knowledge and its generation without studying the Indian texts.

Finally, the Indian texts on mathematical astronomy written in Sanskrit and Persian in north India between about 1500 and 1900 will provide historians, once they have been edited and studied, with a wonderfully complete documentation of the way in which these advanced scientific systems—the traditional Indian, the Muslim adaptation of Ptolemy, and the western descendent of them both—interacted with and influenced each other, and of how the western variant was ultimately (for non-scientific as well as scientific reasons) the dominant science. The unraveling of this process, which is just beginning, promises again to illuminate more fully the inevitably close connections between culture and science.

NOTES

1. Barton (1994) includes a study of Greek science in the period of the Roman Empire.
2. An accounting of this enormous and largely unpublished Indian literature in the exact sciences is being provided in Pingree (1970-), where bibliographies concerning the individual scientists mentioned in this article will be found. A non-technical survey can be found in Pingree (1981).
3. See, for instance, Bag (1979, 52-102).

4. Recent surveys of Indian geometry include Bag (1979, 103-174, 229-285) and Sarasvati (1979).
5. For algebra see Bag (1979, 175-228).
6. See Kusuba (1993).
7. The work of this Kerala school has been the subject of much discussion ever since it was re-examined by Marar and Rajagopal (1944); for the later bibliography see Pingree (1981, 65-66, n. 62) and Gold and Pingree (1991).
8. See Plofker (1995) and the articles by R.C. Gupta, T. Hayashi, T. Kusuba, and M. Yano listed in the bibliographies to Pingree (1970-).
9. See the articles by Pingree listed in the bibliographies to Pingree (1970-) and Pingree (1993).
10. See Pingree (1978)

REFERENCES

Bag, A.K. 1979. *Mathematics in Ancient and Medieval India.* Varanasi: Chaukhamba Orientalia.

Barton, Tamsyn S. 1994. *Power and Knowledge.* Ann Arbor: Univ. of Michigan Press.

Gold, David, and David Pingree. 1991. "A Hitherto Unknown Sanskrit Work concerning Madhava's Derivation of the Power Series for Sine and Cosine." *Historia Scientiarum* 42: 49-65.

Kusuba, Takanori. 1993. *Combinatorics and Magic Squares in India: A Study of Narayana Pandita's "Ganitakaumudi," Chapters 13-14.* Unpublished doctoral dissertation, Brown University.

Marar, K. Mukunda and C.T. Rajagopal. 1944. "On the Hindu Quadrature of the Circle." *Journal of the Bombay Branch of the Royal Asiatic Society,* New Series 20: 65-82.

Pingree, David. 1970-. *Census of the Exact Sciences in Sanskrit,* Series A, vols. 1-5. Philadelphia: American Philosophical Society. To be continued.

———. 1978. "History of Mathematical Astronomy in India." *Dictionary of Scientific Biography.* New York: Charles Scribner's Sons. 15: 533-633.

———. 1981. *Jyotihsastra-Astral and Mathematical Literature.* Wiesbaden: Otto Harrassowitz.

———. 1993. "Aryabhata, the Paitamahasiddhanta, and Greek Astronomy." *Studies in History of Medicine and Science.* New Series 12: 69-79.

Plofker, Kim. 1995. *Mathematical Approximation by Transformation of Sine Functions in Medieval Sanskrit Astronomical Texts.* Unpublished doctoral dissertation, Brown University.

Sarasvati Amma, T.A. 1979. *Geometry in Ancient and Medieval India.* Delhi: Motilal Banarsidass.

Music

NAZIR ALI JAIRAZBHOY

"In music the influence of India has been even less significant ..."
(Basham 1975). While India's influence on western thought in
the areas of phonetics, comparative philology, comparative religion,
and even folktales are recognized, India's contribution to western
studies in musicology are not generally known. The discovery of a
sophisticated musical theory in ancient India, initially exposed by Sir
William Jones (1784), had little impact in the West—certainly a far
cry from the reactions to the West's discovery of India's religious,
dramatic, and poetic literature. Yet there is reason to believe that
Indian musical thought did have a major impact on the nascent field
of ethnomusicology.

It happened in the 1880s, even before the term "comparative
musicology" (later called ethnomusicology) was invented by Guido
Adler in 1885. Raja Sourindro Mohan Tagore, a "lesser" raja, the
younger of two landowning brothers of an immense estate in Bengal,
chose, during the period of nationalistic awareness in India, to
devote much of his life to propagating Indian music. He was an
enigmatic character. On the one hand, he was devoutly supportive
of the British colonialists and other European monarchies,
entertaining such personages as the Prince of Wales and Leopold II
from Belgium at his family estate. On the other hand, he was also
a nationalist, a scholar, and an aficionado of Indian music, and he
organized elaborate recitals for his western guests. An indication of
the nature of these performances is found in the program notes
from one of his soirees at his palatial residence in Esmerand Bowen,
near Calcutta in 1879.[1] Although this presentation was not put on
for royalty,[2] it was unimaginable in its scope and variety by present-day
standards. The concert was composed of two parts, the first held in
a concert hall on the second floor of Tagore's mansion, the second
in a theater on the first floor. The first part had fourteen different
items, among which were four instrumental solos, on *sur-bahar* and
jalataranga by Mahomed Khan, on *setar* by Babu Ramsabak Misser

and *nyāstaraga* (presumably *nyāstaranga,* a type of kazoo) by Prosonno Bannerjea, and several vocal items, including *dhrupad, telena* (cf. *tarānā*), and *quol*[3] by Gopal Chunder Chuckerburtty and a *kheyal* and *tuppa* sung by Guru Prashad Misser. In addition there were dances, one presumably of Kathak since the song accompanying is given as *thungri* (cf. *ṭhumrī*), a narrative song, *kathakata,* a vocal/ instrumental competition between two parties, called *panchali,* enactments of Krishna episodes, called *rasdhari, jatra* episodes, a boat song, and a type of devotional song, *nagar-kirtun.*

This enormously lengthy and complicated program was followed in the second half by a series of six tableaux depicting the six male *rāgas* with numerous songs and music composed by S.M. Tagore and Khetter Mohun Gossamy.[4]

Raja Tagore's fervent desire to demonstrate the vitality of India's performing traditions is clearly evident in such a production, and this helps to explain some of his other excesses in the promotion of Indian music (discussed below). But one can hardly imagine how such a seemingly endless event would have been received by an uninitiated western audience. In those days Indian music with its continuous drone was generally regarded by many Europeans as being utterly boring.[5] More often than classical music, Europeans heard "ditties, sung by ill-instructed screaming dancing women, at crowded native darbars, marriages and other cermonials ... all sang and played together whatever they pleased, and the clamour of their different tunes, with all their varied accompaniments, was quite indescribable. It is no wonder, therefore, that the English guests stopped their ears, and declared native music to be abominable." (French 1882, 267)

Such attitudes evidently did not deter Raja Tagore in his quest to inform the West of India's musical traditions. The other strategy he adopted was to gift collections of Indian musical instruments and books on Indian music to numerous museums in the western world as well as some in the Far East. Major collections of these instruments are still to be found in many cities in Europe as well as some in the U.S. including in the Metropolitan Museum in New York.[6] The major impact of these magnanimous gifts was, however, in Belgium, where 98 Indian instruments were received at the museum of the Conservatoire Royal de Bruxelles in 1876. Since Indian musical instruments often tend to be rather large, the Director, Monsieur F.-A. Gevaert, must have been rather taken aback by this unexpected acquisition, and feeling unequal to the task of preparing a catalogue for these instruments, he invited Victor Mahillon, the son of an instrument maker and publisher and joint editor of the periodical, *L'Echo Musical*, to undertake this task.

Mahillon is still regarded by many ethnomusicologists as the father of organology (the study of musical instruments) based on the catalogue he produced of this Tagore collection. His main contribution is said to have been the scientific organization of instruments on the basis of the primary sound-producing element. Instruments had been classified in a western-biased functional manner into strings (chordophones), winds (aerophones), and percussion instruments. The logic underlying the percussion instruments deviated from the cordophones and aerophones in that it lumped together instruments on the basis of playing technique rather than on the method of sound production. Mahillon, however, dispensed with percussion as a category and introduced, instead, two new categories, membranophones and autophones (now referred to as idiophones), both of which conform to the concept of the sound producing element.

Gevaert, the Director of the Brussels Museum, fully aware of Mahillon's "new" categories continued to use the traditional classification system in his catalogue of western instruments in the museum on the grounds that membranophones and autophones whose "function is solely rhythmic, have for the most part, little artistic value," whereas the other two (i.e., chordophones and aerophones) he regarded as "the most noble instruments." (Gevaert 1885, 3)

Elsewhere I have argued that the arrival of Tagore's collection of musical instruments, accompanied by various treatises not only inspired the development of the field of organology, but also provided the written Indian sources from which Mahillon directly took his system of classification (Jairazbhoy 1990). The *Nāṭya Śāstra* mentions exactly the same four categories, albeit in a different sequence: *tata, suṣira, avanaddha,* and *ghana,* the exact counterparts of chordophones, aerophones, membranophones, and autophones (idiophones). It is distressing to note, however, that Mahillon failed to give credit to the Indian sources but instead in 1878 published an article by Charles Bosselet in Mahillon's periodical (*l'Echo Musical*) describing his catalogue in which the credit for the invention of this classification system is given solely to Mahillon.[7] For this "invention" Mahillon is regarded as the father of western organology; however, this appellation should surely belong to Bharata, the attributed author of the *Nāṭya Śāstra.*

In 1885 Sir Alexander Ellis' "On the Musical Scales of Various

Nations"[8] was published and had a major impact on the developing field of ethnomusicology, then referred to as comparative musicology. Whereas musical intervals had traditionally been measured in terms of ratios or string lengths, leading to such complex numbers as 243:256 and 289:433, Ellis introduced a new system of measurement that divided the western tempered semitone into 100 equal logarithmic cents. Using this, Ellis was able to give both the theoretical and practical measurements of the scales of many countries ranging from the Scottish highlands to China and Japan. The Indian scale was one of many that he considered, giving both the theoretical intervals (measured in *śrutis*) of the ancient Indian scale given in the *Nāṭya Śāstra*, as well as the measurements of various tunings played by Raja Ram Pal Singh played on the *sitahr* (sic.). In addition, he measured the intervals on two fixed-fretted *vīṇās* that Mahillon loaned from the Tagore collection. Ellis also had access to two of Tagore's works, "Hindu Music from Various Authors" published by Tagore that included a major article of his, as well as a second work, "The Musical Scales of the Hindus," which had been published in 1884. It is thus clear that Ellis had access to ancient Indian musical theory. Although Ellis' section on India does not appear to be of major importance in his work, there is a possibility that Indian musical theory may have inspired him to invent the system of cents, as the concept underlying *śruti* is similar to that of cents; i.e., both are logarithmic units by which musical intervals are measured. The major difference between the two is that Ellis' cents divide a semitone into 100 parts; whereas a semitone was divided into just two *śrutis* in the Indian system. Nevertheless, the *śrutis* and the cents function in exactly the same way, since an interval of 13 *śrutis* represents a perfect fifth wherever it occurs, just as does the Ellis interval of 702 cents.

There is no evidence, however, that Ellis modeled his cent system after *śrutis,* although he certainly availed himself of the Tagore gift in preparing his famous article. It is worth noting that in both instances no intellectual credit was given to Indian scholars or authors, a situation that continues to some extent into the present. A.H. Fox Strangways' book *Music of Hindostan* was published in 1914. It is a work of great depth and perception that treats Indian musical culture with sympathy and understanding. Fox Strangways wanted to communicate his conceptions of Indian music to his countrymen and thus used numerous western music analogies that evidently had little impact on western scholarship as a whole. It did, however, have an impact on the Dutch scholar Arnold Bake who, in the 1930s, stayed at least a year with "Foxie" translating Sanskrit musical treatises for him.

Bake carried out his Ph.D. research on a Sanskrit musical treatise (*Sangīta Darpana*) in Shantiniketan, where he was greatly influenced by Rabindranath Tagore, who drew much of his inspiration from the folk traditions of Bengal, specifically those of the Baul singers, the tribal Santals, and the songs of the boatmen who plied the Ganges and its tributaries. Bake, who was a western classical singer before he became a Sanskritist under the influence of Fox Strangways and Tagore, anticipated the approaches of ethnomusicology by realizing that classical music cannot develop without a contributary support system in the folk culture of the country. He thus set out to study and document all forms of music in the country, ranging from the classical to the most simple non-literate forms as sung by laborers and housewives. His documentation of the devotional and folk/ tribal music in the 1930s and particularly on one fifteen-month fieldtrip in 1938-1939 is perhaps the most important source of visual and auditory information for the recent history of Indian music and performing arts. Although he was universally recognized as an excellent scholar, he did not publish a major work. The main impact of Bake's work was on two of his students, J.R. Marr and N.A. Jairazbhoy at the University of London's School of Oriental and African Studies. Jairazbhoy, realizing the importance of Bake's field recordings of the 1930s, received a grant for copying Bake's old recordings to magnetic audio tape four years after Bake's demise in 1963. In 1988 Jairazbhoy contributed to the copying of Bake's 16 mm. silent films.[9]

One of Jairazbhoy's primary concerns was the fact that foreign scholars had made many recordings with visual documentation that had been taken out of India and housed in other parts of the world, with no copies available in India. This led to the establishment of the Archives and Research Center for Ethnomusicology, a subsidiary of the American Institute of Indian Studies, funded by the Smithsonian Institution and the Ford Foundation, the primary purpose of which was to serve as a repository for audio/visual documentation collected by foreign scholars. This included the returning to India of the Bake materials as well as those collected by Jairazbhoy on his numerous fieldtrips, with funding from the Asian Cultural Council. The major credit for the success of the Archives should be given to the Director-General of the American Institute of Indian Studies, Dr. Pradeep Mehendiratta, and the Research Director of the Archives, Dr. Shubha Choudhury.

The Bake materials have been featured in two major research projects: a continuing project, "Bake Restudy in India," carried out by Jairazbhoy with the collaboration of Dr. Amy Catlin;[10] and a similar project in Nepal by Dr. Carol Tingey.[11] In both these projects, copies of Bake's recordings, films, and photographs were taken to the original sites and played back/shown, whenever possible to the original performers or their families, with a view to collecting further information on them and rerecording the items to assess the elements of continuity and change.

In the 1950s and 1960s the West began to discover the great diversity and fascination of Indian music as several collectors (John Levy, Deben Bhattacharya, David Lewiston, and Genevieve Dournon among others) traveled to different regions of India, recording and releasing as LPs many different genres of Indian music. They undoubtedly served an important purpose by disseminating these materials in the western world, although some Indian musicians and scholars began to question the motives of recordists as being commercial rather than educational. This had a negative impact on some of the western research scholars in the 1960s and 1970s who were occasionally viewed with suspicion. Fortunately, however, the sincerity and dedication displayed by these scholars in the pursuit of their projects, and the generosity of the host country as well as of indigenous musicians and scholars, helped them to overcome such stigmas.

This period also saw the "discovery" of Indian classical music in the West as Ravi Shankar and Ali Akbar Khan gave numerous recitals to enthusiastic audiences. Ravi Shankar's association with the Beatles and his collaborations with Yehudi Menuhin played a major part in convincing the western world that Indian music was indeed a vital world art form. At about the same time, ethnomusicology began to acquire prominence in U.S. universities. Beginning in the University of California at Los Angeles under the leadership of Mantle Hood, and then at other universities (e.g., Wesleyan under Robert Brown and the University of Washington under Robert Garfias), ethnomusicology programs included performances of numerous world music traditions that were taught by native musicians brought to the U.S. specifically for this purpose. India was represented by classical musicians from both south and north India.

Exposure to Indian music was no less significant in Europe and other parts of the world, as a number of Indian musicians toured, giving concerts and offering master classes or lectures even in such remote places as Mauritius and Kabul. Often these musicians were not paid particularly well, but on return to India they received prestige as being "foreign returned," which gave their Indian careers a significant boost (Neuman 1980, 190-191). Some of the musicians stayed abroad or visited regularly for months at a time, giving lessons privately or at educational institutions. Ali Akbar Khan established a music college in the San Francisco Bay area that still continues after more than twenty years, and artistes from India are frequently invited from India to assist in teaching north Indian classical music. Most of the students are westerners, some of whom have achieved remarkable performance abilities, concertize regularly, and also give lessons themselves. Mention must here be made of the late Professor Jon Higgins (d.1984) whose mastery of south Indian vocal classical music has now become legendary. Similar developments were also taking place in Europe, particularly in England (which, of course, has a large Indo-Pakistani population) and other countries, for instance, the Netherlands where the Rotterdam Conservatory of Music has a special world music program featuring Indian music.

The consequence of all this performance activity was that a number of western students went to India to study performance with leading musicians in the traditional *guru-śisya* system, and many have achieved sufficient performance skills to give recitals in both India and the West. At the same time, with the steady burgeoning of western academic programs in ethnomusicology and performance studies, an increasing number of students and scholars began to take advantage of the many different areas available for research in music and the performing arts of India. Although the following lists are by no means comprehensive,[12] they will nevertheless give some indication of the numbers of western scholars involved in such research.[13]

For the purposes of this enumeration, the subject of Indian music and performance is divided into six categories: 1. General works on Indian music, 2. Historical studies, 3. Regional studies, 4. Studies of communities of performers, 5. Studies of musical instruments, and 6. Studies of particular genres.

1. General Works on Indian Music. Since William Jones (1784), Augustus Willard (1834) and the early writings of this century by Fox Strangways (1914), Ethel Rosenthal (1918), H.A. Popley (1921), and Arnold Bake (1957a), most of the general works on Indian music have focused almost entirely on various aspects of classical music. These include works by Howard Boatwright (1963), Jerry Cohn (1966), Robert Brown (1967), Josef Kuckertz (1970), Emmons White (1971), Peggy Holroyde (1972), Nelly van Ree-Bernard (1973),

Emmie te Nijenhuis (1974, 1977), Reginald and Jamila Massey (1977), Bonnie Wade (1979), Dane Rudhyar (1979), Neil Sorrell and Ram Narayan (1980), Leela Floyd (1980), Wim van der Meer (1980, 1982), Alicia Lewis (1989) and traveler's accounts of Indian music, and Deborah Ann Swallow (1982) who treats the subject of comparative music symbolism. There have also been articles in encyclopedias, e.g., *Encyclopedia Britannica* (Nazir Jairazbhoy, 1974) and the *New Grove Dictionary of Music and Musicians* (Harold Powers et al., 1980) in which the coverage is somewhat broadened to include discussion of non-classical genres.

The subject of intonation (*śruti*) in classical music has been a subject of considerable fascination to western scholars and is discussed in many of the general works on Indian music mentioned above. Some of the prominent writers focusing on the subject are E. Clements (1913), A.H. Fox Strangways (1914), Arnold Bake (1957a), Nazir Jairazbhoy and A.W. Stone (1963), Alain Danielou (1968), Mark Levy (1982), and James Arnold and Bernard Bel (1983). An unusual work is that of Anoop Chandola (1988) with his ethnomusico-linguistic approach to music.

The subject of *rāg* (*rāga*) is of particular importance in classical music. Since there is no close parallel to this melodic concept in the West, a number of western scholars have addressed the subject. Among the most prominent works on *rāg* are Walter Kaufman (1968, 1976), Alain Danielou (1968), Janet Way (1969), Harold Powers (1970), Nazir Jairazbhoy (1971), Emmie te Nijenhuis (1976), Patrick Moutal (1987,1991), Joep Bor (1992), Gordon Thompson (1995), and Richard Widdess (1995). The topic of *tāl* (*tālā*) has also received some attention, e.g., Manfred Junius (1983), although this topic is usually subsumed in the works on *tablā* and *mṛdaṅgam.*

2. *Historical Studies.* Many western scholars, beginning with Sir William Jones (1784), have been fascinated by music theory as expressed in the Sanskrit treatises of various periods. Among them should be mentioned A.A. Clements (1912), A.H. Fox Strangways (1914), A.A. Bake (1930, 1957a, 1957b, 1957c), Nazir Jairazbhoy (1958, 1961, 1975), Harold Powers (1958, 1970, 1980), S. Ramanathan (1979), Ranaganayaki Iyengar (1980), Emmie te Nijenhuis (1970), Lewis Rowell (1992), Richard Widdess (1995), and Gordon Thompson (1995). Several of these works, and particularly that of Mark Levy (1982), have attempted to correlate theoretical formulations with present-day practice. An unusual historical presentation is that of Kaufmann et al. (1981) that relies on visual sources. Another

unusual historical presentation is that of J. Andrew Greig (1987), who focused on Persian treatises for his historical research of the Mughals in the 16th and 17th centuries.

3. Regional Studies. Regional studies tend to focus on the social organization of performers rather than on the music per se. They include studies of music in cities, particularly Madras: Milton Singer (1972), Kathleen l'Armand and Adrian L'Armand (1978), and Bruno Nettl (1985) comparing Madras and Tehran. They also include broader studies of states, regions, or linguistic areas, for instance, Uttar Pradesh: Edward Henry (1974, 1977), Laxmi Tewari (1974), Scott Marcus (1989), and Peter Manuel (1988); Gujarat: Gordon Thompson, (1987); Rajasthan: Nazir Jairazbhoy (1977), Joan Erdman (1985), David Roach (in progress), and Daniel Neuman (in progress)[14]; South India (Tamilnadu, Kerala, and Karnataka): Nazir Jairazbhoy and Amy Catlin (1988); Karnataka: Gayathri Kassebaum (1994); and Ladakh: Mark Trewin (1987).

4. Studies of Communities of Performers. Some of these studies focus on the social organization of musicians, e.g., Felix van Lamsweerde (1969), Brian Silver (1976), and Daniel Neuman (1974, 1978, 1980), while musicians' social organization is a subsidiary topic in many other works on performers: the Baul community, Bengal: Joseph Kuckertz (1976) and Charles Capwell (1986); Cochin Jews: Johanna Spector (1967, 1969); Calcutta Jews: Rahel Musleah (1991); the Manganihar community, Rajasthan: Amy Catlin (1977) and Nazir Jairazbhoy (1980b); the Bhat community, Rajasthan: Nazir Jairazbhoy (forthcoming); the Charans of Gujarat: Gordon Thompson (1987, 1991); Gond, Baiga, and Muria tribes: Walter Kaufmann (1941, 1969); the Barela-Bhilala tribe: Engelbert Stiglmayr (1970); a general discussion of tribal music: Carol Babiracki (1990); the Munda tribe, Bihar: Carol Babiracki (1991); the Kota tribe, Tamilnadu: Richard Wolf (in progress); and the Toda tribe, Tamilnadu: Joseph Kuckertz (1978).

5. Studies of Musical Instruments. As a consequence of S.M. Tagore's gifts of collections of musical instruments to numerous museums in the West, and the remarkable series of paintings reproduced in the work of C.R. Day (1891), one would have expected the germination of many individual studies on Indian musical instruments. While A.A. Dick (1984) has dealt extensively with Indian musical instruments in *The New Grove Dictionary of Musical Instruments*, the majority of research has been carried out on just a few instruments of classical music generally with an emphasis on teaching methods and repertoire. Among these are: *sitār*: Ravi Shankar (1968), Allen Keessee (1968), Harold Schramm (1969), Manfred Junius (1974), Stephen Slawek (1987), Annysha Sacchini (1987), James Hamilton (1989), and Allyn Miner (1993); *tablā*: Rebecca Stewart (1974), Frances Shepherd (1976), Gert-Matthias Wegner (1982), Robert Gottlieb (1977,1993), and James Kippen (1988); *sarod*: George Ruckert (1991); *vīṇā*: Karaikuddi Subramanyam (1984), David Reck (1983); *rudra vīṇā*: Thomas Marcotty (1980); *mṛdaṅgam*: Robert Brown (1965); Himalayan folk drumming: Anoop Chandola (1977); *tambūrā*: Kathryn Vaughn (1991); *violin*: Barbara Benary (1971), L. Shankar (1974), Gordon Swift (1990); *ḍholak*: David Roach (in progress); *nāgasvaram*: William Skelton (1971), Yoshihiko Terada (1992); and *shahnā'ī*: Nazir Jairazbhoy (1970, 1980a), Reis Flora (1983), Alastair Dick (1984). Mention should also be made of Roderick Knight's article on the only remnant of the ancient "*harp*" *vīṇā* (1985) and of Walter Kaufman's article on tribal musical instruments in Bastar, Madhya Pradesh (1961).

6. Studies of Particular Genres. Many of these studies are focused on classical and semi-classical music: *ālāpana*: T. Viswanathan (1974, 1977); *dhrupad*: Indurama Srivastava (1977); *khyāl*: Bonnie Wade; *kṛti* and *pallavi*: Ranganayaki Ayyangar (1965), Amy Catlin (1980, 1985, 1991), and David Reck (1983); *thumrī*: Peter Manuel (1989); music of Bharata Natyam: Jon Higgins (1993); *padam*: Mathew Allen (1992); *qawwālī*: Nazir Jairazbhoy (1968), Regula Qureshi (1983, 1986); and *ghazal*: Peter Manuel (1979).

Genres of religious and devotional (bhakti) music have attracted several western scholars. Among them are: Vedic chant: Nazir Jairazbhoy (1968), Lewis Rowell (1977), Wayne Howard (1977, 1986); Bengali *Krishna bhajans*: Edward Dimock (1967); *Radha-Krishna bhajans*: Milton Singer (1972); south Indian *bhajans*: Robert Simon (1975, 1984); *kīrtan*, Stephen Slawek (1986); Emmie te Nijenhuis (1987); *Namdev bhajans*: Winand Callewaert; and *Vallabhācārya bhajans*: Meilu Ho (in progress). There have also been a number of studies of the dramatic forms that have arisen from the religious/devotional environment emphasizing Hindu heroic legends: *terrukūttu*: Richard Frasca (1990); Yaksagana: Martha Ashton (1977); *nautaṅki*: Kathryn Hansen (1992); *ālhā* epic: Laxmi Tewari (1974); *birahā*: Scott Marcus (1989, 1994); and *kaṭhputlī* puppetry: Nazir Jairazbhoy (forthcoming). Other genres that have been studied include: Tamil bow song (*villupāṭṭu*): Stuart Blackburn (1980, 1986); *bhārud, vāghyā-murali*, and *daf gān*: B.C. Deva and Joseph Kuckertz (1981); and *tāyampaka*: Rolf Groesbeck (1995). There have also been studies of popular musical forms, e.g., *lāvnī*: Kristen Rao (1985); street bands (*nānkhatai*): Gregory Booth (1990); Telugu courtesan songs: A.K. Ramanujan et al. (1994); *filmī gīt*: Teri Skilman (1986), Alison Arnold (1988, 1991); and 'popular' music: Gregory Booth (1991), Peter Manuel (1993).

It must be emphasized that this is not by any means a complete enumeration of the western scholars who have carried out research in India; nor is it intended to provide a complete list of subjects researched. Even so, it must convey an impression of the versatility as well as the vitality of music and performance in India that has drawn so many western scholars to its study. There still remain innumerable other topics for music and performance studies in India, which speaks to the boundless creativity of its inhabitants. Much credit, however, must also go to the Government of India for providing such a hospitable climate for research, and to the masters and indigenous scholars of the performing arts for giving so much of their time, energy, and knowledge to western scholars for their research knowing that their compensation would be relatively minimal, as it has been in most cases.

The major insight to be gained from this range of studies is the validation of the ethnomusicological approach that endorses a holistic view in the study of music, where history, culture, and the organization of society all interact to create a musical product. The art traditions are merely the top of the iceberg that could never have developed without the underlying strata. No part of the world illustrates the ethnomusicological hypothesis better than does India, which still continues to maintain, simultaneously, the old and the new, the simple and the complex, the "little and the "great." Some scholars are of the opinion that it is only a matter of time before these traditions "grey" out—and indeed, there is some justification for this view, since some music traditions have either disappeared or adopted modern musical forms. But in India there are factors mitigating against wholesale musical change—for instance, the way in which music is integral to religion and ritual. Until religious practices change and the rituals are abandoned, music will continue in whatever alternative form the future might impose.

Many of the scholars who have written on Indian music are established in the western academic scene, and the impact of their studies in India will be felt for many years. Just how this will shape future western scholarship (as, indeed, it must) remains to be seen, but there can be no question that these scholars' contributions to the understanding of India's music in the West have already been considerable.

NOTES

1. The full program, translated into French with fascinating descriptions of the items, is published in *L'Echo Musical* (July 5, 1879).
2. The guests of honor in this instance were M. and Mme Grant (ibid.).
3. Described as being a Mahomadan religious song generally composed in Arabic (ibid.). Spellings of instruments and genres are as given in *L'Echo Musical.*
4. K.M. Goswamy was a famous music scholar of his time and the author of *Sangita Sara* (1868).
5. "Indian harmony is mostly confined to a monotonous repetition of the key-note during the flights of their vocal or instrumental melody." Anonymous writer describing Captain Augustus Willard's treatise, "Music of Hindustan", in the *Journal of the Asiatic Society*, vol. 15, 1834. Reprinted in Sourindo Mohun Tagore. 1882. *Hindu Music from Various Authors*, 1-122.
6. "There is hardly a capital in Europe whose museums or libraries have not received (from Raja Sourindro Mohun Tagore) instruments or written works, treasures of an inestimable value for the history of music ..." *L'Echo Musical* 10:21 (October 1878). Translated from the French by Amy Catlin.
7. The wording of Charles Bosselet's passage is quite unequivocal (translation by Amy Catlin): "But the types of information which initiate us into the musical customs of the Hindus and other less well-known peoples, however interesting they may be, still do not form the most remarkable feature of this catalogue. We appreciate, above all, the method of classification based upon the different natures of the bodies employed as the source of sonority which allows in one clearly defined category, every instrument which enriches the collection. This classification, *which we believe to be entirely new* (present writer's emphasis), is accompanied and explained by a succinct and clear theory concerning all the methods of producing sound, which constitutes a veritable course in the history of instrumental organography." *L'Echo Musical* 10:17 (August 17, 1878).
8. *Journal of the Society of Arts* 33 (March 27, 1885).
9. Copies of Bake's materials are housed in the School of Oriental and African Studies, London, the University of California at Los Angeles, and the Archives and Research Center for Ethnomusicology in New Delhi.
10. The first restudy, carried out in India in 1984, has been published as a videotape ("Bake Restudy 1984") with an accompanying monograph and has been discussed in Jairazbhoy (1991).

11. *The Nepalese field-work of Dr. A. A. Bake: A Guide to the Sound Recordings.* Unpublished master's thesis, Goldsmiths College, London.
12. Partly because some of these scholars have not yet published the results of their research.
13. This discussion does not include indigenous Indian scholarship or that of non-European countries. It does include, however, scholars of Indian descent and other non-European scholars living or trained in the West.
14. Neuman's Musical Atlas of Rajasthan, prepared in collaboration with Komal Kothari and Shubha Chaudhury, is designed as an interactive CD-Rom.

REFERENCES

Allen, Matthew H. 1992. *The Tamil Padam: A Dance Music Genre of South India.* Unpublished doctoral dissertation, Wesleyan University.,

Arnold, Alison E. 1988. Popular Film Song in India: A Case of Mass-market Musical Eclecticism." *Popular Music* 7:2.

————. 1991. *Hindi Filmi Git: On the History of Commercial Indian Popular Music.* Unpublished doctoral dissertation, University of Illinois.

Arnold, James E. and Bernard Bel. 1983. "A Scientific Study of North Indian Music." *National Centre for the Performing Arts Quarterly Journal* 12:2&3.

Ashton, Martha and Bruce Christie. 1977. *Yaksagana: A Dance Drama of India.* New Delhi: Abhinav.

Ayyangar, Ranganayaki Veeraswamy. 1965. *Analysis of the Melodic, Rhythmic, and Formal Structure of Karnatic Kriti as exemplified in the Kritis of Sri Syama Sastri, Sri Muttuswami Diksitar and Sri Tyagaraja.* Unpublished master's thesis, University of Hawaii.

————. 1980. *Gamaka and Vedanabheda: A Study of Somanatha's Ragavibodha in Historical and Practical Context.* Unpublished doctoral dissertation, Pennsylvania State University.

Babiracki, Carol M. 1990. "Music and History of Mundari-Caste Interaction." In *Ethnomusicology and Modern Music History,* ed. S. Blum, P.V. Bohlman and D.M. Neuman. Urbana: Univ. of Illinois Press.

————. 1991. *Musical and Cultural Interaction in Tribal India: The Karam Repertory of the Mundas of Chotanagpur.* Unpublished doctoral dissertation, University of Illinois.

————. 1991. "Tribal Music in the Study of Great and Little Traditions of Indian Music." In *Comparative Musicology and Anthropology of Music,* ed. Bruno Nettl and Philip V. Bohlman. Chicago: Univ. of Chicago Press.

Bake, Arnold A. 1930. *Bydrage tot de Kennis der Voot-Indische Muziek.* [Damodara's *Sangita Darpana,* ch.1 and 2. Sanskrit text with English translation]. Parys: Paul Geuthner.

————. 1957a. "The Music of India." In *The New Oxford History of Music.* London: Oxford Univ. Press.

————. 1957b. "Indische Musik." In *Die Musik in Geschichte und Gegenwart.* 6. Kassel: Baerenreiter-Verlag.

————. 1957c. "Bharata's Experiment with the Two Vinas." *Bulletin of the School of Oriental and African Studies* 20.

Basham, A.L. 1959. *The Wonder That Was India: A Survey of the Culture of the Indian Sub-continent Before the Coming of the Muslims.* New York: Grove.

Benary, Barbara. 1971. *The Violin in South India.* Unpublished master's thesis, Wesleyan University.

Blackburn, Stewart H. 1980. *Performance as Paradigm: The Tamil Bow Song Tradition.* Unpublished doctoral dissertation, University of California, Berkeley.

————. 1986. "Performance Markers in an Indian Story-Type." In *Another Harmony: New Essays on the Folklore of India,* ed. Stuart H. Blackburn and A.K. Ramanujan. Berkeley: Univ. of California Press.

Boatwright, Howard. 1963. *Indian Classical Music and the Western Listener.* Bombay: Bharatiya Vidya Bhavan.

Booth, Gregory. 1990. "Brass Bands: Tradition, Change, and the Mass Media in Indian Wedding Music." *Ethnomusicology* 34.

————. 1991/1992. "Disco Laggi: Modern Repertoire and Traditional Performance Practice in North Indian Popular Music." *Asian Music* 23(1).

Bor, Joep. 1987. "The Voice of the Sarangi." *National Centre for the Performing Arts Quarterly Journal* 25-26.

Bor, Joep with Phillipe Bruguiere. 1992. *Meister des Raga.* Berlin : Haus der Kulturen der Welt.

Brown, Robert E. 1965. *The Mṛdāṅga: A Study of Drumming in South India.* Unpublished doctoral dissertation, University of California at Los Angeles.

————. 1967. "India's Music." In *Chapters in Indian Civilization, vol. II, British and Modern Period,* 367-403. Reprinted in *Readings in Ethnomusicology,* ed. McAllester, David P. 1971. New York, London: Johnson Reprint Corporation.

Callewaert, Winand M., and Mukund Lath. 1989. *The Hindi Songs of Namdev.* Leuven: Department Orientalistiek.

Capwell, Charles. 1986. *Bauls: Music of the Bauls of Bengal.* Kent, OH: Kent State Univ. Press.

————. 1988. "The Popular Expression of Religious Syncretism: the Bauls of Bengal as Apostles of Brotherhood." *Popular Music* 7:2, Cambridge.

Catlin, Amy Ruth. 1977. "Whither the Manganihars? An Investigation into Change Among Professional Musicians in Western Rajasthan." *Bulletin of the Institute of Traditional Cultures.* Madras.

————. 1980. *Variability and Change in Three Karnataka Kritis: A Study of South Indian Classical Music.* Unpublished doctoral dissertation, Brown University.

————. 1985. "Pallavi and Kriti of Karnatak Music: Evolutionary Processes and Survival Strategies." *National Center for Performing Arts Journal.* Bombay.

————. 1990. *The Bake Restudy.* See Nazir Jairazbhoy and Amy Catlin.

————. 1991. "Vatapi Ganapatim: Sculptural, Poetic and Musical Texts in a Hymn to Ganesa." In *Ganesh: Studies of an Asian God,* ed. Robert L. Brown. Albany: State Univ. of New York Press.

Chandola, Anoop. 1977. *Folk Drumming in the Himalayas: A Linguistic Approach.* New York: AMS Press.

————. 1988. *Music as Speech: an Ethnomusicolinguistic Study of India.* New Delhi: Navrang.

Clements, E. 1913. *Introduction to the Study of Indian Music.* London: Longmans Green. Reprint (n.d.) Allahabad: Kitab Mahal Private Ltd.

Cohn, Jerry. 1966? *An American Student and North Indian Music.* Delhi: Motilal Banarsidass.

Danielou, Alain. 1968. *The Rāgas of North Indian Music.* 2 vols. London: Barrie & Rocklif. Reprint 1980, New Delhi: Munshiram Manahorlal.

Day, C.R. 1891. *The Music and Musical Instruments of Southern India and the Deccan.* Reprinted 1977, Delhi: B.R. Publishing.

Deva, B. Chaitanya and Joseph Kuckhertz. 1981. *Bharud, Vaghya-Murali, and Daff-Gan of the Deccan: Studies in the Regional Folk Music of South India: A Research Report.* Munich: E. Katzbichler.

Dick, Alastair A. 1984. *The New Grove Dictionary of Musical Instruments,* ed. Stanley Sadie. New York: Macmillan.

————. 1984. "The Earlier History of the Shawm in India." *Galpin Society Journal* 37.

Dimock, Edward C., Jr. 1967. *In Praise of Krishna: Songs from the Bengali.* New York: Doubleday.

Erdman, Joan. 1985. *Patrons and Performers in Rajasthan: the Subtle Tradition.* Delhi: Chanakya.

Flora, Reis W. 1983. *Double-Reed Aerophones in India to A. D. 1400.* Unpublished doctoral dissertation, University of California at Los Angeles.

Fox Strangways, A.H. 1914. *The Music of Hindoostan.* Oxford: Clarendon.

Frasca, Richard A. 1990. *The Theater of the Mahabharata: Terukkuttu Performances in South India.* Honolulu: Univ. of Hawaii Press.

French, P.T. 1882. *Catalogue of Indian Musical Instruments: Hindu Music from Various Authors.* Tagore, S.M., compiler. Reprinted 1965. Varanasi: Chowkhamba Sanskrit Series: 49.

Gottlieb, Robert S. 1977. *The Major Traditions of North Indian Tabla Drumming.* Munich: Musikverlag Emil Katzbichler.

————. 1993. *Solo Tabla Drumming of North India: Its Repertoire, Styles, and Performance Practices.* Delhi: Motilal Banarsidass.

Greig, John Andrew. 1987. *Tarikhi Sangita: The Foundations of North Indian Music in the Sixteenth Century.* Unpublished doctoral dissertation, University of California at Los Angeles.

Groesbeck, Rolf. 1995. *Pedagogy and Performance in Tayampaka: A Genre of Temple Instrumental Music in Kerala, India.* Unpublished doctoral dissertation, New York University.

Hamilton, James Sadler. 1989. *Sitar Music in Calcutta: An Ethnomusicological Study.* Calgary: Univ. of Calgary Press.

Hansen, Kathryn. 1992. *Grounds for Play: The Nautanki Theater of North India.* Berkeley: Univ. of California Press.

Henry, Edward O. 1974. *The Meanings of Music in a North Indian Village.* Unpublished doctoral dissertation, Michigan State University.

————. 1976. "The Variety of Music in a North Indian Village: Reassessing Cantometrics." *Ethnomusicology* 20(1): 49-66.

————. 1977. "The Ethnographic Analysis of Four Types of Performance in Bhojpuri-Speaking India." *Journal of the Indian Musicological Society* 8(4): 5-22.

————. 1988. *Chant the Names of God: Musical Culture in Bhojpuri-Speaking India.* San Diego: San Diego State Univ. Press.

Higgins, Jon. 1993. *The Music of Bharata Natyam.* American Institute of Indian Studies. New Delhi: Oxford Univ. Press

Howard, Wayne. 1977. *Samavedic Chant.* New Haven: Yale Univ. Press.

————. 1986. *Veda Recitation in Varanasi.* Delhi: Motilal Banarsidass.

Jairazbhoy, Nazir A. 1958. "Bharata's Concept of Sadharana." *Bulletin of the School of Oriental and African Studies,* 21: 54-60.

————. 1961. "Svaraprastara in North Indian Classical Music." *Bulletin of the School of Oriental and African Studies,* 24: 307-325.

————. 1963 (with A.W. Stone). "Intonation in Present-Day North Indian Classical Music." *Bulletin of the School of Oriental and African Studies,* 26: 119-132.

————. 1968a. "Le chant vedique." In *Encyclopedie des Musiques Sacrees.* Paris: Editions Labergerie.

————. 1968b. "L'Islam en Inde et au Pakistan." In *Encyclopedie des Musiques Sacrees.* Paris: Editions Labergerie.

————. 1970. "A Preliminary Survey of the Oboe in India." *Ethnomusicology* 26: 63-81.

————. 1971. *The Rags of North Indian Music.* London: Faber and Faber. New Edition 1995, Bombay: Popular Prakashan.

————. 1974. "Music" under "South Asian Peoples, Arts." In *Encyclopedia Brittannica.*

————. 1977. "Music in Western Rajasthan: Stability and Change." *Yearbook of the International Folk Music Council* 9: 50-66.

————. 1980a. "The South Asian Double-Reed Aerophone Reconsidered." *Ethnomusicology* 24(1): 147-55.

————. 1980b. "Embryo of a Classical Music Tradition in Western Rajasthan." *Communication of Ideas.* 10th ICAES 3: 99-109.

————. 1984. *Folk Musicians of Rajasthan.* Videotape with accompanying monograph. UCLA Program in Ethnomusicology.

————. 1988 (with Amy Catlin). *Bake Restudy 1984.* Videotape with accompanying monograph. Van Nuys: Apsara Media.

————. 1990. "The Beginnings of Organology and Ethnomusicology in the

West" *Selected Reports in Ethnomusicology* 7: 67-80.

———. 1991. "The First Restudy of Arnold Bake's Fieldwork in India." In *Comparative Musicology and Anthropology of Music,* ed. Bruno Nettl and Philip V. Bohlman. Chicago: Univ. of Chicago Press.

———. Forthcoming. *The World of Kathputli Puppeteers.* Washington: Smithsonian Institution Press.

Jones, William. 1784 (expanded 1882, reprinted 1965). "On the Musical Modes of the Hindoos." *Hindu Music from Various Authors.* Tagore, S.M. compiler. Varanasi: Chowkhamba Sanskrit Series: 49.

Junius, Manfred M. 1974. *The Sitar: The Instrument and its Technique.* Berlin: International Institute for Comparative Music Studies and Documentation.

———. 1983. *Die Talas der Nordindischen Musik.* Munchen: Musikverlag E. Katzbichler.

Kassebaum, Gayathri Rajapur. 1994. *Katha: Six Performance Traditions and the Preservation of Group Identity in Karnataka, South India.* Unpublished doctoral dissertation, University of Washington.

Kaufmann, Walter. 1941. "Folk Songs of the Gond and Baiga." *Musical Quarterly* 17(3).

———. 1960. "The Songs of the Hill Muria, Jhoria Muria and Bastar Muria Gond Tribes." *Ethnomusicology* 4(3).

———. 1961. "The Musical Instruments of the Hill Maria, Jhoria and Bastar Muria Gond Tribes." In *Ethnomusicology* 5(1).

———. 1968. *The Ragas of North India.* Bloomington, Indiana: Indiana Univ. Press.

———. 1976. *The Ragas of South India.* Bloomington, Indiana: Indiana Univ. Press.

Kaufmann, Walter, Joep Bor, Wim van der Meer, and Emmie te Nijenhuis. 1981. "Altindien." *Musikgeschichte in Bildern* 2(3). Leipzig: Deutscher Verlag fur Musik.

Keesee, Allen. 1968. *The Sitar Book.* New York: Oak Publications.

Kippen, James. 1988. *The Tabla of Lucknow: A Cultural Analysis of a Musical Tradition.* Cambridge: Cambridge Univ. Press.

Knight, Roderic. 1985. "The Harp in India Today." *Ethnomusicology* 29(1).

Kuckertz, Joseph. 1970. *Form und Melodiebildung der Karnatischen Music Sudindiens im Umkreis der Vorderorientalischen und der Nordindischen Kunstmusik.* Wiesbaden: Otto Harrasowitz.

———. 1976. "Origin and Construction of the Melodies in Baul Songs of Bengal." In *Yearbook of the International Folk Music, Congress VII.*

———. 1978. "Songs of the Todas of the Nilgiris." *Sangeet Natak* 50. New Delhi.

———. 1981. See B. Chaitnya Deva and Joseph Kuckertz.

Lamsweerde, Felix van. 1969. "Musicians in Indian Society: An Attempt at a Classification." *Tropical Man* 2(7).

L'Armand, Kathleen and Adrian L'Armand. 1978. "Music in Madras: The

Urbanization of a Cultural Tradition." In *Eight Urban Musical Cultures: Tradition and Change*, ed. Bruno Nettl. Urbana: Univ. of Illinois Press, 115-145.

Leela, Floyd. 1980. *Indian Music*. London: Oxford Univ. Press.

Lentz, Donald A. 1971. *Tones and Intervals of Hindu Classical Music*. Lincoln: Univ. of Nebraska.

Levy, Mark. 1982. *Intonation in North Indian Music*. New Delhi: Biblia Impex.

Lewis, Alicia. 1989. *Traveller's Accounts of Indian Music: A Computer-accessed Bibliographic Coded Database*. Unpublished master's thesis, University of Washington.

Mahillon, Victor C. and Charles Bosselet Jr., eds. 1869-1897. *L'Echo Musical*. Brussels.

Manuel, Peter L. 1979. *The Light-Classical Urdu Ghazal-Song*. Unpublished master's thesis, University of California at Los Angeles.

———. 1986. "The Evolution of Modern Thumri." *Ethnomusicology* 30(3): 470-490.

———. 1988. "Popular Music in India: 1901-86." *Popular Music* 7(2).

———. 1988. "Social Structure and Music: Correlating Musical Genres and Social Categories in Bhojpuri-speaking India." *International Review of Aesthetics and Sociology of Music*. Zagreb.

———. 1989. *Thumri in Historical and Stylistic Perspectives*. Delhi: Motilal Bararsidass.

———. 1993. *Cassette Culture: Popular Music and Technology in North India*. Chicago: Univ. of Chicago Press.

Marcotty, Thomas. 1980. *The Way-Music: How to Conjure with Sounds?: Rudra Veena, the Theory and Technique of Tantric Music*. Lugano, Switzerland: Decisio Editrice.

Marcus, Scott. 1989. "The Rise of the Folk Music Genre, Biraha." In *Culture and Power in Benares: Performance Community and Environment 1800-1980*. Berkeley, CA.

———. 1994-1995. "Parody-Generated Texts: The Process of Composition in Biraha, a North Indian Folk Music Genre." *Asian Music* 26(1).

Meer, Wim van der and Joep Bor. 1980. *Hindustani Music in the 20th Century*. The Hague: Martinus Nijhoff.

———. 1982. *De roep van de Kokila: Historische en Hedendaagse Aspecten van de Indiase Muziek*. The Hague: Martinus Nijhoff.

Miner, Allyn. 1993. *Sitar and Sarod in the 18th and 19th Centuries*. New York: F. Noetzel.

Moutal, Patrick. 1987. *Hindustani Raga Sangita: Une Etude de Quelques Mecanismes de Base*. Paris: C.E.M.O., U.E.R. de Musique et de Musicologie.

———. 1991. *A Comparative Study of Selected Hindustani Ragas: Based on Contemporary Practice*. New Delhi: Munshiram Manoharlal Publishers.

Musleah, Rahel. 1991. *Songs of the Jews of Calcutta*. Cedarhurst, NY: Tara.

Nettl, Bruno. 1985. "Two Cities." In *The Western Impact on World Music: Change, Adaptation and Survival*. New York: Schirmer.

Neuman, Daniel M. 1974. *The Cultural Structure and Social Organization of Musicians in India: The Perspective from Delhi.* Unpublished doctoral dissertation, University of Illinois, Urbana.

———. 1978. "Gharanas: The Rise of Musical 'Houses' in Delhi and Neighboring Cities." In *Eight Urban Musical Cultures: Tradition and Change,* ed. Bruno Nettl. Urbana: Univ. of Illinois Press, 186-222.

———. 1979. "Country Musicians and Their City Cousins." In *Proceedings of the XIIth Congress of the International Musicological Society.* Kassel: Barenreiter Verlag.

———. 1980. *The Life of Music in North India.* Detroit: Wayne State Univ. Press.

———. 1984. "The Ecology of Indian Music in North America." *Bansuri* 1: 9-15.

Neuman, Daniel M., Komal Kothari and Shubha Choudhuri. In progress. *The Ethnographic Atlas of Music Cultures in West Rajasthan.* CD-Rom.

Nijenhuis, Emmie te. 1970. *Dattilam: A Compendium of Ancient Indian Music.* Leiden: Brill.

———. 1974. *Indian Music: History and Structure.* Leiden: Brill.

———. 1976. *The Ragas of Somanatha.* Leiden: Brill.

———. 1977. *Musicological Literature.* (In the series, *A History of Indian Literature*). Wiesbaden: Harrassowitz.

Nijenhuis, Emmie te and Sanjukta Gupta. 1987. *Sacred Songs of India: Diksitar's Cycle of Hymns to the Goddess Kamala.* Wimterthur, Schweiz: Amadeus.

Pesch, Ludwig. 1993. *Ragadhana: An Alpha-numberical Directory of Ragas.* Kerala: Natana Kairali.

Popley, H.A. 1921 (3rd edition 1966). *The Music of India.* Madras: Modern Book Printers.

Powers, Harold S. 1958. *The Background of the South Indian Raga-system.* Unpublished doctoral dissertation, Princeton University.

———. 1970. "An Historical and Comparative Approach to the Classification of Ragas (with an appendix on ancient Indian tunings)." *Selected Reports* 1(3).

———. 1980. "India, Subcontinent of." In *The New Grove Dictionary of Music and Musicians.* London: Macmillan.

Qureshi, Regula. 1969. "Tarannum: The Chanting of Urdu Poetry." *Ethnomusicology* 13(3): 425-468.

———. 1972. "Indo-Muslim Religious Music, an Overview." *Asian Music* 3(2).

———. 1983. "Qawwali: Making the Music Happen in the Sufi Assembly." *Performing Arts in India: Essays on Music, Dance, and Drama,* ed. Bonnie Wade. Berkeley: Center for South and Southeast Asia Studies, University of California.

———. 1986. *Sufi Music of India and Pakistan: Sound, Context and Meaning in Qawwali.* Cambridge: Cambridge Univ. Press.

Ramanathan, S. 1979. *Music in Cilappatikaram.* Madurai, Tamilnadu: Madurai Kamaraj University.

Ramanujan, A.K., Velcheru Narayana Rao, and David Dean Shulman. 1994. *When God is a Customer: Telugu Courtesan Songs by Ksetrayya and Others.* Berkeley: Univ. of California Press.

Rao, Kristen. 1985. *Lavni of Maharashtra: A Regional Genre of Popular Music.* Unpublished doctoral dissertation, University of California at Los Angeles.

Reck, David. 1983. *A Musician's Tool-kit: A Study of Five Performances by Thirugokarnam Ramchandra Iyer.* Unpublished doctoral dissertation, Wesleyan University.

Ree-Bernard, Nelly van. 1973. *Introduction to the Construction of Hindustani Music.* Amsterdam: Broekmans & Van Poppel.

Rowell, Lewis. 1977. "A Siksa for the Twiceborn." *Asian Music* 9(1).

———. 1992. *Music and Musical Thought in Early India.* Chicago: Univ. of Chicago Press.

Ruckert, George. 1991. *Introduction to the Classical Music of North India* . Staunton, VA: East Bay Books.

Rudhyar, Dane. 1979. *The Rebirth of Hindu Music.* New York: S. Weiser.

Sacchini, Annysha. 1987. *Il Sitar e la Musica Indiana.* Milano, Italy: Sugar.

Schramm, Harold. 1969. *Traditional Melodies for the Sitar.* New York: Southern Music Publishing Co.

Shankar, L. 1974. *The Art of Violin Accompaniment in South Indian Classical Music.* Unpublished doctoral dissertation, Wesleyan University.

Shankar, Ravi. 1968. *My Music, My Life.* New York: Simon and Schuster.

Shepherd, Frances. 1976. *Tabla and the Benares Gharana.* Unpublished doctoral dissertation, Wesleyan University.

Silver, Brian. 1976. "On Becoming an Ustad: Six Life Sketches in the Evolution of a Gharana." *Asian Music* 7(2).

Simon, Robert L. 1975. *Bhakti Ritual Music in South India: A Study of the Bhajana in its Cultural Matrix.* Unpublished doctoral dissertation, University of California at Los Angeles.

———. 1984. *Spiritual Aspects of Indian Music.* Delhi: Sundeep.

Singer, Milton. 1972. "The Radha-Krishna Bhajanas of Madras City." In *When a Great Tradition Modernizes: An Anthropological Approach to Indian Civilization,* ed. Milton Singer, 199-244. New York: Praeger.

Skelton, William. 1971. "The Nagaswaram and the South Indian Hindu Festival." *Asian Music* 2(1).

Skilman, Teri. 1986. "The Bombay Hindi Film Song Genre." *Yearbook for Traditional Music* 18: 133-44.

Slawek, Stephen M. 1986. *Kirtan: A Study of the Sonic Manifestations of the Divine in the Popular Hindu Culture of Banaras.* Unpublished doctoral dissertation, University of Illinois, Urbana.

———. 1987. *Sitar Technique in Nibaddh Forms.* Delhi: Motilal Banarsidass.

Sorrell, Neil and Ram Narayan. 1980. *Indian Music in Performance: A Practical Introduction.* Manchester: Manchester Univ. Press.

Spector, Johanna. 1967. "Samaritan Chant." *Journal of the Music Academy, Madras* 38: 103.

————. 1969. "Shingli Tunes of the Cochin Jews." *Journal of the Music Academy, Madras* 40: 80-88.

Srivastava, Indurama. 1977. *Dhrupada: A Study of its Origin, Historical Development, Structure and Present State.* Utrecht: Drukkerij Elinkwijk B.V.

Stewart, Rebecca. 1974. *The Tabla in Perspective.* Unpublished doctoral dissertation, University of California at Los Angeles.

Stiglmayr, Engelbert. 1970. *The Barela-Bhilala and their Songs of Creation.* Eien: Engelbert Stiglmayr (Series title: *Acta Ethnologica et Linguistica*, 20. Series Indica).

Subramanian, Karaikudi S. 1984. "An Introduction to the Vina." *Asian Music.* 16(2).

Swallow, Deborah Ann. 1982. *Symbolism in the Music Theories of China and India: A Comparative Analysis.* Unpublished masters thesis, University of California at Los Angeles.

Swift, Gordon N. "South Indian Gamaka and the Violin." *Asian Music* 21(2).

Tagore, Sourindro Mohun, compiler. 1882 (reprinted 1963). *Hindu Music from Various Authors.* Varanasi: The Chowkhamba Sanskrit Series Office.

Terada, Yoshitaka. 1992. *Multiple Interpretations of a Charismatic Individual: The Case of the Great Nagasvaram Musician, T.N. Rajarattinam Pillai.* Unpublished doctoral dissertation, Wesleyan University.

Tewari, Laxmi G. 1974. *Folk Music of India: Uttar Pradesh.* Unpublished doctoral dissertation, Wesleyan University.

Thompson, Gordon R. 1987. *Music and Values in Gujurati-Speaking Western India.* Unpublished doctoral dissertation, University of California at Los Angeles.

————. 1991. "The Carans of Gujarat-Caste-identity, Music and Cultural Change." *Ethnomusicology.* 35(3).

————. 1995. "What's in a Dhal? Evidence of Raga-like Approaches in a Gujarati Musical Tradition." *Ethnomusicology.* 39(3).

Tinge, Carol. *The Nepalese Field-work of Dr. A.A. Bake: A Guide to the Sound Recordings.* Unpublished master's thesis. Goldsmiths College, London.

Trewin, Mark and Susan M. Stephens. 1987. *The Music Culture of Ladakh: An Ethnomusicological Study Conducted in the Himalaya of North-Western India.* London: The City Univ. Ladakh Expedition 1986.

Vaughn, Kathryn. 1991. *Perceptual and Cognitive Implications of the Tambura Drone: Figure-Ground Interaction with Ten North Indian Scale Types.* Unpublished doctoral dissertation, University of California at Los Angeles.

Viswanathan, T. 1974. *Raga Alapana in South Indian Music.* Unpublished doctoral dissertation, Wesleyan University.

————. 1977. "The Analysis of Rag Alapana in South Indian Music." *Asian Music* 9(1).

Wade, Bonnie C. 1972. "By Invitation Only: Field Work in Village India." *Asian Music* 3(2).

————. 1972. "Songs of Traditional Wedding Ceremonies in North India." *Yearbook of the International Folk Music Council* 4.

————. 1979. *Music in India: The Classical Traditions*. Englewood Cliffs, NJ: Prentice-Hall.

————. 1985. *Khyal: Creativity Within North India's Classical Music Tradition*. Cambridge: Cambridge Univ. Press.

Way, Janet Madelaine. 1969. *Correlations between Raga and Rasa in Indian Music*. Unpublished master's thesis, University of California at Los Angeles.

Wegner, Gert-Matthias. 1982. *Die Tabla im Gharana des Ustad Munir Khan (Laliyana): Studien zum Trommelspiel in der Nordindischen Kunstmusik*. Hamburg: K.D. Wagner.

White, Emmons E. 1971. *Appreciating India's Music; An Introduction, with an Emphasis on the Music of South India*. Boston: Crescendo.

Widdess, Richard. 1995. *The Ragas of Early Indian Music*. Oxford: Clarendon.

Willard, Augustus N. 1834 (reprinted 1882). "A Treatise on the Music of Hindoostan." In *Hindu Music from Various Authors*. Tagore, S.M., compiler. Varanasi: Chowkhamba Sanskrit Series 44.

Philosophy

KARL H. POTTER

'There is a problem in talking about Indian philosophy. It is doubtful there is any term in an Indian language that translates the English term "philosophy" at all adequately. The Sanskrit term that is usually translated into English as "philosophy" is *darśana*, a term that literally means a "view." In India, when one speaks of *darśanas*, one usually refers to views about ultimate things. Most classical Indian[1] texts on *darśana* concern the problem of karma and rebirth and how to attain liberation from them. Thus the branches of philosophy, so understood, are Nyāya-Vaiśeṣika, Sāṃkhya, Yoga, Mīmāṃsā, Advaita Vedānta, and the several systems of Buddhist and Jain thought.

There is also a problem in talking about western "philosophy." Literally the term "philosophy" should mean "love of wisdom," and very possibly any thoughtful person is a lover of wisdom (at least perhaps a striver for it) and thus a philosopher. Nevertheless, at least in present times, philosophy has become a standard "science" (in the broad sense of that term), and its practitioners, largely those who teach it in institutes of higher education, devote their attention to subjects usually thought of as central areas of the philosophical discipline, areas such as logic, epistemology, ethics, metaphysics, philosophy of language, of politics, of religion, of history, of art ("aesthetics"), and many others. Indeed, philosophy has been characterized in the West as the "queen of the sciences," and in that capacity there is a philosophy corresponding to every science, the study of which deals with the assumptions underlying the questions being addressed by that science.

There is, then, a sense in which there is no such thing as "Indian philosophy." The Indian branches of *darśana* have no counterparts in the West, and the topics that comprise philosophy in the West, though they are certainly addressed in India, are not considered in India to constitute a distinct discipline and subject matter. Furthermore, those topics, when they are addressed in the *darśana* literature of India, tend to be addressed as aspects of the ultimate concern of liberation.

As a result of this disparity between *darśana* and philosophy, the analyses of large portions of science, while recognized and practiced in India, are not counted as *darśana* there. The subjects westerners classify as philosophy, aesthetics, ethics, political science, philosophy of history, philosophy of science, etc. are not *darśana* in India. Likewise, large portions of the subjects addressed in the *darśana* literature are not counted as distinctively philosophical in the West. Rather, they are regularly classified in the West under religion, despite the fact that most of the Indian *darśanas* are atheistic.[2] This seems anomalous to the Indians (and to me), and it also raises qualms among western religionists who, viewing God as central to any religion, are not altogether happy to include avowedly atheistic accounts of things under the rubric of religion.

Nevertheless, the literature on Indian philosophy is vast (Potter 1995), and the subject is sometimes taught in colleges in the western world as well as in India. While in many cases the subject of the classes largely concerns matters deemed religious, there is, nevertheless, a small but vitally important group of sciences that are recognized as philosophical in India and not standardly classified by westerners as religion. We might call them the peculiarly philosophical sciences. In a sense they constitute a sort of middle ground or meeting-point of philosophy and *darśana*, dealing with questions that are crucial if one is seriously to consider disciplining oneself for liberation, and that are also central to philosophy as understood in the western world, the centrality being traceable to their fundamental position among the questions answers to which are presupposed in any inquiry at all.

These peculiarly philosophical sciences include: logic, epistemology, and ontology. I reiterate: these do not constitute the *raison d'etre* of the *darśanas*. What each system is concerned with is describing and analyzing the nature of bondage, defending the possibility of achieving liberation, rehearsing the means of attaining that end, and resisting attacks on the analysis being given, attacks that stem from skeptics as well as from rival systems' accounts. The reason why these three peculiarly philosophical sciences have a special position is their centrality to the debates thus produced among the schools. Logic (*nyāya*) in the Indian context is not "formal logic" but rather the science of debate, of how to tell good reasons from bad ones for a thesis proffered by one school in criticism of another's. Epistemology has to do with the nature of truth (*pramā*) and falsity, with the means (*pramāṇa*) for arriving at knowledge and for rejecting the mistaken views of other schools. Metaphysics or ontology deals with the categories of the things that exist, with identifying the referents of the true beliefs that constitute knowledge and criticizing the claims of other schools on that score. Because of the centrality of these three topics, and also since other concerns that one might deem crucial will be taken up in other sections of the present collection of essays, I shall concentrate on these topics, i.e., logic, epistemology, and ontology.

Before dealing with these three topics, however, it will be helpful to give an overview of the *darśanas*, the literature of which constitutes the source of the analyses to be reviewed, thus introducing the characters in the play I am about to present. The review I propose below was first presented in a paper published in the *Journal of Asian Studies* over thirty years ago (Potter 1961), and it is the basic plan I use in my *Presuppositions of India's Philosophies* (Potter 1963). It has the advantage of locating the positions of the various philosophical systems in a kind of grid that locates their positions on key philosophical questions in a way that provides understanding of why each system takes the view it does on each question. And the questions themselves are among the central ones falling within the three peculiarly philosophical sciences just now referred to, and with which the most insightful studies published within the last fifty years deal.

Classical Indian thought locates humans in a chain of living beings extending from the smallest insects (even perhaps plants) up to the gods. To the extent that these beings are capable of action (*karman*) they are capable of producing karmic results, traces (*saṃskāra*) which are held to be laid down and preserved in the agent until such time as s/he performs an action that "works off" such a trace. This fundamental karmic doctrine is basic to all the *darśanas*. They differ over how they view the relation of the cause— an action—to the effect—the production of one trace and the working off of another, and the relation of that working off to subsequent actions and further traces.

The basic question is: What is the nature of the relation between cause and effect? A thing C is a cause of effect E just if, when C occurs, E always occurs. But if C, an action, is itself an effect of the trace of some other action B, and B of A, etc., can there be any possibility of liberating oneself from all traces? Yet it is precisely such liberation that is the acknowledged aim of Indian philosophers.

One implication of this that does not bother Indian thinkers is the problem of beginninglessness. It would seem that the causal sequence must go on backwards in time forever; if it doesn't, that means that there is at least one thing, the first cause, that is not the effect of a cause, one action that is not the result of a trace. This idea of a first cause, celebrated in theistic western medieval philosophy, is not to be found in Indian thought; in Indian thought it is universally accepted that the universe is beginningless, that there was no first event. Not that it would much help if there were; the problem goes in the other direction. If the C that causes E is itself the effect of B, and B of A, etc. how can one possibly make it the case that the cause-effect series stops? Causation has already started, indeed has been happening forever; the question is how to escape it.

Next, then, let us peer more closely at this cause-effect relation. When we say that C causes E, do we mean that C constrains things so that E must occur, that C is sufficient in itself to produce E? If so, and especially since we now realize that (according to Indian assumptions) there have been Cs and Es beginninglessly, there is no hope of avoiding E—E will have to occur, since C, which is sufficient itself to produce E, is unavoidable, given past occurrences that are themselves sufficient to produce C. The things that have happened in the past are sufficient to limit the possibilities of present occurrence to precisely one, namely, E. E could not have failed to occur. This we usually think of as fatalism, and it is a view that existed in India in the Buddha's time; indeed, he is held to have studied with one of its main proponents.

If fatalism is true, there is no possibility of liberation. Thus the relation of cause to effect had better not be understood as one of being a sufficient condition. But the other extreme is no better. Suppose that our view of things being connected as cause and effect were merely the results of chance, merely accidental associations. Then any attempt to stop the causal series is again doomed to failure, since we have no way of being sure that what we do actually brings about the annulment of an unwanted future event. The relation between cause and effect would be so loose as to make any plan of action defeasible; we could never be sure that, whatever we do to block E from occurring, it will fail to occur. This, then, is skepticism about causation, the denial that there is a sufficient condition of E.

Fatalism and skepticism are not really philosophical views at all, but rather antiphilosophy, the denial that liberation is possible. Still, since they do constitute possible views about action and liberation, they must be counted within views broadly considered. The rest of the views that constitute Indian philosophy avoid these two extremes by assuming that the relation between a C and an E is not so strong as to lead to fatalism, but not so weak as to lead to skepticism. There are three possible ways of viewing that assumed relation between C and E, and these three ways generate a basic classification of the remaining *darśanas*.

The classification is generated in this way. On close inspection, a causal sequence characteristically consists of a number of causal factors conspiring to produce a certain result of a certain kind. Thus, if there is appropriate soil, moisture, oxygen, and a seed, one can expect that (provided other countervailing factors are not present) a sprout will grow up in due course. Now why (or how) is it that a particular set of factors produces that particular result? One possible answer to this is that within the set is one crucial factor, namely the presence of the sprout in potency, and that what happens is that the other "causal factors" combine to provide the occasion for the potency to become actual, for the sprout to arise. A second possible answer is that this talk of "potency" is empty, but that it is just the case that when those kinds of factors (soil, moisture, oxygen, seed) occur together, another kind of thing, a sprout, regularly occurs immediately thereafter. A third kind of answer is that all sorts of things happen when these kinds of causal factors occur together, and among them is the sprout, but that we think of it as "the effect" only because we choose at least for the moment to ignore the other results.

Now the first answer, which goes under the unwieldy rubric of *satkāryavāda* in Sanskrit, is the answer propounded by Sāṃkhya, Yoga and Advaita Vedānta. They apply their preferred analysis to the question of worldly causality in this way: Just as the sprout in potency becomes actual when other factors occur, so an action in potency actualizes when other factors occur, the other factors here being the presence at the appropriate time and place of the relevant features comprising an occasion for the action. Thus the causal process is one-many, a single causal nexus (sprout in potency) being the producer of a sequence of several occurrences comprising the result, viz. the seed's growing.

The second answer, of *asatkāryavāda*, is espoused by Nyāya-Vaiseṣika, Purvamīmāmsākas, and Buddhist philosophers. On their view the effect—the sprout—is a completely new entity, not present even in potency before the moment of causation. Causation is a many-one relation, a number of occurrences (a moment in the history of each of the soil, the moisture, etc.) occurring together being followed by a momentary occurrence that we call the first moment in the history of the sprout. Thus it is the entire collection of factors that constitutes the sufficient condition for the arisal of this particular effect.

Finally, there is the third position, held by the Jains. As they see it, nothing is merely a single entity; our identification of a thing as a sprout, say, is merely our penchant for singling out for attention just one of the aspects of a multifarious collection that constitutes the effect in a given causal occurrence. The cause in that occurrence is likewise multifarious; its being identified as the cause in a given case is a result of our singling it out for attention. Thus everything is both many and one—many in actuality, but one considered in its relevance to a particular explanatory account that someone is interested in. Thus the two other positions just reviewed, of the satkāryavādins and the asatkāryavādins, are viewed from the Jain standpoint as partial truths; the complete truth comprises both kinds of relationships.

If, then, one arranges these three positions with the asatkāryavādins on one side, say the left, and the satkāryavādins on the right, with the Jain position between them, one has a kind of map of those philosophical systems that take causation seriously and make it central to the understanding of how things are. And the map is useful in that it provides a kind of rationale for understanding the positions the various systems take on topics arising within the three that I called peculiarly philosophical sciences, i.e., logic, ontology, and epistemology.

1. Logic. Fifty years ago takes us back to 1945, when the study of Indian logic in the U.S. was still in its infancy. Discussions of inference in the early part of the 20th century were strongly geared toward trying to assimilate Indian models to what were presumed to be more advanced western logical procedures. What caused trouble in this line of analysis was the assumption that Indian philosophers, like westerners, were working under the basic paradigm of a deductive syllogism, that is, the sort of inference Aristotle taught that was improved by the use of mathematical and geometrical models developed by such figures as Peano, Boole, and Frege. On this assumption, the standard example of an Indian inference such as: "That mountain is on fire because it is smoking" is seen as an instance of the deductive syllogism "All smoking things are on fire; that mountain is smoking; therefore that mountain is on fire," a valid syllogism of the Barbara type as viewed under Aristotelian assumptions.

It became apparent more recently, however, that this interpretation of the Indian argument fails to account for certain features usually found in Indian arguments. For one thing, the Aristotelian syllogism is purely formal, in the sense that its truth is guaranteed by the mere form of the inference regardless of the particular meanings of the terms involved. Plug in other terms in place of "smoking things," "fire," and "that mountain." If the form of the three parts of the syllogism remain as they are, the syllogism must be true regardless of what the terms are and how the things they refer to are in fact related. Yet, as an Indian understands an inferential argument, it must contain what are termed "examples," the specification of a thing other than that mountain which is both smoky and fiery (say, a kitchen), as well as the specification of a type of thing that, not being fiery, is not smoky (say, a lake). If the argument is syllogistic, what is the need of examples? Is this merely a confusion born of failure to recognize the purely formal character of an inference, a confusion traceable to the Indians' failure to appreciate the formal nature of the syllogism? For another thing, Indian logical analysis, when it turns to consideration of fallacious reasoning, does not locate mistakes in reasoning only in failure to adopt valid patterns of argument. Indian logical analysis also includes as fallacies false empirical claims, the use of ambiguous language, as well as failure to recognize the context.

These anomalies between syllogistic reasoning and the nature and context of Indian inference (*anumāna*) grew on early western students of Indian logic, and occasioned various techniques for handling them. Some of the accounts offered by J.F. Staal (Staal 1960a, 1960b), for example, attempted to capture the peculiarities of Indian logic by extending symbolic logical methods through the invention of special devices to be built into the kind of symbolism pioneered by, for example, Gottlob Frege, Bertrand Russell, Alfred North Whitehead, and Ludwig Wittgenstein. However, the result of this appeared to be greater complexity rather than clarity. As time went by, it became clear that the differences mentioned in the preceding paragraph were fundamental ones, signifying that *anumāna* should not be assimilated to the syllogistic model of deductive logic, but rather to a different model, that of hypothetico-deductive reasoning used in an everyday argument, the sort of procedure that Charles Sanders Peirce called "abduction," though the relevance of Peirce's insight has only recently been appreciated (Factor 1983).

That the proper paradigm for *anumāna* is abductive reasoning rather than deductive logic is confirmed by a number of facts about the Indian way of studying inference. I have mentioned already two of them. (a) In Indian philosophy what is sought is not merely formal validity but empirical truth. Thus, if any of the premises in an Indian inference are found to be false, the inference is then rendered unsound and dispensable, even though it may be formally valid. For example, "all cows are dogs; all cats are cows; therefore all cats are dogs" is formally valid, but since its premises and conclusion are false, it will be rejected on Indian inferential grounds. (b) The presence of the examples in an Indian inference becomes easy to understand when one stops viewing the proposition "all smoky things are fiery things" as merely an element in a formally valid inference schema and starts taking it as what it most naturally is, a claim about a lawlike relation in the empirical world. The "major premise" in the Indian "syllogism" is, in fact, a claim that the relation expounded is a natural law, a true empirical generalization, and the examples function initially to provide evidence for that claim. That smoke and fire are found together in at least some kitchens makes it plausible that smoke and fire go together regularly in the world, and the absence of both in a body of water also suggests, though it does not entail, the truth of the claimed law of nature. (c) The "fallacies" studied in Indian logic are not to be thought of as mistakes in deductive procedure, but rather as including all sorts of errors that can arise in the course of an empirical investigation of an alleged law of nature and the procedures involved in establishing the law and its implications. Thus the fallacies falling under this classification are not formal at all; rather, they constitute various kinds of mistakes that can be committed in the process of empirical investigation and presentation. Indeed, the formal relation between the law of nature appealed to and the particular instance of it that is being claimed to hold in the world (e.g., between "all smoky things are fiery things" and "this smoking mountain is on fire") is taken for granted and not found in the list of things relevant to fallaciousness. What is required is, rather, the truth of "this mountain is smoking," for instance, as well as the truth of the alleged law of nature itself. Other "fallacies" noted in Indian analyses include mistakes in the examples proposed (of kitchen and lake in the case studied; to offer a hearth as a case where smoke and fire are both always absent is a "fallacy," though one correctable by substituting a different, satisfactory example). Another interesting fallacy is that of empty terms. If one offers an inference involving a term no cases of which are accepted by one's addressee as present in the actual world, the argument stops, at least until the existence of such a thing is independently established. Again, to offer as one's reasons for a conclusion a proposition denied by the person to whom one is speaking is ruled out of court, i.e., is deemed a fallacy.

2. *Ontology*. Each of the systems appearing in the model I described above provides a fundamental list of what there is, the things that actually exist in the world, especially those things that play a part in the process of achieving liberation from karmic rebirth. And each system views its list as the correct one and rejects the lists of the others, citing reasons. In the past this too has not been regularly appreciated. Again, there is a history to be told here about scholarship in the field and early misapprehensions to which scholars were prone.

Toward the end of the nineteenth century in Europe, absolute idealism was at its zenith, having been promulgated by influential writers such as Hegel, Bradley, Bosanquet, and others. Thus it is not surprising that those westerners who first happened upon Indian philosophy were prone to find parallels between idealism and certain aspects of Indian thought. One of the early authors conveying Indian philosophy to the western world was Paul Deussen (Deussen 1907), and the philosophy he conveyed was Advaita Vedānta, which he found to be in close agreement with idealistic thinking in that it taught one ultimate *Brahman*, itself the seat of all consciousness, as the only reality, reminding Deussen of the idealist's conception of the Absolute. Deussen viewed Advaita as the pinnacle of Indian philosophy, and he tended to regard it as the only Indian system worthy of extended explanation. Advaitins, in fact, had already pioneered the way to this understanding. They taught a view of the several Indian schools of philosophy in which their own view represented the highest achievement of Indian thought, presenting what it claims is the correct analysis of the meaning of what they take to be the most authoritative texts, the *Upaniṣads*. Early explorations into Buddhist thought by, for example, the Russian scholar Theodor Stcherbatsky (Stcherbatsky 1930) found in Buddhist thought another instance of absolutistic thinking. Thus the most influential early western interpreters of Sanskrit learning conveyed a view of the Indian philosophical situation that was skewed in a direction that was at that time naturally favored in any case.

Again, it has taken many decades for scholarship to overcome the weight of these initial leanings. Although scholars were aware from the outset that there were other schools of thought in Indian philosophy besides Advaita Vedānta, they were too easily caught up in the self-serving classifications advanced by proponents of that school which, not necessarily wittingly, downgraded the status of other systems. A spate of English introductions to Indian philosophy have appeared through the 20th century. Perhaps the most influential of these, by Sarvepalli Radhakrishnan (Radhakrishnan 1927), at one time the President of India, is typical among them in revealing to the western world the true complexity of Indian thought and the large number and divergent assumptions of the various systems indigenous to it. But it is also typical in its implicit, sometimes explicit, acceptance of the Vedāntins' view of the hierarchical relations among those systems. A rather fairer assessment is found in Surendranath Dasgupta's five-volume history (Dasgupta 1922-1925), although in this case the work comprises mainly summaries of texts thrown together in a rather haphazard manner without any consistent attempt to organize and interrelate the several systems of thought.

It is not possible here to review the details of the categories proposed by the various systems. But what has been said already is suggestive of how these schools differ in their assumptions. Thus the many-one schools on the left—Buddhists, Naiyāyikas, and Mīmāṃsākas—tend to distinguish into many varieties the kinds of things there are in actuality. A fundamental difference separates the Buddhists from the others: The Buddha taught that there are no persistent entities and, in particular, no self (ātman), a doctrine that requires us to class all ordinary thinking about persistent entities such as ourselves within the category of error, a basic misunderstanding of the nature of things. The Buddhist view, in fact, squares rather well with current assumptions in physics, where apparently persistent entities are taught to be actually fleeting bits of energy. The Nyāya and Mīmāṃsā position is more commonsensical. For them there are both persistent and momentary types of things; for example, selves and material atoms are persistent, but sensory qualities are momentary. For these two systems the causes of bondage are analyzable into substances, qualities, etc., and the analysis of these categories, when carefully done, reveals the causes of our karmic bondage and rebirth as well as what can be done to stop those causes from recurring, thus providing a path to liberation. For the Buddhists, by contrast, since the assumption of physical continuance is mistaken, our bondage is revealed as based in misunderstanding. Liberation from bondage is taught to be found through meditation on this underlying truth and the consequent abandonment of ways of thinking that take selves and material things as persistent.

For the one-many schools on the right—Sāṃkhya-Yoga and Vedānta—there are a small number (two in Sāmkhya, one in Vedānta) of basically real entities. In Sāmkhya-Yoga every physical and mental thing emanates from a fundamental category called *prakṛti*, and the emanations arc vicwcd as rcal entities of a changed nature, on the analogy of milk really, not just apparently, turning into curds. Thus liberation is not merely a matter of changing one's views. One has to take steps to stop the evolutionary flow leading from the unmanifest *prakṛti* that perennially exists (even during the period between cosmic ages) to the selves, minds, bodies and experiences that constitute natural existence. That flow, which stems from the karmic traces stored in that portion of *prakṛti* that is associated with a particular person (*puruṣa*), can be stopped by learning how to act without laying down further karmic traces. The procedure involved is what is termed yoga.

For Advaita Vedānta there is really only one self, the Self that is identified in the *Upaniṣads* as *Brahman*, the sole reality. The illusion that I am an embodied soul distinct from you and others is an aspect of our karmic bondage, and the process of gaining deliverance from that bondage involves coming to realize fully that it is an illusion. This is a process that essentially involves full appreciation of the truths taught in the *Upaniṣads*. While the process can be helped along by philosophical speculation about categories or by devotion to a chosen deity or by yoga, it is eventually only by study of the *Upaniṣads* that liberation can be achieved.

3. Epistemology. The views of these various systems about what constitutes knowledge are hopefully suggested by what has been said above. The question remains: Why should one believe one of these views among the others? This leads to the question of what constitute good reasons for believing in anything, of what are called *pramāṇas* in classical Sanskrit. Each school has its own list of what are counted as good reasons: lists generally include perception, inference, and verbal authority. We discussed inference above, and in what was just said about Vedānta one can see the importance of the authoritative texts such as the *Upaniṣads*. Since it is difficult to produce belief in a doctrine that flatly contradicts what all people can see with their own eyes, perception is generally counted as authoritative unless one can find reason to think there is some sort of illusion occurring. But this brief paragraph of comments covers a topic to which a great amount of attention is paid in the philosophical literature.

The proliferation of writing on Indian thought has increased in vast proportions, as can be seen by counting the entries in the "Bibliography" of Indian Philosophies (Potter 1995) for recent years as contrasted to the period ending fifty years ago. Nevertheless, despite many attempts to bring Indian philosophy into the purview of philosophy as understood in the western world, it· remains ignored by professional philosophers of Europe and America, except as a curiosity to be studied by specialists. Perhaps this is unavoidable. The problem addressed in India, which stems from the assumption that actions lay down karmic traces that generate constant rebirths, is an assumption not shared by westerners, and hence the literature and thinking addressed to that problem is naturally disregarded by western philosophers. Nevertheless, a broader view would note that the background assumptions of what they consider to be uncritical religious commitments do not lead those very same philosophers to deem medieval thinkers such as Anselm and Aquinas as being beyond the purview of philosophy; so it is unclear why the presence of background assumptions in itself should suffice to expunge a tradition from the class of philosophies. I think the cause of western philosophers' ignoring Indian thought has rather to do with less academic and abstract matters. The languages in which Asian philosophies are written are difficult to master, and translations, sometimes difficult to procure, are disparate in their style and in the manner in which technical terms are translated. All considered, it is simpler to ignore Indian contributions to the understanding of things, trusting to specialists to provide whatever can be made of it. Of course, a less charitable view might be that western philosophers have somehow come to the conclusion that Indian thought is generally nonsense and not worthy of serious philosophical analysis. One hopes that this is not the way professional philosophers in the western world currently think, since Indian philosophers discovered many things that have only recently become clear to westerners,[3] and such a dismissive attitude certainly does not put western philosophers in an attractive light. I prefer to think that western philosophers take the easy way out, given the perceived difficulty of properly understanding what is going on in Indian thought. But if that is so, improving the availability of Indian materials for western readers should, in time, bring academicians in U.S. philosophy departments into contact with Indian thinking, so that in due course one may hope to see an introductory course in philosophy dealing with worldwide materials, not just Anglo-American thinking.[4]

NOTES

1. By "Classical Indian" I refer primarily to Indian thought after Vedic times and before modern times, thus approximately from the time of the Buddha to the 7th century CE.

2. Although several Indian *darśanas* recognize an entity they call "God" (*iśvara*), in most of them God's function is limited. Notably, most systems view a good part of what actually occurs from moment to moment as determined basically by the karmic residues of the beings inhabiting (or seeming to inhabit) the world at that moment. God's function is limited to providing the arena in which these karmic traces can be worked out. For example, God may (as in Nyāya-Vaiśesika) be counted the initiator of the first movement of the atoms at the creation of the world, but God's function is limited to giving the first push. The cause of how atoms actually combine and what they form as a consequence is determined by the karmic residues of the individual souls, who require an appropriate arena to perform further actions in the course of working off the traces laid down by their past doings. And in many systems—in Buddhism, Jainism, Mīmāmsā, and Sāṃkhya, for example—while gods (*deva*) are acknowledged, no God is.

3. As an example, consult Ingalls (1951, 65-66), who shows that De Morgan's law, well-known to students of symbolic logic, was used by Gaṅgeśa in his *Tattvacintāmani* around 1350 CE. Ingalls notes that De Morgan's law was also known to Petrus Hispanus in the Middle Ages. Ingalls shows a number of other instances in which Gaṅgeśa utilizes principles supposed to have been discovered in modern logic.

4. For an interesting effort to provide a textbook for such a course involving philosophies of both East and West, see Russell T. Blackwood and Arthur L. Herman 1975.

REFERENCES

Blackwood, Russell T. and Arthur L. Herman, eds. 1975. *Problems in Philosophy, West and East.* Englewood Cliffs, NJ: Prentice-Hall.

Dasgupta, Surendranath. 1922-1925. *A History of Indian Philosophy.* 5 vols. Cambridge: Cambridge Univ. Press.

Deussen, Paul. 1912. *The System of the Vedanta.* tr. Charles Johnston. Chicago: Open Court.

Factor, R. Lance. 1983. "What is the 'Logic' in Buddhist Logic?" *Philosophy East and West* 33:2 (April): 183-188.

Ingalls, Daniel H.H. 1951. *Materials for the Study of Navya-Nyaya Logic.* Harvard Oriental Series 40. Cambridge: Harvard Univ. Press.

Potter, Karl H. 1961. "A Fresh Classification of India's Philosophical Systems." *Journal of Asian Studies* 21: 25-32.

————. 1963. *Presuppositions of India's Philosophies.* Englewood Cliffs, NJ: Prentice-Hall.

————. 1995 (3rd revised edition). "Bibliography." *Encyclopedia of India's Philosophies.* vol. 1. Delhi: Motilal Banarsidass.

Radhakrishnan, Sarvepalli. 1927 (rev. edition). *Indian Philosophy.* 2 vols. New York: Macmillan.

Staal, J. Frits. 1960a. "Correlations Between Language and Logic in Indian Thought." *Bulletin of the School of Oriental and African Studies.* 23: 109-122.

————. 1960b. "Formal Structure in Indian Logic." *Synthese* 12: 279-286.

Stcherbatsky, Theodore. 1930. *Buddhist Logic.* 2 vols. Leningrad: Bibliotheca Buddhica.

Political Science

JOHN ECHEVERRI-GENT

The study of Indian politics offers a formidable challenge to political scientists. Good political analysis must be firmly rooted in relevant empirical data while being informed, and ultimately advancing, the latest developments in the theories of politics. The diversity and distinctiveness that are central to Indian politics means that making sense of Indian politics requires an extraordinary investment in intellectual resources. Collecting the data necessary for good analysis in a society with almost a billion people speaking 15 official languages, practicing all of world's major religions, and acting in a context with unique social and political institutions is a daunting prospect to any scholars, but especially to those primarily interested in making broader theoretical contributions and those non-specialists wishing to compare India's experience with other countries.

The chapter will begin by surveying the areas in which U.S. political scientists have contributed to the study of Indian politics. I provide this overview to show the broad range and richness of U.S. studies. The chapter will then assess the areas in which the study of Indian politics have made outstanding contributions to the discipline of political science. I will argue that the analysis of politics in India has helped political scientists come to better terms with the concept of political development. Furthermore, analysis of India's rich culture has enabled important advances in our understanding the relationships between culture and politics. Finally, I will show how the study of Indian politics has contributed to the broader study of political parties and party systems. Both Indian politics and the discipline of political science have changed considerably in the last few years. In my conclusion, I will contend that innovations in the discipline of political science can advance our understanding of recent developments in Indian politics.

THE TERRAIN OF INQUIRIES

Prior to the 1950s, American political scientists were largely unconcerned with politics in developing countries.[1] They were especially indifferent to politics in the far off and exotic India which, after all, was in the domain of British rule. However, the end of World War II brought the beginning of the "American Century" with its American military hegemony, a concern for preempting the spread of communism, and the United State's rapidly growing international economic interests. Simultaneously, struggles for national independence spread throughout the colonial world liberating much of Africa and Asia from colonial rule, in the process creating "virgin territory" for American idealism and its efforts to remake the world. These circumstances provided the impetus for the Americans' study of politics in what became know as the "Third World."

U.S. programs to study India became institutionalized only in the 1950s, and U.S. scholars began publishing studies of Indian politics by the end of the decade. One of the earliest volumes written by an American on the Indian public administration was by Paul Appleby (1953), a veteran of promoting rural development in the United States through his role as Assistant Secretary in the U.S. Department of Agriculture during the New Deal. Appleby's volume was widely read throughout India. The cold war, communist revolution in China, and India's own communist insurrection in Telengana raised great concern about communist expansion, and two landmark books on the Communist Party of India were published during this period (Kautsky 1956, Overstreet and Windmiller 1959). The most prolific American analyst of Indian politics, Myron Weiner, began his corpus with *Party Politics in India* (1957), a volume that provides an insightful overview of India's major opposition parties and places the evolution of India's party system in a comparative perspective informed by contemporary theories of party politics. Drawing from papers presented in a 1956 seminar at Berkeley, Richard Park and Irene Tinker (1959) edited a volume on the role of political leadership in post-colonial societies. Joan Bondurant (1958) analyzed Gandhian philosophy and political strategy.

U.S. analysis began the 1960s with a concern for the integrity of India. By the end of the decade, despite the war with China, the rise of cultural nationalism in south India and severe drought, the resilience of Indian democracy had earned the respect of most American political scientists. Selig Harrison's highly influential *India: The Most Dangerous Decades* (1960), Myron Weiner's *The Politics of Scarcity* (1962) and his essays in *Political Change in South Asia* (1963) articulately expressed the apprehension that mixing democracy, economic growth, and traditional social institutions could be an explosive combination that threatened the integrity of India. Harrison

and Weiner's concern for the survival of India set an agenda
addressed by much of the work later in the decade. Paul Brass
(1965), Myron Weiner (1967), Stanley Kochanek (1968), and Richard
Sisson (1972) provided analyses that highlighted the importance of
the Congress party in building the new nation by bringing traditional
groups into the democratic process while providing them with a
responsive and stable government. These studies along with Lloyd
and Susanne Rudolph's *The Modernity of Tradition* (1967) and Robert
Hardgrave's (1969) study of the political incorporation of the Nadar
caste into Tamilnadu politics played an important role in
demonstrating that modernity and tradition did not amount to a
volatile confrontation between an irresistible object and an immovable
force but rather were social forces that interacted in ways that might
enhance political stability while producing continuity and change.

Americans began to broaden their investigation of Indian politics
during the 1960s. Weiner (1968) continued the trend concerned
with local politics by editing a volume on state politics. Franda
(1968) conducted a study of Indian federalism. Weiner and Kothari
(1965) edited one of the first volumes to study Indian voting
behavior. This was followed by Craig Baxter's (1969) examination of
district level voting trends. Baxter (1969) also published a study of
the Jana Sangh, and Howard Erdman (1967) published his
examination of the evolution of the Swatantra party. Granville
Austin (1967) completed a masterful study of the writing of India's
constitution. David Bayley (1969) published his very interesting
study of the Indian policy and political development. The 1960s also
saw the publication of the first American academic studies of India's
foreign policy (Harrison 1961, Fisher et al. 1963, Stein 1969).

The tumultuous politics of the 1960s gave rise to a range of
studies examining how Indian politics accommodated the radical
forces that confronted it. Marcus Franda (1971) examined radical
politics in West Bengal and then co-edited with Paul Brass (1973) a
volume analyzing radicalism in other states. Lewis Fickett (1976)
completed a study of India's socialist parties. Important work was
also completed by Das Gupta (1970), Brass (1974), and Barnett
(1976) on the politics of cultural nationalism with special attention
paid to language policy.

Some of the most interesting U.S. work on Indian politics during
the 1970s examined public policy and how it reflected and in turn
shaped state-society relations. Francine Frankel's (1971) study of
India's Green Revolution and her magisterial study of India's political
economy (1978) were important examples of this trend. Many of the

chapters in *Education and Politics in India* (Rudolph and Rudolph 1972) used local-level studies to generate insights about how the interaction between social groups and policymakers affected the formation of education policies. Stanley Kochanek's (1974) investigation of the role of organized business associations provided illuminating insights into the historical evolution of India's best organized interest group and its surprisingly limited influence over Indian policy. Donald Rosenthal (1976, 1977) completed two volumes that investigated the role of local elites in urban and rural politics. Meanwhile Stanley Heginbotham's (1975) and James Bjorkman's (1979) books provided in-depth examinations of the workings of Indian bureaucracy.

During the 1970s scholars based in the United States, at times collaborating with Indian scholars, provided some of the most thorough and sophisticated analyses of Indian voting behavior (Franda and Field 1974, Bhagwati 1975, Barnett 1975, Field 1977, Palmer 1975, Weiner 1978, Eldersveld and Ahmed 1978, and Blair 1979). Stephen Cohen published his important study of the Indian army (Cohen 1971). Americans continued to study Indian foreign policy (Barnds 1972). They provided assessments of Indira Gandhi's extraordinary political leadership with evaluations that ranged from sympathetic (Carras 1979) to critical (Hart 1976).

Many of the most innovative U.S. contributions to the study of Indian politics during the 1980's followed the lead of Francine Frankel (1978) in investigating the ways in which Indian democracy accommodated social inequality. Ron Herring's *Land to the Tiller* (1983) used an insightful comparison of agrarian reform in Kerala with reforms in Sri Lanka and Pakistan to make a sophisticated normative argument for radical land reform. Marshall Bouton (1985) examined the development of rural radicalism through a detailed ecological analysis of the agrarian structure in Tamilnadu. Leslie Calman (1985) analyzed the forces behind the rural poor to mobilize and protest against inequity. Atul Kohli's (1987) comparative analysis of rural poverty alleviation in three states found the nature of political parties to be a key variable in explaining the efficacy of poverty alleviation efforts. Holly Sims' (1988) comparative study of agricultural policy in Indian and Pakistani Punjab demonstrated how India's democratic regime promoted more equitable and effective development than did Pakistan's authoritarian regime. The Social Science Research Council's project on South Asian Political Economy produced a volume edited by Desai, Rudolph, and Rudra (1984) that included contributions of political scientists as well as economists, historians, and anthropologists from India and the United States and demonstrated the complex contingency of the impact of agrarian structure on agricultural productivity in India.

The economic issues and interests highlighted by these studies arise in a societal context where caste hierarchies shape the structure and dynamics of inequality. Weiner and Katzenstein (1981) and Galanter (1984) completed studies of India's affirmative action programs. Paul Brass (1983, 1985) published a collection of his essays in two volumes that provide us with a nuanced analysis of the impact of caste on electoral competition in northern India. In these volumes, Brass compares India's political parties with those of western Europe and contends that Indian parties have been distinctively "ideological in principle but opportunistic in practice." In addition, he provides extensive documentation of his argument that in northern states the Congress Party based its support on a coalition of elite castes (especially Brahmans and Rajputs), Muslims, and Scheduled Castes and Scheduled Tribes. When read with his two chapters in Gould and Ganguly (1993), they provide a cogent analysis of the reasons for the decline of the Congress (I) Party in northern India.

Before the end of the 1980s, three works appeared that were especially impressive in their empirical scope and theoretical contribution. The collection of essays by U.S., Indian, and British scholars jointly edited by Francine Frankel and M.S.A. Rao (1989, 1990) analyzed how, as democratic practice eroded the power and legitimacy of the Brahmanical social order, India's increasingly assertive backward castes were incorporated into its democratic order through different patterns of interaction among its caste, religious, and political institutions. Atul Kohli's (1987) edited volume assembles essays that examine how the spread of political participation has shaped the evolution of India's political institutions. Lloyd and Susanne Rudolph's *In Pursuit of Lakshmi* (1987) demonstrated the importance of the state institutions both as objects of political contestation and as independent actors shaping the political process.

In addition to the concern for the dynamics of state-society relations, U.S. political scientists pursued other areas of research. Two of the more innovative works investigated the interface between India's domestic and international political economy. Joseph Grieco (1984) conducted an interesting study of India's encounter with the international computer industry, and Dennis J. Encarnation (1989) examined India's efforts to limit the presence of foreign multinationals. Lloyd Rudolph (1984) edited a suggestive volume exploring the impact of public policy on cultural change. Raju Thomas (1986) examined international and domestic variables in his study of India's security policy. Ziring (1982) edited a volume on India's foreign relations with its neighbors. While Lloyd and Suzanne Rudolph (1980) edited a volume on India's relations with the United States.

U.S. work in the 1980s extended previous work in a number of areas. Field (1980) and Myron Weiner (1983) published studies of India's elections and electoral behavior. Wood (1984) edited a volume on state politics in India. Sisson and Wolpert (1988) edited a collection of essays on the Indian National Congress prior to Independence. Anderson and Damle (1988) published a remarkably well-researched study of the history of the Rastriya Swayamsevak Sangh.

During the 1990s much of the best U.S. work on Indian politics employed innovative comparative research strategies to conduct more tightly focused investigations of key issues in comparative politics. Atul Kolhi's *Democracy and Discontent* (1990) replicated Myron Weiner's (1967) study of the Congress party to demonstrate that the deterioration of party organization in the face of increased political mobilization of the Indian public had contributed to a crisis of governability. Amrita Basu (1992) explored the advantages and disadvantages of political activism in political parties and NGO's by comparing women's activism in the Communist Party of India (Marxist) and women's activism in the Shramik Sangathana. John Echeverri-Gent (1993) investigated the relative effectiveness of implementing rural poverty alleviation programs through government departments and through panchayats by comparing implementation of the Employment Guarantee Scheme in Maharashtra with the Jawahar Rozgaar Yojana in West Bengal. Paul Brass (1997) compared the ways in which five incidents of collective violence have been interpreted in order to investigate the ways in which the politics of interpretation promote and subvert various understandings of the incidents.

The effort to use comparative methods to examine more rigorously examine Indian politics during the 1990s has led to important attempts to incorporate India into cross-national comparisons. By comparing India's public policies with those of other countries in the domains of education and child labor, Myron Weiner's *The Child and the State in India* (1991) demonstrated how distinctive social and cultural features of India have contributed to India's underemphasis on primary education. In an effort to understand better the politics of affirmative action, Sunita Parikh (1996) compares the evolution of India's programs to reserve jobs, education, and political representation for underprivileged castes with affirmative action programs in the United States. John Waterbury's (1993) study of public sector enterprises in India, Mexico, Egypt, and Turkey highlighted the parallels between the problems of India and those of the other countries. Waterbury's concludes that the problems of public sector enterprises in developing countries are intrinsic to public ownership rather than to country-specific historical and cultural variables. By contrasting the development of the computer industry in India, Korea, and Brazil, Peter Evans' book, *Embedded Autonomy* (1995) develops an important critique of neo-liberal economic policies, contending that the key issue regarding industrial development is not *whether* the state should intervene to promote industrial development but *how* should it intervene.

During the 1990s Leslie Calman (1992) published an important study of women's politics. Dennis Dalton (1993) reevaluated Mahatma Gandhi's political strategy of civil disobedience. Gould and Ganguly (1993) edited a volume of studies of India's general elections in 1989 and 1991. There were also important works on India's foreign relations with the United States (Gould and Ganguly 1993), India's role in the Bangladesh independence struggle (Rose and Sisson 1993), India's relations with its neighbors (Babbage and Gordon 1992), and the conflict in Kashmir (Ganguly 1997).

CONTRIBUTIONS FROM THE STUDY OF
INDIAN POLITICS TO POLITICAL SCIENCE

Study of Indian politics during the last fifty years has challenged scholars to investigate the politics of change. At least through the early 1980s, political scientists analyzed political change through the concept of political development. Whether due to an interest in making the world safe for the United States or simple ethnocentrism, most American political scientists viewed political development as advancing along the path from traditional to modern polities, almost uniformly understood as western liberal democracy. In their thinking, all good things—capitalist development, secularism, liberalism, and democratic institutions—went together. Deviations from the path were viewed as setbacks to development.

Scholars analyzing Indian politics were among the first to criticize this conventional wisdom. Selig Harrison and Myron Weiner asserted that democracy could derail development. Harrison's *India: The Most*

Dangerous Decades (1960) traces how India's democracy in the 1950s gave birth to groups whose demands threatened the integrity of the country. For Harrison, traditional India was characterized by an overwhelming array of parochial interests that made India's contemporary political unity an exception to the complex mosaic of political authority that had prevailed on the subcontinent throughout most of history. In Harrison's view, if there were any basis for national unity, it was the Brahmanical sanskritic culture that transcended the regions. However, the mobilization of the lower castes under Indian democracy threatened to undermine Brahmanical traditions. Harrison's prescient work highlighted issues that, in one form or another, have confronted India to this day. Efforts to accommodate demands of traditionally subordinated groups continue to be divisive, and regions on the periphery of the Hindi-heartland continue to assert demands for greater autonomy. In retrospect, Harrison was unduly pessimistic about the capacity of Indian democracy to accommodate conflict. India survived its dangerous decades because of, not despite, its democracy, and Harrison provides us with few analytic insights to understand how.

Myron Weiner's *The Politics of Scarcity* (1962) joined in highlighting the contradictions of political development. Weiner concluded that economic development, by promoting the organization of new interest groups, often disrupts rather than facilitates political development (238). As Weiner noted, many in India and abroad viewed the organization of new interests in India with considerable disdain. In their view, the new interests were parochial and disruptive. At a time when India's national leaders looked to technocratic expertise to resolve the nation's problems, democracy obstructed technocracy. Weiner shows how the government turned to authoritarian measures—e.g., the Preventive Detention Act, the Press (Objectionable Matter) Act, President's Rule, the Industrial Disputes Act, and the Maintenance of Essential Services Act—in an effort to restrain disruptive demands. However, Weiner puts little stock in authoritarianism which, he asserts, may radicalize the new groups. Instead, he advocates a strategy of "accommodation and absorption" based on his appreciation of the fact that India's democratic institutions can be altered so as to accommodate better the demands of the new groups.

Works like those of Harrison and Weiner prefigure later seminal work by Samuel Huntington (1968) and Crozier, Huntington, and Watanuki (1975) who argued that "premature" or "excessive" political mobilization can lead to a "crisis of democracy." Along similar lines,

Mancur Olson (1982) conceptualized economic development as a collective-action problem in which the particularistic interests articulated by interest groups conflicted with the "national interest." For Olson, the conflict was an important cause of economic stagnation and the "decline of great nations." By the late 1960s, U.S. political scientists drew from India's experience to demonstrate that democratic states had much greater powers of accommodation and resilience than had been anticipated.

Theories of political development during the 1960s were preoccupied with national integration. They exalted the nation-state and posited identification with it as a teleological endpoint of political development (Emerson 1962). Ethnic and religious identities were viewed as being "traditional" and parochial. They were therefore divisive impediments to "modern" national integration (Geertz 1967). Lloyd and Susanne Rudolph (1967) criticized the conventional dichotomy between tradition and modernity and contended that traditional forms of social organization could facilitate integration into modern polities. The Rudolphs argued that the distinction between tradition and modernity was based on crude ideal-types that created an artificial gap between the two. The "imperialism of categories" and false dichotomies obscured the variations and potentialities of societies. It was the Rudolphs' contention that the continuities between tradition and modernity, or the "modernity of tradition," facilitated rather than impeded political development. Caste was not an anachronistic social institution; it was a vehicle for incorporating citizens into the democratic polity. Mahatma Gandhi was neither traditional nor modern but rather a political leader who used traditional symbolism to fashion a modern political movement. The Rudolphs cogently observed that the crude analytical categories and synchronic comparisons that were characteristic of political science in the 1960s were insensitive to the dynamics of political change. While their analysis is open to the criticism that the dialectic of tradition and modernity that they posited understated the problems of political development, their analytical framework was one of the first to suggest that political development, rather than diminishing the salience of caste and religion, might perpetuate or increase it.

Paul Brass's *Language, Religion and Politics in North India* (1974) further advanced our understanding of political development by disabusing political scientists of the notion that modern democratic polities were confronted with a choice between cultural amalgamation or political secession. By distinguishing between political integration and nationalism, Brass demonstrated that multiple nationalisms or subnationalisms could coexist within a single state. His study of Sikh nationalism, in particular, showed political parties, rather than exacerbating conflict among nationalities, can help to accommodate ethic conflict either by accommodating different nationalities within their organization or by entering into alliances with other parties representing different ethnic groups. Furthermore, he demonstrated that states have a range of policy alternatives to accommodate subnationalisms. Brass's study of India advanced our understanding of the possibilities and prospects for multinational states.

Brass's analysis contains an ingenuous research design that enabled him to advance an important model of ethnic/religious mobilization. By examining the abortive Maithili regional movement, the successful Sikh mobilization to establish a Sikh majority state, and the permutations of Muslim politics in Northern India, Brass is able to develop a sophisticated theory of ethnic mobilization that was a major contribution to the field. He levels a profound criticism of primordialist views of ethnicity by arguing that the "objective marks of group identity, such as language or religion are not 'givens' ... but are themselves subject to variation" (45). Brass stresses the agency of elites in constructing ethnic identity. He contends that elites initiate ethnic movements by attaching symbolic value to certain objective characteristics of a group. They create a myth of group history or destiny, and they communicate that myth to the defined population (43-44). In contrast to prevalent theories at the time (e.g., Deutsch 1966), Brass maintains that politics plays a central role in constructing ethnic identity. In his view, political organizations do not necessarily arise spontaneously to reflect the demands of ethnic groups; rather they often precede the existence of group identity and play a critical role in shaping it (38). Elites use different symbols in attempts to mobilize support, and ethnic mobilization often becomes part of a multi-layered struggle for power—the outcome of which affects ethnic identity and culture. Additionally, Brass found that public policy plays an important role in affecting identities and conflicts.

In later work, Brass (1985, 1991) added to our understanding of ethnic conflict by highlighting the role of the state in ethnic conflicts. He asserted that the state is an important factor in ethnic conflict. Brass argued that modernizing states, through their promotion of secularism, centralization, meritocracy, and democracy, pose a threat to local elites that can spur them to mobilize their communities. The state also may incite conflict because its programs in effect distribute resources among different social groups, and the leaders of some groups may protest apparent inequities in the resource distribution by the state. Finally, the state often becomes an object of struggle because it is a source of limited resources—jobs, revenues, education, legitimation of values, etc.—that are sought after by different ethnic groups. Brass's study of the role of the state in ethnic conflict contributed to the development of institutionalist approaches to politics that have gained currency among social scientists in the last decade (Evans, Reuschemeyer and Skocpol 1985; Steinmo, Thelen, and Longstreet 1992).

Brass's (1997) most recent work on communal violence is a logical extension of his work on ethnic conflict. He observes that the multiplicity of interpretations of communal violence make it virtually impossible to arrive at an "objective" understanding of what are ambiguous events to begin with. The search for objective understanding, according to Brass, misses the most important point. Different interpretations of events are constructed by various political interests. Indeed, Brass regards communal violence as profoundly political, not simply in the sense that they involve a politics of meaning, but also because their incidence is a consequence of political agency and therefore can generally be prevented. Despite criticizing ecological explanations, Brass asserts that communal violence occurs at sites where there are "institutionalized riot systems," political actors with vested interests in transforming local conflicts into communal violence, and failures of local and state authorities to act decisively to prevent such transformations. Brass's discussion of the politics of interpretation not only adds to our understanding of communal violence in India, it also contributes to recent literature on the framing of social movements (McAdam et al. 1996).

The study of Indian political parties has also contributed to better understandings of parties in the broader discipline of political science. The personalistic nature of India's parties has served a useful purpose in limiting generalizations based on observations from industrialized societies. For instance, Myron Weiner (1957) argues that the personalistic basis of party organization makes India's party system a counter-example to Duverger's law (1954) according to which first-past-the-post elections produce two-party systems. Similarly, Brass draws from the Indian experience to counter prevalent arguments that political instability in party systems arises from ideological claims made by political parties with disciplined organizations and strong ties to different groups of supporters. Brass shows that in India indisciplined party organizations, lack of institutionalized ties to various social groups, and consequently defections from parties are primary sources of instability. In addition, Brass takes on Samuel Huntington's (1968) argument that political instability is caused by institutional decay in the face of rapid social mobilization by showing that in India it is in the areas of rapid mobilization where party institutions are strongest.

Myron Weiner's (1965, 1967) study of the Congress party incited him to be an early proponent of the position that effective political parties can insulate democratic institutions from political instability. Brass (1974) later showed that political parties can play an important role in accommodating the demands of ethnic groups. Arend Lijphart (1996) uses the Indian experience to extend his theory of consociational democracy. He asserts that the Indian case illustrates how power-sharing arrangements in pluralistic societies, usually reached through accommodations between parties, can be achieved within the organization of single parties.

There is an irony to exalting the virtues of the Congress party in face of its steady decline over the last decade. Atul Kohli (1990) used his incisive study of Congress party decay to develop an alternative perspective to those who have argued that centralization of power enhances its efficacy (e.g., Haggard 1990). Kohli demonstrated how centralization of power within the Congress (I) and the central government ultimately landed Rajiv Gandhi in a situation of powerlessness. This insight contributed to the recent reassessment of an institutionalist perspective, based on the realization that linkages to society, rather than diminishing state autonomy and power, can play an important role in enhancing state capacity to achieve its policy objectives (Evans 1995, Migdal et al. 1994, Echeverri-Gent 1993).

CONCLUSION

Although the study of Indian politics is a formidable challenge for U.S. political scientists, it has produced substantial rewards. While Americans' far-ranging research on Indian politics has made important contributions to advance the general understanding of Indian politics, the breadth and depth of knowledge gained through the study of Indian politics has also enabled these observers of U.S. politics to add insights to the development of the field of comparative politics. In particular, the study of Indian politics has been fruitful in its contributions to the fields of political development, ethnic and religious conflict, and political parties.

Indian politics and the discipline of political science have undergone important changes in recent years. These changes have generated new potential synergies in the study of Indian politics. The decline of the Congress party and the fragmentation of India's party system have created ample scope for applying recent theoretical developments in the study of political coalitions (Laver and Shepsle 1996, Mershon 1996, Enelow and Hinich 1990, Strom 1990) to analyze the new dynamics of India's partisan competition. India's budget has become the most important forum for economic policy statements during the period of economic reform, but there has been very little study of the politics of the budgetary process in India. Studies of budgetary politics have been quite extensive in the United States (Wildavsky and Caiden 1997, Schick 1990, Savage 1988), and the theoretical insights of such studies offer possible departure points for analyzing India's budgetary process.

One of the most important theoretical trends among American political scientists has been renewed interest in the study of political institutions (Shepsle and Weingast 1995, Steinmo et al. 1992, March and Olson 1989, and Evans et al. 1985). From the perspective of this "new institutionalism," many important political institutions in India have been understudied. There is substantial scope for theoretically-informed studies of such well-established Indian institutions as Parliament, the Prime Minister's office, and the police.

Recent transformations in the Indian state have created a new set of institutions that remain largely unstudied. We are witnessing a transformation in the regulation of the Indian economy as direct government intervention is curtailed and more independent regulatory agencies are created. New agencies like the Stock Exchange Bureau of India do not intervene to determine market outcomes as did the old regulatory agencies but instead regulate the procedures of market transactions. U.S. experience with economic deregulation and re-regulation (Mucciaroni 1995, Derthick and Quirk 1985) and roughly comparable independent regulatory agencies may provide U.S. scholars with the intellectual resources to advance our understanding of India's new regulatory institutions.

At the same time new institutions are being established, old institutional arrangements are being transformed. Indian federalism is of particular interest in this regard. As economic reform limits economic intervention by the central government, it enhances the relative importance of provincial governments in providing infrastructure, attracting domestic and foreign investment, and implementing social-sector programs such as primary health and education. Greater capital mobility increasingly pits India's states in competition with one another. Will this competition result in more efficient state government or beggar-thy-neighbor inter-state competition? The ongoing exploration of these issues in the U.S. context (Weingast 1995, Brace 1993, Eisinger 1988, and Foster 1988) may give U.S. political scientists distinctive perspectives to contribute to discussions of India's changing federalism.

By bringing a comparative perspective to the study of Indian politics, U.S. political scientists have drawn interesting parallels between politics in India, the United States and other countries. Their comparative work also has enabled them to understand better what is distinctive about Indian politics. During the last fifty years the work of U.S. political scientists has added to our understanding of Indian politics and has also enriched the broader discipline of political science. Given the knowledge base that has already been accumulated, the next fifty years promise deeper and even more extensive insights.

NOTE

1. The literature survey in this section is limited to a review of major books written or edited by authors from the United States. I have identified these authors according to two criteria: those whose graduate training was in the United States, and those whose professional employment has been primarily in the United States.

REFERENCES

Anderson, Walter K. and Shridhar D. Damle. 1987. *The Brotherhood in Saffron: The Rashtriya Swayamsevak Sangh and Hindu Revivalism.* Boulder: Westview.

Appleby, Paul H. 1953. *Public Administration in India—Report of a Survey.* Delhi: Manager of Publications, Government of India.

Austin, Granville. 1967. *The Indian Constitution: Cornerstone of a Nation.* Oxford: Clarendon.

Babbage, Ross and Sandy Gordon, eds. 1992. *India's Strategic Future: Regional State or Global Power?* New York: St. Martins.

Barnds, William J. 1972. *India, Pakistan and the Great Powers.* New York: Praeger.

Barnett, Marguerite Ross. 1975. *Electoral Politics in the Indian States: Party Systems and Cleavages.* Delhi: Manohar.

———. 1976. *The Politics of Cultural Nationalism in South India.* Princeton: Princeton Univ. Press.

Basu, Amrita. 1992. *Two Faces of Protest: Contrasting Modes of Women's Activism in India.* Berkeley: Univ. of California Press.

Baxter, Craig. 1969. *District Voting Trends in India: A Research Tool.* New York: Columbia Univ. Press.

————. 1969. *The Jana Sangh: A Biography of an Indian Political Party.* Philadelphia: Univ. of Pennsylvania Press.

Bayley, David H. 1969. *The Policy and Political Development in India.* Princeton: Princeton Univ. Press.

Bhagwati, Jagdish N. 1975. *Electoral Politics in the Indian States: Three Disadvantaged Sectors.* Delhi: Manohar.

Bjorkman, James W. 1979. *Politics of Administrative Alienation in India's Rural Development Programs.* Delhi: Ajanta.

Blair, Harry W. 1979. *Voting, Caste, Community, Society.* New Delhi: Young Asia.

Bondurant, Joan. 1958. *Conquest of Violence: The Gandhian Philosophy of Conflict.* Princeton: Princeton Univ. Press.

Bouton, Marshall. 1985. *Agrarian Radicalism in South India.* Princeton: Princeton Univ. Press.

Brace, Paul. 1993. *State Government and Economic Performance.* Baltimore: Johns Hopkins Univ. Press.

Brass, Paul R. 1965. *Factional Politics in an Indian State: The Congress Party in Uttar Pradesh.* Berkeley: Univ. of California Press.

————. 1974. *Language, Religion, and Politics in North India.* London: Cambridge Univ. Press.

————. 1983. *Caste, Faction, and Party in Indian Politics.* vol 1: *Faction and Party.* Delhi: Chanakya.

————. 1985. *Caste, Faction and Party in Indian Politics.* vol 2: *Election Studies.* Delhi: Chanakya.

————. 1985. "Ethnic Groups and the State." In *Ethnic Groups and the State,* ed. Paul R. Brass, 1-56. Totowa, NJ: Barnes and Noble.

————. 1991. *Ethnicity and Nationalism: Theory and Comparison.* New Delhi: Sage.

————. 1997. *Theft of an Idol: Text and Context in the Representation of Collective Violence.* Princeton: Princeton Univ. Press.

Brass, Paul R. and Marcus Franda. 1973. *Radical Politics in South Asia.* Cambridge: MIT Press.

Calman, Leslie J. 1985. *Protest in Democratic India.* Boulder: Westview.

————. 1992. *Toward Empowerment: Women and Movement Politics in India.* Boulder: Westview.

Carras, Mary C. 1972. *The Dynamics of Indian Political Factions: A Study of District Councils in the State of Maharasthra.* Cambridge: Cambridge Univ. Press.

————. 1979. *Indira Gandhi: In the Crucible of Leadership: A Political Biography.* Boston: Beacon Press.

Cohen, Stephen P. 1971. *The Indian Army: Its Contribution to the Development of a Nation.* Berkeley: Univ. of California Press.

Crozier, Michel, Samuel P. Huntingon, and Joji Watanuki. 1975. *The Crisis of Democracy.* New York: New York Univ. Press.

Dalton, Dennis. 1993. *Mahatma Gandhi: Nonviolent Power in Action.* New York: Columbia Univ. Press.

Das Gupta, Jyotindra. 1970. *Language Conflict and National Development.* Berkeley: Univ. of California Press.

Derthick, Martha and Paul J. Quirk. 1985. *The Politics of Deregulation.* Washington: Brookings.

Deutsch, Karl. 1966. *Nationalism and Social Communication: An Inquiry into the Foundations of Nationality.* Cambridge: MIT Press.

Duverger, Maurice. 1954. *Political Parties.* London: Methuen.

Echeverri-Gent, John. 1993. *The State and the Poor: Public Policy and Political Development in India and the United States.* Berkeley: Univ. of California Press.

Eldersveld, Samuel J. and Bashiruddin Ahmed. 1978. *Citizens and Politics: Mass Political Behavior in India.* Chicago: Univ. of Chicago Press.

Emerson, Rupert. 1962. *From Empire to Nation: the Rise of Self-Assertion of Asian and African Peoples.* Boston: Beacon Press.

Encarnation, Dennis J. 1989. *Dislodging Multinationals: India's Strategy in Comparative Perspective.* Ithaca: Cornell Univ. Press.

Enelow, James M. and Melvin J. Hinich. 1984. *The Spatial Theory of Voting.* Cambridge: Cambridge Univ. Press.

Erdman, Howard L. 1967. *The Swatantra Party and Indian Conservatism* Cambridge: Cambridge Univ. Press.

Evans, Peter. 1995. *Embedded Autonomy: States and Industrial Transformation.* Princeton: Princeton Univ. Press.

Evans, Peter B., Dietrich Rueschemeyer, and Theda Skocpol, eds. *Bringing the State Back In.* Cambridge: Cambridge Univ. Press.

Field, John O. 1980. *Consolidating Democracy: Politicization and Partisanship in India.* New Delhi: Manohar.

Fickett, Lewis P. Jr. 1976. *The Major Socialist Parties of India: A Study in Leftist Fragmentation.* Syracuse: Maxwell School of Citizenship and Public Affairs, Syracuse University.

Field, John O. 1977. *Electoral Politics in the Indian States: The Impact of Modernization.* Delhi: Manohar.

Fisher, Margaret W. and Joan V. Bondurant. 1956. *The Indian Experience with Democratic Elections.* Berkeley: Institute of International Studies, University of California.

Fisher, Margaret W., Leo E. Rose, and Robert A. Huttenback. 1963. *Himalayan Battleground: Sino-Indian Rivalry in Ladakh.* New York: Praeger.

Foster, Scott, ed. 1988. *The New Economic Role of American States.* New York: Oxford Univ. Press.

Franda, Marcus F. 1968. *West Bengal and the Federalizing Process in India.* Princeton: Princeton Univ. Press.

————. 1971. *Radical Politics in West Bengal.* Cambridge: MIT Press.

Frankel, Francine R. 1971. *India's Green Revolution: Economic Gains and Political Costs.* Princeton: Princeton Univ. Press.

————. 1971. *Radical Politics in West Bengal.* Cambridge: MIT Press.

————. 1978. *India's Political Economy, 1947-77: The Gradual Revolution.* Princeton: Princeton Univ. Press.

Frankel, Francine R. and M.S.A. Rao, eds. 1989, 1990. *Dominance and Social Order.* 2 vols. Delhi: Oxford Univ. Press.

Galanter, Marc. 1984. *Competing Inequalities: Law and Backward Classes in India.* Berkeley: Univ. of California Press.

Ganguly, Sumit. 1986. *The Origins of War in South Asia: Indo-Pakistani Conflicts Since 1947.* Boulder: Westview.

———. 1997. *The Crisis of Kashmir.* Cambridge: Cambridge Univ. Press.

Geertz, Clifford. 1967. "The Integrative Revolution: Primordial Sentiments and Civil Politics in the New States." In *Old Societies and New States: the Quest for Modernity in Asia and Africa,* Clifford Geertz, ed., 105-157. New York: Free Press.

Gould, Harold A. and Sumit Ganguly, eds. 1992. *The Hope and the Reality: U.S. India Relations form Roosevelt to Reagan,* Boulder: Westview.

——— and ———, eds. 1993. *India Votes: The Quest for Consensus, 1989 and 1991,* Boulder: Westview.

Grieco, Joseph M. 1984. *Between Dependency and Autonomy: India's Experience with the International Computer Industry.* Berkcley: Univ. of California Press.

Haggard, Stephan. 1990. *Pathways from the Periphery: The Politics of Growth in the Newly Industrializing Countries.* Ithaca: Cornell Univ. Press.

Hardgrave, Robert L. Jr. 1969. *The Nadars of Tamilnad: The Political Culture of a Community.* Berkeley: Univ. of California Press.

Harrison, Selig. 1960. *India: The Most Dangerous Decades.* Princeton: Princeton Univ. Press.

Harrison, Selig, ed. 1961. *India and the United States,* New York: Macmillan.

Hart, Henry C., ed. 1976. *Indira Gandhi's India: A Political System Reappraised.* Boulder: Westview.

Heginbotham, Stanley J. 1975. *Cultures in Conflict: The Four Faces of Indian Bureaucracy.* New York: Columbia Univ. Press.

Herring, Ron. 1983. *Land to the Tiller: The Political Economy of Agrarian Reform in South Asia.* New Haven: Yale Univ. Press.

Huntington, Samuel P. 1968. *Political Order in Changing Societies.* New Haven: Yale Univ. Press.

Kautsky, John. 1956. *Moscow and the Communist Party of India.* New York: John Wiley.

Kochanek, Stanley A. 1968. *The Congress Party of India: The Dynamics of One-Party Democracy.* Princeton: Princeton Univ. Press.

———. 1974. *Business and Politics in India.* Berkeley: Univ. of California Press.

Kohli, Atul. 1987. *The State and Poverty in India.* Cambridge: Cambridge Univ. Press.

———. 1988. *India's Democracy: An Analysis of Changing State-Society Relations.* Princeton: Princeton Univ. Press.

———. 1990. *Democracy and Discontent: India's Growing Crisis of Governability.* New York: Cambridge Univ. Press.

Laver, Michael and Kenneth Shepsle. 1996. *Making and Breaking Governments.* Cambridge: Cambridge Univ. Press.

Lijphart, Arend. 1996. "The Puzzle of Indian Democracy." *American Political Science Review* 90:2 (June): 258-268.

McAdam, Doug, John D. McCarthy, and Mayer N. Zald, eds. 1996. *Comparative Perspectives on Social Movements: Political Opportunities, Mobilizing Structures, and Cultural Framings.* Cambridge: Cambridge Univ. Press.

March, James G. and Johan P. Olson. 1989. *Rediscovering Institutions: The Organizational Basis of Politics.* New York: Free Press.

Mershon, Carol A. 1996. "The Costs of Coalition: Coalition Theories and Italian Governments." *American Political Science Review* 90:3 (September): 534-555.

Migdal, Joel S., Atul Kohli, and Vivienne Shue, eds. 1994. *State Power and Social Forces: Domination and Transformation in the Third World.* Cambridge: Cambridge Univ. Press.

Mucciaroni, Gary. 1995. *Reversals of Fortune: Public Policy and Private Interests.* Washington: Brookings.

Oldenburg, Philip. 1976. *Big City Government in India: Councilor, Administrator, and Citizen in Delhi.* Tucson: Univ. of Arizona Press.

Olson, Mancur. 1982. *The Rise and Decline of Nations: Economic Growth, Stagflation, and Social Rigidities.* New Haven: Yale Univ. Press.

Overstreet, Gene D. and Marshall Windmiller. 1959. *Communism in India.* Berkeley: Univ. of California Press.

Palmer, Norman D. 1975. *Elections and Political Development: The South Asian Experience.* Durham: Duke Univ. Press.

Palmer, Norman D. 1984. *The United States and India: The Dimensions of Influence.* New York: Praeger.

Parikh, Sunita. 1996. *Politics of Preference: Democratic Institutions and Affirmative Action in the United States and India.* Ann Arbor: Univ. of Michigan Press.

Park, Richard L. and Irene Tinker, eds. 1959. *Leadership and Political Institutions in India,* Princeton: Princeton Univ. Press.

Rose, Leo E. and Richard Sisson. 1992. *War and Secession: Pakistan, India and the Creation of Bangladesh.* Berkeley: Univ. of California Press.

Rosenthal, Donald B. 1977. *The Expansive Elite: District Politics and State Policy-Making in India.* Berkeley: Univ. of California Press.

Rudolph, Lloyd I. and Susanne H. Rudolph. 1967. *The Modernity of Tradition: Political Development in India.* Chicago: Univ. of Chicago Press.

———— and ————. 1987. *In Pursuit of Lakshmi: The Political Economy of the Indian State.* Chicago: Univ. of Chicago Press.

Rudolph, Lloyd I. and Susanne H. Rudolph, eds. 1980. *The Regional Imperative: The Administration of U.S. Foreign Policy Toward South Asian States Under Presidents Johnson and Nixon.* Atlantic Highlands: Humanities Press.

Rudolph, Susanne H. 1957. *Some Aspects of Congress Land Reform Policy.* Cambridge: Center for International Studies, MIT.

Rudolph, Susanne H. and Lloyd I. Rudolph, eds. 1972. *Education and Politics in India.* Cambridge: Harvard Univ. Press.

Savage, James D. 1988. *Balanced Budgets and American Politics.* Ithaca: Cornell Univ. Press.

Schick, Allen. 1990. *The Capacity to Budget.* Washington: Urban Institute Press.

Shepsle, Kenneth A. and Barry R. Weingast, eds. 1995. *Positive Theories of Congressional Institutions.* Ann Arbor: Univ. of Michigan Press.

Sims, Holly. 1988. *Political Regimes, Public Policy and Economic Development: Agricultural Performance and Rural Change in Two Punjab.* Thousand Oaks, CA: Sage.

Sisson, Richard and Ramashraya Roy, eds. 1990. *Diversity and Dominance in India Politics*, vol. 1, *Changing Bases of Congress Support.* New Delhi: Sage.

Sisson, Richard and Stanley Wolpert, eds. 1988. *Congress and Indian Nationalism: The Pre-Independence Phase.* Berkeley: Univ. of California Press.

Stein, A.B. 1969. *India and the Soviet Union: The Nehru Era.* Chicago: Univ. of Chicago Press.

Steinmo, Sven, Kathleen Thelen and Frank Longstreet, eds. 1992. *Structuring Politics: Historical Institutionalism in Comparative Perspective.* Cambridge: Cambridge Univ. Press.

Strom, Kaare. 1990. *Minority Government and Majority Rule.* Cambridge: Cambridge Univ. Press.

Thomas, Raju G.C. 1986. *Indian Security Policy.* Princeton: Princeton Univ. Press.

Varshney, Ashutosh. 1995. *Democracy, Development and the Countryside: Urban-Rural Struggles in India.* Cambridge: Cambridge Univ. Press.

Weiner, Myron 1957. *Party Politics in India: The Development of a Multi-Party System.* Princeton: Princeton Univ. Press.

———. 1962. *The Politics of Scarcity: Public Pressure and Political Response in India.* Chicago: Univ. of Chicago Press.

———. 1963. *Political Change in South Asia.* Calcutta: Firma K.L. Mukhopadhyay.

———. 1967. *Party Building in a New Nation.* Chicago: Univ. of Chicago Press.

———. 1978a. *India at the Polls: The Parliamentary Elections of 1977.* Washington: American Enterprise Institute.

———. 1978b. *Sons of the Soil: Migration and Ethnic Conflict in India.* Princeton: Princeton Univ. Press.

———. 1983. *India at the Polls, 1980: A Study of Parliamentary Elections.* Washington: American Enterprise Institute for Public Policy Research.

———. 1989. *The Indian Paradox: Essays in Indian Politics.* New Delhi: Sage.

———. 1991. *The Child and the State in India and Pakistan: Child Labor and*

Education Policies in Comparative Studies. Princeton: Princeton Univ. Press.

Weiner, Myron ed. 1968. *State Politics in India,* Princeton: Princeton Univ. Press.

Weiner, Myron and Mary Katzenstein. 1981. *India's Preferential Policies: Migrants and the Middle Classes, and Ethnic Equality.* Chicago: Univ. of Chicago Press.

Weiner, Myron and Rajni Kothari, eds. 1965. *Indian Voting Behavior: Studies of the 1962 General Elections,* Calcutta: Firma K.L. Mukhopadhyay.

Weingast, Barry R. 1995. "The Economic Role of Political Institutions: Market-Preserving Federalism and Economic Development." *Journal of Law, Economics and Organization* 11(1): 1-31.

Wildavsky, Aaron B. and Naomi Caiden. 1997. *The New Politics of the Budgetary Process.* New York: Longman.

Wood, John R., ed. 1984. *State Politics in Contemporary India: Crisis or Continuity,* Boulder: Westview.

Ziring, Lawrence, ed. 1982 (rev. edition). *The Subcontinent in World Politics: India, Its Neighbors, and the Great Powers.* New York: Praeger.

Religious Studies:
Vedic and Classical Hinduism

MARY MCGEE

The past fifty years of religious studies involving Vedic and classical textual sources have been marked by a development beyond the original focus on the texts themselves. In particular, our knowledge of Hindu religious traditions has been enriched by growing attention to modern religious practices and to a more active awareness of other textual sources, including texts in vernacular Indian languages as well as in classical Indian languages other than Sanskrit (such as Tamil, Pali, and Prakrit). This enlarged framework of classical sources, beyond the traditional attention to *śruti* and *smṛti* texts, has greatly enhanced our understanding of religious life in India, enabling us to examine the interaction with parallel and subsequent features of Indian life. The current state of religious studies in U.S. scholarship concerning the contribution of Vedic and classical sources to our understanding of Hinduism is the result primarily of three converging circumstances that have influenced our study of Indian religious traditions during the past fifty years: 1. Evolving concerns in the academic study of religion. 2. Increased access of U.S. scholars to Indian sources, particularly through field research in India and tutelage by Indian scholars and *paṇḍits*. 3. Shifts of emphasis in indological studies. I will consider each of these threads in this brief essay, interweaving them as I go. In my conclusion I will introduce some new threads of intellectual inquiry that are already beginning to shape the next fifty years of scholarship related to our understanding of the *Vedas* and Hinduism.

EVOLVING CONCERNS IN THE ACADEMIC STUDY OF RELIGION

In the brief history of the academic study of religion, scholars have shown a particular fascination with texts; indeed, many early scholars of comparative religion sought to find the equivalent authority to the "Bible" in their study of other religious traditions. The study of

Hinduism until very recently was dominated by philological studies of Vedic and classical texts that resulted in the translations of significant Sanskrit texts such as the *Ṛg Veda*, the *Upaniṣads*, the *Manu-smṛti* and the *Bhagavad Gītā*; every anthology of "Hindu Scriptures" and almost every textbook entry on Hinduism provides a testimony to our dependence on these texts for teaching and representing Hinduism. After World War II, the academic study of religion broke out of its dependence on texts and archaeological findings, and new orientations and inquiries emerged, largely inspired by the social sciences. The influence of anthropology, sociology, and psychology introduced new techniques, tools, and theories to the study of religion, and such trends as structuralism, functionalism, analytic philosophy, and new linguistics were each brought to bear on the interpretation of *homo religiosus*. Louis Dumont's *Homo Hierarchicus*, that analyzes the Indian caste system, is a product of the structuralist influence of Durkheim. The more recent scholarship of Veena Das (Delhi), Madeleine Biardeau (Paris), and Alf Hiltebeitel (George Washington), all influential scholars in shaping our contemporary understanding of the structures of Hinduism, is in this intellectual lineage. A more Weberian approach to Indian religion and culture is evident in the scholarship of the late Milton Singer (Chicago) and of J.C. Heesterman (Leiden), whereas the utilitarian or empiricist interpretation is represented by scholars from the previous generation such as A.B. Keith, Monier-Williams, and A.L. Basham.

In addition to these intellectual trends, which engaged and stimulated the developing scholarship of the academic study of religion so as to make religious studies a truly interdisciplinary enterprise, two other concerns emerged shortly after World War II that still continue to influence our study of Hinduism in particular. One was the increased attention to iconographic materials and other art forms (and for Hinduism we are in debt to the scholarship of Ananda Coomaraswamy and Stella Kramrisch); the other was the concern with the relationship between popular religion and "official" or "orthodox" religion. The terms "great tradition" and "little tradition" emerged out of this trend to refer respectively to the Sanskrit, Brahmanical culture and to the popular, vernacular folk culture. The process of "Sanskritization," identified by M.N. Srinivas, explicated how a lower caste community advanced its status by taking on the "marks" of a higher caste (e.g., vegetarianism, non-widow remarriage, study of Sanskrit, observing strict rules concerning intermarriage and inter-dining, etc.). Louis Renou noted a similar phenomenon, which he called "Vedicization," in which private or domestic rituals were modeled on public sacrificial rituals in their form and language. More recently scholars such as Vasudha Narayanan (Florida) and Philip Lutgendorf (Iowa) are investigating how vernacular texts and performance traditions have modeled themselves on the *Veda* in an effort to tap into the authoritative power attributed to the *Veda*.

Perhaps one of the most profound changes in the academic study of religion in the last fifty years, and particularly for those of us who study Hindu traditions, has to do with the expanding of religious studies to include not only historical traditions but also living traditions. The study of active, living religious communities by anthropologists and sociologists has required scholars of religion to develop new and different ways of study than had been applied to historical religious traditions and texts. It has also provided an opportunity to examine the relationship between text-based Hinduism and practiced Hinduism. This approach, articulated and advocated by Wilfred Cantwell Smith in his 1962 Canadian radio talks (later published as *The Faith of Other Men*),[1] sought to understand Hindus rather than "Hinduism." This new orientation in the study of religion shifted many scholars' focus from texts to the significance of texts and other religious phenomena in the individual lives of persons of faith; the emphasis of the inquiry was on describing and analyzing religious experience. Increased opportunities to study in India allowed this approach to be cultivated by a new generation of scholars. These experiences of learning in India provided surprises for many young scholars whose formative studies in Indian religions, based on Vedic and classical texts, had led them to expect India to be populated largely by yoga-practicing ascetics. This generation of scholars, troubled by the lack of resemblance between textbook Hinduism and the observed experience of living Hindu traditions, has begun to question how we interpret and represent Hinduism, and whether western scholarship has somehow misrepresented the complexities of Hinduism by privileging certain texts and interpretations, thereby creating a misleading authoritative history. After years of interpreting Hinduism using categories and tools developed within western scholarship and derived historically from the study of Judaism and Christianity, several scholars are beginning to ask, and investigate seriously, what a concept of religion, or a sociology or phenomenology of religion, would look like if we started from within Hindu culture instead of outside of it. Recent work on the hermeneutical traditions of Indian intellectual traditions by such scholars as Francis X. Clooney (Boston College) and Sheldon Pollock (Chicago) is making an important contribution to this inquiry.

As our academic knowledge of Hindu traditions has deepened during the past fifty years, it has also influenced the western academic enterprise of the study of religion. We have begun to question the adequacy of our western-based theories and methods for interpreting Hinduism (as well as other religious traditions), and we are reexamining our academic categories such as "scripture," "canon," and "revelation" in light of the problematic application of such terminology to aspects of Hindu religious phenomena and experience. I should add that the academic study of religion is historically a western enterprise and has not found a home in most Indian universities. On the one hand, we might argue that the study of Indian religions has often been thwarted by the lack of parallel academic inquiries and institutions in India; on the other hand, U.S. scholars have benefitted greatly from their affiliations with both traditional and contemporary centers of study and research in India, such as Banaras Hindu University in Varanasi; Kuppuswami Shastri Research Institute and the University of Madras in Chennai; Bhandarkar Oriental Research Institute, Deccan College Post-Graduate Institute, Vaidik Samshodhan Mandal, and the Centre for the Advanced Study of Sanskrit at the University of Poona, all in Pune; and the Prajna Pathshala in Wai. At such places we have had the chance to work with traditional *paṇḍits* such as Yudhisthira Mimamsaka and Agnihotra Ramanuja Tatachariar of Madras; Tarkatirtha Laxmanshastri Joshi of Wai; Vaman Shastri Bhagwat of Pune; and Pandit Ambika Datta Upadhyaya of Varanasi as well as noted scholars such as V. Raghavan, T.M.P. Mahadevan, and S.S. Janaki in Madras; R.N. Dandekar, G.U. Thite, and D.D. Kosambi in Pune; and Veena Das, T.N. Madan, and Romila Thapar in Delhi, to name only a few of the distinguished and generous Indian scholars who have mentored U.S. scholars.

INCREASED ACCESS OF U.S. SCHOLARS TO INDIAN SOURCES

The ever-increasing contact that opened up with India after Independence has resulted in the exposure of western scholars interested in the religious traditions of Vedic and classical India to a much larger range of source materials and connections. This contact has also had a significant impact on the ways we go about our study of the religious traditions of Vedic and classical India. No longer are scholars of religion limited to deciphering the meaning of words on a page; since India's independence increasing numbers of western scholars have had the opportunity to sit at the feet of traditional Indian *paṇḍits* and have benefitted from the knowledge and interpretation transmitted by an expert of a particular religious or philosophical text. We have also had the privilege of observing the preparation and performance of Vedic *yajñas*, smarta *saṃskāras*, and puranic *pūjās*. Indologists such as William Dwight Whitney and Otto Boehtlingk never visited India; how much richer might their nonetheless significant contributions to our understanding of Indian religious history have been if they had studied in India. Daniel H.H. Ingalls' opportunity to study with M.M. Sri Kalipada Tarkacharya and to observe a living shastric tradition, opened up a whole new chapter of our understanding of Indian philosophy, and resulted in his 1951 ground-breaking *Materials for the Study of Navya-Nyaya Logic*,[2] one of the first fruits of post-Independence U.S. indological scholarship.

One of the results of the greater access to India and interaction with Indian scholars, *paṇḍits*, and religious leaders has been our increased awareness of more sources of information such as different recessions of Vedic texts and vernacular variations of the Sanskrit stories and teachings. This in turn has led to a greater appreciation of the multi-cultural complexity of the Indian religious landscape, and to a reassessment of what is meant by the terms "Veda," "Vedic," and "Hindu."

The opportunity to study in India has also exposed more scholars to traditional pedagogical techniques and hermeneutics. In particular, scholars have become fascinated with the orality, transmission, and memorization of religious texts. This cultural immersion in India has led more scholars to an appreciation and study of the performance and ritual aspects of the Vedic tradition: the research of David Knipe (Wisconsin), Frederick Smith (Iowa), Christopher Minkowski (Cornell), and especially Frits Staal (Berkeley)—whose study of the *agniṣṭoma* sacrifice included the production of a film, *Altar of Fire*, that documented the recreation of this ancient fire sacrifice—comes to mind. Field research on *pūjā*, pilgrimage, and *vrata* rituals by such scholars as Richard Davis (Bard), Gudrun Bühnemann (Wisconsin), Diana Eck (Harvard), and Mary McGee (Columbia) have enhanced their interpretations of the classical treatises on these ritual forms. The new perspectives gained from this approach of interrelating text and performance have enriched our understanding of the relationship between Vedic and Hindu forms, not to mention our understanding of the religious experience of Hindus. The advance in technology over the past fifty years has increasingly allowed us to film and record the recitation of texts and performance of rituals, permitting scholars and students to undertake a range of new comprehensive and comparative research projects. New computer technology is also allowing us to recreate the no longer extant ritual structures and spaces detailed in Vedic texts. The CD-Rom on *yajñas* in preparation by Frederick Smith (Iowa) is an example of the kinds of pedagogical and research tools being developed that make use of ancient texts, footage from contemporary ritual performance, digital animation, and hypertext technology.

SHIFTS OF EMPHASIS IN INDOLOGICAL STUDIES

Lectures given by two prominent indologists in the spring of 1951 provide us with a good overview of the state of western scholarship on Indian religion and philosophy by which we might gauge our intellectual progress, and access the scholarly trends and cornerstones that have emerged in the past fifty years. In March of 1951, Walter E. Clark, Wales Professor of Sanskrit at Harvard University, delivered the presidential address, entitled "The Future of Indian Studies,"[3] to the American Oriental Society, which met in Philadelphia that year. Two months later, Louis Renou, Professor of Sanskrit and Indian Literature at the Sorbonne, presented the Jordan Lectures at the School of Oriental and African Studies in London on the subject of religions of India. Renou's lectures were subsequently published in a book entitled *Religions of Ancient India*,[4] which, taken together with the two-volume study Renou authored with Jean Filliozat, *L'Inde Classique*[5] (still today a most valued piece of scholarship), offer us an excellent presentation of the depths and range of indological studies, particularly in Europe, some fifty years ago.

In his opening Jordan lecture on "Vedism," Renou observed that there had been a recent shift in scholarship from a focus on Vedic studies (which produced monographs, translations, and critical editions) to a foregrounding of concerns about "cultural influences and points of contact between civilizations" (Renou 1968, 2). Clark noted a similar shift, opening his address with this remark: "Until the present generation Indian studies in this country have been very closely connected with linguistics and comparative philology and with old Vedic literature" (209). Clark went on to acknowledge a growing interest in modern India and Indian cultural history, due to India's emergence "into the main current of world history," but expressed a concern about the subsequent production of "students of modern India who know little or nothing of the languages and little or nothing of India's past history" (209). He insisted that scholars dealing with modern India should have a reading knowledge of one of the national languages and a "good knowledge of India's past cultural history and some knowledge of Sanskrit" (209). Among the four areas of Indian studies that Clark singled out in 1951 as those expected to have the greatest strides in scholarship in the years to come was the study of Hinduism. Clark called for a more detailed study of Hinduism, and specifically for more attention to the female principle in Hindu thought, more editions and studies of the *āgamas* and *saṃhitās*, a closer look at the relationship between Vedic *yajña* and Hindu *pūjā*, and the production of a *Reallexikon* that would draw on such neglected texts as the *Artha Śāstra* in order to get more information about "the practical affairs of life," thereby complementing the almost exclusive scholarly attention to "philosophical and religious texts and belle lettres" (Clark 1951, 211). In Renou's lectures we see some similar concerns and ideas expressed; in one of his lectures, Renou refers to a historical reconstruction of a Vedic ritual he witnessed in Pune, sponsored by a Vedic research institute, that was undertaken more for the sake of scholarly study than for religious merit. For both Clark and Renou, philological studies were critical to the study of Vedic and classical Indian traditions, and the learning of Sanskrit was a necessary tool, but they realized the need to complement these approaches with new avenues of intellectual inquiry.

While Clark and Renou both remarked on the shift away from philological studies some fifty years ago, we have seen in subsequent years a continuation of philological and linguistic analyses, particularly in Vedic studies. Scholars of Vedic linguistics and Sanskrit philology, such as Michael Witzel (Harvard), Stanley Insler (Yale), Joel Brereton (Missouri), Madhav Deshpande (Michigan), and Ashok Aklujkar (British Columbia), and earlier Franklin Edgerton (Yale), have made important contributions to our understanding of Vedic culture and religion. The *History of Indian Literature* series under the editorship of Jan Gonda (Utrecht), with its detailed overview of Vedic and classical texts and in its multiple footnotes and references, has served as a starting point for many a doctoral dissertation. These more philologically-oriented studies have been complemented by a growing body of scholarship that focuses more on intertextuality and the content, meaning, and use of the texts.

While the production of critical editions has been less enthusiastic among U.S. scholars than some other scholars, U.S. research is nonetheless in great debt to such undertakings as the critical edition of the *Mahābhārata* that was completed with the publication of the *Harivaṃśa*, 1969-1971. That project, inaugurated in 1919, was based at Bhandarkar Oriental Research Institute in Pune, and involved an impressive team of Indian *paṇḍits* and Sanskritists. Franklin Edgerton, best known for his translation of the *Bhagavad Gītā*, was the only western scholar to edit a volume in the series. This critical edition has proved to be an invaluable tool for many scholars by providing more reliable access to an older text. The monumental task of critically editing the text has been complemented by a different but still daunting project undertaken by U.S.-based scholars, that being the translation into English of the critical edition of the *Mahābhārata*. Begun by the late Dutch scholar J.A.B. van Buitenen, the translation project, based at the University of Chicago, continues today. A similar project—the translation of a critical edition of Valmiki's Sanskrit *Rāmāyaṇa*—has also been undertaken under the editorship of a U.S. Sanskritist, Robert Goldman (Berkeley). Both of these endeavors have contributed greatly to our understanding of the social, mythic, and historical worldviews represented in these two great Indian epics. The religious poetry, didactic passages, heroic legends, and stories of divine interventions found in these texts provide scholars of religion with insights into the fundamental values, tensions, and beliefs of the classical tradition. Our teaching of Vedic and classical Hinduism has also been greatly aided by new translations of significant texts, among them Wendy Doniger's widely-used translations of the *Ṛg Veda*,[6] puranic myths,[7] and the Laws of Manu (done with Brian K. Smith).[8] Most recently Patrick Olivelle (Texas) has provided us with a much-needed and elegant new translation of the principal *Upaniṣads*.[9]

Clark's desideratum that more attention be given to the female as we developed a more sophisticated presentation of Hinduism has indeed come to pass, though there remains much more work to be done in this area. The first significant contribution to gender concerns was A.S. Altekar's *The Position of Women in Hindu Civilization: From Prehistoric Times to the Present Day,* first published in 1938 then revised in 1959.[10] While Altekar's text continues to be widely consulted, much new research on women in India offers us a corrective to some of his interpretations, for example, the careful textual studies of Stephanie Jamison and Julia Leslie (London School of Oriental and African Studies) have given us important insights on women's roles and gender dynamics in Vedic and Brahmanical texts. A popular interest in goddess traditions has yielded a range of recent studies that contribute to gender studies as well as to our understanding of *śakti* theology; among these works are Thomas Coburn's analysis of the *Devi Mahātmya*[11] and Tracy Pintchman's research on the rise of the goddess tradition as evidenced in Vedic and classical Sanskrit texts.[12]

The need for more scholarly attention to texts such as the *Artha Śāstra* to illuminate our understanding of Hinduism, another hope of Clark's, has received less attention. While Patrick Olivelle, Richard Larivicre (Texas), Ludo Rocher (Pennsylvania), and others have made significant contributions to our understanding of *dharmaśāstra*, as did Robert Lingat, J. Duncan M. Derrett and Julius Jolly before them, these texts, including the encyclopedic *dharma-nibandhas*, are still largely untapped sources of research for our understanding of classical Hinduism, not to mention the "practical affairs of life" referred to by Clark. I think we have grown too dependent on Manu and especially on P.V. Kane's much-consulted *History of Dharmaśāstra*.[13] The 1997 publication of a comprehensive index to Kane's five-volume study testifies to our reliance on this encyclopedic reference work, published between 1932 and 1955.

The philosophical texts of classical Hinduism continue to be an important focus in both research and teaching about Hinduism, though the tendency has been to privilege Vedānta and Śaṅkara over other philosophical schools and thinkers. This inquiry into the philosophical traditions has benefitted significantly from the work of scholars such as Karl Potter (Seattle), Surendranath Dasgupta, B.K. Matilal (Oxford), M. Hiriyanna, Phyllis Granoff (McMaster), Eliot Deutsch (Hawaii), Gerald Larson (Indiana), Wilhelm Halbfass (Pennsylvania), and the collaborative effort of S. Radhakrishnan and Charles Moore, which produced a still widely-used *A Source Book in Indian Philosophy* (1957).[14]

Perhaps one of the most significant contributions to indological studies in the past fifty years, and one that has augmented our sources for the understanding of Hinduism as well as of other religious traditions of India, has been the attention to classical sources other than those of the Brahmanical Sanskrit communities. I am thinking especially of classical Tamil literature, which grew up alongside of—and in contact with—Sanskrit classical literature, and the importance of which has been so carefully elucidated in the scholarship of George Hart (Berkeley) and others. Increasing attention has also been given to the interaction between Brahmanical communities and Jains (see the work of Padmanabh Jaini, Kenneth Folkert, and John Cort), as well as with Buddhists (relying on the classical works of such authors as Bhartṛhari). Warren Clark would be pleased to know that the *āgamas*, which he thought were underrepresented among the classical sources for our study of Hinduism, have begun to receive the attention they deserve thanks to the research of scholars like Douglas Brooks (Rochester), Alexis Sanderson (Oxford), Vasudha Narayanan (Florida), and the late A.K. Ramanujan and Agehananda Bharati, among others.

In looking at new trends that are emerging in the study of Vedic religion and classical Hinduism, we must not forget the foundational and comprehensive work done by Louis Renou and the many contributions of W. Norman Brown, both of whom were influential in shaping indological studies and benefitted greatly from the increased connections with India after Independence. While the production of critical editions, translations, and indices (projects widely undervalued in the humanities) has made a significant contribution to our study and teaching about Vedic and classical Hindu religious traditions in the past fifty years, other types of interpretative projects have made an effort to unlock the meaning of these texts. Scholars like Ronald Inden (Chicago) have been able to make connections between the political information found on copper-plate inscriptions and social and cultural information found in puranic texts; and Paul Younger (McMaster) has drawn on temple inscriptions and evidence from art history, as well as contemporary fieldwork, to elucidate the centrality of the temple in south Indian society. Scholars have brought different hermeneutical tools and emphases to their study of Vedic and classical sources: For example, Heesterman's research aims at reconstructing the world to which the texts point, while Brian K. Smith's work tries to discern the intention of the authors of these texts. Some scholars are concerned with finding an organizing principle through which to understand Hindu society and religion. For Biardeau, that organizing principle has been sacrifice; for Dumont, it has been the discourse between the renunciant and the "man-in-the world." Most recently some scholars have brought the concerns of subaltern studies and gender studies to bear on the interpretation of these Vedic and classical texts; these scholars join the structuralists, mythologists, deconstructionists, psychologists, philologists, phenomenologists, historians, and comparativists who have each brought their particular theories and tools to the attempt to open new windows of understanding.

The shift in emphasis in indological studies, which both Renou and Clark noted was in process some fifty years ago, has had an impact on both the scholarship and the teaching of historians of religion, though course syllabi have been slow to reflect this change. The Hinduism that has been taught in the United States, until very recently (and still in many places), has been largely the Hinduism of the Vedic and classical texts. Our authoritative texts have been the *Ṛg Veda*, the *Upaniṣads*, the *Manu-smṛti* and the *Bhagavad Gītā*, and the authoritative voices have been, for the most part, Sanskrit-speaking Brahman males. As modern indology has sought to represent the *Vedas* in their proper historical perspective (rather than attempting to trace all of Indian or Hindu culture back to the *Vedas* as in the earlier approach), and to balance the evidence from Sanskrit Brahmanical texts with perspectives from vernacular texts and traditions, teachers of Hinduism have struggled not only with how much emphasis to give to the *Vedas* but even with where to introduce them in the syllabus. Similarly, teachers are increasingly experimenting with how to structure a course on Hinduism, trying alternatives to a chronological approach while being sensitive to indigenous categories of thought. Some have divided the course along the lines of the *Bhagavad Gītā*'s three yogas (*jñāna, karma,* and *bhakti*); others have used the four *puruṣārthas* (*dharma, artha, kāma, mokṣa*) as an organizing theme. Efforts to include more material related to women have usually resulted in a section of the syllabus carved out especially for attention to women, but more of us are trying to integrate multiple perspectives, among them the role of women, into each unit of a course's syllabus.

Perhaps the most recent intellectual challenge to those of us who teach and study Hinduism has been a serious reconsideration of the definition of Hinduism and a critical examination of the extent to which the academic definition of Hinduism has been shaped by western concepts and religious categories, and by scholars' dependence on Sanskrit textual traditions in examining the phenomenological and philosophical aspects of Hinduism. Brian K. Smith (California) in recent writings has walked us through the intellectual struggle of defining Hinduism, reaching his own definition that Hinduism is defined by its relationship to "the authority of the Veda." He and other scholars, such as Barbara Holdrege (Santa Barbara) and Laurie L. Patton (Emory), have sought to explicate further the nature of that authority. Is it based on the text, the word, the sound, the ritual, the structure, or the idea of *Veda*? Learning that the concept of *Veda* as held by many practicing Hindus does not necessarily correspond to our academic idea of *Veda* as a corpus of ancient texts has motivated us to rethink our academic categories and paradigms for the study of religion.

A significant impetus to this reexamination of our portrayal of Hinduism has been the opportunity for scholars of my generation to do prolonged research in India, to work with Indian scholars and *paṇḍits*, and to be immersed in the daily life of Hindus, thanks to fellowships from the American Institute of Indian Studies and Social Science Research Council, and to Fulbright grants. Many of us have experienced an incongruity between U.S. textbook Hinduism and the Hindu traditions we have encountered in India, which has driven us to reconsider our definitions, interpretations, and presentations of Hinduism. My guess is that the textbooks and sourcebooks on Hindu traditions will look significantly different fifty years from now (not merely in their technological presentation but in their content as well).

NEW TECHNOLOGIES WEAVING TOGETHER
ANCIENT TEXTS AND NEW INTERPRETATIONS

While we have been especially concerned in the last ten years to incorporate more subaltern and vernacular voices into our study of Hinduism, the study of the Vedic and Brahmanical traditions as represented by Sanskrit texts will always continue to be an important part of our academic enterprise as scholars of religion. Computer technology is already easing the traditionally tedious process of creating indices and critical editions through the manipulation of digitized texts. Already, thanks especially to Japanese colleagues, one can access the *Mahābhārata* and many other major texts through the Internet. The Internet is allowing more collaborative research among scholars both nationally and internationally, as evidenced by the number of electronic networks such as Indology and RISA-L (Religion in South Asia), which are designed for the exchange of information among scholars. On-line journals devoted to indological studies are allowing for greater access to new scholarly interpretations, and personal as well as institutional web-pages are devoted to sharing wisdom about the religious and intellectual traditions of India. This new technology is already having a significant impact on how we use, learn, and teach about sources for the study of Hinduism. Two phenomena that scholars of religion and indology are already beginning to examine, but which will surely be of growing importance to studies in our field during the next fifty years, are the increasing Hindu diaspora outside of India, and Hindu nationalism. Related to these two concerns, we will want to understand how traditional texts such as the *Vedas* and epics are used and understood by these communities, for political as well as religious purposes. Another significant change that, I think, will expand and enrich our understanding of Hindu texts and traditions in the years to come is the growing number of students from South Asian and Hindu backgrounds who are choosing to do graduate work in the academic study of religion. Their perspectives will add a welcome dimension to the shape of religious studies in the 21st century.

NOTES

1. Smith, Wilfred Cantwell. 1963. *The Faith of Other Men.* New York: New American Library.
2. Ingalls, Daniel H.H. 1951. *Materials for the Study of Navya-Nyaya Logic.* Harvard Oriental Series 40. Cambridge: Harvard Univ. Press.
3. Clark, Walter E. 1951. "The Future of Indian Studies." *Journal of the American Oriental Society* 71(4): 209-212.
4. Renou, Louis. 1968. *The Religions of Ancient India.* New York: Schocken.
5. Filliozat, Jean. 1947. *L'Inde Classique: Manuel des Etudes Indiennes.* Paris: Payot.
6. Doniger, Wendy. 1981. *The Rg Veda: An Anthology: One-Hundred and Eight Hymns.* Harmondsworth: Penguin.
7. Doniger, Wendy. 1975. *Hindu Myths: A Sourcebook.* Harmondsworth: Penguin.
8. Doniger, Wendy and Brian K. Smith. 1991. *The Laws of Manu.* Harmondsworth: Penguin.
9. Olivelle, Patrick. 1996. *Upanishads.* New York: Oxford Univ. Press.
10. Altekar, A.S. 1959 (2nd ed.). *The Position of Women in Hindu Civilization: From Prehistoric Times to the Present Day.* Delhi: Motilal Banarsidass.
11. Coburn, Thomas. 1984. *Devi-Mahatmya: The Crystalization of the Goddess Tradition.* Delhi: Motilal Banarsidass.
12. Pintchman, Tracy. 1994. *The Rise of the Goddess in the Hindu Tradition.* Albany: State Univ. of New York Press.
13. Kane, P.V. 1930-1962. *History of Dharmaśāstra.* Poona: Bhandarkar Oriental Research Institute.
14. Radhakrishnan, Sarvepalli and Charles Moore. 1957. *A Source Book in Indian Philosophy.* Princeton: Princeton Univ. Press.

Religious Studies: Medieval Hinduism

JOHN STRATTON HAWLEY

Butler Library, the hulking structure that has anchored the central quadrangle of Columbia University since 1934, solemnly announces the glories of the past. The upper margins of this great mausoleum bear a ribbon of stone names—Homer, Herodotus, Sophocles, Plato, Aristotle, Cicero, Demosthenes, Virgil, and if one turns the corner, onward to Dante. These are the men upon whom were thought to hang the cultural edifice we call western civilization.

At commencement in the Spring of 1989, however, everything changed. On that day one of the graduates, Laura Hotchkiss Brown, unfurled a great white banner that blotted out these names, replacing them all with women. Sappho led this guerrilla brigade, but we advanced quickly beyond Greece and Rome to a more modern cohort. Before long the banner project became a standing University tradition, and its protest was not just against biases of gender, but of culture as well. So it was that in 1994, as I gazed across the quandrangle at Butler, I was pleased to see the name of Mirabai staring back.

Fifty years ago it would have been inconceivable to find the name of a sixteenth-century Hindu saint emblazoned on a typical U.S. university library, even for a day. But much has changed. Back when India and Pakistan became independent nations, the study of religion in western universities was typically the study of Christianity, and was modeled on the disciplines found in the Christian seminaries where most faculty members had commenced their graduate education. There was also an interest in the generic study of religion, as represented by courses on the philosophy, psychology, and sociology of religion, but the subject matter rarely extended farther afield than Judaism. Then during the early 1960s came a real shift. One indication of it was that the National Association of Biblical Instructors refashioned itself as the American Academy of

Religion, an organization clearly dedicated to the study of religion generically, and in time its membership grew to exceed that of the older, more narrowly-focused Society of Biblical Literature. The basic paradigm for composing an undergraduate curriculum in religion also changed. Increasingly after 1970 the typical introductory course turned from being an exploration of the scripture, history, and theology of Christians and Jews to a course in world religions. And there was a similarly Copernican revolution in the way basic textbooks on religion were written.

A scholarly engagement with India did much to hasten these developments. That engagement did not begin, of course, with the subcontinent's release from colonial rule in 1947. In the field of religion one could look back, for example, to huge British projects such as *The Sacred Books of the East,* edited by Max Müller, that commenced in 1879 with his own translations of selected *Upaniṣads* and *Āraṇyakas*; or to the series on Non-Christian Religious Systems of the Society for Promoting Christian Knowledge, that included Monier Williams' *Hinduism,* published in 1877. Here was Oxford looking east, and primarily through a classicist lens. But the change in geopolitical circumstances after World War II definitely had an effect. In India's struggle for independence, the ongoing power and inventiveness of religion in South Asia became very clear, and when Gandhi emerged as the premier modern saint, there was an automatic destabilizing of Judeo-Christian hegemony.

Obviously the study of medieval Hinduism per se played only a small role in this change, yet that study was more influential than has sometimes been noticed. Max Müller and Monier Williams were Sanskritists, and Sanskrit was also the language that claimed the main attention of the person most responsible for producing the great paradigm shift in the American study of religion from Christianity (with a footnote to Judaism) to world religions. This was Mircea Eliade, who became professor of the history of religions in the University of Chicago in 1958. He had worked primarily with Sanskrit texts to produce his volumes on yoga and shamanism, but his interest in the *realia* of Indian religion exposed him also to vernacular expressions, especially in Bengali, via Surendranath Dasgupta. Hence the sources he used for his study *Yoga: Immortality and Freedom* (first edition in French, 1936; revised English version, 1958) went far beyond Patañjali to Gorakhnath and modern practice. The generic phenomenological approach to religion that he institutionalized at Chicago, published in works such as *Patterns in Comparative Religion* (French, 1949; English, 1958), and expressed through the journal *History of Religions,* which he helped found in 1961, drew importantly on his experience with India.

An engagement with the vernacular languages and cultures of India was still more important to two other figures who exerted a fundamental force on the study of religion in North America. Both Wilfred Cantwell Smith and A.K. Ramanujan respected the importance of lived religion, a magnet that has drawn many scholars to the vernacular classics that emerged in medieval India. It was Smith who gave definition to Harvard's graduate program on the study of religion after joining the faculty in 1964. Smith was primarily an Islamicist, but his experience of living in Lahore and Aligarh from 1940 to 1946 contributed much to his appreciation of the fundamental importance of interactions between religious communities and to his sense that no "system of belief," as the going phrase had it, really defined the religiousness of living, breathing people. Both insights found expression in his formative article on "The Crystallization of Religious Communities in Mughal India" (1969).[1] In other works he reacted against others' Protestant disparagement of the distance between scripture and practice in the religious styles of both Muslims and Hindus living in South Asia, insisting that what turns a text into a scripture is precisely its success in the realm of practice—the way in which it is intoned, interpreted, and reinterpreted over the centuries. Smith's own interests were directed intensely toward speech and writing, but the absence of a single Sanskrit analogue to the *Qur'an* in lived Hinduism and the richness of vernacular expressions of Hindu faith raised deep questions in his mind about the overconfident scripturalism that had channeled the western study of religion. Since the idea of religion in European languages was tied fundamentally to text and creed, this also informed his growing conviction that the concept "religion" was a relatively recent western invention. Smith's insights have profoundly redirected scholarship on religion in the last twenty-five years.

A.K. Ramanujan was a very different sort of scholar—a poet, translator, linguist, and literary critic who did not even think of himself as a scholar of religion by profession. In fact, one of his deeply charming (and, indeed, charismatic) qualities was that he thought of himself very little in professional terms at all. Yet Ramanujan's engagement with Tamil and Kannada poetry dating from the sixth century CE to the twelfth fundamentally altered the shape of Hindu studies and of religious studies more broadly. As a translator, Ramanujan evolved a spare "vertical" mode for rendering

Dravidian poetry that answered well to the expectations created by English blank verse and has been widely adopted by other translators in the field, many of them his own students at Chicago. The works of Ramanujan and his "atelier" demonstrated, by their aggregate weight, that the fields we customarily demark by the names poetry and religion are not at all so distinct as most twentieth-century English speakers tend to think.

In part because of his personal qualities, Ramanujan seemed to exemplify the sort of personal engagement that was taught theoretically in the various *bhakti* schools. Of course, the question "What is a person?" remains primary, but this is precisely the sort of question that an engagement with *bhakti* poet-saints forces upon us, and Ramanujan's refined interest in the personhood and poetry produced within the broad span of medieval *bhakti* has drawn considerable attention to the field in international circles. In forums such as the annual meetings of the American Academy of Religion, he and those who followed him into medieval Hindu studies have engaged with specialists on poetry and hagiography in other religious traditions, raising in broad terms the question of why or whether saints must be poets—or poets, saints. Similarly, Ramanujan's probing the boundaries between classic and vernacular, "great" and "little"— all categories he was eager to move beyond—has encouraged religionists to take the popular or folk aspects of religion as seriously as the clerical or classical, and to study multiform interactions between the two. Moreover, his work with McKim Marriott and others on "indigenous categories," like the series of publications initiated and inspired by Kapila Vatsyayan at the Indira Gandhi National Centre for the Arts in Delhi, has helped western students of religion to examine the familiar furniture of their intellectual living rooms.

Many other students of medieval Hindu texts have had similar, if perhaps less powerful (Ramanujan is hard to match!), effects on readers outside India in the last fifty years. One thinks especially of Monika Boehm-Tettelbach for German, David Lorenzen and his colleagues at the Colegio de Mexico for Spanish, and Charlotte Vaudeville and Francoise Mallison for French. In English, Deben Bhattacharya, Clinton Seely, and Rachel McDermott come to mind for Bengali; David Shulman, Indira Peterson, K.V. Zvelebil, Norman Cutler, and Vasudha Narayanan for Tamil; Velcheru Narayana Rao and David Shulman for Telugu; Kenneth Bryant, Linda Hess, Winand Callewaert, and Philip Lutgendorf for Hindi; Anne Feldhaus, Eleanor Zelliot, and Vinay Dharwadkar for Marathi; and a host of others, including the derivative but nonetheless noteworthy Robert Bly. For Sanskrit texts of the period, one can hardly bypass Barbara Stoler Miller's translation of the *Gīta Govinda*. In a number of cases, these same scholars have also investigated the performative dimensions of the texts they treat, and have thereby made an important contribution to international scholarship, where the boundary between text and performance is increasingly seen as a frail, even false, one. Here the study of medieval Hindu texts is particularly illuminating, since critical scholarship often shows them to be far less clearly defined as written works than is the norm for either earlier or more modern texts within India, let alone other religious traditions. With medieval religious texts, questions of canon and authority are hard to avoid, and the boundaries between poem and song, and between written and oral transmission, are frequently hard to draw.

Investigations of these matters by scholars of medieval Hinduism do not seem to have drawn the same international attention that has come to similar efforts by post-modern scholars working on more recent materials. Perhaps this is natural. In the colonial and post-colonial fields, English paves a wide thoroughfare, and agonizing, fascinating questions of its use in fashioning or suppressing Indian identities come quickly to the surface, especially in the thinking of Indians themselves. But the same questions of performance, position, and power that are so close to the heart of colonial/post-colonial debates also arise in many pre-modern contexts. Simply moving away from English (a move required by pre-modern studies) confronts one with huge vistas of "subaltern" work that have been remarkably neglected by many who hold high the banner of subaltern studies.

In that regard let us return to Mirabai, with whom we began. As a medieval figure, with all the problems of access implied by that word, she provides a telling index for patterns of cultural exchange between India and the West. There is little doubt that Mirabai is on the threshold of attaining a firm place in the world canon of cultural "greats." We already know of her place on the feminist banner that periodically obscures the cultural forefathers etched into the facade of Butler Library, but she also appears in the newly expanded edition of *The Norton Anthology of World Masterpieces* (1995).[2]

Anyone who thinks seriously about the Butler banner or those Mira pages in the "Norty" faces a series of questions that also affect certain other celebrities recently enrolled in the emerging international canon of classics. For example, what credentials count? We have good manuscript evidence for poetry attributed to a number of north Indian saints (all of them men) from Mira's period. But for her we have only five poems up to the mid-seventeenth century. What makes her a more credible classic than many of them? For the early period, her hagiographical record is much stronger than her literary one, yet her story changes a good bit depending on who is telling it, and she shares whole chunks of her life with other poet-saints. Does she really have a history of her own? Mira became a symbol of struggle in certain parts of the Indian nationalist movement. Does that add to her value or make it suspect? Finally, she is the only female among the major poet-saints of north India, a "tokenism" we also find in the hagiological families of south and west India, as well as in Kashmir. As the only woman, she has all too easily been made to represent womanhood with a capital "W," and, partly as a result, the life and poetry attributed to her relate even more closely to music, dance, and theatricality than those of comparable male saints. Not only that, her cinematic career is far more impressive than theirs. Do these facts mean that she is not really an individual in the sense we might expect in a secular canon of the sort the *Norton Anthology* projects?

As one can see, with Mirabai we are entering what is, from the point of view of much western literary and historical criticism, a morass. Yet for many modern Indians she is the cardinal representative of "medieval" Hinduism, whether as a heroine of inner devotion, a paragon of religious and social commitment, or a leading protagonist in a global narrative of resistance to the oppressions of caste, imperialism, gender, and, yes, religion. How do scholarship and canonical veneration interact?

In regard to the matter of history and historicity, the answer is clear: uneasily. Indian Marxist scholars, apparently accustomed to the more ample documents available for the colonial and post-colonial periods, have sometimes seemed impatient with—or simply unaware of—the constraints imposed by slimmer and often more problematic sources relating to the medieval period. Kumkum Sangari's widely read essay "Mirabai and the Spiritual Economy of Bhakti," which betrays no knowledge of manuscripts relating to Mirabai, has therefore been criticized by Parita Mukta in her recent book *Upholding the Common Life.*[3] Mukta's approach displays a subtler marshalling of methods that bear on the historical study of religion, and opens the way to a better use, in sociological context, of nitty-gritty textual work such as has been pursued by Kalyansimh Shekhavat, Winand Callewaert, and Nancy Martin. In Mukta's work, as in Callewaert's, we begin to see how important are the musical and ethnomusical contexts in which religious traditions are remembered and reshaped. And in Mukta's and Martin's work we see how hard it is to separate out the "medieval" from the "modern" in the history of hagiography, poetry, and community that make Mirabai who she "is." It does seem that Mira is considerably more important as a twentieth-century figure than as a sixteenth-century one, but this news is hardly unexpected in the field of religious studies, which concerns itself as much with the impact of collective memory as with the issue of historical fact. Hence the best scholars of Mira are medievalists who also report on more modern and contemporary manifestations, or vice versa. And the very figure of Mirabai—embedded as she is in the web of text, context, and performance—forces us to ask hard questions about the salience of the category "medieval."

Two matters relating to the status of Mirabai have become particularly critical to the study of religion as it has developed in the West in recent years: issues of religious nationalism and of gender. In regard to religious nationalism (or fundamentalism, the more common but possibly pejorative term), studies of medieval India have played a surprisingly major role. The best known controversy swirls around the New Zealand scholar W.H. McLeod, whose attempts to deploy methods of textual and historical criticism originally developed to analyze the Bible and the classics of Greece and Rome have been interpreted by certain vocal Sikhs as an open attack on their faith.[4] At least three major issues are involved: the right of an outsider to consider the canonical writings of any religious community; the relation of revelation to historical evolution; and the connection between one religious community and another. The third issue concerns us particularly, because McLeod, joining western scholars such as Charlotte Vaudeville and Sikh scholars such as J.S. Grewal and Fauja Singh, laid considerable stress on major continuities between the thoughts and expressive modes of Guru Nanak, on the one hand, and those of his Hindu and Muslim contemporaries, on the other. Considering that influential Sikhs from the late nineteenth century onward had precisely tried to create a clear demarcation between Sikhs and Hindus, this was seen as incendiary. It also raised new questions about distinctions between Sikh gurus and non-Sikh *bhagats* (i.e., *bhaktas*) that had been developed early in the formation of the Sikh canon.

In part because it echoes other confrontations between "traditional" believers and "modern" scholars, the heated affair surrounding the work of McLeod and those associated with him has had a considerable impact on religious studies. McLeod's scholarship is of sufficient eminence in its own terms to have qualified him for selection as the American Council of Learned Societies lecturer on the history of religions for 1986-1987.[5] But the controversy in which he was embroiled undoubtedly had something to do with his being chosen for that honor, as it became clear how important were his work and personal situation for the field at large. Since McLeod wrote *The Religion of Guru Nanak* (1968) and *The Evolution of the Sikh Community* (1975), a number of other works have appeared in Sikh studies and in the study of medieval Hinduism more broadly that have challenged boundary definitions that gained wide acceptance in subsequent periods. Notable among them are Harjot Oberoi's *The Construction of Religious Boundaries* (1994), Gurinder Singh Mann's *The Goindwal Pothis* (1996), David Lorenzen's studies of the Kabir Panth, Charlotte Vaudeville's work on the Vaisnavization of Braj and Maharashtra, and Peter van der Veer's study of parallel formations of Islamic and Hindu communities in *Religious Nationalism: Hindus and Muslims in India* (1994).

These studies have been controversial in two ways. On the one hand, they have shown, contrary to the view that reigns in certain circles of South Asia scholarship, that to blame the British for creating clear (but false) divisions between Muslims, Hindus, and Sikhs is vastly to overstate the case. Deep tensions, especially between Hindus and Muslims, existed long before the British became involved. On the other hand, these studies have challenged "essentialisms" such as those one familiarly encounters in the rhetoric of religious nationalism, whether Hindu, Muslim, or Sikh. For example, new epigraphic and archival work by Tarapada Mukherjee and Irfan Habib (as in Margaret Case, ed., *Govindadeva: A Dialogue in Stone*, 1996) clearly demonstrates that the great Vaisnava institutions dating back to the sixteenth century in Braj came into being because of close cooperation between Muslims and Hindus, namely, the Mughal emperors and their Rajput generals. Given that these are some of the major religious formations to have persisted in north India from medieval times into the present (with various attempts to reconfigure and even obscure their history along the way), we see, as with Mirabai, that medieval and modern realities are intimately inter-twined. As some of these studies, especially van der Veer's, have become well known, they have sensitized specialists in other areas of religious studies to the subtleties involved. Broader works such as *The New Cold War?: Religious Nationalism Confronts the Secular State* (1993), written by Mark Juergensmeyer, who is himself a student of religious interactions in north India and of the medieval roots of Radhasoami, have brought some of these issues to the attention of the general public.

A second issue that comes to light in relation to Mirabai and her complex legacy is the importance of gender in the study of religion. Again this is a field where an engagement with India has been of fundamental importance to the study of religion broadly. It seems fair to say that the major force behind the drive to understand and challenge the often unconscious gender-dependency of religious ideas and norms has come from feminist scholarship in the West, and the major target has been the notoriously androcentric religious traditions of the West itself. Patriarchalism in India has scarcely gone unnoticed, either by western students of religion or by their Indian counterparts. But probably the main way in which the study of Hindu religion has contributed to the current international discussion is by showing what a multigendered religious tradition looks like, both conceptually and in practice. Few argue that the presence of females in the Hindu pantheon erases a bias in favor of men in much Hindu religious life. In fact, many hold that the correlation is more often inverse than direct. Yet the variousness of Hindu approaches to the divine and to religious practice, from the point of view of gender, has been a real resource in discussions that often begin in religious contexts far from India.

One could point to the work of many scholars who have enabled this to happen, but few have been as influential as Wendy Doniger, whose studies of the elaborate permutations of gender identity developed in Hindu myths, particularly those found in the medieval Sanskrit *puranas*, have been widely read. Among her many books, one might especially cite *Siva, the Erotic Ascetic* (1973), *Hindu Myths* (1975), *Women, Androgynes, and Other Mythical Beasts* (1980), and her forthcoming opus *Sexual Masquerades*.

Studies of individual goddesses, many based on medieval texts, have also been important. I have learned with pleasure that my own most frequently-cited work is a book I edited with Donna Wulff called *The Divine Consort* (1982, 1986), a collection of essays on Radha and other Hindu goddesses. A sequel called *Devi: Goddesses of India* (1996) has just been issued. In these books contributors such as Thomas Coburn, Diana Eck, Kathleen Ernst, Shrivatsa Goswami, Cynthia Humes, David Kinsley, Frederique Marglin, Vasudha Narayanan, and Rachel McDermott delve into the "medieval" background of modern, multigendered Hinduism. Most of them have written book-length studies themselves. Meanwhile scholars such as Mary McGee, with her examination of the disparity between medieval textual prescriptions relating to vows (*vratas*, a familiar feature of women's religion) and their observance by actual women living today, keep us aware that concept and practice are not always the same. The works of Julia Leslie and Anne Pearson have also been important in this regard, and many Indian feminist scholars, such as those who contribute to the journal *Manushi*, point in a similar direction. This is a set of concerns that relates in a number of ways to the figure of Mirabai, who is sometimes depicted as a goddess, sometimes as a human, sometimes as a being who inhabits mythical space, sometimes as a creature of history, and sometimes—a special feature of her being positioned as "medieval"—as a bit of both. Not surprisingly, therefore, Mirabai has appeared a number of times in the pages of *Manushi*, which has a growing international readership.

In writing the above, I have accepted the editors' challenge to think about the ways in which scholarship on India has affected "scholarship throughout the world" in my field. I have allowed this to mean western scholarship, and U.S. scholarship in particular. Yet I want to make it clear that I do not think such an impact, however great, is the true or main payoff that comes from studying medieval Hinduism. The primary significance of scholarship in this area is the light it sheds on India itself, both medieval and modern. As I have tried to stress, one of its most interesting effects of scholarship in this area is to question the distinction between tradition and modernity that lies just beneath the surface when we contrast "medieval" and "modern." In taking Mirabai as my special focus, I hope to have raised this issue with particular force, and to suggest that if she succeeds in becoming a major figure in the international canon of literature and religion that is now being fashioned, that is because she is at least as important in contemporary India as she was a half millenium ago. It is an axiom of current scholarship that traditions are invented realities, and Mirabai is no exception to the rule. We carry her with us today—perhaps more than ever before.

NOTES

1. Smith, Wilfred Cantwell. 1969. "The Crystallization of Religious Communities in Mughal India." In *Yad-Name-ye-Iraini* [sic]-*ye Minorsky*, ed. Motjaba Minovi and Iraj Afshar, 197-220. Tehran: Itisharat Daneshgah.
2. Mack, Maynard, gen. ed. 1995. *The Norton Anthology of World Masterpieces.* New York: W.W. Norton.
3. Mukta, Parita. 1994. *Upholding the Common Life: The Community of Mirabai.* Delhi: Oxford Univ. Press. 32-34.

4. McLeod summarizes and responds to some of these criticisms in "The Study of Sikh Literature." See W.H. McLeod. 1993. *Studying the Sikhs: Issues for North America*, ed. John Stratton Hawley and Gurinder Singh Mann, 47-68. Albany: State Univ. of New York Press. McLeod's student, Pashaura Singh, also working on the early—i.e., "medieval"— period in Sikh scriptural history, has been similarly attacked, as for instance in Bachittar Singh Giani, ed. 1994. *Planned Attack on Aad Sri Guru Granth Sahib: Academics or Blasphemy* [sic]. Chandigarh: International Centre of Sikh Studies.

5. These lectures were published as W.H. McLeod. 1989. *The Sikhs: History, Religion, and Society.* New York: Columbia Univ. Press.

Religious Studies:
Modern Hinduism/Jainism

What does "modern" actually mean? In the realm of Indian religions the term cannot be exactly synonymous with "contemporary," for much that is contemporary in Indian religions is in fact very ancient—hardly modern by anyone's definition. For present purposes let it suffice to say that by *modern* Hinduism and Jainism we refer merely to elements of these traditions that have, during this century and especially during the post-Independence period, undergone important transformations. In what follows, I describe some examples of such changes in Hindu and Jain traditions and some of the responses they have evoked among students of Indian religions. The moral of the story is the tenuousness of boundaries—boundaries between old and new, international boundaries, and the boundaries of confessional communities. Modern Hinduism and Jainism are at once old and new, Indian and global, and far less definable as discrete cultural entities than is commonly supposed. In fact, the study of religious modernity in India has raised new questions about the status of Hinduism and Jainism, old or new, as bounded traditions.

There are at least three functional domains—shared by most religious systems—in which to look for change. First, religious traditions must be socially reproduced and propagated, which requires that technical means exist for their *transmission*. Second, religious systems are embedded in *social contexts* by which they are shaped in fundamental ways. And, third, religious systems are often (perhaps always) implicated in the legitimization of *authority*.

Although these three characteristics of religious systems are obviously linked and interdependent, keeping them distinct will enable us to view religious modernity in India from significantly different points of view.

TRANSMISSION

A leading edge of technological change in this century—in India, as everywhere—has been in the technology of mass communications, and India has incontestably undergone a genuine media revolution. Few visitors to India from other countries can fail to notice the extraordinary degree to which electronically amplified sound and visual images projected by chromolithography, film, and television have become part of the Indian sensory surroundings, especially in India's cities. These developments are the latest manifestations of a trend that began in the late nineteenth century with the general spread of printing technology in India, a trend that has had profound implications for the way religious traditions have been transmitted and reproduced.

At issue is distance and its diminution. In abstract terms, the media revolution can be characterized as a progressive enhancement of the mobility of symbols (of which religious symbols are one type) in a society. In part, this is a question of physical mobility. When information of whatever kind is carried by modern communications technologies—especially those involving the modulation of electro-magnetic radiation (i.e., radio or television broadcasting)—even subcontinental distances shrink into relative insignificance. But probably more important than the reduction of physical distance has been the dramatic impact of new communications technology on traditional cultural and social barriers to the transmission of tradition. Symbols, including religious symbols, can be said to move through social as well as physical space, and the speed with which they do so, and the distance they are able to travel, is determined by the amount of social or cultural "friction" they encounter along the way. Bottlenecks imposed by the monopolization of the means of symbol-transmission by cultural elites, the exclusion by tradition of some groups from contact with important traditions, and so forth, are the sources of such friction, and barriers of this sort are radically challenged by new communications technologies.

When physical and social distances are reduced by new media technology, a process we might call "cultural amplification" occurs. By this I mean the process by which formerly parochial or obscure symbols, images, or ideas come to be shared by, and even normative for, large populations. This is undoubtedly one of the most important general effects that modern communications media have had on societies and cultures everywhere.

In India, the amplification effect of new media has been powerfully evident in the realm of religious culture. A spectacular example is the impact of commercially reproduced religious poster art on Hindu traditions. In a recent analysis of this phenomenon, Stephen Inglis (1995) shows how one gifted artist's conception of the visual appearance of certain Hindu deities has become, by means of the extraordinary reproductive capacities of photo-offset printing, the way these deities are actually visualized throughout south India and beyond. He suggests that we are currently witnessing the emergence of an Indian "national aesthetic" in which Hindus everywhere are increasingly participating in a common vision of sacred beings.

The most famous example of media-amplification in Hinduism, however, is the film, *Jai Santoshi Ma*. Although the classical Hindu film has been on the wane in recent decades, *Jai Santoshi Ma* defied the trend when it was released in 1975. It was a hit film, and drew audiences of urbanites as well as the villagers who are the usual audiences for explicitly religious films. The film concerns the heroine's devotion to a goddess named Santoshi Ma ("Satisfaction Mother"), a daughter of the deity Ganesh. From what oral tradition this goddess originally came is unclear, but, according to Stanley Kurtz (1992, 13), printed versions of the myth of a goddess called Santoshi Ma and instructions for her worship began to appear in the early 1960s. The film presented a polished and cinematically gussied-up version of the bazaar-pamphlet myth, and ultimately became a vehicle for the explosive spread of the cult of the goddess Santoshi Ma across northern India (Erndl 1993, 141-152). In effect, Santoshi Ma was a movie-created goddess.

A more recent and highly sensational example of electronic amplification of religious culture was the televised serialization of the *Rāmāyaṇa*. This series, the first of its kind, was a national phenomenon and cultural-historical event of the first magnitude. Beginning in January 1987, and continuing for a total of seventy-eight Sunday-morning installments (plus a later sequel), the series ultimately became the most widely-watched program ever shown on Indian television. The show was produced and directed by Ramanand Sagar, a Bombay filmmaker who seems to have few pretensions to high art, but clearly possesses a genuine love of the *Rāmāyaṇa*, especially the *Rāmcaritmānas* of Tulsidas, and an instinctive understanding of popular taste. The televised *Rāmāyaṇa* revealed a deep cultural divide between average viewers and India's cosmopolitan cultural elites. Most Sunday-morning aficionados found the material presented and the manner of its presentation deeply satisfying, but educated and cosmopolitan critics tended to deride the series as tasteless, vulgar, culturally inauthentic, and demeaning to Indian tradition.

The televised *Rāmāyaṇa* certainly looked like something truly new on the religious scene. Here was a "traditional" text conveyed by a purely modern medium, and here was a version of the epic that seemed to be undergoing an unprecedented degree of universalization, leaping over every kind of physical and social barrier by means of electronic technology. Observers also noted what seemed to be the emergence of a new mode of worship in which an electronic device was actually slipping into the role of an object of worship. On Sunday mornings, some viewers would bathe and avoid eating before episodes began, much as they would as a prelude to temple worship. Television sets were installed in altar-like surrounds, complete with incense and other accouterments of image-worship; and, at the show's conclusion, sanctified food (*prasād*) was sometimes distributed to the viewers, which is the standard final act in much Hindu worship.

But how much of a real difference did any of this make? That is, to what degree is the religious culture transmitted by new media technologies actually transformed into something new? This is a question that must be asked by those who seek to understand "modern" religion, and the answer turns out to be more complex and ambiguous than one might have supposed. Is it the case, for example, that media amplification is, by a process of selection of some symbols and images at the expense of others, standardizing religious culture in a way that it never was before? Maybe. Religious poster art standardizes images, but it also reproduces images of regional deities, and the pictures themselves enable devotees to combine and recombine deities and other religious symbols in culturally various and, indeed, idiosyncratic ways (Inglis 1995, Smith 1995). Is the cult of Santoshi Ma really an innovation? This goddess *looks* new, but Stanley Kurtz shows that in truth there is little new about her. His respondents refused to differentiate her from other goddesses for the simple reason that her character is really only a new permutation of various older elements that belong to the character of the generic Hindu goddess (1992, 13-19; for a somewhat different view, see Das 1980).

And, finally, what if anything was really new about Ramanand Sagar's *Rāmāyaṇa*? Not, it seems clear, the "video-latry" (Lutgendorf's apt term). If the setting of worship was new—the knobs, the flickering glass screen, and all the rest—the actual ritualizations were quite standard; here was sacred viewing, *darśan*, merely transposed to a new setting. And although critics condemned the series on the grounds of cultural inauthenticity, Lutgendorf's analysis reveals it to have been one among many versions of the epic, a culturally authentic retelling utilizing a new performance medium. There was, however, one new—and perhaps sour—note. This was the series' stress on the notion of the *Rāmāyaṇa* as "a symbol of national unity and integration" (Lutgendorf 1995, 222), a theme to which we shall return.

My own very unsystematic observations suggest that the media revolution has been somewhat slower to have an impact on Jainism than Hinduism. It is true that Jains are also eager consumers of mass-reproduced framing pictures on specifically Jain themes. Jain versions of the famed *Amar Chitra Katha* comic series (on the series itself, see Hawley 1995 and Pritchett 1995) have appeared in recent years, as have audio and video cassettes on religious themes. Nonetheless, a media repackaging of Jainism on the same scale that we see among Hindus still lies in the future.

SOCIAL CONTEXTS

The social structures within which religious traditions are produced, embedded, channeled, and reproduced in India are complex and multi-layered. Families, castes, villages, and other local groupings— the social structures of day-to-day life—have played this role. So has the state. And so have the various structures associated specifically with religious and ritual life—the monastic and sectarian orders, the specialist-complexes flourishing at major temples and pilgrimage destinations, and so on. Has any of this changed? It all has, at least to some degree, and in this sense it can be said that in the late twentieth century the entire social context of religion in India has undergone vast changes with results that have yet to be fully understood or even registered.

Among the modern transformations of Indian society to which students of Indian religions have given special attention is the rise of new urban classes and lifestyles that have engendered religious responses. Unfortunately, the work that has been done thus far in this area is extremely lopsided in favor of the religious proclivities of urban elites. Little significant work has been done on the religious movements of the urban proletariat of India, despite the fact that an excellent model for such work exists in the Sri Lanka studies of Gombrich and Obeyesekere (Gombrich and Obeyesekere 1988, Obeyesekere 1981). In India, middle-class (and for the most part upper-caste) movements have gotten most of the attention.

David Knipe refers to the rise of middle-class religious movements as "acaryization" (1991, 148-149), and in doing so he highlights an important fact. Although these movements arise within a modern social milieu, at their core we find an institution that is very ancient. This is the dyad of guru and disciple, a simple pairing that can be seen as the atomic minimum of the social organization of Indic religious traditions. This dyad endures still; most middle-class religious movements in India emanate primarily from charismatic individuals. We live in a time of jet-age holy men and women. For this very reason, most of these movements have serious succession problems.

The gurus of India's modern middle classes are a heterogeneous group. Some are very famous. Others, the majority, operate in obscurity; Kirin Narayan's *Swamiji* (1989), for example, would have been known only to a small group of devotees were it not for the accident of Narayan's connection with him. Some, such as the many gurus in the Radhasoami tradition (see Juergensmeyer 1991), emerge from well-established disciplic lineages. Others, such as Sathya Sai Baba, project their own lineages. They promulgate no single message or doctrine.[1] Many, though not all, tend to be highly ecumenist. Most try to differentiate their teachings from older traditions deemed to be in some sense obsolete or "unscientific." Notably, too, many are vigorous pursuers of international clienteles, a point to which we shall return.

To what degree is acaryized Hinduism distinctively new? This is a key question for the student of modern Hinduism. We found before, in the case of modern media, the answer is by no means obvious. Sathya Sai Baba, arguably the premier "godman" of post-independence India, is a good case in point. On the one hand, his constituency is certainly "modern" by most understandings of the term (Babb 1986). Many of his followers are cosmopolitan and sophisticated; some, indeed, are distinguished scientists. Although he himself has not traveled to the West, he has a large number of western devotees. And the version of the Hindu tradition he offers to his followers is streamlined and stripped down, a simplified version suited to the religious tastes and sensibilities of persons who at least to some degree have been culturally uprooted. Despite all this, Sathya Sai Baba's teachings and the persona he projects cannot be said to be culturally inauthentic. The miracles he is so famous for performing are embedded in cultural assumptions about the activities of divine beings, and much of the symbolism he deploys in his self-presentation is drawn directly from Shaivite traditions. In this case, and probably in others, we find less cultural novelty than first meets the eye.

One feature of many of these middle-class movements, however, does indeed seem new, and this is their strong (and often evangelistic) transnationality. In many cases the internationalizing impulse arose initially from the desire for the domestic legitimization conferred by acceptance in the West. This has substantially changed, for these movements are now becoming more rooted in overseas Indian communities. The globalization of Hinduism can be seen as a specific response to a worldwide trend in which human and cultural flows across international frontiers are becoming ever less inhibited. It seems safe to say, therefore, that the study of modern Hinduism is increasingly going to be the study of global Hinduism.

Similar trends can be seen in Jainism. An important modern Jain movement is the Kanji Svami sect. It was founded in the 1930s by an apostate Sthanakvasi monk—Kanji Svami—who preached a form of Digambara Jainism that stressed soteriological concerns and de-emphasized ritualism and the role of initiated ascetics (Dundas 1992, 227-232). This formula has proven immensely successful among Jains, both in India and abroad. This latter point is crucial. Jain monks and nuns are not supposed to use mechanical modes of transportation, which historically has confined Jainism to the Indian subcontinent. Because of its strong lay-orientation, the Kanji Svami sect probably has a bright future within the large and growing Jain community in the Indian diaspora.

One of the most modernistic faces of Jainism in the post-independence period has been the Anuvrat movement (Ibid. 223-224). This movement was founded in 1949 by Acarya Tulsi, the energetic and charismatic ninth *ācārya* of the Terapanthis (a reformist Svetambara sect established in the eighteenth century). He began the movement as a means of promoting Jain values outside the Jain community, and from this base has grown a transnational educational, meditational, and proselytizing movement headquartered at Ladnun in Rajasthan. Among the movement's most important innovations is the development of a new class of Jain ascetics who are allowed to use artificial means of transportation, and are thus permitted to travel and proselytize abroad. As with the Kanji Svami sect, this may prove an augury of future success among Jains outside of India.

Indeed, future studies of modern Jainism would do well to focus on diaspora communities, for these communities are likely to continue to grow, and—precisely because of the ritual restrictions on travel by monks and nuns—are likely as well to become centers of innovation in Jainism. This is an ironic modern twist, considering the former subcontinental confinement of Jainism. The late Acharya Sushil Kumarji—a controversial and nontraditional ascetic who not only traveled by jet but also established an ashram in Blairstown,

NJ—may thus represent a future paradigm for religious leadership among Jains.

THE STATE

There is nothing new about the fusion of politics and religion in India. As it was idealized in classical Indian civilization, the state was ruled by the *kṣatriya* king whose exercise of sovereignty was legitimized by his sponsorship of sacrifice. The performer of the sacrifice was the *brāhmaṇ* priest, and thus *brāhmaṇ* and *kṣatriya*—priest and warrior/ king—were co-participants in the project of the state, which itself was seen as a political/ritual order. But the modern Indian state is another matter. It was intended to be a secular state, by which was meant that the Republic of India would neither favor nor promote any religion, or interfere with the practice of any religion. In recent years this commitment has come under challenge from Hindu nationalists, a challenge that has reflected in the 1992 destruction of the Babri Masjid in Ayodhya and the periodic electoral successes of Hindu nationalists.

This essay is not the place to trace the history of this challenge or to explore its current political implications; our interest, rather, is in the questions it has raised for students of Indian religions in particular, and students of any religions in general. These question are many. To what degree, for example, do new media lend themselves to the projects of any nationalism, including Hindu nationalism? In this connection it is certainly worth noting that the televised *Rāmāyaṇa* seems to have been an important ingredient in the symbolic run-up to the events at Ayodhya. Another crucial issue is how religious-nationalist world views have appropriated older ritual constructions of group identity, territoriality, and history (van der Veer 1994). And, finally, an issue that will certainly continue to provoke hot debate is whether, or to what degree, the categories employed by religious nationalists are colonial constructions or indigenous constructions. This question emerges with particular clarity in controversies concerning the status of that complex entity known as "Hinduism," but it also emerges in controversies outside India concerning the status of Buddhism, Islam, Judaism, Confucianism, Protestantism, and Catholicism.

The notion of Hinduism has for so long been taken for granted that it requires a certain effort of will to remind ourselves that its meaning is deeply problematical. When it became current in the nineteenth century, the English term "Hinduism" had no exact or established equivalent in Indic languages (Hawley 1991). The word

"Hindu" was originally used by Muslims as an ethnographic term, denoting the inhabitants of the lands beyond the Indus. Its marriage to the English morpheme "ism" was performed by orientalist scholars, who were looking for an Indic "religion." The resulting union was welcomed by nationalist intellectuals, who were looking for a culturally plausible response to the challenges of Christianity and colonial rule.

The reality obscured by this modern reification was, and remains, endlessly various and complex, a multi-leveled and diverse patchwork of sects and traditions. Of course it must be stressed that few would claim that Hinduism does not exist in any sense at all. The traditions so designated bear common traits such as the concept of rebirth, the linked idea of karmically-determined destiny, and the goal of the liberation of the soul from the cycle of transmigration, seen as a concatenation of karmic effects. An admiration for the world renouncer is also a feature of most of these traditions, as are some common modes of worship. These and other shared features may be said to underlie "family resemblances" common to many Hindu traditions, and in this sense "Hinduism" certainly exists. But when some nationalist politicians speak of a "Hindu majority," an abstraction becomes concrete, and the impression is lent that there actually is a united and monolithic Hindu community that has been cheated out of its "majority" rights by the Indian state.

"Hinduism" has been a word in common parlance and an entrenched analytical category in Indian studies (and indeed religious studies), but with the rise of what Romila Thapar (1985) calls "syndicated" Hinduism, it has also become an actual political force. This is a form of politically-organized Hinduism that embodies the idealization of Hinduism as a Semitic-style religion, a monolithic and timeless entity that is an authentic expression of Indian nationhood. Associated largely with the outlook and interests of the urban middle classes and rural rich, it overlaps to some degree, though not entirely, with the Hinduism promulgated by the acaryized movements mentioned earlier. And because of its relationship with globalized Hinduism, and also because of its dependence on international networks of material support, it is—despite its focus on India itself—highly transnational. This, indeed, may be the most "modern" Hinduism of all.

At this point theories about the unity or lack of unity of Hinduism acquire more than merely academic interest. All of sudden, one's conception of what Hinduism is becomes a political as well as a religious-historical or ethnographic idea. This being so—and regardless of one's political proclivities—the issue of the relationship between religion and group boundaries has to come to the fore. The revival of the issue of the status of "Hinduism" by Thapar (Ibid.), Frykenberg (1989), and others, thus emerges as an important contemporary turning point in the study of Indic religions. In this sense it can be said that the rise of "new" Hinduism has, by a circuitous route, generated searching questions about the true nature of "old" Hinduism.

Similar issues, though not as politically fraught, arise with respect to Jainism. Here, too, it is no longer as clear as it once seemed to be that "Jainism" is an unproblematic cultural reality. The emergence of "Jain" as a prominent category of self-identification seems to be a relatively recent development, and Jains commonly reported themselves as "Hindu" in early British censuses (Dundas 1992, 3-6). Many Jains worship at Hindu temples and participate in Hindu festivals. Jains and Hindus frequently intermarry. To this very day uncertainty persists about the boundaries between the Jain and Hindu worlds, and Jains must therefore continue to negotiate (as must Hindus) their religious and social identities. Currently the general tendency seems to be for Jains to stress the separateness of their identity, but this separation is not complete and probably never will be. As in the case of Hinduism, we see that the student of modern Jainism must return to basic questions regarding religious and group boundaries. The same questions of permeable, continually-redefined boundaries and of the unity or lack of unity of religions that have become apparent in the study of modern Hinduism and Jainism have become apparent elsewhere in the world. In India itself many of the same issues arise regarding groups such as the Sikhs and the neo-Buddhists. In Pakistan similar questions of boundaries arise regarding Sufis and Christian Protestants. In Israel they arise between different groups of Jews and between Jews and Palestinians. And among Christians in the United States they arise between Black and White congregations, affirming and non-affirming congregations, and evangelical and non-evangelical congregations. Insights obtained from the study of modern Hinduism and Jainism in India can and do shed light on the study of modern religions elsewhere in the world.

NOTE

1. In my opinion Bharati's study (1970) of the shared subculture of these movements has yet to be improved upon.

REFERENCES

Babb, Lawrence A. 1986. *Redemptive Encounters: Three Modern Styles in the Hindu Tradition.* Berkeley: Univ. of California Press.

Bharati, Agehananda. 1970. "The Hindu Renaissance and Its Apologetic Patterns." *The Journal of Asian Studies* 29: 267-287.

Das, Veena. 1980. "The Mythological Film and Its Framework of Meaning: An Analysis of Jai Santoshi Ma." *India International Centre Quarterly* 8: 43-56.

Dundas, Paul. 1992. *The Jains.* London: Routledge.

Erndl, Kathleen M. 1993. *Victory to the Mother: The Hindu Goddess of Northwest India in Myth, Ritual, and Symbol.* New York: Oxford Univ. Press.

Frykenberg, Robert E. 1989. "The Emergence of Modern 'Hinduism' as a Concept and as an Institution: A Reappraisal with Special Reference to South India." In *Hinduism Reconsidered,* ed. Gunther D. Sontheimer and Hermann Kulke. 29-49. New Delhi: Manohar.

Gombrich, Richard and Gananath Obeyesekere. 1988. *Buddhism Transformed: Religious Change in Sri Lanka.* Princeton: Princeton Univ. Press.

Hawley, John S. 1991. "Naming Hinduism." *The Wilson Quarterly* (summer): 20-34.

_____. 1995. "The Saints Subdued: Domestic Virtue and National Integration in Amar Chitra Katha." In *Media and the Transformation of Religion in South Asia,* ed. Lawrence A. Babb and Susan S. Wadley, 107-134. Philadelphia: Univ. of Pennsylvania Press.

Inglis, Stephen R. 1995. "Suitable for Framing: The Work of a Modern Master." In *Media and the Transformation of Religion in South Asia,* ed. Lawrence A. Babb and Susan S. Wadley, 51-75. Philadelphia: Univ. of Pennsylvania Press.

Juergensmeyer, Mark. 1991. *Radhasoami Reality: The Logic of a Modern Faith.* Princeton: Princeton Univ. Press.

Knipe, David M. 1991. *Hinduism: Experiments in the Sacred.* San Francisco: Harper.

Kurtz, Stanley N. 1992. *All the Mothers are One: Hindu India and the Cultural Reshaping of Psychoanalysis.* New York: Columbia Univ. Press.

Lutgendorf, Philip. 1995. "All in the (Raghu) Family: A Video Epic in Cultural Context." In *Media and the Transformation of Religion in South Asia,* ed. Lawrence A. Babb and Susan S. Wadley, 217-253. Philadelphia: Univ. of Pennsylvania Press.

Obeyesekere, Gananath. 1981. *Medusa's Hair: An Essay on Personal Symbols and Religious Experience.* Chicago: Univ. of Chicago Press.

Narayan, Kirin. 1989. *Storytellers, Saints, and Scoundrels: Folk Narrative in Hindu Religious Teaching.* Philadelphia: Univ. of Pennsylvania Press.

Pritchett, Frances W. 1995. "The World of Amar Chitra Katha." In *Media and the Transformation of Religion in South Asia,* ed. Lawrence A. Babb and Susan S. Wadley, 76-106. Philadelphia: Univ. of Pennsylvania Press.

Smith, H. Daniel. 1995. "Impact of 'God Posters' on Hindus and Their

Devotional Traditions." In *Media and the Transformation of Religion in South Asia*, ed. Lawrence A. Babb and Susan S. Wadley, 24-50. Philadelphia: Univ. of Pennsylvania Press.

Thapar, Romila. 1985. "Syndicated Moksha?" *Seminar* 313 (September): 14-22.

van der Veer, Peter. 1994. *Religious Nationalism: Hindus and Muslims in India.* Berkeley: Univ. of California Press.

Religious Studies:
South Indian Hinduism/
Buddhism/Jainism

PAULA RICHMAN AND
NORMAN CUTLER

During the last half-century scholars of Indian culture and religion have come to rethink, transform, and sometimes reject theories, categories, and methodologies formulated in the West. This has come about at least partially as a result of their study of south Indian religious texts and practices. We cannot highlight all of these innovations in this short essay; instead we chart some of the most fruitful trends in the study of south Indian religions. These include: 1. Balancing views derived from Sanskrit textual sources with others derived from oral and written texts in Tamil, Kannada, Malayalam, Telugu, and Tulu,[1] and acknowledging interactions among these different linguistic realms. 2. Recognizing ways in which religious and political/social practices are intertwined. 3. Attending to the ways religious texts are deployed in specific performative contexts. 4. Exploring ways in which gender shapes the diversity of religious beliefs and practices. 5. Charting interactions and congruencies between seemingly different religious traditions. In the essay that follows we selectively review scholarly projects that touch upon these themes from two somewhat different perspectives, perspectives that reflect differences in our training and in the trajectory of our academic careers. In the first part of the essay, Paula Richman examines ways in which scholarship on religion in south India has had an impact on the discipline of history of religions. In line with this orientation, her starting point is the work of Mircea Eliade. In the second part of the essay, Norman Cutler adopts a perspective governed more by areal interests, choosing as his starting point the well-known one-volume *A History of South India from Prehistoric Times to the Fall of Vijayanagar* by K.A. Nilakanta Sastri.

I. THE VIEW FROM THE HISTORY OF RELIGIONS

The field of study called "History of Religions" achieved scholarly momentum and prominence in the academy under the direction of Mircea Eliade, who came to teach at the University of Chicago in 1956.[2] In the early 1930s Eliade studied for three years with Surendranath Dasgupta, Principal of the Sanskrit College in Calcutta, who had published widely in the field of Indian philosophy, especially on yoga as a system of thought and form of religious practice.[3] In addition to living with Dasgupta's family in Bengal for some time, Eliade spent six months visiting ashrams. He later published the fruits of his research in *Yoga: Immortality and Freedom*,[4] a work that introduces themes he developed more fully in his later writings.

Eliade's forward to *Yoga* comments on some motivations and methodological concerns of his study of the "various cultural adventures" (xiii) of India. He notes that western philosophers have recently focused their energies on understanding "the *human condition*, and above all the temporality of the human being," a subject that, Eliade claims, India has applied itself to analyzing "with a rigor unknown elsewhere" (xvi). Eliade identifies the major sources for his book as Sanskrit and Pali texts, especially the major texts on yoga. Since Dasgupta had written a comprehensive study of classical yogic philosophy as expounded in Patanjali, Eliade concentrates on less-explored aspects of yoga, thus positioning himself as a mediator between western philosophers and the lesser-known yogic texts.

The organization of *Yoga* provides an explicit framework for examining aspects of the yogic tradition in India. Eliade structures the first chapters to set out what he takes to be the two defining aspects of yoga: a set of ideas about the nature of religious liberation (chap. 1) and the practices that lead to liberation (chap. 2). Each remaining chapter examines the beliefs and practices of a particular religious tradition, ranging from Brahmanism and Buddhism to tantrism, alchemy, and aboriginal practices.

Periodically, however, Eliade directs his attention to the meaning of selected religious symbols within the yogic tradition. Here he reveals his propensity to treat specific themes culled from Indian texts as manifestations of universal patterns that structure religious experience. For example, he sees the process of mythmaking as a way whereby human beings reenact archetypal actions of their deities in order to recreate "the sacred" and bring meaning to human actions that would otherwise be "profane." He also regards religious myth as a means by which humans can transcend history to return ritually to primordial time, *illo tempore,* before the dualities of human life existed.

Eliade's method of studying religion paid scant attention to particular ethnographic details of religion as practiced in specific locales. Symptomatically, Eliade identified the views he had constructed from Sanskrit and Pali texts, as well as from a somewhat idiosyncratic selection of secondary works on alchemy, Gopi Chand, and "obscure religious cults," as *the* Indian view of things. He proclaims, for example, "From the Upanishads onward, India has been seriously preoccupied with but one great problem—the structure of the human condition" (xvi).

Several times in *Yoga,* Eliade tells us that particular symbols are common to all "archaic" societies. For example, he says, " ... this nostalgia for the primordial completeness and bliss is what animates and informs all the techniques that lead to the *coincidentia oppositorum* in one's own being. We know that the same nostalgia, with an astonishing variety of symbolisms and techniques, is found almost everywhere in the archaic world" (272). Eliade assumes that certain recurrent motifs can be read into religious systems found in diverse geographical regions, because they all share a universal set of symbolic patterns. He also sets up a dichotomy between "archaic man" and "modern man." According to Eliade, the mythic life of "modern man" has become impoverished; so he needs to sate his spiritual hunger through "cultural adventure" among the 'Other.' For Eliade, the 'Other' is represented by, among others, the writings of Indian ascetics and mystics. Especially as Eliade moved from writing about particular yogic systems to writing about universal religious patterns, he did not feel the need to test his interpretation of the "true" meaning of religious symbols through fieldwork. [5] Fortunately, from the late 1950s onward, the increasing number of graduate students studying Indian religions coincided with initiatives to provide instruction in Indian regional languages and new anthropological studies of Indian civilization. Gradually, insights that emerged from examining religious texts in languages other than Sanskrit, fieldwork on the role of texts in cultural performance (rather than just in a written textual lineage), and a critical mass of people studying regionally-based Indian languages, made it possible for historians of religions to develop more sophisticated and less reductionistic approaches to the study of Indian religions. These translated into greater awareness of regional religious practices, including those of south India.

CULTURAL PERFORMANCES OF RELIGIOUS TEXTS

When, as part of one major initiative in anthropology, Milton Singer surveyed cultural performances in the city of Madras, his methodology and results challenged scholars in anthropology and religious studies to rethink their analytical categories. First, Singer emphasized the anthropological study of religion in cities, whereas previously anthropologists had conducted fieldwork almost exclusively in Indian villages. He also demonstrated that participant observation helped one to understand rituals as performed by ritual actors and received by an audience, rather than simply as described in texts.[6] Singer did not neglect texts, but, unlike his predecessors, he examined how religious texts are used in *situ* before theorizing about their significance and reach.

Singer interviewed a range of religious practitioners and respected their differing views of theological and ritual issues, rather than attempting to arrive at some "essential" or "representative" construct of religious meaning. He talked to people conversant with "classical" and "non-classical" Sanskrit texts (e.g., *pūjā* manuals and astrological guides), as well as to people familiar with regional texts in Tamil and Telugu. By including in his spectrum of cultural performances classical music and dance festivals run primarily by Smarta Brahmans, as well as religious discourses by non-Brahman Śaiva Siddhānta leaders, folk performers who travelled to the city from rural areas, Siddha medical healers, and non-Brahman teachers of temple dancers, Singer suggested some of the diversity of religious performance in south India.

Scholars who followed Singer investigated more fully both Sanskritic and non-Sanskritic texts in south India. Carman and Narayanan's *The Tamil Veda*, for example, explores a corpus of Tamil religious texts, attributed with the status and authority of the Sanskrit *Vedas*, and commentary on them in Manipravalam (a language with Tamil linguistic structure but a preponderance of Sanskrit vocabulary).[7] In *Poems to Siva*, Indira Peterson examines how her informant, an *ōtuvār* (non-Brahman singer), inflects the performance of Shaivite hymns through repetitions and rearrangements of the text, as well as through ornamentation of particular lines. Her work shows how recitation of a Tamil hymn entails subtle forms of interpretation.[8]

Other scholars developed and refined Singer's emphasis on ritual performance within the context of a specific religious configuration of beliefs, paying particular attention to how religious specialists use oral exegesis to frame verses from written texts. For example, Margaret Trawick describes how Themozhiyar, a traditional teacher of Śaiva Siddhānta philosophy, develops ideas about gender and personal identity through oral exegesis of a written text, and she also relates these ideas to her observations of interactions and expressions of love in Themozhiyars' own joint family.[9] Other insights about textual exegesis emerge in Stuart Blackburn's study of a puppet performance tradition located near the border of Kerala and Tamilnadu. The puppeteers frame selected verses from Kampan's twelfth century *Irāmavatāram*, an erudite and accomplished Tamil rendering of Ram's story, with extensive improvised commentary in colloquial Malayalam/Tamil. Blackburn shows how reciting Kampan's verses enables puppeteers to voice their own ethical concerns and convey practical wisdom.[10]

Building on the work of Singer, who studied folk performers who came to Madras for certain festivals and Madrasi virtuosos who went on tour in the countryside, other anthropologists began to chart the intriguing transformative cultural performances in south India that involved religiously sanctioned movement, namely pilgrimage. For example, E. Valentine Daniel's account of a pilgrimage to Lord Ayyapan's temple, in the hills of central Kerala, records how pilgrims' view of the nature of knowledge changed as they climbed to the hilltop shrine. He charts how the process of enduring hardship encourages pilgrims to turn away from mere analytic knowledge of the Ultimate, move through a state in which classifications of the Ultimate dissolve, and finally reach a state where they no longer perceive clear distinctions between self and other. Thus, the cultural performance of pilgrimage dramatically shapes the religious experiences of the participants.[11]

Emphasis on religious performance in south India has broadened the scope of the history of religions, lessening the discipline's dependence on Sanskrit texts. It has become clear that textual diversity derives, in part, from performers' selective emphasis on certain textual passages, how they enact that emphasis, and how exegesis emerges from, or frames, "root" texts. Attending to cultural performance as an expression of religious transformation also brings anthropologists closer to understanding the depth and range of religious experiences. Ritual takes different forms in, and en route to, specific temples and shrines in south India.

GENDER AND RELIGION IN SOUTH INDIA

Referring to Eliade's call for efforts to understand "religious man," Caroline Bynum wrote in 1986, "Until recently the field of comparative religion dealt with homo religiosus—the religious experience of man ... It is no longer possible to study religious practice or religious symbols without taking gender—that is, the cultural experience of being male or female—into account."[12] Most early scholarly studies discussing relationships between women and the Hindu tradition were based on selected Sanskrit *Dharma Śāstra* texts that legitimated women's subordination to their husbands and to other elders in the joint family. Although an earlier generation of scholars had paid some attention to Hindu myths about goddesses described as powerful vessels of *śakti*, the relationship between texts and women's religious practices remained unclear. Anthropologists of south India were among those who helped enlarge history of religions from a study of man's religious experiences to a study of the religious experiences of men and women.

Some scholars did so by looking at how women viewed the relationship between norms of female subordination and the exercise of women's power in the religious sphere. For example, Trawick recorded autobiographical accounts from women who had experienced intense suffering in their lives. These women believed that they had been granted extraordinary powers, either to bring fertility or to become the site of possession by a goddess who would help to heal illness, because they had subordinated their own desires for the sake of their family. Although they took for granted the ideology of female subordination to a certain extent, these women had also achieved autonomy as religious vessels of divine power.[13]

Exploring the relationship between subordination and women's power from another angle, Sheryl Daniel has demonstrated that, within a single village, more than one ideological explanation of power and hierarchy could be invoked by the same people, depending upon the context.[14] On certain occasions, villagers invoked the Chidambaram Temple, in which Lord Shiva exercises dominance over his wife Parvati, as a model for explaining the dynamics of marital life. On other occasions, however, the same villagers would invoke the Meenakshi Temple, in which Goddess Meenakshi reigns as the tutelary goddess of the city (with her husband's shrine being of lesser significance) as a model for how, in order for a family to flourish, the wife must take the upper hand in a marital context. Thus, the *dharmaśāstraic* view represents just one way that people explain experiences they encounter in daily life. To assume that the *dharmaśāstraic* view is the only form of explanation is an oversimplification.

In other writings, scholars have begun to explore women's religious traditions that provide space and times for women to voice their own concerns. For instance, Velcheru Narayana Rao's essay, "A

Ramayana of Their Own"[15] shows how songs of Telugu Brahman women tell the *Rāmāyaṇa* story in a way that omits references to warfare. Instead, they concentrate on episodes of greater interest to a female audience: Ram's mother's morning sickness and the pain of childbirth, Sita's dowry, Sita's relations with her mother-in-law, and her difficulties raising her two sons in Valmiki's ashram.

Even when men and women are each perceived as saints within a religious community, important differences occur in how their religious experiences are represented. For example, A.K. Ramanujan has shown that, according to south Indian hagiographical accounts, female saints tend to develop their devotion to a chosen deity early in their lives, need either to avoid marriage or to escape from its demands, and actively defy societal expectations. In contrast, male saints tend to experience a turning point in their adult lives at which time they embrace a life of devotion. Also, men do not find that devotion conflicts with spousal duties to the same extent that women do.[16]

Attention to gender differences, as well as to those linked to caste status,[17] provide new perspectives on the range of religious beliefs and actions in south India. The religious experience of men and women within the same community may differ; the way that religious experience comes to be expressed may differ; the way texts narrate those experiences may differ. Furthermore, people in the same community may, depending upon the context, invoke differing mythic explanations to describe religiously sanctioned behavior, such as marital duties. Recognition of these differences allows historians of religions to move beyond the Eliadean tendency to essentialize Indian religion.

SOUTH INDIA AS A MULTI-RELIGIOUS REGION

In her study of Muslims and Christians in south Indian society, Susan Bayly asserts, "There are no fixed or 'traditional' identities in south Asia."[18] Building on this premise, Bayly explains how various groups negotiated their own and others' diverse and changing social and religious identities in the eighteenth and nineteenth centuries. Recent research suggests that investigating how Buddhists, Jains, and Hindus negotiated their own and others' changing identities will help to understand the complex relations between the three groups. Earlier studies tend to view Jain and Buddhist traditions either as movements that spring up in times of "social crisis," or as "heterodox" intrusions into the "bastion" of Hindu orthodoxy; but recent scholarship shows that it is more useful to view the boundaries between the multiple south Indian religious traditions as relatively permeable.

Some of the oldest extant religious and ethical texts portray relatively fluid interchanges between members of different religious communities. Consider, for example, the Tamil "twin epics," *Cilappatikāram* (c. 5th century CE) and *Maṇimēkalai* (c. 6th century CE). Recent scholarship has noted that *Cilappatikāram* portrays a Jain nun as the spiritual mentor to the heroine, who eventually is deified as a goddess who possesses great powers.[19] *Maṇimēkalai*'s Buddhist affiliation is unmistakable. Its heroine renounces her hereditary occupation in order to become a Buddhist nun; the text contains hymns of praise addressed to the Buddha; and it expounds highly technical Buddhist philosophy. Yet, in so doing, the text's author draws upon the classical Tamil poetic tradition, a shared legacy for poets of multiple religious affiliations.[20] As additional evidence of the permeability of religious categories, consider the Kannada version of the *Rāmāyaṇa* by Pampa (12th century CE), who reinterpreted the story of Ram from a Jain point of view while receiving the patronage of a Hindu monarch.[21]

Although Buddhism has all but died out in south India, a community of Jains is active, especially in northern Karnataka.[22] Only recently, however, have scholars of Indian religions moved away from viewing Jainism as a self-contained religious tradition and towards a perspective that sees Jains as involved in debate and dialogue with members of other religious groups. John Cort's edited volume *Open Boundaries: Jains in Indian History and Culture,* provides insights into interactions among Jains, Hindus, and Buddhists in south India. For example, Leslie Orr demonstrates how both Jain and Hindu women played important roles as cultural patrons in medieval Tamilnadu; Richard Davis develops the idea of similarities and mutual influence between Jain and Hindu traditions; while Indira Peterson analyzes how Tamil Shaivite saints cast Jains as the 'Other' against which they constructed a Tamil Shaivite identity.[23]

Recent studies of the construction of south Indian identities have shown how an agenda that rejects Hindu Brahmanical authority and glorifies ancient Tamil culture has revived interest in Buddhist and Jain works. For instance, Norman Cutler has shown how the putative Jain authorship of *Tirukkuṟaḷ* and the non-sectarian quality of its moral teachings have contributed to this text's popularity as an icon of a Dravidian cultural tradition that owes little to Brahmanical texts.[24] Similarly, some south Indians have sought intellectual roots in ancient Buddhism.[25]

Thus, scholars have begun to study the region of south India, once viewed stereotypically as the "seat of Hindu orthodoxy," as a region of multiple religious traditions, each contributing to regional religiosity in its own way. Most recently, as scholars have begun to criticize the notion of India as a unified "nation," the status of south India as a region has come under closer scrutiny. A new journal, *South India Studies*, proclaims in its statement of goals, "The agenda of rethinking the region must engage, first and foremost, in the crucial task of widening and deepening knowledge of the region ... In order to rethink the region, scholars must transgress the borders of disciplines to develop new languages that will adequately represent the histories and aspirations of the region."[26] In the last fifty years the study of south Indian religiosity has merged insights from textual studies, literature, anthropology, and gender studies in order to deepen the knowledge of Indian religions and the region of south India.

II. THE VIEW FROM SOUTH INDIAN STUDIES

Shortly after India's independence, K.A. Nilakanta Sastri, under the title *A History of South India from Prehistoric Times to the Fall of Vijayanagar*, published "a brief general survey of the ancient history of South India to the middle of the seventeenth century A.D." that would "give a general idea of the main lines of movement in the history of politics and culture" (Nilakanta Sastri 1955, 1).[27] At that time south India, defined by Sastri as "all the land lying south of the Vindhyas" (1), received little attention in the available general histories of India. Once Sastri's volume filled this void, it remained the preeminent authority on the history and culture of south India at least well into the 1970s. Like other histories of India written around the same time, Sastri's work is largely devoted to a chronological account of the rise and fall of dynasties that wielded political power in the region, followed by several chapters devoted respectively to Social and Economic Conditions, Literature, Religion and Philosophy, and Art and Architecture. In these latter chapters Sastri sketches "the social and economic conditions that prevailed in South India from the sixth to the seventeenth centuries A.D.," and traces in outline "the principal movements of culture in the spheres of literature, religion, and art" (313).

In his chapter on Religion and Philosophy, Sastri maps the south Indian religious landscape according to distinctions between Hindu, Buddhist, Jain, and other "first-order" religious traditions, with the

greatest space devoted to Hinduism. Hinduism, in turn, is represented
as a host of sects, most of which are contained within the rubrics of
Vaishnavism and Shaivism. Sastri is not very explicit about the
sources of his narrative of south Indian religious life, but he treats
the literatures of the various south Indian "religious movements" in
the preceding chapter on Literature. His chapter on Literature is
organized in five sections devoted respectively to Sanskrit, Tamil,
Kannada, Telugu, and Malayalam. In words that his critics are fond
of quoting,[28] Sastri deems Sanskrit to be "the magic wand whose
touch alone raised each of the Dravidian languages from the level
of a patois to that of a literary idiom" (340). Leaving aside Sastri's
often contested propensity to emphasize Sanskrit's primacy in south
Indian culture, suffice it to say that Sastri's treatment of south Indian
literature (religious literature being no exception) remains divided
into discrete, language-specific compartments, despite his own
aknowledgement that there was interaction not only between Sanskrit
and the Dravidian languages but also among the Dravidian languages
themselves.

George Hart, in his book *The Poems of Ancient Tamil*, argues that
Sastri exaggerates the degree to which early Tamil literature and
institutions were influenced by northern/Sanskritic prototypes.[29]
Hart is primarily concerned with the texts and cultural milieu of the
earliest Tamil poems, usually dated around the first through third
centuries CE, a period that predates Sastri's narrative of south
Indian religion. To the relatively small degree that Sastri attends to
Hart's period, Sastri views religious beliefs and practices as a composite
of Aryan and pre-Aryan elements and gives precedence to the
former.

Like Sastri, Hart reads the corpus of early Tamil poems, which
are most immediately the creations of an aesthetic sensibility, as
historical documents (in a broad sense), but he attempts a much
"deeper" reading of the evidence. While Sastri is primarily concerned
with finding evidence for empirically observable practices, Hart
attempts to elicit from the poems an indigenous conceptualization
of "the sacred." Hart's reading of the poems highlights the role of
the sacred in early Tamil culture that stands in stark contrast to
northern, Sanskritic conceptions. Hart explains:

for the Tamils, the sacred was primarily manifested not through a number
of discrete deities, each of which had an extensive mythology associated
with it, as in North India, but rather through a power thought to inhere in
certain objects and persons and to be activated in certain situations.
Moreover, this *ananku*, as the Tamils called it, was not a force that worked

for human welfare, but rather was capricious and potentially malevolent; therefore it had to be carefully controlled lest, like fire, it bring destruction. (Hart 1975, 81)

In Hart's reconstruction of an early Tamil religious milieu, kings, women, and members of certain low castes are especially important by virtue of their special relationship to sacred power.

Hart's work on ancient Tamil poetry departs from the epistemological and methodological presuppositions of an earlier generation of scholars in ways that foreshadow some of the most significant recent scholarship concerned with south Indian religion. By identifying the king as one of the most important loci of "the sacred," Hart implicitly calls into question arbitrary boundaries, not always compatible with the south Indian data, between the domains of "religion" and "politics." Further, while Hart is clearly partisan to Tamil, he consults both Tamil and Sanskrit sources in order to explore the interaction of Tamil and Sanskrit literary conventions, unlike Sastri who pays mere lip service to these interactions. In pursuit of his aim to demonstrate that, contrary to the conventional wisdom (in 1975), many literary conventions found in Sanskrit poetry probably originated in Old Tamil poetry, Hart initiates a move away from the prevailing tendency among scholars to treat the literatures of different South Asian languages as essentially autonomous domains.

Crossing linguistic boundaries is crucial to Friedhelm Hardy's methodology in his *Viraha-Bhakti: The Early History of Krsna Devotion in South India,* a monumental study of the genesis of emotional Krishna *bhakti.*[30] Axiomatic to Hardy's study is the distinction between intellectual *bhakti* as documented in, for example, the *Bhagavad Gītā,* and emotional *bhakti* as expressed for the first time in Sanskrit in the *Bhāgavata Purāṇa.* He observes that for scholars of an earlier generation, who approached the study of South Asian religion almost exclusively through Sanskrit texts, the "sudden" appearance of a new kind of emotional *bhakti* in the *Bhāgavata Purāṇa* remained a mystery. The missing link, Hardy argues, is to be found in the Tamil poetry of the *āḻvārs.*

In the late 1990s it may not come as a revelation that many South Asian literary and religious cultures are multilingual and cannot be fully understood if this basic truth is not addressed. Increasingly Sanskritists are acknowledging that the authors of Sanskrit texts were also speakers of India's regional languages and that their regional linguistic/cultural identities and their participation in the world of Sanskrit arts and letters were not mutually exclusive. Hardy's

Viraha-Bhakti is important, among other reasons, for overcoming the limitations imposed by a monolingual perspective in a study of depth and philological rigor.

While Hardy's project in *Viraha-Bhakti* helps dismantle the artificial linguistic boundaries that have tended to limit scholarly perspectives on south Indian religion, the category of "religion" as a domain of human thought and experience remains for the most part unproblematized in his work. For instance, he categorizes the Sanskrit, Prakrit, and Apabhramsa sources that contribute to the mythological blueprint for emotional Krishna *bhakti* as secular, epic, and puranic. Judging from the kind of texts and subject matter Hardy incorporates into his project, his sense of the category "religion" and its contents is not very different from Nilakanta Sastri's. That is to say, most of the texts Hardy examines could be comfortably situated in Sastri's chapter devoted to "Religion and Philosophy," and most of the others, such as *kāvya* poetry, Hardy labels "secular."

In contrast, the works of scholars such as Arjun Appadurai, David Shulman, V. Narayana Rao, and Joanne Punzo Waghorne, to name just a few, implicitly challenge the notion that in the south Indian context one can identify a religious domain that is distinct from other domains of human activity and experience. The problematic status of the boundary between religion and politics in particular is highlighted in recent studies that focus on ideologies and practices centered on south Indian kings and temples.

In *Worship and Conflict Under Colonial Rule*,[31] Arjun Appadurai raises the question, "What is the relationship between the economic and political domains of South Asian society and South Asian ideas concerning such things as salvation, pollution, ritual, and worship?" He further points out that "most anthropologists and sociologists working on South Asia have approached this issue in terms of (culturally inappropriate) dualistic categories" including the dualism of secular vs. sacred (Appadurai 1981, 6). Appadurai argues that in south India the Hindu temple is a useful locus from which to consider this and other related issues (8), and he notes the absence in the extant scholarly literature of a coherent analysis "of the temple *as such*, as a total functioning institution viewed from the 'inside'." (9)

Appadurai offers a view of the temple as an institution closely imbricated with kingship and social relations that is situated in a culture that does not make a clear separation between the economic/political domain and the religious/cultural domain (8). Rather than uncritically assigning the Hindu temple to the domain of "religion" and kingship to the domain of "politics," Appadurai describes a set of institutional structures and practices that resist this sort of categorization. Not only does he characterize the deity enshrined in the Hindu temple as a paradigmatic sovereign, he goes on to describe ways in which the human and the divine sovereign each require the other to fulfill his role in the cultural system:

In purely cultural terms ... we can see in the relationship of human kings to temple deities in South India an elegant and symbiotic division of sovereignty. The sovereign deity is the paradigm of royal authority. By serving the deity ... and by protecting the redistribution process of the temple, human kings share in this paradigmatic royalty. By being the greatest servant of the sovereign deity, the human king sustains and displays his rule over men. (51)

Appadurai's primary sources are inscriptions, administrative records, and court cases. The importance of kingship for the study of "religion" in south India is also evident in several studies that are based on sources of a more "literary" nature. In *The King and the Clown in South Indian Myth and Poetry*,[32] David Shulman utilizes a great number and variety of sources, primarily in Tamil and Sanskrit, to elicit images of medieval south Indian kingship. By unearthing images of kingship found in these sources, Shulman seeks to unearth the "inner reality, the linkages, the motivations" (Shulman 1985, 24) that underlie the surface features of the south Indian state as described by historians such as Burton Stein.

The question arises, in what way is Shulman's study of medieval south Indian kingship "from the inside" relevant to the study of religion, if indeed it is possible to continue to speak of religion in south India at this time as a distinctive area of inquiry? In the kingdom of the imperial Cholas, a king's right to rule is legitimated both by endowing Brahmans, as in earlier times, and, more prominently, by endowing temples and their deities. Even more relevant to Shulman's interests, "nature's struggle and the internal dynamic of kingship are ... seen as homologous. A necessary drive toward containment within highly ordered boundaries is pitted against the urge to make contact with life's forces in their raw, unlimited state" (54). Similarly, Shulman observes:

the king's exilic identity, expressed in shadow and disguise, is in no way less authentic than his normally "ordered" self; in fact it is the latter ... that is constituted by a series of royal masks, while in exile the king is brought into contact with an area of experience perhaps ultimately *more* "real" than any prescribed role. (218)

If "religion" retains meaning as an area of inquiry, it surely must include such attempts to make contact with a transcendent reality.

In collaboration with V. Narayana Rao and Sanjay Subramanyam, Shulman continues his exploration of south Indian kingship in *Symbols of Substance: Court and State in Nayaka Period Tamilnadu.*[33] Pooling their linguistic competencies, the authors make use of primary sources in Tamil, Telugu, and Sanskrit including courtly dramas, *kāvya* texts, chronicles, learned literature, and "minor" works. If *The King and the Clown* exposes the underbelly of the iconic (read "dharmic") image of kingship that prevailed in south India during the reign of the imperial Cholas (late 9th-12th centuries CE), *Symbols of Substance* shows how this iconic image had changed by the time of Nayak rule based in Madurai, Tanjavur, and Senji (approximately mid-16th - late 17th centuries CE).

The authors of *Symbols of Substance* emphasize that during the period of Nayak rule the values of *bhoga* ("enjoyment") largely overshadow the values of dharma in the dominant image of kingship. This transformation involves a much more explicit attribution of divinity to the king, further conflating the domains of religion and politics. Evidence for the divinization of the king appears in a number of forms, such as a Telugu literary genre called *abhyudayamu*, which takes as its subject a day in the life of the king. " ... the abhyudayamu genre is articulated in a *pūjā* mode of worship, with the king cast as the divine subject, his daily routine a framework of ritualized revelation" (59). Readers of this study encounter a large body of literary evidence that iterates the theme of king/god identity. The authors of *Symbols of Substance* argue that if the spheres of religion and polity were symbiotically interconnected in the cultural system that prevailed under the Cholas, the spheres should also be interconnected under the cultural system of the Nayaks.

The authors of *Symbols of Substance* also make a related methodological point. They question the linear logic of much Indian historical writing whereby "periods of economic dislocation and political fragmentation are *simultaneously* seen as characterized by cultural crisis and decline" (313). Rao, Shulman, and Subramanyam offer the Nayak period as a counter example to this conventional wisdom; here we find a period characterized by a certain precariousness in developing economic and political structures accompanied by movement, innovation, and rapid growth in the cultural sphere (314). More fundamentally, they question "the dualism inherent in the very distinction between 'material' and 'cultural' ... " They tell us, "in part, our study has aimed at showing the mutual constitutive power of domains that we conventionally keep separate, to little purpose—say, politics and poetics, or money and metaphysics" (313).

This brings us to the most recently published work treated in this survey, Joanne Punzo Waghorne's *The Raja's Magic Clothes: Re-Visioning Kingship and Divinity in England's India.*[34] Waghorne's work reiterates and extends a major organizing theme for this essay: The disruption of methodologies and perspectives founded on fixed linguistic and disciplinary boundaries. Waghorne focuses on the "little kingdom" of Pudukkottai, one of the princely states during the days of the British raj, located in present-day Tamilnadu. She calls her study an "ethno-theology," that is to say, a study of the nature of divinity within a particular historical moment (Waghorne 1994, 5).[35]

As a self-identified historian of religions, Waghorne argues that the nature of kingship/divinity in Pudukkottai poses a serious challenge to long-held understandings of Indian religiosity by western scholars. She traces these understandings to 19th century orientalist scholarship with its tendency to privilege the Advaita Vedānta tradition and to locate "true" Indian religion in the inner realm of the spiritual in stark opposition to the outer realm of the material. Waghorne argues that the opposition between inner-spiritual and outer-material is ill-suited to her material. Religiosity in Pudukkottai more appropriately belongs to "the world of the iconic—the location of beingness not in the essence of things but in their *pūrṇā*, their fullness, their overflow into image, into form that exists in full view of the human imagination" (255). Waghorne feels that largely through the influence of Victorian scholars like Max Müller and James Frazer, the comparative study of religion became blinded to this kind of sacredness, much to its own loss, and she offers her own work as a contribution to a much-needed corrective.

Waghorne also parts ways with an earlier generation of scholars in her choice of source material. She contends that "historians of religions have too long looked only at words" (11). Although Waghorne's primary sources include archival records, temple histories, songs of praise for the king, and other texts made from words, she places particular emphasis on visual texts such as photographs and paintings of members of the Pudukkottai royal family, the Pudukkottai court in durbar, and architectural details of the Pudukkottai palace. Perhaps exaggerating a little, she claims that her study "depends primarily on an analysis of images, not of concepts. The argument is created not through a progression of ideas but in a chronological progression of portraits and photographs, a play of images" (12). If other work discussed in this essay is noteworthy for crossing linguistic boundaries, Waghorne's work might be said to go the further step of crossing the boundary between verbal and visual media.[36]

SUMMING UP

Using as a baseline the scholarship of Eliade and Nilakanta Sastri, this relatively brief and necessarily selective review of scholarship on south Indian religion reveals that this area of inquiry has undergone some profound changes during the last fifty years. Taking a long view of these changes, we find two trends that have affected scholars' understanding of both the object and the method of their inquiry. On the one hand, we find a movement away from reductionist, homogenized representations of Indian religion, based, for the most part, on decontextualized readings of Sanskrit texts. Scholars have addressed this distortion caused by reductionism by being sensitive to the ways in which language, region, gender, and social environment contribute to religious experience. On the other hand, we find a questioning of the disciplinary boundaries and phenomenological categories that until recently have prevailed in the western academy. Perhaps most striking in this regard is how scholarly engagement with India in general and with south India in particular has contributed to the demise of such dualisms as 'secular and sacred,' and 'material and spiritual.' This trend also has resulted in a blurring of perceived boundaries between, for example, the domains of religion and politics, or even between "different" religious traditions. In conjunction, these trends have resulted in a radical reconsideration of the nature of religious experience. Instead of being seen as a domain unto itself, "religion" has come to be seen as intertwined with other forms of cultural expression. In this sense recent studies of south Indian religion contribute to the ongoing remaking of the humanities, a remaking that has implications for how "religion," politics, and even "different" religious traditions are viewed in the West by westerners.

NOTES

1. We do not cover scholarship concerned with Tulu sources in this essay, but we refer the reader to Peter Claus's noteworthy contributions in this area.
2. Davis, Richard H. 1985. *South Asia at Chicago*, Chicago: Committee on Southern Asian Studies, University of Chicago. 10-11.

3. In addition to his five-volume history of Indian philosophy, Surendranath Dasgupta also published *The Study of Patanjali*. 1920. Calcutta: Univ. of Calcutta, and *Yoga as Philosophy and Religion*. 1924. London: Kegan, Paul, Trench, Trubner and Co. among other works.

4. Mircea Eliade's *Yoga: Immortality and Freedom* (henceforth abbreviated as *Yoga*) 1958. Princeton: Princeton Univ. Press. It was originally published in French in 1954. Page numbers for citations will immediately follow quotations.

5. Eliade's tendency to divide cultures into "archaic" and "modern" becomes particularly pronounced in later books such as *Myth and Reality* (1963. New York: Harper and Row). Increasingly he deals with India only as one of a number of places where common symbols reappear, and concentrates, as he puts it in *Cosmos and History: The Myth of the Eternal Return* (1959. New York: Harper Torchbooks), on the "universal patterns" that form part of his "philosophy of history" (xi). Furthermore, in addition to overgeneralizing in his textual analysis, Eliade's "fieldwork methodology" leaves much to be desired in terms of cultural and ethical sensitivity. If we accept his account of his stay in the home of his Indian guru, he had sexual relations with his guru's daughter and then wrote a sensationalized novel based on this episode. See Mircea Eliade, *Bengal Nights* (French, 1950) and the response by the guru's daughter, Maitreyi Devi, *It Does Not Die* (Bengali, 1974). Both works were republished in English. 1995. Chicago: Univ. of Chicago Press.

6. Milton Singer. 1972. *When a Great Tradition Modernizes: An Anthropological Approach to Indian Civilization*. New York: Praeger. Milton Singer's work on cultural performances grew out of a project on the "Comparative Study of Civilizations" initiated by Robert Redfield. V. Raghavan greatly influenced Singer's research trajectory in Madras.

7. Carman, John and Vasudha Narayanan. 1989. *The Tamil Veda: Pillan's Interpretation of the Tiruvaymoli*. Chicago: Univ. of Chicago Press.

8. Peterson, Indira Viswanathan. 1989. *Poems to Siva: The Hymns of the Tamil Saints*. Princeton: Princeton Univ. Press. 59-75.

9. Trawick, Margaret. 1990. *Notes on Love in a Tamil Family*. Berkeley: Univ. of California Press.

10. Blackburn, Stuart. 1996. *Inside the Drama-House: Rama Stories and Shadow Puppets in South India*. Berkeley: Univ. of California Press.

11. Daniel, E. Valentine. 1984. *Fluid Signs: Being a Person the Tamil Way*. Berkeley: Univ. of California Press. Chap. 7.

12. Bynum, Caroline, Stevan Harrell, and Paula Richman, eds. 1986. *Gender and Religion: On the Complexity of Symbols*. Boston: Beacon Press. 1-2.

13. Egnor, Margaret (nee Trawick). 1980. "On the Meaning of Sakti to Women in Tamil Nadu." In *The Powers of Tamil Women*, ed. Susan S. Wadley, 1-34. Syracuse: South Asian Series no. 6, Foreign and Comparative Studies Program, Maxwell School, Syracuse University.

14. Sheryl B. Daniel, "Marriage in Tamil Culture: The Problem of Conflicting 'Models'." In *The Powers of Tamil Women,* ed. Susan S. Wadley, 61-91. Ibid. The articles by Egnor and Daniel were first presented on the panel "Conceptions of Woman and Power in Tamil Culture" at the annual meeting of The Association for Asian Studies in 1978.

15. Narayana Rao, Velcheru. 1991. "A Ramayana of Their Own: Women's Oral Tradition in Telugu." In *Many Ramayanas: The Diversity of a Narrative Tradition in South Asia,* ed. Paula Richman. 114-136. Berkeley: Univ. of California Press and 1993. New Delhi: Oxford Univ. Press.

16. Ramanujan, A.K. 1982. "On Women Saints." In *The Divine Consort: Radha and the Goddesses of India,* ed. John S. Hawley and Donna Wulff, 316-324 and 365-367. Berkeley: Berkeley Religious Studies Series, Graduate Theological Union.

17. Other essays in this volume will deal more specifically with the interactions between caste identities and religious identities.

18. Bayly, Susan. 1989. *Saints, Goddesses, and Kings: Muslims and Christians in South Indian Society, 1700-1900.* Cambridge: Cambridge Univ. Press. 2.

19. See R. Parthasarathy. 1993. *The Cilappatikaram of Illanko Atikal: An Epic of South India.* New York: Columbia Univ. Press. 332-337. See also Sally Noble. 1990. *The Tamil Story of the Anklet: Classical and Contemporary Tellings.* Unpublished doctoral dissertation, University of Chicago.

20. See, for example, Paula Richman. 1988. *Women, Branch Stories, and Religious Rhetoric in a Tamil Buddhist Text.* Syracuse: South Asian Series no. 12, Foreign and Comparative Studies Program, Maxwell School, Syracuse University, chaps. 4 and 6; Paula Richman. 1992. "Gender and Persuasion: The Portrayal of Beauty, Anguish, and Nurturance in an Account of a Tamil Nun." In *Buddhism, Sexuality, and Gender,* ed. José Ignacio Cabezón, 111-136. Albany: State Univ. of New York Press; and David Shulman. 1996. "Cattanar's Dream Book." In *Buddhism and Manimekalai,* ed. Peter Schalk. Uppsala: History of Religions, Uppsala University.

21. See Lewis Rice, ed. 1882. *The Pampa Ramayana or Ramachandra Charita Purana of Abhinava Pampa, An Ancient Jain Epic in the Kannada Language.* Bangalore: Mysore Government Press.

22. See Michael Carrithers and Caroline Humphrey, eds. 1991. *The Assembly of Listeners: Jains in Society.* Cambridge: Cambridge Univ. Press. 12.

23. See Leslie C. Orr. 1997. "Jain and Hindu 'Religious Women' in Early Medieval Tamilnadu," Richard H. Davis. "The Story of the Missing Jains: Retelling the Saiva-Jain Encounter in Medieval South India," Indira Peterson, "Sramanas against the Tamil Way: Jains and Buddhists in the Hymns of the Tamil Saiva Saints." In *Open Boundaries: Jains in Indian History and Culture,* ed. John E. Cort. Albany: State University of New York Press.

24. See Norman Cutler. 1984. "The Fish-eyed Goddess Meets the Movie Star: An Eyewitness Account of the Fifth International Tamil Conference." In *Cultural Policy in India,* ed. Lloyd I. Rudolph, 105-125. Delhi: Chanakya.

25. See the articles in Section VII (Southern Languages) of *Buddhist Themes in Modern Indian Literature,* ed. Shu Hikosaka and G. John Samuel. 1992. Madras: Institute of Asian Studies.

26. *South Indian Studies,* 1 (January-June 1996): iii.

27. Nilakanta Sastri, K.A. 1966 (3rd edition). *A History of South India from Prehistoric Times to the Fall of Vijayanagar.* London: Oxford Univ. Press (1st ed., 1955).

28. For example, see George L. Hart, III. 1975. *The Poems of Ancient Tamil: Their Milieu and Their Sanskrit Counterparts.* Berkeley: Univ. of California Press, 10.

29. Ibid., 10-12.

30. Hardy, Friedhelm. 1983. *Viraha-Bhakti: The Early History of Krsna Devotion in South India.* Delhi: Oxford Univ. Press.

31. Appadurai, Arjun. 1981. *Worship and Conflict under Colonial Rule: A South Indian Case.* Cambridge: Cambridge Univ. Press.

32. Shulman, David. 1985. *The King and the Clown in South Indian Myth and Poetry.* Princeton: Princeton Univ. Press.

33. Narayana Rao, Velcheru, David Shulman, and Sanjay Subrahmanyam. 1992. *Symbols of Substance: Court and State in Nayaka Period Tamilnadu.* Delhi: Oxford Univ. Press.

34. Waghorne, Joanne Punzo. 1994. *The Raja's Magic Clothes: Re-visioning Kingship and Divinity in England's India.* University Park, PA: Pennsylvania State Univ. Press.

35. In an interesting parallelism, Appadurai describes his methodological approach as "ethnohistorical."

36. This is not to say that Waghorne is the only scholar treated in this essay who makes use of visual resources. Hardy, Shulman, and Narayana Rao all refer to visual documents. However, visual documentation plays a much more prominent role in Waghorne's work.

Religious Studies:
Theories of Comparison[1]

JOSÉ IGNACIO CABEZÓN

Asia in general, and India in particular, have traditionally served for the western scholar principally as sources of data. Both social scientists and scholars of the humanities have tended to look to the subcontinent to provide them with the information that they then expose to the various methodologies of western critical scholarship. Hence, India provides western scholars with facts, but the West furnishes the theory. Of course, there are exceptions to the rule. Some scholars have consciously drawn on Asian material for theoretical insights (Campany 1992), and even those who have not cannot help but be theoretically influenced by the material (the data) that they study. But as a rule western scholars have tended, whether consciously or not, to eschew Indian thought—at least classical Indian thought—as a source of theoretical insight. This essay should be viewed as a challenge to this trend. Its goal is to suggest that classical Indian philosophical speculation concerning comparison (*upamāna*) is valuable in the more general methodological task of formulating theories of cross-cultural comparison.

Most Buddhologists/Tibetologists (like myself) have received a good deal of background in Sanskrit and Indian studies as part of their training. This is natural, given the fact that India is the birthplace of Buddhism, and that Indian Buddhism has exerted such a strong influence on other Asian Buddhist countries like Tibet. This training has justifiably been seen as a necessary prerequisite—a kind of essential grounding—to serious scholarship in the field of Buddhist studies (regardless of geographical area of specialization). Indian history and philosophy have, however, rarely been utilized by Buddhologists and Tibetologists apart from their direct application to their respective field of study, e.g., contextualizing a particular Buddhist movement or school, describing Buddhists' adversaries, and so forth. Having found positions in academic (especially religious studies) departments, however, my experience has been that many of us have extended our interest in the Indian texts over and above that required by our discipline. This has certainly been true in my case.

This renewed interest in the Indian sources has, at least initially, been fueled by a number of what might be termed academic sociological factors.[2] Buddhologists and Tibetologists employed in departments of religious studies and theology (it seems as though the majority of us are) have found ourselves responsible for India, and occasionally for all of Asia (Cabezón 1995). For those of us whose interests lie outside of India proper, this has meant broadening the scope of our teaching to include the subcontinent. For some, this state of affairs has been an unwelcomed intrusion on more deeply focused research. For most of us, however, the obligation to cover India as part of our teaching responsibilities has added new dimensions to our research. This obligation has led, on one hand, to an interest in the classical Indian philosophical tradition as a system of thought deserving attention in its own right and, on the other hand, to an interest in comparative issues. How, for example, does the Indian philosophical tradition relate to other systems of thought?

In my own case, this obligation to cover India has also led to an exploration of questions concerning the very nature of the comparative enterprise. What does it mean to compare two things? What kind of knowledge is the knowledge born from comparison? Are there criteria for judging comparisons? Initially, my research into this more theoretical field of inquiry led me to read the classical and contemporary western literature on comparison in disciplines as diverse as comparative philosophy/religion, anthropology, comparative literature, and cross-cultural psychology. At a certain point, however, I realized that many of the issues addressed in the western sources were also issues that had been of concern to classical Indian philosophers. It was at this point that I recognized that India had a great deal to offer those of us concerned with the methodological questions regarding the nature of cross-cultural comparison as a form of knowledge. It is obviously beyond the scope of this essay to cover this very complex topic in any great detail. It is, nonetheless, my hope that the remarks that follow will suggest ways in which classical Indian philosophical thought can be mined for theoretical insight, and in this way will help dispel the notion that the Euro-American academy is the sole purveyor of theoretical truth. This essay, then, is part of a more general study whose goal it is to shed light on the nature and function of comparison itself. The present paper is part of a larger study on Indian theories of comparison. Although my original intention was to cover the theories of comparison of the three major Indian philosophical schools that treat the issue (Nyāya, Mīmāṃsā, and Advaita), constraints of space force me to focus on only one of these, the Nyāya.

Indian texts typically treat the issue of comparison (*upamāna*) as an epistemological one. Aside from the most basic questions concerning the nature and function of comparison, the Indian sources are preoccupied with questions such as the following: Is *upamāna* a distinct way of knowing (*pramāṇa*) different from other ways of knowing? If so, how does it differ from valid testimony (*śabda*), from perception (*pratyakṣa*), and from inference (*anumāna*)? Is comparative knowledge useful, and if so to what use can it be put? This epistemological premise does not imply that ontological issues do not play a part in the analysis of comparison. For example, the question of where similarity resides is one that is sometimes found in the discussion. But, overall, speculation concerning comparison is epistemological in tone. This, in itself, is interesting.

Upamāna, variously translated as "comparison" or "analogy,"[3] is one of the *pramāṇas* or "methods of knowledge" of classical Indian philosophy. Though rejected as a separate method of knowing by some schools, who categorize it variously as either perception,[4] a form of valid testimony,[5] or, in some instances, a kind of inference,[6] it came to be accepted as a distinct *pramāṇa* by the Nyāya, Mīmāṃsā, and Advaita schools. Mentioned in some early medical works,[7] it becomes the object of sophisticated philosophical speculation for the first time in the *Nyāya Sūtras* (2nd-3rd century CE?). There *upamāna* is defined as "that which establishes for one knowledge of something through its similarity to something else that is already known to one."[8] The example given is the classical one in which a person, having heard from a forester that a wild cow (*gavaya*) is like a cow (*go*), goes to the forest and sees an actual wild cow. The person remembers having heard of such a thing in the past and arrives at the conclusion that the animal now being seen is a wild cow, and names it as such. This is the *upamiti*, the knowledge derived from comparison. Vātsyāyana, commenting on this verse in the *Nyāya Sūtras* (Sastri 1976, 23-24), tells us that comparison functions to give one knowledge of the relationship between a word ("wild cow") and the object denoted by it (the wild cow actually being perceived for the first time).[9] According to this interpretation, then, the comparative method (*upamāna*, lit. the means of acquiring comparative knowledge) consists of (a) gathering verbal knowledge (*atideśa vākya*) of the similarity between two objects (one known and one unknown), (b) perceiving the unknown object and its similarity (*sādṛśya*) to the known one, and (c) recalling the statement of similarity previously expressed to one linguistically. Though involving three distinct cognitive functions (verbal testimony, perception, and memory), the Naiyāyikas claim that comparison cannot be reduced to any of these, whether individually or in combination.[10] Actual comparative knowledge (*upamiti*), the end product of these three steps, is knowledge of the denotative power of a word (*śaktigraha*) ("wild cow"). It is the ability to name something that, though heard of previously, had never been seen. It is the capacity to apply the previously heard name ("wild cow") to the object now being perceived for the first time.

Later in the text of the *Nyāya Sūtras* (2.1.45-46)[11] an interesting objection to the general possibility of comparison is raised by an unidentified opponent, an objection that is subsequently answered. The opponent claims that comparison is impossible because there is no fixed measure of similarity necessary to generate comparative knowledge. If two things have to be similar in all respects in order to be compared (like this cow and this cow), then comparison would be tantamount to tautology. If they are only slightly similar (like the mustard seed and the mountain), then anything could be compared to anything else, making the process useless. In between these two extremes, the opponent states, there are no fixed upper and lower limits of similarity to which one can point and say that this is the measure within which comparison can function.

The issue raised by the opponent is interesting because of its similarity to a question that has vexed western students of the comparative method: Is comparison more like a science or more like an art? Though framed differently in the *Nyāya Sūtras*, the demand of the Naiyāyika opponent, that some fixed measure of similarity is necessary for comparison to function as a way of knowing, is analogous to the western, especially the Enlightenment, impulse to find strict standards modeled on those of science.

Now the Naiyāyika response to this conundrum is just as interesting as the question. What is important for comparison to function, says the Naiyāyika, is not the *extent* of the similarity of the two comparanda. That is something that has yet to be ascertained. What is crucial, instead, is that the person have thorough knowledge of the known element in the comparison and that the known comparandum have the ability to shed light (specifically denotative light) on the unknown element.[12] It is interesting that for the Naiyāyikas the exploration of the extent of similarity does not belong to the realm of comparison per se. Comparison instead seems to be viewed as the first moment, or impetus, for that exploration. Once comparison has yielded the ability to name the new object, it ceases to be comparison. For example, according to Vātsyāyana (Sastri 1976, 121), the foresters who inform us about the similarity of the wild cow to the domesticated cow arc *not* themselves engaged in the act of comparison, since they already know the denotative relationship between the word "wild cow" and the actual beast. Hence, though comparison requires that we rely on the expertise of others—on their testimony—that expertise is not itself comparison, and that is why comparison is said to be only for the sake of others (*parārtha*). Put another way, comparison requires a certain kind of ignorance on the part of the comparer. Once the objects denoted by the two comparanda are known, even if minimally (the merest glimpse of a wild cow), the act ceases to be comparison. Knowledge of the relationship between word and unknown object is the *terminus ad quem* of comparison. Any subsequent investigation of the similarities of the two comparanda falls outside the range of comparison proper, since such knowledge lacks the ability to establish for oneself (*svārtha*) knowledge of the naming of the unknown object.

Be that as it may, no fixed standard regarding the extent of the similarity is required. Hence, knowing comparatively is for the Naiyāyika a process to be gauged qualitatively rather than quantitatively. I have come to wonder, in my readings of these texts, if the attempt to make of comparison or analogy a separate way of knowing is not in part motivated by a nostalgia for proto-philosophy, i.e., for a simpler and more analogical philosophy of a bygone age. That Indian philosophy begins analogically, using the known phenomena of the conventional world as a means of explicating new and unknown metaphysical entities, is hardly a novel idea (Dixit 1971, 33 passim). Might it not then be the case that the canonization of comparison as a *pramāṇa* represents in part latter-day philosophers' attempts to preserve a method that was operative during a time when philosophical speculation was of a "kinder and gentler" sort? It leads one to pause. To suggest that this is so, however, is at best speculation as to the subconscious motivation of the Naiyāyikas. By the time of the *Nyāya Sūtras* there is little direct evidence of any such nostalgia. If anything, early Nyāya can, in its systematization of *upamāna*, be accused of having decontextualized the notion of comparison to such an extent that it is hardly recognizable.

Even in the Indian sources it has not gone unnoticed that the Naiyāyika interpretation of comparison is a fairly trivial way of knowing. There is arguably nothing very profound about learning to name an object. Jayanta (c. tenth century CE) himself realizes this and attempts to demonstrate the usefulness of *upamāna* so understood (*Nyāyamañjarī*, 383-384), citing, for example, the necessity (*prayojana*) of employing comparison in identifying certain species of herbs and plants. In the end, however, one must conclude, together with their later critics, that the early Naiyāyikas' interpretation of comparison trivializes the concept.

Although one may find the end product of the Nyāya analysis somewhat vacuous, the *process* of philosophical speculation leading to the final (albeit questionable) Nyāya conclusions is not without its claims. These claims, it seems to me, are worthy of the contemporary comparativist's attention. The claims include:

1. The question of how comparison functions is best treated epistemologically. How does one *know* comparatively? What are the cognitive steps that culminate in comparative knowledge? What role does previous experience of the comparanda play? What is the role of memory in the process? What is the end result—comparative knowledge itself—like? How is this knowledge different from other forms of knowledge? Though one may disagree with the Naiyāyikas' answers to these questions, one can hardly deny that the questions themselves are fundamental to any theoretical treatment of the subject of comparison.

2. The degree of similarity between the comparanda (an ontological issue) is irrelevant to comparison. This is a most interesting Nyāya claim. It shifts the focus of discussion from ontology to epistemology, for if there is no minimum level of similarity required for the emergence of comparative knowledge, this means that, like beauty, comparison is in the eye of the beholder. The condition for the emergence of valid comparative knowledge, according to the Naiyāyikas, is not ontological (involving some threshold of similarity) but epistemological. What is required is that the person engaging in the comparison perceive some (quantitatively unspecified) similarity between some newly encountered, unknown object and something that is well known.

3. Comparison requires knowledge of one of the comparanda

and a certain level of ignorance in regard to the other one of the comparanda. This claim, though apparently bordering on the banal, is nonetheless interesting. For comparison to function, (a) the person engaged in the comparison must have some body of knowledge on which to draw; (b) there must be something intriguing (e.g., some wild cow) that is as yet unknown; and (c) the known body of knowledge must illuminate that which is unknown through the perception of similarity.

The Nyāya theory of comparison is not all insight. There are limitations to its conclusions, some evident to the Naiyāyikas and their contemporaries, some only to contemporary westerners in search of a different kind of *mokṣa*. I have already mentioned one limitation: The apparent trivialization of comparison by making of it nothing but a process of naming. Let me point out three more limitations that vitiate the usefulness of the Nyāya theory of *upamāna* for western theorists of the comparative method.

1. In a real sense, the Naiyāyikas cease their speculation on comparison where it becomes most interesting, i.e., in the exploration of the similarities (and differences) between two objects that are already partially known. For the Naiyāyika, it is the unidirectional illumination of the unknown by the known (culminating in knowledge of the denotative relationship) that constitutes comparison. For the western comparativist this is *at most* the beginning of the comparative process. To the western comparativist it is the mutual, bi-directional, illumination of two partially known categories— the exploration of the nexus of similarities and differences, and the increased knowledge of both comparanda that this yields—that constitutes the process of comparison.
2. The Nyāya theory delimits the source of the original information concerning the similarity of the two comparanda to the valid testimony of an expert. Might this be too rigid for western purposes? Would not the western theorist wish greater flexibility than this in regard to what constitutes the onset of the process of comparison? A further limitation of the Nyāya theory is apparent in the seemingly arbitrary and rigidly prescribed order of the steps that lead to comparative knowledge. Why, for example, must the foresters' valid testimony of the similarity of a wild cow to a domesticated

cow always precede the encounter with the real wild cow in order for the process to be considered an instance of comparison? Why is it not possible for a direct encounter with an unknown object to yield a subsequent understanding of similarity, and, if this is possible, why should this not be considered an instance of comparison?

3. What is perhaps the greatest limitation of the Nyāya (and indeed of all other Indian) theories of comparison is the fact that they seem to be fixated on the need for sense perception of the unknown object as part of the process. The wild cow, the unknown herb, must be *seen* in the forest. In a single blow this eliminates most of what comparativists do. Given the abstract nature of the objects comparativists investigate (God, ritual, and even comparison itself) it is not as though a simple trip to the forest will do. Conceptual constructs, the comparanda of the philosopher, simply do not live in forests.

Now the Mīmāṃsā and Advaita theories of *upamāna* are more interesting than that of the Nyāya. For them comparison, rather than culminating in a naming process, culminates in the actual cognition of similarity. *Upamāna,* as the means of knowing, consists of the understanding that the wild cow is similar to the cow; whereas the *upamiti,* comparative knowledge itself, is the understanding of the converse relationship, namely that the domesticated cow is similar to the wild cow. The implications of this interpretation of *upamāna* are various and profound. To name just one, this interpretation raises the issue of whether or not the relationship we know as similarity is reflexive—that is, whether or not A's similarity to B implies (either logically or epistemologically) B's similarity to A. The Mīmāṃsā and Advaita theories of comparison cannot be treated here in detail. Suffice it to say that they present an alternative to the Nyāya view that is at once more intuitively cogent and more fruitful as an object of reflection for the contemporary theorist.

The time is ripe for western scholars to begin the process of seriously investigating the nature of comparison as a method. In so doing, however, such scholars must avoid the imperialistic pitfall that sees the western academy as the sole source of theory. People of other places and times have thought critically about the issues of comparison, and it would be foolhardy to disregard their contributions. The breakdown of western intellectual imperialism continues to occur in stages. The comparativists of previous generations showed us that westerners were not the sole possessors of religion. Coming generations will demonstrate that westerners are not the sole purveyors of theory. My goal here was to demonstrate (a) that Indian philosophers developed sophisticated theories of comparison, ones worth contemplating, and (b) that such theories, though not without their limitations, are useful in the second order task of elucidating the process through which comparativists understand other cultures. I end with the hope that this essay has in some small way managed to convey the sophistication and importance of what some classical Indian theorists have had to say about processes of comparison, processes in which western scholars of subjects as diverse as anthropology, folklore, literature, psychology, and religion are currently actively engaged.

NOTES

1. The research for this essay was funded in part by a grant from the Association for Theological Schools' faculty research grant program.
2. On the need to take into account the sociological workings of the academy in explaining such things as directions of research, see, for example, Rabinow (1986, 234-261).
3. Kuppuswami Sastri (1961, 250-252) translates the term as "assimilation" and A. Foucher and D.H.H. Ingalls as "identification" because of the linguistic or "naming" quality of comparison as expounded by the early Naiyāyikas (see below). Although perhaps appropriate in the Nyāya context, the term "assimilation" fails to convey the broader meaning of the term *upamāna* as it is interpreted by Mīmāṃsākas and Advaitins.
4. This is the position of the Sāṃkhyas, who maintain that comparative knowledge arises upon the perception of the similarity of the wild cow to the domesticated cow, which occurs when the wild cow is perceived for the first time. See Vacaspati's *Tattvakaumudi*, commentary on *Sāṃkhyakārikā*. For an Advaitin critique of this position see Satprakashananda (1965, 154).
5. Jayanta Bhatta (1969, 374-375) sets forth this position as that of an opponent and then goes about refuting it. In general, the *Nyāyamañjari* contains one of the longest and most interesting expositions of *upamāna*. An English translation, lacking critical apparatus but somewhat useful nonetheless, is to be found in Janaki Vallabha Bhattacharya (1978, vol. 1, 295-312).
6. It is the Sāṃkhyas, Vaiśeṣikas and some Buddhists who subsume *upamāna* within the category of inference (*anumāna*). For the Nyāya defense see *Nyāya Sūtras* 2.1.47-49 (Sastri numeration) and *Nyāyamañjari* (1969, 381, 385-386). For an Advaitin argument against this view that *upamāna* can be reduced to inference, see Satprakashananda (1965, 154).

7. Caraka (first century CE), in *Saṃhita* (III, 8), speaks of *aupamya*, a variant of the word *upamāna*. See Dasgupta (1975, vol. 1, 302).

8. *Prasiddhasadhārmyāt sādhyasādhanam upamānam/sūtra* 1.1.6; Vidyabhusana (1981, 4).

9. *Saṃjñasaṃjñisambandha.* This position of Vātsyāyana is followed by some later Naiyāyikas, e.g., Annambhaṭṭa (twelfth century). See Mehendale (1980, 23-24, 32). But see also *Nyāyamañjarī* (1969, 374), where Jayanta attributes this position to the older (*vṛddha*) Naiyāyikas.

10. On a controversy concerning which of these three factors predominates as the actual cause of comparative knowledge, see Chattopadhyaya and Gangopadhyaya (1968, 82-83).

11. Sastri (1976, 119-120). For a translation see Chattopadhyaya and Gangopadhyaya, (1968, 81-83) where the enumeration of the verses is different.

12. *Prasiddhasadhārmyāt sādhyasādhanabhāvamāsrityopamānaṃ pravartate.* Vātsyāyana's gloss of 2.1.46; Sastri (1976, 120).

REFERENCES

Bhattacharyya, Janaki Vallabha, tr. 1978. *Jayanta Bhatta's Nyāya-Manjari: The Compendium of Indian Speculative Logic.* Delhi: Motilal Banarsidass.

Cabezón, José Ignacio. 1995. "Buddhist Studies as a Discipline and the Role of Theory." *Journal of the International Association of Buddhist Studies.* 18(2):231-268.

Campany, Robert. 1992. "Xunxi and Durkheim as Theorists of Ritual Practice." In *Discourse and Practice,* ed. Frank Reynolds and David Tracy, 197-231, Albany: State Univ. Of New York Press.

Chattopadhyaya, Debiprasad and Mrinalkanti Gangopadhyaya, tr. 1968. *Nyaya Philosophy: Literal Translation of Gautama's Nyāya-sutra and Vātsyāyana's Bhasya. Part II: Second Adhyaya.* Calcutta: Indian Studies Past and Present.

Dasgupta, Surendranath. 1975. *A History of Indian Philosophy.* Delhi: Motilal Banarsidass.

Dixit, K.K. 1971. *Jaina Ontology.* Ahmedabad: L.D. Institute of Indology.

Dwarikadas Sastri, Swami, ed. 1976. *Nyayadarsanam: Nyaya Sutras of Maharsi Gautama and Bhasya of Maharsi Vatsyayana.* Varanasi: Bauddha Bharati.

Jayanta Bhatta, ed. 1969. *Nyayamanjari,* ed. K.S. Varadacharya. Mysore: Oriental Institute.

Kuppuswami Sastri, S. 1961 (3rd edition). *A Primer of Indian Logic According to Annambhatta's Tarkasamgraha.* Mylapore, Madras: Kuppuswami Sastri Research Institute.

Mehendale, K.C., ed. 1980. *Tarkasamgraha.* Varanasi: Bharat Bharati.

Rabinow, Paul. 1986. "Representations are Social Facts: Modernity and Postmodernity in Anthropology". In *Writing Culture: The Poetics and Politics of Ethnography,* ed. James Clifford and George E. Marcus, 234-261. Berkeley: Univ. of California Press.

Satprakashananda, Swami. 1965. *Methods of Knowledge: Perceptual, Nonperceptual and Transcendental, According to Advaita Vedanta.* Calcutta: Advaita Ashrama.

Vidyabhusana, Satis Chandra. 1981 (rev. edition). *The Nyaya Sutras of Gotama.* Delhi: Motilal Banarsidass.

Religious Studies: Islam

BRUCE B. LAWRENCE

This essay is framed by two artificial boundaries. One limits agency; it suggests that the study of South Asia in the U.S.A. should somehow be cordoned off from its study elsewhere in the world. The absurdity of applying this stricture to South Asian Islam becomes apparent as soon as one begins to think of subfields and major scholarly figures. Can one imagine pre-modern Indian Sufism without the works of the British polymath Simon Digby or the Indian paragon K.S. Nizami? Can one conceive of linguistic studies involving Persian, Urdu, and Punjabi without the labor of the Britishers Ralph Russell and Christopher Shackle, or Mughal history without the special role of the Indian Marxist and metacritic Irfan Habib?

And so while the limit of agency imposed on this essay is necessary, to conform to the overall purposes of the edited volume in which it appears, the limit is also artificial. All U.S. scholarship stands beside, or stands on, the shoulders of other scholars both European and South Asian; without them there would not be a coherent field of study called South Asian Islam.

The other boundary, no less artificial, concerns the topic: Islam. How can one consider only Islam without immediately raising the perennial question: By Islam do we mean Islamic identity (that is, a creedal/liturgical norm with ethical and juridical dispositions that separate Muslims from other South Asian religious groups), or do we mean the Muslim community (that is, Muslims defined by others, specifically British others, and acknowledged as one among several census-driven categories from the colonial period)? Islamic identity and Muslim community overlap, but they are not identical. One relates to religious perceptions and pursuits, the other to civil society and political expediency.

A major scholar has even suggested that both kinds of Islam, at least in the South Asian context, are too restrictive as a locus of study. Barbara Metcalf has proposed that among South Asianists we "need scholars who, unlike my generation, do not study Muslims alone."[1] It is strange to think of Richard Eaton and Carl Ernst, David Gilmartin and Sandria Freitag—all senior historians with productive careers in South Asian culture generally and Muslim social, political and religious life in particular—as concerned only with the study of South Asian Muslims. Yet Metcalf's appeal comes at a time when many feel all boundaries should be redrawn, and she makes her appeal with telling force from her post as retiring president of the Association for Asian Studies.

I think that there is a greater danger than either overloading the study of Islam or looking with blinders at Muslims alone. It is the danger of inflating the value of academic labor as a corrective to popular understanding. Nowhere is this more evident than in the study of South Asian Islam, and I will try to recall what has already been done as a corrective and also what remains to be done.

Merely by limiting the essay to South Asia/Islam/Religious Studies does not remove us from the obligation to link our topic with other parts of South Asia that are non-Muslim and also with other approaches to Islam that are non-South Asian. All good scholarship treats topical tropes as entry points, not as conclusive judgements. In what follows I will draw attention to the overlaps between Muslims and others, between South Asians and other Asians. I will also point out the ambiguities and contradictions these overlaps entail. At the same time, I will try to offer a perspective, admittedly my own and only my own, on what the study of South Asian Islam has contributed to the subfield of Islamic studies in late 20th century U.S.A., and also on the impact the study of South Asian Islam might have, but has not yet had, on popular perceptions of Islam and Muslims.

Had I been free to choose the title of this essay, I would have chosen "From Ajmer to Middle America." The two spaces are as unrelated to most Indians or most Americans as they are intimately entwined for all who take South Asia to be central to the notion of Islamic identity. Ajmer represents not just a city in Rajasthan but also the pilgrimage site for a most illustrious Muslim standard bearer and Sufi master, Shaykh Mu'in al-din Chishti Ajmeri. P.M. Currie, a British student of Simon Digby, has written the most recent, exhaustive work on both the saint and his legacy: *The Shrine and Cult of Mu'in al-Din Chishti of Ajmer*.[2] Originally an Oxford D.Phil. dissertation completed in 1978, it conforms to a starkly positivist methodology that one could easily fault, but more important lessons are the limits that Currie's book places on any effort to make too great a claim for

U.S.—and U.S. only—studies of South Asian Islam during the past half-century.

The temptation, after all, is to make an essay like this into a triumphalist account. One could, for instance, list off an impressive bibliography that highlights books, essays, and articles from U.S. scholars (many of them funded by AIIS fellowships) that have changed the way that Islam in the Asian subcontinent has been perceived since 1947. Consider just one major reference: Joseph Schwartzberg's A Historical Atlas of South Asia.[3] Though the atlas deals with much more than Islamic empires or Sufi movements, its range complicates the notion of a single Muslim presence in India more than any other contemporary piece of scholarship, and so it deserves as much pride of place in assessing the AIIS contribution to Islamic studies as it does in assessing several other academic domains.

On the other side of the spectrum from Schwartzberg and similar reference works, there are a profusion of articles, essays, and book chapters. They cover virtually every topic of concern to regionalists in general and Islamicists in particular. To cite but one issue, the gnarled issue of conversion, it is possible now to consult a range of essays on the conversion of indigenous Indians to Islam. Few of these articles, essays, and chapters share the same perspective. They defy easy summation. Yet collectively they challenge the still prevalent notion that Muslims converted either by the threat of the sword or by the suasion of Sufi emissaries. Five such essays are: 1. John F. Richards, "Islamic Expansion into South Asia."[4] 2. Bruce Lawrence, "Early Indo-Muslim Saints and Conversion."[5] 3. Richard M. Eaton, "The Political and Religious Authority of the Shrine of Baba Farid in Pakpattan, Punjab."[6] 4. Richard M. Eaton, "Approaches to the Study of Conversion to Islam in India."[7] 5. Stephen Dale, "Trade, Conversion and the Growth of the Islamic Community in Kerala, South India."[8]

Eaton's two essays also demonstrate how a single author's work can be traced through early articles or book chapters in edited volumes to later solo-authored books. Though his subject matter changed significantly, some of his early insights about the social formation of Islamic identity are amplified in his recent monograph, The Rise of Islam and the Bengal Frontier, 1204-1760[9], itself a major revision and advance in historical thinking about the emergence of Bengali Muslim loyalties. Though narrower in scope, another monograph by a South Asia scholar trained at the University of Chicago also deals with the issue of conversion. Looking at one part of south India (Tamilnadu), Abdul Malik Mujahid traces the controversial shift to a Muslim identity by a particular untouchable community.[10]

Beyond the subject of conversion, monograph after monograph have appeared on numerous topics of interest to social and intellectual historians, cultural critics, anthropologists, and sociologists concerned with Islam. It would be impossible to do justice to the vast and impressive output of U.S. scholars during the past fifty years. But even a minimum, selective list would have to include the following:

ON MUGHAL INDIA AND ADJACENT POLITIES

Begley, Wayne and Ziauddin Desai. 1990. *The Shah Jahan Nama of Inayat Khan.* New York: Oxford Univ. Press.

Blake, Stephen P. 1991. *Shahjahanabad: The Sovereign City in Mughal India, 1639-1739.* Cambridge: Cambridge Univ. Press.

Eaton, Richard M. and George Michell. 1992. *Firuzabad: Palace City of the Deccan.* New York: Oxford Univ. Press.

Findly, Ellison B. 1993. *Nur Jahan: Empress of Mughal India.* New York: Oxford Univ. Press.

Hambly, Gavin. 1968. *Cities of Mughal India: Delhi, Agra, and Fatehpur Sikri.* New York: Putnam.

Michell, George, ed. 1986. *Islamic Heritage of the Deccan.* Bombay: Marg.

Richards, John F. 1993. *The Mughal Empire.* Cambridge: Cambridge Univ. Press.

Richards, John F., ed. 1981. *Kingship and Authority in South Asia.* Madison: Center for South Asia, University of Wisconsin.

Streusand, Douglas. 1989. *The Formation of the Mughal Empire.* New York: Oxford Univ. Press.

Thackston, Wheeler. 1995. *The Baburnama: Memoirs of Babur, Prince, and Emperor.* Washington, DC: Freer Gallery of Art: Arthur M. Sackler Gallery, Smithsonian Institute.

ON THE BRITISH COLONIAL PERIOD AND ITS SIGNIFICANCE FOR MUSLIM IDENTITY

Barnett, Richard B. 1980. *North India Between Empires: Awadh, the Mugals and the British, 1720-1801.* Berkeley: Univ. of California Press.

Brass, Paul R. 1974. *Language, Religion and Politics in North India.* London: Cambridge Univ. Press.

Cole, Juan R.I. 1988. *Roots of North Indian Shi'ism in Iran and Iraq:*

Religion and State in Awadh, 1722-1859. Berkeley: Univ. of California Press.

Dale, Stephen F. 1980. *Islamic Society on the South Asian Frontier: The Mappilas of Malabar, 1498-1922*. Oxford: Clarendon.

Ewing, Katherine P., ed. 1988. *Shariat and Ambiguity in South Asian Islam*. Berkeley: Univ. of California Press.

Fisher, Michael H. 1987. *A Clash of Cultures: Awadh, the British and the Mughals*. New Delhi: Manohar.

Gilmartin, David. 1988. *Empire and Islam: Punjab and the Making of Pakistan*. Berkeley: Univ. of California Press.

Jones, Kenneth W. 1989. *Socio-Religious Reform Movements in British India*. Cambridge: Cambridge Univ. Press.

Jones, Kenneth W., ed. 1992. *Religious Controversy in British India: Dialogues in South Asian Languages*. Albany: State Univ. of New York Press.

Kopf, David. 1969. *British Orientalism and the Bengal Renaissance: The Dynamics of Indian Modernization, 1773-1835*. Berkeley: Univ. of California Press.

Kozlowski, Gregory C. 1985. *Muslim Endowments and Society in British India*. Cambridge: Cambridge Univ. Press.

Lelyveld, David. 1978. *Aligarh's First Generation: Muslim Solidarity in British India*. Princeton: Princeton Univ. Press.

McLane, John R. 1993. *Land and Local Kingship in 18th-century Bengal*. Cambridge: Cambridge Univ. Press.

Metcalf, Barbara D. 1982. *Islamic Revival in British India: Deoband, 1860-1900*. Princeton: Princeton Univ. Press.

Metcalf, Thomas R. 1994. *Ideologies of the Raj*. Cambridge: Cambridge Univ. Press.

Minault, Gail. 1982. *The Khilafat Movement: Religious Symbolism and Political Mobilization in India*. New York: Columbia Univ. Press.

Oldenburg, Veena Talwar. 1984. *The Making of Colonial Lucknow, 1856-1877*. Princeton: Princeton Univ. Press.

Sanyal, Usha. 1996. *Devotional Islam and Politics in British India: Ahmad Riza Khan Barelwi and His Movement, 1870-1920*. Delhi: Oxford Univ. Press.

ON SUFIS, CORRELATIVE SPIRITUAL GROUPS, AND THEIR CRUCIAL ROLE IN SEVERAL PERIODS

Eaton, Richard M. 1977. *Sufis of Bijapur, 1300-1700: Social Roles of Sufis in Medieval India*. Princeton: Princeton Univ. Press.

Ernst, Carl W. 1992. *Eternal Garden: Mysticism, History, and Politics at a South Asian Sufi Center.* Albany: State Univ. of New York Press.

Ernst, Carl W. and Grace Martin Smith, eds. 1994. *Manifestations of Sainthood in Islam.* Istanbul.

Kassam, Tazim R. 1995. *Songs of Wisdom and Circles of Dance: Hymns of the Satpanth Ismaili Muslim Saint, Pir Sham.* Albany: State Univ. of New York Press.

Lawrence, Bruce B. 1978. *Notes from a Distant Flute: The Extant Literature of Pre-Mughal Indian Sufism.* Tehran: Imperial Iranian Academy of Philosophy.

Lawrence, Bruce B., tr. 1992. *Nizam ad-din Awliya: Morals of the Heart: Conversations of Shaykh Nizam ad-din Awliya.* New York: Paulist Press.

Metcalf, Barbara D., ed. 1984. *Moral Conduct and Authority: The Place of Adab in South Asian Islam.* Berkeley: Univ. of California Press.

Nanji, Azim. 1978. *The Nizari Ismaili Tradition in the Indo-Pakistan Subcontinent.* Delmar, NY: Caravan Books.

ON THE ISSUES OF WOMEN'S ROLES AND REPRESENTATIONS

While there are fewer books than one would like, there are still the magnificent and unsurpassed essays/chapters in:

Forbes, Geraldine H. 1996. *Women in Modern India.* Cambridge: Cambridge Univ. Press.

Kandiyoti, Deniz, ed. 1991. *Women, Islam, and the State.* Philadelphia: Temple Univ Press.

Metcalf, Barbara D., tr. 1990. *Perfecting Women: Maulana Ashraf 'Ali Thanawi's Bihishti Zewar: A Partial Translation with Commentary.* Berkeley: Univ. of California Press.

Papanek, Hannah and Gail Minault, eds. 1982. *Separate Worlds: Studies of Purdah in South Asia.* Delhi: Chanakya.

ON POLITICS SINCE INDEPENDENCE INVOLVING MUSLIMS AS BOTH AGENTS AND VICTIMS

Brass, Paul R. 1994 (2nd edition). *The Politics of India Since Independence.* Cambridge: Cambridge Univ. Press.

Douglas, Ian H. 1993. *Abdul Kalam Azad.* Oxford: Oxford Univ. Press.

Embree, Ainslee T. *Imagining India: Essays on Indian History,* ed. Mark Juergensmeyer. Delhi: Oxford Univ. Press.

Jalal, Ayesha. 1995. *Democracy and Authoritarianism in South Asia: A Comparative and Historical Perspective.* New York: Cambridge Univ. Press.

Nasr, Seyyed Vali Reza. 1994. *The Vanguard of the Islamic Revolution: The Jama'at-i Islami of Pakistan.* Berkeley: Univ. of California Press.

_____. 1996. *Mawdudi and the Making of Islamic Revivalism.* Oxford: Oxford Univ. Press.

Wolpert, Stanley. 1997. *A New History of India.* New York: Oxford Univ. Press.

OTHER MONOGRAPHS TOO BROAD TO CATEGORIZE OR PARTICULARIZE

Ahmad, Syed Nesar. 1991. *Origins of Muslim Consciousness in India: A World System Perspective.* New York: Greenwood.

Babb, Lawrence A. and Susan Wadley, eds. 1995. *Media and the Transformation of Religion in South Asia.* Philadelphia: Univ. of Pennsylvania Press.

Breckenridge, Carol A. and Peter van der Veer, eds. 1993. *Orientalism and the Postcolonial Predicament: Perspectives on South Asia.* Philadelphia: Univ. of Pennsylvania Press.

Freitag, Sandria B. 1989. *Collective Action and Community: Public Arenas and the Emergence of Communalism in North India.* Berkeley: Univ. of California Press.

Galanter, Marc, ed. 1989. *Law and Society in Modern India.* Delhi: Oxford Univ. Press.

Metcalf, Barbara D., ed. 1996. *Making Muslim Space in North America and Europe.* Berkeley: Univ. of California Press.

van der Veer, Peter, ed. 1995. *Nation and Migration: The Politics of Space in the South Asian Diaspora.* Philadelphia: Univ. of Pennsylvania Press.

OTHER MONOGRAPHS GOING FAR BEYOND SOUTH ASIA YET INCLUDING MUCH MATERIAL RELEVANT TO BOTH MUSLIM SOCIAL LIFE AND RELIGIOUS EXPRESSION IN THE SUBCONTINENT

Adas, Michael, ed. 1990. *Islamic and European Expansion: The Forging of a Global Order.* Philadelphia: Temple Univ. Press.

Burke, Edmund III, and Ira M. Lapidus, eds. 1988. *Islam, Politics, and Social Movements.* Berkeley: Univ. of California Press.

Cole, Juan R.I., ed. 1992. *Comparing Muslim Societies: Knowledge and the State in a World Civilization*. Ann Arbor: Univ. of Michigan Press.

Eickleman, Dale and James Piscatori, eds. 1990. *Muslim Travellers: Pilgrimage, Migration and the Religious Imagination*. London: Routledge.

Eickelman, Dale and William Roff, eds. 1987. *Islam and the Political Economy of Meaning: Comparative Studies of Muslim Discourse*. Berkeley: Univ. of California Press.

Esposito, John L. 1987 (rev. 2nd edition). *Islam and Politics*. Syracuse: Syracuse Univ. Press.

Juergensmeyer, Mark. 1993. *The New Cold War?: Religious Nationalism Confronts the Secular State*. Berkeley: Univ. of California Press.

Lapidus, Ira M. 1988. *A History of Islamic Societies*. New York: Cambridge Univ. Press.

Levitzion, Nehemia and John O. Voll, eds. 1987. *Eighteenth-Century Renewal and Reform in Islam*. Syracuse: Syracuse Univ. Press.

Despite all the advance that the above books represent, and despite the absence of attention to major articles and essays that would supplement the scholarly achievement they represent, there remains a major problem in the academy. Part of it is the legacy from prior generations that resists all efforts at recasting and rethinking either Muslim experience or Asian history. As I wrote in 1995, there remains:

... a vast, and numbingly circular, literature on Islam in South Asia. It is characterized by sweeping narratives, mostly focused on dynastic histories into which economic, social, cultural, and religious history is spliced. It is also rigidly diachronic: the unspoken assumption is that all history must be teleological, that we begin at the beginning (with Muslim raids, conquests, and empire-building) and then move through the centuries toward some putative end. In the case of South Asian Islam, it is always a grim end, since the advent of the West and the bitterness of the colonial/postcolonial eras confirm the prejudgement that Islam is in political decline and, with few exceptions, reduced to a hopeless, private sphere of personal piety.[11]

Although that judgement does not apply to most of the studies cited above, one still has to ask the blunt question in a summary overview such as this: Is the glass half full or half empty? Do we rest content with praising those U.S. scholars who have contributed so much to the academic assessment of Islam in the subcontinent? Or do we also have to ask the related, but cautionary, question: What has been the influence of all these studies taken together on the view that Americans, both in and beyond the academy, both in scholarly and popular circles, have of Islam? How far do we go from Ajmer to Middle America? Do Americans at the end of the 20th century think differently about Islam than they did at the middle of this century? If so, do they think differently because they perceive South Asian Muslims to be a major component of the global Muslim community to a larger degree than was the case fifty years ago?

I call this second question the proportionality question. Unmasking all pretense that scholarly labor can produce, or has yet produced, a collective advance in popular consciousness, it asks: For most Americans at the end of the 20th century, do Muslims today appear to be Asian as much as Arab, and if they appear to be Asian, do they appear to be South Asian rather than Central or Southeast Asian?

There are few readers who would hesitate either to smirk or to wince when asked this question. They would smirk at its absurdity; they would wince at its impossibility. For despite the fact that the largest Muslim community in the world (numbering over 300 million persons) is South Asian, and despite the fact that excellent scholarship, much but not all from Americans, has highlighted the nature of this community, the standard perception—popular as well as academic—remains what it was fifty or one hundred years ago: Islam is first of all Arab, secondly Persian or African, and only thirdly Asian or South Asian. For most Americans the distinctive role, and the special place, of South Asian Muslims in a global profile of the one-billion-member Muslim community remains mute. It is not that the academy has failed, or that the AIIS has not given enough grants to scholars working on Muslim topics, though some might be willing to advance both points. Rather, it appears to be the case that cartoons and headlines still shape perceptions in and beyond the academy far more than do ground-level facts or researched monographs.

As a subgroup of U.S. scholars who define ourselves as Asianists with a particular interest in Islam and above all in the cultural legacy of South Asian Muslims, we can claim that we have come a long way in the harsh and often disappointing 20th century. We have come a long way toward bringing out the versatility and richness, the nuance and excitement of Islamic experience in the Asian subcontinent. But, as this century ends, we have to admit to failure on the popular front. We have not changed the overall popular or academic assessment of our chosen subject.

The greatest opportunity, I believe, is to mount a still more earnest campaign to pluralize Islamic identity. The next generation of South Asian scholars should not simply cease to study Muslims alone; rather they should pluralize such study both within and beyond South Asia. At the same time they should not lose sight of what Muslims themselves often claim to be a singular and unifying global vision of Islamic loyalty. They should be vigilant in trying to understand that complex set of indices that mark Muslims as Muslims and not as some other collective identity or family resemblance, and to value the Muslim "difference" not as confrontation but as complementarity.

For the next generation of U.S. scholars who look at the crescent in the subcontinent, especially for those who continue to benefit as we gray-haired ones have benefitted from the AIIS, the benchmark for vigilance remains the hope, which was also the warning, voiced by Marshall Hodgson over 25 years ago. According to Hodgson, such scholars should not opt for criteria of equality or even-handedness, since Muslims in the Republic of India, as in the world at large, remain a minority. Minorities never gain equal treatment. In Hodgson's own words, the hope for Indian Muslims is to recognize "the new opportunities for exploring the relevance of Islam in a multi-religious society."[12] That challenge flies in the face of calls for a repudiation of victimhood, as if damage and loss, grievance and betrayal, are the sole legacy of Indian nationalism for the minority Muslims of the Republic of India. Neither politicians nor academics, whether in Asia or the U.S.A., can preempt the nationalist virus provoked with new fervor since the end of the Cold War. If there is to be a future worthy of the AIIS (and of those who study Indian Muslims under its aegis), there will be new ways to recall the plea of Hodgson and continue to challenge the stubborn disparity between who South Asian Muslims are and how they are perceived.

The best message for the future goes beyond the hysteria of cultural difference, now raised by Cold Warriors retreaded as academic soothsayers. It joins all Muslims, including the several South Asian Muslim communities, to the collective plea for resacralizing the fractured, polluted, overpopulated, war-torn space we call the globe. As one Muslim scholar has astutely observed, there is no divide between Islam and the West:

The tendency of some Muslims to posit a conflict between 'Islam and the West' simply plays into the hands of those opponents of Islam who hope to minimize its influence by making it appear too alien and outmoded to be relevant to modern society. In fact, the ethical and religious values expressed in the Qur'an have much in common with those of the so-called

'West' ... Dialogue with Christians, Jews, Buddhists, and philosophical Hindus would reveal to Muslims (and also to those with whom they dialogue) that all world religions face a similar challenge in modern times—not that of the "modern world" or the West per se, but the general desacralization of existence that contemporary man has produced.[13]

The Muslim difference becomes a way of furthering the Islamic contribution to the resacralization of life in the 21st century, from South Asia as well as from Malaysia, from Dakar (in Senegal) to Djakarta (in Indonesia). If scholars as well as Islamic advocates work toward that common goal, even popular perceptions will eventually change, replacing the Arab terrorist (the Muslim the West loves to hate) with the Asian pluralist (the Muslim among muslims, the lower case 'm' signaling all humankind who acknowledge the superior, unifying force behind and within the cosmos).

NOTES

1. See Barbara D. Metcalf. 1995. "Presidential Address: Too Little and Too Much: Reflections on Muslims in the History of India." *Journal of Asian Studies.* 54:4 (November): 964.

2. Currie, P.M. 1989. *The Shrine and Cult of Mu'in al-Din Chishti of Ajmer.* Oxford: Oxford Univ. Press.

3. Schwartzberg, Joseph E. 1992 (2nd impression). *A Historical Atlas of South Asia.* New York: Oxford Univ. Press.

4. Richards, John F. 1973. "Islamic Expansion into South Asia." *South Asia III, Journal of South Asian Studies.*

5. Lawrence, Bruce. 1984. "Early Indo-Muslim Saints and Conversion." In *Islam in Asia,* vol. 1. *South Asia,* ed. Yohanan Friedmann, 109-145. Boulder: Westview.

6. Eaton, Richard M. 1984. "The Political and Religious Authority of the Shrine of Baba Farid in Pakpattan, Punjab." In *Moral Conduct and Authority: The Place of Adab in South Asian Islam,* ed. Barbara Metcalf. Berkeley: Univ. of California Press.

7. Eaton, Richard M. 1985. "Approaches to the Study of Conversion to Islam in India." In *Approaches to Islam in Religious Studies,* ed. Richard C. Martin, 106-123. Tucson: Univ. of Arizona Press.

8. Dale, Stephen. 1990. "Trade, Conversion and the Growth of the Islamic Community in Kerala, South India. *Studia Islamica.* 71:155-175.

9. Eaton, Richard M. 1993. *The Rise of Islam and the Bengal Frontier, 1204-1760.* Berkeley: Univ. of California Press.

10. Mujahid, Abdul Malik. 1989. *Conversion to Islam: Untouchables' Strategy for Protest in India.* Chambersburg, PA: Anima.

11. Lawrence, Bruce B. 1995. "Islam in South Asia." In *The Oxford Encyclopedia of the Modern Islamic World,* ed. John L. Esposito. New York: Oxford Univ. Press, vol. 2, 284.

12.   Hodgson, Marshall G.S. 1974. *The Venture of Islam: Conscience and History in a World Civilization*. Chicago: Univ. of Chicago Press. vol. 3, 441.

13. Cornell, Vincent J. 1994. "Towards a Cooperation among People of Different World Religions: Muslim/NonMuslim Cooperation— Perspectives from History and Religious Studies." In *Towards a Positive Islamic World-View: Malaysian and American Perceptions,* ed. Abdul Monir Yaacob and Ahmad Faiz Abdul Rahman. Kuala Lumpur, Malaysia: Institute of Islamic Understanding, 99.

Sanskrit

ROBERT P. GOLDMAN

na hi suśikṣito'pi naṭabaṭuḥ svaskhandam adhiroḍhuṃ paṭuḥ/
"Even if you train him well, an actor's child will never be clever
enough to stand on his own shoulders."

The role of the AIIS in the development of Sanskrit studies in U.S.
over the last thirty years and the place of Sanskrit scholarship in the
larger project of the Institute are major elements in the narrative of
the complex relationships between U.S. and Indian students of India
that have arisen during the half century since Indian independence.

What is especially remarkable about this powerful interrelation
is the surprising degree to which Sanskrit—in some circles virtually
a metaphor for the dead, the dry, and the hopelessly arcane—has
proven to be a particularly vital force in the growth and expansion
of America's (and the world's) scholarly understanding of South
Asia in its broadest contexts, historical, social, regional, and cultural.
For our knowledge of India has increased dramatically under the
aegis of the AIIS in virtually all areas of the humanities and social
sciences, spanning an enormous chronological sweep of nearly five
millennia from the archaeology of the ancient Indus valley to the
statistical analysis of the latest Indian elections and a vast geographical
territory covering the entire Indian subcontinent and radiating from
it to include the worldwide diffusion of its many cultures and the
diaspora—as some would term it—of its peoples.

The relative prominence of Sanskrit studies in the broad
interdisciplinary melange that is Indian or South Asian Studies in
the United States has had a powerful and, I believe, a largely salutary
effect on the direction and morphology of the field. For it has, in
many cases, led to an integrative approach that is capable of
assessing modern and even contemporary phenomena of India's
social, political, and cultural life in terms of critical aspects of the
pre-modern tradition, much of which is recorded in Sanskrit texts.

By the same token, studies of ancient and medieval traditional texts have often been examined—cautiously, in the best instances—in the light of later expressions of the traditions in question. In this way the larger field of Indian Studies, as fostered by the Institute and practiced by its Fellows and former Fellows, has combined the worlds of traditional philologically-based Indology with that of the rather different concerns of contemporary "South Asianists," whose scholarly focus has tended to be on the social sciences as they approach contemporary phenomena of the region.

All of this may appear obvious and unremarkable to many scholars, especially those of the younger generation. If this is so, I believe it is a tribute to the success of the Institute in bringing together what were earlier in this country (and continue to be in some countries) two quite different universes of discourse. This separation, still quite pronounced in some European scholarly circles, is not entirely absent, of course, from U.S. Indian Studies. It has taken on an institutional reality, for example, in the formation of, on the one hand, the indological section of the American Oriental Society (AOS) and, on the other hand, the South Asia section of the Association for Asian Studies (AAS).

South Asia Scholars who are members of the American Oriental Society have traditionally concerned themselves largely with the recovery of what they took to be the most primal level of Indo-Aryan thought and culture. They occupied themselves chiefly in subjecting written texts to meticulous and minute philological analysis and the purgation from them of all elements these scholars felt to be later accretions. The principal goal of such scholarship has been—in large measure—to reveal these ancient texts and the cultures that created them in their purest and most "uncorrupted" if not actually "original" forms. This style of indological scholarship, which reached its highest expression, perhaps, in the work of the great nineteenth century European philologists and Vedic scholars, is perhaps best exemplified in the careers of some of these savants, who, although they devoted their whole careers to the arduous study of Indian texts, languages, religions, and philosophies, often cared little for the contemporary cultures of the Indian subcontinent and—in many cases—disdained to visit India. Such scholarship has been of enormous value in determining the nature and antiquity of much of the textual record. Indeed, it has been one of the foundation stones of indological research. None the less, as has been demonstrated by numerous scholars in the generation since the appearance of Edward Said's influential *Orientalism*,[1] this work was itself a product of a particular world-view that may have contributed to distortions as well as illuminations of the Indian tradition.

On the other hand, South Asia scholars involved in the creation of the Association for Asian Studies, a group concerned largely with contemporary matters, were more concerned with the social sciences and those areas of the humanities that, to a greater or lesser extent, use the methodologies and share the concerns of those social sciences, particularly anthropology and sociology. Such studies, which we tend to call "South Asia(n) Studies," are in general empiricist in outlook, positivist in ideology, and contemporary in focus, relying in more recent times heavily on "participant-observation" and other non-textual methodologies. U.S. academics engaged in these studies have sometimes regarded Sanskrit as of strictly antiquarian interest, with little or no bearing on the study of even modern folk, literary, and religious texts, to say nothing of the contemporary economic, social, and political life of India.

That the gap between these two types of South Asia scholars has in many cases narrowed rather than widened is, I would argue, largely to the credit of the AIIS. For, in making it possible for two generations of U.S. Sanskrit scholars to spend considerable amounts of time living and studying in India and working with contemporary Indian scholars and institutions, the Institute has accomplished two things that bear on this issue. It has, of course, exposed Sanskritists to many aspects of contemporary Indian life, learning, and culture. At the same time, through its encouragement of significant numbers of younger U.S. Sanskrit scholars to continue on in their rather marginalized and under-funded field, it has created an intellectual climate in which Sanskrit Studies have been effectively represented at all levels at most of the academic and scholarly institutions that support and carry on Indian Studies in the United States.

It is my belief that it is in no small part a consequence of the work of the Institute that in the early 1970s, the time when the first generation of AIIS Junior Fellows was joining the faculties of American colleges and universities, we began to see scholars with memberships in both the AOS and the AAS and, more importantly, the first scholarly panels at the annual meetings of the latter body that not only addressed Sanskrit Studies, but did so in a way quite different from that generally adopted by their elders, infusing the analysis of Sanskrit texts with the insights and methodologies of such contemporary fields as literary criticism, psychoanalysis, women's studies, etc. These are matters that I will discuss in greater detail below.

Another striking feature of Indian Studies in the United States in the era since the founding of the AIIS is the extent to which Sanskrit scholars, always a small minority even by the standards of a small field, and often regarded by their colleagues as a somewhat rarefied if nor frankly unworldly group, have taken prominent and active administrative roles in the critical academic institutions and agencies around which the study of India—contemporary as well as traditional—is organized in this country. Thus an examination of the various academic departments and research centers and institutes at U.S. universities that have housed and maintained South Asia Studies programs in the years since the foundation of the Institute will show that a surprisingly high percentage—often a majority—of them have been headed by Sanskrit scholars. At several periods during the past ten years or so as many as six or seven of the ten federally funded national Resource Centers for South Asia have had Sanskritists as their directors. This phenomenon becomes even more striking when one compares South Asian Studies Centers with the other major Language and Area Centers. In those fields, areas such as East Asia, Latin America, Eastern Europe, Africa, etc., it has been rare indeed for centers to be directed by a humanist, let alone a classicist. Overwhelmingly these units have been directed by political scientists, historians, and economists at whose hands humanistic and pre-modern studies have generally taken a secondary position at best. What can account for this striking difference?

There can be little doubt that a good deal of the particular character of the field as it has developed in the U.S. during the era of the AIIS can be traced to the influence and the example of the Institute's founder and early guiding spirit, the late W. Norman Brown. For Brown was in many respects the archetype of the "crossover" Sanskritist who combined a rigorous training in Vedic and Sanskrit philology with a broad range of interests in the contemporary life of India. Although Brown had had a "classical" training at the feet of Maurice Bloomfield, his experience of growing up in India as the child of missionary parents and his own lively curiosity about all things South Asian led him to explore not only the conundrums of the Vedic ṛṣis, but the folklore, arts, and general culture of the region as well. Moreover, his service with the Office of Strategic Services during World War II helped further develop his interest in Indian political affairs, and he was one of the very few U.S. Sanskritists to have published in such areas as American foreign policy towards the modern nation states of South Asia as well as the folklore, art history, philosophy, and linguistics of the region.

There is little doubt that it was the very breadth and catholicity of Brown's interest in, and experience, of India that both inspired and infused his vision of an American Institute whose mission would be to enable American scholars to advance knowledge about all aspects of India's past and present, including the humanities, the social sciences, and the performing arts. It is equally clear that his great love for Sanskrit, and his sense that Sanskrit learning lay at the root of much of traditional India's universe of knowledge, was a potent factor in the Institute's encouragement of both senior and junior Sanskrit scholars and their continuing significant representation among its Fellows.

As a result of the integrative approach to Indian Studies that was so close to Brown's heart and has been followed by his successors at the Institute, the AIIS came to be the single greatest central source for the support of Sanskrit Studies in America. In the thirty or so years since the founding of the Institute, dozens of Fellows have spent, collectively, many decades of research time in India and have greatly enriched the corpus of scholarly work on Sanskrit and related disciplines with hundreds of learned articles, monographs, books, and translations.

With this as a background, then, I would like to discuss some of the notable developments in U.S. Sanskrit Studies that have occurred in the last thirty or so years, the period during which the AIIS and its Fellows have been active in the field.

Perhaps the first and most significant characteristic of much of the best of recent U.S. Sanskrit studies is the extent to which they constitute a fruitful blending of the scholarly traditions of India and the West. To a large extent many of the works are in a sense truly collaborative efforts. For U.S. Sanskritists of the past three decades have, in the main, been far more respectful of the traditions of *paṇḍita* and *śāstraic* learning than any preceding generation of western scholars since the era of the British orientalist scholar-administrators of the late eighteenth and early nineteenth centuries. Whereas students of Sanskrit such as Jones, Colebrook, Wilson and their like were, in effect, absolutely dependent on the *paṇḍits* in their employ to learn the rudiments of the language and the nature and extent of its literary corpus, many of their successors, particularly those from continental Europe, were either unconcerned with, or utterly dismissive of, the learned Sanskrit scholiasts of the past or their heirs who continued to carry on the tradition of high scholarship in the modern era. It is thus that in indological works produced in the latter half of the nineteenth and the first half of the twentieth centuries we so often find a disregard amounting often to contempt for the work of the "native" commentators on Sanskrit texts and for the philosophical rigor, religious cogency, and aesthetic values of the texts themselves.

Even the great founding fathers of western Sanskrit studies mentioned above worked with traditionally trained scholars primarily out of sheer necessity and in keeping with a larger project that was as much a function of the exigencies of colonial administration as of the demands of any form of "disinterested" scholarship. Their successors, especially those from countries with no considerable political or economic interests in India, tended—with only the relatively rare, distinguished exception—to pursue their philological investigations and textual reconstructions in all but total isolation from any traditional hermeneutic.

This practice began to break down in the post-Independence era in India when distinguished U.S. Sanskrit scholars such as Brown and Daniel H. H. Ingalls began setting an example of respectful collaboration for their students, many of whom, with the support of the newly founded AIIS, spent years in India studying daily at the feet of *paṇḍits* and *śāstrins* at many of the centers for Sanskrit learning in that country.

What is particularly noteworthy, I think, about much of the work of the generation of scholars who trained with such Sanskritists is that it is significantly integrative along both of the major methodological axes referred to above (the one between older philological and newer social and cultural studies) and the one between western analytical or "etic" and traditional Indian or "emic" approaches .

For at the same time that American Sanskrit students were immersing themselves in the world of the *paṇḍita* tradition, a profound paradigmatic change was beginning to sweep through those scholarly disciplines that centered themselves on the study of cultural artifacts and especially those that concerned themselves with the cultures of the non-western world. Thus it happened that just as scholars trained in the western critical traditions of philological indology were beginning seriously to confront and learn from Indian approaches to the study of India's intellectual and cultural heritage, the quiet positivist schools of ethnology, anthropology, religious studies, and literary criticism were being convulsed by the onslaught of radically new approaches that attacked the very foundations of the older disciplines, approaches such as those inspired by structuralism and post-structuralism, deconstructionism, feminism, women's and gender studies, subaltern historiography, and the like, many of which had their roots in the nineteenth century radicalism of theorists such as Marx and Freud.

This is not to say that efforts to move along these axes have been tremendously widespread among U.S. Sanskritists, or that they have been universally welcomed. Far from it, many, especially older, scholars often continued to attend the annual meetings of the oriental societies and read the established journals, giving scant attention to contemporary theoretical developments in the study of texts and cultures, often oblivious and sometimes hostile to the intellectual upheavals going on around them.

On the other hand, non-Sanskritist South Asianists often tended to immerse themselves enthusiastically in the new cultural studies, writing passionately of re-visioning, liminality, hegemony, resistance contestation of discourse, the 'Other,' constructions of gender and the body, powers of women, subalternism, feminism, Orientalism, and power relations in general without the least regard for the fundamental linguistic and philological skills upon which an informed study of a culture must finally rest.

In fact, one might say that the last few decades have witnessed something of a cultural war between these two kinds of Asianists, the nature of which is perhaps most clearly brought out in the following excerpt from the presidential address delivered to the American Oriental Society at that organization's 202nd annual meeting in 1992:

Unfortunately, we live in times when history and tradition have become debased coinage and our enterprise has come to signify at best an arcane kind of scholarship, heavily invested in philology and other outmoded intellectual discourses. There is also a less kind view of the American Oriental Society, its activities and its partisans—the view that holds Orientalist culpable for engaging in a conspiracy to rob other civilizations of their cultural integrity. This claim would be silly if it were not so patently self-serving and deliberately mischievous. Even our overly confident forbears, the Orientalists of the past century, had too much integrity, too much scholarly acumen, certainly too wide a learning for that accusation to be taken seriously ... It is often the detractors of the orientalist enterprise who inscribe their own values on the "other" and on past and present alike. In doing that, they obscure rather than clarify while at the same time they denigrate the very civilization and cultures whose integrity they claim to uphold.[2]

Although tensions such as those alluded to in this passage are by no means fully resolved, there has been a great deal of Sanskrit

scholarship done in the era since the inauguration of the AIIS that
has tended to bridge the gaps between traditional and modern
scholarship both in the Indian and the western contexts.

In doing so, I should like to call attention to a related and
significant development in the demographics of the field in North
America that has coincided closely with the shifts influenced by the
work of the Institute. I am referring, of course, to the infusion of
scholars of Indian origin and training into the ranks of North
American Sanskritists that began to occur in the late 1960s and early
1970s. These scholars, many of whom had completed their doctoral
work at U.S. universities, substantially enriched the field with their
various kinds of expertise and their own unique perspectives that
had been shaped by their education in the two systems of learning.
Notable among them are such scholars as Ashok Aklujkar, Madhav
Deshpande, Padmanabh Jaini, and the late Bimal Krishna Matilal.

As a result of the rich and complex mix of methodological,
theoretical, and intellectual elements that came during this period
to be characteristic of Sanskrit studies as they are practiced in
America, the field, although still minuscule by the standards of most
humanities areas, has come—at least in some quarters—to exhibit
an impressive diversity and a liveliness of debate rarely found in
connection with what many people still think of as a "dead" language.

Let me turn now to a consideration of some of the products of
the kinds of cross-fertilization I have mentioned above. To begin let
me mention some notable examples of outstanding scholarly work
in the field that reflect their authors' extraordinary success in
integrating the best elements of the western and traditional Indian
systems of learning. Let me choose two examples, one of a scholar
who brought his early grounding in the Indian tradition to bear on
his later training in western methodology and scholarly concerns,
and the other who has traced, in a way, the opposite trajectory, using
a traditional western scientific methodology as a context in which to
frame a later, more traditional reading of the relevant *śāstra*.

The first of these is the late Bimal Krishna Matilal, Spalding
Professor of Eastern Religion and Ethics at Oxford. Matilal, who
came to North America in the 1960s to study Sanskrit and philosophy
at Harvard and who taught at universities in the United States and
Canada before shifting to Oxford, had had an unusually solid
traditional *śāstraic* education at the feet of such scholars as Tarkatirtha
Herambanath Sastri of Calcutta and had taught for some time at
Presidency College in Calcutta before coming to the United States
to train with scholars like Ingalls and Quine. As a result of this

unusual trajectory, he commanded an extraordinary insider's grasp of both Indian and western philosophy with a particular depth in Logic. Following in the footsteps of his teacher Ingalls, who had earlier provided western Sanskritists with considerable impetus towards the serious study of Indian logic with his 1951 *Materials for the Study of Navya-Nyaya Logic*,[3] and the footsteps of his *naiyāyika* gurus in Calcutta, Matilal made an important impact on the study of Indian philosophy in the West. Convinced that western philosophers would be attracted by the rigor and rationality of the classical Indian (Buddhist and Jain as well as Hindu) logicians, Matilal set out through publications such as his *Buddhist Logic and Epistemology : Studies in the Buddhist Analysis of Inference and Language,* (1986. Boston: Reidel), *The Central Philosophy of Jainism (Anekanta-Vada)* (with Arindam Chakrabarti, eds. 1994. Boston: Kluwer Academic), *Epistemology, Logic, and Grammar in Indian Philosophical Analysis* (1971 The Hague: Mouton), *The Navya-Nyaya Doctrine of Negation: The Semantics and Ontology of Negative Statements in Navya-Nyaya Philosophy* (1968. Cambridge: Harvard Univ. Press), and *Perception: An Essay on Classical Indian Theories of Knowledge* (1986. Oxford: Clarendon), and the *Journal of Indian Philosophy*, which he founded and edited, to shift discussion of India's philosophical heritage away from the areas of theology and mysticism that had hitherto, Matilal felt, tended to dominate western discourse on the subject. In this he became part of an important shift in the scholarly appreciation of classical Indian thought whose direction he shared with contemporaries such as Mohanty, Potter, and Staal.

The second example is that of George Cardona who, trained as a Sanskritist and a linguist at Yale, went on to spend years studying Panini and the tradition of *vyākaraṇaśāstra* at the feet of the late and immensely learned Pt. Raghunath Sharma of Varanasi. Through his teaching at the University of Pennsylvania and published works such as *Linguistic Analysis and Some Indian Traditions* (1983. Poona: Bhandarkar Oriental Research Institute), and *Panini: His Work and Its Traditions* (1988. Delhi: Motilal Banarsidass), Cardona became part of a revival of interest in Sanskrit Grammar as a subject of intellectual investigation and set a high standard of mastery of both Indian and western theories of language. So great was Cardona's reputation as a *vaiyākaraṇa*, that Penn came to be a kind of Mecca for students interested in this field, some of whom, like Deshpande and the late Jayshree Gune, came there from noteworthy Indian centers of grammatical learning such as Pune.

While some scholars were bringing together the best of the

Indian and western scholarly traditions into a productive harmony, others of their generation were experimenting with the application of theories drawn from other human sciences to the analysis of some of the central documents of the Sanskritic and early Indian tradition. Worthy of mention here is the work of a loosely constituted group of scholars who had received their early Sanskrit training at U.S. universities only to go on to spend some years in India studying with traditionally trained scholars through the support provided by the AIIS. Some of these scholars began to explore the psychological significance of some of the great themes of traditional Sanskritic culture, themes such as renunciation, asceticism, and the whole constellation of attitudes towards sexuality, the body, society, and authority that came early on to characterize both the Brahmanic and śramaṇic sub-cultures. In so doing, they began to apply various elements and insights drawn from Freudian psychoanalysis to the study of Sanskrit texts and were probably the first of those who have attempted this actually to control both subjects fully.

Noteworthy in this connection is the work of Jeffrey Masson, who began his career as a Sanskritist studying alaṃkāraśāstra, first with Ingalls at Harvard, and, later, with such outstanding Indian scholars as V. Raghavan and M.V. Patwardhan. In this connection Masson made important contributions to the study of Indian aesthetics with his scholarly studies and annotated translations of Abhinavagupta's great commentaries, the Abhinavabhāratī and the Dhvanyāloka. Masson later turned his abiding interest in people's inner lives to a series of studies of the forces and factors in traditional cultures that lead to a cultural predilection for such phenomena as childhood fantasies, the mortification of the senses, and the flight from the emotions that characterize much of the religious literature of early India. This study resulted in a series of fascinating and revolutionary—if highly controversial—articles on such topics as the psychology of the ascetic, the childhood of Krishna, Hanuman as an imaginary companion, and the hidden psychic forces underlying the Rāmāyaṇa's construction of the fratricidal rivalry between the monkeys Valin and Sugriva. This phase of Masson's indological work culminated in his volume entitled The Oceanic Feeling: The Origins of Religious Sentiment in Ancient India (1980. Boston: Reidel). Masson's work, with its controversial themes and conclusions (among which were the assertion that every ascetic had been a victim of some form of abuse in his or her childhood and that the career of the Buddha was thus as much a product of profound melancholia as of spiritual enlightenment) was, not unexpectedly, somewhat shocking to practitioners of both western and eastern approaches to indic texts and aroused no little reaction from its readers. None the less Masson was in many ways a pioneering effort to plumb an important aspect of the traditional culture that had been largely ignored by Sanskrit scholars and thus to expand significantly our understanding of the mechanisms of traditional culture both in India and elsewhere.

Psychological and psychoanalytic studies of Sanskrit texts have also been pursued by other scholars with significant experience of both the Indian and western traditions of Sanskrit learning. The late A.K. Ramanujan produced an influential study on the "Indian Oedipus," while S.J. Sutherland-Goldman published some of the first scholarly papers to be informed by a training in both Indic philology and western feminist theory with her analyses of prominent female characters in the Sanskrit epics and the construction of femininity in traditional Indian culture. I myself have essayed a number of psychologically-oriented studies or such topics as parricide and karma theory in the Sanskrit epics and *purāṇas*, and the theme of transsexualism in the Indian tradition.

Such studies were not, initially, always well received by more traditionally oriented indologists who saw them as, perhaps, exceeding the boundaries of philology, but gradually this kind of research has gained acceptance, and examples of it are now not infrequently found in even the more conservative of the scholarly journals that serve the field while panels involving such themes are have now become commonplace at the meetings of the scholarly societies engaged in Asian Studies.

Another provocative and highly promising area of Sanskrit scholarship (in which a profound mastery of the Sanskritic tradition is combined with a facility with current theoretical developments in the areas of contemporary scholarly discourse on power and power relations) has begun—again somewhat against the grain of traditional Indic philology—to examine normative Sanskrit texts and their discursive strategies in light of the history of power and of social and communal relations in the subcontinent. Most noteworthy here, in my estimation, is the work of Sheldon Pollock on the political and communal applications of the *Rāmāyaṇa* and the relationships between traditionalist modes of theorization and the realities of social and political practice.

Yet another area in which U.S. Sanskrit scholars have made significant and distinctive progress during the past three decades is that of translation. Translation has, of course, been at the heart of the indological project since its inception in the eighteenth century, and the intervening years have seen the production of a vast corpus of translations of Sanskrit texts into the languages of Europe and Asia as well as other indic languages. Many of these have been excellent and have helped to make several important texts (that had not been translated in several decades or whose translations had been less than readable by the non-specialist) accessible to a new generation of scholars and lay readers as well. In this category one might mention such highly readable translations of the *Bhagavad Gītā*[4] as well as of the poetry of Bhartrihari,[5] Bilhana,[6] Jayadeva[7] produced by the late Barbara Stoler Miller, the plays of Kalidasa rendered by Edwin Gerow[8] and the scholarly, annotated translation of the legal text, the *Nārada Smṛti*, by Richard Lariviere.[9]

What is new (at any rate since the days of the early orientalists mentioned above) in respect to some of these translations is the degree to which the translators have been willing seriously to engage the best of traditional Indian scholarship on these texts both in the form of Sanskrit commentaries and in the exegeses of contemporary scholars.

At the risk of indulging in the reprehensible practice of *ātmastuti*, I should like to illustrate this by referring to the ongoing collaborative project on the translation and annotation of the critical edition of the *Vālmīki Rāmāyaṇa* with which I have been connected, for it is the translation project with which I am most familiar. This work has been truly a cooperative effort in which I have been fortunate and privileged to have had the opportunity to work closely with a group of extraordinary Sanskritists including Sally Sutherland Goldman, Rosalind Lefeber, Sheldon Pollock, and Bart van Nooten, and the well-known poet Leonard Nathan. One of the things that has distinguished this effort from previous translations of this seminal text is our insistence on consulting all available Sanskrit commentaries on the epic text and bringing to our reading and annotation the benefit of the collective wisdom of the outstanding scholars who composed these commentaries between the twelfth and eighteenth centuries. In addition, many of the most problematic passages in the text and in the commentaries were re-read over the past twenty years with learned Sanskrit scholars in India, people of the likes of the late V. Raghavan, Pt. Srinivas Shastri, Mr. K. Venugopalan, Dr. Nilmadhav Sen, the late Dr. V.W. Paranjpe, and many others. Our understanding of the great epic and its role in the formation of traditional Indian culture and society, as well as our translation, owes much to the wisdom of these authorities.

One should not, I think, close even so sketchy a survey of

Sanskrit studies during the past several decades without at least some reference to some important innovations in the teaching of the language to new generations of U.S. students.

Sanskrit students who trained in the United States up to the sixties were generally forced to do so through the so-called "inductive" method. What this meant in practice was that one was given a descriptive grammar of the language such as that of William Dwight Whitney, and an annotated reader with a glossary, such as that of Charles R. Lanman. These texts were by then somewhat dated in that they used a rather archaic set of linguistic terms and generally assumed a solid background in Latin and Greek on the part of the students. Students were taught only to read (although decipher might be a more accurate term). Scant if any attention was given to the pronunciation of the language or to its all-important prosody. None whatever was given to Sanskrit as a spoken medium of daily communication or of intellectual discourse. In short, Sanskrit was taught as if it were a dead language of antiquity, with a history not much different from that of, say, Sumerian.

It was only when U.S. students—largely under the auspices of the AIIS—traveled to India and began to study with traditionally trained *paṇḍits*, many of whom spoke the language fluently, recited its poetry beautifully, and were deeply versed in its own, uniquely suitable system of grammar, that they began to realize the deficiencies of the method according to which they themselves had been trained.

Many of these younger scholars, returning to take up teaching positions in the United States, found the texts and techniques through which they had learned Sanskrit to be too limiting and generally inadequate. In response to their perception of the great disparity between the way Sanskrit was taught and learned in the West and the way they had been privileged to learn it in India, several of them undertook to prepare and publish their own new teaching materials which, they hoped, would combine the western philological method with the traditional training and love of the language as a medium of communication and a site of aesthetic pleasure they had acquired through their study in India.

Several such teaching texts have appeared over the past decades, authored by scholars such as Ashok Aklujkar, George Hart, Sally Sutherland Goldman, and myself who, despite their varying backgrounds and approaches, were united in a love of the Sanskrit language and a desire to instill that love in the hearts of their students. In this area too, I believe, U.S. Sanskrit studies have benefitted by the fruitful contact between western and traditional

Indian approaches in a way that would have been difficult to imagine without the support and institutional facilities made available by the AIIS.

In the above brief and sketchy survey I have attempted to skim the surface of the complex and diverse world of Sanskrit studies in America as it stands towards the close of the twentieth century. In so doing I have had, perforce, to touch lightly on only a few of the trends that have struck me as significant and as exhibiting something, at least, of a distinctive flavor when compared, on the one hand, with the scholarship of earlier generations, and on the other, with contemporary Sanskrit scholarship being carried out in other countries. What remains now is to speculate briefly on what the future may hold for U.S. indology as we enter the twenty-first century.

In some ways the future, at least the short-term future, promises to be more challenging for Sanskritists than even the past fifty years have been. The challenges I foresee will be the result of a number of changes that are occurring in a number of realms that intersect at this point: the state of higher education in the U.S., the nature of governmental support for scholarly research in the humanities, the availability of resources for the study of India, and, finally, the conditions for sustaining and transmitting the great tradition of Sanskrit learning in India today.

In all of these areas there are, I believe, reasons for concern. As is now widely understood, higher education, particularly in the public sector, has been in a period of crisis for a number of years. Increasing costs and dramatically declining inputs, especially from governmental sources, have forced some institutions to the point of insolvency from which they have been saved, if at all, only by dramatic measures including sharply curtailing programs and significant reductions in faculty, often though aggressive early retirement programs. In such an environment, college and university administrators have increasingly been forced to look at their "bottom lines" and have, in many cases, sought to rescue or stabilize popular programs in the sciences, engineering, and the professional schools by whittling away at the funding base for humanities programs, especially those that are seen as obscure or outside the mainstream. This is, of course, a climate in which programs such as Sanskrit and Indian Studies cannot thrive. Sanskrit scholars need to be active and vigilant, ensuring that their colleagues and administrators understand clearly the importance of India and of Indian Studies to the humanities and social science curricula of those universities with claims or pretensions to world-class status. Moreover, they must accustom themselves to leaving their studies to engage themselves actively in fund-raising efforts among donors such as the members of the Indo-American community who fully appreciate the richness, depth, and importance of Sanskrit and the vast literary, historical, religious, philosophical, political, and scientific culture of which it is the medium.

At the same time that the U.S. academy has been struggling to survive, there has been a severe decline in foundation and governmental support for humanistic research. The domination of the discourse of public funding of scholarship by conservative voices has been very marked in the past several years, and this too bodes ill for Sanskrit and Indian Studies as for many other areas. For example, the National Endowment for the Humanities, which over the past two decades has provided much-needed support for Sanskrit Studies along with many other areas of humanistic scholarship, has in the past two years essentially ceased to exist as a source of support for research in any field.

These developments have come at a particularly bad time for Sanskrit and Indian Studies, as they coincide with the ending of the US-India Fund that has been the major source of the money that the AIIS has, since its inception, invested in indological research. This funding has been critical as the AIIS has, as noted above, been undoubtedly the largest and most consistent American agency active in the support and encouragement of high quality scholarship on India. These funds will be difficult to replace, and the Institute and American scholars must work closely with private, corporate, and governmental sources in the United States and India to develop strategies to offset their loss.

Finally, what may be the most daunting and irremediable problem of all may be the waning of the *śāstraparamparā*, the indigenous traditions of Sanskrit learning that have made this language one of the world's great intellectual and cultural treasures. I have been working for the past several years (with the support of the AIIS, needless to say) on a study of the state of the *paṇḍita* tradition in today's India, and my observations, like those of many other concerned scholars, are far from encouraging. The simple fact is that the political, economic, and social conditions that have sustained Sanskritic learning in India since quite ancient times no longer exist. As a result, the best and brightest of India's youth, some of whom have traditionally followed their family traditions to become *paṇḍits*, no longer have the incentives to do so. Whether they emigrate to the

West or remain in India, they are increasingly forced by economic and political circumstances to abandon Sanskrit Studies for more practical and remunerative fields such as science, medicine, engineering, and business. Today's older generation of traditionally-trained, Sanskrit-speaking scholars may well be the last in India's long history, for changing times have made it all but impossible for their children to follow in their footsteps. When this generation passes from the scene—and their numbers diminish daily—a vast tradition of learning will all but vanish from the earth.

Now it is neither possible nor even desirable to arrest the course of history. None the less, I feel that some kind of bi-national effort must be made to preserve at least some elements of this tradition; and it is here that the AIIS should take a major role. For not only has it been a major force in the support and strengthening of Indian Studies in America in general, but it has also been a potent factor in the fruitful interaction of western and Indian traditions of scholarship for the last three-and-a-half decades and has thus enabled the production of the kinds of eclectic and intercultural scholarship discussed above that have become characteristic of the best in U.S. Sanskrit scholarship. Through its group of American alumni, its Indian Advisory Board, and its excellent contacts in the scholarly, foundation, corporate, and governmental agencies of both India and the United States, the AIIS is uniquely situated to recruit and marshal the scholarly, administrative, and financial resources to insure that the proud tradition of Sanskrit scholarship remains vibrant in both these great countries.

Like the proverbial actor's child mentioned in the title of this piece, Sanskrit studies in America cannot support itself on its own shoulders. If it is to continue and to thrive, Sanskrit studies will take the continued support of organizations such as the AIIS and others in the world of government and education in India as well as in the U.S.A. For without such support this vital and productive field of scholarship that has done so much to enhance the mutual understanding between India and the U.S. must—*śāntaṃ pāpam* — slowly but surely begin to fade from the American academic scene.

NOTES

1. Said, Edward. 1978. *Orientalism.* New York: Random House.
2. Lassner, Jacob. 1994. "'Doing' Early Islamic History: Brooklyn Baseball, Arabic Historiography, and Historical Memory." *Journal of the American Oriental Society.* 114:1 (January-March): 1-10.
3. Ingalls, Daniel H.H. 1951. *Materials for the Study of Navya-Nyaya Logic.*

Harvard Oriental Series 40, Cambridge: Harvard Univ. Press.

4. Miller, Barbara Stoler. 1986. *The Bhagavad-Gita: Krishna'a Councel in Time of War.* New York: Bantam.

5. Miller, Barbara Stoler, tr. 1967. *Bhartrihari: Poems.* New York: Columbia Univ. Press. See also Barbara Stoler Miller, tr. 1978. *The Hermit and the Love-Thief: Sanskrit Poems of Bhartrihari and Bilhana.* New York: Columbia Univ. Press.

6. Miller, Barbara Stoler, tr. 1971. *Phantasies of a Love-Thief: Caurapancasika Attributed to Bilhana.* New York: Columbia Univ. Press.

7. Miller, Barbara Stoler, tr. 1977. *Love Song of the Dark Lord: Jayadeva's Gitagovinda.* New York: Columbia Univ. Press.

8. Gerow, Edwin, tr. 1971. "Malavika and Agnimitra: A Translation of Kalidasa's Play." *Mahfil* 7(3/4): 67-128.

9. Lariviere, Richard, tr. 1989. *The Naradismrti: A Critical Edition.* Philadelphia: Dept. Of South Asian Regional Studies, University of Pennsylvania.

Sociology

JOSEPH W. ELDER

Of the three main founders of the discipline of sociology (Karl Marx, Max Weber, and Emile Durkheim), two focused considerable attention on India.

For Karl Marx (1818-1883) India provided a basis of comparison with the West. Marx maintained that Asia and India retained one of the world's earliest forms of property after societies had evolved from their archaic periods. This Asiatic/Indian form of property was characterized by communal property possessed (but not "owned") privately by individuals *as members of communities or clans.*[1] According to Marx, the strictest clan form was "the caste-order, in which one [caste] is separated from the other, without the right of intermarriage, quite different in [degrees of] privilege; each with an exclusive, irrevocable occupation."[2]

Marx contrasted India with Europe. According to Marx, Europe, after evolving from the archaic period, had undergone a series of "pressing contradictions" (*aufheben*) whereby European societies had moved from communal property possessed (but not "owned") privately by individuals as members of communities or clans to "the ancient, the feudal and the modern bourgeois modes of production as so many epochs in the progress of the economic formation of society."[3]

India, however, had not experienced Europe's "pressing contradictions." Nor had India moved through change epochs. Instead India had, since "the remotest times," developed a village system made up of family-communities containing a peculiar combination of "hand-weaving, hand-spinning and hand-tilling agriculture which gave them self-supporting power" and left them almost impervious to change.[4] Lest such village communities seem too attractive, Marx added:

... we must not forget that these idyllic village communities, inoffensive though they may appear, had always been the solid foundation of Oriental despotism, that they restrained the human mind within the smallest possible compass, making it the unresisting tool of superstition ... We must not forget that these little communities were contaminated by distinctions of caste and by slavery ... that they transformed a self-developing social state into never changing natural density ... [5]

Marx predicted that the self-supporting village economies could be destroyed only by external factors. "Modern industry, resulting from the railway system, will dissolve the hereditary divisions of labour, upon which rest the Indian castes, those decisive impediments to Indian progress and Indian power."[6] England's positive role in this destruction could not be overlooked. According to Marx:

England ... in causing a social revolution in Hindustan, was actuated only by the vilest interests ... But that is not the question. The question is, can mankind fulfil its destiny without a fundamental revolution in the social state of Asia? If not, whatever may have been the crimes of England she was the unconscious tool of history in bringing about that revolution.[7]

For Max Weber (1864-1920) India also provided a basis of comparison with the West. Unlike Marx, who focused on the political-economy and its shaping of social and cultural superstructures, Weber's interpretive sociology focused on humans' need for meaning. Weber identified religions—especially salvation religions—as providing major sources for such meaning as well as recommending ethical behavior related to such meaning. According to Weber:

... a quest for salvation in any religious group has the strongest chance of exerting practical influences when there has arisen ... a systematization of practical conduct resulting from an orientation to certain integral values.[8]

After examining a variety of salvation religions, including Catholicism, various Protestant sects, Hinduism, Jainism, and Buddhism, Weber concluded that:

The decisive historical difference between the predominantly oriental and Asiatic types of salvation religion and those found primarily in the Occident is that the former [i.e., the oriental and Asiatic] usually culminate in contemplation [i.e., resignation] and the latter [i.e., the occidental] in asceticism [i.e., efforts at active mastery].[9]

Emile Durkheim (1858-1917), a third founder of the discipline of sociology, wrote very little about India. His basic evolutionary model envisioned societies moving from low division of labor, low inter-dependence, and strong collective conscience to high division of labor, high inter-dependence, and weak collective conscience as a result of greater concentrations of population, the formation of cities, increases in the number and rapidity of ways of communication and transportation, and/or some changes in collective values.[10]

Durkheim's model did not fit India very well. For centuries, if not millennia, in many of India's villages, multiple castes had lived together with a high division of labor and high inter-dependence, a phenomenon to be expected *after*—rather than before—greater concentrations of population, the formation of cities, and increases in the number and rapidity of ways of communication and transportation.

Virtually from the start, then, Marx, Weber, and Durkheim identified Indian society as differing in significant ways from societies in the West. How significant are those differences, and what implications those differences hold for the discipline of sociology were matters that would be debated by sociologists for many decades.

PAST AND PRESENT GOVERNMENT CONSTRUCTIONS
OF INDIA'S CASTE SYSTEM

"Caste" is not an Indian word. The Portuguese used their term "casta" to describe the lineages they found living along the western and southern shores of India. The Portuguese and Spaniards had already been using the term "casta" in the New World to identify people according to the different proportions of their "blood" (White, Indian, Black, Creole, Mestizo, Mulatto, etc.).[11] In a technical sense, the Portuguese were in error when they applied the term "casta" to the endogamous lineages in India that did not identify themselves according to proportions of different "blood." But the term "casta" prevailed. Its derivative "caste" became the term the British applied to India's kinship groups. As Britain expanded its administrative control over India, it found itself increasingly responsible for operationalizing and legally defining castes and their boundaries. An early vehicle for such caste definitions was the census.

The British gathered their first census of India between 1867 and 1872 and continued to take censuses every ten years at the start of each decade (1881, 1891, 1901, 1911, etc.). From the beginning they faced two conceptual problems: How to identify a person's caste and distinguish it from that person's tribe, sub-caste, section, sub-section, etc. And how to construct an overall census hierarchy to apply to all of India. For the 1901 census Sir Herbert Risley defined caste as:

... a collection of families or groups of families, bearing a common name which usually denotes, or is associated with, a certain occupation, claiming descent from a mythical ancestor, human or divine, professing to follow the same calling, and considered by those who are competent to give an opinion as forming a single homogeneous unity.[12]

A series of British census commissioners documented their efforts to distinguish castes from tribes, as well as from sub-castes, sections, and sub-sections.[13] But in the end the distinctions were frequently arbitrary; census enumerators often had a strong voice in how given groups were categorized. In 1911, for example, the census office in the United Provinces prepared a caste index that included:

not only a list of castes (with localities where found, chief occupations, religious affiliation, and possible sources of error), but also a list of indefinite or variant names that are *not* to be used. With such aids it is possible both to secure fairly good enumeration and to correct bad returns after they are received in the provincial office.[14]

Constructing an overall census hierarchy to apply to all of India proved equally difficult for the British census takers. The British accepted the classical four-*varṇa* Hindu framework as a starting point. In the 1901 census for Madras Presidency, for example, they organized the 378 recorded castes into fourteen categories from top to bottom as follows: I. Brahmans and Allied Castes. II. Kshatriyas and Allied Castes, III. Vaisyas and Allied Castes. IV. Sat-Sudras or Good Sudras. V. Sudras who habitually employ Brahmans as purohits [family priests], and whose touch pollutes to a slight degree. VI. Sudras who occasionally employ Brahmans as purohits and whose touch pollutes. VII. Sudras who do not employ Brahmans as purohits, and whose touch pollutes. VIII. Castes which pollute even without touching but do not eat beef. IX. Castes which eat beef but do not pollute except by touch. X. Castes which eat beef and pollute without even touching. XI. Castes which deny the sacerdotal authority of the Brahmans. XII. Cases in which caste was insufficiently indicated. XIII. Castes foreign to the Presidency. XIV. Caste not stated[15]. The vague distinctions between many of the fourteen categories underscores how arbitrary must have been the assignment of many Madras-Presidency castes to one of these fourteen categories during the 1901 census.

Some castes contested their census-assigned categories, maintaining the census-takers were in error. Some castes presented evidence that their group should have been assigned to a higher category. Other difficulties emerged. Castes that identified themselves with one name in one census identified themselves with another name in the next census ten years later, some of them in the hope that they could thereby be assigned to a higher category . Finally M.W.M. Yeatts, Superintendent of the 1931 Madras census, declared that it was no longer possible to obtain accurate caste returns. The 1931 census was the last one in which caste data were gathered from India's entire population.

Although after 1931 the government census no longer gathered caste data for most of India's population, caste data continued to be gathered for one sector of India's population—the "Untouchables" (less demeaningly referred to as the "Depressed Classes"). In 1930, at the first London Round Table Conference, Dr. B.R. Ambedkar, a leader of the Depressed Classes, called for special electoral rights for the Depressed Classes. His call triggered a series of responses including the 1932 "Communal Award" by Prime Minister Ramsay MacDonald, a life-threatening fast by Mahatma Gandhi, and the compromise Poona Pact.[16] The Poona Pact provided for primary elections by eligible voters belonging to the Depressed Classes. That meant that census figures had to be gathered throughout India of the "Depressed Classes."

By 1936 the government of India had prepared an all-India official list (i.e., schedule) of castes suffering from the "contempt and aversion of higher caste Hindus" and such disabilities as being refused access to village wells, being barred from certain roads and temples, and being regarded as directly or indirectly polluting. The particular forms of "contempt and aversion" that were experienced varied from caste to caste, region to region, and even district to district. The fact that people from the same caste were identified as "Scheduled" in certain districts of a province and *not* "Scheduled" in other districts reflected both the complexity of caste as a phenomenon and the arbitrariness of census-takers' assignments of castes to specific categories.

By 1936 the Government of India had also prepared an all-India list of "Backward Tribes." In India's 1937 election, the "Scheduled Castes" and "Backward Tribes" played a part in the election outcomes. And "Untouchables" and "Depressed Classes" were now officially referred to as "Scheduled Castes."

India achieved its independence in 1947. By 1950 the government had drawn up official lists of "Scheduled Castes" and "Scheduled Tribes".[17] The stage was set for the Indian constitution's "abolition of untouchability"[18] and India's post-Independence policies of "protective discrimination" granting (on ten-year-renewable bases) reserved electoral seats and reserved central-government jobs to members of the Scheduled Castes and Scheduled Tribes. During the succeeding decades the lists of Scheduled Castes and Scheduled Tribes were revised, often amidst argument and acrimony. Some of the acrimony concerned the eligibility of ineligibility for benefits of Christian, Buddhist, Sikh, and Muslim members of Scheduled Castes and Scheduled Tribes.

In the 1970s and 1980s additional government lists were drawn up, this time of "Backward Classes," i.e., disadvantaged but not "scheduled" castes.[19] In Article 15 (4) the Indian Constitution had stated that the State can, if it wants, make "special provision" for the advancement of any socially and educationally backward class of citizens ..." However, the Constitution was silent as to how a socially and educationally backward class was to be identified. In 1978 the B.P. Mandal Commission was assigned this task by the Government of India. In 1980 the Mandal Commission submitted its seven-volume report recommending that, in addition to jobs reserved for Scheduled Castes and Scheduled Tribes, 27% of central government jobs should be reserved for socially and educationally backward classes. The Mandal Commission report included (in volume six) an index of 3,743 Hindu and non-Hindu castes designated as "Other Backward Classes."[20]

No immediate action was taken on the Mandal Commission Report. Then, ten years later, in 1990, the V.P. Singh National Front government declared it was prepared to implement the recommendations.[21] Shortly thereafter, V.P. Singh and his government fell—in part because of widespread upper-caste agitation against the Mandal Commission Report. In the 1991 election the Congress Party returned to power. In 1992 the Supreme Court ruled favorably on the constitutionality of the Mandal Commission recommendations and on the acceptability of castes being used for purposes of identifying socially and educationally backward classes. In addition, the Supreme Court ruled that the "creamy layer" (i.e., the wealthier members) of the Backward Classes were ineligible for special benefits. In 1993 Prime Minister Narasimha Rao and his Congress Party government began implementing the recommendations of the Mandal Commission. Members of hundreds of newly-eligible castes began receiving preferential appointments to central-government jobs.

Castes have been, and continue to be, legal as well as social entities in India. Today an Indian citizen, on the basis of administratively-constructed caste categories, can claim preferential treatment from the government based on her or his membership in those constructed categories. Castes have also become significant voting-, and even decision-making-, components of political parties whose agendas support those castes' specific concerns (see also Echeverri-Gent, this volume).

PRE-1947 U.S. SOCIOLOGISTS' PERCEPTIONS
OF INDIA'S CASTE SYSTEM

During the first half of the twentieth century, U.S. sociologists and anthropologists continued to use India for purposes of implicit and explicit comparisons with the West. In 1937 John Dollard published *Caste and Class in Southern Town* in which he identified Whites and Negroes as two separate castes, one superior, the other inferior, each with distinctive psychologies, both subject to barriers against social contact and prohibitions against legitimate descent.[22] W. Lloyd Warner, following his 1930s "Yankee City" research, stated that in caste-organized societies the males and females of two uniting families must be members of the came caste; whereas in a class society a positive sanction is placed on marrying up, and a negative sanction is placed on marrying down.[23] Kimball Young, in his 1942 sociology textbook, wrote:

... we may arrange the various forms of inherited group status along a continuum from the highly rigid caste system to the flexible and loosely ordered open-class system such as that which emerged in 19th century America.[24]

Young went on to define a caste as an endogamous and hereditary group occupying a relatively fixed place on a scale of superior-inferior status, with no approved opportunity for an individual to change caste or to move from one level to another. Young described castes in Mexico, Peru, Polynesia, Samoa, and New Zealand. He then described castes in India as follows:

The Hindu word for caste is *varna*, meaning color, and there is little doubt that in India, as elsewhere, color and racial differences have had some part in setting up caste lines ... Castes are formed in terms of occupation, sectarian groups, races, tribes, and other associations of people with distinctive culture traits or social functions.[25]

Kimball Young's assumption that the term *varna* had something to do with color or race resonated with widely-held views in India. Young referred to the laws of Manu that assigned occupational tasks to India's "four chief castes" (i.e., *varnas*): *brāhmans, kṣatriyas, vaiśyas,* and *śūdras.* He described these four "castes" (i.e., *varnas*) as "but the skeleton of a highly complex system of castes and sub-castes;"[26] thereby providing U.S. sociological legitimation to widely-held (but largely untested) assumptions in India regarding contemporary castes evolving from the four classical *varṇas*.[27]

Decades were to pass before those assumptions were seriously challenged by increasing amounts of evidence that castes (i.e., endogamous lineages) emerged from many sources, that castes negotiated/were assigned ranks in the *varṇa* system through various social mechanisms, and that castes could not be distinguished on the basis of race/color.[28]

POST-1947 U.S. SOCIOLOGISTS' PERCEPTIONS OF INDIA'S CASTE SYSTEM

Following India's emergence as an independent nation and the increasing flow of western scholars to India for field research, sociologists and anthropologists began to raise questions about the ability of western sociological concepts to describe Indian social phenomena. M.N. Srinivas pioneered in using the created term "Sanskritization" to describe adoption of "the customs, rites, and beliefs of the Brahmins, and the adoption of the Brahminic way of life by a low caste."[29] Other unique-to-India terms such as "Rajputization" and "Bollywoodization" began to enter sociological discourse.

At the forefront of the western questioners was the French scholar Louis Dumont. In the opening pages of his book *Homo Hierarchicus: An Essay on the Caste System*[30] Dumont cautioned his western readers of their possible deeply-embedded assumptions:

We, in our modern society, have adopted the principle ... of ... moral and political egalitarianism ... and condemn outright anything which departs from it ... For the moment, our first aim is to come to understand the ideology of the caste system [i.e., the ideology of hierarchy]. This ideology is directly contradicted by the egalitarian theory which we hold ... [W]e shall see that our modern denial of hierarchy is what chiefly hinders us in understanding the caste system.[31]

Identifying the roots of the caste system to lie in India's classical past as described in Sanskrit texts, Dumont stated:

The decisive step in [the caste system's] historical establishment was probably when the Brāhmaṇs were attributed the monopoly of religious functions as against the king. From this flowed two fundamental facts: the existence of the pure type of hierarchy, completely separated from that with which hierarchy is usually mixed, namely power; and the form of this hierarchy, namely the opposition between pure and impure.[32]

Enlarging on his point, Dumont pointed out that for centuries in India there had existed:

... an absolute distinction between priesthood and royalty. Comparatively speaking, the king has lost his religious prerogatives: he does not sacrifice, he has sacrifices performed ... Status and power, and consequently spiritual authority and temporal authority, are absolutely distinguished ... this relationship has never ceased to obtain and still does ... This fact is older than the castes ... it is only once this differentiation [between status and power] has been made that hierarchy can manifest itself in a pure form.[33]

According to Dumont, India's caste system is sociologically unique. Sociologists who claim that western systems of social stratification are the same as India's caste system reveal their "naive egalitarianism" and "smug sociocentricity."[34]

In order to decide whether one can speak of a caste system in a society, one must ask: are status and power completely dissociated, can one find the equivalent of the Brahman/Kshatriya relationship? ... the supremacy of the priest is an Indian fact which has remained unexportable.[35]

McKim Marriott and Ronald Inden of the University of Chicago, like Louis Dumont, criticized western sociology's perceptions of South Asian caste systems:

[Western sociology's] typifications of these systems remained sociocentric, reflecting modern western society's assumptions about essential elements and processes while reversing some cherished Western values. It did not attempt to base its understanding closely upon the cognitive assumptions actually prevalent in South Asia.[36]

Like Louis Dumont, Marriott and Inden turned to classical Sanskrit texts in order to grasp those cognitive assumptions:

The organization of South Asian society is premised on the ancient and continuing cultural assumption that all living beings are differentiated into genera, or classes, each of which is thought to possess a defining coded substance. One of the commonest words for genus in most Indian languages, *jāti*, is derived from an Indo-European verbal root meaning "genesis," "origin," or "birth." ... Every human genus (and therefore every caste) is thought to have as the shared or corporate property of its members a particular substance (e.g., *śarīra*, "body," *rakta*, "blood") embodying its code for conduct (*dharma*). Each caste's inborn code enjoins it to maintain its substance and morality, its particular occupation, and its correct exchanges with other castes ... These units make up a single order, one that is profoundly particularized.[37]

In addition to differing from Dumont in observing a single (rather than Dumont's dual) ranking system in Indian society,

Marriott and Inden differed from Dumont in their observation that caste systems "need not be thought of as unique to South Asia or its emigrants."[38]

In 1957 Louis Dumont called for a "sociology of India,"[39] and he and David Pocock began editing a publication titled *Contributions to Indian Sociology*. *Contributions* became a lively forum for intellectual debates. Notable among these debates was an exchange between T.N. Madan and Louis Dumont over the nature and scope of a "sociology of India." Madan questioned Dumont's stress on classical indological texts to provide the explanations "from within" of Indian sociological phenomena. Madan also questioned Dumont's statement that sociological understanding is more advanced by the sociologist looking at foreign societies rather than by looking at her or his own society. In response, Dumont commented:

If there were no "external view", no comparison, no objectivity, then there might be as many "sociologies" as there are different civilizations. But, when Dr. Madan deplores the fact that Indian scholars have merely "imitated" the Westerners in the matter of sociology, the statement is ambiguous. Does he mean that Indian scholars could have made an original contribution within the framework of ("Western") sociology, and failed to do so—which may be true—or does he mean that they should have built up a sociology of their own, basically different from (Western) sociology—in which case he would be entirely wrong? A Hindu sociology is a contradiction in terms ...[40]

In his reply to Dumont, Madan wrote, "There cannot be many sociologies, but sociological understanding must take account of social specificity ... the fault of the Indian sociologist has not been that he has not built a Hindu sociology, but that he has not made a significant contribution to the development and refinement of sociological concepts."[41]

In 1976 the Social Science Research Council (SSRC) in the United States decided to encourage the development of South Asian conceptual systems in all fields of the social sciences and humanities. Subsequently the Joint Committee on South Asia of the SSRC and the American Council of Learned Societies launched a project on "Karma and Rebirth" that led to a series of workshops[42] and conference panels.[43]

In 1990 in a chapter calling for the development of Indian ethnosocial sciences, McKim Marriott observed:

Constructing a theoretical social science for a culture ... requires developing words and measures that can be used rigorously for description, analysis and explanation within that culture; and it especially requires developing deductive strategies that can generate hypotheses for empirical tests in order that the science may criticise itself and grow. It requires doing all this in terms that will be analytically powerful enough to define all the major parameters of living in that culture without violating the culture's ontology, its presuppositions, or its epistemology.[44]

The volume in which Marriott's chapter appeared included seven other chapters written by authors aiming "to expand the world repertory of social sciences" by looking "through Hindu categories" at such phenomena as Hindu periods of death impurity, explanations of a fire in a Hindu village, the "heating" and "cooling" of two Hindu deities, and the construction of a Hindu house.[45] In 1993 Bradley Hertel and Cynthia Humes edited a volume entitled *Living Banaras: Hindu Religion in Cultural Context*[46] in which ten scholars (including three sociologists, an anthropologist, and a socio-linguist) presented their observations of life in Varanasi, drawing extensively on conceptual categories of the city's residents. In 1995 T.K. Ooman published *Alien Concepts and South Asian Reality: Responses and Reformulations*[47] in which he, as an Indian sociologist, "confronted" twelve western sociological concepts or theoretical propositions including the rural-urban continuum, charisma, community power structure, voluntary associations, student power, agrarian classes and political mobilization, political alienation, movements and institutions, everyday behavior, religion and development, a futuristic agenda, and processual linkages between ethnies (people who share a common culture but do not occupy their homeland), states (entities with political sovereignty over a clearly-defined territory), and nations (people who share a common territory and form of communication). In his "confrontations," Ooman described what he perceived to be the validity and limitations of each western concept when used to try to understand South Asian "reality."

In 1994 Murray Milner of the University of Virginia published *Status and Sacredness: A General Theory of Status Relations and an Analysis of Indian Culture*. Reversing the more-usual process of applying western sociological concepts to Indian society, Milner applied Indian concepts of social status, symbolic or cultural capital, and stratification to social groups elsewhere in the world.[48] His hope was that "the intensity and extensiveness of status mechanisms in India" would enable him "to identify the principles that underlie these processes *in all social groups.*"[49] Recommending a "provisional resource structuralism as a theoretical framework for the analysis of status and sacral relationships,"[50] Milner concluded his book with a series of succinct sociological propositions categorized under "resources and alienability" and "resources and expansibility." In

1996 the American Sociological Association honored Milner with its Distinguished Scholarly Publications Award, a tribute indirectly to the usefulness of applying Indian sociological concepts to phenomena outside of India.

By 1997 sociologists in the United States could generally agree that the term "caste" as it appeared in India-related writings could refer to at least three different socially-constructed phenomena: the *varnas* of the classical texts, the castes listed in government documents and schedules, and the lineages of related families from which parents arrange their children's marriages. With the term "caste" thus clarified, the way was open for continuing speculation and data-gathering about the relationships between the three phenomena, and relationships between the three phenomena and other sociological processes and entities.[51]

U.S. SOCIOLOGISTS' RESEARCH IN INDIA

The space restrictions of this chapter severely limit describing what U.S. sociologists have learned from India during the past fifty years. India's receptivity to foreigners' research (in addition to enabling U.S. sociologists to perceive more clearly the workings of India's caste system, and providing such sociologists with culturally-specific concepts like "Sanskritization" and "Rajputization") has offered venues for a wide variety of sociological research topics. In the remainder of this chapter, I shall look briefly at five such research topics: Economic Development, Landlessness, Urbanization, Education, and Peace Studies.

Economic Development

In the years immediately following India's independence, U.S. sociologists and other social scientists generally agreed that "traditional" cultural and social factors in countries such as India inhibited, if indeed they did not actually obstruct, economic development. In 1960 Bert Hoselitz suggested that "underdeveloped" societies needed to transform certain traditional institutions—perhaps even their family system—if they were going to "advance."

A change in the pattern of family organization has been observed to accompany all really far-reaching instances of economic growth ... It may even be argued that the abolition of certain aspects of the traditional joint family is necessary, because with them the demands of the new economic order could not be adequately met.[52]

In 1961 David C. McClelland identified an attitudinal variable he labeled "Need Achievement" that he believed was the product of child-rearing and was significantly associated with economic growth. He conducted a "Need Achievement"-enhancement training project in Kakinada, India with a group of businessmen. He then contrasted with a control group of other Kakinada businessmen the subsequent economic performance of his "Need Achievement"-enhanced businessmen. The contrast was significant.[53]

In 1962 Everett Hagen wrote:

A society is traditional if ways of behavior in it continue with little change from generation to generation. Where traditionalism is present ... behavior is governed by custom, not law. The social structure is hierarchical ... and at least in the traditional state so far in the world's history, economic productivity is low.[54]

Gunnar Myrdal, in his 1968 three-volume *Asian Drama*, described the clash between "modernization ideals" and "traditional valuations." Myrdal maintained that when certain traditional valuations were held by members of government and those participating in shaping government planning, they acted as *inhibitions* to development. When those valuations were held by the majority of a country's citizens, they became *obstacles* to development.[55]

In 1974 Alex Inkeles and David W. Smith published *Becoming Modern: Individual Change in Six Developing Countries,*[56] presenting the case for "modern" attitudes being both useful antecedent conditions for economic development and measures of successful outcomes of economic development.

Data were already beginning to appear that challenged the propositions of social scientists like Hoselitz, McClelland, Hagen, Myrdal, and Inkeles and Smith. Helen Lamb, in a series of publications, reported on how the profit-oriented calculations of certain Indian merchants readily enabled them to become entrepreneurs.[57] In 1962 I observed a significant rise in agricultural yields and villagers' investments in irrigation wells following the government's consolidation of their landholdings.[58] In 1965 Richard Lambert published *Workers, Factories, and Social Change in India*[59] in which he identified three types of factories in Poona and the different characteristics of their labor forces. In 1965 Morris Morris published *The Emergence of an Industrial Labor Force in India: A Study of the Bombay Cotton Mills, 1854-1947*[60] describing the changing composition of the Bombay cotton mills' labor force over the decades. In 1966 George Rosen published *Democracy and Economic Change in India*[61] analyzing India's planned economic programs and identifying gains and losses in urban and rural areas. In 1967 Lloyd and Susanne Rudolph described ways in which presumably-traditional caste associations invested in high schools, colleges, hostels, and scholarships for the future benefit of their castes' children, provided low-interest loans for caste-fellows' business ventures, and engaged in political activities to increase their castes' collective opportunities.[62] In 1968 James Silverberg edited *Social Mobility and the Caste System in India: An Interdisciplinary Symposium* that provided additional case studies of caste associations engaging in activities to improve their castes' economic and political leverage.[63] In 1968 Frederick Fliegel and his colleagues found evidence of widespread agricultural innovations in Indian villages.[64] The collection of chapters in Helen Ullrich's 1973 edited volume *Competition and Modernization in South Asia* illustrated varied ways in which social conflict could "transform and modernize the lifeways and social structure of villages, kin groups, castes, and religious fraternities."[65] By the late 1970s the proposition that, as a rule, traditional values and institutions inhibited or actually obstructed economic development had been laid to rest on the basis of accumulated empirical evidence.[66]

In later decades, sociological research on economic development in India followed a variety of paths. One such path looked at the ways in which voluntary grassroots organizations contributed to economic development—especially sustainable development. Shashi Pandey's 1991 *Community Action for Social Justice: Grassroots Organizations in India*[67] described a number of rural development experiments, their linkage with community action groups, and their applicability to global development. Another path looked at how rural-based groups organized resistance to centrally-conceived plans that appeared to threaten their survival and/or well-being, as in William Fisher's 1994 *Toward Sustainability Development: Struggling Over India's Narmada River*.[68] Still another path noted the effects of world competition on India's industrial development, as in the case of Joseph Grieco's 1984 *Between Dependency and Autonomy: India's Experience with the International Computer Industry*.[69] Following India's adoption of economic liberalization policies in July 1991, entire new avenues opened up for sociological research related to economic development in India.

Landlessness

Most ethnographies of Indian villages refer at least in passing to village residents with little or no land.[70] Several social scientists have chosen to focus on the landless. In 1974 Tomasson Januzzi described the difficulties facing landless villagers in Bihar, even as efforts were being made to improve their lot through Vinoba Bhave's Gandhian-style land reforms[71]. Also in 1974 E. Kathleen Gough described Indian peasant uprisings.[72] In 1977 Joan Mencher reported on the emergence of agricultural labor unions among the landless, and in 1978 she identified relationships between landlessness and other aspects of social structure in Tamilnadu.[73] In 1978 Miriam Sharma described landlessness and conflict in an Uttar Pradesh village.[74] Ronald Herring, in his 1983 *Land to the Tiller: The Political Economy of Agrarian Reform in South Asia*[75] directly addressed problems regarding the implementation of land reform programs in India. In 1985 Marshall Bouton reported on the potential and actual explosiveness in rural Thanjavur district in Tamilnadu in his *Agrarian Radicalism in South India.*[76] In 1982 Gail Omvedt edited a book titled *Land, Caste and Politics in Indian States,*[77] and in 1993 she published *Reinventing Revolution: New Social Movements and the Socialist Tradition in India*[78] that included a major section on the farmers' movement. Many of these movements were led not by the landless or sharecroppers fighting landlords but by "independent commodity producers"—"peasants caught up in the throes of market production, dependent on the state and capital for their inputs of fertilizer, pesticide, seeds, electricity, and water and for the purchase of their products."[79] In both books Omvedt identified strengths and weaknesses in applying Marxist analyses to India's data. In a separate article Omvedt analyzed the usefulness of traditional Marxist categories to understanding South Asian data—especially rural data.[80] In 1994 Bina Agarwal included the issue of gender in the subject of landholding and landlessness in her *A Field of One's Own: Gender and Land Rights in South Asia.*[81]

Urbanization

Among the early post-1947 U.S. studies of the urban scene in India was Roy Turner's 1962 edited volume *India's Urban Future: Selected Studies from an International Conference Sponsored by K. Davis, R.L. Park, and C.B. Wurster.*[82] This volume pointed to various promising directions for future urban research in India. Among the early U.S. studies of an urban occupational group in India was Harold Gould's 1965 analysis of rickshawalas and their social organization in Lucknow.[83] For many unskilled males migrating from villages to cities, pedaling a rickshaw was one of the most-available first-employment opportunities. The active involvement of American social scientists in urban projects in India generated a number of publications dealing with urbanization. In 1966 Marshall Clinard published *Slums and Community Development: Experiments in Self-Help*,[84] based on his experiences as a consultant to India's urban development program— a program that attempted, with some success, to apply rural community development principles to urban slums. In 1967 Owen Lynch challenged universal sociological distinctions between "urban" and "rural" in his description of on-going village-like neighborhoods in the city of Agra.[85] In 1970 Richard Fox brought together a number of authors in his *Urban India: Society, Space and Image*.[86] In 1971 Leo Jakobson and Ved Prakash published *Urbanization and National Development*,[87] drawing on their years of professional experience with the Calcutta Metropolitan Planning Project. Allen Noble and Ashok Dutt, in their 1977 *Indian Urbanization and Planning: Vehicles of Modernization*,[88] discussed India's efforts to deal on a national level with the processes and goals of urban planning. Subsequent analyses of the impact of urbanization on Indian social institutions include such wide-ranging studies as Sylvia Vatuk's 1972 *Kinship and Urbanization: White-Collar Migrants in North India*[89] reporting on her research in Meerut; Milton Singer's 1972 *When a Great Tradition Modernizes: An Anthropological Approach to Indian Civilization*[90] describing the vitality of Hinduism in Madras; Marc Katz's 1993 study in Varanasi, *The Children of Assi: The Transference of Religious Traditions and Communal Inclusion in Banaras*;[91] and Sara Dickey's data from Madras described in her 1993 *Cinema and the Urban Poor in South India*.[92]

Education

For at least a century and a half education has been a major channel for upward mobility in India. After India's independence, a number of U.S. social scientists have carried out research on the dynamics of educational processes in India. Some of them have focused on the structures of India's educational institutions and their relationships with aspects of government policies. Published research has included Donald Smith's 1963 *India as a Secular State*,[93] Frederick Harbison's and Charles Myers' 1964 *Education, Manpower and Economic Growth; Strategies of Human Resource Development*,[94] Robert Gaudino's 1965 *The Indian University*,[95] and Amrik Singh's and Philip Altbach's edited 1974 *The Higher Learning in India*.[96] Other research has focused on student politics on Indian campuses. Examples of these include Margaret Cormack's 1962 *She Who Rides a Peacock: Indian Students and Social Change, a Research Analysis*,[97] Philip Altbach's 1968 edited *Turmoil and Transition: Higher Education and Student Politics in India*,[98] and Joseph DiBona's 1969 *Change and Conflict in the Indian University*.[99]

Other research has dealt with education as an open or closed avenue for upward mobility by the lowest castes; examples include Alan Sable's 1977 *Paths Through the Labyrinth: Educational Selection and Allocation in an Indian State Capital,*[100] and Vahid Motamedi and Lelah Dushkin's 1996 article "Dependency Theory and Education in India."[101] For a brief review of the sociology of education in India, see my 1993 article titled "Education in India."[102]

Peace Studies

Since India's independence, a number of U.S. social scientists have been interested in policies implemented by Mohandas K. Gandhi. Joan Bondurant's 1958 *Conquest of Violence: The Gandhian Philosophy of Conflict*[103] launched what has been a continuing series of social scientists' studies of Gandhian policies—especially his policy of *satyāgraha* ("truth-force," non-violent engagement in a struggle for truth). Bondurant's book included a detailed analysis of five of Gandhi's *satyāgraha* campaigns and concluded with a chapter entitled "The Gandhian Dialectic and Political Theory." In 1968 Thomas Schelling published *Civilian Resistance as a National Defense: Non-Violent Action Against Aggression,*[104] in which he said, "Disciplined nonviolence—an overriding unwillingness to comply—has this unique defensive quality ... If it is known that no sanctions, no penalties, no inducements can make one behave, then *purposive* threats are to no avail."[105] In 1973 Gene Sharp, drawing extensively on Gandhi's concept of *satyāgraha,* published *The Politics of Nonviolent Action.*[106] Echoing Gandhi's distinctions, Sharp wrote,"Careful consideration of actual response to social and political conflict requires that all responses to conflict situations be initially divided into those of *action* and those of *inaction,* and not divided according to their violence or lack of violence. In such a division nonviolent action assumes its correct place as *one* type of *active* response." In his book Sharp went on to "de-mythologize" nine "misconceptions" about nonviolent action, and to identify (and provide historical illustrations of) 198 different methods of nonviolent action.

Sharp's continuing interest in Gandhi and *satyāgraha* led him in 1985 to publish *Making Europe Unconquerable: The Potential of Civilian-based Deterrence and Defense.*[107] In 1986 he co-edited *Resistance, Politics, and the American Struggle for Independence, 1765-1775*[108] that presented the startling suggestion that the thirteen American colonies had almost won their independence from Great Britain through nonviolent action before General Washington and his militia ever became involved. Had they *not* become involved, and had the thirteen colonies won their independence through nonviolent means, U.S. (and even world) history might have been different.

Other sociologists and social scientists became interested in conflict, nonviolence, conflict resolution, and conflict regulation. In 1979 sociologist Elise Boulding, with others, produced a *Bibliography on World Conflict and Peace*,[109] while contributing her efforts to organizing the American Sociological Association's Section on Peace and War. In 1979 Paul Wehr wrote *Conflict Regulation*.[110] His book was followed by Roger Fisher and William Ury's 1981 *Getting to Yes: Negotiating Agreement Without Giving In*,[111] Louis Kriesberg's 1982 *Social Conflicts*,[112] Dean Pruitt's co-authored 1986 *Social Conflict: Escalation, Stalemate, and Settlement*,[113] Louis Kriesberg's co-edited 1989 *Intractable Conflicts and Their Transformation*,[114] Elise Boulding et al.'s 1991 *Peace Culture and Society: Transnational Research and Dialogue*,[115] Jacob Bercovitch's 1996 *Resolving International Conflicts: The Theory and Practice of Mediation*,[116] and Lester Kurtz and Jennifer Turpin's co-edited 1997 *The Web of Violence: From Interpersonal to Global*.[117]

Had Gandhi never enunciated and implemented his principles of *satyāgraha*, U.S. sociologists might have written some of these books (or books similar to them) anyway. The fact that Gandhi *did* enunciate his principles of *satyāgraha* meant that U.S. social scientists received from India a concept that has proved to contain on-going, significant research and implementation potential.

NOTES

1. Marx, Karl. 1973. *Karl Marx: Grundrisse: Foundations of the Critique of Political Economy*. New York: Vintage, 477 (emphasis added).
2. Ibid. 478.
3. Hobsbawm, Eric J., ed. 1964. *Karl Marx: Pre-Capitalist Economic Formations*, New York: International Publishers, 19.
4. Marx, K. and F. Engels. 1959. *The First Indian War of Independence, 1857-1859*. Moscow: Progressive Publishers, 18.
5. Ibid.
6. Ibid. 33.
7. Ibid. 18-19.
8. Weber, Max. 1964. *The Sociology of Religion*. Boston: Beacon Press, 149.
9. Ibid. 177.
10. Durkheim, Emile. 1984. *The Division of Labor in Society*. New York: Free Press, 200-225.
11. See *Artes de Mexico: Nueva Epoca, La Pintura de Castas*, 8 (May, June) 1990. This issue includes late-1700s paintings by Miguel Cabera and José de Páez representing (and labeling) the formation of such "castas" as "albinos," "mestizos," "moriscos," and "mulatos" through

matings of Spanish or White men with women from different racial groups (e.g., Indians, Blacks, etc.). These paintings also represent the formation of further "castas" from different combinations of Spanish or White men with Indians, "albinos" "mestizos," "mulatos," etc. Page 79 lists fifty Mexican "castas" and includes their presumed racial (or mixed-racial) origins.

12. Chailly, J. 1910. *Administrative Problems of British India*. London: Macmillan, 96.
13. See E.A.H. Blunt. 1931. *The Caste System of Northern India*. London: Oxford Univ. Press. See also John H. Hutton. 1946. *Caste in India*. Cambridge: Cambridge Univ. Press.
14. Davis, Kingsley. 1951. *The Population of India and Pakistan*. Princeton: Princeton Univ. Press, 163.
15. India (Country), Census Commissioner. 1902. *Census of India, 1901*, Madras: Government Press, vol. 15, chap. 8, 136ff.
16. For a description of these events, see Marc Galanter. 1984. *Competing Equalities: Law and the Backward Classes in India*. Berkeley: Univ. of California Press, 29-40.
17. For further details about the Scheduled Tribes, see Marc Galanter. 1984. Ibid. 147-153.
18. Article 17—"'Untouchability' is abolished and its practice in any form is forbidden. The enforcement of any disability arising out of 'Untouchability' shall be an offence punishable in accordance with law." Article 15 (2)—"No citizen shall, on grounds only of religion, race, caste, sex, place of birth or any of them, be subject to any disability, liability, restriction or condition with regard to—(a) access to shops, public restaurants, hotels and places of public entertainment; or (b) the use of wells, tanks, bathing ghats, roads and places of public resort maintained wholly or partly out of State funds or dedicated to the use of the general public."
19. For details see Marc Galanter, op. cit., 121-187.
20. India (Republic), Backward Classes Commission, 1980. 1984. 7 vols. *Report or the Backward Classes Commission*. Delhi: Controller of Publications.
21. For further details, see Kameshwar Choudhary. 1990. "Reservation for OBCs: Hardly an Abrupt Decision." *Economic and Political Weekly*, Sept. 1-8, 1929-1935.
22. See John Dollard. 1949 (3rd edition). *Caste and Class in a Southern Town*. New York: Doubleday, 62-64.
23. Warner, W. Lloyd, J.O. Low, Paul S. Lunt, Leo Srole. 1961 (one-volume abridged edition). *Yankee City*. New Haven: Yale Univ. Press, 47.
24. Young, Kimball. 1942. *Sociology: A Study of Society and Culture*. New York: American Book Company, 813.
25. Ibid. 815-816.
26. Op.cit. 815.

27. Jawaharlal Nehru, for example, in his widely-read *The Discovery of India*, wrote: "What were the main castes? If we leave out for a moment those who were considered outside the pale of caste, the untouchables, there were the Brahmins, the priests, teachers, intellectuals; the Kshatriyas or the rulers and warriors; the Vaishyas or merchants, traders, bankers, etc.; and the Shudras, who were the agricultural and other workers ... There was always a continuous process of new castes being formed as new occupations developed ... These processes have continued to our day." (266)

28. See Irawati Karve. 1968 (2nd edition). *Hindu Society—An Interpretation.* Poona: Deshmukh Prakashan.

29. Srinivas, M.N. 1952. *Religion and Society Among the Coorgs of South India.* New York: Asia, 30.

30. Published in the original French in 1966. It was translated into English by Mark Sainsbury and published by the University of Chicago Press in 1970. A completely enlarged version of *Homo Hierarchicus: An Essay on the Caste System* was published in 1980, translated by Mark Sainsbury, Louis Dumont, and Basia Gulati, again by the University of Chicago Press.

31. 1970, 2-20.

32. Ibid. 213.

33. Ibid. 71-72.

34. Ibid. 214.

35. Ibid. 215-216.

36. Marriott, McKim and Ronald B. Inden. 1974. "Caste Systems." *Encyclopaedia Britannica, macropaedia* 15th ed., 3:983.

37. Ibid. 983. For further details of Marriott's observations regarding coded substances see McKim Marriott. 1968. "Hindu Transactions: Diversity Without Dualism." In *Transaction and Meaning: Directions in the Anthropology of Exchange and Symbolic Behavior,* ed. Bruce Kapferer, 109-142. Philadelphia: Institute for the Study of Human Issues.

38. Ibid. 991.

39. Dumont, Louis. 1957. "For a Sociology of India," *Contributions to Indian Sociology,* 1: 7-22.

40. Dumont, Louis. 1967. *Contributions to Indian Sociology, new series 1* (December): 92.

41. Ibid. 92.

42. Including workshops at Lake Wilderness, Washington in October 1976; Pasadena, California in January 1978; and Philadelphia, Pennsylvania in April 1980. These workshops stimulated a series of publications including Wendy Doniger O'Flaherty, ed. 1980. *Karma and Rebirth in Classical Indian Traditions.* Berkeley: Univ. of California Press, and Charles F. Keyes and E. Valentine Daniel, eds. 1983. *Karma: An Anthropological Inquiry.* Berkeley: Univ. of California Press (dealing with popular ideas of karma).

43. Including panels on ethnosociology at the 1983 meetings of the

American Anthropological Association and the 1984 University of Wisconsin's Annual Conference on South Asia.

44. Marriott, McKim. 1990. "Constructing an Indian Ethnosociology." In *India Through Hindu Categories,* ed. McKim Marriott, 1-39. New Delhi: Sage.

45. The authors of the seven other chapters in *India Through Hindu Categories* include Nicholas Dirks, Diane Mines, Melinda Moore, Manuel Moreno, Gloria Raheja, A.K. Ramanujan, and Susan Wadley and Bruce Derr. This collection of writings appeared initially in 1989 as a special issue of *Contributions to Indian Sociology* titled *Toward an Ethnosociology of India* 23:1 (January-June).

46. Hertel, Bradley and Cynthia Humes, eds. 1993. *Living Banaras: Hindu Religion in Cultural Context.* New York: State Univ. of New York Press.

47. New Delhi: Sage.

48. Milner took as his initial point of departure Pierre Bourdieu and Jean-Claude Passeron's 1977 *Reproduction in Education, Society and Culture.* Beverly Hills: Sage. A major point they make is that both the placement of individuals and the ability of privileged groups to reproduce themselves, although frequently depending on physical or economic capital, cannot be understood without also recognizing symbolic capital or, more specifically, social status.

49. Milner, Murray, Jr. 1994. *Status and Sacredness: A General Theory of Status Relations and an Analysis of Indian Culture.* New York: Oxford Univ. Press, 12 (emphasis added).

50. Ibid. 237.

51. Elder, Joseph W. 1996. "Enduring Stereotypes About Asia: India's Caste System." *Education About ASIA* 1:2 (Fall): 20-22.

52. Hoselitz, Bert. 1960. *Sociological Aspects of Economic Growth.* Glencoe: Free Press, 45.

53. McClelland, David C. 1961. *The Achieving Society.* Princeton: D. Van Nostrand.

54. Hagen, Everett. 1962. *On the Theory of Social Change.* Homewood, IL: Dorsey, 83-84.

55. Myrdal, Gunnar. 1968. *Asian Drama.* New York: Pantheon. vol. 1, 73.

56. One of these countries was India. See Alex Inkeles and David W. Smith. 1974. *Becoming Modern: Individual Change in Six Developing Countries.* Cambridge: Harvard Univ. Press.

57. See Helen B. Lamb. 1954. "The Development of Modern Business Communities in India." In *Labor, Management, and Economic Growth; Proceedings of a Conference on Human Resources and Labor Relations in Underdeveloped Countries, November 12-14, 1953,* ed. Robert L. Aronson and John P. Windmuller, 106-121. Ithaca: Cornell Institute of International Industrial and Labor Relations. See also Helen B. Lamb. 1959. "The Indian Merchant." In *Traditional India: Structure and Change.* ed. Milton Singer, 231-240. Philadelphia: American Folklore Society.

58. Elder, Joseph W. 1962. "Land Consolidation in an Indian Village: A Case Study in the Consolidation of Holdings Act in Uttar Pradesh." *Economic Development and Cultural Change* 11:1 (October): 16-40.

59. Lambert, Richard D. 1963. *Workers, Factories, and Social Change in India.* Princeton: Princeton Univ. Press.

60. Morris, Morris David. 1965. *The Emergence of an Industrial Labor Force in India: A Study of the Bombay Cotton Mills, 1854-1947.* Berkeley: Univ. of California Press.

61. Rosen, George. 1966. *Democracy and Economic Change in India.* Berkeley: Univ. of California Press.

62. Rudolph, Lloyd I. and Susanne Hoeber Rudolph. 1967. *The Modernity of Tradition: Political Development in India.* Chicago: Univ. of Chicago Press.

63. Silverberg, James, ed. 1968. *Social Mobility and the Caste System in India: An Interdisciplinary Symposium.* The Hague: Mouton.

64. Fliegel, Frederick C., Prodipto Roy, Lalit K. Sen, and Joseph E. Kivlin. 1968. *Agricultural Innovations in Indian Villages.* Hyderabad: National Institute of Community Development.

65. Ullrich, Helen E., ed. 1975. *Competition and Modernization in South Asia.* New Delhi: Abhinav.

66. Elder, Joseph W. 1972. "Cultural and Social Factors in Agricultural Development." In *The Political Economy of Development,* ed. Norman T. Uphoff and Warren F. Ilchman, 46-55. Berkeley: Univ. of California Press.

67. Pandey, Shashi. 1991. *Community Action for Social Justice: Grassroots Organizations in India.* New Delhi: Sage.

68. Fisher, William. 1994. *Toward Sustainable Development: Struggling Over India's Narmada River.* Armonk, NY: M.E. Sharpe.

69. Grieco, Joseph M. 1984. *Between Dependency and Autonomy: India's Experience with the International Computer Industry.* Berkeley: Univ. of California Press.

70. See, for example, E. Kathleen Gough. 1962. "Caste in a Tanjore Village." In *Aspects of Caste in South India, Ceylon and North-West Pakistan.* ed. E.R. Leach, 11-60. Cambridge: Cambridge Univ. Press. See also Joseph W. Elder. 1962. Op. cit.

71. Januzzi, F. Tomasson. 1974. *Agrarian Crisis in India: The Case of Bihar.* Austin: Univ. of Texas Press.

72. Gough, E. Kathleen. 1974. "Indian Peasant Uprisings." *Economic and Political Weekly.* 9:32-34, 1391-1412.

73. See Joan Mencher. 1977. "Agricultural Labor Unions: Some Socioeconomic and Political Considerations." In *The New Wind: Changing Identities in South Asia,* ed. Kenneth David, 309-336. The Hague: Mouton. See also Joan Mencher. 1978. *Agriculture and Social Structure in Tamil Nadu: Past Origins, Present Transformations, and Future Prospects.* Bombay: Allied.

74. See Miriam Sharma. 1978. *The Politics of Inequality: Competition and Control in an Indian Village.* Honolulu: Univ. of Hawaii Press.

75. Herring, Ronald J. 1983. *Land to the Tiller: The Political Economy of Agrarian Reform in South Asia.* New Haven: Yale Univ. Press.

76. Bouton, Marshall M. 1985. *Agrarian Radicalism in South India.* Princeton: Princeton Univ. Press.

77. Omvedt, Gail, ed. 1982. *Land, Caste and Politics in Indian States.* Delhi: Authors Guild.

78. Omvedt, Gail. 1993. *Reinventing Revolution: New Social Movements and the Socialist Tradition in India.* Armonk, NY: M.E. Sharpe.

79. Ibid. 101.

80. Omvedt, Gail. 1974. "Marxism and the Analysis of South Asia." *Journal of Contemporary Asia* 4(4): 481-501.

81. Agarwal, Bina. 1994. *A Field of One's Own: Gender and Land Rights in South Asia.* Cambridge: Cambridge Univ. Press.

82. Turner, Roy, ed. 1962. *India's Urban Future; Selected Studies from an International Conference Sponsored by K. Davis, R.L. Park, and C.B. Wurster.* Berkeley: Univ. of California Press.

83. Gould, Harold. 1965. "Lucknow Rickshawalas: The Social Organization of an Occupational Category." *International Journal of Comparative Sociology* 6: 24-47.

84. Clinard, Marshall B. 1966. *Slums and Community: Experiments in Self-Help.* New York: Free Press.

85. Lynch, Owen M. 1967. "Rural Cities in India: Continuities and Discontinuities." In *India and Ceylon: Unity and Diversity,* ed. Philip Mason, 142-158. New York: Oxford Univ. Press.

86. Fox, Richard G., ed. 1970. *Urban India: Society, Space and Image.* Durham, NC: Monograph and Occasional Paper Series no. 10, Program in Comparative Studies on Southern Asia, Duke University.

87. Jakobson, Leo and Ved Prakash. 1971. *Urbanization and National Development.* Beverly Hills: Sage.

88. Noble, Allen G. and Ashok K. Dutt. 1977. *Indian Urbanization and Planning: Vehicles of Modernization.* New Delhi: Tata McGraw-Hill.

89. Vatuk, Sylvia. 1972. *Kinship and Urbanization: White-Collar Migrants in North India.* Berkeley: Univ. of California Press.

90. Singer, Milton. 1972. *When a Great Tradition Modernizes: An Anthropological Approach to Indian Civilization.* New York: Praeger.

91. Katz, Marc J. 1993. *The Children of Assi: The Transference of Religious Traditions and Communal Inclusion in Banaras.* Goteborg: Dept. of Religious Studies, University of Goteborg.

92. Dickey, Sara. 1993. *Cinema and the Urban Poor in South India.* New York: Cambridge Univ. Press.

93. Smith, Donald E. 1963. *India as a Secular State.* Princeton: Princeton Univ. Press.

94. Harbison, Frederick H. and Charles A. Myers. 1964. *Education, Manpower*

and Economic Growth; Strategies of Human Resource Development. New York: McGraw-Hill.

95. Gaudino, Robert L., 1965. *The Indian University.* Bombay: Popular Prakashan.

96. Singh, Amrik and Philip G. Altbach, eds. 1974. *The Higher Learning in India.* Delhi: Vikas.

97. Cormack, Margaret L. 1962. *She Who Rides a Peacock: Indian Students and Social Change, a Research Analysis.* New York: Praeger.

98. Altbach, Philip, ed. 1968. *Turmoil and Transition: Higher Education and Student Politics in India.* Bombay: Lalvani.

99. DiBona, Joseph E. 1969. *Change and Conflict in the Indian University.* Durham, NC: Program in Comparative Studies on Southern Asia, Duke University.

100. Sable, Alan. 1977. *Paths Through the Labyrinth: Educational Selection and Allocation in an Indian State Capital.* New Delhi: S. Chand.

101. Motamedi, Vahid and Lelah Dushkin. 1996. "Dependency Theory and Education in India." *Asian Profile* 24:5 (October): 425-432.

102. Elder, Joseph W. 1992. "Education in India." In *Columbia Project on Asia in the Core Curriculum; Asia: Case Studies in the Social Sciences: A Guide for Teaching.* ed Myron L. Cohen, 493-503. Armonk, NY: M.E. Sharpe.

103. Bondurant, Joan V. 1958. *Conquest of Violence: The Gandhian Philosophy of Conflict.* Princeton: Princeton Univ. Press.

104. Schelling, Thomas. 1968. *Civilian Resistance as a National Defense: Non-Violent Action Against Aggression.* Harrisburg, PA: Stackpole Books.

105. Ibid. 304.

106. Sharp, Gene. 1973. *The Politics of Nonviolent Action.* Boston: Porter Sargent, prepared under the auspices of Harvard University's Center for International Affairs.

107. Sharp, Gene. 1985. *Making Europe Unconquerable: The Potential of Civilian-based Deterrence and Defense.* Cambridge: Ballinger.

108. Conser, Walter H., Jr., Ronald N. McCarthy, David J. Toscano, and Gene Sharp, eds. 1986. *Resistance, Politics, and the American Struggle for Independence, 1765-1775.* Boulder: Lynne Rienner.

109. Boulding, Elise, J. Robert Passmore, and Robert S. Gassler. 1979. *Bibliography on World Conflict and Peace.* Boulder: Westview.

110. Wehr, Paul. 1979. *Conflict Regulation.* Boulder: Westview.

111. Fisher, Roger and William Ury. 1981. *Getting to Yes: Negotiating Agreement Without Giving In.* Boston: Houghton Mifflin.

112. Kriesberg, Louis. 1982 (2nd edition). *Social Conflicts.* Englewood Cliffs, NJ: Prentice-Hall.

113. Pruitt, Dean G. and Jeffrey Z. Rubin. 1986. *Social Conflict: Escalation, Stalemate, and Settlement.* New York: Random House.

114. Kriesberg, Louis, Terrell A. Northrup, and Stuart J. Thorson, eds. 1989. *Intractable Conflicts and Their Transformations.* Syracuse: Syracuse Univ. Press.

115. Boulding, Elise, Clovis Brigagao, and Kevin Clemente, 1991. *Peace Culture and Society: Transnational Research and Dialogue.* Boulder: Westview.
116. Bercovitch, Jacob, ed. 1996. *Resolving International Conflicts: The Theory and Practice of Mediation.* Boulder: Lynne Rienner.
117. Kurtz, Lester R. and Jennifer Turpin, eds. 1997. *The Web of Violence: From Interpersonal to Global.* Urbana: Univ. of Illinois Press.

Theatre

RICHARD SCHECHNER

No one writing in, on, or about India can hope to get even a fair proportion of anything about anything. The place is too vast conceptually and historically, too varied demographically and linguistically, too dynamic intellectually and artistically, too fractious politically and religiously to admit of summaries. The most one can hope for is to play the role of a respectful blind person with a couple of fingers on the elephant reporting what one feels. Furthermore, an American writing about India is under the constraints of post-colonialism and orientalism, whatever her/his personal politics and scholarly outlook.

This is the case with me here. I have a long experience of India, for a non-Indian, dating back to 1971. But I have never lived there for more than 11 months at a time, and most of my encounters have been much briefer. Nor do I speak any language but English. I have, either in turn or simultaneously, been in India as a researcher, a working artist, a conference-goer, a tourist, and a passenger-in-transit. I have friends in India, but the masses of people, the villagers, the urbanites both poor and working class, the desperate and the fabulously wealthy, the political leaders—I do not know, except as a spectacle passing before my eyes or a din or a song in my ears or some tantalizing or disgusting flavor in my nose and mouth. At one point I converted to Hinduism,[1] not out of over-riding belief, but from curiosity and the desire to experience the initiation and to enter temples in the south unhindered. Yet, lest I appear too much the cynic, I learned yoga in Madras in 1971 and have practiced it since—not only *āsanas* and *prāṇāyāma* (poses and breathing)—but something that can only be called spiritual-intellectual. I do not read Sanskrit, but I have been affected in my thinking and writing by Bharata's *Nāṭya Śāstra*, its commentators, and *rasa*-theory. My experience of/with Ram Lila of Ramnagar has changed me; nor is that over yet: I am in India on my way to Ram Lila as I finish this writing.

MY OWN JOURNEYS TO INDIA, BRIEFLY RECOUNTED

I went to India in 1971 to find out about its theatre.[2] I began by meeting Dr. Suresh Awasthi, at that time Secretary of the Sangeet Natak Akademi. The Akademi had the responsibility of preserving and documenting the many genres of traditional performance existing in the subcontinent. But Awasthi was also very interested in the "modern theatre," those writers, actors, directors, producers, and venues making and staging dramas in the western sense. As in much of Asia (and for that matter, in the rest of the post-colonial world), the "problem" of modern theatre persisted and persists. That is, the question of whose theatre is it, and how long, and under what circumstances do practices introduced by the colonizers become localized—no longer signaling adherence to colonial ideals but even its opposite: resistance to outside influence, the assertion of national desires and identities, the recounting of local experiences, and the expression of indigenous arts. The British brought modern theatre to the subcontinent as part of the colonizing process to entertain the Europeans and as something Indians might emulate. Many Indians practicing modern theatre have studied in the U.K., Russia, and the U.S.A. Others have studied in India at the National School of Drama, modeled in the early 1960s by its founder Ebrahim Alkazi as an amalgam of the British and the Russian approaches to theatre as this approach might be applied to India in the formation of a "national theatre."[3] But these influences do not mean that Indian modern theatre is western. Not only are the subjects of the drama Indian, but through the "roots movement" (of which I will speak shortly) a number of the most influential modern Indian theatre people have drawn in unique ways on traditional Indian genres of performance. To put it another way, what might have been European at first has long since become distinctly Indian.

Awasthi passionately campaigned to link the modern and the traditional by introducing directors and writers to the panoply of traditional performances he himself had seen, patronized, and was attempting to preserve; and by bringing traditional artists to Delhi. He was, in this sense, an early and effective champion of "interculturalism,"[4] what Awasthi dubbed "roots," consciously or not taking off from the popular American TV series about the roots of the African experience in Africa. Awasthi, a wiry, boundlessly enthusiastic man, not only knew a great deal about the various kinds of Indian theatre, he was eager to share what he knew in the most practical and useful way. "I will show you myself. And where I can't go, I will make the arrangements." Awasthi's support made all the difference: his roadmap was my first guide to Indian performance.

Thus in 1971 I encountered Kathak, Odissi, Jatra, Tamasha, Yakshagana, Bharata Natyam, Kuchipudi, Manipuri, Bhand Pather, Teyyam, Kathakali ... and more, including modern theatre, some in English, some in Hindi, Bengali, Marathi, Gujarati, and other languages —but most of it (in my view) stale proscenium stuff. An exception was a thrilling performance by the Repertory Theatre of the National School of Drama of John Osborne's *Look Back in Anger*, with Surekha Sikri and Manohar Singh, both of whom I later had the pleasure of working with when in 1983 I directed Chekhov's *Cherry Ka Baghicha (The Cherry Orchard)* with the National School of Drama's Repertory Theatre (NSD Rep).

Among my destinations in 1971 was Calcutta, where I met Badal Sircar and Shyamanand Jalan. I arrived in Calcutta just as the Indo-Pakistan war broke out, at the height of the Naxalite rebellion, during a period of explosive Bengali cultural expression.[5] After the surging cultural life of Calcutta, I went to Madras, a blissfully peaceful place at that time. There I studied yoga for a month with Krishnamacharya and observed Bharata Natyam, Manipuri, and other kinds of dance-theatre at Kalekshetra. Then I meandered down the coast to Kanyakumari and into Kerala, stopping by the way at temples including Chidambaram and Mahabalipuram. In Kerala I visited the Kathakali Kalamandalam where I met, watched the work of, and spoke to some of the great performers of Kathakali and Kutiyattam. I also saw Teyyam and Kalarippayattu. Then I worked my way up into Karnataka where I met Martha Ashton who was researching what was to become *Yaksagana: A Dance Drama of India* (1977). I proceeded to Bombay, before leaving India via Delhi for Sri Lanka and other parts of Asia.

My second Indian journey filled nearly the whole of 1976. It began in February with The Performance Group's production of Bertolt Brecht's *Mother Courage and Her Children* touring to Delhi, Lucknow, Calcutta, Sinjole (a village near Calcutta), and Bombay.[6] Touring a professional production put me in touch with a very wide range of Indian theatre people, from well-known directors such as B.V. Karanth (who was then the artistic director of the Rabindra Bhavan in Bhopal) to workmen and truck drivers setting up our environments and transporting actors, technicians, and goods. Most audiences and theatre professionals were enthusiastic about *Mother Courage*, recognizing in it not only contemporary experimental theatre, but something akin to the folk theatres of India. This coincidence was partly just that and partly the result of my earlier exposure to Indian performance. Environmental theatre has many sources, one of them my knowledge both historically and anthropologically of participatory rituals and ritual dramas staged in site-specific locations. What I saw in India confirmed and reinforced my own theoretical and artistic tendencies.

After the run of *Mother Courage,* I and some other members of The Performance Group stayed on in India each going our separate ways. I remember strongly the National School of Drama's Repertory Theatre's (NSD Rep's) splendid production of Mohan Agashe's *Ade Adhure.* But my main interest was to deepen my studies of traditional, folk, and ritual forms. I spent part of March-April shuttling from Seraikella to Mayurbanj to Purulia observing the three types of Chhau during the Chaitra Parva celebrations.[7] In July I observed, and to a small degree participated in, the summer training program at the Kathakali Kalamandalam. In August I went to Vrindaban for Ras Lila. And in September I saw, for the first time, the Ram Lila of Ramnagar. Then I left India for other parts of Asia—returning in January 1977 for the Maha Kumbhamela in Prayag (Allahabad). Ram Lila took me by storm. I had never experienced such a combination of environmental theatre, devotion-audience participation, myth-making, song, text, drama, and spectacle. I began what was to become a long if intermittent study of Ramnagar Ram Lila which I continued in 1978, 1983, and 1997. This work I am not yet finished with.[8]

In 1983 I returned to New Delhi to direct *Cherry Ka Baghicha* with the NSD Rep. The Rep's acting style was a combination of British, Stanislavskian, and Brechtian influences modified by the Indian life-experiences of Rep members. I was not the only person in the Rep for whom Hindi was a foreign language. The production was, at its very core, intercultural. I worked closely with Nissar Allana who designed the theatrical environments and Amal Allan who designed the costumes. The production was environmental theatre. Each act was performed in a different space in and around the outdoor theatre at Delhi's Rabindra Bhavan. Working on the inside of an Indian professional company, following through on the details of a production, coaching the actors, debating important artistic decisions, inventing a *mise-en-scene,* meeting audiences—this way of learning aspects of a culture cannot be acquired by observation alone.

Since 1983, and until a two-and-a-half month research trip focused on Ram Lila in 1997, I visited India only briefly, for a few days, in 1989.

SOME QUESTIONS

Awasthi wanted to introduce traditional Indian performance to modern Indian theatre makers, writers, and directors. Awasthi's work was parallel to that of Habib Tanvir who was actually fusing folk theatre and modern techniques. In 1971 I was not familiar with the complex conversations going on in India—arguments still not resolved as the twenty-first century approaches: Is there one India or many? Can local forms thrive, or even exist without direct help from by the "center" (the national authorities in New Delhi). How ought the former colonial powers, the United Kingdom especially, but also the U.S.A.[9] and (to lesser degrees, depending upon where one looked from) France and Portugal, be regarded? And what about "minorities" and "Scheduled Castes," not to mention the enormous Muslim population, persons who did not identify with the Sanskritic tradition. Add to this the "language question" and all it implied. Did Hindi replace, or stand next to, English as an alien even "colonial language?" How could the various Indian languages thrive without also dooming India to Babelism? These questions and many others revolved around the central dilemma of how to make one "nation" out of many cultures.

In India I encountered performing arts, rituals, and scholarly approaches at odds with themselves, organized into overlapping and contradictory categories—classical, folk, popular, traditional, ritual, tribal, modern. Why are Odissi, Kathak, and Bharat Natyam "classical" while Jatra is "popular" and Teyyam "folk" or "ritual"? What is the difference between "tribal" theatre and "folk" theatre? Does the conscious introduction of codification and systematic training promote a genre from "folk" to "classical," as Sadir Natch was promoted into Bharata Natyam through the work of Rukmini Devi and others? Does a provable link to the *Nāṭya Śāstra* make a difference? And what is a "provable link" anyway? Do the sculptures at Chidambaram prove that the movements represented in the stone karanas, the sadir nac of the devadasis, the dancing of the "Tanjore Quartet," and today's bharatanatyam are part of the same line of development? What relationship does caste, language, geography, and the colonial experience have to theatre? Where does modern theatre fit into it all? What is the relationship between English and the other Indian languages? In what ways can India be conceptualized? Through the notion of "Ram raj" as narrated in Vālmīki's *Rāmāyaṇa*, in the model of empire as conceived by the Mughal conquerors or the British colonialists? As a democratic, multicultural entity as dreamed of by Nehru, Gandhi, and other revolutionary leaders?

At the very local level, many discussions with artists showed me that the practitioners of this or that form often did not see beyond what they themselves were doing. Their very strength as artists and cultural performers depended on their nearly total immersion in what they were doing. India was not one world, but many, seen from myriad localities. Even, from the Hindu perspective, the underlying Sanskritic tradition was, it turned out, a "restored behavior," as much in debt to European scholarship as it was to any kind of uninterrupted tradition reaching back towards Vedic times.[10] This condition was more than simply not having traveled outside their own areas. It was an expression of what Clifford Geertz later called "local knowledge." The "national scale" of things simply did not interest people like Seraikella Chhau maskmaker Mahapatra or Seraikella Chhau dance guru Kedar Nath Sahoo. In fact, neither Mahapatra nor Sahoo were much interested even in the other kinds of Chhau, no less Kutiyattam in very far-away Kerala or Bhand Pather in Kashmir. This local-centricity I found repeated again and again, even when encountering extremely sophisticated and commercially aware artists such as the Jatra performers and producers I met in Calcutta.

The impetus to merge and fuse genres, spurred by Awasthi and his supporters, found able practitioners in artists such as Mohan Agashe in his production of Vijay Tendulkar's *Ghashiram Kotwal* and directors such as Tanvir, K.N. Panikkar, and B.V. Karanth. This work was made possible by an impetus coming from the Sangeet Natak Akademi and the National School of Drama. The NSD became an "all-India" presence. Actors and directors came to Delhi, trained there, and then worked in all parts of the country (though, in some persons' opinion, too many of them remained in urban centers or went to work in Bollywood). Noteworthy is the fact that the concerns of the School's founder, Ebrahim Alkazi, were extremely cosmopolitan, reaching out to, and beyond, western European theatre. Nor was Alkazi bound to the Hindu tradition by ties of belief but rather by means of respect and knowledge. He was very interested in Urdu literature and Moghul culture. Students came to the National School of Drama from all over India, where English (as much as Hindi) was a language of instruction. Since Alkazi's departure in 1977, the National School of Drama has had a number of directors some of whom have been more responsive than others to indigenous Indian concerns, languages, and theatrical techniques. Over time, through its graduates, faculty, and productions, the National School of Drama has had an enormous impact on Indian theatre and film.

TWO PATHS

When I arrived in Calcutta, Awasthi was already there. He mapped
out my program which included both Bengali- and Hindi-speaking
theatre workers. Two especially, each in his own very particular way,
have had a long-term impact on me: Badal Sircar and Shyamanand
Jalan. When I met him, Sircar had already achieved all-India fame
with his 1965 play, *Evam Indrajit*, a drama about the angst of both
the Indian middle class and the artists who were writing about it. But
Sircar was totally unhappy with not only fame but the theatre in
which he was famous. He felt that the modern theatre was reaching
only a small fraction of Indians, those already acculturated mostly
toward western things. He wanted to speak to people in villages,
people on the streets. He was also drawn to experiments in
environmental theatre, the work of the Living Theatre, and of Jerzy
Grotowski.

In 1967 Sircar founded Satabdi, a group he still leads. Joan
MacIntosh and I led a brief workshop with that group in 1971.
Sircar, MacIntosh, and I were drawn to each other through our
theatrical ideals and techniques. In the summer of 1972 Sircar came
to Vancouver to work with The Performance Group, getting more
than a taste of our approach to environmental theatre and actor
training. That approach was influenced by my work in 1967 with
Grotowski. The work in Vancouver helped Sircar in his efforts in the
streets and non-ordinary performing spaces of Calcutta and beyond
into villages in the Bengali countryside. Sircar's relation to Calcutta
is best told in his own words:

Calcutta. The city I was born and raised in. An artificial city created in the
colonial interests of a foreign nation. A monster city that grew by sucking
the blood of a vast rural hinterland which perhaps is the true India. A city
of alien culture based on English education, repressing, distorting, buying,
promoting for sale the real culture of the city. A city I hate intensely. A city
I love intensely. (1982, 51)

Sircar began writing plays specifically for non-theatre venues, for
the outdoors, for villages. Thus were *Bhoma, Micchil, Stale News* and
other dramas born:

Yes our theatre has become a theatre of change ... We came out of the
proscenium stage in 1972 ... The immediate reason was that of
communication—we wanted to break down the barriers and come closer to
the spectators, to take full advantage of direct communication that theatre
as a live-show offers ... But in taking that course we also found our theatre
outside the clutches of money. We could establish a free theatre, performing
in public parks, slums, factories, villages, wherever the people are, depending

on voluntary donations from the people for the little expenses we needed. [...] We concentrated on the essentials—the human body and the human mind. Our theatre became a flexible, portable, and inexpensive—almost free—theatre. (1982, 56)

To the best of my knowing, Sircar still lives by these principles in his work with Satabdi. *Third Theatre* is a 1996 film by Amshan Kumar about Sircar's work from the 1970s to the 1990s.[11] Seagull Books has recently brought out Sircar's *Beyond the Land of Hattamala* and *Scandal in Fairyland* (1994). Sircar's work is political, even if it is not in the service of a particular political party. His work is linked to that of Tanvir and to that of Safdir Hashmi who founded Janam, a political street theatre group in the Delhi area. On 1 January 1989 during a performance of *Halla Bol* (Attack!) for industrial workers in Jhandapur, Hashmi was dragged from the performance and murdered by goons (see Van Erven 1989).

Shyamanand Jalan took me under his wing in the most direct way possible: He invited me to live in his house as he introduced me to both the Bengali and the Hindi branches of Calcutta theatre. From the 1960s, Shyamanand Jalan has been a shaker-mover. He is a leader of Anamika Kala Sangam, a Hindi-speaking Calcutta arts group. Since 1972 he has been the founder-director of Padatik. An attorney by trade, Shyamanand Jalan has wide-ranging abilities including those of film and television actor, director, and producer, theatre director, and publisher. If Sircar focused more and more sharply on the particular people and spaces of the urban masses and villagers, Shyamanand Jalan branched out ever more widely. In a certain sense, Sircar represented India's inward-looking aspect, its attention to particular cultural units and populations while Jalan represents the equally powerful Indian penchant for inclusivity and globalism. It is not true to say that "real India" is in the villages; or in the cities; or anywhere. "Real India" is in the multiplicities of Indias, including the ever-swelling, influential diaspora.

Shyamanand Jalan is part of Calcutta's Hindi-speaking business-oriented Marwari community, originally from Rajasthan. The Marwaris are very culturally active. Shyamanand Jalan was a principal organizer of several conferences on the relationship between traditional and modern theatre. He was instrumental in starting Seagull Books, an important English-language publisher, as well as the publisher of *Seagull Theatre Quarterly,* today India's most adventurous theatre journal (I am speaking only of what's in English). Shyamanand Jalan's work in relating traditional and modern Indian themes and techniques is perhaps best demonstrated in his 1995 production,

Ram Katha, Ram Kahani, choreographed by Chetna Jalan, his wife. The Jalans' approach is, can I say it? post-modern. As Ruben Banerjee wrote in *India Today*:

Ram, Hindi film music. World Wrestling Federation (WWF), pop music, fashion shows ... Another MTV promo? Not really. Only Ramayan moving into the 21st century ... Calcutta-based Chetna Jalan goes where no one has dared before. She is telling the tale, as *Ramkatha-Ramkahani,* through Kathak: her troupe, Padatik, dances to Hindi film hits, ghazals, rap, rock and qawwali: interspersed are WWF, the drug problem, fashion shows ... But why Ramayan? Jalan says the idea struck her at the Sahmat conference in Ayodhya. "Strains of *Ram naam* drifted from every lane," she says, "yet the town was strife-torn. I was appalled." It was to rediscover Ram and spread his message of love in "a language that all understand" that she decided to make *Ramkatha-Ramkahani.* (1995, 183)

Shyamanand Jalan himself is more skeptical, as recorded in his "Director's Notes":

Do I believe in God? ... Though there is no clear answer, yet I have a vague feeling that I do. Not in Rama or Krishna or Vishnu or Shiva, but in an unknown force which controls us ... But I wish I did believe in Rama, that I did love him, that I had faith in him. This would have made life simpler ... There is a thing called Indianness. The difference is the same as between Bharata and Aristotle, 'Rasa' and Catharsis, Hinduism and Christianity. ... It is very difficult to define that Indianness, yet we feel it all the time, when women sob in a Hindi commercial movie, in the informality of the Durga Puja celebrations and in people trying to speak with Zarda Pans in their mouth ... Which is the theatre I must now do? And I am not talking about that theatre which is beneficial to the Society ... The theatre in which an average Indian from any background or level can walk in and enjoy himself—a theatre which may or may not impress, may or may not instruct but which does entertain. And what could be that theatre? It could be the 'total' theatre—with drama, dance and music; it must be the theatre which touches emotions whether it imparts a thought, an idea or not.

Jalan's belief in karma, the "unknown force which controls us" propels him as a restless, always-inquisitive searcher. *Ram Katha, Ram Kahani* is "roots," post-modern, experimental, and popular. As the *Times of India* said: "The pantheon-sized *Ram Katha Ram Kahani* quilts together an incredible range of ethno-cultural diversity. The result may not be seamless, but the audacity leaves you breathless. Kathak, rap, and Batman, the melodrama of Parsi theatre and the coquetry of Umrao Jaan, even the telescoping of the title to *RKRK* as though it were *HAHK* may seem profane in the retelling of India's most sacrosanct legend. But they all enrich the epic's style, update the message, and bowl a goodly to those who are determined to tar our rainbow heritage with one monochromatic brush" (17 December 1995, 14). I would add that *RKRK* is traditional because it is part of the longstanding and ongoing tradition of updating and popularizing the *Rāmāyaṇa*, from Tulsidas' *Rāmcaritmānasa* to Ram Katha reciters to the Doordarshan TV series. And I note that purists—both scholarly and cultural—take a dim view of works such as *RKRK*.

AMERICAN SCHOLARLY WRITING ON INDIAN PERFORMANCE

The great preponderance of American scholarly writing about Indian performance is about stuff that is presumed to be "really Indian": the so-called classical, ritual, traditional, and/or folk genres. There is no doubt that U.S. scholars desire to work on material that is not "tainted" by western or globalizing influences. But, on close examination, these performances prove to be examples of restored behavior, invented traditions under strong pressure to update and change. What else could one expect? There are no "untouched" or "pure" rituals or performances in India or anywhere else. In fact, there never were any such. Indian culture, from its very inception, from Mohenjo-Daro and Harappa, was already and always infiltrated, invaded, and affected by what was coming from outside. But every external influence was "domesticated," fused with what was already there. These fusions do not exist in a cultural archeology, one distinct layer on top of another, piling up from pre-historic times to the present. Rather, if one seeks a metaphor, the *rasa* ("flavor") is more appropriate—an infiltration of essences; cultures that are always simultaneously performed and hybrid, dynamically mixing into new concoctions.

The amount written by U.S. scholars about Indian performance is enormous. I have neither the encyclopedic knowledge nor the surveyor's gift to overview so much excellent work including Ph. D. dissertations, only some of which have been revised into books. I cannot in this writing even list or summarize most of what has been done since Independence, no less discuss any particular writing in critical detail. But I can suggest a categorization into "generations" of scholars and interests. Along the way I will nominate a few of my own personal favorites and raise certain questions.

In 1962 and 1966 Balwant Gargi, an Indian, published in America, *Theatre in India* and *Folk Theatre of India*, two books that introduced U.S. theatre people to the wide range of Indian theatre. Gargi's work was improved upon by Kapila Vatsyayan's *Traditional Indian Theatre: Multiple Streams* (1980) and theorized by Suresh

Awasthi in *Drama: The Gift of the Gods: Culture, Performance, and Communication in India* (1983). In 1970 Clifford R. Jones and Betty True Jones brought out *Kathakali: An Introduction to the Dance-Drama of Kerala*, a theatrically oriented description of preparations, acting techniques, music, and choreography as well as a summary of narratives. The Gargi and Jones books were superficial, to be sure, but they opened a lot of peoples' eyes, especially in the theatre community.

Gargi and the Joneses were harbingers, but the two "parents" of recent U.S. scholarship on Indian performance are Milton Singer and Norvin Hein. Singer's *When a Great Civilization Modernizes* and Hein's *The Miracle Plays of Mathura* both appeared in 1972. Singer, developing the work of Robert Redfield, proposed the notion of "cultural performances" which:

could be regarded as the most concrete observable units of Indian culture, the analysis of which might lead to more abstract structures within a comprehensive cultural system. Looking at performances from this point of view, it soon became evident that the rites and ceremonies performed as ritual obligations, usually by domestic or temple priests, had many elements in common with the more secular cultural performances in the theatre, concert hall, radio programs, and films and that these linkages revealed not only the outlines of a cultural structure but also many indications of the trend and process of change in that culture. (1972, 64)

In other words, participant-observation of a wide range of performative activities is the key to understanding not only the structure of Indian societies, but also the processual and historical changes driving them historically. An interrelated network of performances—urban and village, artistic and religious, individually authored and collective, expressing both "great" and "little" traditions—comprise a single, processual system. In the villages and in village-like enclaves in the cities (and the cities are latticed with such enclaves), social life, religious life, political life, family life, and artistic life are closely knit to each other. If at one extreme India presents a complex nexus of individual units, at the other extreme it offers, again in Singer's words, "'a ladder of abstraction' that leads from these units to holistic constructs" (1972, 65). This holistic approach has been followed by many scholars who refuse the mostly-western division into high and low arts, fenced off genres, and isolatable social units.

If Singer sought to make connections, Hein in his work on the Ras Lilas of Vrindavan provided a model of a closeup study of a particular nexus of performances. Beginning, in Hein's own words, "as a literary search for traces of obscure religious drama, on the supposition that North India's instruments of oral education may have included traditions of popular theatre which had never been recorded" (1972, 1), Hein soon found himself on the ground in the Braj-speaking district of Mathura observing Ras Lilas. *The Miracle Plays of Mathura* includes a lot of linguistic analysis as well as chapters on Kathak, Bhaktamal Natak, and Ram Lila but its center is Ras Lila. Exploring an avenue opened by Hein, David Kinsley in *The Divine Player* (1979) takes an historical and theoretical approach, investigating the ideas of *Maya Lila*, also very brilliantly explored by Wendy Doniger O'Flaherty in *Dreams, Illusions, and Other Realities* (1984). Hein's study also influenced Hawley's excellent *At Play With Krishna* (1981) as well as Philip Lutgendorf's *The Life of a Text* (1991), an examination of how Tulsidas' *Rāmcaritmānasa* remains dynamic by means of story-telling (*kathā*), theatre (Ram Lila), and media.[12] William S. Sax explores various lilas while raising important theoretical questions in *The Gods at Play: Lila in South Asia* (1995). The *Oral Epics in India* (1989), edited by Stuart H. Blackburn, Peter J. Claus, Joyce B. Flueckiger, and Susan S. Wadley combines fieldwork with careful historical and linguistic research. Taken collectively, the oral epics are practiced in a great many areas of India connecting local heroes with the great figures of the Sanskrit epics and *purāṇas*.

Although there are too many books on specific performance genres to name even a fraction of them, some need mention here because of their excellence and/or their priority in time. Ashton's and Christie's *Yaksagana: A Dance Drama of India* (1977) is based largely on Ashton's grasp of Yakshagana through taking lessons in dancing, drumming, make-up, and costuming After Ashton, many of those who studied Indian performance took very seriously the "participant" side of their research. Richard A Frasca worked this way from 1977 to 1982 as he researched *The Theatre of the Mahabharata* (1990). In his introduction, Frasca writes: "I balanced my data collection with actual performance training in the genre. I have always felt that an active involvement with the performing arts facilitated research on them ..." (xiii). Frasca also studied Karnatak vocal music, Bharata Natyam, and *mṛdaṅgam* (a drum). Take also, in the best Hein mode, *Inside the Drama-House: Rama Stories and Shadow Puppets in South India* (1996) by Stuart Blackburn, a finely-knit study of the textual and the contextual. Blackburn's work brings to the fore the too often overlooked Indian puppetry tradition.

Phillip Zarrilli is a scholar who deserves special attention because of how he combines-extends the Hein and Singer models. Zarrilli's scholarship, practical work, theorizing, and artistic endeavors are exemplary. He has done more than anyone writing in English to probe what he calls the "Kathakali complex,"[13] a related set of performance events and genres of Kerala. Kathakali stands at the apex of a whole complex of performance events and genres that includes (but is not wholly limited by) Kutiyattam, Teyyam, and Kalarippayattu. All these kinds of performances continue to exist in Kerala. Kutiyattam precedes Kathakali both historically and conceptually; Teyyam is a key part of the ritual underpinning of Kathakali; and Kalarippayattu informs the rigorous Kathakali training. But it would be a most grievous error to conclude, therefore, that Kutiyattam, Teyyam, and Kalarippayattu exist "for" Kathakali, analogous to the farm team system of U.S. baseball. Kutiyattam, Teyyam, and Kalarippayattu are wholly independent genres, bringing together in their own unique ways ritual, theatre, music, dance, martial arts, and yogic/ayurvedic conceptions of what Zarrilli correctly calls the "bodymind." Nor is Kathakali just one thing. There is government-sponsored Kathakali, the training-to-performance operation at the Kalamandalam in Cheruthuruthy, Kathakali performed in temples and for various ritual and religious festivals and occasions, Kathakali in secular and highly aestheticized situations, Kathakali on tour in India and abroad, Kathakali experiments including the staging of Shakespeare's plays ... and so on. In the U.S.A., the Kalamandalam brand of Kathakali is the best known. Is this because it is the finest kind? Or is it more attributable to converging patronage, publicity, centrality—and because the Kalamandalam from its founding decades ago by Vallathol has been open to westernized standards of schooling and presentation? No single or simple answer can be given. Even the terms "western" and "Indian" are very slippery. Historical origin does not determine cultural affinity. An operation that begins as an importation or a hybrid may in a generation or two become entirely of the place it was brought to or formed in. In this regard, the Kalamandalam is an Indian-Keralan-Cheruthuruthian operation, whatever its origin. So also for English, which, as Salmon Rushdie and others have pointed out, thrives as an Indian language alongside of many other Indian languages.[14]

Zarrilli's work demands special commendation because he has not only done excellent scholarship, he has also, through extended and rigorous training and practice, become a master of Kalarippayattu which he teaches not only for its own sake but also as a basis for performer training. In other words, Zarrilli has entered into an extraordinarily fruitful relationship with a key determinant of Keralan performance culture, and he has found a way to use what he has learned without being either reductive or exploitative. His research, writing, and practice have served as a beacon for others working in Kerala.[15]

IN SEARCH OF THE HOLY (SANSKRIT) GRAIL

Europeans first became interested in Indian culture when research indicated the existence of the Indo-European family of languages. These scholars "found" an India of *Vedas, Upaniṣads,* epics, dramas of Kalidasa, Bhasa, and ruins—lots of ruins: temples, murals, palaces, tombs. The Indias of the present were not so fascinating to these men as was the "glorious" India of the past. The quest for remnants of old India, and attempts to revive and revitalize aspects of it, continue. This quest takes three principle forms: making modern productions using as texts classic Sanskrit dramas or the epics; the search for surviving rituals and theatre from Sanskrit and/or Vedic times; the investigation and application of the performance theories of the *Nāṭya Śāstra.*

Sanskrit Drama in Performance (1981), edited by Rachel Van M. Baumer and James R. Brandon, was the fruit of a 1974 conference on the "Art of Sanskrit Drama in Performance" held at the University of Hawaii. The conference, and the book, focus on how Sanskrit dramas are performed "today" (in the 1970s). Along with this are essays by both Indian and western scholars on the origins of Sanskrit drama, on *rasa* theory, and on the movement styles of Sanskrit drama. Any number of attempts have been made, both in India and the U.S.A., to contemporize Sanskrit dramas. With the appearance of *Theatre of Memory: The Plays of Kalidasa* (1984), edited by Barbara Stoler Miller, playable translations of at least some key dramas exist. In this regard, David Gitomer's *The Catastrophe of the Braid: The Mahabharata in Classical Drama* (in press) works through Sanskrit texts as performance texts. What makes production so difficult, however, is that the theatrical underpinnings of classical Sanskrit drama are far from both modern Euro-American and traditional Indian theatre. Even Kutiyattam, which is played in Sanskrit, most probably does not conform to the production values of Kalidasa's day. Kutiyattam in itself has attracted plenty of attention, with important writings by Farley Richmond and Clifford Jones.

More troubling, from my point of view, has been the attempt to locate surviving so-called Vedic rituals. Most notably this work was carried on with great energy by Frits Staal, who detailed his finding in *Agni: the Vedic Ritual of the Fire Altar* (1983). I critiqued this approach in 1985,[16] pointing out that "survivals," far from being fossils of earlier cultural practice, were both living and changing events as well as, in the agni case that Staal documents, at least partly a creation of the scholars who were supposedly "just watching." In fact, the Heisenbergian principle applies to cultural studies as well as particle physics: Observation is itself a consequential intervention.

I believe that very fruitful work has been done in relation to the *Nātya Śāstra*. The text and its most important commentaries have been probed by a variety of scholars Indian, European, and American.[17] Where the *Nātya Śāstra* lives is in the embodied practice of any number of dance-theatre gurus transmitting the classical genres. Kelucharan Mahapatra in Odissi, Birju Maharaj in Kathak, Kalanidi Narayan in the abhinaya of Bharata Natyam, and Kedar Nath Sahoo in Seraikella Chhau are but four among many. In these masters, the classical *Nātya Śāstra* tradition is combined with martial arts, local knowledge, and personal artistic excellence. In this sense, the *Nātya Śāstra*-as-practice is neither dead, text-bound, nor static.

AN INDIAN PERSPECTIVE

Americans (and those from the European tradition generally) have overwhelmingly concentrated their study and practice on classical, traditional, ritual, and folk forms. Relatively little interest has been shown—either practically or from a scholarly perspective—in modern Indian theatre.[18] The modern theatre is not taken seriously. It is not treated as on a par with what happens in Berlin, Paris, London, or New York. "What could *we* learn from *them* about what is really *ours?*" is the attitude. At best, taking modern Indian theatre seriously would be bringing coals to Newcastle. Orientalist biases die hard. What is "interesting" about India to westerners is precisely what these westerners mark as "non-western." This traditional cultural stuff is received on the practical-artistic level (by Eugenio Barba, Jerzy Grotowski, Peter Brook, and their American cohorts) as "raw material," or as a survival of an old and thought-to-be "more pure and powerful" kind of performance knowledge. On the scholarly level the traditional is regarded as what is most indicative of Indianness, which is, after all what the scholars get their grants to study. But modern theatre is as Indian as Kutiyattam; and Indian performance theory—*rasa* theory especially—informs modern as well as traditional theatre.

The situation is very different when Indians regard their own performance worlds. Take for example, Ananda Lal's recent *Rasa:*

The Indian Performing Arts in the Last Twenty-Five Years (1995), multiply edited and authored, a large-format study of Indian theatre and film issued in Calcutta by the Anamika Kala Sangam. *Rasa* features discussions both of over-arching theoretical, historical, social, and political concerns as well as overviews of the theatres of sixteen language groups, starting with Sanskrit and ending with English.[19] *Rasa's* contributors focus mostly on modern theatre, though with the knowledge that the modern, the experimental, the classical, and the folk are mutually dependent in India. It is well worth citing from Ananda Lal's introduction to *Rasa's* theatre section:

The term "Indian theatre' is so simplistic that it is a misnomer. There is no such homogeneous entry, even if we apply the apparently obvious principle of classifying all theatre within the borders of sovereign India as "Indian." By such a delimitation, what happens to the remarkably large Indian diaspora? ... More academically speaking, no analysis of contemporary Indian theatre can afford to ignore the profound Indian influence on world theatre—as in the eclectic intercultural work of Peter Brook of Jerzy Grotowski ... or in the scholarly thesis suggested by two American professors of theatre [Burnet Hobgood and Thomas Mitchell] in this book, proposing Western receptivity to the subtleties of Sanskrit theatre aesthetics as a corrective to the prevalent scientific approach in occidental theatre practice, or even in the cross-cultural experience of directors such as Vijaya Mehta, when they take an Indian production on tour internationally or stage an Indian text using a European cast ... If the Government really believed in propagating unity in diversity [an official slogan], it would have arranged for a plan by which seminal dramatic texts in Indian languages are translated into all other Indian languages ... [B]ut the Government, as in other matters, has failed to identify this need. (1995, 1,3)

Of *Rasa's* 218 pages devoted to theatre, only seven are exclusively about folk performance and none about classical dance-theatre—yet these are the meat-and-potatoes of U.S. scholarship. Why this striking dissimilarity? First off, there is plenty of Indian scholarship on "class dance-theatre" forms such as Kathakali, Kathak, Bharata Nātyam, and Odissi. As for "folk theatre," the authors of *Rasa* problematize the whole category. As Lal states:

A real problem has arisen in Indian culture recently, of unconsciously discussing and writing about urban theatre as if it is the only sophisticated variety of theatrical expression worthy of attention. Many writers habitually ignore the authentic folk forms, apparently oblivious to the fact that their own city-centric theatre represents the artistic impulses of a minority (albeit powerful) of the Indian population whose productions mostly never reach, nor have relevance for, the rural majority. On the other hand, practitioners have bent over backwards to create "folk-based" performances that appropriate the techniques of traditional forms in a self-righteous and self-conscious search for the "roots" which merely betrays their own poverty of imagination while producing ersatz populist idioms which do well abroad due to their colourful, exotic otherness. How typically "Indian" are these spectacles, one may justifiably ask, compared to their village antecedents which now lie in their death throes ... ? (1995, 1)

Nor are the Indians at all happy about what foreigners write concerning Indian theatre. Take, for example, Lal's devastating critique of the Indian entries in the *Cambridge Guide to Theatre* (1992). All 53 entries on India were written by Farley Richmond, a theatre professor whose main work has been on Kutiyattam. Why would Richmond accept the task of writing *all* the entries on India? In scarcely concealed rage, Lal details both the many errors of fact—from spelling of individual names and genres to dates in the Indian ritual calendar to over-simplifications to fundamental errors regarding Indian history and demographics. Part way through this critique Lal writes: "Lest readers think I am unfairly generalizing from one writer's shortcomings, I should add that he [Richmond] is not the first contemporary indologist to show a blissful ignorance of Indian history and geography" (1995, 26). Perhaps even worse than errors of fact are those of conception and theory. Noting that the overall editor of the *Guide* is Martin Banham of the University of Leeds and that the eight member advisory board are *all* from either the U.S.A., the U.K., or Canada, Lal wonders how the *Guide* can truly claim to represent "world theatre." Lal laments that Richmond's errors are further disseminated because they are repeated in the *Cambridge Guide to Asian Theatre*. The errors, in fact, were present in the Richmond, Swann, and Zarrilli *Indian Theatre: Traditions of Performance* (1990). Faulty scholarship is a robust weed almost impossible to dig up once rooted.

SO WHY THE IMBALANCE?

What is missing from U.S. scholarship are studies of movements, writers, and directors of specific Indian theatres—something for modern theatre comparable to what has been done for traditional forms. As of yet there are no sizable essays I know of, no less books, on persons such as Vijay Tendulkar, Ratan Thiyam, B.M. Shah, Mahesh Elkunchwar, Utpal Dutt, B.V. Karanth, Satyadev Dubey, Girish Karnad, Vijaya Mehta, Sombhu and Tripti Mitra, Mohan Rakesh, K.N. Panikkar, Mohan Agashe, Probir Guha, Badal Sircar, Shyamanand Jalan, Anuradha Kapur, and Anamika Haksar—to name just some. There is no U.S. book focused entirely on modern

Indian theatre. There is no book-length study of Indian colonial theatre. The reason for the imbalance is both obvious and obscure. On the obvious level, U.S. scholars consider modern Indian theatre to be derivative. Only the traditional theatre is regarded as "really Indian." But if we examine this prejudice more carefully, we find something more nettlesome.

What is regarded as "really Indian," the traditional theatre itself—and not only in India—has become a "cultural preserve," existing to a large degree because of official interest and patronage. This interest and patronage ranges from outright subsidy—to help to scholars who want to study traditional forms—to touring opportunities that link folk and traditional performers into a global network. In some cases, as with the late Sanjukta Panigrahi, the outstanding Odissi performer, performers are at ease in the international circuit, exchanging techniques and views across a broad spectrum of interests, from the traditional to the avantgarde. But in other cases, performing on foreign stages transforms ritual and/or aesthetic work into an object of cultural tourism. In our supposedly sophisticated times, the notion of the "colonial exposition" is long-gone. But its ghost hovers over every festival, whether in Delhi on display or at New York's Asia Society or in some prestigious European site. Furthermore, as my colleague Barbara Kirshenblatt-Gimblett pointed out, the work of anthropologists, and anthropo-logically-influenced scholarship, has always been to seek out the exotic, the other, the categorically different. Ironically, as we move into the 21st century, the objects of such study must be artificially preserved. Instead of there being even the appearance of the 'Other' or the "wild" (from the home culture's perspective), per-formance genres, like many other cultural practices, exist in "game parks" or nicely patrolled cultural zoos. My rhetoric appears sardonic, but I for one, tentatively and with much trepidation, support such aspirations and operations. Diversity is a positive value, society and culture are constructions; therefore, let us make the best of it.

The question, of course, demanding but not getting an answer is: Who is "us"?

NOTES

1. See "Jayaganesh and the Avantgarde" in my *the Future of Ritual* (1993).
2. I was accompanied in 1971 and again in 1976 by actress Joan MacIntosh, my partner in the Performance Group and later my wife. We separated in 1978 and divorced a year later.

3. Alkazi himself studied in the U.K. at the Royal Academy of Dramatic Arts. Alkazi was also affected by the Russian master teacher of acting, Michael Chekhov, who was working in the U.K. at that time.

4. "Interculturalism" is a troubled and therefore interesting term signaling not the easy companionship theorized by multiculturalists but the often uncomfortable yet very lively interaction among various tendencies, where cultures collide, interact, and are in dialog with each other. It suggests not "purity" but hybridity, fusion, and the emergence of new forms. One might theorize modern India as an intercultural experiment.

5. See my "Letter from Calcutta" (1974).

6. See "The Performance Group In India: February-April 1976" (1976) in the *Quarterly Journal* of the National Centre for the Performing Arts, Bombay, reprinted in *Performative Circumstances* (1983).

7. See "Restoration of Behavior" in *Between Theatre and Anthropology* (1985) for my discussion of Chhau.

8. I along with my co-researcher in 1978, Linda Hess, have written often on Ramlila. See, for example, our "The Ramlila of Ramnagar" (1977), Hess's "Ram Lila: The Audience Experience" (1983) and her "The Poet, the People, and the Western Scholar" (1988); see also my "Ramlila of Ramnagar" in *Between Theatre and Anthropology* (1985) and "Striding Through the Cosmos" in *The Future of Ritual*. Norvin Hein (1972) and Philip Lutgendorf (1991) both discuss Ram Lila. Anuradha Kapur's *Actors, Pilgrims, Kings, and Gods* (1990) is the only book-length study of the Ramnagar Ram Lila of which I am aware.

9. The U.S.A. never had a colony or territorial concession in India (as it did in China). But U.S. money and influence were certainly present in India, and increasingly so after the British departed. From the point of view of scholarship, the link between PL480 and U.S. citizens researching in India is indisputable. India paid back U.S. loans in rupees, that could not leave India. In time, many of these rupees were spent on supporting U.S. research in India.

10. See, for example, my discussion of both Bharata Natyam and "contemporary" Vedic ritual in "Restoration of Behavior" in *Between Theatre and Anthropology* (1985), first written in 1977 shortly after my return from India, and revised several times thereafter. Also, in terms of performance, Bharata's *Nāṭya Śāstra* was, as a Sanskrit text, more or less "lost" until restored by English scholars. But the underlying impetus of the *Nāṭya Śāstra* was very present in the actual practices of any number of dance and theatre gurus who passed on to their students *ways of performing* that were, it turns out, profoundly (if sometimes not consciously) formed or informed by the principles of the *Nāṭaya Śāstra*. So the question remains, to whom do we "owe" the *Nāṭya Śāstra* as currently theorized and used? The answer is that at least two lines of descent converged in the twentieth century. The first was the oral tradition as practiced by various genres; the second was

the scholarly tradition in which the texts were uncovered and restored to more general use by orientalists. After some time of existing independent of each other, these two traditions are now, and have been since the 1920s or 1930s, in conversation with each other.

11. The film can be obtained from: A.K. Films, 13 Robertson Lane, Mandaveli Madras (Chennai) 600 028.

12. Lutgendorf wonders if the ramkathas are in decline. He thinks not. Some of the vitality he attributes to Hindu fundamentalism, especially surrounding the name and power of Ram, most visible in the bloody struggles over the holy locations in Ayodhya, Ram's putative birth town. Lutgendorf is one of a few scholars who does not bemoan the impact of information technology on traditional performance. Noting that literacy undermines oral traditions, Lutgendorf takes a McLuhanesque approach, suggesting that the newer electronic media may in fact help the traditional Katha and Ram Lila performances. Indeed the 1987-88 television serial of the *Rāmāyaṇa*, corny as it was, played to an enormous audience, a sizable proportion of whom treated the show as a religious experience (see Lutgendorf 1990). However, popularity itself is not a reliable measure of excellence. At any rate, we scholars ought to think twice before sneering at popular culture.

13. Zarrilli has written extensively on the performing arts of Kerala ranging from the aesthetic to the athletic, ritual, and medical. See especially, *The Kathakali Complex* (1984), *When Gods and Demons Come to Play: Kathakali Dance-Drama in Performance and Context* (199TK), his essay, "What Does It Mean to 'Become the Character': Power, Presence, and Transcendence in Asian In-Body Disciplines of Practice" (1990), and *"When the Body Becomes All Eyes": Paradigms, Practices, and Discourses of Power in Kalarippayattu—a South Indian Martial/Medical Art* (in press).

14. Rushdie argues that English is an Indian language, a language of other nations, and a "world language." By claiming English as an Indian language, Rushdie means that a significant and expanding Indian literature exists in English; that many millions of people speak English as their primary tongue; and that English—like Urdu— has firmly established itself on the subcontinent in a locution that is unlike British or American English.

15. See for example, Freeman J. Richardson's 1993. *Performing Possession: Ritual and Consciousness in the Teyyam Complex of Northern Kerala* (Unpublished doctoral dissertation, Anthropology Department, University of Pennsylvania). The dissertation has been condensed into a chapter in *Flags of Fame*, ed. Heidrun Bruckner, Lothar Lutze, and Aditya Malik (1993). See also the writings of Wayne Ashley (who actually began his research at about the same time Zarrilli did), Sarah Caldwell, Rolf Groesbeck, and Deborah Neff.

16. See my "Restoration of Behavior" in *Between Theatre and Anthropology*.

17. I will name only a few of what I consider the most important: Byrski (1974), Kale (1974), Tarlekar in his study of Kutiyattam (1975), and Gupt (1994).

18. A recent exception and, I hope, a harbinger, is the work of Erin. B. Mee. See her "Contemporary Indian Theatre: Three Voices" (1997). Also Richmond, Swann, and Zarrilli devote a section of their *Indian Theatre: Traditions of Performance* (1990) to modern theatre.

19. Sanskrit, presumably the earliest language we know of that was imposed on the peoples of the subcontinent, and English, the most recent, make interesting bookends for the list: Assamese, Bengali, Gujarati, Hindi, Kannada, Kashmiri, Malayalam, Manipuri, Marathi, Oriya, Punjabi, Tamil, Telugu, and Urdu (another imposed language). Even with these 16 languages, *Rasa* editor Lal notes that Konkani, Sindhi, Meghalayan, Sikkimese, Andaman-Nicobarese theatre are not discussed "despite our best efforts to obtain articles about them." (1995, 3)

REFERENCES

Ashton, Martha and Bruce Christie. 1977. *Yaksagana: A Dance Drama of India.* New Delhi: Abhinav.

Awasthi, Suresh. 1983. *Drama: The Gift of the Gods: Culture, Performance, and Communication in India.* Tokyo: Institute for the Study of Languages and Cultures of Asia & Africa.

Banerjee, Ruben. 1995. "Acting Out Our Times," *India Today* 15 December: 183.

Baumer, Rachel Van M. and James R. Brandon, eds. 1981. *Sanskrit Drama in Performance.* Honolulu: Univ. of Hawaii Press.

Blackburn, Stuart H., Peter J. Claus, Joyce Burkhalter Flueckiger, and Susan S. Wadley, eds. 1989. *Oral Epics In India.* Berkeley: Univ. of California Press.

Bruckner, Heidrun, Lothar Lutze, and Aditya Malik, eds. 1993. *Flags of Fame: Studies in South Asia Folk Culture.* New Delhi: Manohar.

Byrski, M. Christopher. 1974. *Concept of Ancient Indian Theatre.* New Delhi: Munshiram Manoharlal.

Dumont, Louis. 1970. *Homo Hierarchicus: An Essay on the Caste System.* Chicago: Univ. of Chicago Press.

Frasca, Richard S. 1990. *The Theatre of the Mahabharata: Terukkuttu Performances in South India.* Honolulu: Univ. of Hawaii Press.

Gargi, Balwant. 1962. *Theatre in India.* New York: Theatre Arts Books.

———. 1966. *Folk Theatre of India.* Seattle: Univ. of Washington Press.

Gitomer, David. In press. *The Catastrophe of the Braid: The Mahabharata in Classical Drama.* New York: Oxford Univ. Press.

Gupt, Bharat. 1994. *Dramatic Concepts Greek and Indian.* New Delhi: D.K. Printworld.

Hawley, John S. 1981. *At Play With Krishna.* Princeton: Princeton Univ. Press.

Hiltebeital, Alf. 1988. *The Cult of Draupadi I: Mythologies.* Chicago: Univ. of Chicago Press.

Hein, Norvin. 1972. *The Miracle Plays of Mathura.* New Haven: Yale Univ. Press.

Jacob, Paul, ed. 1989. *Contemporary Indian Theatre: Interviews with Playwrights and Directors.* New Delhi: Sangeet Natak Akademi.

Jones, Clifford R. and Betty True Jones. 1970. *Kathakali: An Introduction to the Dance-Drama of Kerala.* San Francisco: American Society for Eastern Arts and Theatre Art Books.

Kale, Pramod. 1974. *The Theatric Universe.* Bombay: Popular Prakashan.

Kapur, Anuradha. 1990. *Actors, Pilgrims, Kings, and Gods.* Calcutta: Seagull.

Lal, Ananda, ed. 1995. *Rasa: The Indian Performing Arts in the Last Twenty-Five Years.* Calcutta: Anamika Kala Sangam.

Lutgendorf, Philip. 1990. "Ramayan: The Video," TDR 34, 2:127-76.

———. 1991. *The Life of a Text: Performing the Ramacaritmanas of Tulsidas.* Berkeley: Univ. of California Press.

Mee, Erin B. 1997. "Contemporary Indian Theatre: Three Voices." *Performing Arts Journal* 55: 1-26.

O'Flaherty, Wendy Doniger. 1984. *Dreams, Illusion, and Other Realities.* Chicago: Univ. of Chicago Press.

Richardson, Freeman J. 1993. "Performing Possession: Ritual and Consciousness in the Teyyam Complex of Northern Kerala." In *Flags of Fame: Studies in South Asia Folk Culture,* ed. Heidrun Bruckner, Lothar Lutze, and Aditya Malik, 109-38. New Delhi: Manohar.

Richmond, Farley P., Darius L. Swann, and Philip B. Zarrilli. 1990. *Indian Theatre: Traditions of Performance.* Honolulu: Univ. of Hawaii Press.

Sax, William S. 1995. *The Gods at Play: Lila in South Asia.* Oxford: Oxford Univ. Press.

Schechner, Richard. 1974. "Letter from Calcutta." *Salmagundi.* 25 (Winter): 47-76. Reprinted in *Performative Circumstances* (see below).

———. 1976. "The Performance Group in India: February-April 1976." *Quarterly Journal of the National Centre for the Performing Arts.* Bombay: 9-28. Reprinted in *Performative Circumstances.*

———. 1983. *Performative Circumstances: From the Avante Garde to Ramlila.* Calcutta: Seagull.

———. 1985. *Between Theatre and Anthropology.* Philadelphia: Univ. of Pennsylvania Press.

———. 1993. *The Future of Ritual.* London: Routledge.

Schechner, Richard and Willa Appel, eds. 1990. *By Means of Performance.* Cambridge: Cambridge Univ. Press.

Singer, Milton. 1972. *When a Great Tradition Modernizes: An Anthropological Approach to Indian Civilization.* London: Pall Mall.

Sircar, Badal. 1982. "A Letter from Badal Sircar." *The Drama Review* 26(2): 51-58.

———. 1983. *Three Plays.* Calcutta: Seagull.

————. 1994. *Beyond the Land of Hattamala and Scandal in Fairyland.* Calcutta: Seagull.

Tarlekar, G.H. 1975. *Studies in the Natyasastra.* Delhi: Motilal Banarsidass.

Vatsyayan, Kapila. 1980. *Traditional Indian Theatre: Multiple Streams.* New Delhi: National Book Trust.

Van Erven, Eugene. 1989. "Plays, Applause, and Bullets." *The Drama Review* 33(4): 32-46.

Zarrilli, Phillip. 1984. *The Kathakali Complex: Actor, Performance, Structure.* New Delhi: Abhinav.

————. 1990. "What Does It Mean to 'Become the Character': Power, Presence, and Transcendence in Asian In-Body Disciplines of Practice." In *By Means of Performance,* ed. Richard Schechner and Willa Appel, 131-148. Cambridge: Cambridge Univ. Press.

————. In press. *When Gods and Demons Come to Play: Kathakali Dance-Drama in Performance and Context.* London: Routledge.

————. In press. *"When the Body Becomes All Eyes:" Paradigms, Practices, and Discourses of Power in Kalarippayattu—A South Indian Martial/Medical Art.* New Delhi: Oxford Univ. Press.

Women's Studies

GERALDINE FORBES

The invitation to contribute to this volume asked me to do three things in relation to the field of women's studies: review what scholars have learned about India in the last fifty years; identify ways that scholars, working with data and systems of conceptualization and articulation in India, have been led to reconsider western-based theories, classification schemes, and methodologies for organizing knowledge; and analyze how scholarship throughout the world has been affected by interchange with India. In the paper that follows I begin by defining the relatively new field called women's studies; trace the study of Indian women from the late 19th century to the present; discuss how one topic, i.e., the study of colonialism, has been challenged and enriched by the research on women/gender in India; and, finally, consider what has been gained and what challenges still lie ahead.

WHAT IS WOMEN'S STUDIES?

The term women's studies was first used in the United States in the 1970s to define clusters of feminist courses on college campuses. As these courses became formalized in inter-disciplinary programs and departments, they articulated two long-range academic goals: transformation of traditional disciplines to include knowledge about women; and establishment of a new discipline focused on gender systems and women's experience. The task of women's studies scholars has been to explain gender systems and recover how women think, write, and act in the world.[1] This effort has close links with disciplines studying social systems and ideas, but its closest tie has been with second-wave feminism. This connection commits women's studies to ambitious social goals: equality, humanitarianism, and peace.

Women's studies scholarship in the United States roughly parallels changes in the feminist movement.[2] In the 1960s the feminist movement's first phase worked to secure equitable treatment for women. In feminism's second phase, the salience of men's rights for women's reality was questioned, and women's culture received new attention. Critics of this theoretical framework, influenced by the rise of ethnic movements and multi-culturalism, pointed out that attention to 'women's culture' led to essentialism and the obliteration of differences among and between women. Corresponding to these shifts, women's studies concentrated first on addressing questions of women's equality, then on recovering women's culture and achievements, and is now dealing with the post-modernist interpretations of difference.

Women's studies in India also began in the 1970s. The Research Center for Women's Studies at Shreemati Nathibai Damodar Thackersey Women's University in Bombay began its work in 1974 with Neera Desai as director. In 1980 the University Grants Commission (UGC) named it a Center for Advanced Research in Women's Studies. That same year the Center for Women's Development Studies opened in Delhi with Vina Mazumdar as director. This Center has studied the status of women and has made policy recommendations to the government. Since then, many universities have established women's centers and research units; in 1996 thirty-two of these centers and research units received some support from the UGC.

Although the development of women's studies courses has been a stated goal of organized academic feminists, most women's studies centers in India concentrate on research rather than teaching. University courses focusing on women and gender do exist, but they are the work of individuals rather than an institutional response to the feminist movement.[3]

At the 1996 Berkshire Conference on the History of Women, Tanika Sarkar spoke of the close relationship in India between writing women's history and becoming politically active. Joining protest movements in the 1970s, practitioners of women's history learned about women's conditions first hand, experienced the exhilaration of action, and looked closely at female subculture. With the rise of the Hindu right in the 1980s and its manipulation of a gendered narrative, many women historians found themselves engaged in a contest over representation. While women historians in the West are attempting to change the narrative, in India they are caught within the dialectics of empowerment and containment.[4]

Women's studies scholars in India who are political and social activists cannot escape the political and social consequences of their scholarship. In the eyes of many India-based women's studies scholars who have had intimate experiences with gendered political agendas, some western-generated scholarship is irresponsible and can be utilized to help reinforce and reinscribe patriarchy. Even though there are tensions between western and indigenous approaches to the study of Indian women, both approaches continue to "interact and inform one another."[5]

WOMEN'S STUDIES SCHOLARSHIP ON INDIA

Long before women's studies was invented, the 'Woman Question' existed in India. The British were obsessed with the treatment of Indian women, labeled them oppressed, and used this 'fact' to confirm their superior status and justify their right to rule. Reform-minded Indian men responded with a new ideology that combined foreign ideas and indigenous concepts to redefine gender relations. Not all Indians, however, agreed their gender system needed modification.

British men, Indian reformers, those opposed to reform, and (from the late 19th century) British and Indian women all wrote about the 'Woman Question.' Consequently, our accounts of Indian women for much of the 19th century are located with discussions of 'social evils:' sati, female infanticide, purdah, prohibitions on widow remarriage and female education, and the low status of widows. These topics dominate the narrative, leaving us relatively uninformed about women's work and occupations, values and emotional lives, and health and physical well-being.

In the late 19th century women began composing their own journals, novels, and autobiographies. By the 1920s women had formed their own organizations to deal with social problems and were writing about education, medical issues, and legal and political rights. The 1930s were a time of heightened concern with the dual issues of feminism and nationalism, a picture complicated by the raj's efforts to pose as the champion of oppressed women. All three voices competed during this period, and books on women's status joined the voices of nationalist leaders, while Katherine Mayo's *Mother India* (1927) turned gender reform issues into a debate about whether or not Indians were fit for self-government.

As women leaders put aside feminist projects to join the freedom struggle, publications about social issues diminished in number. On the eve of India's independence Gandhian and nationalist themes dominated women/gender publications. Books with Gandhi's writings to and about women shared the shelf with books on his wife, Kasturbai, and women 'pioneers.' But women's roles in the economy, their educational progress, professional status, and contributions to the arts and culture were largely ignored.

Following India's independence, biographies of Gandhi's women lieutenants and prominent nationalist women were popular. Most publications applauded women's accomplishments in new India, but Neera Desai, in *Woman in Modern India* (1957), called attention to women's poverty, illiteracy, and lack of opportunity and progress. Kamaladevi Chattopadhyaya, a doyen of the nationalist movement, criticized Desai for her 'feminist' theoretical framework, disapproving of this book that set out to explain how "the old fossilized, oppressive institutional and ideological legacy" worked to prevent women from enjoying rights granted them under India's constitution.[6]

Ignoring Desai's blunt assessment, publications on women/gender in the 1960s continued on a positive note. Manmohan Kaur's *Role of Women in the Freedom Movement 1857-1947* (1968) celebrated women's political achievements. Autobiographies and biographies featuring such prominent women as Sarojini Naidu, Muthulakshmi Reddy, Usha Mehta, and Vijayalakshmi Pandit continued to flow from the press. While articles were appearing that echoed Desai's theme, they were outnumbered by the laudatory accounts of 'great women,' 'pioneers,' and 'brave heroines.' More mundane topics did not attract authors.

Toward Equality: Report of the Committee on the Status Of Women In India, published in 1974, dramatically altered the study of women/gender in India. This was the work of a committee appointed in 1971 by the Ministry of Education and Social Welfare in response to a U.N. request for reports on the status of women for the International Women's Year in 1975. The committee had two tasks: first, to examine "the Constitutional, legal and administrative provisions that have a bearing on the social status of women, their education and employment," and, second, to assess the impact of these provisions.[7]

In preparing this report, the committee commissioned a number of studies and interviewed approximately 500 women from each state in India. These studies were the first major effort to discover the extent to which constitutional guarantees of equality and justice had benefitted women. The authors of the report concluded that women's status had not improved in the twenty-five years since India's independence.

Toward Equality's impact on programs and policies for women and the direction of research on women/gender as well as our reading of the history of women in India from Independence until 1970 has been momentous. Following publication of the report in

1974, the Indian Council of Social Science Research (ICSSR) established an advisory committee on women's studies headed by Dr. Vina Mazumdar. The ICSSR supported further research to discover the conditions under which women lived and worked in contemporary India.

The mid-1970s witnessed the publication of a number of edited inter-disciplinary volumes with 'women' in the title. Alfred de Souza's *Women in Contemporary India* (1975), Devaki Jain's *Indian Women* (1975), and B.R. Nanda's *Indian Women: From Purdah to Modernity* (1976) belong in this category. Articles in these volumes challenged conventional assumptions about women and their history and raised new questions about women's political success, the representation of women in nationalist propaganda, and the nature of women's lives.

This decade also saw the first publications about women revolutionarics and radical women's movements. Participants such as Renu Chakravartty wrote *Communists in Indian Women's Movement, 1940-1950* (1980), while scholar/activists celebrated women's opposition to traditional systems of oppression, see Gail Omvedt's *We Will Smash this Prison* (1979) and Devaki Jain's *Women's Quest for Power* (1980).

This decade was also a period of discovery and recovery. The Nehru Memorial Museum and Library began its oral history project and made an active effort to contact women with private collections of papers and documents. Social scientists working in the field located manuscripts, private papers, collections of journals, and records of organizations in trunks, godowns, and sometimes trash barrels and worked to preserve these in libraries and on microfilm. Shudha Mazumdar's memoir, published as *A Pattern of Life* (1978), was part of this recovery effort. In Madras C.S. Lakshmi sought out little-known periodicals by women and interviewed Tamil writers, singers, dancers, musicians, and others. Other feminist scholars turned to their mothers and grandmothers, and women in their communities to learn of the past.

The investigation into women's social and economic condition that began with *Toward Equality* now generated new questions. Maria Mies' *Indian Women and Patriarchy* (1980) documented the persistence of patriarchy in a time of social change. Researchers questioned the decline of women's employment reported in the 1971 census and explored women's work in marginal industries. Barbara D. Miller looked closely at the census data over time and wrote *The Endangered Sex* (1981), the first monograph to focus on the differential sex ratio. This book stimulated additional research on gender differentials in medical care and nutrition. Micro-studies that explored single industries, traced regional data, and studied neglected populations, created a body of literature that provided the foundation for later synthetic works.

The decade from the mid-1970s to the mid-1980s saw new attention paid to the lives of non-elite women, Leela Gulati published her *Profiles in Female Poverty* (1981) and Malavika Karlekar published her *Poverty and Women's Work* (1982). This was a time of questioning historical paradigms, rediscovering women's struggles, and raising new social and economic issues. Equally important were efforts to recover and preserve women's writings and records of their lives and work.

The decade from the mid-80s to the present is marked by a significant increase in the number of books published, the range of topics considered, and new efforts to develop a theoretical perspective. Significantly, important synthetic works appeared during this period.

Women-centered ethnographies and studies of women's status, marriage and kinship, rural employment, and development and environmental issues have contributed to a new understanding of how the social structure is gendered. Alice Clark's (ed.) *Gender and Political Economy* (1993) brings together new research on production and reproduction, the intensification of economic forces, and development issues. In 1994 two important books were published that drew on recent work as well as the authors' own research to present a more comprehensive picture of women in society: Bina Agarwals' *A Field of One's Own* (1994) and Susan S. Wadley's *Struggling with Destiny in Karimpur, 1925-1984* (1994).

Feminist writings on environmental issues have been especially influential. Vandana Shiva's *Staying Alive* (1988) stands out among these works for its successful integration of a critique of (masculine) colonialism with the retrieval of women's history and the creation of a theory of indigenous feminine ecology. Shiva's work remains central to eco-feminism.

Of all the disciplines, history has been especially productive. The publication of two volumes: *Women in Colonial India* (1989), edited by J. Krishnamurthy, and *Recasting Women* (1989) edited by Kumkum Sangari and Sudesh Vaid, signaled a new direction in reassessing colonialism. Two recent collections of articles have continued the effort to reconsider old questions and introduce new ones: *From the Seams of History* (1995), edited by Bharati Ray, and *Indian Women* (1995) edited by Jasodhara Bagchi.

Simultaneously, scholars began to utilize the new historiography to reread existing sources and/or newly discovered/preserved records. Meredith Borthwick's *The Changing Role of Women in Bengal, 1849-1905* (1984), Malavika Karlekar's *Voices From Within* (1991), and Barbara Southard, *The Women's Movement and Colonial Politics in Bengal, 1921-1936* (1995) are examples of this scholarship. Sumantha Banerjee, author of *The Parlour and the Streets* (1989), is one of the few historians to include an exploration of folk culture in his gendered analysis of tensions between elite and popular cultures in 19th century Bengal. As these examples make clear, much of this new historical literature is dominated by works on Bengal. Historians had neglected what Partition and the 'recovery' that followed Partition meant for women until the *Economic and Political Weekly* devoted its April 24, 1993 issue to this topic with articles by Ritu Menon and Kamla Bhasin, Urvashi Butalia, Karuna Chanana, Ratna Kapur, and Brenda Crossman. Meanwhile, Barbara Ramusack explored the role of foreign women in India, while Antoinette Burton analyzed the role of the 'Indian woman question' in the construction of British feminism. The search for women's voices has also been of major importance in recent times. *Women Writing in India*, v. I (1991) and v. II (1993) edited by Susie Taru and K. Lalita, is one of the most ambitious and valuable collections published to date. Singular memoirs include Kamala Bai L. Rau, *Smrutika: The Story of My Mother as Told by Herself* (1988) and Manmohini Zutshi Sahgal, *An Indian Freedom Fighter Recalls Her Life* (1994), edited by Geraldine Forbes. Sumitra Bhave's *Pan on Fire* (1988) gives voice to Dalit women. These efforts to retrieve women's writings have stimulated reflection on issues of agency/victimhood and women's cultural differences. Gloria Raheja and Ann Gold in *Listen to the Heron's Words* (1994) examine, through women's expressive traditions, an "alternative moral perspective on kinship, gender, and sexuality."[8]

Although women's roles in the struggle for independence have been the subject of numerous monographs, feminist studies of women and politics are rare. Amrita Basu has written on women's activism in Bengal and Maharashtra in *Two Faces of Politics* (1992); Wendy Singer on women as participants in the political process in *India Votes* (1993), edited by Harold Gould and Sumit Ganguly; and Rajeswari Sunder Rajan on Indira Gandhi in her *Real and Imagined Women* (1993). "Women and Religious Nationalism in India," edited by Amrita Basu, a special issue of the *Bulletin of Concerned Asian Scholars* (1993), addresses the rise of the Hindu right and its implications for women. This work can be seen as part of a growing trend to read gender into political issues, the long-term goal of the

Indian feminist periodical *Manushi*. Over the years *Manushi* has included articles about the disturbances in the Punjab, attacks on Muslim minorities, and the Hindu right.

While the persecution of Muslim minorities has received some attention in feminist literature, there are few books on Muslim women. Shahida Lateef's *Muslim Women in India* (1990) is a general history of Muslim women, while the more recent *Forging Identities* (1994), edited by Zoya Hasan, focuses on gendered minority identities. Gail Minault has published a number of articles on the history of Muslim women's education, and Sonia Nishat Amin has published on the education, family life, and literary activity of Muslim women in colonial Bengal. These two historians have monographs forthcoming.

This has been a rich decade for books on gender and Hinduism. Frederique Marglin's *Wives of the God-King* (1985), Lindsey Harlan's *Religion and Rajput Women* (1992), and John Hawley and Donna Wulff's edited *Devi: Goddesses of India* (1995), are only three examples from a much longer list. In comparison, gender and Islam has been neglected. Barbara Metcalf's *Perfecting Women* (1990), a partial translation and commentary of an important document for reformist Islam, stands alone.

A field of growing interest, fueled by the popularity of post-structuralism and post-modernism, is that of cultural studies with its attention to discourse, symbols and representation, the diaspora, and transnationalism. There are a number of works that belong in this category, but Gayatri Spivak's writings on gender and India are fundamental.

Spivak's impact on the study of gender in India derives from her connection with subaltern studies, the challenge to elitist, colonialist, nationalist, and Marxist historiography mounted by Ranajit Guha in the early 1980s. In her essay of introduction to *Selected Subaltern Studies* (1988) Spivak note that the female figures moving through the narratives are "drained of proper identity."[9] In "Can the Subaltern Speak?" Spivak addresses the problem of writing the history of colonial women. She finds that in both colonialist and subaltern historiography, " ... the ideological construction of gender keeps the male dominant." Spivak warns the uncritical historian to beware of the pitfalls of valorizing "the concrete experience of the oppressed." This way of writing history often constitutes an autonomous subject without due recognition of the dual oppression of colonialism and patriarchy, and the further oppression of western scholarship.[10]

Kamala Visweswaran's *Fictions of Feminist Ethnography* (1994) and

Inderpal Grewal's *Home and Harem* (1996) are examples of more recent work of this genre. In a highly self-conscious narrative filled with textual interventions and comments that demand reflection, Kamala Visweswaran moves through accounts of fieldwork to call attention to the politics of representation and to demonstrate how different narrative strategies are authorized. Grewal's *Home and Harem* belongs to transnational culture studies in its concern with linking colonial England and colonized India through the notion of travel and its culture.

STUDYING WOMEN/GENDER IN INDIA AND
RECONSIDERING WESTERN PARADIGMS

Studies of women/gender in India have challenged the conventional wisdom, methodology, and sources of the traditional disciplines and equally important, the assumptions of women's studies. This is best illustrated by a review of some of the writings on colonialism.

Indian women have always played a small but essential part in the narratives of historians from both the colonialist and nationalist schools. Colonialist historians praised the British for their intervention in Indian customs oppressive to women. The historical narrative also took note of British women, first blaming them for driving a wedge between the rulers and their subjects, then praising them as useful appendages. R.C. Mazumdar, representative of nationalist historians, agreed that Indian women's position had fallen to a low state by the beginning of the 18th century. "It was inevitable," he wrote, "that the attention of the Indians should be drawn to these evils by the impact of western civilization." His explanation for this concern with women's issues, to the exclusion of other topics like caste reform, was that these questions touched the reformer's own "kith and kin."[11]

Both colonialist and nationalist accounts share a number of assumptions. First, men assumed they could speak for women. The accounts were male accounts of women's lives male accounts that privileged other male accounts. It was not that women's views were unimportant; many 19th century journals included letters authored by men but 'signed' with women's names. But these were men speaking for women, not women speaking for women. Second, women's silence was an accepted feature of the patriarchal order. Third, men assumed it was their natural duty to protect females and especially female sexuality. Even though the British denounced the *zanānah*, they understood the concerns behind it. Many nationalist historians concurred; they faulted the purdah system for hampering the progress of female education, but continued to valorize female modesty. Nowhere in these historical accounts do modern feminists' concerns with female autonomy and a woman's right to her own body receive attention. Fourth, elitist men shared the notion that their experience should structure the writing of history. Feminist scholarship has challenged all four assumptions.

RECLAIMING WOMEN'S VOICES

In women's studies, 'reclaiming women's voices' is viewed as essential to the task of challenging androcentric theories and narratives. Rosalind O'Hanlon delineates three 'advances' historians have made in addressing questions of social change in colonial Indian society: they have broken with colonial rhetoric about 'tradition' and Indian women; they have gained new understandings of the 'modernizing' woman in late 19th and early 20th century India; and they have acquired new insights into gender and the construction of colonial hegemony. As O'Hanlon points out: "An important if obvious test to our answers to ... [these questions] lies in the extent to which they can encompass and explain women's own expressed views and experience."[12]

In recent years scholars have been engaged in translating, editing, and analyzing women's voices. *Women Writing in India, 600 B.C. to the Present* (1993-1995), edited by Susie Tharu and K. Lalitha, includes works by more than 140 different female authors as well as women's folk songs and other writings by anonymous authors. The editors assembled a collection that would give their readers a taste of what women wrote and hopefully illuminate:

... the conditions in which women wrote ... and help us capture what is at stake in the practices of self or agency and of narrative that emerge at the contested margins of patriarchy, empire, and nation.[13]

The editors explain how difficult it was for them to locate material, find biographical information on the authors, establish publication details, and, finally, develop the context for presenting their findings. This pioneering work will continue to have an impact on scholarship on India and gender issues for many years to come.

Rosalind O'Hanlon's (1994) *A Comparison Between Women and Men* includes a translation from Marathi of Tarabai Shinde's tract, "A Comparison Between Men and Women," originally published in 1882. Tarabai Shinde was enraged by the discussion of Vijaylakshmi, a young Brahman widow sentenced to transportation for life for killing her illegitimate child. Shinde's writing offers new insights into the problems of women and women's consciousness about their own oppression, and enhances our understanding of social change.

In "Chandra's Death" (1987) Ranajit Guha defies conventional historiography in his rescue of a 'fragment:' depositions by people implicated in Chandra's death following an abortion. In his close reading of these few documents from mid-19th century, Guha highlights women's initiative in obtaining and administering the abortion-inducing drug and elaborates on how patriarchy met the challenges posed by the pregnancy, abortion, and death of the unfortunate Chandra. Guha explains the women's actions in terms of gender-empathy, concluding this "tragedy was a measure, for its time, of the strength of women's solidarity and its limitation."[14]

BRINGING WOMEN'S EXPERIENCES TO THE CENTER OF DISCUSSION

Women's studies scholars use a wide range of documents to bring women's experiences, concerns, and ideas to the center of the discussion. 'Women at the center' accounts, with both Indian and British women as subjects, compose the largest number of women/gender studies from the colonial period.

One of the earliest of these histories was Meredith Borthwick's (1985) *The Changing Role of Women in Bengal, 1849-1905* on how the reforms of the modernizing Brahmo Samaj affected women. Borthwick's examination of women's magazines, autobiographical writings, and prescriptive manuals increased our awareness of the richness of these sources and highlighted the persistence of patriarchy in the creation of the 'new woman.'

Geraldine Forbes' work on women's organizations and women's involvement in nationalist politics, in various articles and *Women in Modern India* (1996), focuses attention on how women perceived their world and acted in it. Drawing on women's writings, organizational records, magazines and journals, private papers and letters, Forbes presents socially and politically active upper and middle-class women as thoughtful participants in the events of their time.

Members of the collective Stree Shakti Sanghatana have recorded and edited women's oral histories of armed resistance in Hyderabad in *'We Were Making History ...' Life Stories of Women in the Telangana People's Struggle.* (1989). Their aim was "to analyze and understand the ideological framework in which women struggled, the experiential dimensions of that struggle and its implications for women's questions."[15] The narratives themselves proved challenging: interviewees were unconcerned with the demands of chronological history and often told stories of long-ago as if they happened yesterday. The authors conclude on a contemporary note asking if it is possible to move towards a 'new society' without confronting the politics of patriarchy.

British women have claimed the attention of other historians. Barbara Ramusack was the first historian to look closely at those British women who made India their home and worked for Indian women's rights.[16] Ramusack has categorized British women in India during the late colonial period as 'cultural missionaries,' 'maternal imperialists,' and 'feminist allies.' Her larger questions are about the possibilities of women's collaboration across racial and ethnic lines.

Related to Ramusack's work is that of Antoinette Burton whose 'White Woman's Burden'[17] is a critical view of 19th century British feminists. Burton's *Burdens of History* (1994) reveals the importance of the Indian 'Woman Question' in the development of British feminist ideology and for winning a wider respectability for that ideology. 'Indian women' featured prominently in the British feminist press, and Burton asserts this was:

an example of British feminists' bid for imperial identification—of their belief that feminism must be seen as the truest expression of imperial values because feminists were concerned with colonial women and hence with imperialism.[18]

REASSESSING HISTORY/COMPLICATING THE CATEGORIES

Historians introducing a gendered analysis into their reading of conventional documents represent a third contribution to the literature on gender and colonialism. They have added a significant dimension to women's studies by explaining the "historical processes which reconstitute patriarchy in colonial India."[19] For other disciplines, they demonstrate the richness of a gendered analysis.

Lata Mani, one of the most frequently cited authors, writes about the British abolition of sati—the 'moment in the history' that begins most narratives of women in modern India. Instead of looking at the more conventional topics that have preoccupied historians, namely, why the number of satis increased in certain areas and the social profiles of families involved, Mani 'reads' official documents on sati including the British position, Rammohun Roy's tract favoring abolition of sati, and petitions protesting British efforts to regulate sati. Lata Mani argues that in the course of this debate, "women become emblematic of tradition" so that finally "tradition was thus not the ground on which the status of woman was being contested. Rather, the reverse was true: women in fact became the site on which tradition was debated and reformulated."[20]

Equally influential has been Partha Chatterjee's work on "The Nationalist Resolution of the Women's Question." Chatterjee asks why the 'Woman Question,' so important in early and mid-nineteenth century, diminished (in male discussions) when nationalist issues began to dominate. His answer is that the 'Woman Question' had been safely located in the domestic realm. Even though Indian men pursued science, technology, rational economics, and western political forms, most of them regarded the home as the source of "true identity" that needed protection and strengthening, not transformation.[21]

Mrinalini Sinha's (1995) *Colonial Masculinity: The 'Manly Englishman' and the 'Effeminate Bengali' in the Late Nineteenth Century*, traces colonial and nationalist politics through the idiom of masculinity as it was defined and redefined during four 19th century controversies. Through her close reading of controversial issues, Sinha demonstrates how continued British dominance was justified in terms of the 'natural' hierarchy that prevailed when men controlled and protected women. But she goes much farther than this and explains how Indian males responded with their own version of masculinity. The implications of this work for our discussion of feminism and colonial nationalism are many. Most important, Sinha asserts, "scholarship on the politics of colonial masculinity ... can demonstrate even more conclusively the impossibility of separating the feminist from the anti-colonial nationalist agenda."[22]

By focusing on gender issues rather than 'Women,' these three authors move the discussion in a different direction. People who work to locate and preserve women's writings and those who write about women's experiences do not always relate their work to larger historical debates. Mani's larger agenda is to problematize all debates that use the terms 'tradition' and 'modernity.'[23] Sinha is concerned with recasting "the historiographical unit of both metropolitan and colonial histories to recognize their interaction in the age of imperialism."[24] Chatterjee's project is even larger, he situates his work with other writing arrayed against the "arrogant, intolerant, self-aggrandizing rational subject of modernity ... ."[25]

WHAT HAS THE WORLD LEARNED?

There is a significant body of work that effectively refutes androcentric colonialist and nationalist historians' assumptions that women had no voice other than that given them by men, that patriarchy was unchallenged, that males were protectors of women, and that men's views of the world and experiences should be privileged. Whether one looks at the work of historians or at the work produced in disciplines such as demography and anthropology, one finds compelling arguments for gendered accounts. But, as Alice Clark has noted: "the integration of gender into the mainstream seems tantalizingly out of reach."[26]

In 1984 Hanna Papanek commented on the difficulty of integrating gender into Asian studies, but she also drew attention to an equally difficult problem: integrating an international orientation into feminist scholarship and teaching.[27] In the United States the problem is moving women's studies beyond an orientalist construction of the 'downtrodden' Indian woman. Feminist scholarship on Indian women not withstanding, three journalistic accounts have captured the most attention.

The first, Katherine Mayo's *Mother India*, is found in almost every library. Although published in 1927, it is still used by some women's studies instructors. Mayo, a muck-raking U.S. journalist, used Indian hospital records, official accounts, and personal interviews to condemn Indians for their treatment of women of all ages. She concluded that these social customs explained the weakness of the Indian race and Indians' disqualification for self-rule.

The second widely read book is Mary Daly's book on 'manstrocities,' *Gyn/Ecology: The Metaethics of Radical Feminism* (1978,1990). Her thoughts on India are included in a chapter entitled "Indian S*uttee*: The Ultimate Consummation of Marriage," in a section on the Sado-Ritual Syndrome. Daly's comments are not confined to sati. She discusses other examples of 'female sacrifice:' child marriage, dowry murder, suicide, and the starvation of widows. Ignoring the literature available when she wrote this book, Daly states: "Katherine Mayo stands as a startling exception among scholars who have written about women in India ... ."[28]

Elisabeth Bumiller's journalistic venture into the world of Indian women, *May You Be the Mother of A Hundred Sons: A Journey Among the Women of India* (1990) is a third easily-accessible and widely-cited account. Bumiller, a style reporter for the *Washington Post*, accompanied her husband, a reporter for the *New York Times*, to India where she 'discovered' Indian women. Bumiller, like Daly, was fascinated by Katherine Mayo's account and, although recognizing that Mayo lacked balance, asserts "many of the conditions she reported still exist."[29] Although her narrative includes Indian women who have reached high positions and others who are actively engaged in trying to improve the lot of women, half of Bumiller's book is devoted to social evils: arranged marriage, sati, bride burning, purdah, and sex-selective abortions. According to Chandra Mohanty, this focus on 'downtrodden women' occurs because hegemonic western feminism makes 'Third World women' a monolithic subject. Mohanty examined books in Zed Press' Third World Series and found analytic presuppositions that led to the representation of an "average Third World woman."

This average third world woman leads an essentially truncated life based on her feminine gender (read: sexually constrained) and her being "third world" (read: ignorant, poor, uneducated, tradition-bound, domestic, family-oriented, victimized, etc.).[30]

Put more crudely, India becomes an area of the world (equal to China, 'Africa,' and the 'Middle East') where 'manstrocities' are common.

It is easy to condemn Mayo, Daly, and Bumiller for their orientalism and weak scholarship. It is more difficult to have an impact on women's studies with serious scholarship on women/gender in India. A review of various bibliographies and abstracts that include 'women' and 'women's studies' proved a sobering experience. Aware of the richness of this field, I was both shocked and disappointed at the gaps between what is actually 'out there' and what makes its way into women's studies periodicals. There is no current, comprehensive guide to literature on gender in India. Books on India are not widely reviewed and the only feminist journals published outside of India that included articles on Indian women/gender were: *Genders, Gender and History, Feminist Historiography, Feminist Review, Women's Studies International Forum,* and the *Journal of Women's History.* None of these have included more than two articles on India in the last three years.

Periodicals on women/gender published in India are available in the United States. *Manushi: A Journal About Women and Society* is widely read and often referred to by women's studies scholars who are not India specialists. Another excellent source for a range of topics on women in India is *Economic and Political Weekly.* In addition to bi-annual issues on women's studies, sometimes devoted to a single topic, articles on women and gender appear in every issue. And there are two new Indian journals: *The Indian Journal of Gender Studies,* edited by Malavika Karlekar and published by Sage, and *The Journal of Women's Studies,* published by the Women's Studies Center of Calcutta University. Very soon articles from these journals will be included in *Women's Studies Abstracts* and *Feminist Periodicals,* making them more widely available to interested scholars.

What the study of women/gender in India gives to the world is a rich and growing body of literature that powerfully demonstrates the importance of a gendered analysis to each discipline and to each area of inter-disciplinary inquiry. It is unfortunate that the field of women's studies outside South Asia has not yet integrated the knowledge and approaches found in gendered scholarship about India.

NOTES

1. Coyner, Sandra. 1990. *Transforming the Knowledge Base*. New York: National Council for Research on Women, 6-8.
2. Farganis, Sondra. 1994. *Situating Feminism: From Thought to Action*. London: Sage, 23-24.
3. Desai, Neera. 1986. "Women's Studies in India: An Overview." In *Women's Studies in India*, ed. Maitreyi Krishna Raj. Bombay: Popular Prakashan, 19.
4. Sarkar, Tanika. 1996. Plenary Session: "Gendering Historiography." At the Tenth Berkshire Conference on the History of Women.
5. Clark, Alice W., ed. 1993. *Gender and Political Economy: Explorations of South Asia Systems*. Delhi: Oxford Univ. Press, 5.
6. Desai, Neera. 1974. *Woman in Modern India*. Bombay: Vora and Co., xii.
7. India (Republic), Ministry of Education and Social Welfare. 1974. *Toward Equality: Report of the Committee on the Status of Women in India*. New Delhi: Publications Division.
8. Raheja, Gloria and Ann Gold. 1994. *Listen to the Heron's Words: Reimagining Gender and Kinship in North India*. Berkeley: Univ. of California Press, p. xii.
9. Spivak, Gayatri Chakravorty. 1988. "Subaltern Studies: Deconstructing Historiography." In *Selected Subaltern Studies*, ed. Ranajit Guha and Gayatri Chakravorty Spivak. NY: Oxford Univ. Press, 31.
10. Spivak, Gayatri Chakravorty. 1988. "Can the Subaltern Speak?" In *Marxism and the Interpretation of Culture*, ed. Cary Nelson and Lawrence Grossberg, 271-313. Urbana: Univ. of Illinois Press.
11. Majumdar, R.C., gen. ed. 1965. *British Paramountcy and Indian Renaissance*, Part II. Bombay: Bharatiya Vidya Bhavan, 260.
12. O'Hanlon, Rosalind. 1994. *A Comparison Between Women and Men: Tarabai Shinde and the Critique of Gender Relations in Colonial India*. Madras: Oxford Univ. Press, 3.
13. Tharu, Susie and K. Lalitha, eds. 1993. *Women Writing in India, 600 B.C. to the Present*. Delhi: Oxford Univ. Press, vol. 1, xvii.
14. Guha, Ranajit. 1987. " Chandra's Death." In *Subaltern Studies*. Delhi: Oxford Univ. Press, vol. 5, 165.
15. Sanghatana, Stree Shakti, ed. 1989. *'We Were Making History ...' Life*

Stories of Women in the Telangana People's Struggle. Delhi: Kali for Women, 2.

16. Ramusack, Barbara. 1981. "Catalysts or Helpers? British Feminists, Indian Women's Rights, and Indian Independence." In *The Extended Family,* ed. Gail Minault. Delhi: Chanakya. See also Barbara Ramusack. 1992. "Cultural Missionaries, Maternal Imperialists, Feminist Allies: British Women Activists in India, 1865-1945." In *Western Women and Imperialism,* ed. Nupur Chaudhuri and Margaret Strobel. Bloomington: Indiana Univ. Press.

17. Burton, Antoinette M. 1994. "The White Woman's Burden: British Feminists and 'The Indian Woman,' 1865-1915." In *Western Women and Imperialism.* op. cit. 137-157.

18. Burton, Antoinette. 1994. *Burdens of History: British Feminists, Indian Women, and Imperial Culture, 1865-1915,* p. 100. Chapel Hill: Univ. of North Carolina.

19. Sangari, Kumkum and Sudesh Vaid, eds. 1989. *Recasting Women: Essays in Colonial History.* Delhi: Kali for Women, 1.

20. Mani, Lata. 1989. "Contentious Traditions: The Debate on Sati in Colonial India." In Ibid. 117-118.

21. Chatterjee, Partha. 1989. "The Nationalist Resolution of the Women's Question." In Ibid. 233-253.

22. Sinha, Mrinalini. 1995. *Colonial Masculinity: The 'Manly Englishmen' and the 'Effeminate Bengali' in the Late Nineteenth Century.* Manchester: Manchester Univ. Press, 181

23. Mani, op. cit. 122.

24. Sinha, op. cit. 181.

25. Chatterjee, Partha. 1993. *The Nation and Its Fragments: Colonial and Postcolonial Histories.* Princeton: Princeton Univ. Press, xi.

26. Clark, op. cit. 7.

27. Papanek, Hanna, 1984. "False Specialization and the Purdah of Scholarship—A Review Article." In *The Journal of Asian Studies.* 44:1 (November): 129.

28. Daly, Mary. 1990. *Gyn/Ecology: The Metaethics of Radical Feminism.* Boston: Beacon Press, 127.

29. Burmiller, Elisabeth. 1990. *May You Be the Mother of A Hundred Sons:A Journey Among the Women of India.* New York: Random House, 21.

30. Mohanty, Chandra Talpade. 1991. "Under Western Eyes: Feminist Scholarship and Colonial Discourses." In *Third World Women and the Politics of Feminism,* ed. Chandra Talpade. Mohanty, Ann Russo, and Lourdes Torres. Bloomington: Indiana Univ. Press, 56.

REFERENCES

Agarwal, Bina. 1994. *A Field of One's Own: Gender and Land Rights in South Asia.* Cambridge: Cambridge Univ. Press.

Amin, Sonia Nishat. 1996. *The World of Muslim Women in Colonial Bengal.* Leiden: Brill.

Bagchi, Jasodhara. 1995. *Indian Women: Myth and Reality*. Hyderabad: Sangam Books.

Banerjee, Sumantha. 1989. *The Parlour and the Streets: Elite and Popular Culture in Nineteenth Century Calcutta*. Calcutta: Seagull Books.

Basu, Amrita. 1992. *Two Faces of Politics*. Berkeley: Univ. of California Press.

———, ed. 1993. "Women and Religious Nationalism in India." *Bulletin of Concerned Asian Scholars*. Special Issue. 25: 3. (October-December).

Bhave, Sumitra. 1988. *Pan on Fire: Eight Dalit Women Tell Their Story*. New Delhi: Indian Social Institute.

Borthwick, Meredith. 1985. *The Changing Role of Women in Bengal, 1849-1905*. Princeton: Princeton Univ. Press.

Bumiller, Elisabeth. *May You Be the Mother of A Hundred Sons: A Journey Among the Women of India*. New York: Random House.

Burton, Antoinette. 1992. "The White Woman's Burden: British Feminists and 'The Indian Woman,' 1865-1915." In *Western Women and Imperialism*, ed. Nupur Chaudhuri and Margaret Strobel, 119-136. Bloomington: Indiana Univ. Press.

———. 1994. *Burdens of History: British Feminists, Indian Women, and Imperial Culture, 1865-1915*. Chapel Hill: Univ. of North Carolina Press.

Chakravartty, Renu. 1980. *Communists in Indian Women's Movement,1940-1950*. New Delhi: People's Publishing House.

Chatterjee, Partha. 1989. "The Nationalist Resolution of the Women's Question." *Recasting Women: Essays in Colonial History*. Delhi: Kali for Women.

———. 1993. *The Nation and Its Fragments: Colonial and Postcolonial Histories*. Princeton: Princeton Univ. Press.

Chaudhuri, Nupur and Margaret Strobel, eds. 1992. *Western Women and Imperialism*. Bloomington: Indiana Univ. Press.

Clark, Alice W., ed. 1993. *Gender and Political Economy: Explorations of South Asia Sytems*. Delhi: Oxford Univ. Press.

"Community, State, and Women's Agency." 1993. *Economic and Political Weekly*. 28:17 (April 24):ws2-ws44.

Coyner, Sandra. 1990. *Transforming the Knowledge Base*. New York: National Council for Research on Women.

Daly, Mary. 1978,1990. *Gyn/Ecology: The Metaethics of Radical Feminism*. Boston: Beacon Press.

Desai, Neera. 1977. *Woman in Modern India*. Bombay: Vora and Co.

———. 1986. "Women's Studies in India: An Overview." In *Women's Studies in India: Some Perspectives,* ed. Maitreyi Krishna Raj, 17-22. Bombay: Popular Prakashan.

de Souza, Alfred, ed. 1975. *Women in Contemporary India: Traditional Images and Changing Roles*. Delhi: Manohar.

Farganis, Sondra. 1994. *Situating Feminism: From Thought to Action*. London: Sage.

Forbes, Geraldine. 1996. *Women in Modern India*. Cambridge: Cambridge Univ. Press.

Grewal, Inderpal. 1996. *Home and Harem: Nation, Gender, Empire, and the Cultures of Travel.* Durham: Duke Univ. Press.

Guha, Ranajit. 1987. "Chandra's Death." In *Subaltern Studies V: Writings on South Asian History and Society.* Delhi: Oxford Univ. Press. 135-165.

Gulati, Leela. 1981. *Profiles in Female Poverty.* Delhi: Hindustan Publishing.

Harlan, Lindsey. 1992. *Religion and Rajput Women: The Ethics of Protection in Contemporary Narratives.* Berkeley: Univ. of California Press.

Hasan, Zoya, ed. 1994. *Forging Identities: Gender, Communities and the State.* Delhi: Kali for Women.

Hawley, John and Donna Wulff, eds. 1995. *Devi: Goddesses of India.* Berkeley: Univ. of California Press.

India (Republic), Ministry of Education and Social Welfare. 1974. *Toward Equality: Report of the Committee on the Status of Women in India.* New Delhi: Publications Division.

Jain, Devaki. 1980. *Women's Quest for Power.* Ghazibad, U.P.: Vikas.

Jain, Devaki, ed. 1975. *Indian Women.* New Delhi: Ministry of Information and Broadcasting.

Karlekar, Malavika. 1982. *Poverty and Women's Work: a Study of Sweeper Women in Delhi.* New Delhi: Vikas.

————. 1991. *Voices From Within: Early Personal Narratives of Benguli Women.* Delhi: Oxford Univ. Press.

Kaur, Manmohan. 1968. *Role of Women in the Freedom Movement 1857-1947.* New Delhi: Sterling.

Krishnamurthy, J. ed. 1989. *Women in Colonial India: Essays on Survival, Work and the State.* Delhi: Oxford Univ. Press.

Lakshmi, C.S. 1984. *The Face Behind the Mask: Women in Tamil Literature.* Ghazibad, U.P.: Vikas.

Lateef, Shahida. 1990. *Muslim Women in India.* London: Zed Books.

Majumdar, R.C., gen. ed. 1965. *British Paramountcy and Indian Renaissance. Part II.* Bombay: Bharatiya Vidya Bhavan.

Mani, Lata. 1989. "Contentious Traditions: The Debate on Sati in Colonial India." In *Recasting Women: Essays in Colonial History.* op. cit., 88-126.

Marglin, Frederique. 1985. *Wives of the God-King: The Rituals of the Devadasis of Puri.* Oxford: Oxford Univ. Press.

Mayo, Katherine. 1927. *Mother India.* New York: Harcourt Brace.

Mazumdar, Veena. 1986. "Women's Studies in Indian Perspective." *Women's Studies in India,* ed. Maitreyi Krishna Raj, 23-33.

Mazumdar, Shudha. 1978. *A Pattern of Life.* ed. Geraldine Forbes. Delhi: Manohar.

Metcalf, Barbara. 1990. *Perfecting Women: Maulana Ashraf 'Ali Thawani's Bishti Zewar.* Berkeley: Univ. of California Press.

Mies, Maria. 1980. *Indian Women and Patriarchy: Conflicts and Dilemmas of Students and Working Women.* New Delhi: Concept Publishing House.

Miller, Barbara D. 1981. *The Endangered Sex: Neglect of Female Children in Rural North India.* Ithaca: Cornell Univ. Press.

Minault, Gail. 1981. *The Extended Family: Women and Political Participation in*

India and Pakistan. Delhi: Chanakya.

————. forthcoming. *Secluded Scholars: Women's Education and Social Reform Among Indian Muslims in the Late 19th and Early 20th Centuries.*

Mohanty, Chandra Talpade. 1991. "Under Western Eyes: Feminist Scholarship and Colonial Discourses." In *Third World Women and the Politics of Feminism.* ed. Chandra Talpade Mohanty, Ann Russo, and Lourdes Torres, 51-80. Bloomington: Indiana Univ. Press.

Nanda, B.R., ed. 1976. *Indian Women: From Purdah to Modernity.* New Delhi: Vikas.

O'Hanlon, Rosalind. 1994. *A Comparison Between Women and Men: Tarabai Shinde and the Critique of Gender Relations in Colonial India.* Madras: Oxford Univ. Press.

————. 1988. "Recovering the Subject: Subaltern Studies and Histories of Resistance in Colonial South Asia." *Modern Asian Studies,* 22(2): 184-224.

Omvedt, Gail. 1979. *We Will Smash this Prison.* New Delhi: Orient Longmans.

Papanek, Hanna. 1984. "False Specialization and the Purdah of Scholarship — A Review Article." *The Journal of Asian Studies.* 44:1 (November): 127-148.

Raheja, Gloria and Ann Gold. 1994. *Listen to the Heron's Words: Reimagining Gender and Kinship in North India.* Berkeley: Univ. of California Press.

Rajan, Rajeswari Sunder. 1993. *Real and Imagined Women: Gender, Culture and Postcolonialism.* London: Routledge.

Ramusack, Barbara. 1981. "Catalysts or Helpers? British Feminists, Indian Women's Rights, and Indian Independence." In *The Extended Family: Women and Political Participation in India and Pakistan,* ed. Gail Minault, 109-150. Delhi: Chanakya Publications.

————. 1992. "Cultural Missionaries, Maternal Imperialists, Feminist Allies: British Women Activists in India, 1865-1945." In *Western Women and Imperialism.* op. cit. 119-136.

Rau, Kamala Bai L. 1988. *Smrutika: The Story of My Mother as Told By Herself.* Pune: Dr. Krishnabai Nimbkar.

Ray, Bharati, ed. 1995. *From the Seams of History: Essays on Indian Women* . Delhi: Oxford Univ. Press.

Sahgal, Manmohini Zutshi. 1994. *An Indian Freedom Fighter Recalls Her Life.* ed. Geraldine Forbes. Armonk, NY: M.E. Sharpe.

Sangari, Kumkum and Sudesh Vaid, eds. 1989. *Recasting Women: Essays in Colonial History.* Delhi: Kali for Women.

Shiva, Vandana. 1988. *Staying Alive: Women, Ecology and Survival in India.* Delhi: Kali for Women.

Singer, Wendy. 1993. "Defining Women's Politics in the Election of 1991 in Bihar." In *India Votes,* ed. Harold Gould and Sumit Ganguly, 380-402. Boulder: Westview Press.

————. 1993. "Women's Politics and Land Control in an Indian Election: Lasting Influences of the Freedom Movement in North Bihar." *India Votes.* op. cit. 180-207.

Sinha, Mrinalini. 1995. *Colonial Masculinity: The 'Manly Englishmen' and the 'Effeminate Bengali' in the Late Nineteenth Century.* Manchester: Manchester Univ. Press.

Southard, Barbara. 1995. *The Women's Movement and Colonial Politics in Bengal, 1921-1936.* Delhi: Manohar.

Spivak, Gayatri Chakravorty. 1988. "Subaltern Studies: Deconstructing Historiography." In *Selected Subaltern Studies,* ed. Ranajit Guha and Gayatri Chakravorty Spivak. pp. 3-43. NY: Oxford Univ. Press:

———. 1988. "Can the Subaltern Speak?" In *Marxism and the Interpretation of Culture.* ed. Cary Nelson and Lawrence Grossberg. Urbana: Univ. of Illinois Press.

Stree Shakti Sanghatana, ed. 1989. *'We Were Making History ...' Life Stories of Women in the Telangana People's Struggle.* Delhi: Kali for Women.

Tharu, Susie and K. Lalitha, eds. 1993-1995. *Women Writing in India, 600 B.C. to the Present.* 2 vols. Delhi: Oxford Univ. Press.

Visweswaran, Kamala. 1994. *Fictions of Feminist Ethnography.* Minneapolis: Univ. of Minnesota Press.

Wadley, Susan S. 1994. *Struggling with Destiny in Karimpur, 1925-1984.* Berkeley: Univ. of California Press.

Contributors' Institutional Affiliations

Catherine B. Asher	University of Minnesota-Twin Cities
Lawrence A. Babb	Amherst College
José Ignacio Cabezón	Iliff School of Theology
Peter J. Claus	California State University, Hayward
Frank F. Conlon	University of Washington
Norman Cutler	University of Chicago
Edward C. Dimock, Jr.	University of Chicago
John Echeverri-Gent	University of Virginia
Joseph W. Elder	University of Wisconsin-Madison
Ainslie T. Embree	Columbia University
Joan L. Erdman	Columbia College and University of Chicago
Geraldine Forbes	State University of New York, Oswego
James W. Gair	Cornell University
Robert P. Goldman	University of California, Berkeley
John Stratton Hawley	Barnard College and Columbia University
Alan Heston	University of Pennsylvania
Nazir Ali Jairazbhoy	University of California at Los Angeles
Bruce B. Lawrence	Duke University
David Ludden	University of Pennsylvania
Mary McGee	Columbia University
Velcheru Narayana Rao	University of Wisconsin-Madison
Maureen L.P. Patterson	University of Chicago
David Pingree	Brown University
Gregory L. Possehl	University of Pennsylvania
Karl H. Potter	University of Washington
Paula Richman	Oberlin College
Richard Schechner	New York University
Joseph E. Schwartzberg	University of Minnesota-Twin Cities
Herman H. Van Olphen	University of Texas at Austin
Susan S. Wadley	Syracuse University

Index